AMERICA'S RECENT PAST

AMERICA'S RECENT PAST

EDITED BY

FRANKLIN D. MITCHELL
University of Southern California

RICHARD O. DAVIES
Northern Arizona University

John Wiley & Sons, Inc.

New York · London · Sydney · Toronto

Library of Congress Catalog Card Number: 76-76059
Cloth: SBN 471 61125 5 Paper: SBN 471 61126 3
Printed in the United States of America

To Richard S. Kirkendall

PREFACE

This book is largely the result of the experiences we encountered while teaching courses in modern American history during the past several years. Our classroom efforts have convinced us that the undergraduate student needs an interpretative framework to guide his study, that he needs to become familiar with the best of current historical scholarship without getting bogged down in the subtle nuances of interpretation, and that he needs to work with contemporary sources in order to gain a sense of participation in the historical process. This collection is designed to accomplish these major goals. As such, it should supplement formal lectures and assigned paperbacks and texts, stimulate classroom discussion, and serve as a guide to independent reading.

Hopefully, this volume will help overcome such all-too-frequent student complaints that the study of history constitutes merely the memorization of a maze of seemingly unrelated names, events, and dates. Moreover, because the familiar "problems" approach was avoided, the selections have not been restricted to an artificially narrow framework. We have thus been free to draw upon a much wider—and richer—body of historical literature so that the student might appreciate the variety and complexity of the historical process. By bringing together in one volume both significant interpretative essays by distinguished scholars and illuminating contemporary sources, we have sought to overcome the limitations inherent in many existing readings books that exclusively feature either secondary or documentary materials.

This collection features what we consider to be the significant central themes of America's recent past: the liberal reform tradition from progressivism to the Great Society; the Negro's struggle against discrimination; the origins, nature, and consequences of war; the paradoxes in American life of prosperity and depression, of affluence, and poverty; the growing involvement of the United States in world affairs; the frustrations and responsibilities of a nuclear power in the Atomic Age; and the growing complexity of life in a highly technical, industrial, and urban society. Introductory essays to each section, as well as headnotes to each essay and contemporary sources, will point up these recurring themes and serve as guides to study. Although each of the six sections stands alone, there are threads of continuity that bind the entire volume together. By recognizing these unifying themes, the student will gain an appreciation of the broad sweep of history and will come to understand that history is much more than a confused congeries of disjointed events.

As the student reads these pages, he will quickly recognize that the many perplexing problems and issues confronting contemporary American society are deeply rooted in America's recent history. The past is but a prologue to the present, and the study of that past should enable him to view the present and future with the all-important perspectives that can be derived only from an intelligent understanding of history.

Several persons contributed substantially to the development of this volume. Our first acknowledgement must go to the authors and publishers who extended permission to reprint copyrighted material. We have also benefited from the many constructive suggestions made by our students. Several of our friends and colleagues offered a variety of useful opinions, and we are particularly grateful to Monte M. Poen (Northern Arizona University), Ernest B. Bader (Washburn University), Alonzo M. Hamby (Ohio University), and Richard M. Dalfiume (State University of New York at Binghampton). We are indebted to Professor Loren Baritz (Rochester University) for the numerous ideas that enabled us to improve immeasurably the variety and quality of our selections and saved us from many errors. We also thank our student assistants who relieved us of many time-consuming chores: Sandy Jones, Margaret Oursler, Richard Valentine, and Gary Emmanuel. Several members of the staff of John Wiley & Sons assisted us at every stage of production. William L. Gum, in particular, guided the project from start to finish with unfailing good humor and wise counsel. Appreciation is also due Sharon Davies for her encouragement and patient forebearance. Our greatest debt is to our teacher and friend, Richard S. Kirkendall, to whom this volume is dedicated.

Franklin D. Mitchell
Richard O. Davies

CONTENTS

AMERICA'S RECENT PAST

PART I

The Progressive Movement

THE final decades of the nineteenth century marked the emergence of a new America. Post-Civil War industrialization elevated the United States to prominence as the leading industrial power in the world. Mass immigration swelled and diversified the country's predominately old-stock Protestant population with the arrival of non-Protestant "new immigrants" from southern and eastern Europe. The swift settlement of the trans-Mississippi frontier and the growth of the cities in every section of the nation indicated both the passing of the old agrarian order and the coming ascendancy of the cities. A highly industrialized, ethnically diverse, and rapidly urbanizing society characterized the new America at the beginning of the twentieth century.

The transforming forces of industrialization, immigration, and urbanization altered in a profound way most aspects of national life. Large corporations, railroads, and banks wielded unprecedented power, much to the disadvantage of smaller and less powerful groups, and the still greater disadvantage of unorganized citizens. The proliferation of urban slums and grimy industrial yards outpaced the best efforts of planners and designers of the "city beautiful." At the same time the disparity between the rich and the poor clearly compromised the ideal of America as a land of opportunity and plenty. The ideal of equality and brotherhood was blemished, too, by the cultural antagonisms that existed among the old-stock Americans, new immigrants, and ethnic minorities. Government at all levels was marred by political corruption; more important, the machinery and structure of government were inadequate for solving the problems that had overwhelmed honest officials and private citizens. The long-accepted concepts of a competitive economy, individual self-reliance, and limited government, which had seem-

1

ingly worked well in an agrarian society, were no longer adequate guides for life in complex, modern America.

The reform responses to these and other conditions that confronted American society was the progressive movement. From about 1900 until the nation entered World War I in 1917, the reform spirit to make America over occupied the minds and hearts of millions as progressivism dominated political and social life. Progressivism, however, is not easily defined because of the diversity and complexity of the movement. The progressives themselves were a highly heterogeneous lot that included small-town gentry and the laboring classes of the city, farmers and urban professional classes, large and small businessmen. As might be expected from such diverse groups, progressives disagreed frequently over both reform methods and goals. Most reform-minded citizens resorted to political action for the solution of economic and social problems; others emphasized nonpolitical means of reform, such as education, to secure desired objectives. Ultimately, the progressives were determined to create orderly change—to reform, not revolutionize—American society. To this end they pursued three major lines of reform: public regulation and control of big business; the amelioration of social distress; and the democratization of government. Many of the reformers employed a variety of techniques to gain one—or a dozen—goals, and their arenas of action ranged from the small neighborhoods of countless cities to the national government in Washington.

The diversity of reform and reformers, as well as the paradoxical qualities of American life that called the progressive movement into being, was especially evident in the cities. Indeed, for the progressives, the city was both the hope and despair of America. Here could be found the efficient factory and the wretched slums; the corrupt political boss and nonpartisan civic reformers; the saloon and the settlement house. In the cities, corporation lawyers, bankers, railroad executives, and industrial magnates contended for power with reform-minded journalists, ministers, social workers, educators, and labor leaders. Some businessmen joined the ranks of the reformers and, occasionally, even a few pragmatic bosses felt compelled to throw their support behind progressive programs. During the first decade of the twentieth century, urban reformers, following the examples of Jane Addams of Chicago and Mayor Tom Johnson of Cleveland, produced meaningful housing, labor, and public health legislation and introduced Americans to the advantages of municipal ownership of such vital services as water, gas, electricity, and transportation. Thus it was in the cities that progressives first routed the persistent doctrine of laissez-faire. Many cities also adopted new forms of political organization in an attempt to modernize local government. City manager and commission forms of government won wide adoption in the progressives' search for honest and efficient urban government.

By 1910, the scope of progressivism embraced every section of the nation. In the forefront of the states was Wisconsin, elevated to national prominence by her energetic reform governor, Robert M. La Follette. When La Follette moved from the governorship to the United States Senate in 1906, Wisconsin had adopted such democratic reforms as the direct primary, antilobbying laws, corrupt practices legislation, and civil service. Railroads, corporations, and insurance companies all felt the power of state regulatory commissions and new tax laws. While the variety and vitality of progressivism in Wisconsin was never quite equalled by other states, reform elsewhere demonstrated convincingly that state government was receptive to experimentation and change and capable of providing social and economic services for all.

The Presidency of Theodore Roosevelt inaugurated progressivism at the federal level. In his first annual message to Congress in December of 1901, Roosevelt set forth an ambitious reform program; subsequent messages during his administration provided an agenda of reform not only for T.R., but supplied some ideas for his successors as well. Congress, dominated by "Old Guard" interests, did not do all that Roosevelt wanted, but before leaving office in 1909, T.R.'s legislative achievements included effective railroad rate regulation, a major conservation act, a federal meat inspection act, and a pure food and drug law.

Even more impressive accomplishments came in Roosevelt's vigorous assertion of presidential powers and his efforts to elevate the authority of the federal government over private business interests. His trust policy, essentially a program of federal regulation rather than "trust-busting," was formulated not only to curb the harmful practices of the supercorporations but also to make the federal government a neutral as well as the most powerful arbiter in the country. Presidential intervention in the anthracite coal strike of 1902 exemplified this policy by bringing the recalcitrant mine operators to the arbitration table; thus Roosevelt assisted the long-range trend toward the subordination of all special interests to the interests of the general public. The President capitalized further upon the power and prestige of his office to advance the cause of conservation in the White House Conference of 1908. All of these actions served to enhance and enlarge the powers of the Presidency, thus enabling the nation's Chief Executive to function more effectively in the interest of all the people.

The bold exercise of executive power by Roosevelt produced forceful, if not always effective, foreign policies. He won the Nobel Prize for Peace for his successful mediation of the Russo-Japanese War of 1904-5, and he arranged the Algeciras Conference in 1906, which ended the European crisis over Morocco, but both efforts left substantially unchanged the precarious balance of power in Asia and Europe. In Latin America, where he could employ the nation's naval power and financial resources effectively, Roosevelt acquired *supreme command*

treaty rights to build the Panama Canal and established hegemony over the weak and debt-ridden states of the Caribbean. In these ways Roosevelt and his successors, imbued with a belief in Anglo-Saxon superiority and the "white man's burden," sought to make the United States a world power and a "civilizing force" in the international arena. His willingness to use the "big stick," especially in Latin America, actually created much bitterness toward the United States, which would be mollified neither by William Howard Taft's "dollar diplomacy" nor Woodrow Wilson's moralistic interventionism in Mexico and the rest of the hemisphere.

The course of domestic reform during the Taft administration was characterized by a curious mixture of successes and failures. Congress responded to Taft's request for a strengthened Interstate Commerce Commission, with the passage of the Mann-Elkins Act of 1910. The ICC gained new rate-making powers over the railroads and, for the first time, brought the rates and services of telephone and telegraph companies under its purview. The federal government took on additional responsibilities with the establishment of a postal savings system and the Children's Bureau; labor gained an independent voice in the federal government when the Department of Labor was separated from the Department of Commerce. Taft's Attorney General initiated more antitrust suits than any of his predecessors and Taft, unlike Theodore Roosevelt, attempted to secure tariff reform through provisions of the Payne-Aldrich Tariff of 1909. Like T.R., Taft supported the conservation of natural resources; during his administration, several million acres of land were reserved for the public's future use. Political ineptitude and cautious reserve, however, marred Taft's performance in such vital matters as antitrust action, tariff legislation, and conservation policies, and he managed to alienate reformers in both parties. Insurgent Republicans were particularly unhappy with Taft's record of reform, and they persuaded the not-unwilling Roosevelt to seek the G.O.P. nomination in 1912. When the conservative Republican forces renominated Taft that year, Roosevelt led disgruntled progressives out of the convention to form the Progressive ("Bull Moose") party.

The presidential campaign of 1912 became a four-cornered contest with the candidacy of Socialist Eugene V. Debs. Taft and Debs received considerable support, but major interest was focused upon Roosevelt and the Democratic nominee, Woodrow Wilson. Proclaiming a program that he called the New Nationalism, Roosevelt advocated federal regulation of big business and comprehensive social justice benefits for deserving citizens. In contrast, Wilson advocated the New Freedom, a program designed to restore to the nation's expectant capitalists the condition of economic opportunity within a competitive framework. Wilson seemed to assume that his New Freedom would provide individuals the means of obtaining social and economic justice for themselves, thereby precluding the need for an elaborate social welfare program by the government; he conceded, however, that the government should assist individuals in their efforts to organize for collective action in the pursuit of social justice.

The New Freedom concept of reform came to the fore in the national government with Wilson's election triumph in 1912. A Democrat-controlled Congress, called into special session by the new President, responded to Wilson's call for legislation that would implement his program. In 1913, for the first time since the Civil War, the tariff was significantly lowered, and much-needed banking reform was accomplished with the establishment of the Federal Reserve System. Passage of the mild Clayton Antitrust Act and the creation of the Federal Trade Commission in 1914 rounded out Wilson's program of economic reform. Accordingly, in a letter to Secretary of the Treasury William G. McAdoo, Wilson publicly announced in November the fulfillment of the New Freedom.

Progressives of the New Nationalist school and advocates of social justice were swift to challenge the President's views, as they had opposed certain features of his New Freedom reforms. The advocates of a powerful trade commission, however much they liked the establishment of a federal agency to regulate business practices, were sorely disappointed when Wilson appointed conservative businessmen to that body. Progressives were also aghast at the probusiness representatives Wilson named to the Federal Reserve Board. Farm organizations that desired long-term rural credits, civil rights groups anxious to strike down segregation laws and practices, and suffragettes were angry and upset when the President steadfastly refused to embrace their program of advanced progressivism.

With the approach of the presidential election of 1916, however, a number of considerations moved Wilson to the left and more in step with the demands of the agrarians and social justice progressives. Wilson was confronted with the knowledge that a united Republican party, strengthened by the return of Roosevelt to the party fold, could overwhelm the Democrats and prevent him from obtaining a second term. Republicans at the time charged that expediency had brought about Wilson's conversion. Wilson's biographer, Arthur S. Link, has written that "nowhere did he come out and say that his desire to maintain the Democrats in power was responsible for the commitment he made to advanced progressivism in 1916." In any event, Link adds, Wilson "became almost a new political creature, and under his leadership, a Democratic Congress enacted the most sweeping and significant progressive legislation in the history of the country up to that time." That year Congress passed a rural credits bill, a child labor law, a measure granting legislative autonomy and a larger degree of administrative power to the Philippines, and an eight-hour day for railroad workers. Wilson could therefore boast in 1916 that the Democratic party had enacted nearly every major plank in the Progressive platform of 1912. When peace advocates and advanced progressives came to his support in the election, Wilson had behind him a Democratic coalition capable of returning him to office for another four years.

Presidential politics had given progressivism a new lease on life in 1916, but international events profoundly influenced the course of reform during Wilson's second administration. When Wilson asked Congress for a resolution of war against Germany on April 2, 1917, he indicated that progressivism would be translated into a broad international context to "make the world safe for democracy." The harnessing of the nation's economy for war production completed Wilson's shift to the policies of the New Nationalism as the government assumed an unprecedented amount of direct control over the basic industries, railroads, and farmers. The exigencies of war brought other reforms to fruition, giving progressives of the collectivist-democratic school reason at the time to regard favorably the prospects for democracy's advance.

Before the Armistice, however, these reformers were to assess the experience of war differently. Gradually they had come to view the war as a few unconvinced progressives and peace advocates had maintained all along: that war is the nemesis of reform. While the forces of progressivism had secured some of their goals during the European conflict, the war and the ill-fated peace conference released more powerful forces of reaction. An undercurrent of progressivism would survive, but conservatism replaced the reform spirit and was the dominant impulse of American society from the last years of Wilson's administration until the Presidency of Franklin D. Roosevelt.

Observers at the time, and since, have asked a crucial question about the progressive movement: was progressivism modern enough for the new America? While some reformers looked longingly to the past and regarded advanced progressivism as either inappropriate or inadequate for the America they envisioned, most believed that they had done much to make possible, through public and private action, the means for continued improvement of life in an urban-industrial society. Progressives generally took satisfaction in the fact that they had achieved a middle ground between the extremes of the radical left and the conservative right and thus had preserved both capitalism and democracy. To this end the liberal reformers relied upon government for the regulation of monopoly and the provision of social welfare programs within a capitalistic framework. Such measures as workmen's compensation, women and child labor laws, minimum wages for women, and old-age pensions stand as monuments to the labors of the social justice advocates. The credit for these reforms of the progressive years belong primarily to local and state governments; yet the passage of the Sixteenth Amendment in 1913—giving constitutional sanction for income tax legislation—made possible the future development of the welfare state by the federal government. "The modern democratic social service state," George Mowry has written, "probably rests more upon the income tax than upon any other single legislative act."

What the progressives did not accomplish through legislation was sometimes secured by exhortation. The rhetoric of reform, Richard Hofstadter has observed, motivated many businessmen to adopt a system of private welfare capitalism, in preference to the welfare programs secured by laws or by the efforts of workers fortunate enough to have the power of organized unions behind them. Consequently, many companies embarked upon a reform program that included such measures as factory safety, profit-sharing, group health and life insurance benefits, and even retirement plans. Thus the progressives' antibusiness rhetoric can not be dismissed lightly.

The record of the progressives in cultural liberalism is a checkered one; in some respects the promise of achievement was the only thing mitigating the actuality of neglect and intolerance in the area of human relations. Many progressives of old-stock Protestant, middle-class background, adhering to a set of illiberal and narrow cultural values, demonstrated their parochialism in the advocacy of prohibition and the restriction of immigration based on a system of discrimination against the non-Protestant new immigrants. Yet these middleclass reformers also discovered the poverty-stricken residents of urban slums and supported welfare programs that benefited old and new immigrant alike. Many social workers appreciated the value of Old World customs and traditions of the new immigrants and welcomed their contributions to American life. The newcomers, in addition to furthering the development of cultural liberalism through the practical and fine arts, were important in securing reforms that directly concerned their lives in the industrial cities; thus they helped to humanize the harsh and impersonal features of urban-industrial society.

The plight of black Americans during the era of reform actually worsened as evidenced by the record of lynching, disfranchisement, and segregation. White racism took its worst form in the South, but all sections of the country subjected the Negro to discrimination and injustice. The much-publicized visit of Booker T. Washington to the White House during the first administration of Theodore Roosevelt lost whatever value it had as a symbolic gesture of friendliness and goodwill when Roosevelt acted summarily in dismissing without honor three companies of Negro soldiers involved in a riot in 1906 at Brownsville, Texas. Roosevelt further alienated black Americans when he endorsed the "lily-white" policy of his southern supporters in the presidential campaign of 1912. Woodrow Wilson contributed further to the Negro's nadir during the progressive era by inaugurating the segregation of black federal employees in Washington. The newly formed National Association for the Advancement of Colored People protested Wilson's action, but to no avail.

The NAACP did, however, register some progress in its educational and legal campaign for the redress of racial injustice. *The Crisis*, the official monthly publication of the association, swiftly gained a circulation of 100,000 and, through the incisive editorials of W.E.B. DuBois and the articles of liberals, crusaded against lynching and mob law. The NAACP legal committee assailed the constitutional and legal barriers to equality and gained its first success in 1915 when the United States Supreme Court, in the case of *Guinn vs. United States*, struck down the grandfather clauses in the Maryland and Oklahoma constitutions. The slow advancement of racial minorities had begun, but given the scope and magnitude of the task—intensified and made more difficult by white progressives who were either ingrained conservatives or reactionaries on racial matters—it was the promise of progress, not the performance, that held some hope for the future.

The full significance of the progressive movement ranges beyond the years of its ascendancy, for the failures and successes of that period have had much influence on the liberal reform movements of subsequent years. The selections that constitute this section and other portions of this reader will allow the reader to probe deeply the nature and significance of modern liberal reform in America. For better or worse, the course charted by the progressives has been the main traveled road in our recent past. Has this made all the difference?

SECONDARY SOURCES

1. DEWEY W. GRANTHAM, "THE PROGRESSIVE ERA AND THE REFORM MOVEMENT"

IT is a truism that each generation writes its own history. The first comprehensive history of the progressive movement, Benjamin Parke De Witt's The Progressive Movement: A Non-Partisan, Comprehensive Discussion of Current Tendencies in

SOURCE. Dewey W. Grantham, "The Progressive Era and the Reform Movement," in *Mid-America*, Vol. 46, No. 4, October 1964, pp. 227–251. Copyright 1964 by Dewey W. Grantham. Reprinted by permission of the author.

American Politics, *clearly reflected the optimistic mood of the reformers. Writing near the end of the movement's forward thrust, De Witt had gained little perspective for a history of the recent past, but he enjoyed the advantage of a fresh recollection of the personalities and events then shaping human affairs. Contemporaries greeted De Witt's book with approval and, even today, his study provides a useful survey of the reform era.*

Less than a decade later, however, the journalist William Hard asked the readers of his column in The Nation *to assist him in formulating an answer to the question, "what is 'progressivism'?" The responses that Hard's question elicited reflected not only the changing course of progressivism since 1915, but also the broadened concerns and viewpoints of the respondents. The task of gaining an understanding of progressivism by the scholars of the Twenties was no simple undertaking; perhaps the most conclusive outcome of their labors was to show the complexity of the reform movement.*

The historical quest for an understanding of progressivism has continued to occupy the energies of scholars. Now almost fifty years removed in time from that era of reform, Dewey W. Grantham, Jr., Professor of History at Vanderbilt University, offers the following account of progressivism. Grantham cogently describes and analyzes the various reforms that constituted the progressive movement. Especially valuable is his assessment of the progressive temper, the assumptions of the reformers, the motivations that prompted reform action, and the movement's basic tendencies. His thoughtful conclusions point up progressivism's shortcomings as well as its relevance for later-day liberalism.

One of the most notable features of American scholarship during recent years is the attention being given to the so-called progressive period, an epoch in the nation's history which falls roughly into place between the tumultuous 1890's and American entry into war in 1917. For the student of recent America those years have an obvious meaning: they dominate the era in which the modern nation began to take shape on the basis of an industrialized economy, an urbanized and differentiated society, and an international power and prestige. But the great tides that caused the economic, social, and political currents in America to flow into their modern channels are not alone responsible for the historical significance of the progressive era. It stands out as a major period in the history of American reform. "Th' noise ye hear is not th' first gun iv a rivolution," said the inimitable Mr. Dooley to his friend Hennessy. "It's on'y th' people iv th' United States batin' a carpet." It is that "national housecleaning," that movement of searching inquiry and social amelioration, that gives the age its special meaning for so many students. To speak of the progressive movement is to speak of the spirit of an age, for, like Jacksonian democracy, it was extraordinarily diffuse in its origins, pervasive in its impact, and seminal in its heritage. *not developed, embryonic, rudimentary*

It is difficult if not impossible to define a movement which, according to the leading student of American progressivism, was nothing less than "a social quest . . . [that] attempted to find solutions for the amazing number of domestic and foreign problems spawned by the great industrial, urban, and population changes of the late nineteenth century."[1] The dominant character of this remarkably comprehensive effort will be revealed more clearly perhaps in the analysis that comprises the main part of this paper. In the meantime, it would be well to identify some of the more apparent attributes of progressivism in order to facilitate the description of its evolution. In the first place, the progressive movement was never recognizable as a distinct organization or single campaign. Despite the widely-shared and unifying principles that supported progressivism, it manifested itself in no single movement, political party, geographical section, or social class. As Thomas H. Greer has written, "Here was a social reform movement with no set leadership, no single platform, no disciplined organization, and no planned means of action."[2]

Secondly, nothing was more characteristic of progressivism than its ambivalent attitude toward the organizational revolution of this period. At heart the movement was a revolt against the new industrial discipline and, in the words of Richard Hofstadter, "the complaint of the unorganized against the consequences of organization."[3] But if the organizational revolution did much to call protest movements into being, it also became the vehicle for the adoption of innumerable reforms sought by one group or another. Reformers discovered that organization was the *sine qua non* in the realization of their hopes. At the same time businessmen, farmers, and industrial workers, combining in the interest of their own special economic and political well-being, frequently contributed to the attainment of "progressive" goals. The resentment and protest that inspired much of this organizational activity are important in any valid interpretation of the progressive movement. There was unquestionably a broad spirit of moderation in the progressive milieu, but we miss one of the principal operative elements in progressivism if we minimize the vigorous theme of protest that ran through the movement. One finds it everywhere—in the antimonopoly crusades, in the writings of the muckrakers, in the organization of the settlement houses, and in the formation of the Progressive party. If the progressives were conservative in many of their basic assumptions, they were nevertheless critics, and a note of indignant protest, of moral fervor, of radical expectations permeates the documents of the period.

A third tendency of the reform movement was the increasing resort to

[1] George E. Mowry, *The Era of Theodore Roosevelt, 1900–1912*, New York, 1958, p. xv.

[2] Thomas H. Greer, *American Social Reform Movements: Their Pattern Since 1865*, New York, 1949, 93.

[3] Richard Hofstadter, *The Age of Reform: From Bryan to F.D.R.*, New York, 1955, 214.

politics, to legislative and administrative solutions. Although the growth of a humanitarian spirit and the broadening quest for social justice revealed themselves in many private and nongovernmental areas, the most important issues of the progressive years almost always became focused as issues in the nation's politics. Legislation sometimes became so important as a means that it emerged as an end in itself, encouraging many Americans to believe that the passage of a law would automatically exorcise almost any social evil. Thus Henry Cabot Lodge, a conservative, warned on the floor of the Senate in 1910, against the propensity so widespread in the progressive period "to bring in laws for everything, for everything that happens, to try and find a remedy by passing a statute, and to overlook the fact that laws are made by men and that laws do not make men."

Finally, there was a tendency for most progressive crusades to develop into national crusades. As the period advanced, the nationalizing of reform efforts became more and more conspicuous. In part this was a concomitant of the organizational revolution and of a kind of multiplier effect resulting from the appeal of countless reform movements for the help of leaders, groups, and areas not immediately involved. It also reflected the peculiar nature of American federalism and the inability of reformers to deal with problems at the state and local levels. In its political phases the progressive movement influenced all facets of American politics more or less simultaneously, but its first notable impact was evident in municipal reform, then at the state level, and finally in national affairs.

Of all the problems that confronted Americans in the late nineteenth century, none was more acute than the breakdown of administrative efficiency and honest government in the great urban centers whose rise played such a vital role in the economic transformation of the nation. Swollen by the growing stream of native migrants and the arrival of millions of foreign immigrants, the American municipalities sought to employ the administrative machinery and the political practices of an earlier and simpler day to the problems of a new and complicated age. Even if the city governments had been administratively efficient and socially responsible, they would have been hard put to provide adequate transportation, police and fire protection, lighting and sanitation, and education, not to mention the difficulty of dealing with the problems of disease, congestion, vice, and poverty that hovered like a specter over the mushrooming slums. But the situation was complicated by the widespread existence of bribery, corruption, and crime that flourished as a result of the alliance between politics and privilege. Businessmen who wanted utility franchises and municipal contracts, vice operators who sought protection for illegal activities, and others who could afford to pay for special privileges or immunity from regulation or taxation dealt with a kind of "invisible government" that dominated many of the large cities. These municipalities had come under the control of "machines" which directed what Lincoln Steffens called "the System." Supported by patronage and loyalty, political bosses like Edward R. Butler of St. Louis had moved into the chaos of administrative inadequacy and archaic city government to rationalize politics to the advantage of political insiders and vested interests.

Steffens and other muckrakers during the early years of the twentieth century convincingly documented "the Shame of the City." The muckrakers were not the first, however, to publicize the urban problem. The defects and limitations of American municipal government began to receive national attention in the 1890's, with the appearance of serious articles on urban problems in popular and scholarly magazines and the organization of nonpartisan reform clubs and "good government" leagues in various cities. As George E. Mowry has pointed out, "At a time when Bryan and his grassrooted agrarian disciples were leading the national reform to defeat under the Democratic banner, these nonpartisan organizations were conducting a national campaign of education in street-corner politics."[4]

As a result of this campaign and the spectacular revelations of the muckrakers, the progressive movement at the municipal level was well under way by 1903. The campaign against "bossism" and special privilege, and the crusade to modernize and democratize local government were launched in city after city: Toledo, Cleveland, St. Louis, Minneapolis, Jersey City, Galveston, Memphis, San Francisco, and Los Angeles. In Toledo Samuel M. ("Golden Rule") Jones, following his election as mayor in 1897, repudiated the local machine and startled contemporaries by administering the city in accordance with his interpretation of the Golden Rule. He established an eight-hour day for municipal workers, introduced free kindergartens, and provided public playgrounds and free concerts. In St. Louis a fighting district attorney named Joseph W. Folk received nation-wide attention for his exposure of sensational scandals in that city. In Milwaukee a Socialist mayor was elected in 1910, initiating a long period of efficient and honest government in that municipality. And so it went all across the land.

The most famous of the municipal progressives was Tom L. Johnson, mayor of Cleveland from 1901 to 1909. A former street railroad magnate who had been influenced by reading Henry George's *Progress and Poverty*, Johnson attempted to equalize taxes, reduce streetcar fares, secure municipal ownership of public utilities, and obtain home rule for his city. Although he was prevented by state interference from carrying out all of these plans, he did much to publicize municipal problems, and under his administration and that of his successor Cleveland won a reputation as the best governed city in the United States. Johnson brought together a group of able and

---

[4] Mowry, *The Era of Theodore Roosevelt*, 61.

dedicated young reformers who saw in "the challenge of the city" not only a situation that demanded "social planning" but also a marvelous opportunity to revitalize American democracy. Wrote Frederic C. Howe in 1905:

The city is not only the problem of our civilization, it is the hope of the future. In the city democracy is awakening, it is beginning to assert itself. Here life is free and eager and countless agencies cooperate to create a warmer sympathy, a broader sense of responsibility, and a more intelligent political sense.[5]

The urban reformers did not always succeed in their efforts to destroy the power of political bosses and the corrupt influence of vested interests. Yet their accomplishments in this and in other respects were considerable. They were responsible for the first significant labor, housing, and public health legislation in the United States. The "battle with the slums" led to the introduction of housing reforms, community playgrounds, baby clinics, and juvenile courts. Pioneers like Judge Ben Lindsey of the Denver Juvenile Court were active along a broad municipal front in developing new practices in dealing with the problems of women, children, criminals, and unfortunates generally. Under the leadership of urban progressives the commission and city manager plans were adopted by hundreds of cities, home rule was provided by a dozen states, nonpartisan political tickets were approved, the merit system was extended, "gas and water socialism" was employed by some cities in supplying utilities, bureaus of municipal research were established, the public letting of contracts was instituted, and the direct primary and various types of direct democracy were adopted.

Almost all of the municipal progressives learned sooner or later that urban problems could not be completely solved at the local level. The local machines they fought were usually elements in a state "ring," and the lack of home rule made it possible for state legislatures and conservative courts to frustrate many municipal reforms. Furthermore, the public utility corporations were often too large and powerful to be regulated by the cities. Consequently, many of the city reformers moved on to the state level, and in the case of some states, among them California, the progressive movements at that level grew directly out of the drive for municipal reform. Such a reformer as Joseph W. Folk, who became the outstanding progressive governor of Missouri, first became a progressive while participating in a local reform movement.

Politics at the state level also reflected the pervasive influence of corruption and special privilege, undemocratic political machines, and inefficient and socially backward governments. Railroads and other powerful corporations allied with state machines dominated many state governments, and an

[5] From Howe's *The City: the Hope of Democracy* (1905), quoted in Otis Pease (ed.), *The Progressive Years: The Spirit and Achievement of American Reform*, New York, 1962, 48.

appalling system of bribery and "boodle" characterized much legislative and administrative action. Nominations for public office were usually made by party caucuses in which the voters had little influence. In the main, state governments approached the new social and economic problems in a spirit of conservatism and negativism.

In an effort to change this state of affairs the progressives proposed a program that contained three essential parts. Armed by a strong antipathy toward monopoly and a mounting distrust of the economic and political power wielded by large corporations, they sought to use the state to regulate railroads, insurance companies, and other giant business units. Believing that this could be accomplished only through a more representative politics, they attempted to broaden democracy and to make government more responsible and more efficient by introducing a variety of new democratic forms of government. Increasingly aware of the need for public action to insure greater social justice, they hoped to enact legislation for the benefit of workers, farmers, and other disadvantaged groups.

Although sporadic state reform movements such as those led by John Peter Altgeld of Illinois and Hazen S. Pingree of Michigan occasionally appeared in the 1890's, it was not until after the turn of the century that progressivism on the state level began to distinguish American politics. One of the first progressive leaders in state politics and unquestionably the outstanding representative of the type, was Robert M. La Follette of Wisconsin. A Republican, like many other midwestern reform leaders, he waged a long struggle against the conservatives in his party and the railroad and lumber interests with whom they were allied. After he finally won the governorship in 1900, he was twice re-elected before moving on to the national stage as a United States Senator in 1906. By that time he was convinced that to be genuinely effective the reform movement must be national in scope.

Nevertheless, La Follette had built up a strong machine of his own in Wisconsin, based on small farmers, urban workers, and middle class elements, and he had made the "Wisconsin Idea" what Theodore Roosevelt aptly described as "the laboratory of democracy," the leading example of state progressivism. Seeking to destroy the alliance between corporations and "the bosses," he secured the regulation of railroads, insurance companies, and other business enterprises. His administration reorganized the state's system of taxation; increased corporation taxes; enacted health, education, and agricultural legislation; created a conservation program; and secured legislation establishing a workmen's compensation system, the regulation of child labor, and other protection for workers. While making use of experts from the state university in planning and implementing these reforms, La Follette administered the state government along more democratic lines. A primary election system was inaugurated, and corrupt practices legislation and a civil service act were also added to the statute books.

During the half dozen years following 1906 the progressive movement at the state level entered its most vigorous stage. But the movement had begun in a number of states almost as early as La Follette introduced the "Wisconsin Idea." For example, Albert B. Cummins was elected governor of Iowa in 1901 on an anticorporation and low-tariff platform. During the next seven years he led the progressive forces in that state, before joining La Follette in the Senate. Joseph W. Folk was elected as a reform governor of Missouri in 1904, and in the same year John A. Johnson initiated a moderate reform program in Minnesota. In the years that followed the pattern of progressivism spread throughout the Midwest.

The pattern was not restricted to the Midwest, however. Regulatory campaigns achieved some success in New Hampshire and Vermont. In New York, Charles Evans Hughes was elected governor in 1906, because of his role in the investigation of scandalous corruption in the operation of the great insurance companies. Hughes was able to secure several important changes in New York's insurance laws, as well as a strong public utilities commission and other reforms. Under Woodrow Wilson's leadership in 1911–1912, New Jersey, notorious as a corporation stronghold, enacted a series of laws regulating corporations and enlarging the democracy of that state. A movement led by Hiram W. Johnson rescued California from the control of the Southern Pacific Railroad and reconstructed the state along progressive lines during the years 1910–1916. Several western states introduced electoral changes and new political devices such as the initiative and referendum during the late nineties and the early part of the new century. The leading advocate of direct democracy was William S. U'Ren of Oregon. Meanwhile, the pioneer use of the direct primary occurred in the South, and such southern states as North Carolina, Georgia, Alabama, and Texas had joined the progressive crusade for stronger railroad and insurance regulation, moral legislation, and other reforms.

By 1912 almost all of the states had had a progressive governor or at least a significant reform faction supporting this kind of state action. Many of the states had established vigorous utility commissions and had endeavored in numerous ways to regulate the rates and services of railroads and utility corporations, insurance companies, and financial institutions. Most of them had attempted to democratize and modernize their governments through the adoption of the primary system, antilobbying and corrupt practices laws, the short ballot, and civil service rules. The direct primary was being used in thirty-seven states by 1915, some form of the initiative and referendum had been ratified by twenty states by 1920, and woman suffrage had been provided by a dozen commonwealths by 1914. A majority of the states had compelled the popular choice of United States Senators well before the Seventeenth Amendment made their direct election mandatory throughout the nation. Several states adopted new constitutions during the progressive era, and hundreds of constitutional changes made by the states during this period served to increase the powers of the executive, to centralize administration, and to make government more responsible and more democratic.

By 1920 most of the states had instituted some kind of workmen's compensation, and legislation regulating the labor of women and children, wages and hours, and safety and health standards had been widely adopted despite strong judicial restraints. Embryonic programs in such areas as aid to dependent children and old age pensions had begun to appear. In addition, progressivism at the state level produced a host of measures providing agricultural aid, conservation laws, educational reforms, and prohibition. "So successful were the progressive leaders in the several states by 1912," writes Arthur S. Link,

that all observers agreed that a thoroughgoing revolution had been accomplished since 1900. In most states the power of the bipartisan machines had been shattered or else curtailed. State governments were more representative of the rank and file and more responsive to their economic and social needs. Even more important, moreover, was the fact that by 1912 progressivism had spread into the arena of national politics, subverted ancient party loyalties, and caused such a political commotion as the country had not seen since 1896.[6]

During the years 1906–1912, when the progressive movement among the states was reaching its peak, the movement at the national level was steadily gathering force. By 1912, when the national election revealed the vigor and breadth of the movement in a momentous national debate, many of the state and local progressives had moved on to Washington, either as political leaders in the national arena or as advocates of myriad good causes whose ultimate accomplishment now seemed to necessitate national action. The climax of the national movement came during the eventful administration of Woodrow Wilson.

The first progressive President was Theodore Roosevelt. Although he failed to achieve an impressive program of domestic reform, it was his leadership that brought the first significant political innovations and the first important regulation of the economic system. Widely acclaimed as a trustbuster, he sought through the Bureau of Corporations and in other ways to deal with the problem of economic monopoly at a more fundamental level. He contributed importantly to the introduction of effective national railroad control. He called for a "square deal" for labor, worked energetically for the conservation of natural resources, and successfully urged the passage of a meat inspection act and pure food and drug legislation. Withal, he was an excellent administrator and he did much to strengthen the Presidency. In 1912 he led a

---

[6] Arthur S. Link, *American Epoch: A History of the United States Since the 1890's*, New York, 1955, 88.

new party appropriately named the Progressive party. As President, Roosevelt's greatest contribution to progressivism was the way in which he publicized and dramatized the reform movement.

Meanwhile, William Jennings Bryan, who may rightfully be considered the first national progressive, was constantly agitating for more effective business regulation and the adoption of "anything that makes the government more democratic, more popular in form, anything that gives the people more control over the government." William Howard Taft, the amiable but politically inept successor to Roosevelt in the Presidency, continued some of the progressive reforms initiated under T.R. His administration launched ninety suits against large corporations and enacted more effective railroad regulation. But Taft could not prevent the disruption of his administration precipitated by the swelling tide of Republican insurgency and the bitter controversies surrounding such issues as the tariff and conservation.

With the Republican party in a shambles and progressivism a powerful if inchoate force in national politics, Woodrow Wilson quickly demonstrated his own right to lead the reformers. His administration brought the first real tariff reform since the Civil War, created the Federal Reserve System, enacted important anti-trust legislation, established a program to provide long-term agricultural credit, and enacted several significant labor laws. Wilson made his party a disciplined instrument for national reform, became the leader of "social justice" and advanced progressive groups, and brought together a progressive coalition that made possible his re-election in 1916.

Having outlined the course of the progressive movement in politics and indicated some of its accomplishments, it may be possible to reach some tentative conclusions about the movement's general character and philosophy. While it is impossible to explain so amorphous a phenomenon in a few generalizations, the essential elements of the progressive temper can be suggested. They include a faith in democracy, a concern for morality and social justice, an exuberant belief in progress, a susceptibility to the revelations of journalistic "truths" and the efficacy of education, a middle class and urban outlook, a quest for efficiency, and an entrepreneurial strain.

Typically, the progressive was a democrat, and the long arm of Jeffersonian democracy stretched across the generations to make him an ardent advocate of individual freedom, popular rights, private property, and equality of opportunity. In an age of organization and increasing social differentiation, progressives had an almost mystical faith in the collective good sense and fundamental decency of the "people." Believing in the fundamental goodness of man, the progressive reformers saw in the regenerated individual a moral agent and in public opinion a reflection of moral law. The way to rescue politics from the clutches of the "bosses" and purify it of corruption and special privilege was to "give the government back to the people!" This became a slogan and a rallying cry among the reformers, and it explains their infatuation with devices of direct democracy, with simplified forms of government and more popular participation as a means of revolutionizing public life.

To most progressives the problem of securing good government boiled down to the fundamental necessity of getting men of good moral character in politics. "If bad men control the nominations," declared Robert M. La Follette, "we cannot have good government. . . . The life principle of representative government is that those chosen to govern shall faithfully represent the governed." Yet, while urging an expansion of democracy and return of the government to the "people," the progressives could not trust the masses unreservedly. Social problems might be rooted in environment, but character was still of inestimable importance. All men were not of good moral character and the "people" could not always resist the blandishments of demagogues and sinister influences. It was best to rely on strong leaders of proven character and ability to point the way to progress. It was this attitude that led to the worship of strong leaders by the reformers. But there were also other factors. As Professor Mowry has written, "That worship of the unfettered individual, the strong pride of self, the strain of ambition, and the almost compulsive desire for power ran through progressive rhetoric like a theme in a symphony."[7]

Nor did the progressive as Jeffersonian exhaust the roles played by the early twentieth-century reformers. In fact, they undermined one of Jefferson's maxims, limited government. For, while seeking to broaden the base of democracy, they demanded an extension of governmental activities in many new areas. They did much to subvert the nineteenth-century tradition of laissez faire.

Progressivism also contained a strong moral flavor, a passion for righteousness, and much of the traditional humanitarian spirit. The campaign for "morality in politics" and the plea for new standards of honesty and justice in public and private life pointed up this attitude. Progressive leaders were usually moral crusaders and, like most of their followers, were strongly interested in "moral reforms." Indeed, many people first joined the progressive ranks as a part of antiliquor and antivice campaigns. Few reforms of the period open a more revealing window on the spirit and operative motif of progressivism than the drive for temperance and prohibition. It discloses the stress many progressives placed on conduct, on cultural conformity; it demonstrates the importance of organizations like the Women's Christian Temperance Union and the Anti-Saloon League in the triumph of reform; and it illustrates the growing resort to public policy to achieve

[7] Mowry, *The Era of Theodore Roosevelt*, 88.

moral reforms and the way in which such efforts moved steadily to the national level.

A kind of apocalyptic spirit permeated progressive thought. Life was a morality play. "Urban reform," writes Roy Lubove,

like abolition, was a great moral drama. In Act I the participants must become conscious of their personal guilt for the evils which surrounded them. In Act II this scene of guilt must merge with a conviction of personal responsibility for the eradication of evil. Act III would witness the transvaluation of values—consummation and salvation.[8]

These currents of thought owed a great deal to the institutionalization of humanitarian efforts. A widespread movement for social justice had been developing for decades. While often divorced from the movement for political reforms during the progressive era, this movement was of transcendent importance in creating the progressive milieu. Nothing revealed more plainly the stricken conscience of the middle class over the condition of the poor. The organization of large-scale philanthropy, the creation of state and national organizations, the establishment of settlement houses, and the professionalization of social workers were all part of this movement. Beginning in the neighborhood as charity workers and settlement house residents, the social workers moved on to the city and state levels, eventually organizing such nation-wide associations as the National Conference of Charities and Correction, the National Women's Trade Union League, the National Child Labor Association, and the National Consumers' League. The influence of women, who organized for their own emancipation and for the alleviation of problems in the church, the school, and the home, was of vital importance in the campaigns for child labor legislation, penal reform, and prohibition and other moral crusades.

The social reformers turned increasingly to investigations of the conditions of industrial employment and the need for the regulation of economic life, attacking child labor, seeking to protect women in industry, and urging the establishment of workmen's compensation systems. Emphasizing the environmental origin of social evils, the social justice movement pointed toward the eradication of such evils through men of good will—through the application of Christian principles in the solution of social "sins." "The under dog bothered us all," recalled William Allen White.

We were environmentalists. We believed faithfully that if we could only change the environment of the under dog, give him a decent kennel, wholesome food, regular

[8] Roy Lubove, "The Twentieth Century City: The Progressive as Municipal Reformer," MID-AMERICA, XLI (October, 1959), 206.

baths, properly directed exercise, cure his mange and abolish his fleas, and put him in the blue-ribbon class, all would be well.[9]

Closely allied with the secular crusade for social justice was an organized reform movement in the churches. Challenged by the new immigrants, the slums, and the "labor problem," which threatened to rend Protestantism apart, church leaders slowly began to apply Christianity to the new social problems. More and more of them decided that sin was not theological but sociological. The Social Gospel and the institutional church spread throughout most of the major Protestant denominations, profoundly altering the thrust of American Protestantism. Walter Rauschenbusch, an outstanding spokesman for the new social Christianity, once declared: "The purpose of all that Jesus said and did and hoped to do was always the social redemption of the entire life of the human race on earth." A new "church for the churchless," the Salvation Army, was dedicated to the social salvation of the slums and the urban dispossessed. American Catholicism also began, more slowly, to respond positively to the new social problems. As one Social Gospel leader put it, "Man is called in the providence of God to build on earth the city of God. There are no necessary evils. There are no insoluble problems. Whatever is wrong cannot be eternal, and whatever is right cannot be impossible."[10] The transformation of religious attitudes contributed a mighty force to the progressive movement.

Another component of the progressive impulse was an implicit belief in the onward and upward progress of man. So universal was this attitude that it may be doubted whether many Americans seriously questioned its validity during the progressive period: the whole history of the nation seemed to make it self-evident. Americans did not agree, of course, on the source or nature of progress. Some thought progress resulted from the discovery of natural law, others from the unrestrained competition of the economic system, and still others from a benevolent and purposeful God directing the human race. But, characteristically, the reformers steered clear of any automatic escalator to progress—progress was possible but it depended upon man's acting and thinking rationally, courageously, and in a spirit of social justice. The peculiar contribution of the American progressives was the way in which they humanized and broadened the meaning of progress. As Clarke A. Chambers has written,

To the eighteenth-century belief in man's rationality and goodness, and in the existence of an all-encompassing moral order, was added a nineteenth-century

---

[9] *The Autobiography of William Allen White*, New York, 1946, 389–390.

[10] Samuel Z. Batten, quoted in Clarke A. Chambers, "The Belief in Progress in Twentieth-Century America," *Journal of the History of Ideas*, XIX (April, 1958), 200.

romantic belief in the soundness and benevolence of man's emotions, and a Transcendental faith in his infinite perfectibility.[11]

Proud of the nation's accomplishments, the progressive was nevertheless disturbed by the apparent breakdown of moral standards, the rapid growth of centralization and power in American industry and finance, the new urban problems, the increasing disparities in wealth and class divisions, and the widespread existence of poverty and misfortune in the midst of agricultural and industrial plenty. Yet the bedrock of his confidence in the nation's continued progress was as solid as ever. "Implicit in the disgust which the Progressives felt for the corruption and power lust of the Gilded Age," observes Carl Degler, "and fundamental to the reforms which they advocated was a vague vision of what America should be."[12]

Some of the more advanced progressives were keenly aware of their role in pointing the way toward a radically new America. In its essence, however, the progressive movement was more a culmination than a beginning, and this was pre-eminently true in the case of the theoretical framework that supported the reformers' faith in progress. The creation of this framework had long been under way, and its creators included a numerous and diversified band: political philosophers, sociologists, and economists ranging from Henry George and Lester Frank Ward to J. Allen Smith and Charles A. Beard; spokesmen for the new liberal Protestant theology and the Social Gospel; and English liberals and German social scientists. The structure also owed a good deal to the very absence of a self-conscious ideology in the practice of social reform in America and to the example of European social democracy. Whether consciously or not, however, American progressivism developed an ideology of its own. In part it represented an assault on traditional authority, an attack on formalism, an effort to escape from a static and deterministic cosmology that gave man himself almost no part in the progress of the universe. The progressives steadily undermined the ancient truths associated with laissez faire, social Darwinism, and extreme individualism. Nor was that all. While destroying much of the old system based on determinism, they stood social Darwinism on its head and, using what Eric F. Goldman calls "Reform Darwinism," proceeded to place man in the center of a universe bounded by his own creative intelligence and good will. This progressive ideology rested less on Darwinian concepts and pragmatism, perhaps, than upon traditional postulates, but, in any case, it emphasized the efficacy of man's will, his capacity for rational behavior, and his instinct for co-operation and love.

[11] Chambers, "The Belief in Progress," 202.
[12] Carl N. Degler, *Out of Our Past: The Forces that Shaped Modern America*, New York, 1959, 368.

The work of the muckraking journalists in the years after 1902 is of central importance in any interpretation of the progressive movement. This is true not because the literature of protest and exposure led directly to the accomplishment of many progressive objectives, although it shocked millions of Americans into a greater awareness of the nation's problems, but rather because it reveals one of progressivism's most fundamental assumptions. "It is hardly an exaggeration," writes Richard Hofstadter, "to say that the Progressive mind was characteristically a journalistic mind, and that its characteristic contribution was that of the socially responsible reporter-reformer."[13] The vogue of muckraking revealed the public hunger for information, while apparently confirming some of the reformers' major suppositions. The muckrakers thought of themselves as "realists," and reality in their eyes and those of most reformers was concealed and distorted by the complexities of modern society, personal iniquities, and the manipulations of selfish interests. In the minds of many rural and sectionally-conscious Americans, these attitudes bordered on a kind of conspiracy theory, involving as they often did a suspicion of the uses of corporate power, of secret and corrupt destruction of competition, of subversion of democratic processes by special interests. If reality were exposed and the people were not denied their right to know, democracy could be restored and social evils remedied. "I was confident," recalled one progressive, ". . . that if we wrote truth enough, it would undoubtedly prevail . . . mind and facts would save the world."[14] When La Follette began a progressive magazine in 1909, he dedicated it, appropriately enough, with a quotation from St. John: "Ye shall know the Truth and the Truth shall make you free."

Implicit in these expressions was the progressives' faith in education. Indeed, the progressive mind was also an educator's mind and, as Lawrence A. Cremin has suggested, the mass school came to be viewed as "an adjunct to the mass press."[15] One of the central themes of many progressive reforms was social uplift through education.

The progressives borrowed many of their methods and some of their philosophy from the agrarian reform movement of the 1880's and 1890's. Their emphasis on the positive state, their antimonopoly bias, their advocacy of popular government, and their resort to politics as a means of dealing with economic and social problems were all reminiscent of Populism. There was certainly a relationship between Populist demands and progressive legislation. One can even detect a broad strain of progressivism, especially in the South and West, that carried over rather directly from agrarian radicalism.

[13] Hofstadter, *The Age of Reform*, 185.

[14] Frederic C. Howe, quoted in Judson A. Grenier, "Muckraking and the Muckrakers: An Historical Definition," *Journalism Quarterly*, XXXVII (Autumn, 1960), 556.

[15] Lawrence A. Cremin, *The Transformation of the School: Progressivism in American Education, 1876–1957*, New York, 1961, 89.

William Allen White once remarked that the progressive Republicans "caught the Populists in swimming and stole all their clothing except the frayed underdrawers of free silver." The progressives were bent on preserving traditional values, including many associated with an agrarian way of life, and progressive thought contained strong overtones of the agrarian myth, a yearning for an older, pastoral, and undifferentiated society. One side of progressivism feared and envied the city, distrusting the new urban proletariat and revealing a nativistic dislike of the unassimilated masses in the large cities. This attitude was not altogether absent even from those reformers who accepted the city on its own terms, as their emphasis on the process of Americanization reveals.

Nevertheless, the progressives were friendlier toward the city than were the Populists, closer to the industrial laborer and to the immigrant. Progressivism in general was characterized by an urban and middle class rather than a rural and agrarian outlook and leadership. Even in the more rural areas of the country, it was usually the urban middle classes—the lawyers, journalists, clergymen, teachers, and small businessmen—who dominated the reform movements. This does much to explain the larger movement's respectable and rather benign character. The settlement houses, the organizations for social workers, the feminists in the progressive ranks, the trade and labor movements, and the municipal reform crusaders all were centered in the city. Nor should the influence of the Yankee-Protestant ethos associated with the role of the middle class in the progressive movement be exaggerated. One can catch the first glimmer of an acceptance of a pluralistic society. Moreover, Joseph Huthmacher has recently shown that historians have overlooked the contributions to progressivism made by the non-Anglo-Saxon immigrant masses in the process of entering the stream of American mobility.[16] The city was for many progressives the major problem in civilization. Yet the progressives, as Roy Lubove has written, were "the first group in the American liberal tradition to embrace the city lovingly."[17]

One of the major problems that confronts the student of the progressive movement is how to account for the reform-mindedness of great sections of the middle class, of many wealthy men, and of numerous businessmen, who for the most part had been arrayed against progressive politics in the 1880's and 1890's. One answer obviously lies in the telling impact of humanitarianism. As William Allen White remembered:

Some way, into the hearts of the dominant middle class of this country, had come a sense that their civilization needed recasting, that their government had fallen into

[16] J. Joseph Huthmacher, "Urban Liberalism and the Age of Reform," *Mississippi Valley Historical Review*, XLIX (September, 1962), 231–241.

[17] Lubove, "The Twentieth Century City: The Progressive as Municipal Reformer," *loc. cit.*, 199.

the hands of self-seekers, that a new relation should be established between the haves and the have-nots, not primarily because the have-nots were loyal, humble, worthy and oppressed—Heaven knows we knew that the under dog had fleas, mange and a bad disposition—but rather because we felt that to bathe and feed the under dog would release the burden of injustice on our own conscience. We should do it even unto the least of these.[18]

Richard Hofstadter has argued that a "status revolution" was the principal factor in causing the spiritual descendants of the nineteenth-century Mugwumps to take up the cudgels for reform.[19] Although this explanation is not altogether satisfactory, it is clear that by the turn of the century a growing suspicion of corporate power and, sometimes, of labor organization was spreading rapidly through the broad reaches of the nation's middle classes. Professor Mowry sums it up in a paragraph full of insight:

Emotionally attached to the individual as a causative force and to an older America where he saw his group supreme, assaulted economically and socially from above and below, and yet eager for the wealth and the power that flowed from the new collectivism, the progressive was at once nostalgic, envious, fearful, and yet confident about the future. Fear and confidence together for a time inspired this middle-class group of supremely independent individuals with a class consciousness that perhaps exceeded that of any other group in the nation.[20]

They were eager to fill the role of mediators between the rich and the poor, eager to offer the standards of "culture," morality, and Americanism that would make for social harmony and progress. Furthermore, "the middle class" in America was so diffuse and so ill defined yet so central to the culture that it was almost a state of mind, a state of mind to be fought for and perpetuated.

The manner in which the urban reformers approached such things as specialization, the interdependent character of modern economic life, and the advantages of organization and co-operation suggests another aspect of the progressive rationale. This is what Samuel P. Hays has called "the gospel of efficiency." Although this emphasis sometimes came close to a kind of elitism and in its concern for social planning was far from being a universal desideratum among progressives, it was evident in some degree in almost every part of the movement. It was apparent in the effort to improve administrative efficiency at all levels of government; in the creation of public utility

[18] *The Autobiography of William Allen White*, 429.

[19] Hofstadter, *The Age of Reform*, 131–172. Hofstadter interprets progressivism as essentially genteel, proper, and safe. His concern for social background and social status leads to his emphasis on what he sees as an upheaval in status, and an element of psychological determinism. For a perceptive critique of Hofstadter's volume, see Andrew M. Scott, "The Progressive Era in Perspective," *Journal of Politics*, XXI, (November, 1959), 685–701.

[20] Mowry, *The Era of Theodore Roosevelt*, 103.

commissions staffed by experts and designed to develop modes of regulation and control based on scientific methods and factual data; in the movement for the conservation of natural resources; in the progressives' penchant for strong executive leadership; and in the general tendency to turn to the expert as a disinterested person who would divest himself of narrow class or parochial loyalties.

The gospel of efficiency (as well as such themes as democracy and social justice) frequently collided with another component of progressivism, its entrepreneurial strain. If many reforms during the progressive era grew out of middle and upper class humanitarianism, it is also true that numerous less privileged groups found in progressivism a means of economic, social, and political self-advancement. The movement reflected a strong nostalgia for economic individualism and a determination to maintain economic opportunity. La Follette, Bryan, Wilson, and Brandeis, among other national progressives, were bemused with the notion of restoring and regulating competition. Woodrow Wilson wanted "to set business free." "I am fighting," he once said, "not for the man who has made good, but for the man who is going to make good—the man who is knocking and fighting at the closed doors of opportunity." It was this attitude that led Theodore Roosevelt to assert in 1911 that half of the progressives "are really representative of a kind of rural toryism, which wishes to attempt the impossible task of returning to the economic conditions that obtained sixty years ago." And this was at the center of the ideological differences between the New Freedom and the New Nationalism. The more nationalistic progressives like Herbert Croly felt a strong revulsion for the unrestrained competition, the waste, and the undirected economic development which they saw portended in much of the progressive rhetoric and reform. Many of them were also repelled by grassroots movements of a "democratic" nature which were really given force by a hardy entrepreneurial desire to exploit resources and make their planned and efficient use impossible.[21]

Whether seeking to balance the economic scales, as was often true of farm and labor groups, or to achieve an advantage in the market place, as was

[21] Samuel P. Hays argues, in *Conservation and the Gospel of Efficiency: The Progressive Conservation Movement, 1890–1920*, Cambridge, 1959, that conservation was primarily a scientific movement, concerned with rational planning to promote the efficient development and use of all natural resources. He maintains that the conservation ideology stressed a theory of resource *ownership* when in fact the movement was primarily concerned with resource *use*. It was not, he insists, basically a great moral struggle between the virtuous "people" and the evil "interests." For a different interpretation that views the conservation movement as more concerned with social justice and democracy in the handling of resources than with the mere prevention of waste, see J. Leonard Bates, "Fulfilling American Democracy: The Conservation Movement, 1907 to 1921," *Mississippi Valley Historical Review*, XLIV (June, 1957), 29–57.

frequently the case with business organizations, the result in many instances contributed to the reform movement. There was a hard core of economic issues in much progressive legislation: the regulatory movement at all levels of government; tariff, banking, and tax laws; public ownership of utilities; conservation; and agricultural and labor legislation. Businessmen themselves, who differed enormously in size, economic function, and social attitude, often led in the movements for good government and efficiency, as well as in regulatory campaigns and petitions for governmental intervention designed to strengthen their special position in the political economy. Far from representing a monolithic obstacle in the path of reform, they supported the passage of many progressive measures and, ironically, encouraged the undermining of laissez faire and the drift toward political and administrative centralization.[22]

The relationship between economic struggles and the formulation of public policy during the progressive era helps explain the state and regional convolutions of the movement. For much of the legislative and administrative reform of the period resulted from the efforts of disadvantaged groups and areas to use public policy to enhance their competitive position. Thus local and state rivalries of an economic nature were directly involved in the establishment of strong railroad commissions, the passage of stringent insurance laws, and antitrust action which might be used to the advantage of the businessmen and farmers of a particular city or state. In the same way, the colonial character of certain regions contributed powerfully to the effort to use public policy, especially on the national level, to redress the balance by way of legislative restraints and state aid. This tendency may account, along with new economic forces, for the conservative reaction on the part of an advantaged region like New England toward many of the progressive measures designed to regulate the national economy.[23] As Samuel P. Hays has written, "Sectional economic conflict ran deep during the Progressive Era and produced widespread political repercussions."[24]

There were no doubt other important progressive tendencies, but this list should be sufficient to suggest the paradoxical nature of progressivism: its vitality but its lack of focus; its materialistic emphases but its humanistic achievements; its romanticism but its realism; its particularistic purposes but

---

[22] For an excellent treatment of the divisions among businessmen and their reactions toward reform movements, see Robert H. Wiebe, *Businessmen and Reform: A Study of the Progressive Movement*, Cambridge, 1962.

[23] This is the contention of Richard M. Abrams in a paper entitled "The Progressive Movement Considered as a Regional Struggle for Competitive Advantage: The Case of New England," which was read in Omaha at the annual meeting of the Mississippi Valley Historical Association on May 3, 1963.

[24] Samuel P. Hays, *The Response to Industrialism, 1885–1914*, Chicago, 1957, 116.

its nationalistic values. It should not be assumed that any one reformer during the progressive era reflected all of these impulses in his thought and action. The point is that each of these tendencies contributed in some measure to the currents of progressivism, and, taken collectively, they do much to explain the spirit of an age.

Historians have commonly assumed that World War I brought an end to the progressive movement. There is a good deal of truth in this interpretation, but it is not the whole truth. For one thing, the movement had begun to lose its momentum and direction well before 1917, and for reasons that had little or nothing to do with the war. One indication of this was the permanent injury to the reform elements in the Republican party caused by the party's disruption in 1912 and the rapid disintegration and discrediting of the Progressive party during the following four years. Of even greater importance was the fact that progressivism had seemingly achieved most of its goals by 1914, at least on the national level. Indeed, it has been suggested that the traditions, values, and ideals of "middle class" America had become so widely accepted by that time as to constitute "a kind of orthodoxy."[25]

Nevertheless, in many respects the war wrote an epitaph for progressivism. The issues surrounding neutrality, preparedness, and resort to war divided progressives, while involvement in the war itself blunted the force of the anti-corporation movement and other old progressive concerns. While the shift from domestic to international problems was sometimes viewed as a further enlargement of the movement for democracy and social justice (as a fulfillment of the "American mission"), and while many progressives were momentarily exhilarated by the social unity and exalted patriotism produced by the war effort, the end of the struggle brought further division, disappointment, and disillusionment. Wilson's remarkable progressive coalition of 1916 did not survive the war, being fragmented by the alienation of many liberals as well as key farm and labor groups. Furthermore, the middle ranks of American society were disturbed and often repelled by the militancy of organized labor during and after the war. Spiritually tired by the end of the war, many progressives were embittered by the crushing of civil liberties and the ruthless suppression of criticism and dissent, disheartened by the way in which Wilson seemed to compromise the war ideals at Versailles, profoundly shocked by the Red Scare of 1919–20, and appalled by the new age of materialism and cultural aridity that came after the Armistice. As one member of that generation recalled long afterward:

I grew up in an era where almost everyone believed in the golden virtues and also naively believed the whole world was progressing to a more complete acceptance of

[25] Walter I. Trattner, "Progressivism and World War I: A Reappraisal," MID-AMERICA, XLIV (July, 1961), 144.

them. Suddenly the invasion of Belgium and the submarine sinkings warned us that the cycle might be changing. We were, however, still romantic; we volunteered to "make the world safe for democracy"; the democracies did win the First World War. Then, mysteriously—so mysteriously that I still cannot grasp it—a wave or reaction set the stage for the dominance of the brutalizing forces.[26]

The war made it difficult to hold fast to the belief in man's capacity for rational behavior, in his instinct for co-operation and love, and in the inevitability of progress.

Yet progressivism did not entirely disappear from the American scene. It is true that some of these progressive remnants represented the repressive tendencies of the old Protestant drive for cultural conformity, and this was one reason many intellectuals and much of the new middle class were alienated from the reform movement. Prohibition, the anti-evolution crusade, and the moralism of the Ku Klux Klan caused many of these elements to question the wisdom of trying "to moralize private life through public action."[27] But there were other evidences of progressivism in the twenties. For one thing, there were some progressive accomplishments during the last two years of the Wilson administration, including the Transportation Act of 1920, a new child labor statute, water power and conservation legislation, and the constitutional amendments providing for prohibition and woman suffrage. Progressives continued to be influential in Congress, as is revealed in the farm legislation and tax measures of the early twenties and in the Muscle Shoals controversy and long fight throughout the decade over the public ownership or regulation of the rapidly developing electric power industry.[28] The progressives dominated the Federal Trade Commission until 1925.

The emphasis on positive government, even though directed largely toward the interests of the business class, was a far cry from the nineteenth-century tradition of laissez faire, and the public service concept of government embodied in progressivism manifested itself in many state administrations.[29] Meanwhile, there was considerable evidence of administrative reform

[26] John F. Wharton, "Speculations During a White Night," *Saturday Review*, April 6, 1963, 15.

[27] Hofstadter, *The Age of Reform*, 287. Prohibition in the 1920's, writes Hofstadter, "was the skeleton at the feast, a grim reminder of the moral frenzy that so many wished to forget, a ludicrous caricature of the reforming impulse, of the Yankee-Protestant notion that it is both possible and desirable to moralize private life through public action."

[28] For an extremely suggestive article on the relationship between the twenties and the progressive period, see Arthur S. Link, "What Happened to the Progressive Movement in the 1920's?" *American Historical Review*, LXIV (July, 1959), 833–851.

[29] George B. Tindall has demonstrated, for example, that certain of the old progressive tendencies, particularly efficiency and the public service concept of government, were perpetuated and greatly emphasized in the South during the 1920's. He shows that a

on the municipal level, and in the cities and states there was further progress in educational and welfare activities, transportation and recreational facilities, and certain types of labor benefits. Most of this represented a logical extension of the old progressive temper, even though some of the old assumptions had disappeared and some of the old purposes no longer had much potency. But several of the reformers who appeared in city and state politics—and occasionally in Congress—in the twenties were more characteristic of a new kind of reformism which in the thirties would be known as "liberalism."[30]

The Great Depression and the New Deal brought a vigorous revival of the reform movement in the United States. Its spirit and method differed to some extent from that of the progressive movement: it was more thorough-going in its intervention in the economy, more concerned with specific economic and social benefits, more engrossed with planning, less moralistic, and less optimistic. Progressivism, which dominated a relatively prosperous and decidedly hopeful age, represented a kind of voluntarism, while the New Deal, unfolding in the midst of the nation's most devastating depression, represented a kind of compulsory program. Yet in many important ways the extensions of progressivism that ran through the twenties became the headwaters of New Deal liberalism, and in its fundamental values and aspirations the reform movement of the 1930's was much like that of the progressive era. Many of the basic problems and proposed solutions of the New Deal years had had their first currency during the progressive period.

The progressive movement had its flaws, of course, and in some respects its failures were as monumental as its achievements. Not all bosses and machines were destroyed, and the new devices of democracy did not automatically bring more responsible office-holders, or produce better government, or make political manipulation impossible. The reformers were unable to secure the enactment of many of their proposals, and their laws frequently failed the test of administrative efficiency. They defined social justice too narrowly in traditional middle class terms, they could not bring themselves to encourage a strong labor movement, they had little to offer such agrarian elements as the southern sharecroppers, and their approach to alien minority

---

notable expansion of governmental activities occurred in the southern states during this period, featuring administrative reorganization, tax reforms, good roads, better schools, and expanded public health programs. "Business Progressivism: Southern Politics in the Twenties," *South Atlantic Quarterly*, LXII (Winter, 1963), 92–106.

[30] J. Joseph Huthmacher, in his excellent book *Massachusetts People and Politics, 1919–1933*, Cambridge, 1959, suggests how the emergence of a new frontier of American life—the urbanized, industrialized, and immigrantized Newer American civilization—was in some ways a continuation of progressive tendencies and also a powerful influence in the coalescing forces that supported the New Deal. The 1920's witnessed a transformation of Massachusetts politics that had its beginnings in the progressive era and became complete during the New Deal years.

groups and Negroes revealed the limitations of their social vision. And if many liberals of this period freed themselves from the restraining bonds of the old determinism, they often confronted a new dilemma in the moral relativism of an exaggerated environmentalism.

If the progressive movement was full of contradictions, if it attempted to straddle an era by looking both backward and forward, and if it failed to provide realistic answers to many problems of the day, it was nevertheless the first modern reform upsurge, the first comprehensive attempt by modern America to come to terms with the new economic and social realities. It is a mistake, moreover, to attribute the failures and limitations of progressivism entirely to the movement's inherent contradictions and narrowness of view. To dwell too exclusively on those aspects of the progressive movement is to minimize the very real distinctions between the progressives and their opponents. There were genuine and sharp differences of ideology and objectives among Americans during the progressive era. There was a widespread and vigorous conservative movement during the progressive years, and while it was often as divided and as amorphous as progressivism itself, it revealed itself in a fairly clear-cut fashion in almost every reform campaign of the period.

The most important thing about the progressive movement was that it formulated a broad range of social ideals that transcended particularistic interests. Time has shown that some of the naive assumptions of the progressives were ill-founded, and in practice several of their fondest reforms have produced results that would have shocked their original champions. But if part of progressivism has become anachronistic in our own day, a substantial part of progressive thought has demonstrated a long-time relevance in the history of twentieth-century American reform.

2. J. JOSEPH HUTHMACHER, "URBAN LIBERALISM AND THE AGE OF REFORM"

FOR many years the standard interpretation of the origins of progressivism was that advanced by those historians who looked to the American frontier experience as the prime molder of this nation's democratic institutions. Accordingly, the Presidency of Andrew Jackson was seen as the logical culmination of those frontier forces that had emancipated

SOURCE. J. Joseph Huthmacher, "Urban Liberalism and the Age of Reform," in the *Mississippi Valley Historical Review*, Vol. XLIX, September 1962, pp. 231–241. Copyright 1962 by the Organization of American Historians. Reprinted by permission of the *Journal of American History* and the author.

the common man and had given rise to American democracy. The post-Civil War agrarian reform crusades provided further evidence that the egalitarian spirit sprang from the soil of rural America. In this light, the farmers are the intellectual godfathers of twentieth-century political and economic reform.

Challenging this interpretation has been a growing number of historians who believe that progressivism owes little to the agrarian reformers. Instead, they emphasize the contribution of the city to modern-day reform. These urban-oriented scholars, however, have disagreed among themselves as to the leadership and support of progressivism. Historians George Mowry and Richard Hofstadter, in particular, have singled out the urban middle class as the main force of the progressive movement. The urban gentry, these historians contend, feared and resented the status, power, and values of labor leaders, political bosses, and captains of industry. Thus they were motivated to undertake reforms that would restore the middle class to the position they had formerly enjoyed in society.

J. Joseph Huthmacher, Professor of History at Rutgers University, drawing upon his investigation of the so-called "new immigrant" in Massachusetts and New York during the first three decades of the twentieth century, dissents from the "middle class" interpretation of progressivism. The evidence, Huthmacher argues, "suggests that the triumphs of modern liberalism in the Progressive Era, and in subsequent eras, were owed to something more than a strictly middle-class dynamism. It indicates that the urban lower class provided an active, numerically strong, and politically necessary force for reform and that this class was perhaps as important in determining the course of American liberalism as the urban-middle class. . . ." His essay demonstrates the diversity and sometimes contradictory impulses of progressivism and points toward some of the still unexplored aspects of modern liberalism.

Most historians of twentieth-century America would agree that the effective beginnings of the present-day "people's capitalism"—the present-day liberalism—can be traced back to the Progressive Era. And most of them would agree that the essential ingredient which made possible the practical achievement of reforms at that time was the support given by city dwellers who, at the turn of the century, swung behind reform movements in large numbers for the first time since America's rush into industrialism following the Civil War. True, the Populists and other agrarian radicals had done spadework on behalf of various proposals in the late nineteenth century, such as trust regulation, the income tax, and direct election of senators. But their efforts had gone unrewarded, or had been frustrated by enactment of half-way measures. Not until the reform spirit had seized large numbers of urbanites could there be hope of achieving meaningful political, economic, and social adjustments to the demands of the new industrial civilization.

Between 1900 and 1920 American statute books became studded with the results of urban-oriented reform drives. The direct primary, the initiative, the Seventeenth Amendment; the Clayton Act, a revived Interstate Commerce Commission, and the Federal Trade Commission; workmen's compensation, child labor laws, and Prohibition—these and many other achievements testified to the intensity of Progressivism. It is admitted, of course, that not everything done in the name of reform was desirable. Some measures, notably Prohibition, are counted today as being wrong-headed, while some political panaceas like the direct primary elicited an undue degree of optimism on the part of their exponents. Nevertheless, the Progressive Era did witness America's first modern reform upsurge, and much of substantial worth was accomplished. Moreover, it established patterns and precedents for the further evolution of American liberalism, an evolution whose later milestones would bear the markings "New Deal" and "New Frontier."

In accounting for the genesis and success of urban liberalism in the Progressive Era, however, the historians who have dominated its study thus far have concentrated on one population element, the urban middle class, and its Yankee-Protestant system of values. "The great majority of the reformers came from the 'solid middle class,' " Professor George E. Mowry tells us. "If names mean anything, an overwhelming proportion of this reform group came from old American stock with British origins consistently indicated." Professor Richard Hofstadter adds that "the key words of Progressivism were terms like *patriotism, citizen, democracy, law, character, conscience . . .* terms redolent of the sturdy Protestant Anglo-Saxon moral and intellectual roots of the Progressive uprising."[1] The component parts of this amorphous middle class, and the reasons for their new interest in reform at the turn of the century, have been described by various scholars.[2] We have been told about the "white collar" group which saw, in the increasing bureaucratization of big business, the blotting out of its traditional belief in the American "rags to riches" legend. Some writers have dwelt upon the middle-class intellectuals —writers, publicists, ministers, college women, professors—who, in response to changing patterns of social thought represented by the rise of "realism" in literature, religion, and the social sciences, determined to uplift the living conditions of their less fortunate brothers. Others have examined the "Old Aristocracy" threatened by a "status revolution," and fighting to maintain the degree of deference that had been theirs before the rise of the newly rich moguls of business and finance.

Imbued with this mixture of selfish and altruistic motives, reinforced by

[1] George E. Mowry, *The Era of Theodore Roosevelt, 1900–1912* (New York, 1958), 86; Richard Hofstadter, *The Age of Reform* (New York, 1955), 318.

[2] Mowry, *Era of Theodore Roosevelt;* Hofstadter, *Age of Reform;* C. Wright Mills, *White Collar* (New York, 1951); Eric Goldman, *Rendezvous with Destiny* (New York, 1952); Samuel P. Hays, *The Response to Industrialism, 1885–1914* (Chicago, 1957).

the pocketbook-pinching price inflation that got under way in 1897, the urban middle-class reformers set out to right the wrongs of their society. They introduced a variety of new democratic techniques into our political mechanics, in an attempt to break the grip of the corrupt bosses who manipulated irresponsible immigrant voters and unscrupulous businessmen in ways that subverted good government. They augmented the government's role as watchdog over the economy, either to maintain the traditional "small business" regime of competitive free enterprise, or at least to make sure that oligopolists passed on to consumers the benefits of large-scale operation. Through the activities of their philanthropic organizations, coupled with support of paternalistic labor and social welfare legislation, the middle-class reformers also sought to uplift the standards of the alien, slum-dwelling, urban working class to something more closely approximating the Yankee-Protestant ideal. So runs the "middle-class" interpretation of Progressivism, an interpretation which has set the fashion, by and large, for scholarly work on the subject.

There is no doubt, of course, that discontented elements among the urban middle class contributed much to Progressivism, or that the historians who have explored their contributions and their motives deserve the plaudits of the profession. Nevertheless, it may be pertinent to ask whether these historians have not overstressed the role of middle-class reformers, to the neglect or exclusion of other elements—such as organized labor—who have had something to do with the course of modern American liberalism.[3] More particularly, a number of circumstances call into question the assertion that "In politics . . . the immigrant was usually at odds with the reform aspirations of the American Progressive."[4] If such were the case, how does one explain the drive and success of Progressive Era reform movements in places like New York and Massachusetts—states that were heavily populated with non-Protestant, non-Anglo-Saxon immigrants and sons of immigrants? How could reformers succeed at the polls or in the legislatures in such states if, "Together with the native conservative and the politically indifferent, the immigrants formed a potent mass that limited the range and the achievements of Progressivism"?[5] Moreover, how does one explain the support which individuals like Al Smith, Robert F. Wagner, James A. Foley, James Michael

[3] The suggestions made in this and the following paragraphs stem primarily from the author's research for *Massachusetts People and Politics, 1919–1933* (Cambridge, Mass., 1959), and for a projected biography of Senator Robert F. Wagner of New York. Senator Wagner's papers are deposited at Georgetown University, Washington, D.C.

[4] Hofstadter, *Age of Reform*, 180–81. It is clear, of course, that Professor Hofstadter is referring not only to the first-generation immigrants themselves, but to the whole society which they, their offspring, and their culture were creating within our industrial, urban maze.

[5] *Ibid.*, 181.

Curley, and David I. Walsh gave to a large variety of so-called Progressive measures in their respective office-holding capacities?[6] Surely these men do not conform to the middle-class, Yankee-Protestant "Progressive Profile" as etched by Professor Mowry.[7]

If the Progressive Era is to be considered a manifestation of the Yankee-Protestant ethos almost exclusively, how does one explain the fact that in the legislatures of New York and Massachusetts many reform bills received more uniform and consistent support from representatives of the urban lower class than they received from the urban middle-class or rural representatives? Some of the most effective middle-class reformers, such as social worker Frances Perkins, realized this fact at the time and charted their legislative strategy accordingly.[8] It may be pointed out also that, even when submitted to popular referendums, typically Progressive measures sometimes received more overwhelming support in the melting-pot wards than they received in the middle-class or rural constituencies. This was the case, for example, in Massachusetts when, in 1918, the voters passed upon a proposed initiative and referendum amendment to the state constitution. Such circumstances become especially compelling when we remember that reform measures, no matter how well formulated and publicized by intellectuals, cannot become effective in a democracy without skillful political generalship and—even more important—votes.

Marshaled together, then, the foregoing evidence suggests that the triumphs of modern liberalism in the Progressive Era, and in subsequent reform eras, were owed to something more than a strictly middle-class dynamism. It indicates that the urban lower class provided an active, numerically strong, and politically necessary force for reform—and that this class was perhaps as important in determining the course of American liberalism as the urban middle class, about which so much has been written.

Today's liberals look to the "northern" Democrats and the "eastern"

[6] Oscar Handlin, *Al Smith and His America* (Boston, 1958); Joseph F. Dinneen, *The Purple Shamrock: The Honorable James Michael Curley of Boston* (New York, 1949); Dorothy G. Wayman, *David I. Walsh: Citizen Patriot* (Milwaukee, 1952). See also Arthur Mann, *La Guardia: A Fighter against His Times* (Philadelphia, 1959). Among the measures which Robert F. Wagner introduced as a New York state senator between 1909 and 1918 were the following: a bill to provide for direct election of United States senators; a bill to authorize a twenty million dollar bond issue for conservation and public development of state water power; a direct primary bill; a short-ballot bill; a resolution to ratify the federal income tax amendment; a bill establishing the Factory Investigating Commission; a civil rights bill; a woman suffrage amendment to the state constitution; numerous bills for child labor regulation; a bill to extend home rule to municipalities; a bill to establish a minimum wage commission for women; a bill limiting the issuance of labor injunctions; a bill to authorize municipal ownership of power plants; and a corrupt practices bill.

[7] Mowry, *Era of Theodore Roosevelt*, chap. 5.

[8] Frances Perkins, *The Roosevelt I Knew* (New York, 1946), 12–26.

Republicans—those whose elections are due largely to the votes of the urban working class—for support of their proposals. If, as is contended, this phenomenon of urban lower-class liberalism can be traced back beyond the election of 1960, beyond the New Deal, and to the Progressive Era, then the probing of its chronological origins and the operational details of its emergence present wide fields for fruitful research. In the process of such studies, many other questions will present themselves to the investigator. What were the sources of lower-class interest in reform? How did its sources affect its nature, specific content, and practical effects? How, if at all, did urban lower-class liberalism differ in these respects from urban middle-class liberalism? At the risk of premature generalization, tentative suggestions, indicated by research thus far conducted, may be set forth regarding these matters.

The great source of urban working-class liberalism was experience. Unlike the middle-class reformers, who generally relied on muckrakers, Social Gospelers, and social scientists to delineate the ills of society, the urban working class knew at first hand the conditions of life on "the other side of the tracks." Its members and spokesmen grew to manhood "in the midst of alternately shivering and sweltering humanity in ancient rat-infested rookeries in the swarming, anonymous, polyglot East Side, an international center before the U.N. was dreamed of," where "souls and bodies were saved by the parish priest, the family doctor, and the local political saloonkeeper and boss who knew everyone and was the link between the exploited immigrant and the incomprehensible, distant law."[9] Such people were less imbued than the middle class with the "old American creed" which expounded individualism, competition, and laissez-faire free enterprise as the means of advance from "rags to riches." Their felt needs, largely of the bread and butter type, were of the here and now, and not of the middle-class variety which fastened upon further advancement to a higher station from one already fairly comfortable. Moreover, their constant immersion in the depths of human misery and frailty, and the semi-pessimistic nature of their religious psychology, limited their hopes for environmental improvement within the bounds of reasonable expectation. Their outlook tended to be more practical and "possibilistic" than that of some middle-class Progressives who allowed their reform aspirations to soar to Utopian heights, envisaging a "Kingdom of God on Earth" or a perfect society to be achieved by means of sociological test tubes. Finally, the previous political experience of the immigrant workers, centering about their security-oriented relations with a paternalistic ward boss, conditioned them to transfer the same functional conception to the city, state, and national governments as they became

[9] Robert Moses, "Salute to an East Side Boy Named Smith," *New York Times Magazine* (October 8, 1961), 113.

progressively aware of their ability, through their voting power, to make those governing bodies serve their needs. Consequently, their view of government was much less permeated with fears of paternalism and centralization than that of traditionally individualistic middle-class reformers, many of whom abated their attachment to the laissez-faire principle with only the greatest trepidation.[10]

The influence of these conditioning factors seems clearly discernible in the specific types of reform programs to which the urban lower class and its spokesmen lent greatest support. It is commonplace to say, for example, that the immigrants were not interested in political machinery reforms simply as reforms. Unlike the remaining middle-class "genteel reformers," they did not look upon political tinkering as the be-all and end-all of reform. Yet it is an injustice to imply that the immigrants' attitude on this matter was due to an inherent inability to comprehend the Yankee-Protestant concept of political behavior, and that they were therefore immune to all proposals for political reform. These lower-class voters seemed willing enough to support specific proposals which would enable them to secure the voice necessary to satisfy their economic and social needs, recognizing, quite properly, that the latter were the real sources of society's maladjustment. Since the rural areas of Massachusetts generally controlled the Bay State legislature, the urban working class supported the initiative and referendum amendment which might enable them to by-pass tight-fisted rural solons. Since the same situation prevailed in the New York legislature, the New York City delegation was glad to secure popular election of United States senators. In brief, it would seem that the line-up on such questions depended more upon local conditions of practical politics than upon the workings of a Yankee-Protestant ethos.

In the realm of economic reform, pertaining particularly to the problem of "big business," indications are that the urban lower class tended—unwittingly, of course—to favor the "New Nationalism" approach of Herbert Croly and Theodore Roosevelt over the "New Freedom" of Wilson and the trust-busters. Its members had seldom experienced the white collar group's "office boy to bank president" phenomenon themselves. They had never been part of the "Old Aristocracy," and hence had not suffered a downward revision in status at the hands of big business moguls. They shared few of the aspirations of the industrial "small businessman" and, indeed, recognized that the latter was all too frequently identified with sweatshop conditions. Consequently, the urban lower class was little stirred by Wilsonian cries to give the "pygmies" a chance. To workers the relative size of the employer's establishment was quite immaterial so long as he provided job security and adequate wages and working conditions, and passed some of the benefits of large-scale production on to consumers in the form of lower prices. Governmental stabilization of the

[10] See Hofstadter, *Age of Reform*, chap. 6.

economy and regulation of big business might well prove more successful in guaranteeing these conditions than would government antitrust drives. As a result, we find urban lower-class representatives introducing a large variety of business regulatory measures on the local and state levels during the Progressive Era. And it is symbolic, perhaps, to find Senator Robert F. Wagner introducing the National Industrial Recovery Act in 1933, while Senator David I. Walsh of Massachusetts had sponsored somewhat similar, forerunner, measures in Congress during the 1920's.

What has been said above indicates the basis for urban lower-class interest in the many types of social welfare and labor measures which became novelties, and then commonplace enactments, during the Progressive Era. If the middle class faced the fear of insecurity of status, then the working class faced an equally compelling fear of insecurity of livelihood and living conditions. The precarious condition of the lower class had now become known even to those on the better side of the tracks and, partly for humanitarian reasons and partly to defend their own civilization against a "revolution from below," middle-class reformers had become interested in social justice movements —which involved "doing things for others." But the recipients of this benevolence might surely be expected to show at least an equal interest in such movements—which involved doing something for themselves. That such was the case is clearly indicated by study of the legislative history of measures like workmen's compensation, widows' pensions, wages and hours legislation, factory safety legislation, and tenement laws in the legislatures of New York and Massachusetts during the Progressive years. The representatives of lower-class constituencies were the most active legislative sponsors and backers of such bills and, in collaboration with middle-class propagandists and lobbyists, they achieved a record of enactments which embraced much of the best and most enduring part of the Progressive Era's heritage.

The operations of the New York State Factory Investigating Commission are a case in point. Established by the legislature following the tragic Triangle Shirtwaist Company fire in 1911, the Commission recommended and secured passage of over fifty labor laws during the next four years, providing a model factory code that was widely copied in other states. The Commission's most active legislative members were State Senator Robert F. Wagner and Assemblyman Alfred E. Smith, two products of the East Side, while its most effective investigator and lobbyist was Miss Frances Perkins, a middle-class, college trained social worker. (It should be noted also that the Commission received notable assistance from Samuel Gompers and other leaders of organized labor.) Again it is rather striking to observe that the Social Security Act of 1935, which began the transfer of industrial security matters from the state to the national level, was introduced by Senator Wagner, to be administered by a federal Department of Labor headed by Miss Perkins.

Effective social reform during the Progressive Era, and in later periods, seems thus to have depended upon constructive collaboration, on specific issues, between reformers from both the urban lower class and the urban middle class (with the further co-operation, at times, of organized labor). Of course, such co-operation could not be attained on all proposals that went under the name of social "reform." When, during the Progressive Era, certain old-stock, Protestant, middle-class reformers decided that the cure for social evils lay not only in environmental reforms, but necessitated also a forcible "uplifting" of the lower-class immigrants' cultural and behavior standards to "100 per cent American" levels, the parting of the ways came. Lower-class reform spokesmen had no use for compulsory "Americanization" through Prohibition, the closing of parochial schools, or the enforcement of puritanical "blue laws." Nor had they any use for immigration restriction laws which were based upon invidious, quasi-racist distinctions between allegedly "superior" and "inferior" nationality stocks.[11] To them reform, in so far as the use of government compulsion was concerned, was a matter of environment. The fundamentals of a man's cultural luggage—his religion, his emotional attachment to his "old country" and its customs, his habits and personal behavior—were of concern to himself and his God, and to them alone. The lower-class reformers were products of the melting pot, and most of them took seriously the inscription on the base of the famous statue in New York harbor. True, there were many religious and ethnic differences among the component elements of the lower class, which often resulted in prejudice and violence. But each of these elements resented the Old Stock's contention that all of them were equally inferior to the "real Americans" of Yankee-Protestant heritage, and they resisted the attempts, which grew as the Progressive Era wore on, to enforce conformity to a single cultural norm.

In so far as conformity-seeking "cultural" reforms were enacted in the Progressive years, then, the responsibility must be assigned to urban middle-class reformers, joined in this instance by their rural "bible belt" brethren. The lower class can share no part of the "credit" for reforms like Prohibition. But in resisting such movements, were they not waging an early fight on behalf of what we today call "cultural pluralism"—acceptance of which has become a cardinal tenet in the standard definition of "liberalism" in the modern world? Indeed, it may not be too much to say that in all three fields of

[11] "If the literacy test was not applied to the Irish and the German, why should it now be applied to the Jew, the Italian or the Slav of the new immigration? Like our ancestors, they are now flying from persecution, from ignorance, from inequality; like our ancestors they expect to find here freedom and equal opportunity. Are we going to deny them an equal opportunity? Are we going to withhold from them the equality and opportunities which our fathers enjoyed?" (Excerpt from a speech by Robert F. Wagner in the New York State Senate, on a resolution which he introduced in 1917 petitioning Congress not to pass the literacy test bill. Wagner Papers.)

reform—the political and economic, as well as the social—indications are that the urban lower-class approach was more uniformly "advanced" than that of the middle class, in the sense of being more in line with what has become the predominant liberal faith in modern America. After all, does not the lower-class reform impulse, as outlined above, resemble the "hard-headed," realistic, and pluralistic liberalism for which spokesmen like Reinhold Niebuhr and Arthur Schlesinger, Jr., plead today, so that the "Children of Light" might not fall easy prey to the "Children of Darkness"?[12]

It is not contended, of course, that all members of the urban working class became interested in reform during the Progressive Era, any more than it can be contended that all members of the urban middle class did so. The same "sidewalks of New York" that produced Al Smith and Robert Wagner continued to produce their share of "unreconstructed" machine politicians, whose vision never rose above their own pockets. Nor is it argued that the nature and zeal of lower-class attachment to liberalism remained constant throughout the twentieth century, or that the degree of co-operation attained with other reform minded elements remained unchanging. In the 1920's, for example, mutual suspicion and distrust, based largely on ethnic or "cultural" differences, seem to have displaced the former mood of limited collaboration between lower- and middle-class spokesmen, and in these changed circumstances Progressive-type measures found little chance of enactment. It is also possible that the high level of general prosperity prevailing since 1941 has vitiated urban working-class devotion to economic reform, and that the increasing degree of acceptance enjoyed by ethnic elements formerly discriminated against is causing their members to forget the lessons of cultural pluralism. All of these matters deserve further study.

The last-mentioned problems, dealing with the contemporary scene, may lie more properly within the realm of the political scientist and sociologist. But surely the evolution of America's twentieth-century liberal society, from the Progressive Era through the New Deal, is a province for historical inquiry. It is suggested that the historians who enter it might do better if they modify the "middle-class" emphasis which has come to dominate the field and devote more attention to exploring hitherto neglected elements of the American social structure. Such exploration necessitates tedious research, focusing at first on the local and state levels, in unalluring source materials such as local and foreign-language newspapers, out-of-the-way manuscript collections, and the correlations between the make-up and voting records of small-scale election districts. In the course of this research, however, our conception of the Progressive Era, and of recent American history as a whole, may undergo

[12] See, for example, Reinhold Niebuhr, *The Children of Light and the Children of Darkness* (New York, 1945); Arthur M. Schlesinger, Jr., *The Vital Center* (Boston, 1949).

change. In fact, it may even begin to appear that "old-fashioned" political historians, if they inform their work with up-to-date statistical and social science skills, still have as much to contribute to our knowledge of ourselves as do the intellectual and social historians, who are, perhaps, sometimes prone to over-generalize on the basis of historical psychoanalysis.

3. GABRIEL KOLKO, "THE LOST DEMOCRACY"

JUST how progressive was the progressive movement? Most scholars writing about the reform movement of the Roosevelt, Taft, and Wilson years have concluded that progressivism was a brilliant chapter in twentieth-century liberalism. Some historians have pointed out, however, that alteration and modification of basic economic and political institutions can be essentially conservative. Because the progressives actually preserved capitalism and democracy by correcting some of the defects in these systems, a few scholars are now arguing that progressivism was a "triumph of conservatism."

A recent and highly controversial challenge to the standard liberal interpretation of progressivism has been offered by historian Gabriel Kolko. Kolko asserts that the period from approximately 1900 until the United States' intervention in World War I was really an era of conservatism. Defining conservatism as "the attempt to preserve existing power and social relationships," Kolko argues that businessmen became the initiators of federal regulatory programs to achieve rationalization of the economy. Through the instrument of government, businessmen sought to eliminate internecine competition, stabilize market conditions, minimize the uncertainties of economic planning, and gain protection from the political attacks of their critics. They achieved these goals, Kolko explains, "primarily because no politically significant opposition during the Progressive Era really challenged their conception of political intervention."

The following selection, a section from the final chapter of The Triumph of Conservatism, *sets forth most of the author's conclusions in that work.*

The American political experience during the Progressive Era was conservative, and this conservatism profoundly influenced American society's response to the problems of industrialism. The nature of the economic process in the United States, and the peculiar cast within which industrialism was

SOURCE. Gabriel Kolko, *The Triumph of Conservatism: A Reinterpretation of American History*, New York: The Free Press of Glencoe, 1963, pp. 279–287. Copyright by The Free Press of Glencoe, a Division of The Macmillan Company, 1963. Reprinted by permission of The Free Press of Glencoe and the author.

molded, can only be understood by examining the political structure. Progressive politics is complex when studied in all of its aspects, but its dominant tendency on the federal level was to functionally create, in a piecemeal and haphazard way that was later made more comprehensive, the synthesis of politics and economics I have labeled "political capitalism."

The varieties of rhetoric associated with progressivism were as diverse as its followers, and one form of this rhetoric involved attacks on businessmen—attacks that were often framed in a fashion that has been misunderstood by historians as being radical. But at no point did any major political tendency dealing with the problem of big business in modern society ever try to go beyond the level of high generalization and translate theory into concrete economic programs that would conflict in a fundamental way with business supremacy over the control of wealth. It was not a coincidence that the results of progressivism were precisely what many major business interests desired.

Ultimately businessmen defined the limits of political intervention, and specified its major form and thrust. They were able to do so not merely because they were among the major initiators of federal intervention in the economy, but primarily because no politically significant group during the Progressive Era really challenged their conception of political intervention. The basic fact of the Progressive Era was the large area of consensus and unity among key business leaders and most political factions on the role of the federal government in the economy. There were disagreements, of course, but not on fundamentals. The overwhelming majorities on votes for basic progressive legislation is testimony to the near unanimity in Congress on basic issues.

Indeed, an evaluation of the Progressive Era must concede a much larger importance to the role of Congress than has hitherto been granted by historians who have focused primarily on the more dramatic Presidents. Congress was the pivot of agitation for banking reform while Roosevelt tried to evade the issue, and it was considering trade commissions well before Wilson was elected. Meat and pure food agitation concentrated on Congress, and most of the various reform proposals originated there. More often than not, the various Presidents evaded a serious consideration of issues until Congressional initiatives forced them to articulate a position. And businessmen seeking reforms often found a sympathetic response among the members of the House and Senate long before Presidents would listen to them. This was particularly true of Roosevelt, who would have done much less than he did were it not for the prodding of Congress. Presidents are preoccupied with patronage to an extent unappreciated by anyone who has not read their letters.

The Presidents, considered—as they must be—as actors rather than ideologists, hardly threatened to undermine the existing controllers of economic power. With the possible exception of Taft's Wickersham, none of the major appointees to key executive posts dealing with economic affairs were men likely to frustrate business in its desire to use the federal government to strengthen its economic position. Garfield, Root, Knox, Straus—these men were important and sympathetic pipelines to the President, and gave additional security to businessmen who did not misread what Roosevelt was trying to say in his public utterances. Taft, of course, broke the continuity between the Roosevelt and Wilson Administrations because of political decisions that had nothing to do with his acceptance of the same economic theory that Roosevelt believed in. The elaborate relationship between business and the Executive created under Roosevelt was unintentionally destroyed because of Taft's desire to control the Republican Party. Wilson's appointees were quite as satisfactory as Roosevelt's, so far as big business was concerned, and in his concrete implementation of the fruits of their political agitation—the Federal Reserve Act and the Federal Trade Commission Act—Wilson proved himself to be perhaps the most responsive and desirable to business of the three Presidents. Certainly it must be concluded that historians have overemphasized the basic differences between the Presidents of the Progressive Era, and ignored their much more important similarities. In 1912 the specific utterances and programs of all three were identical on fundamentals, and party platforms reflected this common agreement.

This essential unanimity extended to the area of ideologies and values, where differences between the Presidents were largely of the sort contrived by politicians in search of votes, or seeking to create useful images. None of the Presidents had a distinct consciousness of any fundamental conflict between their political goals and those of business. Roosevelt and Wilson especially appreciated the significant support business gave to their reforms, but it was left to Wilson to culminate the decade or more of agitation by providing precise direction to the administration of political capitalism's most important consequences in the Progressive Era. Wilson had a small but articulate band of followers who seriously desired to reverse the process of industrial centralization— Bryan and the Midwestern agrarians reflected this tradition more than any other group. Yet ultimately he relegated such dissidents to a secondary position—indeed, Wilson himself represented the triumph of Eastern Democracy over Bryanism—and they were able to influence only a clause or amendment, here and there, in the basic legislative structure of political capitalism.

But even had they been more powerful, it is debatable how different Bryanism would have been. Bryan saw the incompatibility between giant corporate capitalism and political democracy, but he sought to save democracy by saving, or restoring, a sort of idealized competitive capitalist economy which was by this time incapable of realization or restoration, and was in any event not advocated by capitalists or political leaders with more power than the agrarians could marshal. Brandeis, for his part, was bound by enigmas in this period. Big business, to him, was something to be ultimately rejected or justified on the basis of efficiency rather than power accumulation. He tried to apply such technical criteria where none was really relevant, and he overlooked the fact that even where efficient or competitive, business could still pose irreconcilable challenges to the political and social fabric of a democratic community. Indeed, he failed to appreciate the extent to which it was competition that was leading to business agitation for federal regulation, and finally he was unable to do much more than sanction Wilson's actions as they were defined and directed by others.

There was no conspiracy during the Progressive Era. It is, of course, a fact that people and agencies acted out of public sight, and that official statements frequently had little to do with operational realities. But the imputation of a conspiracy would sidetrack a serious consideration of progressivism. There was a basic consensus among political and business leaders as to what was the public good, and no one had to be cajoled in a sinister manner. If détentes, private understandings, and the like were not publicly proclaimed it was merely because such agreements were exceptional and, generally known, could not have been denied to other business interests also desiring the security they provided. Such activities required a delicate sense of public relations, since there was always a public ready to oppose preferential treatment for special businesses, if not the basic assumptions behind such arrangements.

Certainly there was nothing surreptitious about the desire of certain businessmen for reforms, a desire that was frequently and publicly proclaimed, although the motives behind it were not appreciated by historians and although most contemporaries were unaware of how reforms were implemented after they were enacted. The fact that federal regulation of the economy was conservative in its effect in preserving existing power and economic relations in society should not obscure the fact that federal intervention in the economy was conservative in purpose as well. This ambition was publicly proclaimed by the interested business forces, and was hardly conspiratorial.

It is the intent of crucial business groups, and the structural circumstances within the economy that motivated them, that were the truly significant and and unique aspects of the Progressive Era. The effects of the legislation were only the logical conclusion of the intentions behind it. The ideological consensus among key business and political leaders fed into a stream of common action, action that was sometimes stimulated by different specific goals but which nevertheless achieved the same results. Political leaders, such as Roosevelt, Wilson, and their key appointees, held that it was proper for an industry to have a decisive voice or veto over the regulatory process within its sphere of interest, and such assumptions filled many key businessmen with confidence in the essential reliability of the federal political mechanism, especially when it was contrasted to the unpredictability of state legislatures.

Business opposition to various federal legislative proposals and measures did exist, of course, especially if one focuses on opposition to particular clauses in specific bills. Such opposition, as in the case of the Federal Reserve Bill, was frequently designed to obtain special concessions. It should not be allowed to obscure the more important fact that the essential purpose and goal of any measure of importance in the Progressive Era was not merely endorsed by key representatives of businesses involved; rather such bills were first proposed by them.

One can always find some businessman, of course, who opposed federal regulation at any point, including within his own industry. Historians have relished in detailing such opposition, and, indeed, their larger analysis of the period has encouraged such revelations. But the finding of division in the ranks of business can be significant only if one makes the false assumption of a monolithic common interest among all capitalists, but, worse yet, assumes that there is no power center among capitalists, and that small-town bankers or hardware dealers can be equated with the leaders of the top industrial, financial, and railroad corporations. They can be equated, of course, if all one studies is the bulk of printed words. But in the political as well as in the economic competition between small and big business, the larger interests always managed to prevail in any specific contest. The rise of the National Association of Manufacturers in the Progressive Era is due to its antilabor position, and not to its opposition to federal regulation, which it voiced only after the First World War. In fact, crucial big business support could be found for every major federal regulatory movement, and frequent small business support could be found for any variety of proposals to their benefit, such as price-fixing and legalized trade associations. Progressivism was not the triumph of small business over the trusts, as has often been suggested, but the victory of big businesses in achieving the rationalization of the economy that only the federal government could provide.

Still, the rise of the N.A.M. among businessmen in both pro- and anti-regulation camps only reinforces the fact that the relationship of capitalists to the remainder of society was essentially unaltered by their divisions on federal intervention in the economy. In terms of the basic class structure, and the conditions of interclass relationships, big and small business alike were hostile to a labor movement interested in something more than paternalism and inequality. In this respect, and in their opposition or indifference to the very minimal social welfare reforms of the Progressive Era (nearly all of which were enacted in the states), American capitalism in the Progressive Era acted in the conservative fashion traditionally ascribed to it. The result was federal regulation in the context of a class society. Indeed, because the national political leadership of the Progressive Period shared this *noblesse oblige* and conservatism toward workers and farmers, it can be really said that there was federal regulation because there *was* a class society, and political leaders identified with the values and supremacy of business.

This identification of political and key business leaders with the same set of social values—ultimately class values—was hardly accidental, for had such a consensus not existed the creation of political capitalism would have been most unlikely. Political capitalism was based on the functional unity of major political and business leaders. The business and political elites knew each other, went to the same schools, belonged to the same clubs, married into the same families, shared the same values—in reality, formed that phenomenon which has lately been dubbed The Establishment. Garfield and Stetson met at Williams alumni functions, Rockeller, Jr. married Aldrich's daughter, the Harvard clubmen always found the White House door open to them when Roosevelt was there, and so on. Indeed, no one who reads Jonathan Daniels' remarkable autobiography, *The End of Innocence*, can fail to realize the significance of an interlocking social, economic, and political elite in American history in this century.

The existence of an Establishment during the Progressive Era was convenient, even essential, to the functional attainment of political capitalism, but it certainly was not altogether new in American history, and certainly had antecedents in the 1890's. The basic causal factor behind national progressivism was the needs of business and financial elements. To some extent, however, the more benign character of many leading business leaders, especially those with safe fortunes, was due to the more secure, mellowed characteristics and paternalism frequently associated with the social elite. Any number of successful capitalists had long family traditions of social graces and refinement which they privately doubted were fully compatible with their role as capitalists. The desire for a stabilized, rationalized political capitalism was fed by this current in big business ideology, and gave many businessmen that air of responsibility and conservatism so admired by Roosevelt and Wilson. And, from a practical viewpoint, the cruder economic conditions could also lead to substantial losses. Men who were making fortunes with existing shares of the market preferred holding on to what they had rather than establishing control over an industry, or risking much of what they already possessed. Political stabilization seemed proper for this reason as well. It allowed men to relax, to hope that crises might be avoided, to enjoy the bountiful fortunes they had already made.

Not only were economic losses possible in an unregulated capitalism, but political destruction also appeared quite possible. There were disturbing gropings ever since the end of the Civil War: agrarian discontent, violence and strikes, a Populist movement, the rise of a Socialist Party that seemed, for a time, to have an unlimited growth potential. Above all, there was a labor movement seriously divided as to its proper course, and threatening to follow in the seemingly radical footsteps of European labor. The political capitalism of the Progressive Era was designed to meet these potential threats, as well as the immediate expressions of democratic discontent in the states. National progressivism was able to short-circuit state progressivism, to hold nascent radicalism in check by feeding the illusions of its leaders—leaders who could not tell the difference between federal regulation *of* business and federal regulation *for* business.

Political capitalism in America redirected the radical potential of mass grievances and aspirations—of genuine progressivism—and to a limited extent colored much of the intellectual ferment of the period, even though the amorphous nature of mass aspirations frequently made the goals of business and the rest of the public nearly synonymous. Many well-intentioned writers and academicians worked for the same legislative goals as businessmen, but their innocence did not alter the fact that such measures were frequently designed by businessmen to serve business ends, and that business ultimately reaped the harvest of positive results. Such innocence was possible because of a naive, axiomatic view that government economic regulation, per se, was desirable, and also because many ignored crucial business support for such measures by focusing on the less important business opposition that existed. The fetish of government regulation of the economy as a positive social good was one that sidetracked a substantial portion of European socialism as well, and was not unique to the American experience. Such axiomatic and simplistic assumptions of what federal regulation would bring did not take into account problems of democratic control and participation, and in effect assumed that the power of government was neutral and socially beneficent. Yet many of the leading muckrakers and academics of the period were more than naive but ultimately conservative in their intentions as well. They sought the paternalism and stability which they expected political capitalism to bring, since only in this way could the basic virtues of capitalism be maintained. The betrayal of liberalism that has preoccupied some intellectual historians did not result from irrelevant utopianism or philosophical pragmatism, but from the lack of a truly radical, articulated alternative economic and political program capable of synthesizing political democracy with industrial reality. Such a program was never formulated in this period either in America or Europe.

Historians have continually tried to explain the seemingly sudden collapse of progressivism after the First World War, and have offered reasons that varied from moral exhaustion to the repression of nonconformity. On the whole, all explanations suffer because they really fail to examine progressivism beyond the favorable conventional interpretation. Progressive goals, on the concrete, legislative level, were articulated by various business interests. These goals were, for the most part, achieved, and no one formulated others that big business was also interested in attaining. Yet a synthesis of business and politics on the federal level was created during the war, in various administrative and emergency agencies, that continued throughout the following decade. Indeed, the war period represents the triumph of business in the most emphatic manner possible. With the exception of a brief interlude in the history of the Federal Trade Commission, big business gained total support from the various regulatory agencies and the Executive. It was during the war that effective, working oligopoly and price and market agreements became operational in the dominant sectors of the American economy. The rapid diffusion of power in the economy and relatively easy entry virtually ceased. Despite the cessation of important new legislative enactments, the unity of business and the federal government continued throughout the 1920's and thereafter, using the foundations laid in the Progressive Era to stabilize and consolidate conditions within various industries. And, on the same progressive foundations and exploiting the experience with the war agencies, Herbert Hoover and Franklin Roosevelt later formulated programs for saving American capitalism. The principle of utilizing the federal government to stabilize the economy, established in the context of modern industrialism during the Progressive Era, became the basis of political capitalism in its many later ramifications.

In this sense progressivism did not die in the 1920's, but became a part of the basic fabric of American society. The different shapes political capitalism has taken since 1916 deserve a separate treatment, but suffice it to say that even Calvin Coolidge did not mind evoking the heritage of Theodore Roosevelt, and Hoover was, if anything, deeply devoted to the Wilsonian tradition in which Franklin Roosevelt gained his first political experience.

CONTEMPORARY SOURCES

4. FREDERIC C. HOWE, "THE CITY FOR THE PEOPLE"

ONLY in recent decades have students come to appreciate the significance of the city in American history. The yeoman farmer ideal, as reinforced by Frederick Jackson Turner's frontier thesis, nurtured a pervasive love for rural life and an intellectual

SOURCE. Frederic C. Howe, *The City: The Hope of Democracy*, New York: Charles Scribner's Sons, 1905, pp. 208–287, 292–293, and 298. Reprinted by permission of Charles Scribner's Sons.

distaste for the city. Americans of the eighteenth and nineteenth centuries (and many of more recent times) concluded that the city represented the bane and despair of the nation.

Much of the progressive crusade dealt with the problems of the city. A host of reform-minded Americans realized that the city represented both challenge and opportunity, and some firmly believed that, once given a chance, urban life would realize a democratic renaissance that would benefit city and country folk alike. Foremost among these progressive visionaries was the prolific and discerning journalist Frederic C. Howe. This excerpt from his book, The City: The Hope of Democracy, *reveals why American cities of the Progressive Era needed reforming. It also demonstrates the optimism with which Howe regarded the prospects of urban life.*

The city is not only the problem of our civilization, it is the hope of the future. In the city democracy is awakening, it is beginning to assert itself. Here life is free and eager and countless agencies coöperate to create a warmer sympathy, a broader sense of responsibility, and a more intelligent political sense. Already the city has attained a higher degree of political responsiveness than has the commonwealth which gave it being and which jealously resents its growing independence. In many instances it is better governed than is the state or the nation at large. It is freer from the more subtle forms of corruption. For the open bribe, the loan, or even the game of poker in which the ignorant councilman is permitted to win a handsome stake are not the only means employed. Self-interest, a class-conscious feeling, the fancied advantage of party may be as powerful a motive for evil as the more vulgar methods with which we are familiar. The sinister influences bent on maintaining the *status quo*, on the prevention of necessary legislation, the control of the party, the caucus, or the convention; methods which are in vogue in national and state affairs, may be even more dangerous to democracy than the acts which violate the criminal code and which are becoming intolerable to public opinion. Moreover, in national affairs, the public is less alert, much less able to act collectively or to concentrate attention upon a given issue. The same is true in state affairs, where the divergent interests of the country and the city render united action well-nigh impossible.

The city is also being aroused to social and economic issues as well as to political ones. It is constantly taking on new activities and assuming new burdens. Everything tends to encourage this, while many things render it imperative. By necessity we are forced to meet the burdens of a complex life. We cannot live in close association without common activities, without abandoning some of our liberties to regulation. Not only do health, comfort, and happiness demand this, self-protection necessitates it.

Some of the activities which the city has assumed, or will assume, have been suggested. Through them many of the losses which the city has created will be made good. By these means the city will become fuller of opportunity than the scattered rural life which it has displaced. A conscious housing policy will be adopted. The tenement will become habitable, comfortable, and safe. Cheap and rapid transit will lure the population from the crowded slum into smaller suburban centres. For the city of the future will cover a wide area.

The same motives that have opened up breathing spots in the form of parks, as well as public baths and gymnasiums, in the crowded quarters will, in time, lead to the establishment of city clubhouses, winter recreation centres, where such advantages as are now found in the social settlement will be offered. About these centres the life of the community will focus for study, play, recreation, and political activity. Here concerts, lectures, and human intercourse will be offered. A sense of the city as a home, as a common authority, a thing to be loved and cared for, will be developed. In the city club the saloon will find a rival. From such centres charity work will be carried on. Here neglected children will be cared for, here the boys and girls will find an opportunity of escape from the street, and the mother and father a common meeting ground which is now denied them. For city life not only destroys the home of the poor, it promotes divorce. The tenement drives its dwellers to the streets and to the saloon. Private philanthropy has done much to relieve this condition through the settlement, but the service it renders is as much a public one as are the parks, the hospitals, or the schools. For the settlement is the equivalent of the outdoor park. Even from a pecuniary point of view it is a good investment to the city. The settlement promotes order, it lessens crime, it reduces petty misdemeanors, and organizes the life and energy of the slum and turns it into good channels. The uniform testimony of police officials is to the effect that a settlement or a playground is as good as a half-dozen policemen.

When the city becomes its own factory inspector, the problem of school attendance will be simplified. Then the city will be able to coördinate its administration and enforce its own ordinances. With reduced cost of transportation, through the public ownership of the means of transit, with free books and possibly free luncheons to school children, compulsory education will become a possibility. For the problem of education is largely economic or industrial. Our cities are now in the illogical position of enforcing school attendance upon those who cannot afford even the insignificant cost of the same.

These reforms will be possible through home rule, through the city-republic. With the city free in these regards it will be able to raise the educational age, adopt manual-training and trades' schools, fit its instruction to local needs, and ultimately elevate the standard of life of all classes. With the city free, the administration of our correctional institutions may be fitted to the crime. Probation courts and city farm schools may then be established and provision made for those of tender years who, in many cities, are still imprisoned with criminals, branded with the mark of crime, a brand which they can never outlive, a memory which they can never forget, an influence that can never be eradicated. Then the city will be able to discriminate between the offences of ignorance and poverty and those of instinct. Today they are all classed together. The poor who have unwittingly violated some local ordinance, such as blocking a sidewalk, driving a garbage cart without a license, failing to remove rubbish, or the like, when arrested, if unable to find bail, are cast into jail to await trial or to serve their time. An examination of the police-court blotter of the average city leads one to wonder if the offences of society against its own do not equal those of the individual against his fellows. Justice, as administered in these courts, probably hurts quite as much as it helps, and society, by its thoughtlessness, creates as much crime as it prevents. The solicitude of the common law for the occasional innocent has not been extended to the thousands of real innocents, to the children, the unfortunate, the ignorant, whom indifference punishes and, in punishing, destroys. Thousands of men and women are sent to the jails, workhouses, and penitentiary every year who should have been sent to the hospital, to an inebriate asylum, to the country, or, much better, given work. Their offence is of a negative sort. It is not wilful. It is industrial or economic; they could not catch on.

By natural processes inability to maintain life in store, factory, or sweatshop produces the outcast woman, just as sickness, irregular employment, hard times yield their unvarying harvest of vagrants, with the sequence of the lodging house, the street, and ultimately a life of petty crime. Such a career is not often taken from choice, but by misfortune. And society often arrests, sentences, and punishes, when it should help and endeavor to reclaim by work, kindness, and assistance.

We have had our public schools for so long that we accept them as a commonplace. But we do not appreciate that the high schools are raising millions of citizens to an educated estate which was known to but a limited number a few years ago. The effect of this infusion of culture into our life is beginning to make itself felt. And in the years to come, when education has, in fact, become compulsory, and the school age has been raised to a higher standard, the effect will be tremendous. Along with the schools go the public libraries. Branches and distributing agencies are extending their influence into every part of the city. Through them opportunity is offered for a continuation of study, even after the door of the school has closed.

Provision for public concerts in summer as well as in winter has already found a place in many municipal budgets. With the development of the city club there will come public orchestras, art exhibitions, and the like that will brighten the life of the community. Something like this is already being done through the libraries which are being constructed with assembly halls and meeting rooms for this purpose. Here and there the idea is taking form of utilizing the public-school buildings as local clubs. The basement, gymnasiums, and assembly rooms are being opened in the evening and during the summer months. In time there will be a modification in their architecture, equipment, and facilities, so that they will be available for a multitude of purposes instead of the limited one of education. In New York City the school buildings are already being erected with roof-gardens, where music, recreation, and a common centre for the life of the locality are offered.

These are some of the things the new city will do. It will also care for the sick, as it now does in many cities, through district physicians or visiting nurses attached to the school departments. It will find work and maintain employment agencies. It will supervise factories, mills, and work-shops. The latter function is now inadequately performed by the state at large, and the inefficiency of its performance is largely attributable to the fact that the state is attempting to supervise a matter of local concern. The regulation of the conditions of employment is as much a city function as is the preservation of the health and well-being of the community. It is also a necessary part of school administration.

All these functions are, in a sense, socialistic. But it is such activities as these, it is the care and protection of the people, that inspire love and affection for the city. For these new activities will enlarge our life, not limit it; will insure freedom, not destroy it; will give to the millions whose life goes to the city's upbuilding something more than ten hours of work, eight hours of sleep, a single room in a tenement for a home, and a few hours in the saloon as compensation for it all. . . .

It is along these lines that the advance of society is to be made. It is to come about through the city. For here life is more active, while the government is close to the people. It is already manifest on every hand. Through the divorce of the city from state control this progress will be stimulated. The city will become a centre of pride and patriotism. Here art and culture will flourish. The citizen will be attached to his community just as were the burghers of the mediaeval towns. Through direct legislation the city will be democratized. Public opinion will be free to act. Then the official will be holden to a real responsibility, while national politics will no longer dominate local affairs, for the test of the candidate for office will be his citizenship in the community which he serves. . . .

. . .The city will cease to be a necessary abyss of poverty. It is our institutions and our laws, not a divine ordinance or the inherent viciousness of humankind, that are at fault. Our evils are economic, not personal. Relief is possible through a change in our laws, in an increase in the positive agencies of the government, and the taxing for the common weal of those values which are now responsible for much of the common woe. It is not personal goodness that is demanded so much as public intelligence. For the worst of the evils under which America suffers are traceable to laws creating privileges. The evils can be largely corrected through their abolition. This is most easily obtainable in the city, for it is in the city that democracy is organizing and the power of privilege most rampant.

5. FREDERIC C. HOWE, "CALLING IN THE EXPERT"

DURING the last two decades of the nineteenth century, American colleges and universities were in intellectual ferment. Scholars, especially social scientists, dissatisfied with the classical mold of education, posed searching questions about the relevance of their professions to practical affairs. One outcome was a new orientation of such fields as anthropology, economics, history, political science, psychology, and sociology. Common to each discipline was an emphasis upon the powerful role of man's environment in shaping the lives of individuals. In addition, the social scientists came to regard government as the instrument through which society might achieve progress. The results of these new currents of thought were twofold: the development of the social service state and the inception of the "service intellectual" (men of academically trained intelligence whose work as intellectuals related closely to active service to their society).

The close relationship between professors of the University of Wisconsin and Wisconsin reform politicians during the Progressive Era constitutes an outstanding example of intellectuals in the service of the state. The state university, located in Wisconsin's capital city of Madison and staffed by some of the nation's leading social scientists, was able to respond to the requests first made of the academic community by Governor Robert M. La Follette. "La Follette," David Shannon has written, "perhaps more than any other figure in twentieth-century political history, was responsible for the now generally accepted practice of government officer-holders seeking the advice and drawing upon the researches by academic experts."

In the following selection, the influential journalist-reformer Frederic C. Howe, himself set on the road to reform by his professors at Johns Hopkins University, reveals how the university functioned as a fourth branch of government alongside the

SOURCE. Frederic C. Howe, *Wisconsin: An Experiment in Democracy*, New York: Charles Scribner's Sons, 1912, pp. 39–48 and 189–191. Reprinted by permission of Charles Scribner's Sons.

traditional legislative, executive, and judicial divisions. According to Howe, Wisconsin's use of the expert largely explains why that midwestern state stood in the forefront of the progressive movement and became the "laboratory of democracy."

Wisconsin is making the German idea her own. The university is the fourth department of the state, along with the judicial, executive, and legislative branches. There is no provision for this in the constitution, no reference to it in the laws. But whether you sit in the office of the governor or of President Van Hise, you see evidences of the most intimate relationship between the two. The university is the nerve centre of the commonwealth, impelling it to action in almost every field of activity. It has been the direct inspiration of many of the progressive laws of the past decade. It has adjusted its teachings to state problems. It loans its equipment and encourages its professors to enter the state service. There is some complaint about this; one hears the suggestion about the state-house that the legislature merely carries out a programme prepared for it on University Hill, at the other end of Madison.

The close union of the university with politics prevented any serious reaction during the years which followed the election of La Follette to the senate. University graduates occupied many of the important state offices, whether elective or appointive. In 1910 there were thirty-five professors and instructors giving part of their time to the public service. President Van Hise and Dean E. A. Birge are members of the conservation commission, state park board, the forestry and fish commissions. John R. Commons, professor of political economy, and now a member of the newly created industrial commission, has promoted much of the industrial, labor, and railway legislation of recent years. Thomas S. Adams, former professor of political economy, is now a member of the tax commission, while Dr. B. M. Rastall is director of the state board of public affairs. Dr. B. H. Meyer, now of the Interstate Commerce Commission at Washington, was a member of the railway commission and at the same time professor of transportation. Charles McCarthy, head of the legislative reference library, is lecturer in political science, and E. M. Griffith, the state forester, is instructor in forestry. C. F. Burgess, professor of mechanical engineering, is on the engineering staff of the railroad and tax commissions, while Richard Fischer, professor of chemistry, is the state chemist. Chauncey Juday, state biologist, is lecturer on zoology. J. G. D. Mack, W. D. Pence, C. G. Burritt, N. P. Curtis, Otto L. Kowalke, H. J. Thorkelson, and J. H. Vosskuehler are all members of the engineering faculty and connected with the railway and tax commissions in the appraisal of property, the investigation of equipment, meters, and conditions of service of the local public utility corporations, and the working out of technical problems connected with the regulation of these industries. Professors in agriculture, in chemistry, in law, and in medicine are identified with other state activities and give a considerable part of their time to public affairs. Groups of students spend their vacations in all kinds of state work and are the most efficient of employees.

Wisconsin has bred a spirit of service that is unique. There is nothing like it in America. It suggests the existence of an instinct for public work that we have rarely offered an opportunity to develop. Men talk about public affairs in Madison; they talk city, state, and nation, the problems of the farmer and the worker, as in no other place I have ever been.

The university is the state research laboratory. Graduate students investigate pending questions, while the seminars in economics, politics, and sociology are utilized for the exhaustive study of state problems. There is scarcely a big legislative measure that was not first thoroughly studied at the university end of Madison before it was placed on the statute books at the other. Wisconsin adopted a state income tax in 1911. For years the subject was studied by advanced students of finance. It was a novel idea. Only two or three states had tried the income tax and in each of them it had been a failure. The students sought for the cause; they studied the federal income tax laws, those of Germany, France, and England, as well as the methods of assessment and collection, and the proper deductions to be made. All these questions were thoroughly worked out by professors and graduate students before the measure was introduced into the assembly. The initiative, referendum, and recall were studied in the same way by the department of politics before resolutions amending the state constitution were approved by the legislature. The wisdom of the experiment was debated, the Swiss and Oregon systems were compared, their details and achievements were analyzed. These measures were discussed all over the state in debating clubs and other societies. Wisconsin was familiar with these new instruments of democracy before they were seriously considered in the statehouse. The commission form of government, home rule for cities, amendments to the direct primary and election laws were studied in the same way. John R. Commons used his department for the study of industrial insurance, child and woman labor, labor exchanges, and factory inspection preparatory to the legislation of 1911. German, French, and English documents were digested and exact information collected for use by the special legislative committee appointed on the subject of workmen's compensation. Mechanical, medicinal, and health problems, the reform of the judiciary and criminal procedure, the care of indigent and criminal classes, the conservation of water-power and forests, all these had been subjects of scientific investigation long before they were imminent as legislation. And when these measures were finally presented, they had nearly a united state behind them.

One of the seminars in political science meets in the state-house, where its members are assigned concrete questions which trouble members of the assembly. Recently six fellowships were created. Not for foreign travel, but for half-time work in the insurance department, the railroad, and tax commissions. Through these fellowships, men secure an actual knowledge of the subjects they are studying. President Charles R. Van Hise awakened the state to an interest in conservation and the preservation of water-powers. His activity aroused the hostility of the electric power interests, which were represented on the board of regents. They resented his activity, as well as the freedom of discussion in the university. This interference with academic freedom ceased in 1911 with a change in the personnel of the board.

Departments far remote from twentieth-century problems are affected by the modern note . . . .

Historians and sociologists interpret their sciences in the light of the needs of present-day Wisconsin. E. A. Ross, the author of "Sin and Society," teaches sociology in terms of the tenement and the farm, rather than in terms of the cave man. He sends students out into the state to learn what the farmer reads, what are his recreations and those of his children, in order that the state may know his needs. He analyzes the crimes of men, of society, of business, the failures of criminal procedure and its punishments, in order that facts may be translated into remedies at the capitol. Sociology in Wisconsin is a science of life, of to-day, of human efficiency.

The utilitarian activities of the university have not interfered with academic standards or high ideals of research and scholarship. For the university encourages research, it maintains high standards of scholarship, and its faculty is filled with men of eminence in their respective fields. While comparisons are difficult, I should say that the achievements and standards of the university are equal to those of the privately endowed universities of the East, and that the publicity given to the agricultural and extension departments has led to more critical standards than would otherwise obtain. The university has made notable contributions to science, while its professors are constantly being called to other institutions. The close contact of the university with the state has vitalized its life. It has done much for the professors; it has done more for the students. There is an atmosphere of enthusiasm, of interest in the things that are, that is different from anything I know in any other institution of learning in America.

A large number of the graduates from the schools of economics and politics enter the public service in Wisconsin, at Washington, and in other states and cities. Requests come to Madison from all over the country for men to fill positions in civil and social work. And apparently graduates prefer public to private work, administrative posts rather than academic ones. Wisconsin has created a new profession, the profession of public service. It has adapted the German idea to American soil.

One of the by-products of the university is the legislative reference library organized by Charles McCarthy of the department of politics. McCarthy observed members of the legislature, untrained to study and bill drafting, drifting about the library seeking information and aid; he saw the mass of conflicting and undigested legislation which went through the mill, and came to the conclusion that legislation has failed, in part at least, because of the absence of any permanent agency for gathering material and the drafting of measures. Most of our state legislatures meet biennially. The session lasts for only a few months. Its members are untrained to law-making and unused to legislative methods. To meet this defect and bring together the various departments of the state, McCarthy evolved a bureau to aid the legislature and translate the work of the expert into law. He became its director. The library occupies quarters in the state-house, where the laws of other states, public reports, monographs, and treatises on current industrial, social, and legal problems are collected. Expert draftsmen are connected with the bureau, as well as a corps of men and women from the university. Members of the legislature come to McCarthy to draft their bills. They bring their local problems or some big constructive proposal. The evil to be corrected is studied, laws of other states are analyzed, and experts from the departments co-operate to make the measure as perfect as possible. The aim is not only exact draftsmanship, but intelligent law-making. McCarthy and his associates work with committees; they aid members in gathering material for speeches, and serve as *ex officio* clerks in the assembly. The bureau occupies a position not dissimilar from the permanent staff of experts in the departments at Washington. It has become a clearing-house of service, not only for Wisconsin, but for the country as well. Into this bureau the political progress of the world is gathered; out of it comes a new chemical compound in the form of progressive legislation. From this laboratory men and women are graduating into similar reference bureaus in cities and states all over the country. . . .

Wisconsin is fortunate in the close identity of the university with the state-house. The reaction of one upon the other has been beneficial to both. The university has been invigorated by its contact with practical problems. Young men have been awakened to an interest in politics. Teaching has been vitalized by the large number of professors, who give a portion of their time to state affairs, to the solution of administrative, legislative, and technical problems. The pioneer work of the state is largely traceable to the bigness of vision that the university has brought to legislation. Laws have been framed with the experience of the world before the legislature. Thoroughness has characterized the laws which Wisconsin has placed on the statute books.

Scientific efficiency is one of the university's contributions to the state, and efficiency is one of Wisconsin's contributions to democracy. It has been carried into almost every department of the commonwealth.

The assumption is not uncommon that democracy involves the common-place, that it means a levelling down, a cheapening, an intolerance of superiority. It is suggested that the people will not stand for generous expenditures, for big deals. Wisconsin proves the contrary. In ten years' time the annual appropriations for the university have increased from $550,000 to $1,700,000. A splendid statehouse, costing $6,000,000, is being erected. Increased provision is being made for new types of normal, agricultural, manual training, and technical schools for the promotion of vocational and extension work. Generous salaries are paid the appointive positions to which the expert is selected, irrespective of his political affiliations.

Democracy not only produced the expert, it elevated him to office. It recognized the necessity of research, of training, of science, in the highly complex business of government. . . .

Democracy, too, began to use its powers to serve, to serve people as well as business, to serve humanity as well as property. Democracy has begun a war on poverty, on ignorance, on disease, on human waste. The state is using its collective will to promote a programme of human welfare.

Wisconsin is dispelling the fears of those who distrusted democracy. It is demonstrating the possibility of using the state as an instrument for the well-being of all people. It is laying the foundations for a commonwealth whose ideal it is to serve.

6. W. E. B. DUBOIS, "THE IMMEDIATE PROGRAM OF THE AMERICAN NEGRO"

WITH the dawn of the twentieth century, black Americans found themselves stripped of those political and social freedoms that they had enjoyed during the era of post-Civil War reconstruction. Following the end of Reconstruction, white Americans of the North and the South had capitulated to racism. In 1896, with its decision in Plessy vs. Ferguson, the United States Supreme Court capped a series of judgments hostile to Negro freedoms by declaring segregation of the races constitutional. State after state in the South resorted to various devices to disfranchise the Negro, thereby eliminating most blacks from the electoral process. An even more flagrant example of racism was the vicious lynching of Negroes; by 1917 more than 1100 colored persons had been murdered by

SOURCE. W. E. B. DuBois, "The Immediate Program of the American Negro," in *The Crisis*, Vol. 9, No. 6, April 1915, pp. 310–312. Copyright 1915 by the National Association for the Advancement of Colored People. Reprinted by permission of the National Association for the Advancement of Colored People.

lawless whites. Negroes thus found themselves not only robbed of political power, but also denied those liberties that are the by-products of economic, educational, and social advancement.

satisfaction for wrong done

Enraged by these developments, a small band of black militants met in 1905 at Niagara Falls, Canada, to draw up a petition of grievances designed to secure the redress of the white man's oppression of the Negro masses. White liberals were also prompted to organize in the Negro's behalf following the 1908 race riot in Springfield, Illinois. That riot, in the city of the final resting place of Abraham Lincoln, was viewed by some to be a portent of racial violence that could sweep the nation. Eventually the black militants and white liberals joined forces, and in May 1910 the National Association for the Advancement of Colored People was organized.

William E. B. DuBois played a major role in the efforts of both the Niagara Movement and the NAACP. DuBois, a mulatto of French Huguenot, Dutch, and Negro ancestry, was educated at Fisk, Harvard, and the University of Berlin; in 1895 he became the first Afro-American to earn a doctorate at Harvard. A prolific writer of political and social tracts concerning the Negro's plight, DuBois became the NAACP's first director of publicity and research, a post he held for nearly a quarter of a century. It was in his capacity as editor of The Crisis, *the official publication of the Association, that DuBois promoted his militant views that Negro self-help and a circumspect distrust of whites was the key to the advancement of the race. Understandably, this position brought DuBois into conflict with conservative members of the Association. Nevertheless, DuBois implored the black masses to join in a cooperative crusade for immediate fulfillment of their human rights, thus outlining a program that, in some respects, differs little from that of the present-day Negro revolution.*

cautious

intermediate The immediate program of the American Negro means nothing unless it is mediate to his great ideal and the ultimate ends of his development. We need not waste time by seeking to deceive our enemies into thinking that we are going to be content with a half loaf, or by being willing to lull our friends into a false sense of our indifference and present satisfaction.

The American Negro demands equality—political equality, industrial equality and social equality; and he is never going to rest satisfied with anything less. He demands this in no spirit of braggadocio and with no obsequious *servile* envy of others, but as an absolute measure of self-defense and the only one that will assure to the darker races their ultimate survival on earth.

Only in a demand and a persistent demand for essential equality in the modern realm of human culture can any people show a real pride of race and a decent self-respect. For any group, nation or race to admit for a moment the present monstrous demand of the white race to be the inheritors of the earth, the arbiters of mankind and the sole owners of a heritage of culture which they did not create, nor even improve to any greater extent than the other great division of men—to admit such pretense for a moment is for the race to write itself down immediately as indisputably inferior in judgment, knowledge and common sense.

The equality in political, industrial and social life which modern men must have in order to live, is not to be confounded with sameness. On the contrary, in our case, it is rather insistence upon the right of diversity;—upon the right of a human being to be a man even if he does not wear the same cut of vest, the same curl of hair or the same color of skin. Human equality does not even entail, as is sometimes said, absolute equality of opportunity; for certainly the natural inequalities of inherent genius and varying gift make this a dubious phase. But there is a more and more clearly recognized minimum of opportunity and maximum of freedom to be, to move and to think, which the modern world denies to no being which it recognizes as a real man.

These involve both negative and positive sides. They call for freedom on the one hand and power on the other. The Negro must have political freedom; taxation without representation is tyranny. American Negroes of to-day are ruled by tyrants who take what they please in taxes and give what they please in law and administration, in justice and in injustice; and the great mass of black people must stand helpless and voiceless before a condition which has time and time again caused other peoples to fight and die.

The Negro must have industrial freedom. Between the peonage of the rural South, the oppression of shrewd capitalists and the jealousy of certain trade unions, the Negro laborer is the most exploited class in the country, giving more hard toil for less money than any other American, and have less voice in the conditions of his labor.

In social intercourse every effort is being made to-day from the President of the United States and the so-called Church of Christ down to saloons and boot-blacks to segregate, strangle and spiritually starve Negroes so as to give them the least possible chance to know and share civilization.

These shackles must go. But that is but the beginning. The Negro must have power; the power of men, the right to do, to know, to feel and to express that knowledge, action and spiritual gift. He must not simply be free from the political tyranny of white folk, he must have the right to vote and to rule over the citizens, white and black, to the extent of his proven foresight and ability. He must have a voice in the new industrial democracy which is building and the power to see to it that his children are not in the next generation trained to be the mudsills of society. He must have the right to social intercourse with his fellows. There was a time in the atomic individualistic group when "social intercourse" meant merely calls and tea-parties; to-day social intercourse means theatres, lectures, organizations, churches, clubs, excursions, travel, hotels,—it means in short Life; to bar a group from such methods of thinking, living and doing is to bar them from the world and bid them create a new world;—a task to which no single group is today equal; it is to crucify them and taunt them with not being able to live.

What now are the practical steps which must be taken to accomplish these ends?

First of all before taking steps the wise man knows the object and end of his journey. There are those who would advise the black man to pay little or no attention to where he is going so long as he keeps moving. They assume that God or his vice-gerent the White Man will attend to the steering. This is arrant nonsense. The feet of those that aimlessly wander land as often in hell as in heaven. Conscious self-realization and self-direction is the watchword of modern man, and the first article in the program of any group that will survive must be the great aim, equality and power among men.

The practical steps to this are clear. First we must fight obstructions; by continual and increasing effort we must first make American courts either build up a body of decisions which will protect the plain legal rights of American citizens or else make them tear down the civil and political rights of all citizens in order to oppress a few. Either result will bring justice in the end. It is lots of fun and most ingenious just now for courts to twist law so as to say I shall not live here or vote there, or marry the woman who wishes to marry me. But when to-morrow these decisions throttle all freedom and overthrow the foundation of democracy and decency, there is going to be judicial house cleaning.

We must *secondly* seek in legislature and congress remedial legislation; national aid to public school education, the removal of all legal discriminations based simply on race and color, and those marriage laws passed to make the seduction of black girls easy and without legal penalty.

Third the human contact of human beings must be increased; the policy which brings into sympathetic touch and understanding, men and women, rich and poor, capitalist and laborer, Asiatic and European, must bring into closer contact and mutual knowledge the white and black people of this land. It is the most frightful indictment of a country which dares to call itself civilized that it has allowed itself to drift into a state of ignorance where ten million people are coming to believe that all white people are liars and thieves, and the whites in turn to believe that the chief industry of Negroes is raping white women.

Fourth only the publication of the truth repeatedly and incisively and uncompromisingly can secure that change in public opinion which will correct these awful lies. THE CRISIS, our record of the darker races, must have a circulation not of 35,000 chiefly among colored folk but of at least 250,000 among all men who believe in men. It must not be a namby-pamby box of salve, but a voice that thunders fact and is more anxious to be true than pleasing. There should be a campaign of tract distribution—short well written facts and arguments—rained over this land by millions of copies, particularly in the South, where the white people know less about the Negro than in any other part of the civilized world. The press should be utilized— the 400 Negro weeklies, the great dailies and eventually the magazines, when we get magazine editors who will lead public opinion instead of following afar with resonant brays. Lectures, lantern-slides and moving pictures, co-operating with a bureau of information and eventually becoming a Negro encyclopedia, all these are efforts along the line of making human beings realize that Negroes are human.

Such is the program of work against obstructions. Let us now turn to constructive effort. This may be summed up under (1) economic co-operation (2) a revival of art and literature (3) political action (4) education and (5) organization.

Under economic co-operation we must strive to spread the idea among colored people that the accumulation of wealth is for social rather than individual ends. We must avoid, in the advancement of the Negro race, the mistakes of ruthless exploitation which have marked modern economic history. To this end we must seek not simply home ownership, small landholding and saving accounts, but also all forms of co-operation, both in production and distribution, profit sharing, building and loan associations, systematic charity for definite, practical ends, systematic migration from mob rule and robbery, to freedom and enfranchisement, the emancipation of women and the abolition of child labor.

In art and literature we should try to loose the tremendous emotional wealth of the Negro and the dramatic strength of his problems through writing, the stage, pageantry and other forms of art. We should resurrect forgotten ancient Negro art and history, and we should set the black man before the world as both a creative artist and a strong subject for artistic treatment.

In political action we should organize the votes of Negroes in such congressional districts as have any number of Negro voters. We should systematically interrogate candidates on matters vital to Negro freedom and uplift. We should train colored voters to reject the bribe of office and to accept only decent legal enactments both for their own uplift and for the uplift of laboring classes of all races and both sexes.

In education we must seek to give colored children free public school training. We must watch with grave suspicion the attempt of those who, under the guise of vocational training, would fasten ignorance and menial service on the Negro for another generation. Our children must not in large numbers, be forced into the servant class; for menial service is still, in the main, little more than an antiquated survival of impossible conditions. It has always been as statistics show, a main cause of bastardy and prostitution and despite its many marvelous exceptions it will never come to the light of decency and honor until the house servant becomes the Servant in the House. It is our duty then, not drastically but persistently, to seek out colored children of ability and genius, to open up to them broader, industrial opportunity and above all, to find that Talented Tenth and encourage it by the best and most exhaustive training in order to supply the Negro race and the world with leaders, thinkers and artists.

For the accomplishment of all these ends we must organize. Organization among us already has gone far but it must go much further and higher. Organization is sacrifice. It is sacrifice of opinions, of time, of work and of money, but it is, after all, the cheapest way of buying the most priceless of gifts—freedom and efficiency. I thank God that most of the money that supports the National Association for the Advancement of Colored People comes from black hands; a still larger proportion must so come, and we must not only support but control this and similar organizations and hold them unwaveringly to our objects, our aims and our ideals.

7. THEODORE ROOSEVELT, "THE TAFT-WILSON TRUST PROGRAMME"

DURING the Progressive Era, controversy swirled around the question of the federal government's proper role regarding the great economic combinations so recently born of advancing, unregulated capitalism. In a number of industrial and financial enterprises, a few private citizens acting as trustees had come to wield immense, monopolistic power over the nation's business. Consequently, a great debate developed concerning the means of subjecting private economic power to the will of the general public. What form should governmental control take? Should the trusts be dissolved or permitted to retain their large-scale organization, submitting only to public regulation?

For Theodore Roosevelt, answers to these questions were self-evident. The economic realities of advanced industrialism, he believed, dictated the development of trusts. If the trusts were controlled by a federal commission in the public interest, he reasoned, they could be beneficial to all.

During the presidential contest of 1912, candidate Roosevelt compared and contrasted

SOURCE. Theodore Roosevelt, "The Taft-Wilson Trust Programme," in *The Outlook*, Vol. 102, September 21, 1912, pp. 105–107.

his position on the trusts with his major opponents, William Howard Taft and Woodrow Wilson. We must read Roosevelt's analysis with caution, however, for although he charged that Wall Street was aligned with his political opponents, a number of big financiers and industrialists looked to T. R. for the preservation of the large business combinations.

During my Administration, and since, I have first directed and tested, and then studied, the working of the Sherman Anti-Trust Law. When I came into office that law was dead: I took it up and for the first time had it enforced.

We gained this much by the enforcement: we gained the establishment of the principle that the Government was supreme over the great corporations; but that is almost the end of the good that came through our law-suits.

Take the Northern Securities case. Under me that suit was brought to a successful conclusion. I at first thought that we had secured a definite and real solution of the difficulties, and my opponents thought so too at first and were very sore; but in the end it proved that all we had actually accomplished was what is said above. As one of the greatest magnates concerned afterwards remarked: "Well, when the smoke cleared away, I found that whereas formerly I had to prove my ownership by one bit of paper, I now have to prove it by two."

Take again the Standard Oil decision. The Standard Oil Company was nominally dissolved as a result of the suit against it. It was divided nominally into thirty-four different companies. For a moment there was a great deal of fright in Wall Street; and under the stress of that fright the big magnates for the time being thought they would come round and advocate the policy of control I had advocated, because, while that control would really control them, would hamper and limit them, at least they thought that they would thereby escape death. Then they found that it was only make-believe death to which they were exposed. And as a result of the suit for dissolution Mr. Rockefeller's property rose in value to a higher degree than it ever had gone before, and to an already sufficient fortune he added some eighty or ninety millions of dollars, while the price of oil went up to the consumer. Men who purchased Standard Oil stock on the curb in New York tell me that the sole difference is that, whereas formerly the broker would give them one slip of paper, now he gives them an envelope containing thirty-seven slips—that's all.

You recollect Mr. Pierpont Morgan said, "You can't unscramble the eggs in an omelet." This particular instance of trying to unscramble them didn't help anybody but the owners of the eggs, for it increased the value of the eggs indefinitely and made the omelet cost more to the general public. Now our proposal is not to try to unscramble the eggs by a mere succession of lawsuits, but to exercise such administrative control by the Government as will prevent the eggs from ever being scrambled.

Mr. Wilson in a recent speech in New York said that "no body of men would have the wisdom necessary to enable them to regulate the industrial processes of the country." I was much interested in that remark because it represents the exact attitude always taken by the respectable ultra-conservative in matters of this nature. Word for word it is what some of the great railway magnates used to say before the passage of the Inter-State Commerce Law. They used to say that "no body of men alive could undertake to regulate the complicated railway business." Other big men used to say the same thing when the proposal was to establish Public Utilities Commissions.

I appeal from the prophet of to-day to the way the facts have refuted the prophets of yesterday. There is no more difficulty in regulating the Standard Oil or the Steel Corporation than in regulating a big railway. We have actually made the Inter-State Commerce Law work. We have found by the test of actual work that the way to control the railways lies through increasing the power, and especially through increasing the application of the power, of the Inter-State Commerce Commission, by regulating and controlling those railways, and not by any development of the Anti-Trust Law. Real control of the trusts can come only by the adoption of similar expedients. What I want to see done with our industrial concerns is to see an Inter-State Industrial Commission established, which shall handle the Standard Oil, the Steel Trust, the Tobacco Trust, and every such big trust, through administrative action, just as the Inter-State Commerce Commission handles the railways, and with a power extended beyond that of the Inter-State Commerce Commission.

And Mr. Wilson need not bother himself about finding men to administer such a law. If he cannot find them, I can and will. I will guarantee to find men who will be able to understand and supervise and regulate the business of those great industrial corporations.

Some of Mr. Wilson's supporters have said that our proposal is to "legalize monopoly" and his to "regulate competition." On the contrary, our proposal is to abolish monopoly and to restore competition where possible, and where this is not possible then absolutely to control the monopoly in the interest of the general public. His proposal is in effect to leave the present system unchanged; and the present system has just resulted in legalizing the monopoly of the Standard Oil and Tobacco Trusts. Substantially this has been the sole result, the only result Mr. Wilson's policy would achieve. His proposal is to do precisely nothing; his proposal is to continue in exactly the same course that the Taft Administration is now continuing; for the differences between the Republican and Democratic platforms on this matter are merely differences of sound and fury, and not of sense.

Mr. Wilson's proposal is to regulate competition by "dissolving" trusts in the way the Standard Oil and Tobacco Trusts were "dissolved." You know the prayer in Wall Street now is, "Give us another dissolution." Wall Street likes to have its property dissolved in that way. Every one of those dissolutions has been accompanied by a great rise in the value of the stocks, has legalized monopoly, and has conferred upon the trust magnates the great boon of being fortified by the law in their intrenchments.

On the contrary, the proposal of the Progressives is to put a stop to the continuance of the Taft-Wilson programme of further legalization of monopoly under the guise of a make-believe assault on monopoly. We propose by administrative action to control the conditions which, if left uncontrolled, lead to monopoly. We propose to restore competition where possible. But where this is not possible, we propose to have a real remedy instead of a sham remedy.

The talk about really controlling the trusts by regulating competition merely by lawsuits along the lines of the Anti-Trust Law, or of any amendment proposed to it by the Stanley Committee or by any one else—all such talk is the veriest nonsense. The proposals in the Democratic platform, so far as they could be enacted into law, would be of no help whatever. They would not change the present situation one little bit, except for the worse.

There is not a Wall Street man engaged in big business of the kind to which our people object, there is not a trust magnate, who doesn't regard with utter derision the talk of interfering with monopolies along the lines indicated by Mr. Wilson and his supporters. The only thing they fear is the kind of regulation that we Progressives propose to give them. Mr. Wilson's proposals are entirely satisfactory to them, quite as satisfactory as the actions of the present Administration; indeed, Mr. Wilson's proposals are so vague that they can hardly be called proposals at all; and the proposals of his supporters are either impracticable to adopt, or, if practicable, would work no real change in the present conditions. Accordingly, the enormous majority of the Wall Street men who have been guilty of the obnoxious practices in connection with trusts, having given up the hope of electing Mr. Taft, are now supporting Mr. Wilson; for they dread us as their only real foes, and know that the policies advocated by Messrs. Taft and Wilson represent, not real hostility, but only mock hostility, to the big crooked trusts—although these same policies do contain a serious menace to every kind of honest business, big or little, which does not rely for protection on adroit use of the chicanery of the law.

I call the attention of those who doubt our ability to regulate big business to what has happened with the insurance companies. Nine years ago the effort was made to limit them in size, much as the Stanley Committee proposes to limit industrial concerns generally. In actual practice this worked so badly that the effort had to be abandoned. At present the insurance companies are not limited in size, but they are supervised and controlled. There is plenty of competition among them, and the policy-holders are so well protected that they are entirely satisfied, those in the big companies more than those in the others.

The sum of the matter, therefore, is this: Mr. Wilson, like Mr. Taft, has no improvement to propose in this matter, for the differences between the proposals in the Republican and the Democratic platforms on the trust question are merely differences of declamation. Both sets of proposals indicate nothing but a vague, puzzled, and hopeless purpose feebly to continue the present futile policy of attempting to regulate the trusts by nothing but a succession of long-drawn and ineffective lawsuits: and if actually put into operation both sets of proposals would produce exactly and precisely nothing.

On the contrary, our proposals are definite and concrete, and are based on successful action along kindred lines in the past. If we are allowed to put them into action, we will immensely benefit the honest business man by making the law certain, and by punishing misconduct and not merely size; and we will effectively, and not merely nominally, curb and control the big trusts which are actually or potentially guilty of anti-social practices.

I do not wonder that, in view of these facts, every big crooked financier is against us and in favor of either Mr. Wilson or Mr. Taft, in order to beat us. I am sorry to say that the great majority of the respectable men of great wealth seem to be against us, not realizing that it is really in their interest that we should exercise supervision over the business use of their great wealth. I feel that every honest and far-sighted business man, big or little, should be with us, for our purpose is to help energy and power in business life, so long as the energy and power are used honestly and the public treated fairly; and all the secondary business men, the moderate-sized business men, should give us their hearty aid.

We are proud of the energy and initiative and success of our business men: we wish to see them prosper and build up American business to the highest pitch of efficiency, both at home and abroad, both in internal trade and in international trade. It is because we war intelligently against dishonesty in business, it is for the very reason that we efficiently oppose crooked business, that we have the right to ask the support of all honest business men; for the Progressive party in its platform offers the only really good platform that the honest business man has had offered him, and makes the only efficient proposals that any party has made for the elimination of evil business practices and the control of big business so that it shall not be used against the interest either of weaker business rivals of the employees and other wage-workers, of the shareholders, or of the general public.

8. WOODROW WILSON, "BENEVOLENCE, OR JUSTICE?"

WHEREAS Theodore Roosevelt's program of New Nationalism maintained that a powerful government should regulate the trusts to achieve social justice for all the people, Woodrow Wilson argued that government owed the people not benevolence, but opportunity and justice. The ideal commonwealth, Wilson believed, was one in which men enjoyed "a free field" for economic endeavor with "special privileges for none." Benevolence, Wilson maintained, whether bestowed by captains of industry or of government, was an ill-advised substitute for the freedoms secured by an enterprising people.

In practice, however, Woodrow Wilson's New Freedom differed little from the economic program espoused by Theodore Roosevelt. Indeed, in his campaign speeches of 1912, Wilson did not promise to dissolve all trusts; rather, he advocated the restoration of competitive conditions to the American economic system. To this end, he subsequently gave his approval to the creation of the Federal Trade Commission, an agency charged with the regulation of business enterprise. Before his first term had ended, Wilson even embraced many of the social justice ideas advanced earlier by Theodore Roosevelt. But at the beginning of his Presidency, as the following hard-hitting partisan speech indicates, Woodrow Wilson was intent in delineating the philosophical gulf that he believed separated him from the sage of Oyster Bay.

The doctrine that monopoly is inevitable and that the only course open to the people of the United States is to submit to and regulate it found a champion during the campaign of 1912 in the new party, or branch of the Republican party, founded under the leadership of Mr. Roosevelt, with the conspicuous aid,—I mention him with no satirical intention, but merely to set the facts down accurately,—of Mr. George W. Perkins, organizer of the Steel Trust and the Harvester Trust, and with the support of more than three millions of citizens, many of them among the most patriotic, conscientious, and high-minded men and women of the land.

The fact that its acceptance of monopoly was a feature of the new party platform from which the attention of the generous and just was diverted by the charm of a social programme of great attractiveness to all concerned for the amelioration of the lot of those who suffer wrong and privation, and the

SOURCE. Woodrow Wilson, "Benevolence, or Justice?", in *The World's Work*, Vol. 25, No. 6, April 1913, pp. 628–640.

further fact that, even so, the platform was repudiated by the majority of the Nation, render it no less necessary to reflect on the significance of the confession made for the first time by any party in the country's history. It may be useful, in order to the relief of the minds of many from an error of no small magnitude, to consider now, the heat of a Presidential contest being past, exactly what it was that Mr. Roosevelt proposed.

Mr. Roosevelt attached to his platform some very splendid suggestions as to noble enterprises which we ought to undertake for the uplift of the human race; but when I hear an ambitious platform put forth, I am very much more interested in the dynamics of it than in the rhetoric of it. I have a very practical mind, and I want to know who are going to do those things and how they are going to be done. If you have read the trust plank in that platform as often as I have read it, you have found it very long, but very tolerant. It did not anywhere condemn monopoly, except in words: its essential meaning was that the trusts have been bad and must be made to be good. You know that Mr. Roosevelt long ago classified trusts for us as good and bad, and he said that he was afraid only of the bad ones. Now he does not desire that there should be any more bad ones, but proposes that they should all be made good by discipline, directly applied by a commission of executive appointment. All he explicitly complains of is lack of publicity and lack of fairness; not the exercise of power, for throughout that plank the power of the great corporations is accepted as the inevitable consequence of the modern organization of industry. All that it is proposed to do is to take them under control and regulation. The national administration having for sixteen years been virtually under the regulation of the trusts, it would be merely a family matter were the parts reversed and were the other members of the family to exercise the regulation. And the trusts, apparently, which might, in such circumstances, comfortably continue to administer our affairs under the mollifying influences of the Federal Government, would then, if you please, be the instrumentalities by which all the humanistic, benevolent programme of the rest of that interesting platform would be carried out!

I have read and reread that plank, so as to be sure that I get it right. All that it complains of is,—and the complaint is a just one, surely,—that these gentlemen exercise their power in a way that is secret. Therefore, we must have publicity. Sometimes they are arbitrary; therefore, they need regulation. Sometimes they do not consult the general interests of the community; therefore, they need to be reminded of those general interests by an industrial commission. But at every turn it is the trusts who are to do us good, and not we ourselves.

Again, I absolutely protest against being put into the hands of trustees. Mr. Roosevelt's conception of government is Mr. Taft's conception, that the Presidency of the United States is the presidency of a board of directors. I am willing to admit that if the people of the United States cannot get justice for themselves, then it is high time that they should join the third party and get it from somebody else. The justice proposed is very beautiful; it is very attractive; there were planks in that platform which stir all the sympathies of the heart; they proposed things that we all want to do; but the question is, Who is going to do them? Through whose instrumentality? Are Americans ready to ask the trusts to give us, in pity, what we ought, in justice, to take?

The third party says that the present system of our industry and trade has come to stay. Mind you, these artificially-built-up things, these things that can't maintain themselves in the market without monopoly, have come to stay, and the only thing that the Government can do, the only thing that the third party proposes should be done, is to set up a commission to regulate them. It accepts them. It says: "We will not undertake, it were futile to undertake, to prevent monopoly, but we will go into an arrangement by which we will make these monopolies kind to you. We will guarantee that they shall be pitiful. We will guarantee that they shall pay the right wages. We will guarantee that they shall do everything kind and public-spirited, which they have never heretofore shown the least inclination to do."

Don't you realize that that is a blind alley? You can't find your way to liberty that way. You can't find your way to social reform through the forces that have made social reform necessary.

The fundamental part of such a programme is that the trusts shall be recognized as a permanent part of our economic order, and that the Government shall try to make trusts the ministers, the instruments, through which the life of this country shall be justly and happily developed on its industrial side. Now, everything that touches our lives sooner or later goes back to the industries which sustain our lives. I have often reflected that there is a very human order in the petitions in our Lord's prayer. For we pray first of all, "Give us this day our daily bread," knowing that it is useless to pray for spiritual graces on an empty stomach, and that the amount of wages we get, the kind of clothes we wear, the kind of food we can afford to buy, is fundamental to everything else.

Those who administer our physical life, therefore, administer our spiritual life; and if we are going to carry out the fine purpose of that great chorus which supporters of the third party sang almost with religious fervor, then we have got to find out through whom these purposes of humanity are going to be realized. It is a mere enterprise, so far as that part of it is concerned, of making the monopolies philanthropic.

I do not want to live under a philanthropy. I do not want to be taken care of by the Government, either directly or by any instruments through which the Government is acting. I want only to have right and justice prevail, so far as I am concerned. Give me right and justice and I will undertake to take care of myself. If you enthrone the trusts as the means of the development of this country under the supervision of the Government, then I shall pray the old Spanish proverb, "God save me from my friends, and I'll take care of my enemies."

Because I want to be saved from these friends. Observe that I say these friends, for I am ready to admit that a great many men who believe that the development of industry in this country through monopolies is inevitable intend to be the friends of the people. Though they profess to be my friends, they are undertaking a way of friendship which renders it impossible that they should do me the fundamental service that I demand—namely, that I should be free and that I should have the same opportunities that everybody else has.

For I understand it to be the fundamental proposition of American liberty that we do not desire special privilege, because we know special privilege will never comprehend the general welfare. This is the fundamental, spiritual difference between adherents of the party that has just taken charge of the Government and those who have been in charge of it in recent years. They are so indoctrinated with the idea that only the big business interests of this country understand the United States and can make it prosperous that they cannot divorce their thoughts from that obsession. They have put the Government into the hands of trustees, and Mr. Taft and Mr Roosevelt were the rival candidates to preside over the board of trustees. They were candidates to serve the people, no doubt, to the best of their ability, but it was not their idea to serve them directly; they proposed to serve them indirectly through the enormous forces already set up, which are so great that there is almost an open question whether the Government of the United States with the people back of it is strong enough to overcome and rule them.

Shall we try to get the grip of monopoly away from our lives, or shall we not? Shall we withhold our hand and say monopoly is inevitable, that all that we can do is to regulate it? Shall we say that all that we can do is to put government in competition with monopoly and try its strength against it? Shall we admit that the creature of our own hands is stronger than we are? We have been dreading all along the time when the combined power of high finance would be greater than the power of the Government. Have we come to a time when the President of the United States or any man who wishes to be President must doff his cap in the presence of this high finance, and say, "You are our inevitable master, but we will see how we can make the best of it?"

We are at the parting of the ways. We have, not one or two or three, but many, established and formidable monopolies in the United States. We have, not one or two, but many, fields of endeavor into which it is difficult, if not impossible, for the independent man to enter. We have restricted credit, we have restricted opportunity, we have controlled development, and we have come to be one of the worst ruled, one of the most completely controlled and dominated, governments in the civilized world—no longer a government by free opinion, no longer a government by conviction and the vote of the majority, but a government by the opinion and the duress of small groups of dominant men.

If the Government is to tell big business men how to run their business, then don't you see that big business men have to get closer to the Government even than they are now? Don't you see that they must capture the Government, in order not to be restrained too much by it? Must capture the Government? They have already captured it. Are you going to invite those inside to stay inside? They don't have to get there. They are there. Are you going to own your own premises, or are you not? That is your choice. Are you going to say: "You didn't get into the house the right way, but you are in there, God bless you; we will stand out here in the cold and you can hand us out something once in a while?"

At the least, under the plan I am opposing, there will be an avowed partnership between the Government and the trusts. I take it that the firm will be ostensibly controlled by the senior member. For I take it that the Government of the United States is at least the senior member, though the younger member has all along been running the business. But when all the momentum, when all the energy, when a great deal of the genius, as so often happens in partnerships the world over, is with the junior partner, I don't think that the superintendence of the senior partner is going to amount to very much. And I don't believe that benevolence can be read into the hearts of the trusts by the superintendence and suggestions of the Federal Government; because the Government has never within my recollection had its suggestions accepted by the trusts. On the contrary, the suggestions of the trusts have been accepted by the Government.

There is no hope to be seen for the people of the United States until the partnership is dissolved. And the business of the party now entrusted with power is going to be to dissolve it.

Those who supported the third party supported, I believe, a programme perfectly agreeable to the monopolies. How those who have been fighting monopoly through all their career can reconcile the continuation of the battle under the banner of the very men they have been fighting, I cannot imagine. I challenge the programme in its fundamentals as not a progressive programme at all. Why did Mr. Gary suggest this very method when he was at the head of the Steel Trust? Why is this very method commended here, there, and everywhere by the men who are interested in the maintenance of the present economic system of the United States? Why do the men who do not wish to be disturbed urge the adoption of this programme? The rest of the programme is very handsome; there is beating in it a great pulse of sympathy for the human race. But I do not want the sympathy of the trusts for the human race. I do not want their condescending assistance.

And I warn every progressive Republican that by lending his assistance to this programme he is playing false to the very cause in which he had enlisted. That cause was a battle against monopoly, against control, against the concentration of power in our economic development, against all those things that interfere with absolutely free enterprise. I believe that some day these gentlemen will wake up and realize that they have misplaced their trust, not in an individual, it may be, but in a programme which is fatal to the things which we hold dearest.

If there is any meaning in the things I have been urging, it is this: that the *incubus* that lies upon this country is the present monopolistic organization of our industrial life. That is the thing which certain Republicans became "insurgents" in order to throw off. And yet some of them allowed themselves to be so misled as to go into the camp of the third party in order to remove what the third party proposed to legalize. My point is that this is a method conceived from the point of view of the very men who are to be controlled, and that this is just the wrong point of view from which to conceive it.

I said not long ago that Mr. Roosevelt was promoting a plan for the control of monopoly which was supported by the United States Steel Corporation. Mr. Roosevelt denied that he was being supported by more than one member of that corporation. He was thinking of money. I was thinking of ideas. I did not say that he was getting money from these gentlemen; it was a matter of indifference to me where he got his money; but it was a matter of a great deal of difference to me where he got his ideas. He got his idea with regard to the regulation of monopoly from the gentlemen who form the United States Steel Corporation.

I am perfectly ready to admit that the gentlemen who control the United States Steel Corporation have a perfect right to entertain their own ideas about this and to urge them upon the people of the United States; but I want to say that their ideas are not my ideas; and I am perfectly certain that they would not promote any idea which interfered with their monopoly. Inasmuch, therefore, as I hope and intend to interfere with monopoly just as much as possible, I cannot subscribe to arrangements by which they know that it will not be disturbed.

The Roosevelt plan is that there shall be an industrial commission charged with the supervision of the great monopolistic combinations which have been formed under the protection of the tariff, and that the Government of the United States shall see to it that these gentlemen who have conquered labor shall be kind to labor. I find, then, the proposition to be this: That there shall be two masters, the great corporation, and over it the Government of the

United States; and I ask who is going to be master of the Government of the United States? It has a master now—those who in combination control these monopolies. And if the Government controlled by the monopolies in its turn controls the monopolies, the partnership is finally consumated.

I don't care how benevolent the master is going to be, I will not live under a master. That is not what America was created for. America was created in order that every man should have the same chance as every other man to exercise mastery over his own fortunes. What I want to do is analogous to what the authorities of the city of Glasgow did with tenement houses. I want to light and patrol the corridors of these great organizations in order to see that nobody who tries to traverse them is waylaid and maltreated. If you will but hold off the adversaries, if you will but see to it that the weak are protected, I will venture a wager with you that there are some men in the United States, now weak, economically weak, who have brains enough to compete with these gentlemen and who will presently come into the market and put these gentlemen on their mettle. And the minute they come into the market there will be a bigger market for labor and a different wage scale for labor.

Because it is susceptible of convincing proof that the high-paid labor of America,—where it is high paid,—is cheaper than the low-paid labor of the continent of Europe. Do you know that about ninety percent of those who are employed in labor in this country are not employed in the "protected" industries, and that their wages are almost without exception higher than the wages of those who are employed in the "protected" industries? There is no corner on carpenters, there is no corner on bricklayers, their is no corner on scores of individual classes of skilled laborers; but there is a corner on the poolers in the furnaces, there is a corner on the men who dive down into the mines; they are in the grip of a controlling power which determines the market rates of wages in the United States. Only where labor is free is labor highly paid in America.

When I am fighting monopolistic control, therefore, I am fighting for the liberty of every man in America, and I am fighting for the liberty of American industry.

It is significant that the spokesman for the plan of adopting monopoly declares his devoted adherence to the principle of "protection." Only those duties which are manifestly too high even to serve the interests of those who are directly "protected" ought in his view to be lowered. He declares that he is not troubled by the fact that a very large amount of money is taken out of the pocket of the general tax-payer and put into the pocket of particular classes of "protected" manufacturers, but that his concern is that so little of this money gets into the pocket of the laboring man and so large a proportion of it into the pockets of the employers. I have searched his programme very thoroughly for an indication of what he expects to do in order to see to it that a larger proportion of this "prize" money gets into the pay envelope, and have found none. Mr. Roosevelt, in one of his speeches, proposed that manufacturers who did not share their profits liberally enough with their workmen should be penalized by a sharp cut in the "protection" afforded them; but the platform, so far as I could see, proposed nothing.

Moreover, under the system proposed, most employers,—at any rate, practically all of the most powerful of them,—would be, to all intents and purposes, wards and protégés of the Government which is the master of us all; for no part of this programme can be discussed intelligently without remembering that monopoly, as handled by it, is not to be prevented, but accepted. It is to be accepted and regulated. All attempt to resist it is to be given up. It is to be accepted as inevitable. The Government is to set up a commission whose duty it will be, not to check or defeat it, but merely to regulate it under rules which it is itself to frame and develop. So that the chief employers will have this tremendous authority behind them: what they do, they have the license of the Federal Government to do.

And it is worth the while of the workingmen of the country to recall what the attitude toward organized labor has been of these masters of consolidated industries whom it is proposed that the Federal Government should take under its patronage as well as under its control.

They have been the stoutest and most successful opponents of organized labor, and they have tried to undermine it in a great many ways. Some of the ways they have adopted have worn the guise of philanthropy and good-will, and have no doubt been used, for all I know, in perfect good faith. Here and there they have set up systems of profit-sharing, of compensation for injuries, and of bonuses, and even pensions; but every one of these plans has merely bound their workingmen more tightly to themselves. Rights under these various arrangements are not legal rights. They are merely privileges which employees enjoy only so long as they remain in the employment and observe the rules of the great industries for which they work. If they refuse to be weaned away from their independence they cannot continue to enjoy the benefits extended to them.

When you have thought the whole thing out, therefore, you will find that the programme of the new party legalizes monopolies and systematically subordinates workingmen to them and to plans made by the Government both with regard to employment and with regard to wages. Take the thing as a whole, and it looks strangely like economic mastery over the very lives and fortunes of those who do the daily work of the Nation; and all this under the overwhelming power and sovereignty of the National Government. What most of us are fighting for is to break up this very partnership between big business and the Government. We call upon all intelligent men to bear

witness that if this plan were consummated, the great employers and capitalists of the country would be under a more overpowering temptation than ever
to take control of the Government and keep it subservient to their purpose.

What a prize it would be to capture! How unassailable would be the
majesty and the tyranny of monopoly if it could thus get sanction of law and
the authority of government! By what means, except open revolt, could we
ever break the crust of our life again and become free men, breathing an air
of our own, living lives that we wrought out for ourselves?

You cannot use monopoly in order to serve a free people. You cannot use
great combinations of capital to be pitiful and righteous when the consciences
of great bodies of men are enlisted, not in the promotion of special privilege,
but in the realization of human rights. When I read those beautiful portions
of the programme of the third party devoted to the uplift of mankind and see
noble men and women attaching themselves to that party in the hope that
regulated monopoly may realize these dreams of humanity, I wonder whether
they have really studied the instruments through which they are going to do
these things. The man who is leading the third party has not changed his
point of view since he was President of the United States. I am not asking him
to change it. I am not saying that he has not a perfect right to retain it. But
I do say that is is not surprising that a man who had the point of view with
regard to the government of this country which he had when he was President
was not chosen as President again, and allowed to patent the present processes
of industry and personally direct them how to treat the people of the United
States.

There has been a history of the human race, you know, and a history of
government; it is recorded; and the kind of thing proposed has been tried
again and again and has always led to the same result. History is strewn all
along its course with the wrecks of governments that tried to be humane,
tried to carry out humane programmes through the instrumentality of those
who controlled the material fortunes of the rest of their fellow-citizens.

I do not trust any promises of a change of temper on the part of monopoly.
Monopoly never was conceived in the temper of tolerance. Monopoly never
was conceived with the purpose of general development. It was conceived
with the purpose of special advantage. Has monopoly been very benevolent
to its employees? Have the trusts had a soft heart for the working people of
America? Have you found trusts that cared whether women were sapped of
their vitality or not? Have you found trusts who are very scrupulous about
using children in their tender years? Have you found trusts that were keen to
protect the lungs and the health and the freedom of their employees? Have
you found trusts that thought as much of their men as they did of their
machinery? Then who is going to convert these men into the chief instruments of justice and benevolence?

If you will point me to the least promise of disinterestedness on the part of the masters of our lives, then I will conceive you some ray of hope; but only upon this hypothesis, only upon this conjecture: that the history of the world is going to be reversed, and that the men who have the power to oppress us will be kind to us, and will promote our interests, whether our interests jump with theirs or not.

After you have made the partnership between monopoly and your Government permanent, then I invite all the philanthropists in the United States to come and sit on the stage and go through the motions of finding out how they are going to get philanthropy out of their masters.

I do not want to see the special interests of the United States take care of the workingmen, women, and children. I want to see justice, righteousness, fairness, and humanity displayed in all the laws of the United States, and I do not want any power to intervene between the people and their Government. Justice is what we want, not patronage and condescension and pitiful helpfulness. The trusts are our masters now, but I for one do not care to live in a country called free even under kind masters. I prefer to live under no masters at all.

I agree that as a nation we are now about to undertake what may be regarded as the most difficult part of our governmental enterprises. We have gone along so far without very much assistance from our Government. We have felt, and felt more and more in recent months, that the American people were at a certain disadvantage as compared with the people of other countries, because of what the governments of other countries were doing for them and our Government omitting to do for us.

It is perfectly clear to every man who has any vision of the immediate future, who can forecast any part of it from the indications of the present, that we are just upon the threshold of a time when the systematic life of this country will be sustained, or at least supplemented, at every point by governmental activity. And we have now to determine what kind of governmental activity it shall be; whether, in the first place, it shall be direct from the Government itself, or whether it shall be indirect, through instrumentalities which have already constituted themselves and which stand ready to supersede the Government.

I believe that the time has come when the governments of this country, both state and national, have to set the stage, and set it very minutely and carefully, for the doing of justice to men in every relationship of life. It has been free and easy with us so far; it has been go as you please; it has been every man look out for himself; and we have continued to assume, up to this year when every man is dealing, not with another man, in most cases, but with a body of men whom he has not seen, that the relationships of property are the same that they always were. We have great tasks before us, and we must enter on them as befits men charged with the responsibility of shaping a new era.

We have a great programme of governmental assistance ahead of us in the coöperative life of the Nation; but we dare not enter upon that programme until we have freed the Government. That is the point. Benevolence never developed a man or a Nation. We do not want a benevolent government. We want a free and a just government. Every one of the great schemes of social uplift which are now so much debated by noble people amongst us is based, when rightly conceived, upon justice, not upon benevolence. It is based upon the right of men to breathe pure air, to live; upon the right of women to bear children, and not to be over-burdened so that disease and breakdown will come upon them; upon the right of children to thrive and grow up and be strong; upon all these fundamental things which appeal, indeed, to our hearts, but which our minds perceive to be part of the fundamental justice of life.

Politics differs from philanthropy in this: that in philanthropy we sometimes do things through pity merely, while in politics we act always, if we are righteous men, on grounds of justice and large expediency for men in the mass. Sometimes in our pitiful sympathy with our fellow-men we must do things that are more than just. We must forgive men. We must help men who have gone wrong. We must sometimes help men who have gone criminally wrong. But the law does not forgive. It is its duty to equalize conditions, to make the path of right the path of safety and advantage, to see that every man has a fair chance to live and to serve himself, to see that injustice and wrong are not wrought upon any.

We ought not to permit passion to enter into our thoughts or our hearts in this great matter; we ought not to allow ourselves to be governed by resentment or any kind of evil feeling, but we ought, nevertheless, to realize the seriousness of our situation. That seriousness consists, singularly enough, not in the malevolence of the men who preside over our industrial life, but in their genius and in their honest thinking.

These men believe that the prosperity of the United States is not safe unless it is in their keeping. If they were dishonest, we might put them out of business by law; since most of them are honest, we can put them out of business only by making it impossible for them to realize their genuine convictions. I am not afraid of a knave. I am not afraid of a rascal. I am afraid of a strong man who is wrong, and whose wrong thinking can be impressed upon other persons by his own force of character and force of speech. If God had only arranged it that all the men who are wrong were rascals, we could put them out of business very easily, because they would give themselves away sooner or later; but God has made our task heavier than that,—he has made some good men who think wrong. We cannot fight them because they are bad, but because they are wrong. We must overcome them by a better force, the genial, the splendid, the permanent force of a better reason.

The reason that America was set up was that she might be different from all the nations of the world in this: that the strong could not put the weak to the wall, that the strong could not prevent the weak from entering the race. America stands for opportunity. America stands for a free field and no favor. America stands for a government responsive to the interests of all. And until America recovers those ideals in practice, she will not have the right to hold her head high again amidst the nations as she used to hold it.

It is like coming out of a stifling cellar into the open where we can breathe again and see the free spaces of the heavens to turn away from such a doleful programme of submission and dependence toward the other plan, the confident purpose for which the people have given their mandate.

Our purpose is the restoration of freedom. We purpose to prevent private monopoly by law, to see to it that the methods by which monopolies have been built up are legally made impossible. We design that the limitations on private enterprise shall be removed, so that the next generation of youngsters, as they come along, will not have to become protégés of benevolent trusts, but will be free to go about making their own lives what they will; so that we shall taste again the full cup, not of charity, but of liberty,—the only wine that ever refreshed and renewed the spirit of a people.

9. PAUL U. KELLOGG, "THE INDUSTRIAL PLATFORM OF THE NEW PARTY"

PROMINENT among the progressives who sought to organize reform on the national level were the social workers. By the century's second decade, leaders of this emerging profession had already made important contributions to local and state movements for better urban housing, the control of disease, and the elimination of industrial hazards. They were now prepared to offer a comprehensive social justice program. Spurned by both the Democratic and Republican party national conventions in 1912, social reformers found their opportunity when Theodore Roosevelt, denied the G.O.P. presidential nomination, stalked out of the Republican convention to place himself as standard-bearer of

SOURCE. Paul U. Kellog, "The Industrial Platform of the New Party," in *The Survey*, Vol. 28, No. 21, August 24, 1912, pp. 668–669.

the new Progressive party. Although some social workers distrusted Roosevelt, doubting that he was a true proponent of social reform, others like Jane Addams and Paul Kellogg endorsed the former Chief Executive when he accepted their platform of industrial minimums as an important plank of the Progressive party.

The following selection contains both a brief history and the basic planks of the new political party's industrial platform. It outlines a legislative program that, although never implemented by Roosevelt's soon-defunct Progressive party, nevertheless gained future acceptance through the sponsorship of both Democrats and Republicans.

The men and women identified with child labor committees, consumers' leagues, charity organization societies, settlements and the like, who drew up at Cleveland in June a series of labor planks which they could stand for collectively, little thought that in less than two months their platform would be adopted bodily as the practical economic gospel of a new political party. Yet that is the way the event has turned.

For three years the National Conference of Charities and Correction has had a committee on standards of living and labor. At the close of this year's session under the chairmanship of Owen R. Lovejoy, those present adjourned as members of the conference (which adopts no resolutions), and as individuals put forward their platform of industrial minimums. There were trade unionists and representatives of employers' associations among them, but for the most part the participants were actively engaged in what we lump as social work. There was a logical sequence in their approach to industrial conditions. The standards they set were clear-cut and they offered the public a new conception of the sphere of governmental concern in industry. They held that the human waste which modern large-scale production throws back upon the community in the shape of trade injuries and occupational disease, overwork and overstrain, orphanage and depleted households gives the public a stake in the human side of industry; that because of this public element, the public is entitled to complete facts as to the terms of work— hours, wages, accidents, etc.; that with these facts and with the advances made by physician and neurologist, economist and engineer, the public can formulate certain minimum standards below which it can be scientifically demonstrated that work can be carried on only at a social deficit; and finally that all industrial conditions falling below such standards should come within the sphere of governmental supervision and control, in the same way that subnormal sanitary conditions because they threaten the general welfare are subject to regulation.

In line with this general principle, certain minimum standards were put out which have won acceptance among those who know labor conditions first hand; and public commissions were called for to investigate wages, factory inspection, social insurance, etc., as a basis for formulating minimums which the public should sanction.

This general program Theodore Roosevelt drafted into his Confession of Faith and on August 6 put it before the Chicago convention of the Progressive Party with characteristic vigor. The same program had been presented by social workers at a hearing of the platform committee, at the earlier Chicago convention; but it left little apparent residuum in the compressed labor paragraph adopted by the Republican Party. The Democratic Party merely reiterated its labor planks of four years ago. . . .

SOCIAL AND INDUSTRIAL JUSTICE

The supreme duty of the national government is the conservation of human resources through an enlarged measure of social and industrial justice. We pledge ourselves to work unceasingly in state and nation for:

Effective legislation looking to the prevention of industrial accidents, occupational diseases, overwork, involuntary unemployment, and other injurious effects incident to modern industry.

The fixing of minimum safety and health standards for the various occupations and the exercise of the public authority of state and nation, including the federal control over interstate commerce, and the taxing power to maintain such standards.

The prohibition of child labor.

Minimum wage standards for working women to provide a "living wage" in all industrial occupations.

The general prohibition of night-work for women, and the establishment of an eight-hour day for women and young persons.

One day's rest in seven for all wage-workers.

The eight-hour day in continuous twenty-four-hour industries.

The abolition of the convict contract labor system; substituting a system of prison production for governmental consumption only, and the application of prisoners' earnings to the support of their dependent families.

Publicity as to wages, hours and conditions of labor; full reports upon industrial accidents and diseases, and the opening to public inspection of all tallies, weights, measures and check systems on labor products.

We pledge our party to establish a department of labor, with a seat in the cabinet, and with jurisdiction over matters affecting the conditions of labor and living. . . .

It is a truism of political history that minority parties ultimately write the platforms for all parties. In time, the causes which they have the temerity to espouse, are taken up by the established organizations when direct appeal to the latter may have proven fruitless. Doubtless this feeling has played a part in leading these and other social workers to throw themselves into the new movement. They have also had a sense of belonging there. They find themselves not in the position of bringing powerful interests round to a new way of thinking but of being met more than half way by men definitely committed to progress in all lines. They see the possibility of a new alignment in American public life which may ultimately lead to a temperamental cleavage between the conservative and progressive and one which is taking shape at a time when another great extension of the suffrage is in process.

However things may turn, the fact remains that in the past month, we have had for the first time in American life a striking hands of political reformers, conservationists and social workers in a piece of national team play; political and industrial insurgency joining forces in a rounded social program. Whatever the outcome of the present campaign or of the third party movement, it may serve to bring forward by fully five years the active discussion of proposals which the public mind has been slow to react upon in the United States, despite the fact that in New Zealand, England and continental Europe they have made large draughts on constructive criticism and statesmanship of the first calibre.

PART II

The Great Crusade

ON the evening of April 2, 1917, a solemn and burdened Woodrow Wilson appeared before a tense Congress to deliver a historic message. Germany's submarine warfare against neutral shipping, the President declared, "constituted warfare against mankind. . . . a war against all nations." Each nation must decide for itself how it would meet the challenge, Wilson said,

> but . . . I advise that the Congress declare the recent course of the Imperial German Government to be in fact nothing less than war against the Government and people of the United States; that it . . . accept the status of belligerent which has been thrust upon it; and . . . exert all its power and employ all its resources to bring the Government of the German Empire to terms and end the war.

The nation's objective, the President asserted, "is to vindicate the principles of peace and justice in the life of the world as against selfish and autocratic power and to set up amongst the really free and self-governed people of the world such a concert of purpose and of action as will henceforth ensure the observance of those principles." Then, in a phrase that captured the idealistic essence of the President's speech, Wilson said, "the world must be made safe for democracy." On April 4, by a vote of 82–6, the Senate adopted a resolution of war and two days later, the House concurred by a vote of 373 to 50. The House action came on the morning of Good Friday; that afternoon, near the hour when Christians throughout the nation would commemorate the death of Christ, the President signed the resolution officially proclaiming the country at war. The Great Crusade had begun.

What happened to the United States during World War I and the immediate postwar period of peacemaking has a significance that far transcends the military aspects of the war. Unquestionably, the United States furnished the Allies with the men and material that provided the margin of victory, but as historian David Shannon has remarked, "apart from the basic conditions of victory or defeat, what happens to a nation economically, politically, socially, and diplomatically during a war has a more lasting impact than the events of conflict." The changes that war and peace produced in America, both domestically and in the relations of the nation to the rest of the world, came with startling swiftness and impact. Some of the developments, of course, were ephemeral and inconsequential; others, however, were more profound and continue to affect the style of national life to this day.

The economic consequences of the war were felt at once, since the financial needs of the belligerents prompted them to liquidate their assets in the United States during the first days of the conflict in 1914. After an initial period of economic distress, most sectors of the economy began to benefit from the war needs of the European combatants. Loans to the belligerents, at first denied them by Secretary of State William J. Bryan on the ground that such transactions were unneutral acts, were later made available to make possible the purchase of American goods. Both loans and commercial intercourse, however, were monopolized almost entirely by the Allied Powers from the early days of the war since the British Navy effectively cut off trade between the United States and the Central Powers. British economic warfare naturally dislocated peacetime markets, but the war orders of the Allies more than offset the loss of trade with the Central Powers. The farmer, no less than the banker and the munitions maker, profited from the purchases of the Allies; by 1915 the prosperity of the nation was inextricably interwoven with the war needs of the Allied Powers.

After the United States entered the war against Germany in 1917, it seemed for a time that the economy, operating under a mixed system of government direction and laissez-faire, would be unable to sustain the war effort. To remedy the situation, the Government established a large number of federal agencies to provide overall direction and coordination. The outcome of this wartime experience was the achievement of an unparalleled degree of national efficiency and unity.

The first steps of the government toward effective mobilization, however, were faltering and unsure. After a series of advisory and supervisory boards headed by a succession of administrators failed to achieve effective industrial production, the Wilson Administration finally organized the War Industries Board in May 1918 and placed it under the direction of the astute financier, Bernard M. Baruch. The W.I.B. established priorities, allocated resources, secured standardization, thus eliminating much waste and duplication and, to some extent, coordinated government purchasing; it was highly successful in mobilizing industry. Moreover, the War Industries Board provided an example for the future. Thirteen years later, when the nation was plunged into depression, Franklin D. Roosevelt would model the National Recovery Administration after the successful War Industries Board and would name old W.I.B. hand, Hugh Johnson, to head it.

To effect the mobilization of agriculture, Congress passed the Lever Act in May 1917, creating the Office of Food Administration. Under the capable direction of Herbert Hoover, this agency assumed the responsibility for coordinating and regulating the production and distribution of food. The Food Administration urged all citizens to practice voluntary rationing and encouraged farmers to expand their crop and livestock enterprises to meet the needs at home and abroad. "The products of the American soil," writes Arthur Link, "were as instrumental in saving the Allies from disaster as were the American doughboys fighting in the trenches." At the same time, the increased crop and livestock production resulted in a general overexpansion of America's agricultural capacity, and the wartime prosperity lured farmers into a false sense of security. When the conflict ended and peacetime market conditions returned, many farmers, unable to meet their fixed operating costs, were forced to leave the farm and seek employment in the cities. Farmers who remained on the land had to struggle throughout the twenties with high mortgages and low commodity and livestock prices. However, the nation's farmers had demonstrated that the food and fiber of America could play a crucial role in world affairs.

In other vital areas of production and distribution, the Wilson Administration adopted wartime nationalization to achieve desired ends. Coal shortages were overcome by the incentive and regulatory policies of the Fuel Administration. Rail transportation bottlenecks were removed and operating difficulties overcome by government management of all the nation's railroads under one integrated system. However, a much less efficient record was achieved in development of a navy and merchant marine. In fact, the Emergency Fleet Corporation, plagued by administrative and other problems, did not function as expected until after the armistice. Yet if the war had lasted for several more months, the record of the Fleet Corporation could be cited as another success story; during the critical months of 1917–1918, government commandeering of foreign and enemy vessels in American ports provided the ships needed to transport both men and supplies to the Allies. Only the Aircraft Production Board was a conspicuous failure; the infant aircraft industry was simply unequal to the task assigned to it by the board and achieved only about one fourth of its goal of 22,000 planes by July 1918.

In order to direct this burgeoning bureaucracy, the government staffed many agencies with "dollar-a-year" businessmen who rendered service to the government for a nominal fee while they maintained their connections with their firms and corporations. No one has fully documented the extent wartime mobilization benefited businessmen but, generally, the public and business itself looked with favor upon the consolidation of industries into large-scale corporations. Congress assisted the development of powerful corporations by passing the Webb-Pomerene Act in January 1918, exempting the foreign operations of business firms from antitrust laws. "At the end of the war," William Leuchtenburg has observed, "business was determined to retain as far as possible the wartime system of operating outside the antitrust laws, and the war experience accelerated the merger movement and the trade-association movement of the 1920's." To a remarkable degree, the businessmen succeeded in achieving their objectives.

If the Wilson Administration placed businessmen in powerful positions within and without the government, it also recognized the necessity of fostering a productive and energetic labor force for the war effort. Two agencies in particular played important roles: the National War Labor Board, established in April 1918, served largely as a judicial body to arbitrate labor-management disputes; the War Labor Policies Board, organized the following month, made studies of the entire labor market with a view toward standardizing wages and hours. The United States Employment Service was established within the Department of Labor to assist the W.L.P.B., especially in registering workers and placing them in vital jobs. The expansion of organized labor, the shortening of the hours of work, the improvement of working conditions, and wage increases were benefits won by labor. However, the workers' wartime gains were not commensurate with those benefits secured by businessmen. When peace came, the government either dismantled or cut back appropriations for the labor agencies, and many of these gains were lost. Nevertheless, the benefits retained by labor provides some evidence that domestic reform was not killed by the war.

Although war was the nemesis of domestic reform generally, its exigencies also hastened the enactment of some long-sought reforms. Prohibition, for example, an old reform of special importance to old-stock moral crusaders of rural and small-town America, gained the impetus it needed to become national policy as a direct consequence of America's involvement in the European conflict. Before the war the drys could not overcome the wet sentiment of the non-Protestant masses of the cities and the objections of local option and state rights advocates who were opposed to making prohibition the policy of the nation. But after April 1917, the prohibitionists had powerful new arguments to advance their cause. By linking prohibition with patriotism, by associating alcohol with German-American ("Hun") brewers, and by stressing the need for the conservation of grain, they achieved their goal. Both the Lever Act and the Selective Service Act of 1917 contained provisions that pleased the drys: the Lever Act prohibited the use of grain for distilling hard liquor and empowered the President to ban the manufacture of other alcoholic beverages; the Selective Service Act forbade the sale of alcoholic beverages at or near military and naval stations. Congress submitted the Eighteenth Amendment to the states on December 18, 1917 and, by January 1919, the requisite number had approved the constitutional change that seemingly made national prohibition and the triumph of the temperance crusade irrevocable and complete.

The war also brought about the last stages of the drive for national women's suffrage. Andrew Sinclair has pointed out that the war assisted the suffrage cause through the good example that most women set in support of the government. Although the first woman to be elected to the Congress, Representative Jeannette Rankin of Montana, had voted against the resolution of war, feminists like Carrie Catt insisted that the "true" women of the country supported the war effort. President Wilson overcame his opposition to women suffrage and asked the Senate in September 1918 to approve the Nineteenth Amendment on the grounds that suffrage was a war measure necessary to make the world safe for democracy. Congressional passage of the amendment finally came in June 1919, and ratification by the states was accomplished by August 1920.

Some progressives such as John Dewey actually came to regard war itself as an instrument of social possibilities. Although Dewey never accepted all the claims that advocates of efficiency had made in behalf of the government's mobilization activities (which in themselves fulfilled the dreams of many progressive followers of Frederick W. Taylor and his program of scientific management), he applauded the support that wartime nationalism and socialism gave to his belief in the merits of public control over private enterprise. Dewey also believed that the war would foster internationalism and thereby break down barriers that hitherto had separated men into quarreling, selfish communities. He observed too that war had demonstrated the potentialities of science to achieve good as well as evil. The pragmatic philosopher became impatient with the pacificists and conscientious objectors who did not recognize and support these social possibilities.

No one offered sharper criticism of Dewey's views on war than the brilliant young intellectual, Randolph Bourne. Bourne was especially chagrined that Dewey believed men might shape the forces of war to achieve socially desirable ends. "War," said Bourne, "determines its own end—victory, and government crushes out automatically all forces that deflect, or threaten to deflect, energy from the path of organization to that end."

This was, in fact, essentially what happened. The government mobilized public opinion behind the war as effectively as it mobilized material resources and manpower. One week after the United States entered the war, President

Wilson authorized the establishment of a Committee on Public Information and placed it under the direction of a Denver journalist, George Creel. The Creel Committee assumed with undiminished vigor its task of selling the war to America. Aided by self-appointed censors, overzealous government officials, and hastily drafted laws, the Committee succeeded in its objective, but not without infringing on the civil liberties of many citizens. The one notable exception to an otherwise bleak period of intolerance was the formation of the American Civil Liberties Union, which understandably had to devote much of its initial energies to a defense of its own existence.

Diplomatically, President Wilson and his followers transmuted the war into a holy crusade that would "make the world safe for democracy." Even before the country entered the war, the President had supported American membership in a postwar league of nations, and in an address to Congress in January 1917, he called for a "peace without victory," and "peace among equals." A year later, after the Bolshevik Revolution had occurred and Lenin had branded the war as an imperialist struggle, Wilson provided a compact formulation of his liberal creed in the Fourteen Points.

The immediate effects of Wilson's liberal principles were to counteract the Bolshevik call for the transformation of the war into a worker's revolution, to infuse the Allied cause with new idealism, and to provide the basis on which the German people could enter into an armistice. Ironically, the Treaty of Versailles and the Covenant of the League satisfied neither liberals nor conservatives; as a consequence, the nation turned in disillusionment from the League of Nations and the long-range, negative effect of the Great Crusade took hold upon the American people. Instead of turning the energies of the nation toward the tasks of domestic and international reform, the "war to end all wars" left men cynical and complacent, little interested in the League of Nations, and content to pursue domestic affairs along conservative lines.

Viewed in the larger context of world history, the consequences of the settlement at Versailles conformed more to the dire prophecies of the pessimists than the bright hopes of the optimists. An embittered and impoverished Germany, saddled with huge reparations, eventually failed to meet even the scaled-down economic demands of the Allies, as the brilliant English economist John Maynard Keynes had predicted in 1919. The depression that overtook Germany and the world in the twenties and thirties not only provoked widespread hardships but also assisted the rise of the militant totalitarian regimes of Mussolini's Italy and Hitler's Nazi Germany. In Asia a restless Japan was to seek the territory and resources that would endow her with the great power status and equality that the Western democracies had denied her at Versailles. The most important legacies of the Great Crusade, however, were the enduring and competing ideologies of the twentieth century: the liberal democratic principles of Wilson and the communism of Lenin. The war and peace of 1917–1919, in spawning the strategies of containment and counterrevolution, helped set the stage for World War II and the subsequent Cold War as well.

SECONDARY SOURCES

1. ROBERT E. OSGOOD, "THE SECOND CRUSADE"

HISTORIANS have been more concerned with the causes of America's entrance into World War I than with the motives of the American people during the years of conflict. Certainly, motives are as difficult to fathom as causes; yet an understanding of the motives that operated in the minds of people and their leaders during the Great Crusade is vital if we are to understand the difficulties that surrounded the waging of war and peace.

One of the most perceptive analyses of the objectives of the American people at war in 1917–1918 is that of Robert E. Osgood, Professor of Political Science at the Center for the Study of American Foreign Policy at the University of Chicago. Osgood has found that although the war objectives advanced by the spokesmen of various groups were quite diverse, by and large the sentiments of the people polarized around the opposing views of President Woodrow Wilson and his chief antagonist, Theodore Roosevelt.

Wilson maintained that the nation's war policy should be one of altruism, with no greater object than that of securing for all mankind a just and lasting peace. The President could on occasion arouse the narrow nationalistic spirit in the masses, but he more consistently appealed to the people to support the war on a higher plane of

SOURCE. Robert E. Osgood, *Ideals and Self-Interest in America's Foreign Relations: The Great Transformation of the Twentieth Century*, Chicago: University of Chicago Press, 1953, pp. 264–281. Copyright by University of Chicago, 1953. Reprinted by permission of the University of Chicago Press and the author.

*idealism. Humanity, not the United States and the Allied Powers, he explained, would
be the victor of the Great War.*

*In his public speeches and private correspondence, a bellicose Theodore Roosevelt
vigorously challenged the benevolent idealism of President Wilson. In sharp contrast
to the lofty objectives of Wilson, Roosevelt asserted his belief in the nation's self-
interest. "First and foremost," he insisted, "we are to make the world safe for ourselves.
This is our war, America's war."*

*Although the Wilsonian dream of a new world order seemed to be in ascendancy
during the last months of the conflict and the early months of the peacemaking that
followed the armistice, millions of Americans shared the realistic reservations of
Theodore Roosevelt. Unfortunately, in the ensuing controversy between idealists and
realists, both groups lost sight of the nation's enlightened self-interest.*

1. The Frustrated Crusade

The way the American people fought World War I and the way they
made peace are two inseparable parts of the same frustrated crusade. As
in 1898, the impact of war wrought changes in America's crusade which
radically altered its entire aspect. Under the stress of war and with the approach of peace, an apparent fusion between egoistic and altruistic impulses
disintegrated in a conflict between divergent attitudes toward the nation's
role in international politics. America's pacific idealists, international reformers, and moral optimists reconciled themselves to violence by setting their
sights on the millennium. America's militant idealists and political realists
tried to counteract the lure of the millennium with the spirit of war, lest
altruism interfere with nationalistic goals. The controversy between these two
groups obscured the objects of enlightened self-interest, for which all factions
might have fought; it confounded the practical expedients of peacemaking,
upon which all might have agreed.

Because neither war nor peace seemed related to any enduring self-interest,
the motives which led to war were not adequate for the prosecution of war,
and the objects for which the nation fought were not sufficiently compelling
to sustain the break with isolation that was necessary for their fulfilment.
Consequently, the great mass of Americans thrilled at a glimpse of utopia,
and then, with the immediate object of victory achieved, lapsed back into
normalcy under the inertia of traditional conceptions of national self interest
and conventional attitudes toward the outside world.

2. America Searches for a Reason to Fight

America began its second crusade with a spirit of resignation to the unavoidable task of vindicating American rights rather than with a spontaneous
burst of moral enthusiasm for waging the battle of humanity. Americans, as

a whole, did not enter the war for the objects that Wilson proclaimed in his addresses of January 22 and April 2. Yet a nation so prone to judge international relations with an ethical yardstick and a nation so reluctant to entangle itself in the world struggle for power could find little inspiration or satisfaction in fighting a war merely for the limited objective of vindicating American rights.

One indication that the motives which led to intervention would not suffice in war was a suggestion of bewilderment and a groping for explanations that crept into popular discussion of the war during the early months of American participation. The American people, having found themselves involved in a war begun and fought for reasons which they believed had nothing to do with their own tangible interests, now began to wonder how it had all happened and what it was all about.

Three weeks after the nation accepted the "challenge to all mankind," the *New Republic* observed that public opinion was curiously placid and unenthusiastic about the war. The people were loyally acquiescent; they had confidence in the President; but they still entertained a suspicion that something had been "put over" on them. Several weeks later the Washington correspondent of the *New York Evening Post* reported that in all parts of the country he found "the opinion that apathy prevails, that there is not much genuine enthusiasm about the war, or the Liberty Loan, but that the people are responding more because of their traditional patriotism than a clear comprehension of what it is all about."

The official explanation of intervention disavowed any hatred or rancor toward the German people and pledged the nation to eschew aggrandizement. At the same time, official and unofficial spokesmen rejected the notion that the United States was committed to the cause of the Allied Powers. So why were Americans fighting?

There was general agreement that the United States had intervened for its own reasons and would fight for its own ends. The *Topeka Capital* thought that America had entered the war "for special reasons, having nothing to do with the dynastic and nationalistic reasons actuating Russia, France, Italy, and England." Oswald Garrison Villard's *New York Evening Post* expressed the opinion of many who had accepted intervention reluctantly when it stated,

It will not do to say that because Americans as a whole sympathize with the Allies, therefore they must lose their identity in a European alliance. Some say that its cause is ours. It may be. But we have never thought of going to war for that reason, and cannot now. If we take up arms against Germany it will be on an issue exclusively between that empire and this republic; and the republic must retain control of that issue from beginning to end.

The *Nation*, another reluctant interventionist but a supporter of Wilson's moral leadership, also expressed the complete independence of America's purpose: "We have no selfish objects in the war. Conquests and indemnities we disclaim in advance. Our battle is solely for the law of nations and for the right of self-government." Therefore, it recommended that the United States withdraw from the war as soon as the original object of the war was achieved.

However, the general tendency to believe that America should fight for its own ends was by no means matched by an agreement upon what those ends ought to be or how they could be attained. It is true that Wilson's phrase "the world must be made safe for democracy" achieved wide currency, but just what that meant in the way of concrete performance was left open to question. Did it mean a peace without victory, a negotiated peace for limited ends, or a crushing military defeat of Germany and a revision of the map of Europe? The one American who, above all others, was in a position to clarify this uncertainty was President Wilson himself.

3. Wilson Explains the War

In the months following the tumultous welcome that Congress showered upon Wilson's War Message, the President scrupulously retained his sober mood of exalted purpose. He would allow no mean or petty selfishness, no unworthy passion, no hate nor vengeance to darken the higher counsel of service to humanity. Self-control and altruism had been the theme of his neutrality policy; they were equally the theme of his war policy.

Two weeks after his War Message the President delivered an appeal to the people. "There is not a single selfish element, so far as I can see, in the cause we are fighting for. We are fighting for what we believe and wish to be the rights of mankind and for the future peace and security of the world." On May 12 he said, "We have gone in with no special grievance of our own, because we have always said that we were the friends and servants of mankind. We look for no profit. We look for no advantage." In a Memorial Day address on May 30 he rejoiced that "in the providence of God America will once more have an opportunity to show to the world that she was born to serve mankind." This religious sense of dedication was even more manifest in his address before the Confederate Veterans on June 5. Proclaiming the American mission, as hundreds of times before, Wilson conjured the people to envision the unfolding of God's majestic plan to use Americans as His chosen instrument to make liberty secure for all mankind, for God had made the nation strong in order to prove, not its selfishness, but its spirit of self-sacrifice.

If this lofty purpose was the primary reason for fighting the war, had Wilson forgotten the loss of American lives on American ships and the long list of Germany's violations of American rights? In a rather heated letter to Congressman Heflin of Alabama, dated May 22, the President answered the critics who accused him of excessive vagueness in explaining the reasons for war. As in his address of April 2, he drew a distinction between the causes and the objects of intervention.

It is incomprehensible to me how any frank or honest person could doubt or question my position with regard to the war and its objects. I have again and again stated the very serious and long continued wrongs which the Imperial German Government has perpetrated against the rights, the commerce, and the citizens of the United States. . . . No nation that respected itself or the rights of humanity could have borne those wrongs any longer.

"Our objects," he continued, "have been stated with equal clearness" in the addresses of January 22 and April 2. "We have entered the war for our own reasons and with our own objects clearly stated, and shall forget neither the reasons nor the objects."

Wilson's distinction between the reasons and objects of intervention was a tacit recognition of the fact that he considered the immediate cause—that is, the violation of American rights and honor—as, in itself, an inadequate justification for war. He was no more willing to justify American intervention than he had been content to press for strict accountability solely in terms of vindicating purely national concerns. In both neutrality and war, only America's mission of bringing peace and democracy to the world elevated the pursuit of American ends far enough above the level of selfishness to satisfy Wilson.

As the war continued, Wilson's "objects" took precedence over his "reasons." This was to win for him the devout support of a vocal group of liberals, intellectuals, and idealists and the determined opposition of America's strong nationalists and militant Realists. It was to involve the great mass of Americans in a momentous crusade, the concrete implications of which they scarcely comprehended.

Throughout 1917 Wilson's objects embellished his public pronouncements as lofty expressions of American righteousness. But, although they received general acclaim, they failed to inspire the nation with overwhelming enthusiasm for the war. There were signs that America wanted more than sermons. If there was little with which one could disagree in Wilson's pronouncements, there was also little that one could solidly grasp. Ordinary people seemed to demand something more concrete, something more down-to-earth to fight for. There was a growing tendency to criticize the nation's apathy, confusion, and lack of fighting spirit. There were demands that the President assert a stronger leadership in order to rally American patriotism. The strong interventionists and nationalists were particularly irritated by Wilson's bland benevolence.

President Wilson seemed to make an effort to meet this situation in his Flag Day address on June 14. It was the most pugnacious statement of the reasons for intervention that he delivered during the entire war. Significantly enough, it was also one of his most popular addresses. There was nothing in this speech about making the world safe for democracy or dedicating the nation to the task of world peace. "It is plain enough how we were forced into the war," Wilson said; and he proceeded to denounce the "military masters of Germany" and their sinister conspiracy against the peace and security of democratic peoples, their flagrant violation of American rights and honor on the high seas and at home, the lies and hypocrisy of their propaganda concerning peace. "For us there is but one choice. We have made it. Woe be to the man or group of men that seeks to stand in our way."

This fighting speech demonstrated Wilson's capacity for militancy. The nation responded to his Scotch combativeness. Yet it was not really his kind of speech. Roosevelt could have done it better. The effect soon wore off. When the President finally rallied American enthusiasm behind his leadership, it was on the basis of ideal goals which had been taking shape in his mind since the beginning of the European conflict. Just as Wilson had initiated a New Diplomacy, so he would lead the people in a new kind of war, one without hatred or bitterness, one for humanity, not just for the United States.

4. The Resurgence of Egoism

Wilson based his moral leadership upon a mystic faith in the altruism of the people, but in the summer of 1917 it became increasingly evident that a powerful faction of the people was determined to wage war in the old way, for tangible and self-interested reasons first, and for universal ideals second. The *Literary Digest* of June 16 noted that there were journals and individuals of unquestioned loyalty "who feel that the official statement of our case, with its emphasis on noble and altruistic ideals, needs to be supplemented by a sharp reminder that this is for us a war of self-defense in which the very soul of our nation is at stake."

Some who had warmly applauded Wilson's statement of American ideals in his War Message became disturbed when it appeared that the welfare of humanity might be stressed to the exclusion of practical self-interest and an unqualified victory over Germany. One such person was "Colonel" George Harvey, editor of the *North American Review*.

In May, 1917, Harvey, who had been Wilson's early political sponsor and was soon to become one of his bitterest political adversaries, had lauded the President's address as a "natural and logical sequence of the Declaration of Independence and the Emancipation Proclamation." He had held that the war was nominally for defense, since it was forced upon the nation by overt acts, but that, in the last analysis, "this war is a continuation of the three-centuries-old strife between the despotic spirit of the Old World and the free spirit of the New."

However, Harvey had also believed that the way to vindicate the cause of democracy was to achieve a crushing military victory. Temperamentally, he had been in Roosevelt's camp. In fact, ever since the *Lusitania* incident his policy had been Roosevelt's rather than Wilson's. In the election of 1916 he had split with the administration because of what he regarded as its timidity in the face of national humiliation.

Therefore, it is not strange that, in the August issue of the *North American Review*, Harvey should have exclaimed, "Peace with complete victory! Peace with unconditional surrender! It is the only way—the only way of living, the only way of righteousness, the only way of mercy." He was dismayed by the lack of fighting spirit in the nation. "The predominant spirit even now is fidelity to the Government rather than to the cause." He warned that this attitude would have to be reckoned with later when American soldiers actually started dying on foreign battlefields and the old query as to why the United States should intervene in a European war arose again. He asserted that the only way to arouse the nation to meet this test was to fight the war on a straight nationalist basis.

It has seemed to us, having in mind the self-interest in human nature, that the most effective method of enlisting the full endeavors of our own people is by convincing them, first, of their own peril and, secondly, of what we believe to be the fact, namely, that if the war is to be won at all America must win it.

Harvey's view was an omen of the same shift toward the aggressive and self-seeking impulses that had marked the imperialists' attitude toward the crusade against Spain. Once more the shock of war was intensifying the antipathy between an altruistic and self-assertive view of national conduct and revealing a fundamental schism among the proponents of the American mission.

The militant idealists of 1917 were on the defensive. They did not speak of the glories of violence, of war's beneficent influence upon human character and the progress of civilization. They did not conjure visions of a Manifest Destiny. They were defending the status quo now. But the temperamental and philosophical basis of their mounting antagonism toward the prophets of self-denial and sweet reasonableness was as evident as in 1898. The validity of universal ideals as a national goal was still, in their minds, contingent upon their coincidence with national self-interest. National benevolence and philanthropy were still valued only incidentally to the vigorous assertion of national power.

5. Roosevelt Repudiates Wilson's War Objectives

. . . in the private correspondence and public pronouncements of Theodore Roosevelt one can trace the shifting course of national egoism and militant idealism. . . .

Under the stress of war it was the underlying difference between these two leaders [Roosevelt and Wilson] which came to the fore.

Three days after Wilson's address Roosevelt wrote his British friend Arthur Lee, "If Wilson will now act in thoroughgoing fashion I shall back him to the limit of my power. I fear it is too late for us to do very efficient work; but thank God we are in, and are able to look men in the eyes without flinching!"

In an article in the June issue of the *Metropolitan*, urging that American troops be sent to France immediately, Roosevelt wrote one of his last passages commending the President in any way.

Thank Heaven, we now have the right to hold up our heads, and look honorable men in the eyes without flinching. The President and the majority of Congress, without distinction of party, earned the gratitude of all self-respecting Americans by their attitude during the first week of April, 1917.

Now we must hit hard, Roosevelt continued. Let us have obligatory military service and conscription. Let us send an expeditionary force to help our comrades in arms. And, finally, let the average citizen get clearly in mind what this war is for. "Let us strive for the peace of justice and of international right." But let there be no peace, he said, until the objects of the war are obtained. Roosevelt listed the peace terms for which the Allies should strive, in principle. They were remarkably similar to those of the subsequent Versailles Treaty, but, significantly, they concerned political and territorial settlements only.

In the July issue of the *Metropolitan* he was still considering the terms of a peace of righteousness, this time in greater detail. He stressed America's unselfish purpose.

The United States does not wish from Germany, Austria, or Turkey a foot of land or a dollar of indemnity. We are in this war partly because it had become impossible for a high-minded nation longer to submit to the intolerable outrages and injuries which for two years we had suffered from Germany; and partly because it was—as it long had been—our clear duty to take an active part in the war for democracy against autocracy, for right against wrong, for liberty against militaristic tyranny, for the cause of the free people against the despotic and oligarchic governments which deny freedom to the peoples.

Roosevelt admitted that it was impossible to devise a peace that would be entirely satisfactory from the standpoint of abstract justice, but substantial justice could be done, and the United States was in the best position to do it. There was little in this article with which Wilson could have disagreed; but the title, "The Peace of Victory for Which We Strive," was an omen of stormier days ahead.

At the same time, Roosevelt's private correspondence expressed a deep and fundamental antagonism toward Wilson and what he stood for. Roosevelt was convinced that Wilson was a pacifist at heart and a selfish partisan and hypocrite into the bargain. He suspected that Wilson would try every way possible to get out of using violence. He despised the sonorous Wilsonian platitudes, and he thought it was the most colossal misfortune of the century that in a time of crisis the President of the United States should be a cold-blooded, unpatriotic rhetorician. He charged that as a result of Wilson's faltering and cowardly leadership Americans had entered the war without really knowing why. To Lord Bryce he wrote, scarcely two weeks after American intervention,

> The perpetual talk and agitation by the International League to Enforce Peace, the announcements that we would welcome peace-without-victory, the hostile notes to England, the endless series, first of condemnatory notes to Germany and then of apologies to Germany, have resulted in the average man being completely puzzled. . . .

Roosevelt's private opinion of Wilson's War Message was anything but favorable. It seemed to him that the only way it could be justified was by unstintingly condemning everything Wilson had done before, when he was spending two and one-half years dulling the American conscience and weakening the nation's moral fiber. To William Allen White he pointed out that there was more justification for going to war immediately after the sinking of the *Lusitania* than in April, 1917. He conceded that it was possible, though not proper, to make some kind of defense "for our going to war on the ground that we were fighting purely for our own interests and rights, and because after two years Germany still adhered to the position about which we had sent her an ultimatum two years previous."

> But what is perfectly impossible, what represents really nauseous hypocrisy, is to say that we have gone to war to make the world safe for democracy, in April, when sixty days previously we had been announcing that we wished a "Peace without victory," and had no concern with the "causes or objects" of the war. I do not regard any speech as a great speech when it is obviously hypocritical and in bad faith; nor do I regard the making of such a speech of service to the world. I regard it as a damage to the cause of morality and decency.

Roosevelt's revulsion from Wilson's persistent idealization of American intervention corresponded with his increasing dissatisfaction with what he considered the administration's half-hearted prosecution of the war. In his mind, winning the war came first; all other objectives depended upon victory. Above all, a sentimental attachment for lofty purposes should not be allowed to distract impressionable minds from the hard and practical dictates of righteousness. With mounting impatience he prodded the administration to fight a full-scale war and field an army of at least five million men. As in his campaign for preparedness, he became obsessed with the profound frustration of his militant idealism at the hands of an insidious form of pseudo idealism he was powerless to combat. His frustration was made doubly intense by Wilson's refusal to accept his offer to lead a Roosevelt Division in the field.

By the end of the summer of 1917 Roosevelt was bending all his energies toward arousing the American people to a fighting pitch, toward opening their eyes to the compelling national interests at stake. Now he said virtually nothing about peace terms or about the vindication of the principles of democracy. In an article entitled "Must We Be Brayed in a Mortar Before Our Folly Depart from Us?" he returned to his life-long theme of preparedness.

> We cannot permanently hold a leading place in the world unless we prepare. But there is far more than world-position at stake. Our mere safety at home is at stake. . . . The probabilities are that the next time we fight a formidable foe we shall not again find allies whose interest it will be to protect us, and to shield us from the consequences of our feebleness and shortsightedness, as France and England have for six months— indeed for three years—been doing.

Thus while Americans in general found increasing consolation in the thought that they were fighting the war to end all wars, Roosevelt was already thinking about the next war; for in his mind force always had been and, in the foreseeable future, would continue to be a persistent element of international relations, which men would ignore at their peril.

It was the basic elements of power and force in the current struggle that Roosevelt aimed to drive home to the American people in his tract *The Foes of Our Own Household*, which he completed in the fall of 1917. America was off on no crusade, he said. "We went to war because for two years the Germans had been murdering our unarmed men, women, and children, and had definitely announced their intention to continue the practice." America's object in the war was not to be defined in terms of any vague pronouncement about making the world safe for democracy. "First and foremost we are to make the world safe for ourselves. This is our war, America's war. If we do not win it, we shall some day have to reckon with Germany single-handed. Therefore, for our own sakes let us strike down Germany."

Recent technological advances in the art of warfare convinced Roosevelt that American isolation was less tenable than ever. He wanted the American people to understand

> that world conditions have changed and that the oceans and even the air have become highways for military aggression. . . . The exploits of the German U-boat off Nantucket last summer . . . showed that if Germany . . . were free to deal with us, the security that an ocean barrier once offered was annihilated. In other words, the battlefront of Europe is slowly spreading over the whole world.

On September 20 Roosevelt set out upon a speaking tour of the West in order to take his message to the people. His speeches bristled with patriotism and bellicosity but said little about the war's ideal objectives. In fact, by way of depreciating these objectives, he seemed anxious to reassert the very reasons for intervention which Wilsonian idealists found most unsatisfactory. At Johnstown, Pennsylvania, he declared,

> We did not go to war to make democracy safe, and we did go to war because we had a special grievance. We went to war, because, after two years, with utter contempt of our protests, [during which] she had habitually and continually murdered our non-combatant men, women, and children on the high seas, Germany formally announced that she intended to pursue this course more ruthlessly and vigorously than ever. This was the special grievance because of which we went to war, and it was far more than an empty justification for going to war. As you know, my own belief is that we should have acted immediately after the sinking of the *Lusitania*.

Clearly, the conception of war as vengeance for a grievance was more compatible with a warlike spirit than Wilson's view of war as an altruistic enterprise. It was consistent with Roosevelt's determination that the war should end in a complete victory, in an overwhelming show of force.

6. WILSON GIVES IDEALISTS A WAR PROGRAM: LASTING PEACE

As Roosevelt's war policy centered more and more upon an appeal to the fighting instincts and the basic imperatives of national power, President Wilson strove to place the war on an ever higher level of morality. On January 8, 1918, he went before Congress and, partly to restore the moral position of the Allies after Russian revolutionists had bared the Czar's archives, announced his memorable Fourteen Points, which soon became one of the most effective war programs in the history of modern nations. Here, at last, was a neat formulation of the idealistic basis for a crusade.

Eight of the points applied to political and territorial settlements in specific areas. These were quite similar to Roosevelt's peace terms of six months before; but the first five points expressed the ideal aspirations which had already seized the imagination of liberal groups in England and the United States, and in Germany as well, and which had even spread among revolutionary groups in Russia and elsewhere: open diplomacy, freedom of the seas, the reduction of economic barriers, the limitation of armaments, and the adjustment of colonial claims on a fair basis. The fourteenth point called for a general association of nations to guarantee the political independence and territorial integrity of great and small nations alike; this was the point dearest to Wilson's heart.

Wilson subsequently elaborated upon the Fourteen Points and added some new points, but it was his original codification of the requirements of a better world that captured the moral fervor of American idealists and became America's war program. However vague and subject to distortion and varied interpretation that program may have been, it had a tremendous impact upon those who yearned for world reform and dreamed of the application of the standards of individual conduct to international society. If war could realize this vision, then it might truly merit the unqualified zeal of men imbued with the gentle spirit of reason and good will.

It was Wilson's moral leadership, under the banner of the Fourteen Points, that finally enabled pacific idealists to reconcile themselves completely to the unpleasant fact of American participation in a world war. In a large measure, it was this final reconciliation to war on the part of men imbued with a strong liberal conscience and a deep-rooted aversion to naked power that consecrated America's second crusade as an altruistic mission. Once these men became convinced that America was going to fight a new type of war, a war to abolish the old diplomacy of power politics, a war to end war, they dedicated their intellects and their souls with unstinting devotion to Wilson's cause. From their ranks came the most skilful, sincere, and enthusiastic propagators of the thesis that America's prime purpose in the war was the disinterested service of the rest of the world. . . .

War is not only a great tragedy; it is sometimes a great opportunity. Only the opportunity for international reform made war bearable for many of America's pacific idealists. When one considers the strength of their inhibitions toward conflict and force, it is understandable that only the loftiest motives could have reconciled them to organized violence. It is no exaggeration to say that for the moral optimists of 1914 Wilson's war aims were a psychological necessity. Naturally, after America intervened these men were hypersensitive to every indication that the war might fall short of achieving these aims.

Of course, this was not true of all liberals and pacific idealists. The *New Republic* had taken a leading part in urging world peace as the basis for American intervention. One of its most influential editors, Walter Lippmann, subsequently had a major influence in the formulation of the Fourteen Points. As Secretary of The Inquiry, a group under the direction of House, which Wilson appointed in the fall of 1917 to prepare a program for peace, Lippmann was responsible for a large share of the abstract ideas which formed the basis of Wilson's war aims and which found their way into a number of Wilson's public speeches. But Lippmann and the editors of the *New Republic* did not base their case for America's participation in the war solely upon Wilson's lofty objects. In their minds intervention was also a practical dictate of national expediency, justified upon grounds of enduring strategic interests; and they regarded membership in an international organization as a means of securing these strategic interests in a larger context.

After the United States intervened the *New Republic* continued to view the idea of a league, not as a dogma, but as a specific arrangement for controlling national power to the best interests of the United States. Because the editors considered the plan for a league as a logical extension of America's reasons for entering the war, rather than as a moral compensation for that distasteful decision, they had no patience with those who, having been reconciled to war solely by the vision of international organization, became seized with doubts when the millennium failed to materialize according to schedule.

In an editorial on October 6, 1917, the *New Republic* joined the doubters in deploring the attempted perversion of America's cause at the hands of the nationalists and the lovers of violence, but it expressed its complete lack of sympathy with those who questioned the wisdom of the declaration of war against Germany on that account. The United States had entered the war because it anticipated the disastrous consequences of a German victory; the editors considered that subsequent events had thoroughly vindicated the wisdom of that calculation.

In a later editorial, taking stock of the political and military changes that had come about during the year since Wilson's War Message, the *New Republic* concluded that interventionists had "abundant reason to congratulate themselves on their decision." The editors regretted the intolerance and hatred that accompanied America's war effort, but they were not disillusioned about intervention, for by that action the United States had prevented a German victory and thereby helped gain the opportunity for establishing a world organization, which might save the nation from future disaster.

In its fusion of realism with idealism the *New Republic* was distinguished from its liberal confrere, the *Nation*, which had accepted intervention reluctantly and which became thoroughly reconciled to America's participation only after it received the assurance of Wilson's Fourteen Points that the war would result in a brave new world. Significantly, it was the *Nation* and not the *New Republic* which placed itself in the vanguard of disillusion when the New World order proved to be a continuation of the Old, after all.

Of course, there were also a few idealists who were never persuaded by Wilson's moral leadership that the glorious end might justify the dreadful means. Oswald Garrison Villard, the editor of the *New York Evening Post* and, after January, 1918, editor of the *Nation*, was one of these holdouts. Randolph Bourne, a brilliant hunchback, who was to become a saint for disillusioned intellectuals after the war, was another. These men—most of them devout pacifists and democratic socialists—were repelled from the war chiefly by a sense of its futility and by an abhorrence of the repercussions of superpatriotism upon reason, decency, and the civil liberties of nonconformists.

As Bourne put it, "The whole era has been spiritually wasted." He charged that the intellectuals had sold their souls to all the rich and reactionary elements of society by abetting the war spirit in order to retain their influence with the nation. In his view the real enemy was War, not Germany. War was the absolute evil, with a will of its own, from which nothing good could result. The real arena of social conflict, he said, was among classes, not among artificial national units. Any idealism attached to the current war was sham and deceit. He pledged himself to purge the war of this deceit. "There is work to be done to prevent this war of ours from passing into popular mythology as a holy crusade."

Bourne was a prophet a few years ahead of his time. For the great majority of liberal intellectuals, humanitarians, and social meliorists the splendor of Wilson's vision remained ample compensation for the seamy side of war—at least as long as the vision did not have to be translated into the realities of international politics. Their efforts in behalf of the war proved once more that a passion for peace and understanding, wedded to the instruments of violence, could produce a crusade of intense, if not lasting, force.

7. WILSON'S PROGRAM AND THE GENERAL PUBLIC

It was Wilson's program of international reform which set the tone of America's crusade. From his speeches the dynamic George Creel, whom Wilson appointed as head of the Committee on Public Information soon after intervention, and his devoted corps of liberal reformers and intellectuals fashioned the verbal magic that cast its spell upon all quarters of the world, elevating the American Messiah to a position of world leadership unprecedented in the annals of the presidency, and, finally, enchanting the German people themselves with the lure of the millennium.

Creel's moral offensive was equally ambitious in America. Five of the famous Red, White, and Blue pamphlets went over the million mark. Creel estimated that over one million of the ubiquitous Four Minute speeches were heard by four hundred million individuals during the eighteen months' life of the Committee on Public Information, while more than seventy-five million copies of war pamphlets, not counting the circulation given to them by the metropolitan dailies, state organizations, and private groups, found their way into American homes.

The Committee's propaganda focused upon the moral issues of the war. A few pamphlets, such as *A War of Self-defense*, written by Secretary Lansing and Louis F. Post, emphasized the threat of German world domination to American security. Pan-German schemes were exposed once more in the *War Books*, written with the co-operation of many of Creel's academic assistants, and published at Princeton and the Universities of Wisconsin, North Carolina, Columbia, Chicago, and Illinois. But even these works were written in the context of German war guilt and depravity rather than in the vein of national expediency.

More typical was the reproduction of Franklin K. Lane's speech "Why We

Are Fighting Germany," included in *The Nation In Arms*, in which he proclaimed, "The world of Christ . . . has come again face to face with the world of Mahomet, who willed to win by force"; or Baker's contribution to the same publication, in which he urged, "Never, during the progress of this war, let us for one instant forget the high and holy mission with which we entered it, no matter what the cost, no matter what the temptation"; or the assertion in *How the War Came to America*, largely the work of Arthur Bullard and approved by Lansing and Wilson, that with the Russian revolution the conviction "finally crystallized in American minds and hearts that this war across the sea was no mere conflict between dynasties, but a stupendous civil war of all the world."

Through this program of holy war America's missionary fervor was aroused once more to the peak of 1898. Once more the nation looked beyond its shores, and out of the fullness of the American tradition of liberty and humanitarianism dedicated its wealth, its military power, and its prestige to the service of the rest of the world.

Yet it would be a mistake to suppose that this crusade, any more than its predecessor, reflected a concerted purpose on the part of the people as a whole to abandon the nation's relative isolation from the stream of world politics or to limit its sovereign independence in its relations with other nations. There is no reason to think that the great mass of Americans, in spite of their altruistic passion, seriously anticipated the sacrifice of a standard of national conduct so firmly established as the tradition of isolation and self-sufficiency for the sake of alleviating the sufferings of foreign peoples.

It is true that Wilson's announcement of the Fourteen Points was received with enthusiasm throughout the country. Hamilton Holt's magazine, the *Independent*, believed that the President had "articulated . . . the very conscience of the American people." The *Literary Digest* reported almost universal approbation of Wilson's address. However, the nation's press virtually ignored the league issue; it was preoccupied with the territorial terms. Apparently, as when John Hay announced the Open Door principle, the American public was basking in the sunshine of its own righteousness, drinking in the gratifying spectacle of the United States advising the unenlightened nations how to straighten out their affairs; but if there was a general desire to undertake any concrete political commitments on behalf of Wilson's pronouncements, the press did not reveal it.

Wilson's mystic faith in his identity with the common people of America was encouraged by the obvious popularity of his war leadership. He never seems to have doubted that the people shared—or soon would share, when they completely understood the matter—his own opinion of the supreme importance of America's participation in a league of nations. Because he was convinced that the people were essentially moral and unselfish, and because he believed that international organization was, at bottom, a moral issue, he was filled with a certain naïve assurance that the great mass of Americans were as fervently and consistently altruistic as he and, therefore, equally attached to his program of international organization.

Perhaps he was right, but it is necessary to recall that while America was at war the league remained a rather vague aspiration, except on the part of those who made international organization their special concern, like the members of the League to Enforce Peace, or those among the band of devout liberals who could reconcile themselves to the fact of war only by saturating their minds in schemes for everlasting peace. There was nothing in the way America's idealistic war program was presented to the nation to produce any more solid attachment to the fourteenth point than was manifested toward Wilson's "steadfast concert for peace" at the time of America's decision to enter the war.

Furthermore, President Wilson intended that this supreme war aim should remain vague until it came time to make peace. During the winter of 1917–18 he took no official steps to start public discussion on the proposed league, lest that divert the people's attention from the war effort and lead to a precise formulation of the fourteenth point, which he might have to oppose later. The demand for a league plan that followed his proclamation of the Fourteen Points led him to ask House to discuss the subject with eminent American advocates, but even then the President remained unwilling to stimulate discussion on constitutional details, for fear that such discussion might ripen into controversy. Even in the summer of 1918, in spite of House's advice that he ought to announce some specific plan so that opinion could crystallize around it, the President blocked public discussion of details and methods because he saw grave dangers in stirring up national sentiments that might endanger solidarity against Germany.

Those who made international organization their special concern continued to publicize the idea and develop its details. The proposals of the League to Enforce Peace continued to elicit an impressive body of favorable comment from political figures, the general public, and the press. In June, 1918, the *New Republic* could observe with satisfaction, "Men who at first sneered at a world made safe for democracy now believe in it without reservation." Yet general approval of a theoretical organization to preserve peace was not the same thing as actual acceptance of the commitments of a specific league of nations.

As long as winning the war remained the immediate, tangible objective in the public mind, the league idea flourished, principally, as a general aspiration for the end of all wars and as an expression of the righteousness of America's cause rather than as a deliberate and reasoned choice of a revolutionary program of participation in world affairs. In fact, American enthusiasm for a league was, in large part, enthusiasm for a world in which the nation could escape a recurrence of its present involvement in the toils of world politics. To this extent the desire for a league arose from the very sentiments that made acceptance of new international commitments unlikely.

Something of the vagueness of the public's understanding of the fourteenth point is reflected in the nature of the publicity campaign of the League to Enforce Peace. In order to identify itself with the war effort and distinguish itself from the "peace-at-any-price" groups the League went out of its way to conform to the requirements of the popular war spirit. Thus the slogan of the League's big national convention in the middle of May, 1918, was "Win the War for Permanent Peace." In the keynote address Taft said that the convention was called to "sound the trumpet of stern implacable war to the end," and speaker after speaker warned against a premature peace. The meeting was reported under such headings as "War to Death Taft's Demand of Peace League," "Peace League to Urge Victory First," and "Carry on War till Victorious Peace Is Forced on Huns." Some editors singled out the league plan for comment, both adverse and favorable; but the emphasis in the press, as in the convention, was upon complete victory.

Like the preparedness campaign, the campaign for a league of nations, as it grew in popularity, broadened in scope and tended to merge with the general stream of patriotic sentiment. While the war was yet to be won, the aim of a league to enforce peace gained strength as a kind of sublimation of the immediate and tangible goal of victory. Yet this very basis of strength would prove a source of weakness when the immediate goal of victory no longer existed. The way in which the league was popularized as a war aim ill prepared the general public to take a strong and consistent stand in the debate between nationalism and internationalism that soon raged around the Versailles Treaty.

2. ARTHUR S. LINK, "WILSON AND THE GREAT DEBATE OVER COLLECTIVE SECURITY"

IN the American democracy, great debates have often preceded national decisions on new and important courses of action. The question of America's entrance into the League of Nations in 1919–1920, historian Arthur S. Link maintains, was an occasion whose significance "was no less important than the great debate of 1787 to 1789 over the ratifica-

SOURCE. Arthur S. Link, *Wilson the Diplomatist*, Baltimore: The Johns Hopkins Press, 1957, pp. 127–156. Copyright by The Johns Hopkins Press, 1957. Reprinted by permission of The Johns Hopkins Press and the author.

tion of the Constitution." Like the earlier debate on the Constitution and its central issue of a weak versus a strong central government, the issue of American participation in the League of Nations involved at its core a controversy over the kind of commitment the United States would make to a universal system of collective security.

The arguments for and against the nation's unqualified or limited participation in the League are clearly presented by Professor Link in the following essay. Years of research for a multivolume biography of Wilson has given Link command of the multitude of factors involved in the League controversy, but he acknowledges that a biographer can only guess why Wilson refused to compromise with the proponents of limited internationalism. He concludes that "the American people were not prepared in 1920 to assume the moral leadership that Wilson offered them, and that the powers of the world were not yet ready to enforce the world-wide, universal system of collective security that the President had created."

Having helped to lay the foundations of a new world order in Paris, Wilson returned to the United States in June, 1919, to face the crucial task of winning the approval of the Senate and the support of the people for the Versailles Treaty, the principal part of the Paris settlement.

During the months following Wilson's homecoming, indeed until the election of 1920, there ensued in the United States a debate no less important than the great debate of 1787 to 1789 over the ratification of the Constitution. At stake in the latter-day discussion was the issue of American participation in a new system of collective security. To a large degree the fate of that experiment and the future peace of the world would depend upon the response that the American people gave.

The facts of the treaty fight are well known, so often and in such detail have historians and biographers told the story of the epic parliamentary struggle between Republicans and Democrats and of the bitter personal controversy between the President and his chief antagonist, Senator Henry Cabot Lodge of Massachusetts. I cannot ignore the forces and factors that cut the channels of the debate and perhaps decisively affected the decisions that the leaders and their followers made. My main purpose in this brief discussion, however, will be to show what has often been obscured by too much concern for dramatic details, namely, the way in which the great debate of 1919–1920 revealed differences in opinion concerning the role that the United States should play in foreign affairs, differences that were fundamental and authentic because they transcended partisanship and personality and have as much relevance for Americans of the mid-twentieth century as they had in Wilson's day.

The lines of battle over ratification of the Treaty of Versailles were first drawn, not after that treaty had been signed, but before Wilson went to Paris, as a consequence of three decisions that he made between October and December of 1918. The first was his decision to issue an appeal to the country on October 25 for the election of a Democratic Congress, and by so doing to make the forthcoming election a specific test of national confidence in his conduct of foreign affairs. The second was his decision to ignore the Senate and the Republican party in discussions of the possible terms of the settlement and in the appointment of the American delegation to the Paris conference, and to name only such men as he thought would be loyal to him and his ideals and subordinate to his direction. The third was Wilson's decision to go to Paris in person, as the head of the American commission. *excessive, notorious*

The first two decisions were certainly egregious mistakes. On the other hand, Wilson was probably right in deciding that he had to go to Paris to take personal leadership in the fight for a liberal peace. However, the important point is not whether Wilson acted wisely or foolishly; it is the way in which his preparations for the peace conference predetermined the shape of the battle over the treaty that would be signed. By appealing for the election of a Democratic Congress on the ground that a Republican victory would imply a repudiation of his leadership in foreign affairs, and by appointing a peace commission composed with one unimportant exception of Democrats, Wilson made a partisan division on the issues of peace inevitable. In other words, he made it certain that Republicans would oppose and Democrats would support whatever treaty he might help to write. Moreover, by first ignoring the Senate in his appointment of the commissioners, and then by going himself to Paris, Wilson made it inevitable that the treaty fight would renew in virulent form the old conflict between the president and the upper house for control of foreign policy.

While Wilson was in Paris there were unmistakable signs at home that he would encounter bitter opposition when he returned with his peace treaty. The most ominous of these was the so-called "Round Robin" resolution that Senator Lodge presented to the upper house on March 4, 1919. Signed by thirty-seven senators, it declared that the Covenant of the League of Nations, "in the form now proposed to the peace conference," was unacceptable. At the same time, frankly isolationist opponents of the League were beginning a furious rhetorical attack in the Senate chamber.

Although there were limits beyond which Wilson would not go in compromise, as he said in a New York address on the eve of his return to France after a brief visit to the United States in late February and early March of 1919, he yielded to the advice of friends who urged him to conciliate his critics. For example, he endeavored to assuage the signers of the "Round Robin" resolution by permitting Henry White, the Republican member of the American peace delegation, to attempt to ascertain from Lodge why the

Covenant was unacceptable to them. Or again, after Lodge had refused to answer specifically, Wilson took the advice of former President William Howard Taft and other Republican supporters of the League and obtained amendments to meet certain American criticisms of the Covenant.[1]

Undertaken reluctantly at best, these measures did little to conciliate the extreme opposition or to conceal Wilson's true feelings about his senatorial critics and his growing determination to defy them. The more he had to concede at Paris during the final months of the conference, the more this determination hardened. By the time he signed the Versailles Treaty, Wilson was obviously sick of making compromises and eager to return to a political arena in which he could fight hard again, without the necessity of giving ground to opponents who had as much power as he. "I have found one can never get anything in this life that is worth while without fighting for it," he told Colonel House, who had urged him to meet the Senate in a conciliatory spirit, on the day that he left Paris.[2]

Arriving in Washington on July 8, the President made no effort to conceal his fighting mood. When a reporter asked him on July 10 whether the Versailles Treaty could be ratified if the Senate added certain reservations, Wilson shot back, "I do not think hypothetical questions are concerned. *The Senate is going to ratify the treaty.*"[3] To cite another example, the French Ambassador, Jules Jusserand, went to the White House at about the same time with a plan that he thought would assure the Senate's approval of the treaty. Conceived by President Nicholas Murray Butler of Columbia University and approved by a large number of Republican senators, this plan envisaged the adoption of certain reservations to the treaty to protect American sovereignty and congressional control over the war-making power. If the President would only accept the reservations, Jusserand urged, there would be no doubt about the treaty's fate in the Senate. "Mr. Ambassador," Wilson replied, "I shall consent to nothing. The Senate must take its medicine."[4]

Wilson was, therefore, in the mood of a triumphant leader presenting his adversaries with a *fait accompli* when he presented the treaty formally to the

---

[1] These amendments provided for the right of members of the League to withdraw after giving due notice, exempted domestic questions from the jurisdiction of the League, permitted member nations to refuse to accept a colonial mandate, and accorded formal recognition to the Monroe Doctrine.

[2] Charles Seymour (ed.), *The Intimate Papers of Colonel House* (4 vols.; New York, 1926–1928), IV, 487.

[3] Quoted in Thomas A. Bailey, *Woodrow Wilson and the Great Betrayal* (New York, 1945), p. 9.

[4] Nicholas Murray Butler, *Across the Busy Years, Recollections and Reflections* (2 vols.; New York, 1939–1940), II, 197–201. [The author adds that if he was writing this chapter again, he would not use this quotation. Wilson made this remark to Jusserand in 1917, in an entirely different context and with a different meaning.]

Senate on July 10. He did not refer to the senators, as he had often done before, as his "colleagues" in the conduct of foreign relations, nor did he use his favorite phrase "common counsel" or talk about the necessity of agreement among reasonable men. On the contrary, after "informing" the senators that a world settlement had been made, he took the highest possible ground to urge prompt and unqualified approval of the treaty. The League of Nations, he exclaimed, was the hope of mankind. "Dare we reject it and break the heart of the world?" He reiterated the answer in an impromptu perora- *concluding portion of an oration* tion at the end:

The stage is set, the destiny disclosed. It has come about by no plan of our conceiving, but by the hand of God who led us into this way. We cannot turn back. We can only go forward, with lifted eyes and freshened spirit, to follow the vision. It was of this that we dreamed at our birth. America shall in truth show the way. The light streams upon the path ahead, and nowhere else.[5]

Many historians have been frankly puzzled by Wilson's refusal even to attempt to build support for the peace settlement in the Senate and the Republican party—among the very men who would have the power of life or death over the Treaty of Versailles. How could an authority on the American constitutional system have forgotten the Senate's jealous role in foreign affairs? How could an intelligent and astute political strategist have done the things best calculated to assure the defeat of plans upon which he thought depended the future happiness of mankind? The dilemma inherent in these *exaggerating* hyperbolic questions is much more apparent than real. In fact, it is not too much to say that Wilson acted in the only way that it was possible for him to act, given his convictions concerning the President's control over foreign relations, his belief in party responsibility, his view of public opinion, and his own temperament. . . .

Wilson believed that the president was a virtual sovereign, responsible only to public opinion and not to Congress, in the conduct of external affairs.[6] In ignoring the Senate in the appointment of the peace commission, in taking personal responsibility for writing the peace treaty, and in standing defiantly in its defense, he was, therefore, simply playing the constitutional role that he thought was proper for the chief executive. Given Wilson's views of party responsibility, moreover, it was inevitable that he should have ignored the Republican opposition in the processes of peace-making, because he could not work in harmony with men whose duty he knew it would be to oppose him at every turn. Given Wilson's urge to dominate and his belief that the Republican leaders, particularly Senator Lodge, represented all the dark forces against which he was battling, it is difficult to imagine him sharing

[5] R. S. Baker and W. E. Dodd, *War and Peace*, i, 548, 551–52.
[6] See above, pp. 22–23.

responsibility or dealing with his opponents on a give-and-take basis after his return from Paris.

These are reasons enough to explain the President's methods and his posture of defiance at the beginning of the treaty fight. There was another reason that was more important than all the rest—Wilson's supreme confidence in his own creation and in the overwhelming support of the American people. He knew not only that he was right, but that the people would know that he was right and would crush any man who dared to obstruct fulfillment of the age-old dream of peace. That was what he meant when he told reporters that of course the Senate would ratify the Versailles Treaty, or when in private he talked about the Senate, that is, the Republican Senate, having to take its medicine.

Actually, the situation was far less simple and reassuring than Wilson imagined at the beginning of the great debate. For one thing, powerful voices were already raised in outright and violent condemnation of the treaty on various grounds. There were the idealists who had thrilled at Wilson's vision of a new world and who now drew back in disgust because the treaty failed to establish a millennial order. There were the so-called hyphenate groups—the German-Americans, who believed that the treaty was a base betrayal of the Fatherland; the Italian-Americans, who were sulking over Wilson's opposition to Italy's demands; and, most important, the several million Irish-Americans, inflamed by the civil war then raging in Ireland, who were up in arms because Wilson had refused to press the cause of Irish independence at Paris and because the treaty allegedly benefited the hated English. There was the powerful chain of Hearst newspapers, marshaling and inciting all the hyphenate protests. There were the out-and-out isolationists, who believed that American membership in the League of Nations would mean entanglement in all of Europe's rivalries and wars. They had powerful advocates in a small group of so-called irreconcilables or bitter-enders in the Senate, led by Hiram Johnson of California, William E. Borah of Idaho, and James A. Reed of Missouri, who opposed the treaty for nationalistic reasons of their own divination.

These were the major groups who opposed ratification of the treaty. In the ensuing debate they were perhaps the loudest and busiest participants of all. They were, however, a minority among the leaders of thought and political opinion, and they spoke for a minority of the people, at least before 1920 if not afterward. This is a simple point but a vital one, because in its important aspects the debate over the treaty was not a struggle between advocates of complete withdrawal on the one side and proponents of total international commitment on the other. It was, rather, a contest between the champions of a strong system of collective security and a group who favored a more limited commitment in international affairs. It was a choice between these alternatives, and not between complete isolation or complete internationalism, that the President, the Senate, and the American people eventually had to make. For this reason, therefore, I propose to let the arguments of the isolationists pass without analyzing them, and to concentrate my attention upon the two main and decisive courses of the debate.

Before we do this, it might be well to remind ourselves of the precise issues at stake. There were differences of opinion in the United States over the territorial and other provisions of the treaty, to be sure, but all of them were insignificant as compared to the differences evoked by the Covenant of the League and its provisions for universal collective security. Those provisions were clear and for the most part unequivocal. There was, of course, Article 10, which guaranteed the political independence and territorial integrity of every member nation throughout the world. There were, besides, Articles 11, 12, 13, 15, 16, and 17, which established the machinery of arbitration for all international disputes susceptible to that procedure and decreed that an act of war against one member nation should "*ipso facto* be deemed to . . . [be] an act of war against all the other Members" and should be followed automatically by an economic blockade against the aggressor and by Council action to determine what military measures should be used to repel the aggression. These were almost ironclad guarantees of mutual security, meant to be effective and unencumbered by the right of any nation involved in a dispute to veto action by the League's Council. Whether such a world-wide system could work, and whether the American people were prepared at this stage of their development to support such a system even if it did—these were the two main issues of the great debate of 1919–1920.

The decisive opposition to the Versailles Treaty came from a group of men who to a varying degree gave negative answers to both these questions. This group included some of the most distinguished leaders in the Senate and out, men like Senator Frank B. Kellogg of Minnesota, Nicholas Murray Butler, former Secretary of State Elihu Root, Charles Evans Hughes, and Herbert Hoover. Most of them were Republicans, because few Democrats active in politics dared to incur the President's wrath by opposing him. They were not isolationists, but limited internationalists who in a varying degree believed that the United States should play an active role in preserving the peace of the world. Most of them favored, for example, arbitration, the establishment of something like a World Court to interpret and codify international law, and international agreements for disarmament, economic co-operation, and the like. Some of them even supported the idea of alliances with certain powers for specific purposes.

On the other hand, all the limited internationalists opposed any such approval of the treaty as would commit the United States unreservedly to such a system of collective security as the Covenant of the League had created.

112 The Great Crusade

Their arguments might be summarized as follows:

First, a system of collective security that is world-wide in operation is not likely either to work or to endure the strains that will inevitably be put upon it, because in practice the great powers will not accept the limitations that the Covenant places upon their sovereignty, and no nation will go to war to vindicate Article 10 unless its vital interests compel it to do so. Such sweeping guarantees as the Covenant affords are, therefore, worse than no guarantees at all because they offer only an illusory hope of security.

Second, the Covenant's fundamental guarantee, embodied in Article 10, is impossible to maintain because its promise to perpetuate the *status quo* defies the very law of life. As Elihu Root put it:

If perpetual, it would be an attempt to preserve for all time unchanged the distribution of power and territory made in accordance with the views and exigencies of the Allies in this present juncture of affairs. It would necessarily be futile. . . . It would not only be futile; it would be mischievous. Change and growth are the law of life, and no generation can impose its will in regard to the growth of nations and the distribution of power, upon succeeding generations.[7]

Third, the American people are not ready to support the Covenant's sweeping commitments and in fact should not do so unless their vital interests are involved in a dispute. They would and should be ready to act to prevent the outbreak of any conflict that threatened to lead to a general war, but it is inconceivable that they would or should assume the risk of war to prevent a border dispute in the Balkans, or to help maintain Japanese control of the Shantung Province or British supremacy in Ireland and India. Unconditional ratification of the treaty by the United States would, therefore, be worse than outright rejection, for it would mean the making of promises that the American people could not possibly honor in the future.

Fourth, unqualified membership in the League will raise grave dangers to American interests and the American constitutional system. It will menace American control over immigration and tariff policies, imperil the Monroe Doctrine, increase the power of the president at the expense of Congress, and necessitate the maintenance of a large standing army for the fulfillment of obligations under the Covenant.

Fifth, and most important, full-fledged participation in such a system of collective security as the Covenant establishes will spell the end of American security in foreign affairs, because it will mean transferring the power of decision over questions of peace and war from the president and Congress to an international agency which the United States could not control.

Voicing these objections day in and out as the great debate reached its crescendo in the autumn of 1919, the limited internationalists made their

[7] Quoted in Philip C. Jessup, *Elihu Root* (2 vols.; New York, 1938), II, 392–93.

purposes and program indelibly clear. They would accept most of the provisions of the treaty unrelated to the League and acquiesce in the ones that they did not like. They would also sanction American membership in the League of Nations. But they would also insist upon reserving to the United States, and specifically to Congress, the power of decision concerning the degree of American participation in the League; and they would make no binding promise to enforce collective security anywhere in the future.

This was also the position of Senator Lodge, the man who devised and executed the Republican strategy in the upper house during the parliamentary phase of the treaty struggle. Personally, Lodge had little hope for the success of the League, a profound personal contempt for Wilson, and almost a sardonic scorn for the President's international ideals. The Massachusetts senator was an ardent nationalist, almost a jingoist, no isolationist, but a believer in a strong balance of power. His solution would have been harsh terms, including dismemberment, for Germany and the formation of an Anglo-Franco-American alliance as the best insurance for future peace. But as chairman of the Foreign Relations Committee and leader of his party in the Senate, it was his duty to sublimate his own strong feelings and to find a common ground upon which most Republicans could stand. That common ground, that program acceptable to an overwhelming majority of Republicans inside the Senate and out, was, in brief, to approve the treaty and accept membership in the League, subject to certain amendments and reservations that would achieve the objectives of the limited internationalists.[8]

Debated all through the late summer of 1919, these amendments and reservations were embodied in the report that the Republican majority of the Foreign Relations Committee presented to the upper house on September 10. During the following weeks the Senate rejected the amendments and adopted most of them in the form of reservations, fourteen in all. Most of them were unimportant, but there was one that constituted a virtual rejection of the system of collective security that Wilson had constructed. It was Reservation 2, which declared that the United States assumed no obligations to preserve the territorial integrity or political independence of any other country, unless Congress should by act or joint resolution specifically assume such an obligation. In addition, the preamble to the reservations provided that American ratification of the treaty should not take effect until at least three of the four principal Allied powers had accepted the reservations in a formal exchange of notes.

This, then, was the program to which most of Wilson's opponents stood committed by the time that the Senate moved toward a formal vote on the

---

[8] My understanding of Senator Lodge has been greatly enlarged by reading John A. Garraty, *Henry Cabot Lodge, A Biography* (New York, 1953).

Versailles Treaty. Whether Lodge himself was an irreconcilable who desired the defeat of the treaty, or whether he was merely a strong reservationist is an important question, but an irrelevant one at this point.[9] The significant fact is that he had succeeded in uniting most Republicans and in commiting them to a program that affirmed limited internationalism at the same time that it repudiated American support of collective security for virtually the entire world.

Meanwhile, despite his earlier show of intransigence, Wilson had been hard at work in preparation for the impending struggle. In an effort to split the Republican ranks, he held a series of conferences in late July with eleven moderate Republican senators who were called mild reservationists because they favored approval of the treaty after the adoption of a few interpretive reservations. On August 19 the President met the Foreign Relations Committee at the White House for a three-hour grilling on all phases of the settlement. In spite of these overtures, there were unmistakable signs that Wilson had failed to win the support of any large number of Republican senators and that the strong reservationists and isolationists were rapidly gaining ground in the debate that was now proceeding in full fury throughout the country.

In response, Wilson made one of the most fateful decisions of his career. It was, as he put it, to go to the people and purify the wells of public opinion that had been poisoned by the isolationists and opponents of unreserved ratification. He was physically weakened by his labors at Paris, and his physician warned that a long speaking tour might endanger his life. Even so, he insisted upon making the effort to rally the people, the sources of authority, who had always sustained him in the past.

Leaving Washington on September 3, 1919, Wilson headed for the heartland of America, into Ohio, Indiana, Missouri, Iowa, Nebraska, Minnesota, and the Dakotas—into the region where isolationist sentiment was strongest. From there he campaigned through the Northwest and the major cities of the Pacific Coast. The final leg of his journey took him through Nevada, Utah, Wyoming, and Colorado, where the tour ended after Wilson's partial breakdown on September 25 and 26. In all he traveled 8,000 miles in twenty-two days and delivered thirty-two major addresses and eight minor ones. It was not only the greatest speaking effort of Wilson's career, but also one of the most notable forensic accomplishments in American history.

Everywhere that he went Wilson pleaded in good temper, not as a partisan, but as a leader who stood above party strife and advantage. He made his

[9] For the conflicting points of view on this question, see Denna F. Fleming, *The United States and the League of Nations* (New York, 1932), and T. A. Bailey, *Woodrow Wilson and the Great Betrayal*, previously cited.

tour, he explained, first of all so that the people might know the truth about the Treaty of Versailles and no longer be confused by the misrepresentations of its enemies. As he put it at Oakland and at Reno:

One thing has been impressed upon me more than another as I have crossed the continent, and that is that the people of the United States have been singularly and, I some times fear deliberately, misled as to the character and contents of the treaty of peace.

Some of the critics . . . are looking backward. . . . Their power to divert, or to pervert, the view of this whole thing has made it necessary for me repeatedly on this journey to take the liberty that I am going to take with you to-night, of telling you just what kind of a treaty this is.[10]

In almost every speech, therefore, Wilson explicitly described and defended the major provisions of the treaty and the purposes of its framers. He defended the severity of the articles relating to Germany, on the ground that her crimes against civilization demanded stern punishment. He answered the critics of the Shantung settlement, first by frankly admitting that he did not like the provisions for Japanese control and next by declaring that he had obtained the only possible settlement that offered any hope for China's eventual recovery of the province. In a similar manner he tried to answer other criticisms, and he concluded, not by denying that there were imperfections in the treaty, but by declaring that they were more than counterbalanced by the constructive achievements.

Wilson's supreme purpose was, of course, not to explain the controverted [disputed] provisions of the treaty relating to territories, colonies, and reparations, but rather to defend the League of Nations against its traducers [slanderers], to explain the system of collective security that its Covenant had established, and to call the American people to the world leadership that he said history now demanded of them.

He began usually by telling how the League of Nations was the fulfillment of an old American dream of peace, how it was an attempt to apply the principles of the Monroe Doctrine to the world at large, how the suggestion of such an organization had come in recent times as much if not more from Republicans than from Democrats, and how he had simply translated American ideas and proposals into statutory form and insisted that they be embodied in the treaty.

The President then proceeded to describe the provisions of the Covenant for collective security, to show how they would work in actual practice, and to attempt to prove that they afforded a system for peace instead of for war. Article 10, he was fond of emphasizing, was the heart of the Covenant and

[10] R. S. Baker and W. E. Dodd, *War and Peace*, II, 265, 327.

the foundation of the new world order. "Article X," he said at Indianapolis, "speaks the conscience of the world."[11] "Article X," he added at Reno,

is the heart of the enterprise. Article X is the test of the honor and courage and endurance of the world. Article X says that every member of the League, and that means every great fighting power in the world, . . . solemnly engages to respect and preserve as against external aggression the territorial integrity and existing political independence of the other members of the League. If you do that, you have absolutely stopped ambitious and aggressive war . . . , [for] as against external aggression, as against ambition, as against the desire to dominate from without, we all stand together in a common pledge and that pledge is essential to the peace of the world.[12]

In answer to critics who had argued that unconditional affirmation of Article 10 would involve the United States perpetually in war, Wilson replied by attempting to demonstrate that future wars would be virtually impossible and almost unnecessary if the collective security provisions of the Covenant implementing Article 10 were observed and enforced by the members of the League. To begin with, nations engaged in a dispute that might lead to war were bound to submit their controversy either to arbitration, the World Court, or the Council of the League. Should any nation go to war in violation of these promises, then all the other members of the League would automatically institute a total blockade, "financial, commercial, and personal," against the aggressor.

As Wilson explained at Kansas City:

We absolutely boycott them [the aggressors]. . . . There shall be no communication even between them and the rest of the world. They shall receive no goods; they shall ship no goods. They shall receive no telegraphic messages; they shall send none. They shall receive no mail; no mail will be received from them. The nationals, the citizens, of the member states will never enter their territory until the matter is adjusted, and their citizens cannot leave their territory. It is the most complete boycott ever conceived in a public document, and I want to say to you with confident prediction that there will be no more fighting after that.[13]

It was possible, of course, Wilson admitted, that war would occur in spite of all these precautions. "Nobody in his senses claims for the Covenant . . . that it is certain to stop war," he said at Indianapolis.[14] If an aggressor flaunted the provisions of the Covenant, and if economic measures did not suffice to stop the aggression, then war would probably occur. If it were a major conflagration, then the United States could not remain neutral in any event. If it were a minor controversy far removed from the Western Hemi-

[11] *Ibid.*, i, 610.
[12] *Ibid.*, ii, 332–33.
[13] *Ibid.*, p. 3.
[14] *Ibid.*, i, 613.

sphere, then the United States would not be directly involved. Enemies of the League had charged that membership in that body would mean American involvement in every dispute everywhere in the world. "If you want to put out a fire in Utah," the President replied at Salt Lake City,

you do not send to Oklahoma for the fire engine. If you want to put out a fire in the Balkans, if you want to stamp out the smoldering flame in some part of central Europe, you do not send to the United States for troops. The Council of the League selects the powers which are most ready, most available, most suitable, and selects them only at their own consent, so that the United States would in no such circumstances conceivably be drawn in unless the flame spread to the world.[15]

To the charge that membership in the League would impair American sovereignty and require the fulfillment of unpleasant duties, Wilson replied that the contention was, of course, true in part. "The only way in which you can have impartial determinations to this world is by consenting to something you do not want to do," he said at Billings, Montana.

Every time you have a case in court one or the other of the parties has to consent to do something he does not want to do. . . . Yet we regard that as the foundation of civilization, that we will not fight about these things, and that when we lose in court we will take our medicine.[16]

It seemed almost superfluous, Wilson added, to argue the necessity of American membership in the League of Nations. There was the obvious fact, he declared at Des Moines, that American isolation had ended,

not because we chose to go into the politics of the world, but because by the sheer genius of this people and the growth of our power we have become a determining factor in the history of mankind, and after you have become a determining factor you cannot remain isolated, whether you want to or not.[17]

The only question confronting the American people was, therefore, whether they would exercise their influence in the world, which could henceforth be profound and controlling, in partnership with the other powers or in defiance of them. Standing alone, he warned, meant defying the world; defying the world meant maintaining a great standing army and navy; and such militarism and navalism meant the end of democracy at home.

There was the additional fact that without American participation and leadership the League of Nations would become merely another armed alliance instead of a true concert of power. "It would be an alliance," Wilson declared at St. Louis,

[15] *Ibid.*, ii, 351.
[16] *Ibid.*, pp. 111–12.
[17] *Ibid.*, p. 18.

in which the partnership would be between the more powerful European nations and Japan, and the . . . antagonist, the disassociated party, the party standing off to be watched by the alliance, would be the United States of America. There can be no league of nations in the true sense without the partnership of this great people.[18]

Without American participation and leadership, therefore, the League would fail. Without the League there could be no effective collective security system. Without collective security, wars would come again. American participation was, therefore, essential to peace, the most vital and elemental interest of the United States. This became increasingly the main theme of Wilson's addresses as he journeyed deeper into the West. Over and over he cried out warnings like these:

Ah, my fellow citizens, do not forget the aching hearts that are behind discussions like this. Do not forget the forlorn homes from which those boys went and to which they never came back. I have it in my heart that if we do not do this great thing now, every woman ought to weep because of the child in her arms. If she has a boy at her breast, she may be sure that when he comes to manhood this terrible task will have to be done once more. Everywhere we go, the train when it stops is surrounded with little children, and I look at them almost with tears in my eyes, because I feel my mission is to save them. These glad youngsters with flags in their hands—I pray God that they may never have to carry that flag upon the battlefield![19]

Why, my fellow citizens, nothing brings a lump into my throat quicker on this journey I am taking than to see the thronging children that are everywhere the first, just out of childish curiosity and glee, no doubt, to crowd up to the train when it stops, because I know that if by any chance we should not win this great fight for the League of Nations it would be their death warrant. They belong to the generation which would then have to fight the final war, and in that final war there would not be merely seven and a half million men slain. The very existence of civilization would be in the balance. . . . Stop for a moment to think about the next war, if there should be one. I do not hesitate to say that the war we have just been through, though it was shot through with terror of every kind, is not to be compared with the war we would have to face next time. . . . Ask any soldier if he wants to go through a hell like that again. The soldiers know what the next war would be. They know what the inventions were that were just about to be used for the absolute destruction of mankind. I am for any kind of insurance against a barbaric reversal of civilization.[20]

Who were the enemies of the League and of the future peace of the world? They were, Wilson declared, the outright isolationists and the men who would destroy the charter of mankind by crippling reservations. They were little Americans, provincials, men of narrow vision. "They are ready to go back

[18] *Ibid.*, i, 640.

[19] At Tacoma, Washington, September 13, 1919, *ibid.*, ii, 173.

[20] At San Diego, California, September 19, and at Denver, Colorado, September 2, 1919, *ibid.*, pp. 291, 391–92.

to that old and ugly plan of armed nations, of alliances, of watchful jealousies, of rabid antagonisms, of purposes concealed, running by the subtle channels of intrigue through the veins of people who do not dream what poison is being injected into their systems."[21] "When at last in the annals of mankind they are gibbeted, they will regret that the gibbet is so high."[22]

One by one Wilson answered the specific criticisms of the Covenant relating to the Monroe Doctrine, the right of members to withdraw, and the question whether the League had any jurisdiction over the domestic affairs of member nations. He told how he had obtained revision of the Covenant to satisfy American doubts about its first draft. These amendments, he continued, were embodied in the Covenant and were written in language as explicit as he knew how to devise. He would not object to reservations that merely clarified the American understanding of these questions. Reservations that in any way changed the meaning of the Covenant were, however, more serious, because they would require the re-negotiation of the treaty.

There remained the greatest threat of all to the integrity of the Covenant, the challenge of the Lodge reservations to Article 10. This reservation, Wilson warned, would destroy the foundations of collective security, because it was a notice to the world that the American people would fulfill their obligations only when it suited their purposes to do so. "That," the President exclaimed at Salt Lake City, "is a rejection of the Covenant. That is an absolute refusal to carry any part of the same responsibility that the other members of the League carry."[23] "In other words, my fellow citizens," he added at Cheyenne,

what this proposes is this: That we should make no general promise, but leave the nations associated with us to guess in each instance what we were going to consider ourselves bound to do and what we were not going to consider ourselves bound to do. It is as if you said, "We will not join the League definitely, but we will join it occasionally. We will not promise anything, but from time to time we may coöperate. We will not assume any obligations." . . . This reservation proposes that we should not acknowledge any moral obligation in the matter; that we should stand off and say, "We will see, from time to time; consult us when you get into trouble, and then we will have a debate, and after two or three months we will tell you what we are going to do." The thing is unworthy and ridiculous, and I want to say distinctly that, as I read this, it would change the entire meaning of the treaty and exempt the United States from all responsibility for the preservation of peace. It means the rejection of the treaty, my fellow countrymen, nothing less. It means that the United States would take from under the structure its very foundations and support.[24]

The irony of it all was, Wilson added, that the reservation was actually

[21] *Ibid.*, p. 235.
[22] *Ibid.*, p. 9.
[23] *Ibid.*, p. 350.
[24] *Ibid.*, pp. 381–82.

unnecessary, *if the objective of its framers was merely to reserve the final decision for war to the American government.* In the case of all disputes to which it was not a party, the United States would have an actual veto over the Council's decision for war, because that body could not advise member nations to go to war except by unanimous vote, exclusive of the parties to the dispute. Thus, the President explained, there was absolutely no chance that the United States could be forced into war against its will, unless it was itself guilty of aggression, in which case it would be at war anyway.

These were, Wilson admitted, legal technicalities, and, he added, he would not base his case for American participation in the League of Nations upon them. The issue was not who had the power to make decisions for war, but whether the American people were prepared to go wholeheartedly into the League, determined to support its collective system unreservedly, and willing to make the sacrifices that were necessary to preserve peace. Wilson summarized all his pleading with unrivaled feeling at the Mormon capital, as follows:

> Instead of wishing to ask to stand aside, get the benefits of the League, but share none of its burdens or responsibilities, I for my part want to go in and accept what is offered to us, the leadership of the world. A leadership of what sort, my fellow citizens? Not a leadership that leads men along the lines by which great nations can profit out of weak nations, not an exploiting power, but a liberating power, a power to show the world that when America was born it was indeed a finger pointed toward those lands into which men could deploy some of these days and live in happy freedom, look each other in the eyes as equals, see that no man was put upon, that no people were forced to accept authority which was not of their own choice, and that out of the general generous impulse of the human genius and the human spirit we were lifted along the levels of civilization to days when there should be wars no more, but men should govern themselves in peace and amity and quiet. That is the leadership we said we wanted, and now the world offers it to us. It is inconceivable that we should reject it.[25]

We come now to the well-known tragic sequel. Following his address at Pueblo, Colorado, on September 25, 1919, the President showed such obvious signs of exhaustion that his physician canceled his remaining engagements and sped the presidential train to Washington. On October 2 Wilson suffered a severe stroke and paralysis of the left side of his face and body. For several days his life hung in the balance; then he gradually revived, and by the end of October he was clearly out of danger. But his recovery was only partial at best. His mind remained relatively clear; but he was physically enfeebled, and the disease had wrecked his emotional constitution and aggravated all his more unfortunate personal traits.

Meanwhile, the Senate was nearing the end of its long debate over the

[25] *Ibid.*, p. 355.

Treaty of Versailles. Senator Lodge presented his revised fourteen reservations on behalf of the Foreign Relations Committee to the upper house on November 6, 1919. Senator Gilbert M. Hitchcock of Nebraska, the Democratic minority leader, countered with five reservations, four of which Wilson had approved in substance before he embarked upon his western tour. They simply sought to make clear the American understanding of Article 10 and other provisions of the treaty. The issue before the Senate was, therefore, now clear—whether to approve the treaty with reservations that did not impair the American obligation to enforce collective security, or whether to approve the treaty with reservations that repudiated all compelling obligations and promised American support for only a limited international system.

Lodge beat down the Hitchcock reservations with the help of the irreconcilables and then won adoption of his own. Now the President had to choose between ratification with the Lodge reservations or running the risk of the outright defeat of the treaty. He gave his decision to Hitchcock in a brief conference at the White House on November 17 and in a letter on the following day: Under no circumstances could he accept the Lodge reservation to Article 10, for it meant nullification of the treaty. When the Senate voted on November 19, therefore, most of the Democrats joined the irreconcilables to defeat ratification with the Lodge reservations by a count of thirty-nine ayes to fifty-five nays. Hoping to split the Republican ranks and win the support of the "mild reservationists," the Democratic leaders then moved unconditional approval of the treaty. This strategy, upon which Wilson had placed all his hopes, failed, as a firm Republican majority defeated the resolution with the help of the irreconcilables by a vote of thirty-eight ayes to fifty-three nays.

It was not the end, for during the following months an overwhelming majority of the leaders of opinion in the United States refused to accept the Senate's vote as the final verdict. In the absence of any reliable indices, it is impossible to measure the division of public opinion as a whole; but there can be little doubt that an overwhelming majority of thoughtful people favored ratification with some kind of reservations, and even with the Lodge reservations, if that were necessary to obtain the Senate's consent.

There was, consequently, enormous pressure upon the leaders in both parties for compromise during the last weeks of 1919 and the early months of 1920. Prominent Republicans who had taken leadership in a nonpartisan campaign for the League, including former President Taft and President A. Lawrence Lowell of Harvard University; scores of editors and the spokesmen of various academic, religious, and labor organizations; and Democratic leaders who dared oppose the President, like William J. Bryan and Colonel House, begged Lodge and Wilson to find a common ground. Alarmed by the possibility of American rejection of the treaty, spokesmen for the British government declared publicly that limited American participation in the League would be better than no participation at all.

Under this pressure the moderate leaders in both camps set to work in late December and early January to find a basis for agreement. Even Lodge began to weaken and joined the bipartisan conferees who were attempting to work out an acceptable reservation to Article 10. But the Massachusetts senator and his friends would not yield the essence of their reservation, and it was Wilson who had to make the final choice. By January he had recovered sufficient physical strength to manage his forces in the upper house. All the while, however, his intransigence had been compounded by personal bitterness and by the growing conviction that rejection of the treaty was preferable to a dishonorable ratification. Consequently, between January and March, 1920, when the final debates and maneuvers were in progress, he rejected all suggestions of yielding on Article 10. Instead, he apparently began to make fantastic plans to run again for the presidency in a campaign that would decide the fate of the treaty. "If there is any doubt as to what the people of the country think on this vital matter," he wrote in a letter to the Democratic party on January 8, 1920, "the clear and single way out is to submit it for determination at the next election to the voters of the Nation, to give the next election the form of a great and solemn referendum."

Thus the parliamentary phase of the struggle moved to its inexorable conclusion when the Senate took its second and final vote on the treaty on March 19, 1920. The only hope for approval lay in the chance that enough Democrats would defy the President, as many friends of the League were urging them to do, to obtain a two-thirds majority for ratification with the Lodge reservations. Twenty-one Democrats did follow their consciences rather than the command from the White House, but not enough of them defected to put the treaty across. The treaty with the Lodge reservations failed by seven votes.

There was a final sequel. The Democratic presidential and vice-presidential candidates, James M. Cox and Franklin D. Roosevelt, tried hard to make the election of 1920 a "great and solemn referendum" on the League. But the effort failed, because so many other issues were involved, because the Republican candidate, Warren G. Harding, equivocated so artfully that no one knew where he stood, and because virtually all the distinguished leaders of the G.O.P. assured the country that a Republican victory promised the best hope of American membership in the League. These promises were obviously not honored. One of the new President's first official acts was to repudiate the idea of membership in the League; one of the new administration's first foreign policies was to conclude a separate peace with Germany.

Virtually all historians now agree that Wilson's refusal to permit his followers in the Senate to approve the treaty with the Lodge reservations was an error of tragic magnitude. Having built so grandly at Paris, having fought so magnificently at home for his creation, he then proceeded by his own hand to remove the cornerstone of his edifice of peace. Why? Were there inner demons of pride and arrogance driving him to what one historian has called "the supreme infanticide"? Did his illness and seclusion prevent him from obtaining a realistic view of the parliamentary situation, or so disarrange him emotionally that he became incompetent in the tasks of statemanship? Or was he simply an idealist who would make no compromises on what he thought were fundamental principles?

The historian, who sees through a glass darkly when probing the recesses of the mind, is not able to give final answers to questions like these. Wilson, for all his high-mindedness and nobility of character, was headstrong and not much given to dealing graciously or to compromising with men whom he distrusted and disliked. Once before, in a violent dispute at Princeton over control of the graduate school, he had revealed these same traits and suffered defeat because he could not work with men whom he did not trust. The sympathetic biographer would like to believe that it was his illness, which aggravated his bitterness and his sense of self-righteousness, that drove Wilson to his fatal choice. Perhaps this is true.[26] He had not always been incapable of compromise; perhaps he would have yielded in the end if disease had not dethroned his reason.

These attempts to extenuate ignore the fact that there were fundamental and vital issues at stake in the controversy over the treaty—whether the United States would take leadership in the League of Nations without hesitations and reservations, or whether it would join the League grudgingly and with no promises to help maintain universal collective security. To Wilson the difference between what he fought for and what Lodge and the Republicans would agree to was the difference between the success or failure and the life or death of man's best hope for peace. This he had said on his western tour, at a time when his health and reasoning faculties were unimpaired. This he believed with his heart and soul. It is, therefore, possible, even probable, that Wilson would have acted as he did even had he not suffered his breakdown, for it was not in his nature to compromise away the principles in which he believed.

If this is true, then in this, the last and greatest effort of his life, Wilson spurned the role of statesman for what he must have thought was the nobler role of prophet. The truth is that the American people were not prepared in 1920 to assume the world leadership that Wilson offered them, and that the powers of the world were not yet ready to enforce the world-wide, universal system of collective security that the President had created.

---

[26] This view has recently been strongly and convincingly supported in Edwin A. Weinstein, "Denial of Presidential Visability: A Case Study of Woodrow Wilson," *Psychiatry* (Washington), xxx (November, 1967), pp. 376–91.

Collective security failed in the portentous tests of the 1930's, not because the League's machinery was defective, but because the people of the world, not merely the American people alone, were unwilling to confront aggressors with the threat of war. As a result a second and more terrible world conflict came, as Wilson prophesied it would, and at its end the United States helped to build a new and different league of nations and took the kind of international leadership that Wilson had called for. But events of the past decade have not fully justified Wilson's confidence in international organization; the only really promising systems of collective security, the regional ones like NATO, have been of a kind that Wilson fervently denounced; and only the future can reveal whether his dream of a universal system can ever be made a reality.[27]

And so it was Wilson the prophet, demanding greater commitment, sacrifice, and idealism than the people could give, who was defeated in 1920. It is also Wilson the prophet who survives in history, in the hopes and aspirations of mankind and in whatever ideals of international service that the American people still cherish. One thing is certain, now that men have the power to sear virtually the entire face of the earth: The prophet of 1919 was right in his larger vision; the challenge that he raised then is today no less real and no less urgent than it was in his own time.

[27] For a provocative reply in the negative, see Robert E. Osgood, "Woodrow Wilson, Collective Security, and the Lessons of History," *Confluence*, v (Winter, 1957), 341–54.

CONTEMPORARY SOURCES

3. ROBERT M. LA FOLLETTE, ADDRESS AGAINST THE DECLARATION OF WAR, APRIL 4, 1917

MUCH of Woodrow Wilson's difficulties with the Congress resulted from his belief that the President was a virtual sovereign in the conduct of foreign affairs. Senator Robert M. La Follette of Wisconsin spoke for many citizens when he disputed the

SOURCE. *Congressional Record*, 65th Congress, 1st Session, pp. 223–226, 228, and 234–237.

President's political philosophy and voiced his opposition to America's entrance into World War I. The will of the people, La Follette asserted, resided in the people themselves, and neither the President nor a majority in Congress could maintain otherwise. In a speech of nearly four hours' duration during the Senate debate on the resolution of war, La Follette reviewed the events leading up to the President's war message and offered several dire predictions on the consequences of American involvement. He insisted that Great Britain no less than Germany had violated American rights. Moreover, he rejected the view that America would be fighting alongside democracy against German autocracy. La Follette voiced his doubts about the ability of the Allied Powers to secure a just peace settlement abroad and expressed his fears that the war would be the nemesis of reform at home. He would be villified many times for his antiwar speeches, and occasionally justly criticized, but few Americans in public life could lay claim to a more courageous stand than that maintained by the progressive senator from Wisconsin.

Mr. LA FOLLETTE. Mr. President, I had supposed until recently that it was the duty of Senators and Representatives in Congress to vote and act according to their convictions on all public matters that came before them for consideration and decision.

Quite another doctrine has recently been promulgated by certain newspapers, which unfortunately seems to have found considerable support elsewhere, and that is the doctrine of "standing back of the President," without inquiring whether the President is right or wrong. For myself I have never subscribed to that doctrine and never shall. I shall support the President in the measures he proposes when I believe them to be right. I shall oppose measures proposed by the President when I believe them to be wrong. The fact that the matter which the President submits for consideration is of the greatest importance is only an additional reason why we should be sure that we are right and not to be swerved from that conviction or intimidated in its expression by any influence of power whatsoever. If it is important for us to speak and vote our convictions in matters of internal policy, though we may unfortunately be in disagreement with the President, it is infinitely more important for us to speak and vote our convictions when the question is one of peace or war, certain to involve the lives and fortunes of many of our people and, it may be, the destiny of all of them and of the civilized world as well. If, unhappily, on such momentous questions the most patient research and conscientious consideration we could give to them leave us in disagreement with the President, I know of no course to take except to oppose, regretfully but not the less firmly, the demands of the Executive.

On the 2d of this month the President addressed a communication to the Senate and House in which he advised that the Congress declare war against

Germany and that this Government "assert all its powers and employ all its resources to bring the Government of the German Empire to terms and end the war." . . .

Mr. President, let me make a suggestion. It is this: That a minority in one Congress—mayhap a small minority in one Congress—protesting, exercising the rights which the Constitution confers upon a minority, may really be representing the majority opinion of the country, and if, exercising the right that the Constitution gives them, they succeed in defeating for the time being the will of the majority, they are but carrying out what was in the mind of the framers of the Constitution; that you may have from time to time in a legislative body a majority in numbers that really does not represent the principle of democracy; and that if the question could be deferred and carried to the people it would be found that a minority was the real representative of the public opinion. . . .

We need not disturb ourselves because of what a minority may do. There is always lodged, and always will be, thank the God above us, power in the people supreme. Sometimes it sleeps, sometimes it seems the sleep of death; but, sir, the sovereign power of the people never dies. It may be suppressed for a time, it may be misled, be fooled, silenced. I think, Mr. President, that it is being denied expression now. I think there will come a day when it will have expression.

The poor, sir, who are the ones called upon to rot in the trenches, have no organized power, have no press to voice their will upon this question of peace or war; but, oh, Mr. President, at some time they will be heard. I hope and I believe they will be heard in an orderly and a peaceful way. I think they may be heard from before long. I think, sir, if we take this step, when the people to-day who are staggering under the burden of supporting families at the present prices of the necessaries of life find those prices multiplied, when they are raised a hundred per cent, or 200 per cent, as they will be quickly, aye, sir, when beyond that those who pay taxes come to have their taxes doubled and again doubled to pay the interest on the nontaxable bonds held by Morgan and his combinations, which have been issued to meet this war, there will come an awakening; they will have their day and they will be heard. It will be as certain and as inevitable as the return of the tides, and as resistless, too. . . .

Just a word of comment more upon one of the points in the President's address. He says that this is a war "for the things which we have always carried nearest to our hearts—for democracy, for the right of those who submit to authority to have a voice in their own government." In many places throughout the address is this exalted sentiment given expression. . . .

Are the people of this country being so well represented in this war movement that we need to go abroad to give other people control of their governments? Will the President and the supporters of this war bill submit it to a vote of the people before the declaration of war goes into effect? Until we are willing to do that, it illy becomes us to offer as an excuse for our entry into the war the unsupported claim that this war was forced upon the German people by their Government "without their previous knowledge or approval."

Who has registered the knowledge or approval of the American people of the course this Congress is called upon to take in declaring war upon Germany? Submit the question to the people, you who support it. You who support it dare not do it, for you know that by a vote of more than ten to one the American people as a body would register their declaration against it. . . .

Had the plain principle of international law announced by Jefferson been followed by us, we would not be called on to-day to declare war upon any of the belligerents. The failure to treat the belligerent nations of Europe alike, the failure to reject the unlawful "war zones" of both Germany and Great Britain, is wholly accountable for our present dilemma. We should not seek to hide our blunder behind the smoke of battle, to inflame the mind of our people by half truths into the frenzy of war, in order that they may never appreciate the real cause of it until it is too late. I do not believe that our national honor is served by such a course. The right way is the honorable way.

One alternative is to admit our initial blunder to enforce our rights against Great Britain as we have enforced our rights against Germany; demand that both those nations shall respect our neutral rights upon the high seas to the letter; and give notice that we will enforce those rights from that time forth against both belligerents and then live up to that notice.

The other alternative is to withdraw our commerce from both. The mere suggestion that food supplies would be withheld from both sides impartially would compel belligerents to observe the principle of freedom of the seas for neutral commerce.

4. JOHN DEWEY, "WHAT ARE WE FIGHTING FOR?"

OUT of the intellectual ferment of the Great Crusade came books and plays and thought-provoking essays on the nature of war. The nation's foremost progressive philosopher, John Dewey, wrote widely about the social possibilities of war. The following essay, published in The Independent *in June 1918, not only offers some inter-*

SOURCE. John Dewey, "What are We Fighting For?", in *The Independent*, Vol. 9, No. 3629, June 22, 1918, pp. 474 and 480–482.

esting speculations about the consequences of new forces called into being by the war, but provides an example of the rationale that many liberals embraced as they came to support the war.

Severally and collectively mankind always builds better or worse than it knows. Even in the most successful enterprizes aims and results do not wholly coincide. In executing our immediate purpose we have to use forces which are outside our intent. Once released, however, they continue to operate, and they bring with them consequences which are unexpected and which in the end may quite submerge the objects consciously struggled for. Such an immense undertaking as the present war is no exception. The will to conquer describes the immediate aim. But in order to realize that end all sorts of activities are set going, arrangement made, organizations instituted, as incidental means. After they have been called into being they cannot be whisked out of existence merely because the war has come to an end. They have acquired an independent being and in the long run may effect consequences more significant than those consciously desired. If, for example, one takes a cross section thru the warring countries at present, one finds a striking rise in power of the wage-earning classes. Thru the necessities of war, their strategic position in modern social organization has been made clear, and the Russian Revolution has brought the fact to dramatic self-consciousness. Is it not conceivable that some future historian may find this consequence outweighing any for which the war was originally fought?

If it is the unintended which happens, a forecast of the consequences of the war seems doubly futile, for it is hard enough to disentangle even the professed aims in such a manner as to make them precise and definite. Yet it is possible to see some of the forces which have been released by the war. Thru fixing attention upon them, we make some guess about the future in its larger outlines. The first result which I see is the more conscious and extensive use of science for communal purposes after the war. Changes which are effected by embodying scientific discoveries in mechanical inventions and appliances endure. The transformations brought about first in industry and then in general social and political life by the stationary steam-engine, the locomotive, the internal combustion engine, etc., have stayed put, while matters which absorbed in their day much more of conscious attention and made much more of a stir in the realm of thought, have sunk beneath waves of oblivion. Mechanically speaking, the greatest achievements of the year have been, of course, the submarine and airplane, the mastery of the undersea and the air. Is it not likely that the combined effects of the two will do more to displace war than all the moralizing in existence? Anticipations of the future are too readily couched in terms of the fantastic rather than of the commonplace; or rather the miraculous, once established, becomes commonplace. But considering the social revolution wrought by steam and electric transportation on land and water in abolishing parochial and provincial boundaries, it seems probable that air navigation will round out their work in obliterating nationalistic frontiers. The war has, in addition to specific inventions, made it customary to utilize the collective knowledge and skill of scientific experts in all lines, organizing them for community ends. It is unlikely that we shall ever return wholly to the old divorce of knowledge from the conduct of social affairs—a separation which made knowledge abstract and abstruse, and left public affairs controlled by routine, vested interest and skilled manipulation. The one phase of Prussianism, borrowed under the stress of war from the enemy, which is likely permanently to remain, is systematic utilization of the scientific expert. Used for the ends of a democratic society, the social mobilization of science is likely in the end to effect such changes in the practise of government—and finally in its theory—as to initiate a new type of democracy. With respect to this alteration, as with respect to the airplane, there is more likelihood of underestimating than of exaggerating the consequences which are to follow.

Another consequence, not directly willed but made necessary as an incident of the war, is the formation of large political groupings. Almost all the nations of the world are now arrayed on one or other of the two sides. Not only is such a world-wide organization including the peoples of every continent a new and unique fact, so much so that the world for the first time is politically as well as astronomically round, but the character of the alliances is quite unprecedented. In order that the military alliance may be made effective, there is in effect if not in name a pooling of agricultural and industrial resources, a conjoint supervision of shipping and hence of international trading, a world-wide censorship and economic blacklist. In addition each nation now has an interest in knowing about other nations, which has put the world as a whole on the map for the citizen of Little Peddlington and Jay Corners. The kind of knowledge and interest that was once confined to travelers and the cultured has become widely distributed. When a million or two young men return from France, the jolt given to our intellectual isolation by the very fact of the war will be accentuated. And Europe, it is safe to say, will have learned as much about us as we about it. The shrinkage of the world already effected as a physical fact by steam and electricity will henceforth be naturalized in the imagination. All of these things mean the discovery of the interdependence of all peoples, and the development of a more highly organized world, a world knit together by more conscious and subtantial bonds. . . .

To say, however, that the world will be better organized is not—unfortunately—the same thing as to say that it will be organized so as to be a better world. We shall have either a world federation in the sense of a genuine concert of nations, or a few large imperialistic organizations, standing in chronic hostility to one another. . . . The choice between these two alternatives is the great question which the statesmen after the war will have to face. If it is dodged, and the attempt is made to restore an antebellum condition of a large number of independent detached and "sovereign" states allied only for purposes of economic and potential military warfare, the situation will be forced, probably, into the alternative of an imperially organized Balance of Power whose unstable equilibrium will result in the next war for decisive dominion.

The counterpart of the growth of world organization thru elimination of isolated territorial sovereign states is domestic integration within each unit. In every warring country there has been the same demand that in the time of great national stress production for profit be subordinated to production for use. Legal possession and individual property rights have had to give way before social requirements. The old conception of the absoluteness of private property has received the world over a blow from which it will never wholly recover. Not that arbitrary confiscation will be resorted to, but that it has been made clear that the control of any individual or group over their "own" property is relative to public wants, and that public requirements may at any time be given precedence by public machinery devised for that purpose. . . .

It may seem a work of supererogation to attempt even the most casual listing of the variety of ways in which the war has enforced this lesson of the interdependence, the interweaving of interests and occupations, and the consequent necessity of agencies for public oversight and direction in order that the interdependence may become a public value instead of being used for private levies. It is true that not every instrumentality brought into the war for the purpose of maintaining the public interest will last. Many of them will melt away when the war comes to an end. But it must be borne in mind that the war did not create that interdependence of interests which has given enterprizes once private and limited in scope a social significance. The war only gave a striking revelation of the state of affairs which the application of steam and electricity to industry and transportation had already effected. It afforded a vast and impressive object lesson as to what had occurred, and made it impossible for men to proceed any longer by ignoring the revolution which has taken place. Thus the public supervision and control occasioned by this war differ from that produced by other wars not only in range, depth and complexity, but even more in the fact that they have simply accelerated a movement which was already proceeding apace. The immediate urgency has in a short time brought into existence agencies for executing the supremacy of the public and social interest over the private and possessive interest which might otherwise have taken a long time to construct. In this sense, no matter how many among the special agencies for public control decay with the disappearance of war stress, the movement will never go backward. Peoples who have learned that billions are available for public needs when the occasion presses will not forget the lesson, and having seen that portions of these billions are necessarily diverted into physical training, industrial education, better housing, and the setting up of agencies for securing a public service and function from private industries will ask why in the future the main stream should not be directed in the same channels.

In short, we shall have a better organized world internally as well as externally, a more integrated, less anarchic, system.

5. *THE NATION,* "PRESIDENT WILSON AS EVANGELIST"

A revealing guide to the idealism and the disillusionment of liberals over the Wilsonian goals of war and the pursuit of peace can be found in the editorials and articles of The Nation. *Through the successive issues of this weekly journal, we can chart the process whereby the initial idealism of the liberals over the Wilsonian war aims yielded to deep and enduring disillusionment. The editors of The Nation charged that the peace settlement was a systematic negation of the liberal principles for which the country had gone to war. Equally severe condemnation was meted out to President Wilson, whom The Nation singled out as a thoroughly discredited man.*

In this editorial of September 13, 1919, published while Wilson was conducting his cross-country tour in a vain effort to rally flagging public support for the League, we find the liberal argument that the new League actually represented the old imperial system. Equally revealing is The Nation's *sense of betrayal by Woodrow Wilson and the journal's determination not to be seduced a second time by the rhetoric of the President. The larger significance of* The Nation's *disillusionment lies in the fact that it constituted the dominant view of liberals toward America's participation in international politics until the approach of World War II.*

The President is apparently doing all that was expected of him as he follows, in a double sense, the Star of Empire westward in behalf of his charter of economic imperialism. He has made several speeches and, as far as we can

SOURCE. Editorial in *The Nation,* Vol. 109, No. 2828, September 13, 1919, p. 360.

learn, has attracted large crowds. Whether this latter phenomenon is due to his personality, his message, local preparation, or popular curiosity towards the headliner is of course uncertain; and speculation about it is of no great value, since all the circumstances invite mixture of motive. As the President warms to his work, he becomes more vehement. His Columbus speech was graceful as usual, was characterized as usual by a great deal of what the old lady from the country called "fluidity," and was quite impersonal; but as he moved westward, he became increasingly severe with his opponents, called them hard names like "contemptible quitters," and indulged himself freely in the questionable luxury of being very personal indeed. Perhaps Mr. Wilson's disposition to abuse those who do not agree with him is an affair of temperament—we hear that it is somewhat common among persons of an artistic turn—and, as such, must be put up with; or perhaps it is a prerogative of those who feel themselves in a position to make a foible of omniscience, and hence is not to be quarrelled with. Possibly, again, it merely follows the old lawyer's advice to his junior, "When you have a bad case, abuse the plaintiff's attorney"; and if so, we can congratulate Mr. Wilson upon the fine appearance of sincerity that he contrives to throw around his practice of this maxim. It is quite as impeccable and convincing as the very best recorded efforts of his professional forbears, Dodson and Fogg.

For his case, also, whether good or bad, Mr. Wilson has accomplished a good deal in other respects. Most of what he said, as usual, will not at all bear disinterested scrutiny; but it must be remembered that he is not reckoning with disinterested scrutiny. He is going on the politician's assumption that the American people can think of only one thing at a time and that they quickly forget everything. His handling of the Shantung matter, for example, is the work of a first-class attorney:

> Great Britain and others, as everybody knows, in order to make it more certain that Japan would come into the war . . . had promised that any rights that Germany had in China should, in the case of the victory of the Allies, pass to Japan. . . . She was to get exactly what Germany had.

Next week *The Nation* proposes to publish the full text of the German-Chinese treaty, which will enable our readers to judge whether Japan gets exactly what Germany had. Mr. Wilson proceeds:

> The only thing that was possible was to induce Japan to promise . . . that she would retain in Shantung none of the sovereign rights which Germany had enjoyed there [the reader will get a precise definition of these "sovereign rights" in the text of the treaty above referred to], but would return the sovereignty without qualification to China, and retain in Shantung Province only what other nationalities had elsewhere; economic rights with regard to the development and administration of the railroad and of certain mines which had become attached to the railway. That is

her promise, and personally I haven't the slightest doubt that she will fulfil that promise.

Nor yet have we; not the slightest. Japan will return that sovereignty promptly and gracefully, having no more use for it than a man who likes oysters has for oyster-shells. If President Wilson were speaking as a man rather than as an attorney, we should wonder whether it were humanly possible for one in his position to be naïve enough not to know that "economic rights" and not political sovereignty determine actual rulership. Those who own rule; and they rule because they own. Give Japan "economic rights with regard to the development and administration," say, of the Pennsylvania Railroad from Pittsburgh to Harrisburg, with economic concessions thirty miles wide on each side of it, and she need not worry about the political sovereignty of the State of Pennsylvania. These "economic rights" in the province of Shantung (according to our own estimate and speaking under correction of those who are better informed) carry enough mineral resources to put a nation which is short only on iron and coal into the position of a first-class military Power.

The President also ventured to say that "this war was a commercial and industrial war, not a political war," and here again we are happy to agree with him. It is quite what many have thought from the beginning. True, the public had it on high authority somewhat earlier that it was, at least as far as our share went, a war to make the world safe for democracy, and to realize other objects of an elevated nature. That was the popular view, and one might perhaps at times have marked a certain tendency in the Administration to enforce that view upon the hesitant, and to stigmatize any other view as improper. But many still held that the war was primarily a squalid squabble over markets and trade-routes; and they now point to the outcome of the Peace Conference as amply justifying their judgment. They persist by strict logical consequence in regarding the treaty as a mere warrant of economic exploitation served by a victorious group upon a defeated group, according to a formula which has prevailed without essential change after every war known to history. They see no more reason, therefore, for accepting the President's indorsement of the treaty than there appears by his own admission to have been for accepting his indorsement of the war. But no doubt the demand for veracity and sincerity under circumstances in which these qualities can by nature have no place is quite enough to brand such persons with the practical politician's white-hot wrath—whether as quitters, pro-Germans, political Bolshevists, or what not.

The attempt to take President Wilson's exhortations seriously has reached the pass of distasteful pretence, and no one should be expected to make it. Which Wilson is the prophet and which the harlequin; and why? Indeed, one may go further and ask which Wilson takes the other seriously, and why. Has the impassioned crusader for democracy any respect for the docile agent of a brazen and unconscionable economic imperialism? Has the author of the Fourteen Points any fellowship of understanding with the promulgator of the peace treaty? Is there any reason why the one should be entrusted with a popular mandate rather than the other, instead of putting both in the category of those whom one looks at and passes by? We knew of none before Mr. Wilson undertook his missionary tour, and we know of none now; and we trust that the residual good sense of the public will withhold its suffrage from Mr. Wilson's present enterprise until one be produced.

PART III

The Twenties

VIEWED from the vantage point of the sixties, the 1920's in America often appear to be a decade crowded with contradiction and paradox. One need only recall some of the labels that historians have affixed to the events of the Twenties, and to the decade itself, to illustrate these perplexing qualities. Although it was the Jazz Era and the time of wonderful nonsense, it was also the decade of sober purpose and noble experiments—prohibition, the outlawry of war, the peace crusade, and the limitation of arms. It was the decade of normalcy and equipoise; of radical dissent and protest; of ballyhoo and brilliant literature; a time of rugged individualism and associational activities; of booming prosperity and financial ruin. It was all of these things and more that have led some to characterize the postwar decade as a paradoxical age.

There is much justification for this opinion, since recent scholarship has given us a deeper and broader understanding of the period than that afforded by the first journalistic histories of the Twenties. The result of numerous studies has been that of demonstrating the contradictions and paradoxes of a period once represented in simple and one-dimensional terms. Today, historians recognize that the Twenties were a time of transition and of significant change, as well as the seedbed of liberalism that would flower in the next decade and beyond. The Twenties were, in the judgment of historian George Mowry, "one of the major formulative epochs in American history."

The persistent impression of the Twenties as a "retreat to isolationism" has itself slowly retreated before mounting evidence of America's extensive far-flung world involvement during the period. The durability of the isolationist thesis, however, is not hard to explain. Because the United States failed to join the League of Nations, erected high tariff barriers, and emphatically ended an era of mass immigration, early histories concluded that the country had embraced political, economic, and cultural isolationism. The postwar nativist slogan "America for Americans" seemed to sum up the case for isolationism.

Yet America had not abandoned her democratic, capitalistic, and Christian mission to the world, nor had she forsaken traditional means to achieve desired ends. What had changed was the degree of economic power that the American policymakers now possessed and the efficacy with which they employed that power in a debt-ridden Europe and an underdeveloped Asia, Latin America, and Africa. The United States had emerged from World War I as a creditor nation, with a surging industrial capitalistic economy, seeking expansionist opportunities abroad. Logically, therefore, Charles Evans Hughes and Herbert Hoover, chief architects of policies in the Departments of State and Commerce, relied heavily on economic rather than political instruments to secure America's overseas objectives.

William Appleman Williams has observed that Herbert Hoover, in his capacity as Secretary of Commerce under Presidents Harding and Coolidge, and later as President, believed that the political aspects of policy were secondary to the economic aspects. That is why Hoover did not campaign for America's entry into the League of Nations. "He felt," explains Williams, "that the right kind of politics would evolve from sound economics"—that proper political consequences would result from "a system of overseas economic expansion envisaged by the strategy of the Open Door Policy." In other words, by keeping the world safe for American investment and trade, Hoover and his political contemporaries expected that the world would, indeed, become safe for democracy.

Just as Hoover believed that economic policies could promote desired political ends, he thought that astute economics could also render war unnecessary as an instrument of national policy. His "goodwill" tour of Latin America as President-elect is a notable example of his rejection of the heavy-handed military and diplomatic intervention practiced there by his predecessors. Hoover's policies thus anticipated both Franklin D. Roosevelt's "Good Neighbor Policy" and John F. Kennedy's "Alliance for Progress."

Secretary of State Charles Evans Hughes had earlier made major contributions to the diplomacy of the dollar by sponsoring the limitations of naval armaments at the Washington Conference of 1921–22, thereby effecting economies and securing for a season the cooperation of Japan in the Far East; and by initiating the Dawes reparations plan of 1923, he aimed to pull Germany into America's orbit. Hughes carried economic diplomacy to its logical conclusion by supporting other arms limitation conferences and reparations schemes of the Twenties.

Overall, the conjoint activities of the federal government and private enterprise succeeded in opening investment and trade opportunities in every quarter of the globe. American capital was put to work in the factories of Europe, in the rubber plantations of West Africa and Southeast Asia, in the oil fields of the Middle East, and in the mines of Latin America. Direct overseas investment of the nation leaped from $94 million dollars in 1919 to $602 million in 1929. Offsetting this success story were some failures in the political realm. Japan was only temporarily deterred from closing the Open Door in Manchuria and parts of China, fascism replaced democracy in Germany, and the hoped-for collapse of communism in the U.S.S.R. proved chimerical. Despite the mixed performance of these policies, America's large involvement in overseas affairs, 1919–1929, renders inaccurate the view of the "isolationist" Twenties.

It is obvious, too, that domestic concerns and world affairs were closely related. The transformation of the Department of Commerce from its central concern with interstate commerce to a new concentration on overseas markets, resources, and loans is the most obvious example of an economic relationship that was as close and vital as it was domestic and international. Moreover, the goals of freedom, prosperity, and peace—the major objectives of Americans in world affairs—were also the major goals at home.

Clearly the business community enjoyed a preponderance of power in both foreign and domestic affairs during the decade. By now, businessmen had generally refurbished their tarnished reputations through public service during World War I; during the Progressive Era their motives had been suspect. In the postwar period the federal government favored business to an extraordinary degree. The Wilson administration, by conferring privileges to big corporations and large banking institutions, had given these powerful groups an advantage over smaller business units. Through legislation of 1918 and 1919, the foreign operations of large businesses were exempted from anti-trust laws, thereby legalizing combinations in restraint of trade in overseas business. "There is ample evidence," David Shannon has written "that corporations which cooperated legally to limit competition abroad found it easier to establish a community of interest for their domestic operations as well."

Another very important type of business combination, initiated by the Wilson administration and given great impetus during the Twenties, was the trade association. Both large and small firms engaged in a particular enterprise were brought into association for mutual advantages. Through cooperation in such vital matters as purchasing, standardization of product, and pricing, the uncertainties born of competition were overcome. Such "associational activities" derived government support largely from Herbert Hoover's Department of Commerce until 1925. That year the Federal Trade Commission, under its conservative chairman William E. Humphrey, accepted Hoover's cooperative program; at the same time, the Supreme Court upheld the constitutionality of the trade association activities. Both actions brought essential unity of policy to the executive and judicial branches of government in regard to the organized powers of business.

The major challenge to the conservative business rule came from a number of southern and western agrarian reformers along with urban liberals in the Congress who managed to keep old reforms alive and to introduce a few new ones. Unfortunately for the progressives, divergent views on several programs —prohibition and immigration restriction in particular—kept the reform forces divided; still other issues such as dissolution of monopolies—the pet proposal of old progressives—failed to excite the young reformers, especially urban liberals like Congressman Fiorello LaGuardia of New York City. The urban reformers were more interested in "bread and butter" progressivism: unemployment insurance, wages and hours legislation, and the like.

When the congressional progressives did unite, as they did against the pro-business tax laws of Secretary of the Treasury Andrew Mellon, they enjoyed success only for a few years. By the mid-Twenties, Mellon was well on the way to gaining most of his tax proposals. One diverse group of progressives was as persistent as Mellon in pursuing their objective of government regulation of the stock market but, unlike Mellon, they failed to achieve their goal. Likewise, the progressives who championed the cause of the farmer through the McNary-Haugen Bill twice actually obtained congressional passage of their plan for a high domestic commodity price and the export of the surpluses abroad, in 1927 and 1928, but their efforts failed. President Coolidge twice killed the proposal with vetoes. Presidential vetoes also doomed for a time the public power proposal envisaged by George Norris, the Nebraska progressive. Norris successfully led the opposition that prevented the sale of the government-owned dam at Muscle Shoals on the Tennessee River during the Twenties, but he had to wait until the New Deal before his dream of a public water development was realized in the Tennessee Valley Authority. Despite the reformers' checkered record, progressivism did survive during the Twenties, although greatly diminished in force. The tangible achievements of the reformers are admittedly few, but the ground was being prepared for the liberal reforms of the Thirties and the subsequent decades.

The dominant mood of the country was expressed not in the rhetoric of criticism and reform proposals initiated by progressives during the Twenties, but in the supreme confidence exuded by the middle class. Bankers, small businessmen, manufacturers, and the white-collar, salaried, and professional people were the most ardent believers in the economics of the "New Era." Advertising and public relations firms, already important before the Twenties, became even more important as the proponents of consumption in an economy of abundance. The praise of these groups for the business civilization was heard and read everywhere—from the pulpit, in the classroom and lecture halls, in popular magazines and best-selling novels, in service clubs, and countless chambers of commerce throughout the nation. If anxieties and fears had once possessed the middle-class mind and motivated the reform impulse of the prewar years, social and economic prestige now gripped the middle classes. Their share in the business civilization gave them security and confidence and made them staunch defenders of the American business system.

The businessman reigned supreme—or almost supreme. A few debunkers had a heyday satirizing the pompous spokesmen of the business civilization and deflating the exaggerated claims made for the new economics. Equally significant criticism was leveled by intellectuals against democracy and some, like H. L. Mencken of the *Baltimore Sun* and the *American Mercury*, lampooned almost every aspect of American life. Mencken had no equal in holding up to ridicule the follies of the masses—the "booboisie" to Mencken. He excoriated the Ku Klux Klan, prohibition, the bigotry and anti-intellectualism of fundamentalists and antievolutionists and thus earned their undying enmity. Other social critics, shocked at the intolerance that surrounded the trial of accused murderers Sacco and Vanzetti, turned the case of the two condemned and subsequently executed anarchists into the great liberal cause of the decade.

But even Mencken found something worthwhile in the cultural life of the Twenties—the literature of the period. We could start with Mencken's own writing, as he once did, and extend the list to include the writers whose work constitutes a brilliant literary renaissance. The brightest stars in the galaxy of the literati were novelists F. Scott Fitzgerald, Ernest Hemingway and, coming into prominence at the end of the decade, William Faulkner; poets Ezra Pound and T. S. Eliot; and playwright Eugene O'Neill. Lesser lights among the novelists were Sinclair Lewis, Theodore Dreiser, John Dos Passos, and Sherwood Anderson. Some treated American themes from afar, as did the expatriates Hemingway in Paris and Eliot and Pound in England and Italy; others like Lewis roamed about mid-America, observing social types and collecting data that would later appear in devastating caricature, as in his treatment of fundamentalist religion in *Elmer Gantry*. Meanwhile, in New York City's Harlem a group of Negro novelists and poets were making substantial contributions to the cultural flowering of the decade. The writings of James Weldon Johnson, Claude MacKay, Langston Hughes, Countee

Cullen, among others, represent the early, brilliant phase of the "Black Renaissance."

In music, the most exciting developments of the decade were the new vocal and instrumental expressions in the blues and jazz idioms. Among the great Negro blues singers were "Blind Lemon" Jefferson, Huddie ("Leadbelly") Leadbetter, and Gertrude "Ma" Rainey. The legendary Bessie Smith became a celebrated figure in the jazz world through her numerous recordings, including some made with jazz artists Louis Armstrong, Fletcher Henderson, and James P. Johnson. Some at the time thought that the improvisations of Louis Armstrong's "Hot Five," "Jelly Roll" Morton, and "King" Oliver were degenerate and vulgar. A young George Gershwin disagreed, and in 1924 he artfully blended jazz and classical styles into the enduring *Rhapsody in Blue*. The new rhythms influenced more than traditional music: the Charleston and other dances of the Jazz Era were inevitable responses to the irresistible beat.

In both art and architecture nothing developed to contrast with the forms of previous decades, although one new art form—the motion picture—made an important technical advance with the introduction of sound in 1927. The movies, along with the radio and phonograph, brought the talents of artistic Americans into the lives of more people at home and abroad than ever before. It truly marked the dawn of mass culture.

Many of the same themes and issues that had aroused or inspired the artists and intellectuals of the Twenties also fueled the heated controversies of American politics. The pervasive disillusionment with world affairs that engulfed so many Americans after the Great War was a major factor in the repudiation of Woodrow Wilson and the landslide victory of the thoroughly conservative Warren G. Harding in the presidential election of 1920. Four years later, Calvin Coolidge, personification of puritan respectability and a model of propriety, led the Republican party to still another victory over the hapless Democrats. The Democrats had narrowly escaped deadlock in that year of 1924 when the rural, old-stock followers of William G. McAdoo and the urban, new-immigrant supporters of Al Smith waged a debilitating battle for control of the party. The delegates finally selected a colorless conservative, John W. Davis, but his nomination did not bring harmony to the party.

The subsequent withdrawal of McAdoo from presidential politics in 1927 gave Smith the Democratic presidential nomination in 1928. But Smith's Republican opponent, the dry, Protestant Herbert Hoover, representative of the old America and architect of the "New Era" prosperity, easily defeated his wet, Irish Catholic opponent. Astute political observers later discovered evidence among the election returns to indicate that the Republican party was losing its hold on the nation's cities and that a new and powerful Democratic coalition was in the making. Few at the time, however, could see that the years of Republican ascendancy and the party's domination of national politics were almost over.

Nor could many detect and properly assess the economic state of the nation in the last year of the "prosperity decade." In retrospect, however, economists can pinpoint those weaknesses in the economy that turned the stock market crash of October 1929 into depression. For one thing, a maldistribution of national income that left the lower-income groups too little with which to buy and the upper-income groups too much with which to invest in new industrial expansion was a major flaw. A workable plan for the relief of agriculture to remedy the disparity between farm income and farm expenses coupled with a more generous share of corporate profits for labor would have done much to correct the poor distribution of income. The steps taken in these directions, however, were either inadequate or too late, or both. The corporate structure with its pyramiding holding companies and trusts possessed certain strengths, but corrupt or irresponsible leadership at the top accentuated weaknesses that eventually brought entire organizations crashing to their foundations. Conversely, the nation's banking institutions, despite the central direction and control effected by the Federal Reserve System, included far too many independent banks incapable of weathering an economic storm. Finally, the country's international credit policies were unrealistic in view of the imbalance of trade—exports persistently exceeding imports—while the debtor status of several important states was not helped by the American refusal to lower tariffs in order to stimulate trans-Atlantic trade. All of the foregoing weaknesses could have been corrected had the policymakers from the President on down possessed the economic intelligence and the tools of the 1960's, but even if Americans of the Twenties had had the ability to discern weaknesses and prescribe remedies for an imperfect economy, there is no assurance that those responsible for policy making would have had the political courage and will to take the necessary action. A wise prophet's warnings would most likely have gone unheeded and unheard, since a lone voice of wisdom could hardly be heard over the din of business activity and innumerable roseate economic forecasts.

In the end, the administration of Herbert Hoover, instead of charting a further advance toward the plateau of permanent national prosperity (as the President had prophesied in his inaugural address in March 1929), watched the long slide into the slough of depression, thereby bringing both Hoover and the Twenties into disrepute. Today, the weaknesses and strengths of Hoover's policies and those of the predepression decade stand out in bold relief.

The men and events of the Twenties continue to command serious attention and interest. The reward of historical inquiry into the perplexities of that decade is to increase our historical consciousness of the present and perhaps make those who master the past more deliberate shapers of the future.

SECONDARY SOURCES

1. WILLIAM A. WILLIAMS, "THE LEGEND OF ISOLATION IN THE 1920'S"

IN recent years historians have come to use the term "isolation" with circumspection, and some have wondered if it has ever had much validity as a concept to explain America's relations to the world. For most scholars writing in the 1920's and 1930's, however, the failure of the United States to enter the League of Nations indicated the adoption of a policy of isolationism. By making participation in the League the measure of the nation's involvement in world affairs, these writers had used a faulty yardstick. The meaningful test of America's international relations during the 1920's was not the extent to which this country acted in concert with other nations in a new world organization, but the extent to which the United States used her instruments of influence to secure the objectives of the old "Open Door" policy throughout the world.

At the forefront of those historians who are presently reexamining the nation's foreign economic and political involvement is William Appleman Williams, professor of American diplomatic history at the University of Wisconsin. Williams is generally recognized as the leader of a school of historians who contend that "the central theme of American foreign relations has been the expansion of the United States."

SOURCE. William A. Williams, "The Legend of Isolation in the 1920's," in *Science and Society*, Vol. 18, No. 1, Winter 1954, pp. 1–20. Copyright Science and Society, Incorporated, 1954. Reprinted by permission of *Science and Society* and the author.

Concerning the post-World War I period, Williams contends that "far from isolation, the foreign relations of the United States from 1920 to 1932 were marked by express and extended involvement with—and intervention in the affairs of—other nations of the world." He elaborates upon his thesis in the following seminal essay.

The widely accepted assumption that the United States was isolationist from 1920 through 1932 is no more than a legend. Sir Francis Bacon might have classed this myth of isolation as one of his Idols of the Market-Place. An "ill and unfit choice of words," he cautioned, "leads men away into innumerable and inane controversies and fancies." And certainly the application of the terms *isolation* and *isolationism* to a period and a policy that were characterized by vigorous involvement in the affairs of the world with consciousness of purpose qualifies as an "ill and unfit choice of words." Thus the purpose of this essay: on the basis of an investigation of the record to suggest that, far from isolation, the foreign relations of the United States from 1920 through 1932 were marked by express and extended involvement with—and intervention in the affairs of—other nations of the world.

It is both more accurate and more helpful to consider the twenties as contiguous with the present instead of viewing those years as a quixotic interlude of low-down jazz and lower-grade gin, fluttering flappers and Faulkner's fiction, and bootlegging millionaires and millionaire bootleggers. For in foreign policy there is far less of a sharp break between 1923 and 1953 than generally is acknowledged. A closer examination of the so-called isolationists of the twenties reveals that many of them were in fact busily engaged in extending American power. Those individuals and groups have not dramatically changed their outlook on foreign affairs. Their policies and objectives may differ with those of others (including professors), but they have never sought to isolate the United States.

This interpretation runs counter to the folklore of American foreign relations. Harvard places isolationism "in the saddle." Columbia sees "Americans retiring within their own shell." Yale judges that policy "degenerated" into isolation—among other things. Others, less picturesque but equally positive, refer to a "marked increase of isolationist sentiment" and to "those years of isolationism." Another group diagnoses the populace as having "ingrained isolationism," analyzes it as "sullen and selfish" in consequence, and characterizes it as doing "its best to forget international subjects." Related verdicts describe the Republican party as "predominantly isolationist" and as an organization that "fostered a policy of deliberate isolation."

Most pointed of these specifications is a terse two-word summary of the diplomacy of the period: "Isolation Perfected." Popularizers have trans-scribed this theme into a burlesque. Their articles and books convey the impression that the Secretaries of State were in semi-retirement and that the citizenry wished to do away with the Department itself. Columnists and commentators have made the concept an eerie example of George Orwell's double-think. They label as isolationists the most vigorous interventionists.

The case would seem to be closed and judgment given if it were not for the ambivalence of some observers and the brief dissents filed by a few others. The scholar who used the phrase "those years of isolationism," for example, remarks elsewhere in the same book that "expansionism . . . really was long a major expression of isolationism." Another writes of the "return to an earlier policy of isolation," and on the next page notes a "shift in policy during the twenties amounting almost to a 'diplomatic revolution.' " A recent biographer states that Henry Cabot Lodge "did not propose . . . an isolationist attitude," but then proceeds to characterize the Monroe Doctrine—upon which Lodge stood in his fight against the League of Nations treaty—as a philosophy of "isolation." And in the last volume of his trilogy, the late Professor Frederick L. Paxton summed up a long review of the many diplomatic activities of the years 1919–1923 with the remark that this was a foreign policy of "avoidance rather than of action."

But a few scholars, toying with the Idol of the Market-Place, have made bold to rock the image. Yet Professor Richard Van Alstyne was doing more than playing the iconoclast when he observed that the "militant manifest destiny men were the isolationists of the nineteenth century." For with this insight we can translate those who maintain that Lodge "led the movement to perpetuate the traditional policy of isolation." Perhaps William G. Carleton was even more forthright. In 1946 he pointed out that the fight over the League treaty was not between isolationists and internationalists, and added that many of the mislabeled isolationists were actually "nationalists and imperialists." Equally discerning was Charles Beard's comment in 1933 that the twenties were marked by a "return to the more aggressive ways . . . [used] to protect and advance the claims of American business enterprise." All these interpretations were based on facts that prompted another scholar to change his earlier conclusion and declare in 1953 that "the thought was all of keeping American freedom of action."

These are perceptive comments. Additional help has recently been supplied by two other students of the period. One of these is Robert E. Osgood, who approached the problem in terms of *Ideals and Self-Interest in American Foreign Relations*. Though primarily concerned with the argument that Americans should cease being naive, Osgood suggests that certain stereotypes are misleading. One might differ with his analysis of the struggle over the Treaty of Versailles, but not with his insistence that there were fundamental differences between Senators Lodge and William E. Borah—as well as between those two and President Woodrow Wilson. Osgood likewise raises questions about the reputed withdrawal of the American public. Over a thousand organizations for the study of international relations existed in 1926, to say nothing of the groups that sought constantly to make or modify foreign policy.

Osgood gives little attention to this latter aspect of foreign relations, a surprising omission on the part of a realist. But the underlying assumption of his inquiry cannot be challenged. The foreign policy issue of the twenties was never isolationism. The controversy and competition were waged between those who entertained different concepts of the national interest and disagreed over the means to be employed to secure that objective. Secretary of State Charles Evans Hughes was merely more eloquent, not less explicit. "Foreign policies," he explained in 1923, "are not built upon abstractions. They are the result of practical conceptions of national interest arising from some immediate exigency or standing out vividly in historical perspective."

Historian George L. Grassmuck used this old-fashioned premise of the politician as a tool with which to probe the *Sectional Biases in Congress on Foreign Policy*. Disciplining himself more rigorously in the search for primary facts than did Osgood, Grassmuck's findings prompted him to conclude that "the 'sheep and goats' technique" of historical research is eminently unproductive. From 1921 to 1933, for example, the Republicans in both houses of Congress were "more favorable to both Army and Navy measures than . . . Democrats." Eighty-five percent of the same Republicans supported international economic measures and agreements. As for the Middle West, that much condemned section did not reveal any "extraordinary indication of a . . . tendency to withdraw." Nor was there "an intense 'isolationism' on the part of [its] legislators with regard to membership in a world organization." And what opposition there was seems to have been as much the consequence of dust bowls and depression as the product of disillusioned scholars in ivory towers.

These investigations and correlations have two implications. First, the United States was neither isolated nor did it pursue a policy of isolationism from 1920 to 1933. Second, if the policy of that era, so generally accepted as the product of traditional isolationist sentiment, proves nonisolationist, then the validity and usefulness of the concept when applied to earlier or later periods may seriously be challenged.

Indeed, it would seem more probable that the central theme of American foreign relations has been the expansion of the United States. Alexander Hamilton made astute use of the phrase "no entangling alliances" during the negotiation of Jay's Treaty in 1794, but his object was a *de facto* affiliation with the British Fleet—not isolation. Nor was Thomas Jefferson seeking to withdraw when he made of Monticello a counselling center for those seeking to emulate the success of the American Revolution. A century later Senator Lodge sought to revise the Treaty of Versailles and the Covenant of the League of Nations with reservations that seemed no more than a restatement of Hamilton's remarks. Yet the maneuvers of Lodge were no more isolationist in character and purpose than Hamilton's earlier action. And while surely no latter-day Jefferson, Senator Borah was anything but an isolationist in his concept of the power of economics and ideas. Borah not only favored the recognition of the Soviet Union in order to influence the development of the Bolshevik Revolution and as a check against Japanese expansion in Asia, but also argued that American economic policies were intimately connected with foreign political crises. All those men were concerned with the extension of one or more aspects of American influence, power, and authority.

Approached in this manner, the record of American foreign policy in the twenties verifies the judgments of two remarkably dissimilar students: historian Richard W. Leopold and Senator Lodge. The professor warns that the era was "more complex than most glib generalizations . . . would suggest"; and the scholastic politician concludes that, excepting wars, there "never [was] a period when the United States [was] more active and its influence more felt internationally than between 1921 and 1924." The admonition about perplexity was offered as helpful advice, not as an invitation to anti-intellectualism. For, as the remarks of the Senator implied, recognition that a problem is involved does not mean that it cannot be resolved.

Paradox and complexity can often be clarified by rearranging the data around a new focal point that is common to all aspects of the apparent contradiction. The confusion of certainty and ambiguity that characterizes most accounts of American foreign policy in the twenties stems from the fact that they are centered on the issue of membership in the League of Nations. Those Americans who wanted to join are called internationalists. Opponents of that move became isolationists. But the subsequent action of most of those who fought participation in the League belies this simple classification. And the later policies of many who favored adherence to the League casts serious doubts upon the assumption that they were willing to negotiate or arbitrate questions that they defined as involving the national interest. More pertinent is an examination of why certain groups and individuals favored or disapproved of the League, coupled with a review of the programs they supported after that question was decided.

Yet such a re-study of the League fight is in itself insufficient. Equally important is a close analysis of the American reaction to the Bolshevik

Revolution. Both the League Covenant and the Treaty of Versailles were written on a table shaken by that upheaval. The argument over the ratification of the combined documents was waged in a context determined as much by Nikolai Lenin's *Appeal to the Toiling, Oppressed, and Exhausted Peoples of Europe* and the Soviet *Declaration to the Chinese People* as by George Washington's Farewell Address.

Considered within the setting of the Bolshevik Revolution, the basic question was far greater than whether or not to enter the League. At issue was what response was to be made to the domestic and international division of labor that had accompanied the Industrial Revolution. Challenges from organized urban labor, dissatisfied farmers, frightened men of property, searching intellectual critics, and colonial peoples rudely interrupted almost every meeting of the Big Four in Paris and were echoed in many Senate debates over the treaty. And those who determined American policy through the decade of the twenties were consciously concerned with the same problem.

An inquiry into this controversy over the broad question of how to end the war reveals certain divisions within American society. These groupings were composed of individuals and organizations whose position on the League of Nations was coincident with and part of their response to the Bosheviks; or, in a wider sense, with their answer to that general unrest, described by Woodrow Wilson as a "feeling of revolt against the large vested interests which influenced the world both in the economic and the political sphere." Once this breakdown has been made it is then possible to follow the ideas and actions of these various associations of influence and power through the years 1920 to 1933.

At the core of the American reaction to the League and the Bolshevik Revolution was the quandary between fidelity to ideals and the urge to power. Jefferson faced a less acute version of the same predicament in terms of whether to force citizenship on settlers west of the Mississippi who were reluctant to be absorbed in the Louisiana Purchase. A century later the anti-imperialists posed the same issue in the more sharply defined circumstances of the Spanish-American War. The League and the Bolsheviks raised the question in its most dramatic context and in unavoidable terms.

There were four broad responses to this reopening of the age-old dilemma. At one pole stood the pure idealists and pacifists, led by William Jennings Bryan. A tiny minority in themselves, they were joined, in terms of general consequences if not in action, by those Americans who were preoccupied with their own solutions to the problem. Many American business men, for example, were concerned primarily with the expansion of trade and were apathetic toward or impatient with the hullabaloo over the League. Diametrically opposed to the idealists were the vigorous expansionists. All these exponents of the main chance did not insist upon an overt crusade to run the world, but they were united on Senator Lodge's proposition that the United States should dominate world politics. Association with other nations they accepted, but not equality of membership or mutuality of decision.

Caught in the middle were those Americans who declined to support either extreme. A large number of these people clustered around Woodrow Wilson, and can be called the Wilsonites. Though aware of the dangers and temptations involved, Wilson declared his intention to extend American power for the purpose of strengthening the ideals. However noble that effort, it failed for two reasons. Wilson delegated power and initiative to men and organizations that did not share his objectives, and on his own part the president ultimately "cast in his lot" with the defenders of the status quo.

Led by the Sons of the Wild Jackass, the remaining group usually followed Senator Borah in foreign relations. These men had few illusions about the importance of power in human affairs or concerning the authority of the United States in international politics. Prior to the world war they supported—either positively or passively—such vigorous expansionists as Theodore Roosevelt, who led their Progressive Party. But the war and the Bolshevik Revolution jarred some of these Progressives into a closer examination of their assumptions. These reflections and new conclusions widened the breach with those of their old comrades who had moved toward a conservative position on domestic issues. Some of those earlier allies, like Senator Albert J. Beveridge, continued to agitate for an American century. Others, such as Bainbridge Colby, sided with Wilson in 1916 and went along with the president on foreign policy.

But a handful had become firm anti-expansionists by 1919. No attempt was made by these men to deny the power of the United States. Nor did they think that the nation could become self-sufficient and impregnable in its strength. Borah, for example, insisted that America must stand with Russia if Japan and Germany were to be checked. And Johnson constantly pointed out that the question was not whether to withdraw, but at what time and under what circumstances to use the country's influence. What these men did maintain was that any effort to run the world by establishing an American system comparable to the British Empire was both futile and un-American.

In this they agreed with Henry Adams, who debated the same issue with his brother Brooks Adams, Theodore Roosevelt, and Henry Cabot Lodge in the years after 1898. "I incline now to anti-imperialism, and very strongly to anti-militarism," Henry warned. "If we try to rule politically, we take the chances against us." By the end of the first world war another generation of expansionists tended to agree with Henry Adams about ruling politically, but planned to build and maintain a similar pattern of control through the use of America's economic might. Replying to these later expansionists,

Borah and other anti-expansionists of the nineteen-twenties argued that if Washington's influence was to be effective it would have to be used to support the movements of reform and colonial nationalism rather than deployed in an effort to dam up and dominate those forces.

[For these reasons they opposed Wilson's reorganization of the international banking consortium, fearing that the financiers would either influence strongly or veto—as they did—American foreign policies] With Senator Albert B. Cummins of Iowa they voted against the Wilson-approved Webb-Pomerene Act, which repealed the anti-trust laws for export associations. In the same vein they tried to prevent passage of the Edge Act, an amendment to the Federal Reserve Act that authorized foreign banking corporations. Led by Borah, they [bitterly attacked the Versailles Treaty because, in their view, it committed the United States to oppose colonial movements for self-government and to support an unjust and indefensible status quo. From the same perspective they criticized and fought to end intervention in Russia and the suppression of civil liberties at home.]

Contrary to the standard criticism of their actions, however, these anti-expansionists were not just negative die-hards. Senator Cummins maintained from the first that American loans to the allies should be considered gifts. Borah spoke out on the same issue, hammered away against armed intervention in Latin America, played a key role in securing the appointment of Dwight Morrow as Ambassador to Mexico, and sought to align the United States with, instead of against, the Chinese Revolution. On these and other issues the anti-expansionists were not always of one mind, but as in the case of the Washington Conference Treaties the majority of them were far more positive in their actions than has been acknowledged.

Within this framework the key to the defeat of the League treaty was the defection from the Wilsonites of a group who declined to accept the restrictions that Article X of the League Covenant threatened to impose upon the United States. A morally binding guarantee of the "territorial integrity and existing political integrity of all members of the League" was too much for these men. First they tried to modify that limitation. Failing there, they followed Elihu Root and William Howard Taft, both old time expansionists, to a new position behind Senator Lodge. [Among those who abandoned Wilson on this issue were Herbert Hoover, Calvin Coolidge, Charles Evans Hughes, and Henry L. Stimson.]

Not all these men were at ease with the vigorous expansionists. Stimson, for one, thought the Lodge reservations "harsh and unpleasant," and later adjusted other of his views. Hoover and Hughes tried to revive their version of the League after the Republicans returned to power in 1920. But at the time all of them were more uneasy about what one writer has termed Wilson's "moral imperialism." They were not eager to identify themselves with the memories of that blatant imperialism of the years 1895 to 1905, but neither did they like Article X. That proviso caught them from both sides, it illegalized changes initiated by the United States, and obligated America to restore a status quo to some aspects of which they were either indifferent or antagonistic. But least of all were they anxious to run the risk that the Wilsonian rhetoric of freedom and liberty might be taken seriously in an age of revolution. Either by choice or default they supported the idea of a community of interest among the industrialized powers of the world led by an American-British entente as against the colonial areas and the Soviet Union.

This postwar concept of the community of interest was the first generation intellectual off-spring of Herbert Croly's *Promise of American Life* and Herbert Hoover's *American Individualism*. Croly's opportunistic nationalism provided direction for Hoover's "greater mutuality of interest." The latter was to be expressed in an alliance between the government and the "great trade associations and the powerful corporations." Pushed by the Croly-Hoover wing of the old Progressive Party, the idea enjoyed great prestige during the twenties. Among its most ardent exponents were Samuel Gompers and Matthew Woll of the labor movement, Owen D. Young of management, and Bernard Baruch of finance.

What emerged was an American corporatism. The avowed goals were order, stability, and social peace. The means to those objectives were labor-management co-operation, arbitration, and the elimination of waste and inefficiency by closing out unrestrained competition. State intervention was to be firm, but moderated through the cultivation and legalization of trade associations which would, in turn, advise the national government and supply leaders for the federal bureaucracy. The ideal was union in place of diversity and conflict.

Other than Hoover, the chief spokesmen of this new community of interest as applied to foreign affairs were Secretaries of State Hughes and Stimson. In the late months of 1931 Stimson was to shift his ground, but until that time he supported the principle. All three men agreed that American economic power should be used to build, strengthen, and maintain the co-operation they sought. As a condition for his entry into the cabinet, Hoover demanded—and received—a major voice in "all important economic policies of the administration." With the energetic assistance of Julius Klein, lauded by the National Foreign Trade Council as the "international business go-getter of Uncle Sam," Hoover changed the Department of Commerce from an agency primarily concerned with interstate commerce to one that concentrated on foreign markets and loans, and control of import sources. Hughes and Stimson handled the political aspects of establishing a "community of ideals, interests and purposes."

These men were not imperialists in the traditional sense of that much abused term. All agreed with Klein that the object was to eliminate "the old imperialistic trappings of politico-economic exploitation." They sought instead the "internationalization of business." Through the use of economic power they wanted to establish a common bond, forged of similar assumptions and purposes, with both the industrialized nations and the native business community in the colonial areas of the world. Their deployment of America's material strength is unquestioned. President Calvin Coolidge reviewed their success, and indicated the political implications thereof, on Memorial Day, 1928. "Our investments and trade relations are such," he summarized, "that it is almost impossible to conceive of any conflict anywhere on earth which would not affect us injuriously."

Internationalization through the avoidance of conflict was the key objective. This did not mean a negative foreign policy. Positive action was the basic theme. The transposition of corporatist principles to the area of foreign relations produced a parallel policy. American leadership and intervention would build a world community regulated by agreement among the industrialized nations. The prevention of revolution and the preservation of the sanctity of private property were vital objectives. Hughes was very clear when he formulated the idea for Latin America. "We are seeking to establish a *Pax Americana* maintained not by arms but by mutual respect and good will and the tranquillizing processes of reason." There would be, he admitted, "interpositions of a temporary character"—the Secretary did not like the connotations of the word intervention—but only to facilitate the establishment of the United States as the "exemplar of justice."

Extension to the world of this pattern developed in Latin America was more involved. There were five main difficulties, four in the realm of foreign relations and one in domestic affairs. The internal problem was to establish and integrate a concert of decision between the government and private economic groups. Abroad the objectives were more sharply defined: circumscribe the impact of the Soviet Union, forestall and control potential resistance of colonial areas, pamper and cajole Germany and Japan into acceptance of the basic proposition, and secure from Great Britain practical recognition of the fact that Washington had become the center of Anglo-Saxon collaboration. Several examples will serve to illustrate the general outline of this diplomacy, and to indicate the friction between the office holders and the office dwellers.

Wilson's Administration left the incoming Republicans a plurality of tools designed for the purpose of extending American power. The Webb-Pomerene Law, the Edge Act, and the banking consortium were but three of the more obvious and important of these. Certain polishing and sharpening remained to be done, as exemplified by Hoover's generous interpretation of the Webb-Pomerene legislation, but this was a minor problem. Hoover and Hughes added to these implements with such laws as the one designed to give American customs officials diplomatic immunity so that they could do cost accounting surveys of foreign firms. This procedure was part of the plan to provide equal opportunity abroad, under which circumstances Secretary Hughes was confident that "American business men would take care of themselves."

It was harder to deal with the British, who persisted in annoying indications that they considered themselves equal partners in the enterprise. Bainbridge Colby, Wilson's last Secretary of State, ran into the same trouble. Unless England came "to our way of thinking," Colby feared that "agreement [would] be impossible." A bit later Hughes told the British Ambassador that the time had come for London's expressions of cordial sentiment to be "translated into something definite." After many harangues about oil, access to mandated areas, and trade with Russia, it was with great relief that Stimson spoke of the United States and Great Britain "working together like two old shoes."

Deep concern over revolutionary ferment produced great anxiety. Hughes quite agreed with Colby that the problem was to prevent revolutions without making martyrs of the leaders of colonial or other dissident movements. The despatches of the period are filled with such expressions as "very grave concern," "further depressed," and "deeply regret," in connection with revolutionary activity in China, Latin America, and Europe. American foreign service personnel abroad were constantly reminded to report all indications of such unrest. This sensitivity reached a high point when one representative telegraphed as "an example of the failure to assure public safety . . . the throwing of a rock yesterday into the state hospital here." Quite in keeping with this pattern was Washington's conclusion that it would support "any provisional government which gave satisfactory evidence of an intention to reestablish constitutional order."

Central to American diplomacy of the twenties was the issue of Germany and Japan. And it was in this area that the government ran into trouble with its partners, the large associations of capital. The snag was to convince the bankers of the validity of the long range view. Hoover, Hughes and Stimson all agreed that it was vital to integrate Germany and Japan into the American community. Thus Hughes opposed the French diplomacy of force on the Rhine, and for his own part initiated the Dawes Plan. But the delegation of so much authority to the financiers backfired in 1931. The depression scared the House of Morgan and it refused to extend further credits to Germany. Stimson "blew up." He angrily told the Morgan representative in Paris that this strengthened France and thereby undercut the American program. Interrupted in the midst of this argument by a trans-Atlantic phone call from Hoover, Stimson explained to the president that "if you want to help the cause you are speaking of you will not do it by calling me up, but by calling

Tom Lamont." Stimson then turned back to Lamont's agent in Europe and, using "unregulated language," told the man to abandon his "narrow banking axioms."

Similar difficulties faced the government in dealing with Japan and China. The main problem was to convince Japan, by persuasion, concession, and the delicate use of diplomatic force, to join the United States in an application of its Latin American policy to China. Washington argued that the era of the crude exploitation of, and the exercise of direct political sovereignty over, backward peoples was past. Instead, the interested powers should agree to develop and exercise a system of absentee authority while increasing the productive capacity and administrative efficiency of China. Japan seemed amenable to the proposal, and at the Washington Conference, Secretary Hughes went a great distance to convince Tokyo of American sincerity. Some writers, such as George Frost Kennan and Adolf A. Berle, claim that the United States did not go far enough. This is something of a mystery. For in his efforts to establish "cooperation in the Far East," as Hughes termed it, the Secretary consciously gave Japan "an extraordinarily favorable position."

Perhaps what Kennan and Berle have in mind is the attitude of Thomas Lamont. In contrast to their perspective on Europe, the bankers took an extremely long range view of Asia. Accepting the implications of the Four and Nine Power Treaties, Lamont began to finance Japan's penetration of the mainland. Hughes and Stimson were trapped. They continued to think in terms of American business men taking care of themselves if given an opportunity, and thus strengthening Washington's position in the world community. Hughes wrote Morgan that he hoped the consortium would become an "important instrumentality of our 'open door' policy." But the American members of the banking group refused to antagonize their Japanese and British colleagues, and so vetoed Washington's hope to finance the Chinese Eastern Railway and its efforts to support the Federal Telegraph Company in China.

In this context it is easy to sympathize with Stimson's discomfort when the Japanese Army roared across Manchuria. As he constantly reiterated to the Japanese Ambassador in Washington, Tokyo had come far along the road "of bringing itself into alignment with the methods and opinion of the Western World." Stimson not only wanted to, but did in fact give Japan every chance to continue along that path. So too did President Hoover, whose concern with revolution was so great that he was inclined to view Japanese sovereignty in Manchuria as the best solution. Key men in the State Department shared the president's conclusion.

Stimson's insight was not so limited. He realized that his predecessor, Secretary of State Frank B. Kellogg, had been right: the community of interest that America should seek was with the Chinese. The Secretary acknowledged his error to Senator Borah, who had argued just such a thesis since 1917. Stimson's letter to Borah of February 23, 1932, did not say that America should abandon her isolationism, but rather that she had gone too far with the wrong friends. The long and painful process of America's great awakening had begun. But in the meantime President Hoover's insistence that no move should be made toward the Soviet Union, and that the non-recognition of Manchuko should be considered as a formula looking toward conciliation, had opened the door to appeasement.

2. WILLIAM E. LEUCHTENBURG, "THE SECOND INDUSTRIAL REVOLUTION"

BY 1920 the American economy had completed a remarkable century of progress. A hundred years before, the country had been slowly taking its first steps as an infant industrializing nation; spurred by the impetus of the Civil War, the steps had become strides and, during the last decades of the nineteenth century, the nation's complex rail and water transport system, along with the formation of an expanding capital and industrial base, readied the economy for the next phase in its drive to maturity. By the third decade of the twentieth century, the significant shift from production of heavy machine goods to mass-produced durable consumer items had occurred. American industry had begun to produce enormous numbers of automobiles, washing machines, electrical appliances, and other items that made modern life more comfortable and convenient. The economy of the Twenties gave Americans the world's highest standard of living.

A standard of living, however, is measured largely in terms of man's basic physical needs: clothing, housing, and food. Still, man also has a capacity for esthetics and non-material things, and a proper living standard ought to include these aspects as well. The economy of the Twenties extended to a large majority of Americans the opportunity to a free education through the eighth grade; for many it provided a high school education, and for a few, college. Public and private development of libraries, hospitals, churches, art galleries, museums, parks, and playgrounds gave additional evidence that gains registered during the decade were not merely in products that could be counted by economists and publicized by every chamber of commerce in the country. At its extreme worst, the system was full of inequities, hollow at its core, and exceedingly base; at its best, the system con-

SOURCE. William E. Leuchtenburg, *The Perils of Prosperity*, Chicago: University of Chicago Press, 1958, pp. 178–203. Copyright by University of Chicago, 1958. Reprinted by permission of The University of Chicago Press and the author.

tained the promise of freeing all men, as it did some, from the drudgery of a machine-age
existence to the enjoyment of leisure activities, including the pursuit of the esthetic and the
spiritual.

William Leuchtenburg, whose book The Perils of Prosperity *is the best interpretive*
survey of the period 1914–1932, impressively demonstrates the pervasive impact of the
"second industrial revolution" upon America. To merely list the ways the economy
influenced the American people and their institutions would be an imposing task, but
Leuchtenburg has done this and more. Thus an understanding of his essay, a chapter
from his book, does much to explain the importance of the Twenties in America.

In the late eighteenth and early nineteenth centuries the industrialization
of England accelerated at such a pace that historians have found no term
adequate to describe it save one usually reserved for violent political change—
revolution. In the late nineteenth century and early twentieth century the
productive capacity of the American economy increased at a rate greater
than that of the Industrial Revolution. After World War I, the United States,
reaping the harvest of half a century of industrial progress, achieved the highest standard of living any people had ever known. National income soared
from $480 per capita in 1900 to $681 in 1929. Workers were paid the highest
wages of any time in the history of the country; essentially unchanged from
1890 to 1918, the real earnings of workers—what their income actually would
buy at the store—shot up at an astonishing rate in the 1920's. At the same
time, the number of hours of work was cut: in 1923 United States Steel
abandoned the twelve-hour day and put its Gary plant on an eight-hour
shift; in 1926 Henry Ford instituted the five-day week, while International
Harvester announced the electrifying innovation of a two-week annual
vacation with pay for its employees.

In 1922 the country, already enormously productive by comparison with
other countries, started a recovery from the postwar depression—a recovery
that maintained prosperity, with slight interruptions, until the fall of 1929.
The key to the piping prosperity of the decade was the enormous increase in
efficiency of production, in part the result of the application of Frederick W.
Taylor's theory of scientific management, in part the outgrowth of technological innovations. In 1914 at his Highland Park plant Henry Ford had
revolutionized industrial production by installing the first moving assembly
line with an endless-chain conveyor; three months later his men assembled an
automobile, down to its smallest parts, in 93 minutes. A year before it had
taken 14 hours. During these same years, machine power replaced human
labor at a startling rate: in 1914, 30 per cent of industry was electrified, in
1929, 70 per cent. The electric motor made the steam engine obsolete;
between 1919 and 1927 more than 44 percent of the steam engines in the

United States went to the scrap heap. Since labor came out of the postwar depression with higher real wages—employers feared a new strike wave if they cut wages as sharply as prices fell—business was stimulated to lower production costs. With more efficient management, greater mechanization, intensive research, and ingenious sales methods, industrial production almost doubled during the decade, soaring from an index figure of 58 in the depression year of 1921 to 110 in 1929 (1933–39 = 100). This impressive increase in productivity was achieved without any expansion of the labor force. Manufacturing employed precisely the same number of men in 1929 as it had in 1919. The summit of technological achievement was reached on October 31, 1925, when Ford rolled a completed automobile off his assembly line every ten seconds.

The physical output of American industry increased tremendously. Between 1899 and 1929 the total output of manufacturing jumped 264 percent. Petroleum products—new oil fields were discovered in Texas, Oklahoma, and California—multiplied more than sixteen times in this period, the basic iron and steel industry five times. The number of telephones installed grew from 1,355,000 in 1900 to 10,525,000 in 1915 to 20,200,000 in 1930. Most impressive was the growth of new industries, some of which did not even exist in 1914. Light metals like aluminum and magnesium experienced a meteoric rise; the output of aluminum more than doubled between 1914 and 1920. American factories turned out a host of new products—cigarette lighters, oil furnaces, wrist watches, antifreeze fluids, reinforced concrete, paint sprayers, book matches, dry ice, Pyrex glass for cooking utensils, and panchromatic motion-picture film.

Many of the new industries were geared to the American home. The American consumed a more varied diet than he ever had before. He thought it commonplace to have fresh fruit and vegetables in midwinter—Louisiana cherries and Arizona melons, Carolina peas and Alabama corn. In 1905, 41 million cases of food were shipped, in 1930, 200 million. Fresh green vegetables, many of them novelties, arrived in northern markets; shipments of lettuce grew from 13,800 carloads in 1920 to 51,500 in 1928, spinach from 2,900 in 1920 to 10,600 in 1927. As people moved into city apartments with kitchenettes, they gave a new spur to the canning industry. Canned fruits and vegetables more than doubled between 1914 and 1929; canned milk almost trebled. In many city homes the family sat down to a meal that started with canned soup, proceeded to canned meat and vegetables, and ended with canned peaches.

The chemicals industry, which started in the 1880's, was enormously stimulated by World War I. The war demonstrated how dependent the country was on foreign supplies of potash, nitrates, and dyes. Potash, essential for fertilizers, had come almost entirely from Germany before the war. When supplies were cut off, prices increased ten times, and this encouraged the creation of a domestic potash industry. When the United States could not import German indigo, the Dow Chemical Company's infant industry spurted. The government contributed more to the development of the chemicals industry than to any other industry. It confiscated German dye patents during the war and turned them over to American firms; it advanced nitrogen development by constructing a plant at Muscle Shoals in the Tennessee Valley and by operating a Fixed Nitrogen Research Laboratory in the War Department; and it gave high tariff protection to domestic chemicals and dyes.

The war also sparked the development of the new synthetics industry. Thousands of by-product ovens were built to produce coke needed in manufacturing explosives; after the war these ovens were used in the production of synthetic chemicals, especially of plastics. Synthetic plastics had been developed as early as 1869, with the creation of celluloid, but it was not until the postwar years that synthetic fibers and plastics became an important industry. The output of rayon, which transformed the textile business, multiplied sixty-nine times between 1914 and 1931. Bakelite, which was developed before the war, proved of enormous importance in the electrical and radio industries. In 1923, lacquers were introduced; easier to apply than paint, giving better protection and offering a wider range of colors, the quick-drying lacquers reduced the time needed to finish an automobile from twenty-six days to a matter of hours. In 1924, Du Pont established a "cellophane" plant in Buffalo; used to wrap everything from bacon to cigarettes, cellophane at least doubled its sales every year for the rest of the decade. In 1925, a Swiss chemist, who had been invited to America by the government during World War I to build a cellulose nitrate plant, placed "celanese" on the market; an artificial silk superior to rayon, celanese was an important step in the development of synthetic textiles. Scientific geniuses like George Washington Carver found new industrial uses for farm products, many of them surplus crops which were glutting the market. From peanuts, Carver extracted everything from shaving lotion to axle grease; from sweet potatoes, he got shoe-blacking, library paste, and synthetic tapioca.

The most important element in the prosperity of the 1920's was the increase in construction, in part because building had been halted during the war, in part to meet the drift from country to city and from city to suburbs. During the decade, New York got a brand new skyline. European travelers who in 1910 had been awed by 20-story skyscrapers returned in 1930 to find them dwarfed by new giants; some of the old structures had even been demolished to make way for 60-story buildings. The Grand Central section of Manhattan was almost entirely rebuilt; Fifth Avenue resounded with the staccato of riveters and the sharp clash of steel beams. High above the city streets, helmeted workers balanced themselves on girders; beneath them, men operated mammoth cranes or turned huge drums of concrete. Taller and taller the buildings soared; toward the end of the decade a race to erect the loftiest skyscraper became a fascinating new outdoor sport. On May 1, 1931, the race ended when the Empire State Building climbed past the Bank of Manhattan's 71 stories and the Chrysler Building's 77 stories. Built in less than a year, the 86-story Empire State Building, topped by a graceful mast, was the tallest building in the world.

What New York had, every interior city had to have too, and those on the prairies erected their own towers. Cities the size of Beaumont, Memphis, and Syracuse boasted buildings of at least 21 stories. Tulsa and Oklahoma City, which did not even exist when the first skyscraper was built, had skylines by by the end of the decade. Cleveland pointed proudly to its 52-story Terminal Tower, Houston to its Petroleum Building, Chicago to its Tribune Tower. The skyscraper was as certain an expression of the ebullient American spirit as the Gothic cathedral was of medieval Europe. Denounced by many American critics as a vulgar evidence of commercialism and an indiscriminate passion for bigness, the skyline was recognized by European observers for what it was—a radiant, defiant display of American energy and optimism. Too often banal in conception, the skyscraper was at its best—as in Raymond Hood's News Building in New York—a symmetrical rectangle of stark beauty.

Outside the great cities, construction went on at an even faster rate, as people fanned out into the suburbs. The borough of Queens, across the East River from Manhattan, doubled its population in the 1920's. Grosse Point Park near Detroit grew 700 percent, Shaker Heights outside Cleveland 1,000 percent, and the movie colony of Beverly Hills 2,500 percent. Save for California, the greatest real estate boom in the country took place in Florida. Flivvers with northern license plates clogged Miami's Flagler Avenue in the 1920's; not only the man of wealth, who headed for Palm Beach or Boca Raton, but the man of moderate income decided to winter in Florida. "Realtors" converted swamps into Venetian lagoons, and much of the population of Florida was engaged in selling lots. In Coral Gables a real estate man hired William Jennings Bryan to sit on a raft under a beach umbrella and lecture on the beauties of Florida climate; Bryan was followed with dancing by Gilda Gray. The land-speculation mania in Florida reached its high point one day in the summer of 1925 when the Miami *Daily News*, crowded with real estate advertisements, printed an issue of 504 pages, the largest in newspaper history. In 1926, after a hurricane had driven the waters of Biscayne Bay over the cottages of Miami, the land boom collapsed. But still the resorts were strung from Jacksonville to Key West. Miami, once a mangrove swamp, grew 400 percent in the decade.

The construction of roads and highways poured fresh public funds into the economy. While Secretary Mellon endeavored to cut back federal spending, state and local governments stepped up spending at a rate which more than offset the Mellon program of deflation. Construction programs for highways and buildings employed more men and spent more money than any single private industry. In 1914, there were almost no good roads outside of the East, and crossing the continent was an adventure. Automobiles sank to their hubs in gumbo muds; travelers crossing Iowa were often forced to wait several days until the roads dried before moving onto the next town. Perhaps because cars were viewed as pleasure vehicles, parsimonious state legislatures were reluctant to vote public funds to improve roads.

The Federal Aid Road Act of 1916 offered federal funds to states which would organize highway departments and match federal grants. Spurred by federal initiative, every section of the country launched ambitious road-building programs in the postwar years. In 1906, local governments appropriated 96 percent of all highway funds; by 1927, they were providing only 53 percent, while the states spent 37 percent, and the federal government 10 percent. Florida built the Tamiami Trail through the swamps of the Everglades; Arizona constructed a road across the desert west of Phoenix; Utah laid a highway over a sea of mud, a relic of ancient Lake Bonneville, near the Nevada line; and in Massachusetts the magnificent Mohawk Trail climbed the Hoosac Range. New York pioneered with the construction of the beautiful Bronx River Parkway which curved its way out of New York City northward through the Westchester countryside. By 1928, the tourist could drive from New York as far west as St. Mary's, Kansas, on paved highways, but it was still not advisable to drive down the Santa Fé Trail southwest of St. Louis in the rainy season, and mountain passes west of Salt Lake City were seldom passable during the winter or early spring.

Without the new automobile industry, the prosperity of the Roaring Twenties would scarcely have been possible; the development of the industry in a single generation was the greatest achievement of modern technology. As recently as 1900, Vermont had enforced a law requiring every motorist to employ "a person of mature age" to walk one-eighth of a mile ahead of him bearing a red flag. That year there was not a single filling station in all the country. In 1902, San Francisco, Cincinnati, and Savannah still maintained speed limits of eight miles an hour. While lawmakers were attempting to keep pace with technology, an enormous change took place within the industry. Ransom Olds started mass production in automobiles; Henry Leland demonstrated that cars could be made with interchangeable parts; and Henry Ford quickly took over both principles and carried them to lengths that left his competitors far behind.

The production of automobiles soared almost at a geometric rate, and the auto industry gave a shot in the arm to the whole economy. In 1900, there had been an annual output of 4,000 cars; by 1929, 4,800,000 automobiles were being produced in a single year, and Americans were driving more than 26 million autos and trucks. In the United States, there was one automobile to each five persons—almost one car per family—as compared to one car to 43 persons in Britain, one to 325 in Italy, one to 7,000 in Russia. In America, the possession of an automobile was not, as in Europe, a class privilege. The auto industry was the most important purchaser of rubber, plate glass, nickel and lead; it bought 15 percent of the steel output of the nation and spurred the petroleum industry to a tremendous expansion. There was scarcely a corner of the American economy which the automobile industry did not touch; it stimulated public spending for good roads, extended the housing boom into the suburbs, and created dozens of new small enterprises from hotdog stands to billboards.

Detroit became the Mecca of the modern world and Ford its prophet. Russian and German scholars talked reverently of "Fordismus," and industrial missions came from all over the world to study American techniques. "Just as in Rome one goes to the Vatican and endeavours to get audience of the Pope," wrote one British traveler, "so in Detroit one goes to the Ford Works and endeavours to see Henry Ford." "As I caught my first glimpse of Detroit," recorded another Briton, "I felt as I imagine a Seventeenth Century traveller must have felt when he approached Versailles." Ford was worshiped as a miracle-maker: a group of college students voted the Flivver King the third greatest figure of all time, surpassed only by Napoleon and Christ. When Ford announced the Model A early in 1928, 500,000 people made down payments without having seen the car and without knowing the price.

Ford personified the farmboy-mechanic who in a single lifetime reached the top. He fulfilled the dream of an acquisitive society committed to a belief in individual advancement. He brought the automobile to the masses of the world; he was the magical tinkerer who revolutionized human life. He was the high priest of mass production, which people the world over saw as more important than any ideological doctrine as a solution to the curse of poverty. His firm was family-owned; he was hostile to Wall Street; he founded, so it was believed, the doctrine of high wages and low prices, of sharing the benefits of his genius with the world—he was, in short, the Good Businessman. He resolved the moral dilemma of a Puritan-capitalist society. He achieved material success without losing his primal innocence.

"Machinery," declared Ford solemnly, "is the new Messiah." Dazzled by the prosperity of the time and by the endless stream of new gadgets, the American people raised business in the 1920's into a national religion and paid respectful homage to the businessman as the prophet of heaven on earth. As government looked only to the single interest of business, so society gave to the businessman social pre-eminence. There was no social class in America to challenge the business class. To call a scientist or a preacher or a professor or a doctor a good businessman was to pay him the most fulsome of compliments, for the chief index of a man's worth was his income. "Brains," declared Coolidge, "are wealth and wealth is the chief end of man." The opinions of a man like Ford, who believed in reincarnation, hated Jews, doctors, Catholics, and bankers, and abominated tobacco (it was "bad for the bowels"), were listened to with reverent respect, not only when he spoke on business matters but also when he made pronouncements on culture and public morals. "The man who builds a factory builds a temple," observed Coolidge, "the man who works there worships there."

Americans had less interest in a hereafter than in salvation on earth. Material comfort became not a means to an end but the final end of life itself. People continued to go to church, but church rituals were accepted less with reverence than with politeness. The functions of the church were gradually replaced by institutions committed to the ideal of service, to "organized altruism." Forced to accommodate themselves, the churches stressed not the divinity but the humanity of Christ. Churches installed swimming pools, game rooms, and gymnasiums with, as one foreign visitor noticed, "the oxygen of good fellowship" permeating everything. When a British journalist visited one American church, its young preacher invited him to "come and inspect his plant."

The classic statement of the secularization of religion and the religiosity of business was Bruce Barton's *The Man Nobody Knows*, a best seller in 1925 and 1926. Barton praised Jesus handsomely as a topnotch businessman. "He picked up twelve men from the bottom ranks of business and forged them into an organization that conquered the world." Jesus was an A-1 salesman, and the parables were "the most powerful advertisements of all time." No one need doubt that business was the main focus of His concern. Why, Jesus Himself had said: "Wist ye not that I must be about my father's business?"

Religion was valued not as a path to personal salvation or a key to the riddles of the universe but because it paid off in dollars and cents. The dean of the University of Chicago Divinity School told a reporter that a man could make more money if he prayed about his business. Reading the Bible, explained another writer, meant money in your pocket. Insurance men were advised that Exodus offered good tips on risk and liability, while a Chicago bond salesman confided that he had boosted his income by drawing arguments from Ezekiel. "Of all the Plenipotentiaries of Publicity, Ambassadors of Advertising and Bosses of Press Bureaus, none equals Moses," said Elbert Hubbard, for it was Moses who "appointed himself ad-writer for Deity." Taught to write advertising copy for their churches, pastors billed their sermons under captions like "Solomon, a Six-Cylinder Sport." Sermons were entitled after a popular cigarette slogan, "They Satisfy," or after a soap advertisement, "Eventually, Why Not Now?" (an appeal for conversion), or "Three-in-One Oil" (the Trinity).

Encouraged by the friendly disposition of the federal government, the concentration of industry stepped up sharply in the postwar years. Although the merger movement had reached its apex before the war, it found new areas like the utilities in the 1920's. Most mergers brought together not competitive firms but companies engaged in the same business in different cities. Between 1919 and 1930, 8,000 businesses disappeared. "So long as I am Attorney General," explained Harry Daugherty, "I am not going unnecessarily to harass men who have unwittingly run counter with the statutes." Despite Daugherty's intentions, the Federal Trade Commission occasionally proved obstreperous and interceded to block consolidations and discourage trade associations. When in 1925 Coolidge appointed the lumber attorney William E. Humphrey to the chairmanship of the commission, large-business interests moved into control of the FTC. Humphrey himself denounced the FTC as "an instrument of oppression and disturbance and injury instead of help to business" and a "publicity bureau to spread socialistic propaganda." After Humphrey's accession, the commission approved trade associations and smiled on business agreements to lessen "cutthroat" competition.

Few businesses grew as rapidly as the electric light and power industry—the chief field for mergers in the 1920's. Between 1902 and 1929, the output of electric power multiplied more than 19 times—from 6 billion kilowatt-hours to 117 billion. Almost as much new hydroelectric power was developed between 1920 and 1930 as in all the years before 1920. As local electric light and power companies, which once served a single town, were interconnected in vast regional grids, financiers used the holding-company device to merge small firms into great utility empires. Between 1919 and 1927 over 3,700 utility companies vanished. Promoters organized a group of utility giants starting with the United Light and Power Company and the American Superpower Corporation in 1923 and ending with the Niagara Hudson Company and the Commonwealth and Southern Corporation in 1929. By 1930 ten holding-company groups controlled 72 percent of the country's electric power.

The most spectacular of the new utility titans was Samuel Insull. Starting as an office boy in London at five shillings a week, Insull rose to the top of a holding-company empire which controlled gas and electric companies in twenty-three states. Operating out of Chicago, he extended his domain over businesses as remote as the Androscoggin Electric Company in Maine and the Tidewater Power Company in North Carolina. Chairman of the board of sixty-five different firms, Insull was involved in business operations in almost every conceivable field, from Mexican irrigation projects to the pathetic attempt to make Port Isabel, Texas, "the Venus of the South." His dairy herd, bathed in ultra-violet rays, was surrounded by electric screens that electrocuted flies. Respected as a philanthropist and a patron of the arts, he built the Chicago Civic Opera, an ornate skyscraper opera house. An intimate of mayors and senators, he was accused of buying political influence and suborning public officials.

The merger movement accelerated rapidly in American banking. The large banks swallowed the little banks or established branch banks which took away their business. In 1920, there were 1,280 branch banks; in 1930, 3,516. The greatest of the branch bankers was a newcomer, Amadeo Peter Giannini, who developed a chain of 500 banks throughout the state of California under a single holding company. His Bank of America National Trust and Savings Association in San Francisco became the fourth largest bank in the country, larger than any bank outside New York. In Manhattan, the National City Bank took over the Farmers Loan & Trust Company; the Guaranty Trust amalgamated with the Bank of Commerce; and the Chase National absorbed the Equitable Trust Company. By 1929, 1 percent of the banks in the country controlled over 46 percent of the banking resources of the nation.

Chain stores grew enormously in the postwar years. Chain-store units rose from 29,000 in 1918 to 160,000 in 1929; between 1919 and 1927 their sales jumped 124 percent in drugstores, 287 percent in groceries, and 425 percent in the clothing business. The Great Atlantic and Pacific Tea Company's chain of red-fronted grocery stores grew from 400 in 1912 to 15,500 in 1932. By the end of the period, the A & P was selling a greater volume of goods than Ford at his peak; its billion dollar a year grocery business accounted for one-tenth of all food sold at retail in the United States. In these same years, the Woolworth "five and tens" crowded out many old neighborhood notion stores; for a dime or less, the customer could buy everything from Venetian Night Incense to Mammoth Tulip Sundaes, Hebrew New Year cards to poker chips, gumdrops to French Guiana stamps. A mammoth holding company, Drug, Incorporated, owned 10,000 Rexall drugstores and 706 Liggett stores, as well as the Owl chain on the Pacific Coast, and owned huge drug companies like Vick Chemical, Bayer Aspirin, and Bristol-Myers. By 1932, chain stores accounted for 22 percent of the retail trade in Baltimore, 31 percent in Atlanta, 37 percent in Chicago. In some places the independent grocery store of 1914 had almost disappeared; Philadelphia bought two-thirds of its food in chain stores.

By the end of the decade the consolidation movement in American business reached boom proportions. In 1919, there were 80 bank mergers, in 1927, 259. In 1928, the Chrysler Corporation took over Dodge Brothers, Postum Company amalgamated with Maxwell House Coffee, and Colgate merged with Palmolive-Peet. Two advertising agencies combined to form the wonderfully sonorous firm of Batten, Barton, Durstine & Osborn. By 1929, the 200 largest non-financial corporations in America owned nearly half the corporate wealth of the nation, and they were growing much faster than smaller businesses. From 1924 to 1928, their assets expanded three times as fast as those of smaller corporations. Four meat packers controlled 70 percent of the production in their industry; four tobacco companies accounted for 94 percent of the output of cigarettes.

Many industries—textiles, clothing, and bituminous coal, in particular—remained boisterously competitive, however. The growth of oligopoly—domination of an industry by a few firms—often meant more rather than less competition. Although consolidation accelerated in the 1920's, there was not as much actual monopoly—that is, domination of an industry by only one company. No longer did a single firm lord it over the steel or the oil industries. Although the chain-store movement spelled national consolidation, it also destroyed the monopoly of the merchant in the small American town.

The benefits of technological innovation were by no means evenly distributed. While workers' income went up 11 percent from 1923 to 1929, corporate profits rocketed 62 percent and dividends 65 percent. Despite the high productivity of the period, there was a disturbing amount of unemployment. Factory workers in "sick" industries like coal, leather, and textiles saw little of the boom prosperity. The Loray Mill in Gastonia, North Carolina, site of a bloody strike in 1928, paid its workers that year a weekly wage of $18 to men and $9 to women for working a 70-hour week. At the height of Coolidge prosperity, the secretary of the Gastonia Chamber of Commerce boasted that children of fourteen were permitted to work only 11 hours a day. Perhaps as many as two million boys and girls under fifteen continued to work in textile mills, cranberry bogs, and beet fields. In 1929, 71 percent of American families had incomes under $2,500, generally thought to be the minimum standard for a decent living. The 36,000 wealthiest families in the United States received as much income as the 12,000,000 American families —42 percent of all those in America—who received under $1,500 a year.

Yet, if one focuses exclusively on farm poverty or on depressed West Virginia coal towns, it is easy to get a distorted picture of life in the 1920's. As Henry May writes, "Sometimes even prosperity—an important fact despite its exception—is belittled almost out of existence." If prosperity was by no means as pervasive as Chamber of Commerce publicists claimed, it was still widespread enough to change markedly the life of millions of Americans. The change resulted less from a considerable increase in income for the average American—by later standards the increase does not seem so impressive—than from the fact that Americans could buy things with their paychecks that they had never been able to get before.

People could get into their automobile—almost everyone owned a car—

and drive into the country or visit neighbors in the next town. For the first time, they saw America, taking trips to distant campsites or historic shrines and most of all discovering the glories of California and Florida. Electricity —all but farm homes had it by the end of the decade—meant not only electric lights but also a wide range of electric appliances. Women could buy vacuum cleaners and washing machines, toasters and electric sewing machines; in 1921, the production of refrigerators was only 0.6 percent of what it was to be in 1929. Women of all classes wore clothing luxuries. They discarded cotton stockings and underwear for silk and rayon (in 1900, 12,000 pairs of silk stockings were sold, in 1930, 300 million), and the American woman became known as "America's greatest fur-bearing animal."

On week ends Americans went to the ballpark. Organized sport in America had captivated the country for decades, but it was not until the 1920's that spectator sports took on a central role in American life. In the Cathedral of St. John the Divine in New York, a bay was built with windows depicting various sports. On July 2, 1921, 91,000 fans at Boyles' Thirty Acres in Jersey City paid more than a million dollars to watch Jack Dempsey fight "gorgeous" Georges Carpentier. Dempsey knocked him out in the fourth round, but more important, the country had seen the first "million dollar gate." It was the Golden Age of Sports—of Babe Ruth, Bobby Jones, and Bill Tilden. It was the era of the Dempsey-Tunney fight, the decade when Ruth hit sixty home runs in a season. The biggest change took place in college football. People who had never been near a college crowded the vast new college stadiums to cheer the Four Horsemen of Notre Dame or the Galloping Ghost of Illinois. On one memorable fall afternoon in Urbana, Harold "Red" Grange scored four touchdowns against Michigan in the first twelve minutes of the game. By the end of the 1920's college football had become a major industry, with gate receipts each year of over $21 million.

People could walk down to the neighborhood theater and see the latest movie. Already flourishing before the war, motion pictures after the war became one of the ten great industries of the country, with an invested capital of a billion and a half dollars. In 1922, movie theaters sold 40 million tickets every week; by 1930, the average weekly attendance was 100 million. The faces of Charlie Chaplin and Harold Lloyd were known in every corner of the globe, and "youngsters playing in the back streets of Hull or Newcastle," noted one British writer, "threatened one another with *the works*." Every respectable American town had its own movie palace. The movie houses became the temples of a secular society. In New York, Roxy's called itself "The Cathedral of the Motion Picture," the Capitol described itself as "The Theater with a Soul," and the Fifty-Fifth Street Theater advertised itself as "The Sanctuary of the Cinema."

Even more intriguing was the new invention of radio. There are many claimants to the honor of being the first station, but radio really arrived on the night of November 2, 1920, when KDKA at East Pittsburgh broadcast the presidential election returns. By 1922 there were radios in three million homes; that year the sale of sets was already a $60 million a year industry. Seven years later $852 million worth of radio sets were sold. Men bought cone-speakers and amplifiers and talked endlessly about how to eliminate static. They introduced a whole new vocabulary and within a few months used the terms—"tune in," "network," "airwaves"—so casually that the words lost their gloss of technological novelty. People clamped on earphones to hear Roxy and His Gang, the Clicquot Club Eskimos, the Ipana Troubadours or the A & P Gypsies. Grantland Rice broadcast the World Series, Floyd Gibbons narrated the news with a machine-gun staccato, and Rudy Vallee warbled the latest songs. From speakers in homes all over America came the sound of the ubiquitous ukelele.

Within a decade the radio and the movie nationalized American popular culture, projecting the same performers and the same stereotypes in every section of the country. In movie theaters everywhere, when olive-skinned Rudolph Valentino carried an impeccably blonde heroine across the burning Sahara and flung her into his tent, women swooned. Men scoffed at the Valentino craze, but barbers reported that men who once had called for bay rum now demanded pomades to make their hair sleek. There was even something of a vogue of sideburns, while dance schools offering the tango did a flourishing business. Endless interviews with Valentino appeared in national periodicals, including one with the inevitable title, "I'm Tired of Being a Sheik."

In the fall of 1929 two former vaudevillians, Freeman Gosden and Charles Correll, began a radio comic strip called "Amos 'n Andy." Within a few months the two blackface comedians, broadcasting over the N.B.C. network, had taken the country by storm. Many people refused to answer their telephone while the program was on the air. Movie theaters in smaller cities were forced to interrupt their show and turn on the broadcast; if they did not, they knew they would lose most of their patrons until the program was over. Millions of Americans followed avidly the affairs of the Fresh Air Taxicab Company, and Madame Queen and the Kingfish became household words. One man inserted an advertisement in a newspaper to ask his friends not to disturb him while the program was being broadcast. Senator Borah referred to Amos and Andy in a debate on the Philippines.

As the country solved the problems of production, greater emphasis was placed on distribution; the old-style manufacturer and tycoon became less important than the salesman and the promoter. In the 1920's the advertising man and the public relations expert came into their own. To staff the agencies of distribution and the "service" industries, a new white-collar class developed in the cities. Together with the civil servant, the salesman, and the salaried manager, these white-collar clerks constituted a "new middle class."

This shift in emphasis produced important changes in the national character. In place of the idea that saving was a virtue, an article of faith as old as the first colonial settlements and the chief conviction of Benjamin Franklin's Poor Richard, a new conviction developed that thrift could be socially harmful and spending a virtue. "We're too poor to economize," wrote Scott Fitzgerald jauntily. "Economy is a luxury." The nineteenth-century man, with a set of personal characteristics adapted to an economy of scarcity, began to give way to the twentieth-century man with the idiosyncrasies of an economy of abundance.

Aggressively optimistic, he was friendlier but had less depth, was more demanding of approval, less certain of himself. He did not knock, he boosted. He had lots of pep, hustle, and zip. He joined the Rotary or Kiwanis, and he believed in "service," a word that was repeated *ad nauseum* during the decade. Sinclair Lewis painted his portrait as George Babbitt, and Babbitt acknowledged that it was a reasonable likeness. "Dare to Be a Babbitt!" urged *Nation's Business*. What the world needed was more Babbitts, "good Rotarians who live orderly lives, and save money, and go to church, and play golf, and send their children to school."

The problem for the twentieth-century man was not the material environment but other people. "Our future," wrote Walter Weyl in 1919, "may depend less on the hours that we work today than on the words or the smile we exchange with some anonymous fellow-passenger in the office-building elevator." Men aimed less at improving their character and more at improving their personality. Neither health nor education nor even one's own "personality" was valued for itself alone, but for what it would do toward making one a "success," success meaning not merely greater income but the social acceptance necessary to stifle self-doubt. The main social knowledge a man had to acquire was how to "sell himself."

The nineteenth-century man coveted individual success; the twentieth-century man sought a place for himself in the bureaucracy. Probably the most important development within corporations during these years was the divorce of ownership from control. In 1900, there were four million owners of stocks; by 1930, twenty million. Control of business policy passed from the hands of owners, many of whom had not the remotest curiosity about or knowledge of the firm in which they held stock, and into the hands of a salaried bureaucracy. By the end of the decade a "managerial revolution" had occurred: plant managers and corporation executives, rather than owners, made the chief decisions. Young men no longer aimed to found their own businesses, to be Carnegies or Vanderbilts; they wanted to rise to a high position as a hired manager or a salaried executive. The businessman was less interested in risk and more in stabilizing his business. Unlike the nineteenth-century tycoon with the attitude of the "the public be damned," the postwar businessman was extremely self-conscious about how he appeared to others.

Business developed ingenious methods to transform anxiety about scarcity into a desire for "luxury consumption of leisure and the surplus product." The advertising man and the salesman assaulted the older virtues of thrift and prudence. Behaviorist psychology, with its manipulative view of man, was perfectly adapted to mass advertising; Watson himself left the Johns Hopkins University under fire to become vice-president of an advertising agency. Advertisers sold not products but qualities like social prestige, which the possession of the products would allegedly secure. With debt no longer regarded as shameful, people bought on installment. Three out of every four radios were purchased on the installment plan, 60 percent of all automobiles and furniture. "You furnish the girl; we furnish the home," advertised one furniture factory. Ten years after the war, conspicuous consumption had become a national mania. When a French perfume would not sell at ordinary rates, the manufacturer raised its price and made a fortune.

Henry Ford had built the Model-T flivver, a sturdy, simply constructed car without grace or beauty, and he had sold millions of them. When he started to lose sales in the 1920's to the more modern General Motors car, he refused to admit that the Model T was no longer marketable. "The customer," he snapped, "can have a Ford any color he wants—so long as it's black." But by the mid-1920's the country had less interest in price than in style and comfort. The purchase of an automobile had been a male prerogative—only men knew what lay under the hood—and men mostly bought cars that offered the soundest mechanical features. As women increasingly decided which car the family would buy, carburetors and gaskets became less important than the color of an automobile and the texture of its upholstery. In May, 1927, Ford surrendered; he halted production on the Model T, and when the Model A came out, it had modern design and construction and could be bought in a choice of colors from Dawn Gray to Arabian Sand.

The Coolidge era is usually viewed as a period of extreme conservatism, but it was thought of at the time as representing a great stride forward in social policy, a New Era in American life. During these years employers embarked on a program of welfare capitalism. They built clean, trim, well-lighted factories, with safety devices to forestall injury. They installed cafeterias, complete with trained dieticians, and formed glee clubs and base-ball teams. The Hammermill Paper Company sold its employees cut-rate gasoline; L. Bamberger and Company provided free legal service; and

Bausch and Lomb set up eye and dental clinics for its workers. In part to avert unionization, employers replaced tyrannical foremen with trained personnel men and organized company unions. They instituted group insurance plans and introduced profit-sharing; probably more than a million workers owned stock by 1929, an innovation which proved of dubious value by the end of the year. "If every family owned even a $100 bond of the United States or a legitimate corporation," declared Franklin D. Roosevelt, "there would be no talk of bolshevism, and we would incidentally solve all national problems in a more democratic way."

Although the new prosperity favored an exceptionally materialistic view of life, it resulted in more than just increased sales of cigarette lighters and kitchen gadgets. The country spent more than twice as much as it had before the war on libraries, almost three times as much for hospitals. The United States in 1928 paid out as much for education as all the rest of the world. In 1900 a child had only one chance in ten of going to high school; by 1931 he had one chance in two. In 1900 he had only one chance in thirty-three of going to college; by 1931 he had better than one in seven. In part the result of increased wealth—which financed research, improved sanitation, and made possible better nutrition—science in the first third of the twentieth century increased American life expectancy from 49 to 59 years, cut infant mortality two-thirds, and slashed the death rate of typhoid from 36 to 2 per 100,000, of diphtheria from 43 to 2, of measles from 12 to 1.

In December, 1928, President Coolidge declared: "No Congress of the United States ever assembled, on surveying the state of the Union, has met with a more pleasing prospect than that which appears at the present time." By 1928, Coolidge had the assent of many of the New Era's former critics. "The more or less unconscious and unplanned activities of business men," noted Walter Lippmann, "are for once more novel, more daring, and in general more revolutionary than the theories of the progressives." "Big business in America," wrote Lincoln Steffens, who had long been a fierce critic of American capitalism, "is producing what the Socialists held up as their goal; food, shelter and clothing for all. You will see it during the Hoover administration."

New Era publicists argued that a new kind of "economic democracy" had been established. The businessman, enjoying high profits, shared them in "high wages" with his worker. The worker himself, by investing in the stock market, open to all, could own a share of industry. "We are reaching and maintaining the position," declared Coolidge as early as 1919, "where the property class and the employed class are not separate, but identical." The consumer, spending his dollars, it was said, cast votes to determine what should be produced. Soundly based on technological innovations, its gains dispersed through high wages, administered by enlightened businessmen, a new civilization appeared to be emerging. Without the class hatred or bureaucratic despotism of communism, the United States, it seemed, was on its way toward the final abolition of poverty.

CONTEMPORARY SOURCES

3. HIRAM MOTHERWELL, "THE AMERICAN EMPIRE"

ALTHOUGH historians have considered the years immediately following the Spanish-American War as the time of great debate between imperialists and anti-imperialists, there has been a continuing controversy over the question of American imperialism. To be sure, the debates through 1930 never quite assumed the dimensions of the turn-of-the-century episode, but much of the intensity and fervor that marked the first controversy characterized the later disputes.

During the Twenties, a few commentators frankly insisted that Americans recognize and take pride in the nation's far-flung empire. It was pointed out that America's protectorates, commonwealths, and colonial possessions, her large overseas investments, and extensive foreign trade, frequent military intervention in Latin America, and the promotion of American ideals abroad all constituted various forms of imperialism. One could, therefore, speak of an American Empire.

The following essay by free-lance writer Hiram Motherwell is a somewhat crude and candidly blunt defense of this American Empire. The tragedy, for Motherwell, was not that America had a record of extensive involvement and frequent intervention in the affairs of foreign nations, but that Americans neither admitted to themselves what they were about nor appreciated the benefits foreigners derived from our benevolent imperialism. Critics of this position would of course question Motherwell's assumptions and contend that the real tragedy of the nation's foreign policy lay in the persistent notion that America could, and should, make the world over in its own image.

I

The phrase, "the American Empire," has become fashionable as a metaphor to describe the growing influence of the United States over her neighbors. But we Americans use it as a metaphor only, with the mental reservation

SOURCE. Hiram Motherwell, "The American Empire," in *The Forum*, Vol. 82, No. 6, December 1929, pp. 372–375.

that the United States is not really an imperialistic nation, but only a big brother to her little friends.

The time has come for us to recognize that the United States is really an imperialistic nation. There really *is* an American empire. We must get used to saying the words aloud, not with tongue in cheek but with clear and confident enunciation. Imperialism is no more disgraceful than weather, and it is just as inevitable at a certain stage of national expansion.

We are all imperialists. Hoover, the Quaker pacifist, is an imperialist when he seeks to flood the world with American goods and capital. You and I, simple citizens who are trying to earn a living and put the boys through college, are imperialists when we cheer for American prosperity based on super-production and gigantic foreign loans. We are profiting from a period of imperial expansion, and we enjoy it.

There is no reason why we should not enjoy it, or why we should be ashamed of it; for American financial imperialism is often beneficial, and rarely needs to be oppressive to other peoples. But there are good reasons why we should no longer try to deny a fact as obvious as a skyscraper, a secret known to the entire world with the exception of the citizens of the United States.

I should like to see every primary school give a course on the American Empire—what it is, how it grew, what it has done and failed to do for its imperial provinces, why and how it is essential to the prosperity of our country. I should like to see every American child grow up taking this empire for granted, just as every English child grows up taking the British Empire for granted.

Public opinion resents the use of the words "imperialist" and "empire" as applied to America's relations with her neighbors. And the United States Government seeks to appease this resentment by explaining that any imperialistic act of the State Department is but a continuation of the old isolation policy, adapted to temporary exigencies. For example, Secretary Hughes said in 1922: "We are not seeking special privileges anywhere at the expense of others. We wish to protect the just and equal rights of American citizens everywhere in the world." Yet the United States has for years been using its influence to prevent other nations from placing important loans in Central America and Caribbean countries; has sought by every possible means to replace outstanding foreign loans in these countries with American money; has repeatedly vetoed concessions or development projects in Cuba and elsewhere in which foreign money was interested; has presented ultimatums to Hayti, Santo Domingo, and other countries, with the marines at hand to enforce them; has forcibly seized control of customs revenues and even shipped customs cash to New York as security for debts in litigation; and has intervened four times in Cuba, five times in Panama, six times in Nicaragua, twice in Mexico, six times in Honduras, once in Colombia, and once in Costa Rica. What is the use of pretending that all this is not imperialistic?

II

And why, on the other hand, assume that such imperialism is necessarily and intrinsically wicked? American financial imperialism means thousands of millions of dollars invested in other countries, developing local wealth, providing jobs for hundreds of thousands of workers, stabilizing national finances, giving large portions of the local populations a stake in peaceful and orderly government. No one will pretend that useful employment, sanitation, roads and railways, and human self-respect are not to be preferred to poverty, disease, and chronic revolution. It is absurd to assert that there is anything sacred in the right of small nations to be governed by a series of military adventurers. If American imperialism improves the condition of the common people at the expense of the local politicians, then it is humanly justified. The question which Americans should ask is not whether America is "imperialistic," but whether, in each instance, American imperialism has really worked for the good of the greatest number, or has bungled its job. Most liberals believe that the United States has bungled its imperial job in many instances, and has senselessly and needlessly oppressed and sometimes slaughtered the local population. But this is no more a condemnation of imperialism than miscarriages of justice are a condemnation of laws and courts.

The trouble with American imperialism comes from the fact that Americans have not the moral courage to admit that it exists. In this the American Government has given them their cue. The State Department has repeatedly explained its imperialistic actions to the public by asserting that they were taken "solely with a view to the welfare of the inhabitants," or "to protect human life," or "to defend American property from bandits." The American Government solemnly asserted its intention to grant complete national freedom to the Philippines and to Cuba, while governing in the one and intervening in the other with a ruthlessness which would have aroused instant rebellion if attempted in any of the states of the Union. In April, 1898, Congress passed a joint resolution declaring that "the people of the Island of Cuba are, and of right ought to be, free and independent, and that the Government of the United States hereby recognizes the Republic of Cuba as the true and lawful government of that island." But in 1919, after four military occupations and almost continuous interference in Cuban administration and finance, the State Department, in a document marked "Confidential: For Official Use Only," sought to reconcile its acts with the original promise by saying:

It would appear that "independence" as a technical term employed in treaties relating to such protected States [as Cuba] does not mean full freedom of action as a positive attribute, but rather the absence of any such restrictions upon the protected State as would amount to an infringement of its international personality and take from it a certain theoretical legal competence to be the arbiter of its own destiny.

How much more candid it would have been to say: "Cuba is free in certain respects; she is not free in others. The United States has certain vital interests in Cuba. She does not propose to permit third nations to gain a military or financial foothold on the island, or to permit irresponsible revolutionists to jeopardize the one and a quarter billion dollars of American investments there. But we can find a way of protecting these interests of ours without jeopardizing the welfare and autonomy of the Cubans."

The reason the State Department is obliged to issue these disingenuous statements is that for a century and a quarter prior to 1898 the American notions of imperialism were molded by the continuous struggle to prevent foreign nations from securing a military foothold in the Western Hemisphere, and to secure the free passage on the seas of the goods with which the United States paid her debts to foreign countries. Hence the dogma of the immorality of imperialism became a fixed part of the political consciousness of the nation.

Now the human animal will submit to any punishment or humiliation rather than be forced to admit that its dogmas are false. Whatever it may do under pressure of necessity, it will passionately seek to reconcile its actions with its dogmas. Hence, although the historic situation to-day is completely reversed and the United States is now a huge exporting, lending, and shipping nation, the government still seeks to make its actions appear harmonious with the old political ethic, which approved of political action abroad only in defense of property and morality.

It was for this reason that Roosevelt said in 1907, to justify his military intervention in Cuba: "I am doing my best to persuade the Cubans that if they will only be good, they will be happy." And Wilson, to justify his intervention at Vera Cruz: "I am going to teach the South America Republics to elect good men."

III

Americans, in their hearts, still imagine that they interfere with other people, in foreign as in domestic affairs, solely in order to make them good. Yet all foreign countries regard the United States not at all as a moral teacher but as a shrewd salesman. They admire and envy, not only our ability to sell good merchandise at a low price, but especially our ability to pretend that we are doing it solely from altruistic motives. No one is deceived by American "altruism" except Americans. As Bertrand Russell has said: "The Americans surpass even the British in sagacity, apparent moderation, and the skillful use of hypocrisy by which even themselves are deceived."

The entire world, with the exception of the United States, believes that there is an American Empire which is fast growing to include the entire

Western Hemisphere, and in some degree Europe and parts of Asia as well. Just what is this empire and where is it?

We might make a map of it—indeed, we may make three maps to distinguish three degrees of American imperial influence. First would come the map showing American "possessions" (a term as yet juridically undefined, but including all territories over which the United States asserts positive political control). These territories would include Porto Rico, the Virgin Islands, Hawaii, Alaska, Guam, Samoa, the Philippines, and the Canal Zone. None of these dominions, save Hawaii and Alaska, fits into the scheme of the American constitution. Hawaii and Alaska are territories, presumably one day to become states. The Philippines are a "possession" presumably one day to become an independent nation. Porto Rico is a territory without any presumption of future citizenship in the Union. Guam and Samoa are simply "owned" by the Federal Government. The Virgin Islands were "purchased" from Denmark and are presumably "owned" by the United States, but the political status of their inhabitants is vague. Whether the Canal Zone is land "leased" or land "owned" is a metaphysical question. But over all these territories the American imperial dominion is absolute and unquestioned.

A second map would include all those territories over which the United States exercises a degree of influence which amounts to effective, although not formal, control over their national lives. These would include Cuba, Haiti, and Santo Domingo; Nicaragua, Panama, and indeed all of North America up to the Rio Grande, except of course British Honduras. Especially Mexico! For that country, after years of playing politics with Great Britain, Japan, and others, has at last come completely within the orbit of American influence so far as its foreign policies and its major domestic policies are concerned. But the map would extend farther. It would include most of the continent of South America. In parts of the South American continent the United States exercises a formal control over the national finances. In other parts American invested capital and American commercial interests are powerful, although Europe enjoys a greater or lesser degree of influence. But whatever influence European nations may have in South America, under the present Monroe Doctrine no foreign power could exercise effective diplomatic control of the foreign policy of any South American nation if the United States Government seriously objected. If it came to a clash, the word of the State Department would be decisive. It is such power to dominate in political crises which is the foundation of empire.

But a third map, variously shaded, would reveal an American empire which casts its shadow over most of Europe and much of Asia. For empire, in modern times, is built on commerce and investment which require political protection. And American merchandise and capital have been flooding these vast areas at a rate unprecedented in the history of the world. Nearly five thousand million dollars worth of American goods and more than one thousand million of American capital annually! Such a penetration cannot continue without creating political implications. And, in times of crisis, American political influence has actually regulated the affairs of Europe through the Dawes Plan and probably the Young Plan, as well as through numerous acts to stabilize European finances, to say nothing of the League of Nations and the Kellogg Pact. At least eight of the leading nations of Europe were financially rehabilitated thanks to money loaned at critical moments under conditions approved by the State Department. All of these nations and most of the others would have to consult Washington before making any major change in national policy. This is dominion. This is a degree of empire.

4. SINCLAIR LEWIS, "OUR IDEAL CITIZEN"

"HIS name was George F. Babbitt. He was forty-six years old now, in April, 1920, and he made nothing in particular, neither butter nor shoes nor poetry, but he was nimble in the calling of selling houses for more than people could afford to pay." This short paragraph introduced thousands of readers to Sinclair Lewis's best-selling novel Babbitt; *in the pages that followed, Lewis sketched a remarkable caricature of the middle class in general and the businessman in particular. Babbittry became synonymous with the crass materialism and chauvinism of the middle class, and Babbitt endures as an archetypal American.*

Critics have catalogued the literary flaws in Lewis's book, but unquestionably Babbitt *deserves critical acclaim as the first business novel to portray the nonproducer, the middleman, who had become the representative figure of the business community after World War I. The novel also makes abundantly clear that America's commercial culture demanded of each individual, at the expense of humane values, pathetic conformity and standardization.* Babbitt, *in the words of Mark Shorer, the biographer of Sinclair Lewis, "is the epic of our 'boom' years, and it remains today as the major documentation in literature of American business culture in general."*

In the excerpt from Babbitt *that follows, one will find much of Babbittry reduced to a few pages. "The Ideal Citizen" is Babbitt himself, speaking at the annual dinner of the Zenith Real Estate Board on such topics as politics, literature and art, business, boosterism, class structure, religion, education, and Americanism. In short, the excerpt*

SOURCE. Sinclair Lewis, *Babbitt*, New York: Grosset and Dunlap, pp. 181–184 and 186–188. Copyright 1922 by Harcourt, Brace & World, Inc.; renewed 1950 by Sinclair Lewis. Reprinted by permission of Harcourt, Brace & World, Inc.

is the novelist's analysis of the sociology of the middle class and America's business culture.

Our Ideal Citizen—I picture him first and foremost as being busier than a bird-dog, not wasting a lot of good time in day-dreaming or going to sassiety teas or kicking about things that are none of his business, but putting the zip into some store or profession or art At night he lights up a good cigar, and climbs into the little old 'bus, and maybe cusses the carburetor, and shoots out home. He mows the lawn, or sneaks in some practice putting, and then he's ready for dinner. After dinner he tells the kiddies a story, or takes the family to the movies, or plays a few fists of bridge, or reads the evening paper, and a chapter or two of some good lively Western novel if he has a taste for literature, and maybe the folks next-door drop in and they sit and visit about their friends and the topics of the day. Then he goes happily to bed, his conscience clear, having contributed his mite to the prosperity of the city and to his own bank-account.

In politics and religion this Sane Citizen is the canniest man on earth; and in the arts he invariably has a natural taste which makes him pick out the best, every time. In no country in the world will you find so many reproductions of the Old Masters and of well-known paintings on parlor walls as in these United States. No country has anything like our number of phonographs, with not only dance records and comic but also the best operas, such as Verdi, rendered by the world's highest-paid singers.

In other countries, art and literature are left to a lot of shabby bums living in attics and feeding on booze and spaghetti, but in America the successful writer or picture-painter is indistinguishable from any other decent business man; and I, for one, am only too glad that the man who has the rare skill to season his message with interesting reading matter and who shows both purpose and pep in handling his literary wares has a chance to drag down his fifty thousand bucks a year, to mingle with the biggest executives on terms of perfect equality, and to show as big a house and as swell a car as any Captain of Industry! But, mind you, it's the appreciation of the Regular Guy who I have been depicting which has made this possible, and you got to hand as much credit to him as to the authors themselves.

Finally, but most important, our Standardized Citizen, even if he is a bachelor, is a lover of the Little Ones, a supporter of the hearthstone which is the basic foundation of our civilization, first, last, and all the time, and the thing that most distinguishes us from the decayed nations of Europe.

I have never yet toured Europe—and as a matter of fact, I don't know that I care to such an awful lot, as long as there's our own mighty cities and mountains to be seen—but, the way I figure it out, there must be a good many of our own sort of folks abroad. Indeed, one of the most enthusiastic Rotarians I ever met boosted the tenets of one-hundred-per-cent pep in a burr that smacked o' bonny Scutlond and all ye bonny braes o' Bobby Burns. But same time, one thing that distinguishes us from our good brothers, the hustlers over there, is that they're willing to take a lot off the snobs and journalists and politicians, while the modern American business man knows how to talk right up for himself, knows how to make it good and plenty clear that he intends to run the works. He doesn't have to call in some highbrow hired-man when it's necessary for him to answer the crooked critics of the sane and efficient life. He's not dumb, like the old-fashioned merchant. He's got a vocabulary and a punch.

With all modesty, I want to stand up here as a representative business man and gently whisper, "Here's our kind of folks! Here's the specifications of the Standardized American Citizen! Here's the new generation of Americans: fellows with hair on their chests and smiles in their eyes and adding-machines in their offices. We're not doing any boasting, but we like ourselves first-rate, and if you don't like us, look out—better get under cover before the cyclone hits town!"

So! In my clumsy way I have tried to sketch the Real He-man, the fellow with Zip and Bang. And it's because Zenith has so large a proportion of such men that it's the most stable, the greatest of our cities. New York also has its thousands of Real Folks, but New York is cursed with unnumbered foreigners. So are Chicago and San Francisco. Oh, we have a golden roster of cities— Detroit and Cleveland with their renowned factories, Cincinnati with its great machine-tool and soap products, Pittsburg and Birmingham with their steel, Kansas City and Minneapolis and Omaha that open their bountiful gates on the bosom of the ocean-like wheatlands, and countless other magnificent sister-cities, for, by the last census, there were no less than sixty-eight glorious American burgs with a population of over one hundred thousand! And all these cities stand together for power and purity, and against foreign ideas and communism—Atlanta with Hartford, Rochester with Denver, Milwaukee with Indianapolis, Los Angeles with Scranton, Portland, Maine, with Portland, Oregon. A good live wire from Baltimore or Seattle or Duluth is the twin-brother of every like fellow booster from Buffalo or Akron, Fort Worth or Oskaloosa!

But it's here in Zenith, the home for manly men and womanly women and bright kids, that you find the largest proportion of these Regular Guys, and that's what sets it in a class by itself; that's why Zenith will be remembered in history as having set the pace for a civilization that shall endure when the old time-killing ways are gone forever and the day of earnest efficient endeavor shall have dawned all round the world!

Some time I hope folks will quit handing all the credit to a lot of moth-eaten, mildewed, out-of-date, old, European dumps, and give proper credit to the famous Zenith spirit, that clean fighting determination to win Success that has made the little old Zip City celebrated in every land and clime, wherever condensed milk and pasteboard cartons are known! Believe me, the world has fallen too long for these worn-out countries that aren't producing anything but bootblacks and scenery and booze, that haven't got one bathroom per hundred people, and that don't know a loose-leaf ledger from a slip-cover; and it's just about time for some Zenithite to get his back up and holler for a show-down!

I tell you, Zenith and her sister-cities are producing a new type of civilization. There are many resemblances between Zenith and these other burgs, and I'm darn glad of it! The extraordinary, growing, and sane standardization of stores, offices, streets, hotels, clothes, and newspapers throughout the United States shows how strong and enduring a type is ours. . . .

Yes, sir, these other burgs are our true partners in the great game of vital living. But let's not have any mistake about this. I claim that Zenith is the best partner and the fastest-growing partner of the whole caboodle. I trust I may be pardoned if I give a few statistics to back up my claims. If they are old stuff to any of you, yet the tidings of prosperity, like the good news of the Bible, never become tedious to the ears of a real hustler, no matter how oft the sweet story is told! Every intelligent person knows that Zenith manufactures more condensed milk and evaporated cream, more paper boxes, and more lighting-fixtures, than any other city in the United States, if not in the world. But it is not so universally known that we also stand second in the manufacture of package-butter, sixth in the giant realm of motors and automobiles, and somewhere about third in cheese, leather findings, tar roofing, breakfast food, and overalls!

Our greatness, however, lies not alone in punchful prosperity but equally in that public spirit, that forward-looking idealism and brotherhood, which has marked Zenith ever since its foundation by the Fathers. We have a right, indeed we have a duty toward our fair city, to announce broadcast the facts about our high schools, characterized by their complete plants and the finest school-ventilating systems in the country, bar none; our magnificent new hotels and banks and the paintings and carved marble in their lobbies; and the Second National Tower, the second highest business building in any inland city in the entire country. When I add that we have an unparalleled number of miles of paved streets, bathrooms, vacuum cleaners, and all the other signs of civilization; that our library and art museum are well supported and housed in convenient and roomy buildings; that our park-system is more than up to par, with its handsome driveways adorned with grass, shrubs, and statuary, then I give a hint of the all-round unlimited greatness of Zenith!

I believe, however, in keeping the best to the last. When I remind you that we have one motor car for every five and seven-eighths persons in the city, then I give a rock-ribbed practical indication of the kind of progress and braininess which is synonymous with the name Zenith!

But the way of the righteous is not all roses. Before I close I must call your attention to a problem we have to face, this coming year. The worst menace to sound government is not the avowed socialists but a lot of cowards who work under cover—the long-haired gentry who call themselves "liberals" and "radicals" and "non-partisan" and "intelligentsia" and God only knows how many other trick names! Irresponsible teachers and professors constitute the worst of this whole gang, and I am ashamed to say that several of them are on the faculty of our great State University! The U. is my own Alma Mater, and I am proud to be known as an alumni, but there are certain instructors there who seem to think we ought to turn the conduct of the nation over to hoboes and roustabouts.

Those profs are the snakes to be scotched—they and all their milk-and-water ilk! The American business man is generous to a fault, but one thing he does demand of all teachers and lecturers and journalists: if we're going to pay them our good money, they've got to help us by selling efficiency and whooping it up for rational prosperity! And when it comes to these blab-mouth, fault-finding, pessimistic, cynical University teachers, let me tell you that during this golden coming year it's just as much our duty to bring influence to have those cusses fired as it is to sell all the real estate and gather in all the good shekels we can.

Not till that is done will our sons and daughters see that the ideal of American manhood and culture isn't a lot of cranks sitting around chewing the rag about their Rights and their Wrongs, but a God-fearing, hustling, successful, two-fisted Regular Guy, who belongs to some church with pep and piety to it, who belongs to the Boosters or the Rotarians or the Kiwanis, to the Elks or Moose or Red Men or Knights of Columbus or any one of a score of organizations of good, jolly, kidding, laughing, sweating, upstanding, lend-a-handing Royal Good Fellows, who plays hard and works hard, and whose answer to his critics is a square-toed boot that'll teach the grouches and smart alecks to respect the He-man and get out and root for Uncle Samuel, U.S.A.!

5. CALVIN COOLIDGE, "A DECLARATION FOR ECONOMIC INDEPENDENCE"

DURING the Twenties, businessmen enjoyed an enviable position. The business community was the most powerful collectivity in American society; by comparison, labor seemed puny, agriculture weak, and the consumer unorganized and unprotected. Moreover,

SOURCE. Calvin Coolidge, "A Declaration for Economic Independence," from an address to the Thirty-seventh Continental Congress of the Daughters of the American Revolution in Washington, April 16, 1928, in *The Nation's Business*, Vol. 16, No. 8, July 1928, p. 19.

the federal government embraced the philosophy that all segments of society would benefit if business prospered. Therefore, government should lower, and keep low, taxes, especially those levied on corporations and high income groups; confer favors upon the business community, but keep its services to others at a minimum; and take action against labor, agriculture, and the consumers whenever those interests sought to alter the status quo or to challenge the "trickle-down" theory of government.

The business community possessed an ardent advocate and powerful friend in Calvin Coolidge who believed that business was the instrument through which government should work to achieve the prosperity and well-being of all. It was an article of faith with the puritan President that government should not, except in a few instances (such as highway construction and flood control), intrude upon the opportunities of private enterprise. America's political democracy, he believed, would collapse if government entered the field of business endeavor.

It did not occur to the idealistic Coolidge that the business community often infringed upon the liberties of the workingman, the farmer, and the consumer, nor did he recognize the many areas where government regulation might further rather than curtail the liberties of the people. Moreover, Coolidge failed to appreciate the difficulty if not the impossibility of every man becoming a property owner.

Coolidge's philosophy was succinctly stated in his address to the Daughters of the American Revolution in the spring of 1928. The approving editors of The Nation's Business, *the journal of the United States Chambers of Commerce, published the speech in their magazine that year.*

We are especially prone to call on the National Government to take over our burdens, and with them our freedom. Through regulations and commissions we have given the most arbitrary authority over our actions and our property into the hands of a few men. Some of this has been necessary to prevent those who are weak from being overcome by those who are strong. But it is a procedure fraught with considerable danger and should only be adopted as a last resort.

There is one field, however, which belongs to the people, upon which they have uniformly insisted that the Federal Government should not trespass. That is the domain of private business.

Society requires certain public activities, like highways and drainage, which are used in common and can best be provided by the Government. But in general the country is best served through the competition of private enterprise. If the people are to remain politically free, they must be economically free. Their only hope in that direction is for them to keep their own business in their own hands.

Our theory of society rests on a higher level than Communism. We want the people to be the owners of their property in their own right. We recognize that they are all capitalists by nature. We want them to be all capitalists in fact. That result is being approached rapidly. Our system is demonstrating by practice that it works.

The theories which are advanced to entice the people into handing their private affairs over to the Government do not take into account all the facts: The fundamental characteristics of humanity are not going to be changed by substituting government action for private enterprise. The individual who manages the one, with all his imperfections and his selfishness, will have to be employed to manage the other.

The very essence of business is the expectation of a profit on the part of those who conduct it. Government is conducted from an entirely different motive. When business is in private hands, it is expected to be run for the benefit of the owners. When the Government steps in, the purchasers, users, and beneficiaries of what the Government undertakes to supply insist that the concern should be conducted for their benefit. It does not eliminate selfishness; it simply transfers it in part from the seller to the purchaser. Under these conditions it ceases to be a real business, becomes lacking in enterprise and initiative, and does not have any motive to provide improved service.

Flowing out of these unavoidable conditions, if the Government gets into business on any large scale, we soon find that the beneficiaries attempt to play a large part in the control. While in theory it is to serve the public, in practice it will be very largely serving private interests. It comes to be regarded as a species of government favor and those who are the most adroit get the larger part of it. Men in public life are besought to secure places of employment for some persons in their locality and favorable contracts for others.

The situation rapidly develops into a position of intrenched selfishness, where a great body of public employes and large outside interests are in virtual control, with the general public paying a high cost for poor service. With all the care that it is possible to exercise, a situation of this kind becomes entangled in favoritism and is always in great danger of causing corruption and scandal.

If it is desirable to protect the people in their freedom and independence, if it is desirable to avoid the blighting effects of monopoly supported by the money of the taxpayer, if it is desirable to prevent the existence of a privileged class, if it is desirable to shield public officials from the influence of propaganda and the acute pressure of intrenched selfishness, if it is desirable to keep the Government unencumbered and clean, with an eye single to public service, we shall leave the conduct of our private business with the individual, where it belongs, and not undertake to unload it on the Government.

6. *THE NATION*, "LA FOLLETTE THE WRECKER"

THE age of normalcy was also a time of vigorous though limited radical political agitation. James Weinstein has shown that during the half-dozen years after World War I, labor and farmer-labor parties contained some promise as a reform alternative to the two older established political parties. Many of those involved in third-party politics at the time looked to the old progressive, Robert M. La Follette, for leadership, and he became their standard-bearer in the presidential election of 1924. Ironically, some radicals of the early Twenties, intent upon the socialization of private enterprise, considered La Follette's reforms entirely too conservative while conservatives regarded the Wisconsin progressive and his presidential program of modest reform as a dangerous threat to the established order.

Differing historical evaluations of La Follette's reform program of 1924 reflect the divided opinion of his contemporaries. "One trouble with La Follette's progressivism," writes John D. Hicks, "is that it had not progressed very far since the times of William Jennings Bryan and Theodore Roosevelt, and had little to offer by way of remedies for the distress that existed among the city masses." But others have pointed out that La Follette's progressivism contained some advanced programs for the urban workers, including abolition of the use of injunctions in labor disputes, collective bargaining, and limitations on child labor. William Leuchtenburg is close to the truth in recognizing that La Follette combined some elements of the old individualistic and evangelical progressivism and the new mass-action, economic liberalism that would emerge under Franklin D. Roosevelt during the 1930's.

The editors of the liberal journal, The Nation, *caught some of the irony and paradox of La Follette's 1924 presidential campaign in a tongue-in-cheek analysis of his platform proposals. Their editorial implies that although there was much that was old about La Follette's program, there was indeed much that was still relevant to the reform of American society.*

How shall we protect the home and fireside, yes, the country, from this man La Follette, whom certain reckless insurgents are about to nominate for the Presidency, thereby jeopardizing the chances of so noble and elevated, so gifted and intellectual a patriot as Calvin Coolidge? We confess our bewilderment, our sense of discouragement. Since 1908 his platforms have regularly been thrown out of the Republican conventions as seditious. He has been

SOURCE. Editorial in *The Nation*, Vol. 119, No. 3079, July 9, 1924, p. 32.

denounced as a wild-eyed radical, a pro-German, a disloyalist. A committee to investigate him nearly drove him from the Senate. He has been pilloried and sent to Coventry, and yet he survives. Our daily press assures us that only the "lunatic fringe" of the country is for him, but there was a majority of 375,000 of the lunatic fringe which voted for him in his own State two years ago. And now he is, despite all his radicalism, all his destructive theories and acts, to be run for the Presidency by the discontented, the down-and-out, the discouraged, and the disappointed.

Let us examine the extent of this man's wrongdoing as set forth in the platform laid before the Republican Convention in Cleveland and indignantly spurned by it. The merest glance at it shows how it plans to strike at the very foundations of our national prosperity—it opposes the Mellon tax plan, would increase inheritance taxes, and would tax excess profits, besides favoring the soldier bonus, thus setting its judgment against Mr. Mellon, who has assured us on his word of honor, as one of the richest men in America, that if his proposals are not accepted there will not be enough loose capital available to carry on the industry of America and further to develop our resources. More than that, the La Follette program calls for the repeal of the Esch-Cummins railroad law and the fixing of railroad rates upon the radical and revolutionary basis of actual prudent investment and cost of service. Then it takes the final plunge of declaring for public ownership of railroads. True, it would sugar-coat this pill by asserting that this must be done with "definite safeguards against bureaucratic control." But we all know what it would mean if the railroads of this country were withdrawn from the control of the combination of capitalists who manage our banks, our public-service corporations, our oil companies, and our mining corporations.

Further to camouflage the menace of these proposals the La Follette platform speaks of collecting the foreign-loan interest and recovering the war stealings—as if to do the latter would not in itself unsettle a good many businesses and disturb many happy and prosperous members of our business world. Again, it would promote cooperation between producers and consumers and thus commit the grave injustice of wiping out in part that large class of invaluable go-betweens, the middlemen. It would further revoke the oil concessions granted in the administration of that noble citizen and soldier in the faith, Warren G. Harding. While it appears to favor super- and water-power systems, to which big business is now in its wisdom turning, it masks behind that its proposal for public ownership of all water-power, another abominable scheme to put the government into private business. Almost worst of all is its declaration in favor of a reduction of the tariff. That is, of course, conceived simply and solely for the purpose of unsettling business and striking a blow at the vested manufactures of the country, built up by the sweat of American labor's brow and the skill of its capitalist directors. Then the Wisconsin wreckers would lay ruthless hands upon the federal-reserve and farm-loan systems, on the excuse of democratizing them in the interest of the farmers. Further to bid for the farmer vote, the La Follette platform promises to protect farmer organizations, to aid them in their collective bargaining, and to reduce freight rates.

When we come to labor questions the full extent of this demagoguery is apparent. La Follette actually proposes to take the workmen's child out of the mills and factories in which it is so much better employed than running around the streets and getting killed by automobiles. Just when so many New England mills have established Southern branches or moved their whole plants to the South to escape the harsh and unjust child-labor laws of New England, comes this other deadly blow at industry, for, though the pending amendment only permits Congress to legislate on the child-labor question, interference with the personal liberty of children over twelve years of age to work as many hours a day as they see fit at any wage would inevitably follow. Again, it is a sop to labor to promise to abolish the injunction in labor disputes, that proved and efficient safeguard to our social structure. From this point it is but a step to the direct nomination and election of Presidents, the federal initiative and referendum, and the nation-wide referendum on war which Mr. La Follette has plainly borrowed from another wicked disturber of business, William J. Bryan.

When it comes to the foreign part of the La Follette policy he is plainly still pacifist, pro-German, unpatriotic, and disloyal. He actually wishes to revise the Treaty of Versailles on the pretense that it should be made to conform to the terms of the armistice to which the United States attached its word. Mr. La Follette would further abolish conscription and reduce armaments. He would strike at the safety of every farm in Iowa and Nebraska by curtailing the $800,000,000 now spent annually for the army and navy. Then Senator La Follette shows his hatred of the war-making branches of the government by desiring to promote treaties to outlaw war and he denounces the all-wise policy of our recent administrations in Washington, both Democratic and Republican, in creating opportunities abroad for American investments and then protecting them by our troops and our ships, by speaking of "the mercenary system of degraded foreign policy . . . which has at times degraded our State Department and its high service as a strong and kindly intermediary for defenseless governments to a trading outpost for those interest- and concession-seekers engaged in the exploitation of weaker nations. . . ."

Fortunately only vapid idealists, silly sentimentalists, and subversive journals like *The Nation* may be counted on to defend such wickedness. The sound common sense of the American people will surely rally to the defense of our Morgans and Garys and Sinclairs and Dohenys and Mellons and prevent this threatened assault upon our established customs, the priceless liberties of the men of business who have made us great and strong. Yes, upon our Government itself.

7. HENRY L. MENCKEN, "THE NEW AGE"

OUTWARDLY, the Twenties seemed to have ushered in a new age for women. The abbreviated dress, constricted bust lines, and bobbed hair were all visible expressions of woman's new freedom and an obvious de-emphasis of the differences between the sexes, as though women were saying that their newly gained suffrage rights under the Nineteenth Amendment had lifted them to a plane of equality with men. One may ask, however, if this decided mannishness in dress was evidence of a new equality experienced by all women or merely the slavish imitation of many to a few bold fashion designers. Or do fashion designers, like other artists, reflect the spirit of an age? Questions such as these deserve the careful attention of scholars.

Although women did enjoy a greater degree of freedom during the Twenties than they had in the past, they were, as they are today, second-class citizens. In the summer of 1968 a report of the President's Advisory Council on the Status of Women reemphasized this point. Although more women are working than ever before, their salaries still lag far behind men's. Property laws throughout the nation generally favor men, and abortion remains a crime in almost every state. Women are still looked upon as intruders and misfits in several professions, and the military academies have yet to accept a female plebe. While more women than men are voting today, the election or appointment of women to high political office remains an infrequent occurrence.

Without claiming too much for the progress achieved by women after World War I, Henry L. Mencken suggested, with considerable insight and characteristic wit, that the key to woman's achievement of equality depended upon her sexual freedom. The following selection from his book, In Defense of Women, *is somewhat prophetic for a generation that is now accepting birth control and is concerned about a population explosion.*

THE TRANSVALUATION OF VALUES

The gradual emancipation of women that has been going on for the last century has still a long way to proceed before they are wholly delivered from

SOURCE. Henry L. Mencken, "The Transvaluation of Values," from *In Defense of Women*, New York: Garden City Publishing Company, n.d., pp. 181–185. Copyright 1922 by Alfred A. Knopf, Inc.; renewed 1950 by H. L. Mencken. Reprinted by permission of Alfred A. Knopf, Inc.

their traditional burdens and so stand clear of the oppressions of men. But already, it must be plain, they have made enormous progress—perhaps more than they made in the ten thousand years preceding. The rise of the industrial system, which has borne so harshly upon the race in general, has brought them certain unmistakable benefits. Their economic dependence, though still sufficient to make marriage highly attractive to them, is nevertheless so far broken down that large classes of women are now almost free agents, and quite independent of the favour of men. Most of these women, responding to ideas that are still powerful, are yet intrigued, of course, by marriage, and prefer it to the autonomy that is coming in, but the fact remains that they now have a free choice in the matter, and that dire necessity no longer controls them. After all, they needn't marry if they don't want to; it is possible to get their bread by their own labour in the workshops of the world. Their grandmothers were in a far more difficult position. Failing marriage, they not only suffered a cruel ignominy, but in many cases faced the menace of actual starvation. There was simply no respectable place in the economy of those times for the free woman. She either had to enter a nunnery or accept a disdainful patronage that was as galling as charity.

Nothing could be plainer than the effect that the increasing economic security of women is having upon their whole habit of life and mind. The diminishing marriage rate and the even more rapidly diminishing birth rate show which way the wind is blowing. It is common for male statisticians, with characteristic imbecility, to ascribe the fall in the marriage rate to a growing disinclination on the male side. This growing disinclination is actually on the female side. Even though no considerable body of women has yet reached the definite doctrine that marriage is less desirable than freedom, it must be plain that large numbers of them now approach the business with far greater fastidiousness than their grandmothers or even their mothers exhibited. They are harder to please, and hence pleased less often. The woman of a century ago could imagine nothing more favourable to her than marriage; even marriage with a fifth-rate man was better than no marriage at all. This notion is gradually feeling the opposition of a contrary notion. Women in general may still prefer marriage to work, but there is an increasing minority which begins to realize that work may offer the greater contentment, particularly if it be mellowed by a certain amount of philandering.

There already appears in the world, indeed, a class of women, who, while still not genuinely averse to marriage, are yet free from any theory that it is necessary, or even invariably desirable. Among these women are a good many somewhat vociferous propagandists, almost male in their violent earnestness; they range from the man-eating suffragettes to such preachers of free motherhood as Ellen Key and such professional shockers of the bourgeoisie as the American prophetess of birth-control, Margaret Sanger. But among them are many more who wake the world with no such noisy eloquence, but content themselves with carrying out their ideas in a quiet and respectable manner. The number of such women is much larger than is generally imagined, and that number tends to increase steadily. They are women who, with their economic independence assured, either by inheritance or by their own efforts, chiefly in the arts and professions, do exactly as they please, and make no pother about it. Naturally enough, their superiority to convention and the common frenzy makes them extremely attractive to the better sort of men, and so it is not uncommon for one of them to find herself voluntarily sought in marriage, without any preliminary scheming by herself— surely an experience that very few ordinary women ever enjoy, save perhaps in dreams or delirium.

The old order changeth and giveth place to the new. Among the women's clubs and in the women's colleges, I have no doubt, there is still much debate of the old and silly question: Are platonic relations possible between the sexes? In other words, is friendship possible without sex? Many a woman of the new order dismisses the problem with another question: Why without sex? With the decay of the ancient concept of women as property there must come inevitably a reconsideration of the whole sex question, and out of that reconsideration there must come a revision of the mediaeval penalties which now punish the slightest frivolity in the female. The notion that honour in women is exclusively a physical matter, that a single aberrance may convert a woman of the highest merits into a woman of none at all, that the sole valuable thing a woman can bring to marriage is virginity —this notion is so preposterous that no intelligent person, male or female, actually cherishes it. It survives as one of the hollow conventions of Christianity; nay, of the levantine barbarism that preceded Christianity. As women throw off the other conventions which now bind them they will throw off this one, too, and so their virtue, grounded upon fastidiousness and self-respect instead of upon mere fear and conformity, will become a far more laudable thing than it ever can be under the present system. And for its absence, if they see fit to dispose of it, they will no more apologize than a man apologizes today.

8. COUNTEE CULLEN, THREE POEMS

THE closing years of World War I marked the emergence of the first brilliant phase of the "Black Renaissance." Through the varied mediums of prose, poetry, drama, and music, a gifted generation of Negro Americans gave eloquent and artistic form to the

SOURCE. Countee Cullen, *Color*, New York: Harper and Brothers, 1925, pp. 4, 15, and 20–21. Copyright 1925 by Harper & Brothers; renewed 1953 by Ida M. Cullen. Reprinted by permission of Harper & Row, Publishers.

aspirations and grievances of the inarticulate colored masses. Much of this literary outpouring originated in Harlem and, for that reason, historians have also designated the Negro contributions to American culture as the "Harlem Renaissance." However, by the end of the Twenties the literary and cultural aspects of the Harlem movement had become national.

One of the talented Negro writers was the young poet, Countee Cullen. A native of New York City, Cullen made his important contribution to poetry at the age of 22 with the publication in 1925 of his first collective work, Color. *Critics have since observed that there is little that is original about Cullen's poetry, and indeed much of his work is derivative. Still there is charm and simplicity about his verse that is captivating. Readers of the poems that follow will easily recognize the poetic expression of "Black is Beautiful" and "Black Power" and sense the humiliation and pain conveyed in the lines about a youthful incident involving racial hatred.*

A Song of Praise
(For one who praised his lady's being fair)

You have not heard my love's dark throat,
    Slow-fluting like a reed,
Release the perfect golden note
    She caged there for my need.

Her walk is like the replica
    Of some barbaric dance
Wherein the soul of Africa
    Is winged with arrogance.

And yet so light she steps across
    The ways her sure feet pass,
She does not dent the smoothest moss
    Or bend the thinnest grass.

My love is dark as yours is fair,
    Yet lovelier I hold her
Than listless maids with pallid hair,
    And blood that's thin and colder.

You-proud-and-to-be-pitied one,
    Gaze on her and despair;
Then seal your lips until the sun
    Discovers one as fair.

Pagan Prayer

Not for myself I make this prayer,
    But for this race of mine

That stretches forth from shadowed places
  Dark hands for bread and wine.

For me, my heart is pagan mad,
  My feet are never still,
But give them hearths to keep them warm
  In homes high on a hill.

For me, my faith lies fallowing,
  I bow not till I see,
But these are humble and believe;
  Bless their credulity.

For me, I pay my debts in kind,
  And see no better way,
Bless these who turn the other cheek
  For love of you, and pray.

Our Father, God, our Brother, Christ—
  So are we taught to pray;
Their kinship seems a little thing
  Who sorrow all the day.

Our Father, God; our Brother, Christ,
  Or are we bastard kin,
That to our plaints your ears are closed,
  Your doors barred from within?

Our Father, God; our Brother, Christ,
  Retrieve my race again;
So shall you compass this black sheep,
  That flushes this wild fruit?

Incident

(For Eric Walrond)

Once riding in old Baltimore,
  Heart-filled, head-filled with glee,
I saw a Baltimorean
  Keep looking straight at me.

Now I was eight and very small,
  And he was no whit bigger,
And so I smiled, but he poked out
  His tongue, and called me, "Nigger."

I saw the whole of Baltimore
  From May until December;
Of all the things that happened there
  That's all that I remember.

9. WILLIAM ALLEN WHITE, "THE FARMER AND HIS PLIGHT"

AGRICULTURE was troubled and depressed during the Twenties. Although some Americans still romanticized the simple and unburdened life of the independent yeoman, the farmer had long before become accustomed to the harsh realities of producing for a commercial market. Under the increasing impact of specialized, commercialized agriculture, farmers simply found themselves beset by a number of problems that did not admit of easy solution. Glutted markets, depressed prices, dietary changes that altered consumer preferences, substitution of synthetic materials for cotton, increased mechanization, higher capital investments, heavily mortgaged property, a scarcity of low-interest credit, and the rising consumer expectations of the farm family all suggest the complexity of the economic problems that plagued the farmers.

Of course, not everyone whose livelihood was linked to agriculture was affected in the same way. Some farmers actually benefited from the change in consumer preferences, especially the well-organized citrus producers of the West, the truck farmers who produced for fresh vegetable markets and canneries, and the dairymen who sold raw milk to metropolitan areas. At the other extreme, faring worst of all, were the day laborers, migrant workers, and sharecroppers. With only their labor services to invest, these groups were especially vulnerable to the landowners' search for greater mechanized efficiency and economy. Caught somewhere in the middle were the farm operators whose capital and labor were invested entirely in land, livestock, and machinery; they could not leave the farm without suffering a large financial loss. This latter group was especially plagued by the concomitants of overproduction. By the end of the decade they had made history by organizing, forming pressure groups, agitating for relief legislation, and in various other ways seeking to obtain cost-plus-profit equality with industry.

It is these farm operators that William Allen White, well-known editor of the Emporia Gazette, *describes in his article of 1929. Writing a few months before the stock-market crash, but nearly a decade after the onset of the agricultural depression of 1920, the Kansas editor outlined the situation of the midwestern livestock and grain producers. White presented little that was new to his farm readers in 1929 (and he failed to recognize that something was necessary to deal with the chronic problem of agricultural surpluses), but his essay offers a useful analysis of the farm operator's plight during the "prosperity" decade.*

SOURCE. William Allen White, "The Farmer and His Plight," in *The Survey*, Vol. 62, No. 5, June 1, 1929, pp. 281–283.

Edwin G. Nourse, writing on economic changes in agriculture for Mr. Hoover's committee, makes it plain that there is before the country a serious farm problem. This problem does not arise from any one cause. It is the result of no malicious conspiracy to oppress the farmer, no ruthless combination to force him down into the level of the European peasantry. The agricultural problem, as Mr. Nourse expounds it, backing up his exposition with statistics and convincing reference, is a problem of the changing times. Economic changes have fallen heavier upon the farmer than upon any other class of American producers because farming is the least flexible of the pursuits of man. Also, by reason of his training and his economic situation, and somewhat by reason of his own desire, the farmer himself is not pliable.

Today, the old farmer whose grandparents told him of the log school-house, the wooden benches, the four-months school, the wood carving, the weaving, the killing and curing of beeves and hogs for home consumption, the preservation of foods for winter use, or ancient contraptions unpatented and unchanged since Ruth and Naomi gleaned in the fields of Moab—this farmer remembers those folktales of his independent, self-sufficient fathers, and they are as strange to him and as meaningless as the yarns in Arabian Nights, chronicles of a day that is passed.

Your American farmer of the present day is a manufacturer. His machinery is a considerable item in his investment. His land has no selling value. He must employ seasonal labor. He must meet a tremendous tax burden to sustain the complicated civilization which has grown up around him and robbed him of his independence. He must keep pace with the new world into which he has been set a pilgrim and a stranger. His children must have an eight-months school and a highschool in every township. Within six miles of the average American farm is a picture show, and in the Mississippi Valley on every farm is a telephone, and on practically every farm is some sort of an automobile. Where there were nearly one hundred thousand tractors sold in the United States in 1918, there are now in use eight hundred thousand. Of the twenty-two million automobiles in America, at least five million are owned by farmers. The combination of the harvester and the thresher, an expensive machine which can be operated economically only upon a farm of five hundred acres or more, is called the combine. Between thirty-five and forty thousand of these machines are in use on American farms today. The radio, part toy and part market reporter supplementing the telephone, will be found in a few years in every farm house. The phonograph is there now, as common as the cabinet organ was in the last quarter of the old century.

These things—farm tools, means of communication, transportation, and diversion—are not luxuries. They are necessities in a new world. The farmer can no more ignore them than he can prosper without hard-surfaced roads. He cannot go back to the older order. He cannot rotate his crops—oats, corn, and meadow land—because the decreasing demand for oats and grass has come inexorably as horses have disappeared from the cities and are disappearing from the farms. What will eat the oats and the hay? He must find other methods of renewing his soil than the old rotation of his fathers. In a mechanical age the farmer cannot defy the machine. And when the machine comes on the farm, it brings with it interest and more taxes and maintenance and care and expert operation.

The farmer is no more independent today than the textile manufacturer. The farmer grows little of his own food. He does not see his wheat, after the combine enters the field. It does not pay his wife even to bake his bread. His cattle are slaughtered a hundred and sometimes a thousand miles from the farm, and no wool has been carded and woven into cloth on a typical American farm for more than two generations. He is lucky if he saves his own cream. And certainly he no longer makes his own cheese. His chickens and eggs are about the only vestige of the farmer's animal food that is grown on the farm.

Behold the industrialist, somewhat laborer, somewhat manufacturer, somewhat borrower in spite of himself, deeply co-operative, his independence gone, his freedom a memory. He turns to the government, and gets only more taxes. He turns to the banker, who is as hard pressed from above as the farmer, and finds his interest rates soaring. The government for the moment turns banker, but relieves the farmer only a little. He looks to the industrial worker and finds him pounding farm prices down that he may have cheaper food. So the farmer, being resentful, frowns on child labor laws which the industrial worker demands that he may keep his children out of the factories.

Because he moves slowly, because he cannot join the tendency of the times and establish high wages, small profits, quick turnover, and mass production, the farmer is like Ishmael. Every man's hand is against the slow-moving unit in a quick-stepping world. He cannot step faster, however he would like to do so. For the farmer requires a year for his crop turnover. Droughts and floods eating into his gross production compel the farmer to seek large profits on his slow turnover, and he must pay small wages if he survives. The loyal independence of his grandfather, the farmer of today has traded off for what?— Isolation! Even in politics he is in the minority. He no longer controls the Congress, and in less than a score of states has he the majority in any legislature.

Yet he must go on. He must fight his fight, adapt himself to the new conditions in a changing world. To tell the truth, and in this chapter on agriculture Mr. Nourse does tell the truth admirably, the farmer has been adapting himself as best he can. He has changed as fast as possible. But, alas, the farmer cannot change as fast as the times are changing. He has speeded up production. He has increased his product and to an extent decreased its cost, but not fast enough to prevent falling prices made necessary by many elements in the economic situation.

The American farmer is competing with European and South American peasants, and he will not be a peasant. He has a standard of living which he must maintain. And there is the battle-ground of the farmer. He will stand and fight for his living standards, which are higher than the standards of any other farmer in the world. He will not take his family to town in a two-wheeled cart. He will not work his family in the fields when the children should be in school. He will not deny them highschool education. He will not clothe them in peasant garb. He will eat what the city man eats, meat two or three times a day, vegetables the year round, sometimes shot full of a thousand miles of rail transportation. He demands his picture show. He *will* listen to the radio. He *will* turn on the phonograph. He *will* talk across the fields to his neighbors and his market town by telephone. He *will* ride in his own car upon a hard-surfaced road, and have his daily paper and his weekly magazine, and his book, and his yearly trip in the family Ford. In these demands for an American living standard, he is only asking what the industrial worker enjoys, what the school teacher, and the preacher, and the country lawyer and doctor require. The American farmer will not be declassed.

He has what no other farmer has ever had before in the age-old struggle of the peasant against the baron. The American farmer has the ballot and he uses it. If he does not control a majority, he makes a balance of power. He forms blocs. He knows the game. He is organized fairly well politically. He does not know how to solve his problem. The farmer's problem will not be solved until he has:

First, cheaper transportation, which probably must come by waterways rather than by reduced rail rates;

Second, better marketing facilities, which will come somewhat through using state and federal agencies to overcome the farmer's traditional inability to organize effectively;

Third, better credit facilities, which will enable him to hold his crops out of glutted markets;

Fourth, new farm methods, which mean the further use of machinery, the saving of waste, the readaptation of land to changing crops and markets;

And fifth, a gradual re-organization of his economic status so that farming will no longer become a way of life as his grandfathers knew it, but a means of living. Farming must be more of a business and less of a career. When the farmer loses his sentimental feeling for the soil, a noble vocation of man will pass, but with its passing will come a more definite economic security. The patrician caste will probably go and a rather cold-blooded business man must come to the American farm.

No one knows how to solve the farmer's problems by ukase or proclamation. Neither business nor government alone can do it. But this the farmer does know, that the answer to his problem cannot come on any other basis than that he must continue to receive his share of the common wealth which his labor makes. He must live up to the American standard. How he can do this, no economist can tell. If the law of supply and demand is to work inexorably, a little figuring will show that the problem cannot be solved in the farmer's favor, but the law of supply and demand has been weakened in America. Our vast economic surplus has enabled us one way or another through public credit or private enterprise, or the benevolences of Croesus, to have what we will, when we will, and how we will, on this continent. And the farmer, embattled behind his ballot box, has no great fear of defeat.

10. *OUTLOOK AND INDEPENDENT,* "THE WICKERSHAM REPORT"

FROM the very beginning of the national prohibition era, some Americans ardently opposed the constitutional ban on the manufacture, distribution, and sale of alcoholic beverages. By 1929 the dissatisfication with and disregard of the Volstead Act, the prohibition enforcement law, had grown to such proportions that the wisdom of such a policy required official review. Accordingly, President Herbert Hoover announced in May 1929 the appointment of the Commission on Law Enforcement and Observance.

The title of the commission and its principal responsibility of investigating the problems of prohibition only within the larger context of law enforcement seemed to many to indicate an unwillingness by the Hoover administration to examine critically a controversial policy. However, the commission's chairman, George W. Wickersham, who had been Attorney General of the United States during the Taft Administration, and the other members of the commission, began work with an announcement that they would investigate all aspects of prohibition.

After months of hearing testimony and collecting evidence, the Wickersham Commission issued an ambiguous report that reflected the nation's divided opinion on the liquor question. While all the members signed the "dry" summary report, separate dissenting "wet" views were incorporated into the full record. The following editorial, written in 1931 soon after the official release of the commission's conclusions, reveals why the report lent itself to so many different interpretations and, more importantly, why the prohibition experiment was unsuccessful.

SOURCE. Editorial in *Outlook and Independent,* Vol. 157, No. 4, January 28, 1931, p. 130.

Of all the absurd reports ever submitted by any investigating body, the report of the Wickersham prohibition commission takes the cake. It is an absurd report because of the terrific anti-climax in which it ends; because, though the body of the report is wet, the recommendations at the close are dry; because, though the commission's conclusions are predominantly against any change in the prohibition experiment, the commissioners record themselves as predominantly in favor of a change in the experiment.

To read the report from beginning to end, without being previously informed of its nature, is to get the surprise of your life. It is packed to the brim with reasons why prohibition as it stands cannot be and should not be enforced. The commission does say, briefly, that the Eighteenth Amendment and the Volstead Act have been followed by certain benefits—"industrial benefits—i.e., increased production, increased efficiency of labor, elimination of 'blue Mondays' and decrease in industrial accidents—increase in savings and decrease in demand upon charities and social agencies." But the bulk of the report is of a distinctly contrary, and incidentally of a distinctly convincing nature.

Thus the commission finds a "widespread and scarcely or not at all concealed contempt for the policy of the national prohibition act." It finds that, "taking the country as a whole, people of wealth, business men and professional men, and their families, and, perhaps, the higher paid working men and their families, are drinking in large numbers in quite frank disregard of the declared policy of the national prohibition act." It finds rampant smuggling of liquor "by land, by water and by air." It finds that "a steady volume of whiskey, much of it of good quality, is put in circulation; and prices at which it is obtainable are a convincing testimony to the ineffectiveness of enforcement" against distillers. It quotes an estimate that nine million gallons of industrial alcohol were diverted in the year ending June 30, 1930.

Thus, again, it finds that necessity compels the abandonment of efforts for effective enforcement against the home production of liquor, even though "it must be recognized that this is done at the price of nullification to that extent. Law here bows to actualities." It finds that, while many speakeasies are closed each year, "the number does not decrease on that account;" that "whiskey of good quality is obtainable substantially everywhere at prices not extravagant for persons of means," while for other persons "a large amount of cheap, poor grade or even poisonous liquor is constantly produced." It finds that in all states there has been a growing tendency to "let the federal government carry the burden of enforcement," while in some states "all attempts at enforcement are substantially precluded by public opinion." It finds flagrant corruptions left and right as well as agitation for the "disregard or abrogation of the guarantees of liberty and of sanctity of the home." It even points out that prohibition's benefits are due less to the present federal experiment than to the closing of the old time saloon. Finally it declares that "We expect legislation to conform to public opinion, not public opinion to yield to legislation," and adds, quite clinchingly, "it is therefore a serious impairment of the legal order to have a national law upon the books theoretically governing the whole land and announcing a policy for the whole land which public opinion in many important centers will not enforce and in many others will not suffer to be enforced effectively."

Yet despite all this, and as incredible as the fact may seem, the commission's report is dry. It is dry because it specifically recommends steps to tighten up enforcement, but does not recommend any important step to liberalize the prohibition laws. Besides advising what should be done to improve enforcement, the commissioners declare that they do not favor the repeal of the amendment or the modification of the Volstead Act; but they lack the courage to say, or rather they are too discreet to say, that they favor the amendment's revision. They therefore merely point obliquely to Henry W. Anderson's plan for the revision of the amendment and do not indorse it. They want the amendment changed so that it will not prohibit the traffic in liquor, but give Congress the power to prohibit or regulate that traffic; in other words, they want liquor laws which will be quickly responsive to a changing public opinion. That is plain not only from the report as a whole, but from the amazing fact that, as shown by their opinions attached to the report, six of the eleven commissioners—that is, a majority—favor the immediate repeal or revision of the Eighteenth Amendment. It is shown again by the fact that, of the five dry commissioners, all but one—Mr. Wickersham himself—as shown in the attached statements, favor revision of the amendment should further trial fail to produce better enforcement. So a commission, which after eighteen months of investigation has become convinced of the necessity for change, submits a report in which no change is recommended.

11. *KANSAS CITY STAR*, "THE OLDER AMERICA WINS!"

THE presidential election of 1928 holds more than usual significance. The campaign waged that year not only marked the first time that a major party had a Catholic candidate, but also the contest between the wet, Irish Catholic Al Smith and the dry, Quaker Herbert Hoover reveals in microcosm the clash between the old and the new America.

SOURCE. Editorial in *Kansas City Star*, Vol. 29, No. 51, November 7, 1928, p. 28.

For years, cultural warfare had raged between rural and urban America, but with the nation's attainment of its urban majority in 1920, the conflict assumed a new intensity. The urban assault upon the cultural values of the older, agrarian America was waged on many fronts, but it was in the political arena that the contending forces fought their battle for control of America.

The landslide victory for Herbert Hoover that year seemed to have settled conclusively such vexatious issues as prohibition, immigration laws, the methods for dealing with the farm problem, and government's policies toward business. Moreover, the country's cultural values seemed to be in safekeeping in the hands of Hoover. This was the interpretation of the Kansas City Star. *Yet little did the* Star's *editor realize how events that lay just over the horizon could demonstrate the inconclusiveness of a presidential election in settling the issues "once and for all." The defenders of the older America would soon discover that the future of American politics lay not in the countryside, but on the urban frontier.*

In the overwhelming election of Herbert Hoover to the presidency the country expressed itself on certain great issues.

The country expressed itself on national prohibition. The big cities may want their liquor. But after seventy-five years of experimenting with every conceivable form of liquor control, including the state dispensary system advocated by Governor Smith, the nation has deliberately made up its mind that national prohibition, with all its defects, offers the great promise to a country that is seeking to abolish poverty through industrial efficiency. Prohibition *is* a noble experiment. The nation recognizes it as such. There will be progress in enforcing the law. No party, after yesterday's lesson, will dare seek its abolition.

(Undoubtedly the religious issue entered into the verdict in certain states. To what extent it is impossible to say. Where the churches took a strong stand prohibition was what they were fighting for. If Smith had been dry instead of wet, it is hard to believe there would have been effective organized opposition to him on religious grounds.)

The country expressed itself on immigration. Mr. Hoover has been one of the leaders for the present restrictions. Governor Smith in his acceptance speech declared for the favorite Tammany proposal of changing the stream of immigration to the South and East of Europe. The proposal met with such criticism that he was silent on it before the campaign had gone far. Under yesterday's verdict immigration restrictions will be tightened rather than loosened.

The country expressed itself on farm relief. Smith sought to sponsor an ambiguous farm program that would capture the West while not alienating the East. He failed. The country, including the farming West, spoke out for entrusting the question of farm relief to the constructive genius of Hoover, with his farm background and his great business experience, rather than to Smith, with his city antecedents and support, and his evident unfamiliarity with agriculture.

The country expressed itself on the general business program offered by Hoover—inland waterways, tariff revision, co-operation of government to promote the interests of legitimate industry, government regulation rather than government in business.

Finally, it must be said that the country expressed confidence in the administrative ability and policies of the Republican organization. There is no getting away from the fact that there is a strong feeling in the country that after all the Republican administration in Washington is pretty competent, is national in outlook, and can be depended on to keep the ship on an even keel.

All these considerations may be summed up in the general statement that the old American tradition is still dominant.

Smith represented the big city, its cosmopolitanism, its impatience with what an eminent New Yorker once called "the moral yearnings of the rural communities," its absorption in itself, its failure to think nationally. Hoover was the embodiment of the qualities and standards of the older and small city America, which still controls the country.

In the election yesterday the newer, urban life clashed with the older tradition, and the older America swept to victory.

12. HOWARD FLORANCE, "WHAT REALLY HAPPENED"

SCHOLARS today place the total number of persons buying stocks in 1929 at a million and a half. Some of the first journalistic accounts of the Great Crash of 1929, however, implied that millions of Americans were stock speculators during the last year of the Big Bull Market. Frederick Lewis Allen, in his widely read survey of the predepression decade, Only Yesterday, *although not too far off in his estimate of the number of persons involved in stock purchases, nonetheless led readers astray through his description of those who were actually buying stock. "All sorts of people" Allen wrote, were in the market,*

SOURCE. Howard Florance, "What Really Happened," in *The Review of Reviews*, Vol. 81, No. 1, January 1930, pp. 118 and 122.

and he listed numerous examples: the rich man's chauffeur, the window cleaner at the broker's office, a Wyoming cattleman, an ex-actress, grocers, motormen, plumbers, seamstresses, and speakeasy waiters.

All sorts of people were indeed in the market but, for the most part, the speculators proved to be men and women who enjoyed adequate incomes, thus enabling them to accumulate modest savings. A typical investor was not the shoeshine boy, but more likely a small businessman who could not resist the speculative urge to hopefully realize a generous return on his investment. Some got in and out of the market at the right time; others bought high and, when the crash came, sold low to salvage something from their original investment. Still others participated by paying less than half of the stock's purchase price, the difference constituting the margin—the amount borrowed from a broker and secured by the stock itself. When the market plunged downward, the indebted speculator and his overextended broker were both in desperate straits. It is the hapless margin-purchaser that the following article analyzes to demonstrate "what really happened."

Let us take a hypothetical person, not unlike many thousands of real ones. Mr. Lamb enters the Street, early in the year 1929, attracted by tales he has heard. He has $1000 of savings, and he has watched a certain stock rise day after day for months. It rose from $30 per share in January, 1928, to $50 in December of that same year. We are using exact figures in this example, though there is no need to name the stock. Mr. Lamb can hold back no longer. He buys. But instead of buying 20 shares at $50 each, he finds that with his thousand dollars he can buy 60 shares! The stock costs $3000, but he buys on a 30 percent margin; that is, he invests his own $1000 and borrows $2000 from a bank through the broker, using the shares themselves as security.

His stock continues to rise. When it reaches 70 he has a 20-point paper profit. It is worth $4200. His profit, if he chooses to sell, is $1200, or more than 100 percent on his investment. But he is not satisfied. He has discovered that he can borrow now a larger sum from his broker, without additional collateral. In other words, he capitalizes his paper profit of $1200, and uses it as the required margin on the purchase of 40 new shares at the prevailing price of 70. This second investment costs $2800, but requires no cash of his. He now owns 100 shares, valued at $7000, on which the broker is willing to lend him up to 70 percent, or $4900. They have cost him $3000 plus $2800 or $5800. He has put in only his original sum of $1000 and has borrowed $4800.

As the price further advances, to 80, our investor buys 35 more shares, still without additional cash. The whole is now worth 135 times $80, or $10,800, on which he has borrowed $7600, or approximately 70 percent of the market value. The three blocks have cost him $3000, plus $2800 plus $2800, or $8600. He paid for them with $1000 cash and $7600 of borrowed money.

Up to this point Mr. Lamb is a successful financier. He "owns" 135 shares of his favorite stock, instead of the 20 that he could have bought outright. When the price rose still further, to 86, he had a paper profit of $4000. In a rising market the thing is quite as simple as it seems. The fact that he owed his broker $7600 did not impress itself. Was he not "worth" 135 times $86, or $11,610?

But our friend had become a speculator; and he soon paid the penalty. . . .

Sales on the New York Stock Exchange were running at the rate of three million shares a day when, on Monday, October 21, they jumped to six million. Even that huge total was exceeded two days later, and on Thursday, October 24, the shares sold approached thirteen millions. Comparative quiet followed. The unexpected can always be expected to happen in Wall Street, however, and after a dull Saturday short session the brokers' offices were flooded with selling orders on Monday morning. Nine million shares were sold, the average decline being the unbelievable sum of $30 per share. On Tuesday, October 29, panic reigned. More than sixteen million shares were dumped. The average price dropped $24 lower—a loss of $54 per share in two days. On the 30th the tide turned; there was buying rather than selling. During the month of October the market value of all shares on the New York Stock Exchange declined from 87 to 71 billion dollars.

PART IV

The Age of the Great Depression

WHEN Herbert Hoover assumed the Presidency in March of 1929, many Americans looked expectantly toward a New Era of enlightened capitalism that would extend the nation's economic abundance to all classes. The new Chief Executive had reached the zenith of a private and public career, which had been distinguished by the greatest of successes. His vaunted abilities were not imaginary; they had been amply demonstrated during an extraordinary career in business and governmental service. Now the American people eagerly awaited the economic fulfillment of the American Dream. In his campaign of 1928 he had told the American voters that, "We in America today are nearer the final triumph over poverty than ever before in the history of the land. The poorhouse is vanishing from among us. We have not reached the goal, but given a chance to go forward with the policies of the last eight years we shall soon, with the help of God, be in sight of the day when poverty will be banished from this nation."

The Great Crash of the stock market in October of 1929 shattered Hoover's dream and, to many, the ensuing depression made a mockery of his campaign promise of "two cars in every garage." (Harry Truman later remarked that he meant "two families in every garage.") Just four years later a new President had to reassure a frightened and bewildered nation that "the only thing we have to fear is fear itself—nameless, unreasoning, unjustified terror which paralyzes needed efforts to convert retreat into advance."

Because the collapse of the world's strongest economy called into question long-established American values and institutions, the Age of the Great Depression constitutes a critical period in American history. Not only did many patriotic and intelligent citizens seriously consider various alternatives to capitalism, but some even came to doubt that democratic political institutions could survive the crisis. The response of the Hoover and Roosevelt administrations demonstrates the critical nature of the situation. Both Presidents conceived of their office as analogous to that of a commander-in-chief in time of war, and they turned to the example of the Wilson Administration's conduct of World War I for guidelines in attacking the depression.

The economic disaster affected all Americans. The most spectacular losses were suffered by those who were caught short in the stock market crash, but independent businessmen, hourly wage earners, and farmers suffered most seriously. The purchasing power of the working man had increased only slightly during the Twenties, and agricultural prices had been depressed throughout the Age of Normalcy. Now, widespread unemployment—which reached the figure of 25 percent of the employable work force by January of 1933—and plummeting farm commodity prices brought disaster to millions. The most devastating aspect of the economic debacle cannot be recaptured by merely examining the appalling statistics of a falling Gross National Product, the spiralling rates of mortgage foreclosures, or the number of families forced on relief. The embarrassment of standing in a breadline, the agony of watching the family homestead sold at a sheriff's auction, the grim apple peddlers on the corner, the overnight appearance of tarpaper shack settlements and tent villages (derisively called "Hoovervilles"), and the futility of searching for a job—these human tragedies all too clearly describe the impact of the depression on the American people.

Inevitably, the nation turned to the White House for leadership. Herbert Hoover's response to the depression was far more complex than the people realized, since he sought to ease the suffering and to work for recovery. His actions deviated sharply from the practices of all previous Presidents faced with similar economic disasters. At first, Hoover relied on simple voluntaristic programs, urging that local government and charity organizations handle the relief problems but, as the depression worsened, he reluctantly utilized more powers of the federal government. While Hoover established several new programs to promote relief and to stimulate recovery, it is questionable whether he moved far enough and fast enough. Historians have frequently observed that while Hoover showed little reluctance to provide long-term loans to big businesses and financial institutions through the Reconstruction Finance Corporation (a "millionaires' dole," cracked Fiorello LaGuardia), he stubbornly resisted with all of his power federal relief for the unemployed. "I am opposed to any direct or indirect federal dole," he said in December

1931. "If the individual surrenders his own initiative and responsibilities, he is surrendering his own freedom and his own liberty."

The American people, however, believed that Hoover had not dealt with the depression with sufficient imagination, and their sentiments were unmistakably demonstrated in the presidential election of 1932. Although few voters knew what Roosevelt's promise of a "new deal" entailed, they were convinced that four more years of Hoover was unthinkable. "They know that they got a man in there who is wise to Congress, wise to our so-called big men," Will Rogers said shortly after Roosevelt's inauguration. "The whole country is with him, just so he does something. If he burned down the capitol we would cheer and say, 'Well, we at-least got a fire started anyhow.' " As Roosevelt himself said in his stirring inaugural address: "This Nation asks for action, and action now . . . We must act and act quickly."

Roosevelt and his phalanx of New Dealers accurately perceived the mood of the nation. Recognizing the demand for immediate action, the Roosevelt Administration pushed through Congress during the first one-hundred days more far-reaching legislative programs for relief, recovery, and reform than had been enacted in the nation's history. The reforms would continue, frequently in short bursts of frenzied legislative activity, until 1938. At first the New Deal sought to provide relief for the unemployed and to promote a general economic recovery, but there soon emerged a social and economic reform program which had a lasting impact on subsequent American life. In 1933 and 1934, reform was concentrated primarily on the economic system, but this period also saw the birth of the Tennessee Valley Authority and the Civilian Conservation Corps. In 1935 came Social Security, the Wagner Labor Act, a more sharply graduated income tax, the Public Utility Holding Company Act, the Banking Act, and the Rural Electrification Administration. These were followed in later years by the beginning of public housing (1937), and a national minimum wage and maximum hours act (1938).

As the New Deal unfolded, action frequently preceded theory. As a result, there was never a grand philosophical design for the New Deal. The programs established were frequently inconsistent, making generalization and interpretation extremely difficult. The New Deal was filled with contradictions, and the student who seeks to compartmentalize it into neat segments will only confuse the problem. This inconsistency is in part the result of the thought processes of its chief architect, Franklin D. Roosevelt. The thirty-second President, one of his long-time associates once remarked, had a "flypaper mind." He continually absorbed a wide variety of ideas and seemingly was not afraid to try new or unusual solutions. "It may be," he said in his first inaugural, "that an unprecedented demand and need for undelayed action may call for temporary departure from that normal balance of public procedure." To what extent he actually departed from tradition, however, remains a crucial question. In retrospect, Roosevelt's commitment to reform and experimentation seems to have been sharply restricted to proposals that would not deviate too far from conventional practice.

Operating essentially what Roosevelt's biographer, James M. Burns, calls a "broker state," in which he sought to placate conflicting points of view or pressure groups, Roosevelt was exposed to a wide spectrum of ideas on how to meet the crisis. Consequently, the New Deal evolved through a series of patchwork solutions; some programs, such as the Civilian Conservation Corps and the Tennessee Valley Authority, worked marvelously; several proved to be partial successes (for example, the National Recovery Administration and the Public Works Administration) and some, like the Resettlement Administration and the Farm Security Administration, failed miserably. Roosevelt, however, was undaunted by setbacks, and with unshakable optimism, invariably moved on to a different approach for the problem at hand. Essentially a pragmatist, he liked to refer to himself as a quarterback who called one play and, if it did not work, would then attempt another approach.

As a result, during the course of the New Deal, both the advocates of Theodore Roosevelt's New Nationalism and Woodrow Wilson's New Freedom had their day in court, as did those calling for a rigid adherence to a balanced budget and those who embraced the new concept of deficit financing of John Maynard Keynes. At the same time, Roosevelt's pragmatism and interest in new ideas had narrow limits. He was not willing to go very far toward the radicalism being promoted by such reformers as the Minnesota governor Floyd Olson, Socialist Upton Sinclair or even the Louisiana Kingfish, Huey P. Long. Conversatives who refused to abandon *laissez-faire* saw in the New Deal the broad outlines of a socialist state in public works, Social Security, the TVA, and economic planning through such agencies as the National Recovery Administration and the Agricultural Adjustment Administration. Yet reformist groups on the political left became equally frustrated with F.D.R. They felt that the New Deal was too conservative, too closely tied to outmoded economic and social doctrines. The presidential candidate of the Socialist Party, Norman Thomas, for example, attacked the Roosevelt program because "The reforms of the New Deal, while by no means negligible, are largely superficial. . . . We still have an army of the unemployed greater than all the rest of the world." Most important, Thomas said, "There have been no very fundamental changes in the structure of a profit-making society."

Still, the manner in which the Great Depression and the New Deal influenced American life is not difficult to determine. The national political structure was changed as the Democratic Party firmly entrenched itself in power on the basis of the new Roosevelt "urban coalition"; the federal government entered the day-to-day affairs of the agricultural and business communities; organized labor came of age and, by 1936, was a potent political force; the size of the government increased dramatically as the New Deal established several programs designed to provide economic security and opportunity for various segments of the population; and perhaps most important of all, many Americans came to expect, even demand, that their government play an active role in protecting them from the vicissitudes of an urban-industrial society.

As a reform movement, however, the New Deal suffered from serious limitations. Despite its numerous relief and public works programs, the New Deal never attempted a meaningful attack upon the sources and conditions of poverty, which had existed in the United States long before the 1930's. Rhetorical concern about "one-third of a nation ill-housed, ill-clad, ill-nourished" notwithstanding, the Roosevelt Administration was far more inclined to aid those persons whose middle-class existence had been temporarily disrupted by the depression. The New Deal was essentially concerned with the middle one-third. The salaried white-collar and the skilled blue-collar workers consequently derived the most benefit from the so-called "radicalism" of the New Deal. Even the business community received much more useful legislation than did the disinherited millions who lived in the shacks of the southern sharecroppers, on remote and forgotten Indian reservations, in the ghettos of the industrial and mining cities, or in the camps of the migrant farm workers.

The New Deal could ignore such groups because they were politically disorganized. Unlike the skilled factory worker or the midwestern farmer, they did not enjoy the benefit of powerful organizations that could effectively bend the government to their advantage. Lacking organizational efficiency, the poor lacked political muscle. Meanwhile the Farm Bureau obtained a lucrative price support program for its member farmers, and the labor unions were rewarded with such welfare guarantees as a minimum wage and Social Security. Although it eventually broke with the New Deal, initially the business community (or at least significant segments of it) was pleased with such business-prescribed legislation as the National Recovery Administration, the Federal Housing Administration, and the Glass-Stegall Banking Act. Conversely, New Deal relief programs never were intended to meet completely the needs of the leaderless and disorganized unemployed, much less to achieve an end to poverty.

The record of the New Deal in aiding America's largest minority group— the Negro—also illustrates the selective nature of New Deal liberalism. Twentieth-century liberalism had not yet embraced civil rights as a major reform objective. The Roosevelt administration contented itself with several symbolic gestures, such as appointing a Negro to a second level administrative position, rather than initiate substantive programs designed to uplift the impoverished Negro masses. Millions of Negroes did, of course, benefit from several of the welfare and relief programs and, in return, they changed their voting allegience to the Democratic Party. But no clear recognition of their particular needs ever emerged, and several New Deal programs actually incorporated racial discriminatory practices. The Civilian Conservation Corps, for example, segregated its members by race, and several of the industrial codes approved by the National Recovery Administration contained two wage scales—one for whites and a lower one for blacks. Indeed, Roosevelt refused to use his influence on behalf of a strong federal antilynching bill in 1937. He was also very reluctant to issue an Executive Order in 1941 abolishing racial discrimination in defense industries until a planned protest march on Washington by 50,000 Negroes threatened to embarrass him and his administration in a world frightened by the racism of Adolph Hitler.

At the same time, the record of the New Deal must be studied from within the context of the 1930's. Despite Roosevelt's lukewarm commitment to civil rights, the Negro made more gains during the decade than in any since Reconstruction; the relief programs might have fallen far short of providing for all the nation's needy, and the existence of hard-core poverty might have been ignored, but in comparison with earlier years, the New Deal relief program was one of overwhelming magnitude.

Because of its central role in shaping contemporary American society, the New Deal has been a major subject for research by historians. The resulting avalanche of books and articles has illustrated the complexities and contradictions of the New Deal, but what is most striking about the New Deal is its strong commitment to traditional American institutions and the desire of its leaders to strengthen them rather than to establish an entirely new set of economic and political relationships. That Roosevelt could have blazed a far more radical trail is readily apparent from his first days in office when he refused to nationalize the banks. The consensus among scholars is that the New Deal was inherently conservative in that it sought to preserve and reform existing institutions rather than create new ones. Capitalism, after all, did survive the depression. With the coming of World War II, free enterprise entered an era of expansion that overshadowed all records made during the 1920's, notwithstanding the fact that the American business system had undergone significant structural and operational reforms.

It was this new role of government that created great controversy in the 1930's, and it is the same issue that continues to excite debate. The following essays and contemporary sources will provide the student with an understanding of the major issues of the era, and should enable him to view the 1930's with sufficient perspective so that he can develop his own conclusions about this important decade.

SECONDARY SOURCES ¹⁷

1. CARL N. DEGLER, "THE ORDEAL OF HERBERT HOOVER"

FEW Presidents ever left office as unpopular as Herbert Hoover. "Democracy is not a polite employer," he later recalled. "The only way out of elected office is to get sick or die or get kicked out." On November 8, 1932, the American people unceremoniously and without regret kicked Herbert Hoover out of the White House. As President, Hoover had been saddled with the responsibility for the depression: "He certainly is a great engineer," one embittered Missouri farmer wrote. "It took him only four years to ditch and drain the whole country."

Hoover's failure as President resulted in part from his inept handling of public relations. No matter how hard he tried, he could not convey to the people his deep concern for the condition of the nation. Hoover's dour and distant personality contributed directly to his failure of leadership; repeated unfortunate predictions that "Prosperity is just around the corner," only further alienated the people. The crisis called for inspirational and imaginative leadership, and Hoover lacked such charismatic qualities. The best that he could muster was an exhortation to remain true to the verities of "rugged individualism" as he weakly attempted to shift the blame for the depression away from his party and administration and toward world economic forces. "I was convinced that efficient, honest administration of the vast machine of the Federal government would appeal to all citizens," he later lamented. "I have since learned that efficient government does not interest the people as much as dramatics."

The President's inability to rekindle hopes for a quick recovery led to the widespread belief that Hoover was not attempting to stimulate recovery and that he was unconcerned about the widespread suffering. This, of course, was not the case and, within the past few years, historians have discovered a "new" Herbert Hoover—one who, although with enormous reluctance, unbalanced the budget, approved public works, provided governmental loans to business, and generally used the powers of the federal government in an

SOURCE. Carl N. Degler, "The Ordeal of Herbert Hoover," in *The Yale Review*, Vol. 52, Summer 1963, pp. 563–583. Copyright 1963 by Yale University. Reprinted by permission of *The Yale Review* and the author.

attempt to solve the paradox of widespread poverty in the midst of plenty. No previous President had ever assumed the responsibility of restoring prosperity in a time of depression.

Yet Hoover was also tied closely to the past and, in many ways, was a prisoner of an economic and political philosophy that had been created during the age of economic individualism. His policies certainly were inadequate, but most historians now admit that he at least labored mightily to reverse the downward plunge of the economy. Hoover, therefore, seems to be a transitional figure *in the White House—on the one hand, his philosophical assumptions look back to the simplistic economic individualism of Calvin Coolidge and William McKinley but, on the other hand, some of his policies anticipated the New Deal. In the following selection, Carl N. Degler, Professor of History at Stanford University, vividly describes the terrible "ordeal of Herbert Hoover."*

In 1958 Herbert Hoover published a book about his old chief entitled *The Ordeal of Woodrow Wilson*. Wilson's struggle for the League was short and his part in it has gained lustre with passing years. Not so with the ordeal of Herbert Hoover. The Great Depression was considerably longer and his reputation has never been free from the memory of that ordeal. Today, in fact, there are two Hoovers. The first is the living man, the former President who has unstintingly and very capably served Democratic and Republican Administrations alike. He is the Hoover of nation-wide birthday celebrations, of rhapsodic editorials, of admiring Republican national conventions. That conception bears almost no relation to the second, the historical Hoover. In the history books his Administration is usually depicted as cold-hearted, when not pictured as totally devoid of heart, inept, or actionless in the face of the Great Depression. Simply because of the wide gulf between the two Hoovers it is time to try to answer the question William Allen White posed over thirty years ago. Writing an evaluation of Hoover's Administration in the *Saturday Evening Post* of March 4, 1933, White closed his piece with following words: "So history stands hesitant waiting for time to tell whether Herbert Hoover . . . by pointing the way to social recovery . . . is the first of the new Presidents . . . or whether . . . he is the last of the old."

The notion of two Hoovers should never have grown up; his life and views were too consistent for that. During Hoover's tenure of office, Theodore Joslin, his press secretary, undertook to examine closely all the President's utterances and writings of the preceding ten or eleven years. "In all of those million-odd words, dealing with every important subject," Joslin reported in 1934, "the number of times he reversed himself or modified an important position could be counted on the fingers of one hand." And so it has remained even after March 4, 1933.

Nor were those principles, to which Hoover held so consistently, simply conservative ones, as has so often been assumed. In 1920, for example, when Hoover's political career began, he was the darling of the progressives who still clustered about the figure of the fallen Wilson. College and university faculties were calling upon Hoover to run for president that year—on either ticket. Indeed, his silence as to which party he belonged to, for a time caused his name to figure as prominently in Democratic primaries as in Republican. For example, he received the most votes by far in the Michigan Democratic primary that year. That year, too, Franklin Roosevelt, who was also a member of Woodrow Wilson's Administration, wrote Josephus Daniels that Herbert Hoover "is certainly a wonder, and I wish we could make him President of the United States. There could not be a better one." (Nor did Roosevelt's enthusiasm cool until much later. In 1928 he refused to write an article against Hoover's candidacy because Hoover was "an old personal friend.")

Hoover's principles were distinctly and publicly progressive. In 1920, for example, he defended the principle of collective bargaining and the right to strike—two very unpopular principles at that date—before a frosty Chamber of Commerce in Boston. As Secretary of Commerce in the Harding Administration he opposed the sweeping federal injunction against the railroad strikers and worked with Harding to have the steel industry abandon the twelve-hour day. In his book of guiding principles, *American Individualism*, which he published in 1922, he was careful to distinguish his views from laissez-faire capitalism. The American way, he insisted, "is not capitalism, or socialism, or syndicalism, nor a cross breed of them." It did include, though, government regulation in order to preserve equality of opportunity and individual rights. "This regulation is itself," he pointed out, "proof that we have gone a long way toward the abandonment of the 'capitalism' of Adam Smith. . . ." While Secretary of Commerce in the 1920's he instituted much needed regulations for the burgeoning radio and airplane industries. It was Herbert Hoover who said in 1922 at the first conference on radio that "the ether is a public medium and its use must be for the public benefit. The use of radio channels is justified only if there is public benefit. The dominant element of consideration in the radio field is, and always will be, the great body of the listening public, millions in number, country-wide in distribution." In the same address, he said, "It is inconceivable that we should allow so great a possibility for service to be drowned in advertising chatter." In 1928 he was recommending that a three billion dollar reserve of public works be built up to serve as an economic stabilizer in times of recession.

In short, though he served both Harding and Coolidge, Herbert Hoover was not of their stripe. As he himself said later in his memoirs, "Mr. Coolidge was a real conservative, probably the equal of Benjamin Harrison. . . .

He was a fundamentalist in religion, in the economic and social order, and in fishing." (The last because Coolidge, the fishing tyro, used worms for bait.) Moreover, unlike Coolidge, Hoover did not publicly ignore the scandals that rocked the Harding Administration. In June 1931, while dedicating the Harding Memorial at Marion, Ohio, Hoover went out of his way to speak of the tragedy of Warren Harding and of the enormity of the betrayal of a public trust by Harding's friends.

Hoover's record as president contains a number of truly progressive achievements. Although he cannot take credit for initiating the Norris-La Guardia Act of 1932, the fact remains that one of the most important prolabor acts in the whole history of American labor was signed by Herbert Hoover. Like other progressives, he sponsored legislation for conservation like the giant Boulder Dam project and the St. Lawrence Seaway.

But perhaps the most striking example of Hoover's willingness to recognize the new role of government in dealing with the complexities of an industrial economy was his breaking precedent to grapple directly with the Depression. From the outset Hoover rejected the advice of his Secretary of the Treasury, Andrew Mellon, who, as Hoover himself said, was a country-banker of narrow social vision. Mellon believed the crash should be permitted to run its course unmolested. His simple formula in a depression, as he told Hoover, was "Liquidate labor, liquidate stocks, liquidate farms, liquidate real estate." A panic, he told the President, was not so bad. "It will purge the rottenness out of the system. High costs of living and high living will come down. People will work harder, live more moral lives. Values will be adjusted, and enterprising people will pick up the wrecks from less competent people."

In contrast, Hoover's anti-depression action was swift in coming. Within a matter of weeks after the great crash of the stock market at the end of October, Hoover called a meeting of prominent business, labor, and farm leaders to work out plans for preventing the market crash from adversely affecting the rest of the economy. A week later he met for the same purpose with railway presidents. The economic leaders agreed to his plan of holding the line on wages and encouraging industrial expansion. In his annual message to Congress in December 1929, Hoover proudly told of these and other efforts his Administration had made to stem the economic decline. These efforts, he said, "must be vigorously pursued until normal conditions are restored." In January he continued to expand public works on Boulder Dam and on highway construction. By the end of July 1930, the Administration had got underway $800 million in public works and the President called upon the states and local units of government to follow the national government's example in order to provide as much employment as possible.

The President was well aware of the unprecedented character of his swift anti-depression action. He said as much in his message to Congress in December 1929; he made the same point more explicitly at the Gridiron dinner in April 1930. The country, he said, had avoided the dole and other unsatisfactory devices to meet unemployment by "voluntary cooperation of industry with the Government in maintaining wages against reductions, and the intensification of construction work. Thereby we have inaugurated one of the greatest economic experiments in history on a basis of nation-wide cooperation not charity."

At first Hoover was optimistic about the effects of his program. Several times during the first year he compared the economic decline with that of 1921–22, usually with the observation that the earlier one was the more difficult. As he told the Chamber of Commerce in May 1930, the amount of public works contracted for was already three times the amount in the corresponding period of the previous "great depression."

Yet his optimism did not keep him from action. One thing he emphasized was the necessity of learning from this Depression about the prevention of future ones. He advocated better statistical measures and reform of the banking structure to prevent the drain of credit from productive to speculative enterprise, such as had led to the stock market boom and crash. Moreover, although he emphasized from the beginning that the Depression was "worldwide" and that its "causes and its effects lie only partly in the United States," he did not use this as an excuse for inactivity. There was no need simply to wait for the rest of the world to recover, he said. "We can make a very large degree of recovery independently of what may happen elsewhere." In October 1930 he told the American Bankers Association that depressions were not simply to be borne uncomplainingly. "The economic fatalist believes that these crises are inevitable and bound to be recurrent. I would remind these pessimists that exactly the same thing was once said of typhoid, cholera, and smallpox." But instead of being pessimistic, medical science went to work and conquered those diseases. "That should be our attitude toward these economic pestilences. They are not dispensations of Providence. I am confident in the faith that their control, so far as the cause lies within our own boundaries, is within the genius of modern business."

Hoover also told the bankers that he could not condone the argument which had been reported from some of them that the people would have to accept a lower standard of living in order to get through the Depression. Such a suggestion, he said, could not be countenanced either on idealistic or on practical grounds. To accept it would mean a "retreat into perpetual unemployment and the acceptance of a cesspool of poverty for some large part of our people." Several times during the Depression Hoover made it clear that the government had a responsibility to employ as many as possible as its contribution to the mitigation of the unemployment which was growing alarmingly.

The failure of the economy to respond to treatment and the loss of many

Republican seats in the elections of 1930 caused Hoover for a while to place new emphasis upon the foreign sources of the Depression. At the end of 1930 he told the Congress that the "major forces of the depression now lie outside of the United States." In fact, though, the real collapse of the European economy was still almost six months away. Hoover was most fearful that the growing Congressional demands for new expenditures would throw the budget out of balance. His concern about the budget and his hostility toward the Congress were both measured in his tactless remark at a press conference in May 1931 that "I know of nothing that would so disturb the healing process now undoubtedly going on in the economic situation" as a special session of Congress. "We cannot legislate ourselves out of a world economic depression; we can and will work ourselves out."

The last sentence, because it was obviously too sweeping to be accurate, was to plague him for years. More important, he quite clearly did not believe it himself, since he later advocated legislation for just the purposes he said it could not serve. In the very next month, for example, he explained at some length to a group of Republican editors just how much the Administration had been doing to extricate the country from the Depression. "For the first time in history the Federal Government has taken an extensive and positive part in mitigating the effects of depression and expediting recovery. I have conceived that if we would preserve our democracy this leadership must take the part not of attempted dictatorship but of organizing cooperation in the constructive forces of the community and of stimulating every element of initiative and self-reliance in the country. There is no sudden stroke of either governmental or private action which can dissolve these world difficulties; patient, constructive action in a multitude of directions is the strategy of success. This battle is upon a thousand fronts." Unlike previous administrations, he continued, his had expanded, instead of curtailing, public works during a depression. Public works expenditures, both by the federal and state governments, he said, continued to increase. Some two billion dollars were being spent, and a million men were employed on these projects. Aid was also being given to farmers in the drought areas of the South and the Middle West.

That Hoover truly favored action over patient waiting for the storm to lift was further shown in his elaborate twelve-point program for recovery presented in his annual message in December 1931. Among his recommendations was the Reconstruction Finance Corporation, which would become one of the major agencies of his Administration and of the New Deal for stabilizing banks and aiding recovery. At a press conference the same month he emphasized anew the desirability of domestic action. "The major steps we must take are domestic. The action needed is in the home field and it is urgent. While reestablishment of stability abroad is helpful to us and to the world, and I am convinced that it is in progress, yet we must depend upon ourselves. If we devote ourselves to these urgent domestic questions we can make a very large measure of recovery irrespective of foreign influences." By early February 1932 the Reconstruction Finance Corporation was in operation. That same month he persuaded the Congress to enact the Glass-Steagall banking bill, which increased the bases for Federal Reserve bank reserves and thus expanded credit and conserved gold. The purpose of the RFC was to shore up failing banks and other financial institutions caught in runs upon their deposits. With the permission of the Interstate Commerce Commission, the RFC could also extend financial aid to railroads.

Beyond these operations, though, the President would not let the lending agency go. Especially did he resist federal aid to the unemployed, although the demands for it were growing monthly. He even opposed Congressional appropriations to the Red Cross on the ground that they would dry up private sources of relief funds. A dole, he said in 1931, must be avoided at all costs because "the net results of governmental doles are to lower wages toward the bare subsistence level and to endow the slacker." He did urge the citizenry generously to support, as he did himself, private charities, like the Red Cross, which were carrying so much of the burden of unemployment relief. At no time, of course, did Hoover object to helping the unemployed; he was no Social Darwinist arguing for the survival of only the fittest. Again and again, using the most idealistic language, he called upon Americans to extend a hand to those fellow citizens in need. But as much as he publicly and privately deplored the suffering which the economic crisis brought, he feared and deplored even more the effects which would be sure to follow if the federal government provided relief to the unemployed. Nowhere was the rigidity of Hoover's highly trained, agile, and well-stocked intellect more apparent than in this matter. Throughout his years as president, despite the cruelest of sarcastic barbs in the press and from the public platform, he held to his position.

Yet surprising as it may seem today, for a long time the country was with him. This was true even during 1931 and early 1932 when it was becoming increasingly evident that private charities, municipal relief funds, and even the resources of the states were inadequate to meet the costs of providing for ten or eleven million unemployed. Already in August 1931 Governor Franklin Roosevelt had told the New York legislature that unemployment relief "must be extended by government—not as a matter of charity but as a matter of social duty." Yet, as late as February 1932 the country was still following Hoover's view of relief and not Roosevelt's. This was shown by the fate of a bill sponsored by liberal Senators Robert M. La Follette, Jr. of Wisconsin and Edward F. Costigan of Colorado to provide federal money to the states for relief. The bill was defeated by a vote of 48 to 35. Democratic Senators made up some forty percent of the votes which killed the measure.

By May 1932, though, the pressure for some federal assistance in relief matters was building up fast. The National Conference of Social Workers, which in the previous year had refused to endorse the principle of federal relief, now switched to supporting it. More important from Hoover's standpoint was the announcement by Senator Joseph Robinson, the conservative Democratic leader in the Senate, that he was joining the liberals in favoring federal relief. Within two days the President announced, after consultation with Robinson, that the RFC would hereafter lend money to the states if their resources for relief were exhausted. The next day the President defended the extraordinary powers of the RFC as necessitated by the economic emergency. In words which sound in retrospect like those of his successor, he said, "We used such emergency powers to win the war; we can use them to fight the depression, the misery and suffering from which are equally great."

Soon thereafter, though, the President demonstrated that he would not take another step toward putting the federal government into the relief field. Two bills by Democrats which went beyond his limits were successfully vetoed. After Congress had adjourned in July 1932, he issued a nine-point program for economic recovery, but most of the items on it were old and the rest were only recommendations for exploratory conferences. By the summer of 1932, then, the Hoover program for recovery had been completed; his principles would permit him to go no further.

As one reviews the actions which Hoover took it is impossible to describe him as a do-nothing president. He was unquestionably one of the truly activist presidents of our history. But he was an activist within a very rigid framework of ideology. Of all American presidents, Herbert Hoover was probably the most singlemindedly committed to a system of beliefs. His pragmatism was well hidden and what there was of it emerged only after great prodding from events. To a remarkable degree, one can observe in his acts as president those principles of individualism which he set forth so simply in his book ten years before. The very same principle, for example, which prevented his sanctioning federal relief to the unemployed, dictated the tone and content of his veto of the bill to create a government corporation to operate Muscle Shoals. The government, he said, should not compete with private enterprise. Moreover, such a project, by being run by the federal government, abrogated the basic principle that all such enterprises should be "administrated by the people upon the ground, responsible to their own communities, directing them solely for the benefit of their communities and not for the purposes of social theories or national politics. Any other course deprives them of liberty." It was this same belief in individual freedom and cooperation which kept him from accepting a governmental system of old age and unemployment insurance. He advocated such measures only when undertaken voluntarily and through private insurance companies.

Even the Reconstruction Finance Corporation, perhaps his most enduring anti-depression agency, was created to assist private business, not to supplant it. True, it was a credit agency in competition with private enterprise, but it was designed to perform tasks which no private institution dared risk; the competition was therefore minimal if not nonexistent. Moreover, although it has been frequently alleged that the RFC lent money to corporations while the Administration denied relief to the unemployed, in Hoover's mind the distinction was crucial and real. The RFC was making loans which would be repaid—and most were—when the banks got back on their feet; it was not making grants. Even when Hoover did permit the RFC to lend money to the states for relief purposes he still insisted that no grants of federal funds be made.

But there was an even more important social justification for agencies like the RFC and the Federal Home Loan Board, which Congress created in July 1932 at the President's request. Hoover recognized as no president had before that the welfare of society was dependent upon business and that government, therefore, must step in. He did this, not because, as some critics said, he favored business over the common people, but because he recognized that if the banks failed the economy would collapse, savings would be lost, and jobs destroyed. The RFC and the Federal Home Loan Board, in effect, socialized the losses of financial institutions by using government to spread their obligations through society. Hoover was not prepared, though, to socialize the losses of the unemployed. That step in ameliorating the impact of the Depression was undertaken by the New Deal through the WPA and other relief agencies. In this respect Hoover was a transitional figure in the development of the government as an active force in the economy in times of depression. He was the first to smash the old shibboleth of government unconcern and impotence.

Perhaps his long-term role was even greater. In the face of great opposition and much outright hostility, he made a determined and even courageous effort to give the business community and voluntary private agencies a chance to show whether they could bring the nation out of a depression. Their failure to do so gave a moral as well as a political impetus to the New Deal. Just as after Munich no one could say the West had not done its utmost to meet Hitler halfway, so after Hoover's Administration no one could say that government had rushed in before other social or economic agencies had been given a try. That this was so goes a long way toward explaining the remarkable consensus among Americans ever since the 1930's that government has the prime responsibility for averting or cushioning the effects of a depression.

A second principle which stopped Hoover from permitting the federal government to provide relief was his conviction that the budget must not be unbalanced. As early as February 1930 he warned the Congress against extravagance and told of his own efforts to economize. Economy was essential, he emphasized, in order to avoid increasing taxes. But as decreasing revenues began to fall behind expenditures, Hoover's concern to keep the budget in balance overcame his reluctance to increase taxes. On July 1, 1931 the deficit was almost $500 million—an astronomical figure in those days when the total federal budget was less than $4 billion. In December of that same year Hoover recommended an increase in taxes. When Congress proved dilatory he told a press conference in March 1932 that a balanced budget "is the very keystone of recovery. It must be done." Anything less would undo all the recovery measures. "The Government," he warned, "no more than individual families can continue to expend more than it receives without inviting serious consequences."

Hoover recommended a manufacturers' sales tax as the chief new revenue device, in which suggestion he was joined by the new Democratic Speaker of the House, John Nance Garner of Texas. Garner enjoyed a reputation for being hostile to business and something of a radical in the old Populist tradition, but in the matter of bringing the budget into balance he stood four-square with the President. Congress did not pass the sales tax, but it did pass one of the largest peacetime tax increases in American history.

Today it seems incredible that in a time of economic slump when consumer purchasing power was the principal requirement for recovery, the nation should elect to take money out of the hands of consumers. Yet this was precisely what the bill recommended and signed by the Republican President and passed by the Democratic House, entailed. In fact, when in the course of the debate the House seemed hesitant about increasing taxes, the Democratic Speaker, John Garner, could not contain his anxiety. Conspicuously forsaking the Speaker's chair, Garner advanced to the well of the House to make an earnest plea for more taxes. At the conclusion of his speech, he asked "every man and every woman in this House who . . . is willing to try to balance the budget to rise in their seats." Almost the whole House, with its majority of Democrats, rose to its feet, to a growing round of applause. When he asked those who did not want to balance the budget to rise, no one did. The overwhelming majority of the newspapers of the country strongly commended the Congress in June 1932 for its efforts to balance the budget through increased taxes.

During the campaign of 1932 the Democrats continued to equal or even outdo Hoover in their slavish adherence to the ideal of a balanced budget. Franklin Roosevelt, for example, unmercifully attacked the Administration for its extravagance and its unbalanced budget, calling the fifty percent increase in expenditures since 1927 "the most reckless and extravagant past that I have been able to discover in the statistical record of any peacetime government anywhere, any time." He promised a cut of 25 percent in the budget if he were elected. Nor was this simply campaign oratory. As Frank

Freidel has observed in his biography, Roosevelt was perfectly sincere in his dismay at the Hoover deficit and he would continue to be regretful about deficits until well after 1933.

From the record, then, it is evident that Democrats were in no better theoretical position to deal with the Depression than Hoover. Leaders of both parties thought of the government as a large household whose accounts must be balanced if national bankruptcy were to be avoided. Neither party could conceive of the central role which government must play in the economy in an industrial society in time of depression. It would take the whole decade of the New Deal and the continuance of the Depression before that fact would be learned by leaders and people alike.

Despite his fixation on the question of the budget, Hoover's conception of the Depression was sophisticated, rational, and coherent; the remedies he suggested were equally so, given his assumptions. In trying to find a way out, Hoover placed most reliance on what modern economists would call the "expectations" of businessmen. If businessmen feel that times are good or at least that they are getting better, they will invest in new plant and equipment, which in turn will employ men and create purchasing power. In substance, the remedies Hoover offered were designed to raise the expectations of businessmen and to maintain purchasing power until the economy picked up again. His first step was securing agreement among businessmen to hold the line on wages in order to keep purchasing power from falling. (And, by and large, as a result of his efforts, wage rates did not fall until the middle of 1931, but employment did, with, unfortunately, the same effect.) A second step in his program was to use government to help out with public work projects and, when private agencies proved inadequate, to provide credit through agencies like the RFC and the Home Loan Board. Finally, as a third arrow in his anti-depression quiver, Hoover sought, through the prestige of his office, to create that sense of confidence and approaching good times which would encourage businessmen to invest. As it turned out, though, he gambled and lost. For with each successive ineffectual statement, the value of his words dropped, until, like the worthless coins of a profligate monarch who debases his own coinage, they were hurled back at his head by a disenchanted press and people.

The Hoover recovery program failed, but probably no government program then thought permissible could have been any more successful. Certainly the New Deal with its more massive injection of government money into the economy succeeded little better. It ended the decade with 9.5 million still unemployed, and industrial production remained below the 1929 level throughout the 1930's except for a brief period in late 1936 and early 1937. On the other hand, most of the countries of Western and Central Europe regained the 1929 level of production by early 1935.

Part of Hoover's ordeal during the Great Depression undoubtedly derived from his personality, which, for a president, was unusual. Indeed, until he became President he had rarely been connected with government other than in an office which was nonpartisan or which he soon made so. Outwardly, at least, he was far removed from the stereotype of the politician: he could not slap a back or utter a guffaw. He appeared shy in public, though stolid was a more accurate description. A bulky man of over 200 pounds, standing almost six feet when he entered the White House, he gave a paradoxical impression of conservative solidity and beaming youth at the same time. His public speech, like his writing, was formal, often stiff, and sometimes bordered on the pedantic. Early in Hoover's Administration, soon after the stock market crash, William Allen White, a Hoover supporter, spotted the new President's weakness. "The President has great capacity to convince intellectuals," he wrote, "He has small capacity to stir people emotionally and through the emotions one gets to the will, not through the intellect." Even Hoover's press secretary recognized that he "experienced the greatest difficulty in interpreting himself and his acts to the public." Indeed, it was characteristic of Hoover that though he found speech writing one of the most laborious of his tasks, he insisted upon writing all his own speeches. The compulsion could be at least enervating, and at worst dangerous to his health. Often he traded sleep for time to work on his speeches and at least once, at St. Paul in the campaign of 1932, he was on the verge of collapse from fatigue. His method of writing was tedious and incredibly time-consuming, involving innumerable drafts, meticulously gone over by himself, only to have still further proofs run off for more rewriting. Yet, after all this effort, his final draft usually was dry, too long, and ponderous.

In view of his poor public image, it is not surprising that for most of his presidency, Hoover's relations with the press were strained when not downright painful. Although he continued the press conferences which Wilson had begun, they were formal affairs with written questions; many reporters were convinced that the President concealed more than he revealed in the meetings. But it was probably Hoover's sensitivity to criticism that worked the real damage. His annual addresses to newspapermen at the Gridiron Club, which, as was customary, mercilessly lampooned his administration, often carried an edge, betraying his sensitivity to the press corps' jibes. Only occasionally did his private wit break through in public. At the Gridiron Club dinner in December 1932, after his defeat for reelection, he puckishly said, "You will expect me to discuss the late election. Well, as nearly as I can learn, we did not have enough votes on our side. During the campaign I remarked that this Administration had been fighting on a thousand fronts; I learned since the campaign that we were fighting on 21 million fronts." (The size of the Democratic vote.) This was one of the rare times that Hoover poked fun at himself in public.

Yet, despite his difficulties as a public figure, in private Hoover was neither phlegmatic nor shy. In fact he was extremely convivial, seeking constant company, whether at the White House or at his retreat on the Rapidan in the Blue Ridge Mountains. His wife told Joslin that the President could not be happy without numbers of people around him. His friends cherished his constant flow of stories and he delighted in his cigars and pipe. He was an outdoor type of man, reveling in fishing and hiking. Although he liked a joke, he rarely laughed out loud, though his friends knew well his soft chuckle. His own brand of humor could be heavy-handed. Thus in January 1931, when addressing the National Automobile Chamber of Commerce, he observed, with a smile, that 3.5 million cars had been sold in the first year of the depression and that consumption of gasoline was up five percent. "This certainly means," he twitted, "that we have been cheerful in the use of automobiles; I do not assume they are being used for transportation to the poorhouse. While I am aware that many people are using the old automobile a little longer it is obvious that they are still using it and it is being worn out. Altogether the future for the industry does not warrant any despondency." Will Rogers was not so sure. Some months later in a radio broadcast, he drawled, "We are the first nation in the history of the world to go to the poorhouse in an automobile."

Part of the reason Hoover resented the barbed comments of the press was that he worked so hard. It was as characteristic of Herbert Hoover that he was the first president to have a telephone on his desk as it was characteristic of Calvin Coolidge that he refused to have one. Hoover rose at 6 A.M. each morning, joined a group of his friends for a brisk half-hour session with a five pound medicine ball on an improvised court on the White House grounds, then went in to breakfast. He was at his desk by 8:30. He worked steadily all day, smoking incessantly, and usually well into the night. Often he would wake up in the middle of the night and pore over papers or write for an hour or two before going back to sleep. Nevertheless, he rose at the same early hour. Subordinates were not always able to keep up with his pace; some had to be dispatched to rest, but Hoover, miraculously, never succumbed to his self-imposed regimen. His secretary reports that he was not sick a single day of the four years he spent in the White House. A few days at the camp on the Rapidan or a short trip usually sufficed to restore his energies and his will to work. But toward the end of his tenure, even the optimism and strength of a Hoover faltered, at least once. He told his secretary, "All the money in the world could not induce me to live over the last nine months. The conditions we have experienced make this office a compound hell."

Aside from the circumstances in which he found himself as President, one of the reasons the office was "hell" was that Hoover was a poor politician. Often it is said that he did not like politics, or even that he was above politics.

Both statements describe the image he held of himself, but many of Hoover's actions while in office are clearly partisan and political. If, for example, he could objectively recognize the weaknesses of the Harding Administration once he was elected president, he could also say during the campaign of 1928 that "the record of the seven and one years" of Coolidge and Harding "constitutes a period of rare courage in leadership and constructive action. Never has a political party been able to look back upon a similar period with more satisfaction." In December 1931, when some voices were calling for a coalition government to deal with the worsening depression, Hoover made it clear that he would have nothing to do with Democrats. "The day that we begin coalition government you may know that our democracy has broken down," he told newspapermen at a Gridiron Club dinner. On the other hand, he could appoint Democrats to office, as he did former Senator Atlee Pomerene to head the RFC when he wanted that office to win support from Democrats. Nor was he devoid of political dramatics. In September 1931 he made a quick descent upon the American Legion Convention in Detroit in a successful effort to stop the Legion from going on record in favor of a bonus for veterans. By going all the way to Detroit, speaking for eleven minutes, and then immediately leaving for Washington again, he demonstrated the importance of his message and the weight of the schedule of work he pursued in Washington. Moreover, as the account written by his Press Secretary Joslin makes clear, he was no more above benefiting from parliamentary trickery in Congress than the next politically-minded president. As Joslin wrote, "It was characteristic of the President to hit back when attacked." Hoover suffered deeply when attacked, and he did not turn the other cheek. As William Allen White, who supported and admired the President, wrote in 1933, "he was no plaster saint politically. He had, during his three years, rather consistently and with a nice instinct chosen to honor in public office men of a conservative type of mind." Moreover, the behind-the-scenes circumstances of his nomination in 1928 and his renomination in 1932, both of which were steam-roller operations, should remove any doubts about his willingness and ability to use devices and tactics quite customary in politics.

No, it was not that he was above politics or that he really despised the operations of politicians. His difficulty was that he was temperamentally incapable of doing what a politician has to do—namely, to admit he could be wrong and to compromise. In the whole volume of his memoirs devoted to the Depression there is not a single mention of a major error on his part, though his opponents are taxed with errors in every chapter. Over a hundred pages of the volume are devoted to the answering of every charge of Franklin Roosevelt in 1932. Nowhere, though, does he notice that in 1932, he himself in his speech at Detroit incorrectly quoted Roosevelt and then proceeded to criticize at length his opponent for something he never said. This inability to admit error, to compromise, William Allen White recognized in 1931 as Hoover's undoing. After all, White wrote, "Politics . . . is one of the minor branches of harlotry, and Hoover's frigid desire to live a virtuous life and not follow the Pauline maxim and be all things to all men, is one of the things that has reduced the oil in his machinery and shot a bearing. . . ." Hoover's inability to admit error and the seriousness with which he viewed himself are both illustrated in another incident during the campaign of 1932. One of the Democrats' favorite sports that year was recalling, with appropriate sounds of derision, Hoover's remarks in 1928 to the effect that the United States was well on the way to abolishing poverty. Hoover, instead of admitting he had been somewhat optimistic, once again donned his hair shirt and stolidly endorsed the earlier statement because, as he said, it expressed the ideals for which Americans stood. Yet this was in the middle of the Depression and he was running for reelection.

In good times, Herbert Hoover's humble birth might have been an asset, but in the Great Depression it was not. Left an almost penniless orphan at nine, Hoover became a world figure and a millionaire before he was forty-five. With such spectacular success behind him it was understandable that he should think, albeit mistakenly, that anyone could achieve at least half as much as he. Undoubtedly his own experience fostered his insistence, throughout his life, that individual initiative was the prime motive force in a good society. What to other men appear as obstacles or handicaps, to the self-made man appear, at least in retrospect, as goads or incentives. Like most such men, Hoover attributed his success to will. When Theodore Joslin once asked him what had been his boyhood ambition, he replied without hesitation, "to be able to earn my own living without the help of anybody, anywhere." To such a man individual effort seems capable of moving mountains unaided; he is loath to see it shunted aside by collective action even in times of economic dislocation. The self-made man can indeed be the wrong man at such times.

Nor was it an accident that the other prominent self-made politician of the time, Alfred E. Smith, was also doubtful about the virtues of government aid to the unemployed, that he should attack Franklin Roosevelt for accusing the Hoover Administration of aiding the corporations and ignoring the poor. "I will take off my coat and vest," Smith vowed in the spring of 1932, "and fight to the end against any candidate who persists in any demagogic appeal to the masses of the working people of this country to destroy themselves by setting class against class and rich against poor." In a short time, Smith's views, like Hoover's, would bring him to outright opposition to the New Deal. It is not without significance in this respect that Roosevelt, who came to represent government benevolence toward the unemployed, was no self-made man, but lived securely and unadventurously on inherited wealth.

The differences in social origins of Roosevelt and Hoover, of course, are only one facet of the divergence between the Hoover Administration and the New Deal. Indeed, since the 1930's it has become commonplace to see Hoover and Roosevelt as opposites. Certainly there are differences—and important ones—between the administrations of the two Presidents, but we are now far enough removed from both to recognize also the real continuity between them that William Allen White was prescient enough to forsee dimly. When the two administrations are seen against the backdrop of previous administrations and earlier social attitudes, the gulf between them shrinks appreciably. Both men, it is worth recalling, were protégés of Woodrow Wilson; both of them, therefore, accepted a role for government in the economy which added up to a sharp departure from laissez-faire. Both, in the course of their respective administrations, drew upon their experiences in the First World War, where they had seen government intervening in the economy. Hoover's RFC, for example, was frankly modeled, as he said, after the War Finance Corporation. Both saw big business standing in need of controls, and, for a while, both believed that cooperation between business and government was the best way to achieve that control. Hoover, for instance, cited the Federal Reserve System as the ideal kind of business and government cooperation for purposes of regulating the economy; Roosevelt in the NRA also placed his trust in controls worked out through business and government cooperation. Moreover, both Roosevelt and Hoover took the view that it was government's responsibility to do something about a depression; neither man was willing to subscribe to the view which prevailed before 1929—namely, that economic declines were simply natural phenomena through which the nation struggled as best it could and that government could not be expected to do much about them.

Finally, it is also worth noticing that the temperament of the two men, their conceptions of America and of its future are much closer than the conventional picture paints them. (It was Roosevelt, during the campaign of 1932, who created the erroneous image of Hoover as the man without faith or hope in the future.) All through the Depression, Hoover's unvarying theme was that all this would pass and the essential vigor of the American economy would reassert itself. Undoubtedly he counted too heavily on the influence of his words to overcome the lack of business confidence, but there is no question of his optimistic outlook. One measure of it was the shock he received when he read Roosevelt's address to the Commonwealth Club in San Francisco. That was the speech in which Roosevelt talked about the frontier being ended and opportunities for economic growth being limited. Hoover took up the challenge, denying "the whole idea that we have ended the advance of America, that this country has reached the zenith of its power, the height of its development. That is the counsel of despair for the future of America.

That is not the spirit by which we shall emerge from this depression." The important point is that such pessimism was really not expressive of Roosevelt's thought, either. Although historians have frequently referred to the Commonwealth Club address as the one clear indication during the campaign of 1932 of the philosophy behind the New Deal, we now know that the speech was neither written by Roosevelt, nor read by him before he appeared before his audience. As Rexford Tugwell has pointed out, the Commonwealth Club address, which Berle and he wrote, did not reflect Roosevelt's true attitude toward the American economic future. Indeed, its very singularity among Roosevelt's campaign speeches demonstrates how foreign it was to Roosevelt's feelings and convictions. The speech belied his abundant enthusiasm for the future, and his deep faith in the country and its capacities. Moreover, he soon contradicted its import in his Inaugural Address, when he electrified the country with the cry, "All we have to fear is fear itself."

How ironical that these words of Roosevelt should be so well known, when it was Herbert Hoover who all along had been saying the same thing—in less graphic and less credible language, to be sure—but saying it nonetheless. That fact, too, contributed to the ordeal of Herbert Hoover.

2. WILLIAM E. LEUCHTENBURG, "THE ¹⁴ ROOSEVELT RECONSTRUCTION: RETROSPECT"

"IT may be that an unprecedented demand and need for undelayed action may call for temporary departure from that normal balance of public procedure," Franklin D. Roosevelt told the American people in his first Inaugural Address. Such a departure, he said, might be necessary to deal with the present emergency: "I am prepared under my constitutional duty to recommend the measures that a stricken Nation in the midst of a stricken world may require. These measures, or such other measures as the Congress may build out of its experience and wisdon, I shall seek, within my constitutional authority. . . . But in the event that the Congress shall fail to take one of these two courses . . . I shall not evade the clear course of duty that will then confront me. I shall ask the Congress for the one remaining instrument to meet the crisis—broad

SOURCE. William E. Leuchtenburg, *Franklin D. Roosevelt and the New Deal, 1932–1940*, New York: Harper & Row, 1963, pp. 326–348. Copyright 1963 by William E. Leuchtenburg. Reprinted by permission of Harper & Row, Publishers and the author.

Executive power to wage a war against the emergency, as great as the power that would be given to me if we were in fact invaded by a foreign foe. . . ."

Just how far and in what manner the New Deal actually departed from tradition has been a major interpretative question for students of the 1930's. Was the New Deal really new, or did it represent merely a logical extension of previously accepted themes and policies of American life?

Those historians who tend to emphasize the evolutionary character of the New Deal point to the protest movements of the late nineteenth century as the seedbed of the New Deal. The depression, they say, merely crystallized the many forces that had been in operation for more than a half century. Out of the ferment of the post-Civil War era came the early stirrings of organized labor, the first halting attempts to regulate business under the Interstate Commerce Act (1887) and the Sherman Anti-Trust Act (1890), and the turbulent Populist movement which saw important segments of the agricultural community assert their demands for wide-sweeping reform. Perhaps most important was the emergence of a strong intellectual movement that successfully challenged the existing order. All of this contributed to the Progressive Era, during which time reform crested at high tide as the determined reformers sought to improve their society. To these historians, the New Deal was the logical culmination of an orderly evolution of a reform movement that had always had as its goal the maintenance of individual liberty and opportunity within an urban and industrial society.

Several prominent scholars, however, strongly disagree with this interpretation. The New Deal, they contend, wrought such fundamental changes in basic governmental policy that it constitutes a "watershed" in American life. The New Deal, Carl Degler has written, was "a revolutionary response to a revolutionary situation." Pointing to several basic discrepancies between the progressive movement and the New Deal, Richard Hofstadter has forcefully argued that the New Deal was a "new departure" in American public policy.

William Leuchtenburg's distinguished history of the New Deal provides one of the best summaries of the "revolutionary" interpretation. Fully aware of the subtleties involved, he readily acknowledges that, "Not only did the New Deal borrow many ideas and institutions from the Progressive era, but the New Dealers and the progressives shared more postulates and values than is commonly supposed. Nevertheless, the spirit of the 1930's seems to me to be quite different from that of the Progressive era." Professor Leuchtenburg's discussion of "The Roosevelt Reconstruction" provides a lucid and sophisticated analysis of the impact of the New Deal on American life.

In eight years, Roosevelt and the New Dealers had almost revolutionized the agenda of American politics. "Mr. Roosevelt may have given the wrong answers to many of his problems," concluded the editors of *The Economist*.

"But he is at least the first President of modern America who has asked the right questions." In 1932, men of acumen were absorbed to an astonishing degree with such questions as prohibition, war debts, and law enforcement. By 1936, they were debating social security, the Wagner Act, valley authorities, and public housing. The thirties witnessed a rebirth of issues politics, and parties split more sharply on ideological lines than they had in many years past. "I incline to think that for years up to the present juncture thinking Democrats and thinking Republicans had been divided by an imaginary line," reflected a Massachusetts congressman in 1934. "Now for the first time since the period before the Civil War we find vital principles at stake." Much of this change resulted simply from the depression trauma, but much too came from the force of Roosevelt's personality and his use of his office as both pulpit and lectern. "Of course you have fallen into some errors—that is human," former Supreme Court Justice John Clarke wrote the President, "but you have put a new face upon the social and political life of our country."

Franklin Roosevelt re-created the modern Presidency. He took an office which had lost much of its prestige and power in the previous twelve years and gave it an importance which went well beyond what even Theodore Roosevelt and Woodrow Wilson had done. Clinton Rossiter has observed: "Only Washington, who made the office, and Jackson, who remade it, did more than [Roosevelt] to raise it to its present condition of strength, dignity, and independence." Under Roosevelt, the White House became the focus of all government—the fountainhead of ideas, the initiator of action, the representative of the national interest.

Roosevelt greatly expanded the President's legislative functions. In the nineteenth century, Congress had been jealous of its prerogatives as the lawmaking body, and resented any encroachment on its domain by the Chief Executive. Woodrow Wilson and Theodore Roosevelt had broken new ground in sending actual drafts of bills to Congress and in using devices like the caucus to win enactment of measures they favored. Franklin Roosevelt made such constant use of these tools that he came to assume a legislative role not unlike that of a prime minister. He sent special messages to Congress, accompanied them with drafts of legislation prepared by his assistants, wrote letters to committee chairmen or members of Congress to urge passage of the proposals, and authorized men like Corcoran to lobby as presidential spokesmen on the Hill. By the end of Roosevelt's tenure in the White House, Congress looked automatically to the Executive for guidance; it expected the administration to have a "program" to present for consideration.

Roosevelt's most important formal contribution was his creation of the Executive Office of the President on September 8, 1939. Executive Order 8248, a "nearly unnoticed but none the less epoch-making event in the history of American institutions," set up an Executive Office staffed with six administrative assistants with a "passion for anonymity." In 1939, the President not only placed obvious agencies like the White House Office in the Executive Office but made the crucial decision to shift the Bureau of the Budget from the Treasury and put it under his wing. In later years, such pivotal agencies as the Council of Economic Advisors, the National Security Council, and the Central Intelligence Agency would be moved into the Executive Office of the President. Roosevelt's decision, Rossiter has concluded, "converts the Presidency into an instrument of twentieth-century government; it gives the incumbent a sporting chance to stand the strain and fulfill his constitutional mandate as a one-man branch of our three-part government; it deflates even the most forceful arguments, which are still raised occasionally, for a plural executive; it assures us that the Presidency will survive the advent of the positive state. Executive Order 8248 may yet be judged to have saved the Presidency from paralysis and the Constitution from radical amendment."

Roosevelt's friends have been too quick to concede that he was a poor administrator. To be sure, he found it difficult to discharge incompetent aides, he procrastinated about decisions, and he ignored all the canons of sound administration by giving men overlapping assignments and creating a myriad of agencies which had no clear relation to the regular departments of government. But if the test of good administration is not an impeccable organizational chart but creativity, then Roosevelt must be set down not merely as a good administrator, but as a resourceful innovator. The new agencies he set up gave a spirit of excitement to Washington that the routinized old-line departments could never have achieved. The President's refusal to proceed through channels, however vexing at times to his subordinates, resulted in a competition not only among men but among ideas, and encouraged men to feel that their own beliefs might win the day. "You would be surprised, Colonel, the remarkable ideas that have been turned loose just because men have felt that they can get a hearing," one senator confided. The President's "procrastination" was his own way both of arriving at a sense of national consensus and of reaching a decision by observing a trial by combat among rival theories. Periods of indecision—as in the spring of 1935 or the beginning of 1938—were inevitably followed by a fresh outburst of new proposals.

Most of all, Roosevelt was a successful administrator because he attracted to Washington thousands of devoted and highly skilled men. Men who had been fighting for years for lost causes were given a chance: John Collier, whom the President courageously named Indian Commissioner; Arthur Powell Davis, who had been ousted as chief engineer of the Department of the Interior at the demand of power interests; old conservationists like Harry Slattery, who had fought the naval oil interests in the Harding era. When Harold Ickes took office as Secretary of the Interior, he looked up Louis

Glavis—he did not even know whether the "martyr" of the Ballinger-Pinchot affair was still alive—and appointed him to his staff.

The New Dealers displayed striking ingenuity in meeting problems of governing. They coaxed salmon to climb ladders at Bonneville; they sponsored a Young Choreographers Laboratory in the WPA's Dance Theatre; they gave the pioneer documentary film maker Pare Lorentz the opportunity to create his classic films *The Plow That Broke the Plains* and *The River*. At the Composers Forum-Laboratory of the Federal Music Project, William Schuman received his first serious hearing. In Arizona, Father Berard Haile of St. Michael's Mission taught written Navajo to the Indians. Roosevelt, in the face of derision from professional foresters and prairie states' governors, persisted in a bold scheme to plant a mammoth "shelterbelt" of parallel rows of trees from the Dakotas to the Panhandle. In all, more than two hundred million trees were planted—cottonwood and willow, hackberry and cedar, Russian olive and Osage orange; within six years, the President's visionary windbreak had won over his former critics. The spirit behind such innovations generated a new excitement about the potentialities of government. "Once again," Roosevelt told a group of young Democrats in April, 1936, "the very air of America is exhilarating."

Roosevelt dominated the front pages of the newspapers as no other President before or since has done. "Frank Roosevelt and the NRA have taken the place of love nests," commented Joe Patterson, publisher of the tabloid New York *Daily News*. At his very first press conference, Roosevelt abolished the written question and told reporters they could interrogate him without warning. Skeptics predicted the free and easy exchange would soon be abandoned, but twice a week, year in and year out, he threw open the White House doors to as many as two hundred reporters, most of them representing hostile publishers, who would crowd right up to the President's desk to fire their questions. The President joshed them, traded wisecracks with them, called them by their first names; he charmed them by his good-humored ease and impressed them with his knowledge of detail. To a degree, Roosevelt's press conference introduced, as some observers claimed, a new institution like Britain's parliamentary questioning; more to the point, it was a device the President manipulated, disarmingly and adroitly, to win support for his program. It served too as a classroom to instruct the country in the new economics and the new politics.

Roosevelt was the first president to master the technique of reaching people directly over the radio. In his fireside chats, he talked like a father discussing public affairs with his family in the living room. As he spoke, he seemed unconscious of the fact that he was addressing millions. "His head would nod and his hands would move in simple, natural, comfortable gestures," Frances Perkins recalled. "His face would smile and light up as though he were actually sitting on the front porch or in the parlor with them." Eleanor Roosevelt later observed that after the President's death people would stop her on the street to say "they missed the way the President used to talk to them. They'd say 'He used to talk to me about my government.' There was a real dialogue between Franklin and the people," she reflected. "That dialogue seems to have disappeared from the government since he died."

For the first time for many Americans, the federal government became an institution that was directly experienced. More than state and local governments, it came to be *the* government, an agency directly concerned with their welfare. It was the source of their relief payments; it taxed them directly for old age pensions; it even gave their children hot lunches in school. As the role of the state changed from that of neutral arbiter to a "powerful promoter of society's welfare," people felt an interest in affairs in Washington they had never had before.

Franklin Roosevelt personified the state as protector. It became common-place to say that people felt toward the President the kind of trust they would normally express for a warm and understanding father who comforted them in their grief or safeguarded them from harm. An insurance man reported: "My mother looks upon the President as someone so immediately concerned with her problems and difficulties that she would not be greatly surprised were he to come to her house some evening and stay for dinner." From his first hours in office, Roosevelt gave people the feeling that they could confide in him directly. As late as the Presidency of Herbert Hoover, one man, Ira Smith, had sufficed to take care of all the mail the White House received. Under Roosevelt, Smith had to acquire a staff of fifty people to handle the thousands of letters written to the President each week. Roosevelt gave people a sense of membership in the national community. Justice Douglas has written: "He was in a very special sense the people's President, because he made them feel that with him in the White House they shared the Presidency. The sense of sharing the Presidency gave even the most humble citizen a lively sense of belonging."

When Roosevelt took office, the country, to a very large degree, responded to the will of a single element: the white, Anglo-Saxon, Protestant property-holding class. Under the New Deal, new groups took their place in the sun. It was not merely that they received benefits they had not had before but that they were "recognized" as having a place in the commonwealth. At the beginning of the Roosevelt era, charity organizations ignored labor when seeking "community" representation; at the end of the period, no fund-raising committee was complete without a union representative. While Theodore Roosevelt had founded a lily-white Progressive party in the South and Woodrow Wilson had introduced segregation into the federal government, Franklin Roosevelt had quietly brought the Negro into the New Deal coalition. When the distinguished Negro contralto Marian Anderson was

denied a concert hall in Washington, Secretary Ickes arranged for her to perform from the steps of Lincoln Memorial. Equal representation for religious
groups became so well accepted that, as one priest wryly complained, one
never saw a picture of a priest in a newspaper unless he was flanked on either
side by a minister and a rabbi.

The devotion Roosevelt aroused owed much to the fact that the New Deal
assumed the responsibility for guaranteeing every American a minimum
standard of subsistence. Its relief programs represented an advance over the
barbaric predepression practices that constituted a difference not in degree
but in kind. One analyst wrote: "During the ten years between 1929 and
1939 more progress was made in public welfare and relief than in the three
hundred years after this country was first settled." The Roosevelt administration gave such assistance not as a matter of charity but of right. This system of social rights was written into the Social Security Act. Other New Deal
legislation abolished child labor in interstate commerce and, by putting a
floor under wages and a ceiling on hours, all but wiped out the sweatshop.

Roosevelt and his aides fashioned a government which consciously sought
to make the industrial system more humane and to protect workers and their
families from exploitation. In his acceptance speech in June 1936, the
President stated: "Governments can err, Presidents do make mistakes, but
the immortal Dante tells us that divine justice weighs the sins of the cold-
blooded and the sins of the warm-hearted in different scales.

"Better the occasional faults of a Government that lives in a spirit of
charity than the constant omission of a Government frozen in the ice of its
own indifference." Nearly everyone in the Roosevelt government was caught
up to some degree by a sense of participation in something larger than themselves. A few days after he took office, one of the more conservative New Deal
administrators wrote in his diary: "This should be a Gov't of humanity."

The federal government expanded enormously in the Roosevelt years.
The crisis of the depression dissipated the distrust of the state inherited from
the eighteenth century and reinforced in diverse ways by the Jeffersonians
and the Spencerians. Roosevelt himself believed that liberty in America was
imperiled more by the agglomerations of private business than by the state.
The New Dealers were convinced that the depression was the result not simply of an economic breakdown but of a political collapse; hence, they sought
new political instrumentalities. The reformers of the 1930's accepted almost
unquestioningly the use of coercion by the state to achieve reforms. Even
Republicans who protested that Roosevelt's policies were snuffing out liberty
voted overwhelmingly in favor of coercive measures.

This elephantine growth of the federal government owed much to the
fact that local and state governments had been tried in the crisis and found
wanting. When one magazine wired state governors to ask their views, only

one of the thirty-seven who replied announced that he was willing to have the states resume responsibility for relief. Every time there was a rumored cutback of federal spending for relief, Washington was besieged by delegations of mayors protesting that city governments did not have the resources to meet the needs of the unemployed.

Even more dramatic was the impotence of local governments in dealing with crime, a subject that captured the national imagination in a decade of kidnapings and bank holdups. In September, 1933, the notorious bank robber John Dillinger was arrested in Ohio. Three days later, his confederates released him from jail and killed the Lima, Ohio, sheriff. In January, 1934, after bank holdups at Racine, Wisconsin, and East Chicago, Indiana, Dillinger was apprehended in Tucson, Arizona, and returned to the "escape-proof" jail of Crown Point, Indiana, reputedly the strongest county prison in the country. Within two days he had bluffed his way out with a wooden gun he had whittled and had driven off in the sheriff's car. While five thousand law officers pursued him, he stopped for a haircut in a barber shop, bought cars, and had a home-cooked Sunday dinner with his family in his home town. When he needed more arms, he raided the police station at Warsaw, Indiana.

Dillinger's exploits touched off a national outcry for federal action. State and local authorities could not cope with gangs which crossed and recrossed jurisdictional lines, which were equipped with Thompson submachine guns and high-powered cars, and which had a regional network of informers and fences in the Mississippi Valley. Detection and punishment of crime had always been a local function; now there seemed no choice but to call in the federal operatives. In July, 1934, federal agents shot down Dillinger outside a Chicago theater. In October, FBI men killed Pretty Boy Floyd near East Liverpool, Ohio; in November, they shot Baby Face Nelson, Public Enemy No. 1, near Niles Center, Illinois. By the end of 1934, the nation had a new kind of hero: the G-man Melvin Purvis and the chief of the Division of Investigation of the Department of Justice, J. Edgar Hoover. By the end of that year, too, Congress had stipulated that a long list of crimes would henceforth be regarded as federal offenses, including not only kidnaping but holding up a bank insured by the Federal Deposit Insurance Corporation. The family of a kidnaped victim could call in the federal police simply by phoning National 7117 in Washington.

Under the New Deal, the federal government greatly extended its power over the economy. By the end of the Roosevelt years, few questioned the right of the government to pay the farmer millions in subsidies not to grow crops, to enter plants to conduct union elections, to regulate business enterprises from utility companies to air lines, or even to compete directly with business by generating and distributing hydroelectric power. All of these powers had been ratified by the Supreme Court, which had even held that a man growing grain solely for his own use was affecting interstate commerce and hence subject to federal penalties. The President, too, was well on his way to becoming "the chief economic engineer," although this was not finally established until the Full Employment Act of 1946. In 1931, Hoover had hooted that some people thought "that by some legerdemain we can legislate ourselves out of a world-wide depression." In the Roosevelt era, the conviction that government both should and could act to forestall future breakdowns gained general acceptance. The New Deal left a large legacy of antidepression controls—securities regulation, banking reforms, unemployment compensation—even if it could not guarantee that a subsequent administration would use them.

In the 1930's, the financial center of the nation shifted from Wall Street to Washington. In May, 1934, a writer reported: "Financial news no longer originates in Wall Street." That same month, *Fortune* commented on a revolution in the credit system which was "one of the major historical events of the generation." "Mr. Roosevelt," it noted, "seized the Federal Reserve without firing a shot." The federal government had not only broken down the old separation of bank and state in the Reserve system but had gone into the credit business itself in a wholesale fashion under the aegis of the RFC, the Farm Credit Administration, and the housing agencies. Legislation in 1933 and 1934 had established federal regulation of Wall Street for the first time. No longer could the New York Stock Exchange operate as a private club free of national supervision. In 1935, Congress leveled the mammoth holding-company pyramids and centralized yet more authority over the banking system in the federal government. . . .

Despite this encroachment of government on traditional business prerogatives, the New Deal could advance impressive claims to being regarded as a "savior of capitalism." Roosevelt's sense of the land, of family, and of the community marked him as a man with deeply ingrained conservative traits. . . . Yet such considerations should not obscure the more important point: that the New Deal, however conservative it was in some respects and however much it owed to the past, marked a radically new departure. As Carl Degler writes: "The conclusion seems inescapable that, traditional as the words may have been in which the New Deal expressed itself, in actuality it was a revolutionary response to a revolutionary situation." . . .

Unlike the earlier Progressive, the New Dealer shied away from being thought of as sentimental. Instead of justifying relief as a humanitarian measure, the New Dealers often insisted it was necessary to stimulate purchasing power or to stabilize the economy or to "conserve manpower." The justification for a better distribution of income was neither "social justice" nor a "healthier national life," wrote Adolf Berle. "It remained for the hard-boiled student to work out the simple equation that unless the national income was pretty widely diffused there were not enough customers to keep the plants going." The reformers of the thirties abandoned—or claimed they had abandoned—the old Emersonian hope of reforming man and sought only to change institutions. This meant that they did not seek to "uplift" the people they were helping but only to improve their economic position. "In other words," Tugwell stated bluntly, "the New Deal is attempting to do nothing to *people*, and does not seek at all to alter their way of life, their wants and desires."

Reform in the 1930's meant *economic* reform; it departed from the Methodist-parsonage morality of many of the earlier Progressives, in part because much of the New Deal support, and many of its leaders, derived from urban immigrant groups hostile to the old Sabbatarianism. While the progressive grieved over the fate of the prostitute, the New Dealer would have placed Mrs. Warren's profession under a code authority. If the archetypical progressive was Jane Addams singing "Onward, Christian Soldiers," the representative New Dealer was Harry Hopkins betting on the horses at Laurel Race Track. When directing FERA in late 1933, Hopkins announced: "I would like to provide orchestras for beer gardens to encourage people to sit around drinking their beer and enjoying themselves. It would be a great unemployment relief measure." "I feel no call to remedy evils," Raymond Moley declared. "I have not the slightest urge to be a reformer. Social workers make me very weary. They have no sense of humor."

Despite Moley's disclaimer, many of the early New Dealers like himself and Adolf Berle did, in fact, hope to achieve reform through regeneration: the regeneration of the businessman. By the end of 1935, the New Dealers were pursuing a quite different course. Instead of attempting to evangelize the Right, they mobilized massive political power against the power of the corporation. They relied not on converting industrial sinners but in using sufficient coercion. New Dealers like Thurman Arnold sought to ignore "moral" considerations altogether; Arnold wished not to punish wrongdoers but to achieve price flexibility. His "faith" lay in the expectation that "fanatical alignments between opposing political principles may disappear and a competent, practical, opportunistic governing class may rise to power." With such expectations, the New Dealers frequently had little patience with legal restraints that impeded action. "I want to assure you," Hopkins told the NYA Advisory Committee, "that we are not afraid of exploring anything within the law, and we have a lawyer who will declare anything you want to do legal."

In the thirties, nineteenth-century individualism gave ground to a new emphasis on social security and collective action. In the twenties, America hailed Lindbergh as the Lone Eagle; in the thirties, when word arrived that

Amelia Earhart was lost at sea, the *New Republic* asked the government to prohibit citizens from engaging in such "useless" exploits. The NRA sought to drive newsboys off the streets and took a Blue Eagle away from a company in Huck Finn's old town of Hannibal, Missouri, because a fifteen-year-old was found driving a truck for his father's business. Josef Hofmann urged that fewer musicians become soloists, Hollywood stars like Joan Crawford joined the Screen Actors Guild, and Leopold Stokowski canceled a performance in Pittsburgh because theater proprietors were violating a union contract. In New York in 1933, after a series of meetings in Heywood Broun's penthouse apartment, newspapermen organized the American Newspaper Guild in rebellion against the dispiriting romanticism of Richard Harding Davis. "We no longer care to develop the individual as a unique contributor to a democratic form," wrote the mordant Edgar Kemler. "In this movement each individual sub-man is important, not for his uniqueness, but for his ability to lose himself in the mass, through his fidelity to the trade union, or cooperative organization, or political party."

The liberals of the thirties admired intellectual activity which had a direct relation to concrete reality. Stuart Chase wrote of one government report: "This book is live stuff—wheelbarrow, cement mixer, steam dredge, generator, combine, power-line stuff; library dust does not gather here." If the poet did not wish to risk the suspicion that his loyalties were not to the historic necessities of his generation, wrote Archibald MacLeish, he must "soak himself not in books" but in the physical reality of "by what organization of men and railroads and trucks and belts and book-entries the materials of a single automobile are assembled." The New Dealers were fascinated by "the total man days per year for timber stand improvement," and Tugwell rejoiced in the "practical success" of the Resettlement Administration demonstrated by "these healthy collection figures." Under the Special Skills Division of the RA, Greenbelt was presented with inspirational paintings like *Constructing Sewers*, *Concrete Mixer*, and *Shovel at Work*. On one occasion, in attempting to mediate a literary controversy, the critic Edmund Wilson wrote: "It should be possible to convince Marxist critics of the importance of a work like 'Ulysses' by telling them that it is a great piece of engineering—as it is." In this activist world of the New Dealers, the aesthete and the man who pursued a life of contemplation, especially the man whose interests centered in the past, were viewed with scorn. In Robert Sherwood's *The Petrified Forest*, Alan Squier, the ineffectual aesthete, meets his death in the desert and is buried in the petrified forest where the living turn to stone. He is an archaic type for whom the world has no place.

The new activism explicitly recognized its debt to Dewey's dictum of "learning by doing" and, like other of Dewey's ideas, was subject to exaggeration and perversion. The New Deal, which gave unprecedented authority to intellectuals in government, was, in certain important respects, anti-intellectual. Without the activist faith, perhaps not nearly so much would have been achieved. It was Lilienthal's conviction that "there is almost nothing, however fantastic, that (given competent organization) a team of engineers, scientists, and administrators cannot do today" that helped make possible the successes of TVA. Yet the liberal activists grasped only a part of the truth; they retreated from conceptions like "tragedy," "sin," "God," often had small patience with the force of tradition, and showed little understanding of what moved men to seek meanings outside of political experience. As sensitive a critic as the poet Horace Gregory could write, in a review of the works of D. H. Lawrence: "The world is moving away from Lawrence's need for personal salvation; his 'dark religion' is not a substitute for economic planning." This was not the mood of all men in the thirties—not of a William Faulkner, an Ellen Glasgow—and many of the New Dealers recognized that life was more complex than some of their statements would suggest. Yet the liberals, in their desire to free themselves from the tyranny of precedent and in their ardor for social achievement, sometimes walked the precipice of superficiality and philistinism.

The concentration of the New Dealers on public concerns made a deep mark on the sensibility of the 1930's. Private experience seemed self-indulgent compared to the demands of public life. "Indeed the public world with us has *become* the private world, and the private world has become the public," wrote Archibald MacLeish. "We live, that is to say, in a revolutionary time in which the public life has washed in over the dikes of private existence as sea water breaks over into the fresh pools in the spring tides till everything is salt." In the thirties, the Edna St. Vincent Millay whose candle had burned at both ends wrote the polemical *Conversation at Midnight* and the bitter "Epitaph for the Race of Man" in *Wine From These Grapes*.

The emphasis on the public world implied a specific rejection of the values of the 1920's. Roosevelt dismissed the twenties as "a decade of debauch," Tugwell scored those years as "a decade of empty progress, devoid of contribution to a genuinely better future," Morris Cooke deplored the "gilded-chariot days" of 1929, and Alben Barkley saw the twenties as a "carnival" marred by "the putrid pestilence of financial debauchery." The depression was experienced as the punishment of a wrathful God visited on a nation that had strayed from the paths of righteousness. The fire that followed the Park Avenue party in Thomas Wolfe's *You Can't Go Home Again*, like the suicide of Eveline at the end of John Dos Passos' *The Big Money*, symbolized the holocaust that brought to an end a decade of hedonism. In an era of reconstruction, the attitudes of the twenties seemed alien, frivolous, or—the most cutting word the thirties could visit upon a man or institution—"escapist." When Morrie Ryskind and George Kaufman, authors of the popular *Of Thee I Sing*, lampooned the government again in *Let 'em Eat Cake* in the fall of 1933, the country was not amused. The New York *Post* applauded the decision of George Jean Nathan and his associates to discontinue the *American Spectator:* "Nihilism, dadaism, smartsetism—they are all gone, and this, too, is progress." One of H. L. Mencken's biographers has noted: "Many were at pains to write him at his new home, telling him he was a sophomore, and those writing in magazines attacked him with a fury that was suspect because of its very violence."

Commentators on the New Deal have frequently characterized it by that much-abused term "pragmatic." If one means by this that the New Dealers carefully tested the consequences of ideas, the term is clearly a misnomer. If one means that Roosevelt was exceptionally anti-ideological in his approach to politics, one may question whether he was, in fact, any more "pragmatic" in this sense than Van Buren or Polk or even "reform" Presidents like Jackson and Theodore Roosevelt. The "pragmatism" of the New Deal seemed remarkable only in a decade tortured by ideology, only in contrast to the rigidity of Hoover and of the Left.

The New Deal was pragmatic mainly in its skepticism about utopias and final solutions, its openness to experimentation, and its suspicion of the dogmas of the Establishment. Since the advice of economists had so often been wrong, the New Dealers distrusted the claims of orthodox theory— "All this is perfectly terrible because it is all pure theory, when you come down to it," the President said on one occasion—and they felt free to try new approaches. Roosevelt refused to be awed by the warnings of economists and financial experts that government interference with the "laws" of the economy was blasphemous. "We must lay hold of the fact that economic laws are not made by nature," the President stated. "They are made by human beings." The New Dealers denied that depressions were inevitable events that had to be borne stoically, most of the stoicism to be displayed by the most impoverished, and they were willing to explore novel ways to make the social order more stable and more humane. "I am for experimenting . . . in various parts of the country, trying out schemes which are supported by reasonable people and see if they work," Hopkins told a conference of social workers. "If they do not work, the world will not come to an end."

Hardheaded, "anti-utopian," the New Dealers nonetheless had their Heavenly City: the greenbelt town, clean, green, and white, with children playing in light, airy, spacious schools; the government project at Longview, Washington, with small houses, each of different design, colored roofs, and gardens of flowers and vegetables; the Mormon villages of Utah that M. L. Wilson kept in his mind's eye—immaculate farmsteads on broad, rectangular streets; most of all, the Tennessee Valley, with its model town of Norris, the tall transmission towers, the white dams, the glistening wire strands, the valley where "a vision of villages and clean small factories has been growing into the minds of thoughtful men." Scandinavia was their model abroad, not only because it summoned up images of the countryside of Denmark, the beauties of Stockholm, not only for its experience with labor relations and social insurance and currency reform, but because it represented the "middle way" of happy accommodation of public and private institutions the New Deal sought to achieve. "Why," inquired Brandeis, "should anyone want to go to Russia when one can go to Denmark?"

Yet the New Deal added up to more than all of this—more than an experimental approach, more than the sum of its legislative achievements, more than an antiseptic utopia. It is true that there was a certain erosion of values in the thirties, as well as a narrowing of horizons, but the New Dealers inwardly recognized that what they were doing had a deeply moral significance however much they eschewed ethical pretensions. Heirs of the Enlightenment, they felt themselves part of a broadly humanistic movement to make man's life on earth more tolerable, a movement that might someday even achieve a co-operative commonwealth. Social insurance, Frances Perkins declared, was "a fundamental part of another great forward step in that liberation of humanity which began with the Renaissance."

Franklin Roosevelt did not always have this sense as keenly as some of the men around him, but his greatness as a President lies in the remarkable degree to which he shared the vision. "The new deal business to me is very much bigger than anyone yet has expressed it," observed Senator Elbert Thomas. Roosevelt "seems to really have caught the spirit of what one of the Hebrew prophets called the desire of the nations. If he were in India today they would probably decide that he had become Mahatma—that is, one in tune with the infinite." Both foes and friends made much of Roosevelt's skill as a political manipulator, and there is no doubt that up to a point he delighted in schemes and stratagems. As Donald Richberg later observed: "There would be times when he seemed to be a Chevalier Bayard, *sans peur et sans reproche*, and times in which he would seem to be the apotheosis of a prince who had absorbed and practiced all the teachings of Machiavelli." Yet essentially he was a moralist who wanted to achieve certain humane reforms and instruct the nation in the principles of government. On one occasion, he remarked: "I want to be a *preaching President*—like my cousin." His courtiers gleefully recounted his adroitness in trading and dealing for votes, his effectiveness on the stump, his wicked skill in cutting corners to win a point. But Roosevelt's importance lay not in his talents as a campaigner or a manipulator. It lay rather in his ability to arouse the country and, more specifically, the men who served under him, by his breezy encouragement of experimentation, by his hopefulness, and—a word that would have embarrassed some of his lieutenants—by his idealism.

The New Deal left many problems unsolved and even created some perplexing new ones. It never demonstrated that it could achieve prosperity in peacetime. As late as 1941, the unemployed still numbered six million, and not until the war year of 1943 did the army of the jobless finally disappear. It enhanced the power of interest groups who claimed to speak for millions, but sometimes represented only a small minority. It did not evolve a way to protect people who had no such spokesmen, nor an acceptable method for disciplining the interest groups. In 1946, President Truman would resort to a threat to draft railway workers into the Army to avert a strike. The New Deal achieved a more just society by recognizing groups which had been largely unrepresented—staple farmers, industrial workers, particular ethnic groups, and the new intellectual-administrative class. Yet this was still a halfway revolution; it swelled the ranks of the bourgeoisie but left many Americans—share-croppers, slum dwellers, most Negroes—outside of the new equilibrium.

Some of these omissions were to be promptly remedied. Subsequent Congresses extended social security, authorized slum clearance projects, and raised minimum-wage standards to keep step with the rising price level. Other shortcomings are understandable. The havoc that had been done before Roosevelt took office was so great that even the unprecedented measures of the New Deal did not suffice to repair the damage. Moreover, much was still to be learned, and it was in the Roosevelt years that the country was schooled in how to avert another major depression. Although it was war which freed the government from the taboos of a balanced budget and revealed the potentialities of spending, it is conceivable that New Deal measures would have led the country into a new cycle of prosperity even if there had been no war. Marked gains had been made before the war spending had any appreciable effect. When recovery did come, it was much more soundly based because of the adoption of the New Deal program.

Roosevelt and the New Dealers understood, perhaps better than their critics, that they had come only part of the way. Henry Wallace remarked: "We are children of the transition—we have left Egypt but we have not yet arrived at the Promised Land." Only five years separated Roosevelt's inauguration in 1933 and the adoption of the last of the New Deal measures, the Fair Labor Standards Act, in 1938. The New Dealers perceived that they had done more in those years than had been done in any comparable period in American history, but they also saw that there was much still to be done, much, too, that continued to baffle them. "I believe in the things that have been done," Mrs. Roosevelt told the American Youth Congress in February, 1939. "They helped but they did not solve the fundamental problems. . . . I never believed the Federal government could solve the whole problem. It bought us time to think." She closed not with a solution but with a challenge: "Is it going to be worth while?"

"This generation of Americans is living in a tremendous moment of history," President Roosevelt stated in his final national address of the 1940 campaign.

"The surge of events abroad has made some few doubters among us ask: Is this the end of a story that has been told? Is the book of democracy now to be closed and placed away upon the dusty shelves of time?

"My answer is this: All we have known of the glories of democracy—its freedom, its efficiency as a mode of living, its ability to meet the aspirations of the common man—all these are merely an introduction to the greater story of a more glorious future.

"We Americans of today—all of us—we are characters in the living book of democracy.

"But we are also its author. It falls upon us now to say whether the chapters that are to come will tell a story of retreat or a story of continued advance."

CONTEMPORARY SOURCES

3. ANDREW M. FAIRFIELD, "MR. HOOVER'S CREDO"

WHEN the depression crashed down upon Herbert Hoover, he reacted by falling back upon the truths which had sustained him during his successful career as an engineer, businessman, and government official. To the unemployed, his lofty appeals to "rugged individualism" and his denunciations of "paternalism" and the "dole" seemed unrealistic. Hoover's most vocal critics, however, were those persons who advocated a more imaginative utilization of the resources of the federal government. The following critique was typical of the attitude of such persons as the depression deepened while Hoover seemed unwilling to act decisively.

SOURCE. Andrew M. Fairfield, "Mr. Hoover's Credo," in *The Nation*, Vol. 133, September 30, 1931, pp. 330–332. Copyright 1931 by *The Nation*. Reprinted by permission of *The Nation*.

The average American President lays no claim to any *Weltanschauung*, any complete social philosophy. He is merely "a good American." He is a Democrat or a Republican, a standpatter or a political progressive of the Roosevelt type. He is blissfully unaware of the existence of hundreds of solid tomes on the questions of government, economics, political science, the philosophy of democracy and representative institutions.

But Herbert Hoover is not supposed to be an average President. He aspires to membership in a different and truly distinguished group—that of Washington, Jefferson, Lincoln, and Wilson. He is an Engineer, a Statistician, an Economist, an Organizer and Administrater *par excellence*. He is the man for the crisis, because he is not a politician or perpetual candidate, but a statesman of ripe and varied experience and sound profound convictions. He is no shifty opportunist; he has clear ideas and a firm faith in first principles. That this is Mr. Hoover's picture and conception of himself, neither his friends nor his foes, nor impartial bystanders, will deny. Let me, then, test Mr. Hoover in the light of his first principles and his philosophy.

He has not failed to supply us with abundant materials and tools for the proposed test. He has written a little book in defense of individualism, and has repeatedly called himself an individualist and an irreconcilable opponent of socialism, collectivism, communism, and bureaucracy. He has lauded "rugged individualism" and has warned us solemnly against "bureaucracy and domination," and against "too much government in business" and too little business method in government. . . .

Of course, no President of the United States could seriously ask Congress to establish and enthrone individualism by statutory law. But a President who really and intelligently espoused and entertained the doctrines and tenets of individualism would certainly feel morally bound to propose legislative steps *toward* the right objective, not steps *away* from it. Mr. Hoover's individualism is, as William Hard has shown in *The Nation*, a monstrous, misshapen, indefensible hodge-podge, a thing of shreds and patches. If he is for any measure, it is consonant with his individualism, and if he is opposed to any proposal, it is branded by him as paternalistic, socialistic, un-American. Intellectual integrity and decent self-respect forbid such playing fast and loose with political science.

But, it may be objected, Mr. Hoover is a defender not of abstract and theoretically consistent individualism, but of the practical, reasonable American variety of that creed and system. But is that variety defensible and worthy of respect and honor? American individualism is plutocratic individualism, the individualism of the fortunate few, the interests in possession, the men and women who control the present order and profit by it. The professed individualism of such predatory groups is a sham and a mockery.

Mr. Hoover affects to contemplate America's false and dishonest individualism with pride and ecstatic veneration. His most intelligible—not intelligent—and frankest exposition of and appeal to the principles of that system will be found in the characteristic and revealing address he delivered at King's Mountain in October, 1930. In that carefully prepared piece Mr. Hoover restated his creed and attempted to define and describe the American social and economic system. What, he asked, was that system and what principles informed and governed it? He declared that he found no name or label at all adequate for it. Liberalism? No, that term had been corrupted by political use. Individualism? No, for it did not permit any class or group to override the equal opportunity of other classes and groups. Capitalism? No, for under it capital was a servant, not a master. Democracy? No, for democratic governments and institutions existed elsewhere under ideals which did not embrace equality of opportunity. Mr. Hoover concluded that the American system was—the American system. A very adroit and acceptable conclusion for a politician. But not for an economist, engineer, and statesman. The sincere thinker knows that there is no such thing as an American "system." A little democracy, a good deal of plutocracy and tyranny, a little pseudo-individualism, a little collectivism—that is the American system.

Mr. Hoover admits it is not perfect. We have, he concedes, some problems to grapple with and solve, but, he asserts, they are problems not of decadence and retrogression, but of growth and progress. This would be important if true. Is the rapid growth of farm tenancy a problem of growth and progress? Are thousands of bank failures an evidence of progress? Is chronic unemployment a monument to progress and equal opportunity? Are business cycles, depressions, crises outward signs of inward grace and sweet harmony? Are the racketeers, bootleggers, political crooks, brutal police officers, profiteers, and monopolists children of health and progress? Mr. Hoover shrinks from pretending that the American system is liberal or democratic. Skyscraper tariffs, Chinese and Japanese exclusion laws, deportation drives and raids, drastic restriction of white immigration, anti-evolution statutes, Volsteadism, Mann Acts, federal and local censorships, Comstock laws are not precisely shining exemplifications of liberalism.

As to the democracy, it exists in some States that have been intelligent enough to modernize their constitutions and to adopt the direct primary, the referendum, the initiative, and the recall. The federal government is autocratic, not democratic. It was meant to be autocratic, and has remained so. The Cabinet is responsible to the President alone. The Senate is more powerful and less amenable to public opinion than any hereditary house of peers. Congressmen are elected and ordered to stay at home about thirteen months, the lame ducks being given four months of control after their repudiation by the electorate—and for no reason or rhyme whatever under present conditions. Five members of the federal Supreme Court veto any really progressive legislation they happen to dislike, and as they are apt to be elderly lawyers of reactionary proclivities, they dislike most legistation designed to correct injustice and to translate Pecksniffian phrases into living realities.

Mr. Hoover is of the opinion that the American democracy is vastly superior to the British, French, or German democracies because its social ideal embraces equality of opportunity. What exactly does he mean by "equality of opportunity"? Opportunity to be and do what? Every college graduate can become a bond salesman, at least when times are good and the security markets active, but is that equality of opportunity? What sort of equality and opportunity are enjoyed by the Negroes, by the women and children in the textile mills, by the coal miners, unionized or non-unionized? What are the opportunities of the aged poor, whose name is legion?

America has no political democracy and never had it, but for many decades it did enjoy social democracy and reasonable equality of economic opportunity. Mr. Hoover must have heard of the era of free land, of the great, wholesome influence of the American frontiers, of the initiative and self-reliance of the pioneers and their contempt for bureaucratic red tape and routine. But his dim notions of the American spirit have little relevance to the conditions of the present age. There are those who say that he has no magnanimity, no sense of social justice, no tenderness or sympathy. They may be right. But what is worse, _he has no sense of actuality_. Facts and statistics, when unpleasant, leave him, the engineer and economist, cold and indifferent. No wonder his tools and hirelings doctor and manipulate statistics and distort painful facts.

Mr. Hoover's distrust and hatred of bureaucracy and bureaucratic domination are natural and commendable. But had he taken the trouble to study the literature of constructive and scientific radicalism, he would not have committed himself to the absurdity that any departure from what he calls Americanism or American individualism necessarily involves an addition to the bureaucracy and all its works. Few enlightened American or European Socialists favor the extension of the functions and powers of the state as it exists. To nationalize this or that industry is no longer tantamount to turning it over to the clumsy and maladroit hands of politicians and bureaucrats. Mr. Hoover should read Norman Thomas's "America's Way Out." Public ownership and operation can and may mean public ownership and operation by the ablest and most efficient men available.

Mr. Hoover, as an engineer and organizer, might do much for genuine individualism and true democracy by opposing, not public ownership and pro-public operation of utilities and other essential industries, but political and bureaucratic operation and management of such enterprises. Under the system extolled by him, governmental business agencies—and there are many of them—are constantly hampered and impeded by office-holders and office-seekers who think more of electioneering and campaign victories than of public assets and administrative efficiency. The Farm Board and its stabilization corporations have been coerced into price-fixing and market-pegging ventures. The heavy deficits in the national postal service are due to political meddling, the spoils system, and rate policies wholly alien to business principles. Mr. Hoover, notwithstanding his devotion to individualism, has never recommended the separation of the postal service from partisan and spoils politics, or its emancipation from "bureaucratic domination." Why not turn it over to a group of capable and alert business executives with instructions to operate it on sound economic principles but, of course, not for private or public profit? The same question arises in the case of Muscle Shoals. Mr. Hoover, the economist and engineer, is willing to waste public assests, but not to call upon public-spirited men of demonstrated capacity to conserve and utilize such assets.

What *is* the matter with Mr. Hoover? My diagnosis is perfectly simple. In the first place, he is ignorant or woefully behind the times. He uses catch phrases and tags, and these serve his purposes with the Babbitts and the plutocrats, big and little. He has no need of clear ideas and no conception of the scientific method as applied to politics and social economics. In the second place, Mr. Hoover is a pedant and doctrinaire. His farcical Children's Charter; his talk about the Home and the Family; his boasts (how sickly and ludicrous they sound now!) in connection with full garages, school attendance, radio sets, the decline and abolition of poverty—all sound hollow. They *are* hollow. Mr. Hoover's whole creed is hollow and shallow. It may impose upon the sentimentalists, but it cannot impress or attract the man or woman who is able to form and entertain his own convictions upon social, economic, and political problems.

A word, finally, about Mr. Hoover's position on the question of federal relief appropriations, or doles. To urge State, county, and city relief organizations and funds is good horse sense. To emphasize *primary* local responsibility and local solidarity under such conditions as now exist is not, however, absolutely to bar federal aid should local efforts prove inadequate. Just what sacrosanct principle enjoins State, county, and municipal doles while forbidding federal doles? And why is character sapped and undermined by federal doles, but not by local doles, or by private charity? Bread lines and soup kitchens, according to Mr. Hoover, nourish and sustain self-respect and dignity, provided private and local public philanthropy alone finance these authentic American institutions. Such reasoning cannot be taken seriously. There is nothing "un-American" in federal aid and relief extended under exceptional and critical situations. If Mr. Hoover fears precedents, a habit of looking to Uncle Sam, he can guard against that peril by insisting on the maximum of effective cooperation between the States and their subdivisions, on the one hand, and the federal agencies on the other. Only a pedant can adhere stubbornly to the indefensible attitude he has adopted on the so-called dole question. And Mr. Hoover is not even a *consistant* pedant since he makes concessions to hated doctrines from political and partisan motives.

4. GEORGE E. SOKOLSKY, "WILL REVOLUTION COME?"

BY the late summer of 1932, with the Battle of Anacostia Flats and the farm strikes firmly etched in the minds of Americans, the question of possible revolution frequently entered into serious political discussions, especially among conservatives. George Sokolsky, a leading conservative newspaper columnist later noted for his hostility toward Franklin Roosevelt, presented a perceptive analysis of the possibility of revolution shortly before the presidential election of 1932. Several historians have since pointed out that the presidential election held out the opportunity for an orderly change in government, thus undercutting revolutionary pressures.

II

Revolution will not come to the United States, because there seems to be in this country an automatic process for the redistribution of wealth and economic power, and because there is no army.

Although Congress is peculiarly unconscious of economic processes at work in the United States, it usually, after much damaging delay, blunders through to an approximation of the needs of the people. If laws are passed which do not fit the times, there is always a Holmes or Hughes or Brandeis or Cardozo to discover the erring comma which saves the country. Thus, the Sherman Anti-Trust Law stands upon the law books of the nation, but who can doubt the existence of trusts in the United States? It is even more important that no one really wants to doubt their existence; no one would want them split up into myriad petty businesses competing against each other, adding to depression a greater confusion.

The very sectionalism of Congress, which irritated and frightened bankers

SOURCE. George E. Sokolsky, "Will Revolution Come?", in *The Atlantic Monthly*, Vol. 150, August 1932, pp. 186–188 and 191. Copyright 1932 by The Atlantic Monthly Company, Boston, Massachusetts. Reprinted by permission of Doubleday & Company, Inc., from George Sokolsky, *Labor's Fight for Power*, and *The Atlantic Monthly*.

criticize, is the saving grace of our Constitution, for the compromise between New York and Oklahoma does avert revolution. New York might become utterly mad on "liquidity," which is economically as sound as the "two chickens in every pot" economics of the boom, but Texas will prevent "liquidity" from driving hungry men frantic. As long as discontent can voice its opinions and win a concession, there will be no fighting.

In 1930, bankers in Wall Street feared a guillotine on the Sub-Treasury steps; in 1932, they are so sure of themselves that they insist on a balanced budget. They are as ill advised in 1932 as they were in 1930. Then men were not yet hungry; therefore there could be no guillotine. Now they are beginning to be hungry; therefore it is wise to listen to Congress.

A demagogue becomes at such a time a safe barometer to follow. He does not sway the populace, but bows to it. He is the willow rather than the oak. When he bends his head low, the wind is blowing fiercely. Those who assume that, because 1930 and 1931 have passed without trouble, 1932 is a good time to call a critic a traitor would be well advised if they took seriously the attitude of La Guardia and Brookhart, who reflect not only voters but people. When they demand drastic action, it means that the people whom they fear demand drastic action. . . .

The sectionalism of Congress gives to the United States an unusual security. It makes it possible to know well in advance, in such times as these, what the hungry man wants and what he will do. The President sits in his White House bird-cage and knows only what he is told by polite friends; the Representative and the Senator hear from the people, who tell them where they get off. I was recently lecturing before a business men's service club in a city in upper New York State. The business men were discontented. They had been led to believe that when the Reconstruction Finance Corporation made the funds of their local banks liquid the banks would pass credits on to them. The bankers, however, held on tightly to their money, forgetful that money has no value of itself, but only in its uses. These business men were mighty sore, but did they march down their main street, seize the bank, appoint a committee to manage it, and give themselves the credits they required to do business? They did not. Instead, they called their Congressman on the long-distance telephone and told him that if he did not get something done he would not be reëlected. This is sound democracy. This is also the sort of thing that prevents revolutions. As long as men telephone to Congress, there will be no street fighting in the United States.

III

As Congress is one valve of safety, so is the redistribution of wealth another. Americans never think in the terminology of economics, and therefore they do not seem to realize that a redistribution of wealth has been taking place in the United States since the beginning of 1930. The full effects of the change are not yet apparent and will not be until the era of depression has given place to what Mr. Harding liked to call "normalcy." . . .

The American people, however, have been bred to abhor all fundamental changes, unless they come on them unaware, like the emancipation of women. Rather than suffer change in form, the American accepts charity. And, curiously enough, the rich in the United States give to charity lavishly, thus taxing themselves for the upkeep of the depressed. This self-imposed charity tax is an indirect method of redistributing wealth. The apparently rich have been stimulated to a type of class consciousness by their leaders, who adjured them to keep revolution from the door by sharing. The country has been covered by "I Will Share" and "Stamp Out Want" signs. Men really sought to share. Their motives were mixed, but the sharing was genuine.

The curves on the chart will not begin to turn upward through sharing by charity or through slogans to stamp out want. The present depression is a correct reaction to unsound economic practices. But as long as those who still possess wealth are willing to distribute their means so that bread becomes available to those who no longer have means, a fundamental economic revolution will not take place. Sharing by charity may, to the unthinking, partake of religious duty, but its economic effect is to keep money moving, so that he who cannot earn may still eat.

What will happen when sharing ceases is quite obvious. The government will be forced to take measures to prevent the law of the hungry stomach from coming into operation. There is a small group in this country which envisages this possibility next winter, and believes that the problem may be solved by an American adaptation of Fascism, by a Presidential appointment of small committees of bankers and lawyers with vast powers who by some magic will do what Congress finds it difficult to do—namely, balance the budget, end the depression, begin a new era of prosperity, and keep the peace. Were the President a Roosevelt or even a Wilson, such a programme might be a palliative, for the men selected would be such as are close to the people; they would know exactly what might be done to curb discontent. . . .

V

Revolution, then, is not for the United States. Revolution requires temper, and the American is without temper. He turns on the radio and listens to the mouthings of Amos 'n' Andy. He can smile at a jest while his children are fed in public schools at the expense, often, of inadequately paid school-teachers. He can vote for Tammany officials in New York in spite of his high rents which their extravagance and dishonesty have made inevitable. He can reëlect the Congressman who voted for a tariff which has reduced his foreign trade and therefore his chances of recovery. He can even grow enthusiastic over bootleg whiskey. He can argue that the depression hits the rich and poor alike. He still scans the stock-market lists and wonders where he can borrow some money to get in on the present low levels. He is carried away by a slogan, "Don't sell America short." He even believes that the repeal of prohibition will save his economic structure.

As simple as a Russian peasant in his intellectual process, he insists on an easy, simplified, quick scheme, summed up in a few words, for reconstruction. Utterly uneducated, he is ready to jump to irrational conclusions. He believed in 1929 that prosperity would last forever in spite of conditions in Europe and Asia which were indicating caution. He believes to-day that political magic will save him. A dozen times he has been disappointed, yet he continues to believe. In 1930, Hoover was the goat; in 1931, Wall Street; in 1932, Congress. The average American can never believe that he is really a stupid fellow, for he has forgotten what his Yankee ancestor knew, and what the French peasant knows to-day—namely, that a nation is prosperous only when its citizens save enough "liquid" assets during boom periods to take up the slack during depressions, and that the safest man, economically, is not the one with a millionaire's equity in paper profits, but the one with a middleman's interest in protected, unspeculative savings.

As long as every American believes that he has as many chances as John D. Rockefeller to become a millionaire, to join a country club, and to get into the upper social brackets, he will not become a revolutionist. Hungry, he will pull in his belt. Annoyed, he will vote for a Democrat. Angry, he will demand beer. Despairing, he will telephone his Congressman. He is what the Russians call a Kerenskyist—a man who takes it on the chin, smiling.

5. *THE NEW REPUBLIC,* "MR. ROOSEVELT'S TASK"

THE gloom created by the depression affected even the normally optimistic liberal journal, The "New Republic." Despite the tremendous response to President Roosevelt's stirring Inaugural Address, the magnitude of the task before the new and untested President caused the editors to view the possibilities for constructive action with considerable pessimism. Quite likely their lack of confidence in the new Chief Executive resulted from the dim view of Roosevelt taken by most liberals during the campaign, when he had coyly resorted to vague generalizations without ever firmly committing himself to far-reaching reform. Walter Lippmann perhaps best summarized the liberals' reservations about Roosevelt early in 1932 when he dismissed him as "a pleasant man who, without any important qualifications for the office, would very much like to be President."

SOURCE. "Mr. Roosevelt's Task," in *The New Republic,* Vol. 74, March 8, 1933, pp. 88–90. Copyright 1933 by *The New Republic.* Reprinted by permission of *The New Republic.*

It is no exaggeration to say that Franklin D. Roosevelt, as he assumes the presidency, is confronted by the most staggering task faced by any man of his generation. The extent to which the hopes of a large part of the entire world are centered upon him is a pathetic reminder of how desperately the people are seeking a Messiah, some mystic and powerful savior who will put everything right.

Such hopes are of course delusive. Even if Roosevelt knew what needs to be done, he has not the power to do more than, say, 20 percent of what is necessary. Some of the further steps require international action, which is hedged about with the enormous difficulties created by nationalistic fear, pride and isolationist economics. Most important of all, some of these steps require a drastic transfer of wealth from the Haves to the Have-nots. And the Marxians are undoubtedly correct in pointing out that the Haves will not give up their possessions without a struggle, even for the sake of creating a better and more orderly society.

Paramount of course among Mr. Roosevelt's immediate obligations is the duty of seeing to it that sufficient money is available to prevent starvation among the unemployed. The $300,000,000 already appropriated by Congress for this purpose is rapidly being exhausted, and vast additional sums will obviously be necessary. Fortunately, Congress now seems to be awake to the necessities of the situation. The Senate has already passed the Wagner bill appropriating an additional $300,000,000 and while we believe the La Follette-Costigan bill was preferable, needless to say, the Wagner bill is a great deal better than nothing. . . .

In the domestic field, the most immediate necessity is to repeat the work of a year ago, and shore up the collapsing national faith in our banking and financial system. Mr. Hoover did this by pouring out vast sums to certain arbitrarily selected institutions; and the inadequacy of his plan is evidenced by the new wave of hoarding and the runs, or threatened runs, which have temporarily closed many or all of the banks in seven states. It seems clear that the Roosevelt administration must adopt some other device than giving more money to men who have demonstrated their incompetence to take care of what they already had; and that federal legislation for unifying and simplifying our banking system is inevitable.

Another subject with which the new President will be forced to deal immediately is the vexed one of inflation versus deflation. An enormous quantity of muddy and biased thinking on this subject has been publicly exhibited of late. The opinions of the bankers who have been crying for "no inflation" may be disregarded as being as short-sighted as they are selfish. The country's debtors have an irresistible case when they claim that the purchasing power of money should be returned to the level where it stood when most of the debts were incurred, or else that the obligations themselves should be scaled down. The weakness of the Hoover policy has been that it permitted deflation in prices already falling the most rapidly, and prevented it in other prices already the more inflexible, throwing the whole system out of balance and causing many patent and glaring injustices. The real question is not whether debtors shall be relieved, but how to do this successfully. *The New Republic* has already indicated its reasons for being skeptical about the efficiency of simple currency inflation. Credit inflation has already been tried, with disappointing results: no one wants to borrow when he does not see how to use the money successfully, and timid bankers hoard their resources and refuse to take even the most reasonable risks.

The best device for the Roosevelt administration to employ, therefore, is one which combines a species of inflation with a direct attack upon the problem of unemployment: a bond issue for the purpose of financing a program of public works as large as the credit of the government will support. It is not sure that such a scheme would be effective, but the chance is certainly worth taking. As our readers know, all the government's efforts in this field heretofore have come to nothing, due to the covert sabotage of Mr. Hoover and the heads of the R.F.C. Congress appropriated one and a half billion dollars for public works, but only about 10 percent of this has been allocated and practically none of it has been spent. To be effective, the new program should involve not less than five billion dollars, to be spent with the greatest rapidity on public works, whether self-liquidating or not, in all parts of the country. Such a program is like the self-starter on an automobile: it is no use unless the engine is in a condition to go on by itself once it has been started. Whether the country is now in such a condition, it is impossible to say without trying. Whether a total as large as this can be floated without injuring the government credit is also uncertain, under present conditions.

With such a program should come a complete alteration of the present R.F.C. policy toward banks and railroads. No aspect of Mr. Hoover's administration has been worse than the policy of pouring out government funds (to the extent of one and a quarter billion dollars) to stave off bankruptcies, "bail out" banks, cover up past mistakes and wrongdoing and continue in office the men who have been guilty of these bad practices. One could ask no clearer example than this of manipulation of public wealth in the interest of a single class. Among Mr. Roosevelt's closest advisers are men who are well aware of the past mistakes of the R.F.C. and what needs to be done to remedy them.

Perhaps the most difficult of the tasks by which the new President is confronted is restoring the purchasing power of the farmer. For generations, American public policy has favored industry as against agriculture, until now the condition is one of crisis. The domestic-allotment plan, as it was originally conceived, would transfer from the pockets of consumers to those of agricultural producers about a billion dollars a year; and by so doing, it would set in motion forces which would not merely redistribute the national wealth, but would increase it. Mr. Roosevelt has in the past favored this plan; and if he should now withdraw his support from it, he could only do so by bringing forward a substitute which would have substantially the same result.

These are but a few of the pressing problems with which the new President will be confronted. Behind them, of course, lie others which are even more fundamental, and will encounter even greater resistances, than these. Our civilization is extremely sick; and the most important cause of its sickness is the maldistribution of income. Mr. Roosevelt is the doctor called in to prescribe for the symptoms while most of the members of the household feverishly hope that he will not touch the underlying malady. Yet if he does not, even his efforts to drive away the surface symptoms can be only momentarily successful. We have seen no evidence as yet that Mr. Roosevelt either understands the fundamental malady or is prepared to deal with it. His actions thus far have been those of one who hopes to patch things up so that they will be better for a while, and will then patch them again and perhaps a little more extensively; and so on. But it is perhaps unfair to judge a President in the week of his inauguration. The larger question, time will answer.

6. FRANKLIN D. ROOSEVELT, "SECOND FIRESIDE CHAT OF 1934"

FRANKLIN D. ROOSEVELT was the first President to utilize radio communications for political advantage. His early "fireside chats" created a great outburst of public support for his policies in 1933, and he continued to use this effective method of reaching the American people throughout his Presidency. The following "chat," presented shortly before the 1934 congressional elections, exemplifies Roosevelt's defense of his administration. It also provides a good example of his facility with the language—a most important weapon in his political arsenal.

SOURCE. Samuel E. Rosenman, ed., *The Public Papers and Addresses of Franklin D. Roosevelt*, New York: Random House, 1938, Vol. III, pp. 413–417 and 420–422. Copyright 1938 by Franklin D. Roosevelt and renewed in 1966 by Elliott Roosevelt, the Honorable James Roosevelt, and Franklin D. Roosevelt, Jr. Reprinted by permission of Random House.

Three months have passed since I talked with you shortly after the adjournment of the Congress. Tonight I continue that report, though, because of the shortness of time, I must defer a number of subjects to a later date.

Recently the most notable public questions that have concerned us all have had to do with industry and labor and with respect to these, certain developments have taken place which I consider of importance. I am happy to report that after years of uncertainty, culminating in the collapse of the spring of 1933, we are bringing order out of the old chaos with a greater certainty of the employment of labor at a reasonable wage and of more business at a fair profit. These governmental and industrial developments hold promise of new achievements for the Nation.

Men may differ as to the particular form of governmental activity with respect to industry and business, but nearly all are agreed that private enterprise in times such as these cannot be left without assistance and without reasonable safeguards lest it destroy not only itself but also our processes of civilization. The underlying necessity for such activity is indeed as strong now as it was years ago when Elihu Root said the following very significant words:

> Instead of the give and take of free individual contract, the tremendous power of organization has combined great aggregations of capital in enormous industrial establishments working through vast agencies of commerce and employing great masses of men in movements of production and transportation and trade, so great in the mass that each individual concerned in them is quite helpless by himself. The relations between the employer and the employed, between the owners of aggregated capital and the units of organized labor, between the small producer, the small trader, the consumer, and the great transporting and manufacturing and distributing agencies, all present new questions for the solution of which the old reliance upon the free action of individual wills appears quite inadequate. And in many directions, the intervention of that organized control which we call government seems necessary to produce the same result of justice and right conduct which obtained through the attrition of individuals before the new conditions arose.

It was in this spirit thus described by Secretary Root that we approached our task of reviving private enterprise in March, 1933. Our first problem was, of course, the banking situation because, as you know, the banks had collapsed. Some banks could not be saved but the great majority of them, either through their own resources or with Government aid, have been restored to complete public confidence. This has given safety to millions of depositors in these banks. Closely following this great constructive effort we have, through various Federal agencies, saved debtors and creditors alike in many other fields of enterprise, such as loans on farm mortgages and home mortgages; loans to the railroads and insurance companies and, finally, help for home owners and industry itself.

In all of these efforts the Government has come to the assistance of business and with the full expectation that the money used to assist these enterprises will eventually be repaid. I believe it will be.

The second step we have taken in the restoration of normal business enterprise has been to clean up thoroughly unwholesome conditions in the field of investment. In this we have had assistance from many bankers and business men, most of whom recognize the past evils in the banking system, in the sale of securities, in the deliberate encouragement of stock gambling, in the sale of unsound mortgages and in many other ways in which the public lost billions of dollars. They saw that without changes in the policies and methods of investment there could be no recovery of public confidence in the security of savings. The country now enjoys the safety of bank savings under the new banking laws, the careful checking of new securities under the Securities Act and the curtailment of rank stock speculation through the Securities Exchange Act. I sincerely hope that as a result people will be discouraged in unhappy efforts to get rich quick by speculating in securities. The average person almost always loses. Only a very small minority of the people of this country believe in gambling as a substitute for the old philosophy of Benjamin Franklin that the way to wealth is through work.

In meeting the problems of industrial recovery the chief agency of the Government has been the National Recovery Administration. Under its guidance, trades and industries covering over 90 percent of all industrial employees have adopted codes of fair competition, which have been approved by the President. Under these codes, in the industries covered, child labor has been eliminated. The work day and the work week have been shortened. Minimum wages have been established and other wages adjusted toward a rising standard of living. The emergency purpose of the N.R.A. was to put men to work and since its creation more than four million persons have been reemployed, in great part through the cooperation of American business brought about under the codes.

Benefits of the Industrial Recovery Program have come, not only to labor in the form of new jobs, in relief from overwork and in relief from underpay, but also to the owners and managers of industry because, together with a great increase in the payrolls, there has come a substantial rise in the total of industrial profits—a rise from a deficit figure in the first quarter of 1933 to a level of sustained profits within one year from the inauguration of N.R.A.

Now it should not be expected that even employed labor and capital would be completely satisfied with present conditions. Employed workers have not by any means all enjoyed a return to the earnings of prosperous times, although millions of hitherto underprivileged workers are today far better paid than ever before. Also, billions of dollars of invested capital have today a greater security of present and future earning power than before.

This is because of the establishment of fair, competitive standards and because of relief from unfair competition in wage cutting which depresses markets and destroys purchasing power. But it is an undeniable fact that the restoration of other billions of sound investments to a reasonable earning power could not be brought about in one year. There is no magic formula, no economic panacea, which could simply revive overnight the heavy industries and the trades dependent upon them.

Nevertheless the gains of trade and industry, as a whole, have been substantial. In these gains and in the policies of the Administration there are assurances that hearten all forward-looking men and women with the confidence that we are definitely rebuilding our political and economic system on the lines laid down by the New Deal—lines which as I have so often made clear, are in complete accord with the underlying principles of orderly popular government which Americans have demanded since the white man first came to these shores. We count, in the future as in the past, on the driving power of individual initiative and the incentive of fair profit, strengthened with the acceptance of those obligations to the public interest which rest upon us all. We have the right to expect that this driving power will be given patriotically and whole-heartedly to our Nation. . . .

Closely allied to the N.R.A. is the program of public works provided for in the same Act and designed to put more men back to work, both directly on the public works themselves, and indirectly in the industries supplying the materials for these public works. To those who say that our expenditures for public works and other means for recovery are a waste that we cannot afford, I answer that no country, however rich, can afford the waste of its human resources. Demoralization caused by vast unemployment is our greatest extravagance. Morally, it is the greatest menace to our social order. Some people try to tell me that we must make up our minds that for the future we shall permanently have millions of unemployed just as other countries have had them for over a decade. What may be necessary for those countries is not my responsibility to determine. But as for this country, I stand or fall by my refusal to accept as a necessary condition of our future a permanent army of unemployed. On the contrary, we must make it a national principle that we will not tolerate a large army of unemployed and that we will arrange our national economy to end our present unemployment as soon as we can and then to take wise measures against its return. I do not want to think that it is the destiny of any American to remain permanently on relief rolls. . . .

In our efforts for recovery we have avoided, on the one hand, the theory that business should and must be taken over into an all-embracing Government. We have avoided, on the other hand, the equally untenable theory that it is an interference with liberty to offer reasonable help when private enterprise is in need of help. The course we have followed fits the American practice of Government, a practice of taking action step by step, of regulating only to meet concrete needs, a practice of courageous recognition of change. I believe with Abraham Lincoln, that "The legitimate object of Government is to do for a community of people whatever they need to have done but cannot do at all or cannot do so well for themselves in their separate and individual capacities."

I am not for a return to that definition of liberty under which for many years a free people were being gradually regimented into the service of the privileged few. I prefer and I am sure you prefer that broader definition of liberty under which we are moving forward to greater freedom, to greater security for the average man than he has ever known before in the history of America.

7. HERBERT HOOVER, "NATIONAL REGIMENTATION"

WITHIN a year after leaving office, Herbert Hoover had become a leading critic of the New Deal. He viewed the Roosevelt program as a direct and serious threat to traditional American liberties and saw in it an attempt to create "national regimentation." Unfortunately, Hoover could offer no alternative to the New Deal other than a restoration of the principles that he had followed and that the voters had convincingly repudiated in 1932. Hoover's viewpoint, however, was also held by millions of Americans who became increasingly apprehensive and angry as the New Deal unfolded. Hoover's appeal to classical liberalism is best summarized in one of the chapters of his book, Challenge to Liberty, *which was published in 1934 in a futile attempt to influence the congressional elections of that year.*

The origins, character, and affinities of the Regimentation theory of economics and government, its impacts upon true American Liberalism, and its departures from it can best be determined by an examination of the actions taken and measures adopted in the United States during recent months.

It is not from oratory either in advocacy of this philosophy or equally in

SOURCE. Herbert Hoover, *The Challenge to Liberty*, New York: Charles Scribner's Sons, 1934, pp. 76–82, 85–89, and 99–103. Copyright 1934 by Charles Scribner's Sons; renewal copyright 1962 by Herbert Hoover. Reprinted by permission of Charles Scribner's Sons.

denial of it that we must search for its significance. That is to be found by an examination of the actual steps taken and proposed.

From this examination we may dismiss measures of relief of distress from depression, and reform of our laws regulating business when such actions conform to the domain of true Liberty, for these are, as I shall indicate, not Regimentation.

The first step of economic Regimentation is a vast centralization of power in the Executive. Without tedious recitation of the acts of the Congress delegating powers over the people to the Executive or his assistants, and omitting relief and regulatory acts, the powers which have been assumed include, directly or indirectly, the following:

To debase the coin and set its value; to inflate the currency; to buy and sell gold and silver; to buy Government bonds, other securities, and foreign exchange; to seize private stocks of gold at a price fixed by the Government; in effect giving to the Executive the power to "manage" the currency;

To levy sales taxes on food, clothing, and upon goods competitive to them (the processing tax) at such times and in such amounts as the Executive may determine;

To expend enormous sums from the appropriations for public works, relief, and agriculture upon projects not announced to the Congress at the time appropriations were made;

To create corporations for a wide variety of business activities, heretofore the exclusive field of private enterprise;

To install services and to manufacture commodities in competition with citizens;

To buy and sell commodities; to fix minimum prices for industries or dealers; to fix handling charges and therefore profits; to eliminate "unfair" trade practices;

To allot the amount of production to individual farms and factories and the character of goods they shall produce; to destroy commodities; to fix stocks of commodities to be on hand;

To estop expansion or development of industries or of specific plant and equipment;

To establish minimum wages; to fix maximum hours and conditions of labor;

To impose collective bargaining;

To organize administrative agencies outside the Civil Service requirements;

To abrogate the effect of the anti-trust acts;

To raise and lower the tariffs and to discriminate between nations in their application;

To abrogate certain governmental contracts without compensation or review by the courts;

To enforce most of these powers where they affect the individual by fine and imprisonment through prosecution in the courts, with a further reserved authority in many trades through license to deprive men of their business and livelihood without any appeal to the courts.

Most of these powers may be delegated by the Executive to any appointee and the appointees are mostly without the usual confirmation by the Senate.

The staffs of most of the new organizations are not selected by the merit requirements of the Civil Service. These direct or indirect powers were practically all of them delegated by the Congress to the Executive upon the representation that they were "emergency" authorities, and most of them are limited to a specific time for the purpose of bringing about national recovery from the depression. . . .

The application of Regimentation to business has made great strides. We now have the important branches of industry and commerce organized into trade groups, each presided over by a committee of part trade and part governmental representatives heading up through an "Administrator" to the Executive. There are a number of advisory boards for various purposes whose personnel is part trade and part bureaucratic. More than 400 separate trades have been so organized, estimated to cover 1,500,000 establishments or about 90 percent of the business of the country outside of farming.

In this organization of commerce and industry the trades were called upon to propose codes of management for their special callings. Parts of each of these codes are, however, imposed by law, whether the trades propose them or not. The determination as to who represents the trade is reserved to the Executive, and in the absence of a satisfactory proposal he may himself make and promulgate a code. He may force deletion of any proposed provision and may similarly impose provisions and exceptions.

Each of the codes is directly or indirectly binding upon every member of the trade whether he was represented in its making or whether he agreed or not. It has the force of statutory law, enforceable by fine and jail through the courts. Originally the Executive could require every member of a trade to take out a license to do business. In this license he could impose the conditions under which persons may continue to do business. The Executive could revoke a license without affording any appeal to or protection of the courts. This licensing power has expired in general industry but still stands as an authority to the Secretary of Agriculture over all producers, processors and dealers in agricultural products. That is a very considerable part of American business. Except as an example of the extent of violation of freedom this licensing provision is not important, as the other provisions and methods are sufficiently coercive without it.

The codes impose minimum wages and maximum hours and provide, further, for collective agreement with labor as to wages and conditions of work beyond the minimums. By far the major use of the codes is, however, devoted to the elimination of "unfair competitive practices." This expression or its counterpart, "fair competition," has been interpreted not alone to cover "unethical" practices, but to include the forced elimination of much normal functioning of competition through reduced production, the prevention of plant expansion, and a score of devices for fixing of minimum prices and trade margins. From so innocent terms as "fair competition" and its counter-part have been builded this gigantic dictation—itself a profound example of the growth of power when once granted. . . .

Over it all is now the daily dictation by Government in every town and village every day in the week, of how men are to conduct their daily lives—under constant threat of jail, for crimes which have no moral turpitude. All this is the most stupendous invasion of the whole spirit of Liberty that the nation has witnessed since the days of Colonial America.

The farmer is the most tragic figure in our present situation. From the collapse of war inflation, from boom, from displacement of work-animals by mechanization, from the breakdown of foreign markets, from the financial debacle of Europe, and from drought, he has suffered almost beyond human endurance.

Instead of temporarily reducing the production of marginal lands by measures of relief pending world recovery, the great majority of farmers were regimented to reduce production from the fertile lands. The idea of a subsidy to a farmer to reduce his production in a particular "staple commodity" was expanded by requiring a contract that he would follow orders from the Secretary of Agriculture in the production of other "staple commodities." Voluntary action was further submerged by threats that if he did not sign up he would have difficulty in obtaining credit.

The whole process has been a profound example both of how bureaucracy, once given powers to invade Liberty, proceeds to fatten and enlarge its activities, and of how departures from practical human nature and economic experience soon find themselves so entangled as to force more and more violent steps.

To escape the embarrassment of the failure to reduce production by these methods, still further steps were taken into coercion and regimentation. Yet more "staples," not authorized by the Congress to be controlled when the contracts were signed, were added to the list. A further step was to use the taxing power on excess production of cotton and to set quotas on sugar. Directly or indirectly, on many farms these devices create a privilege and destroy a right. Since only those who have had the habit of producing cotton and some other commodities may now do so, they are given a monopoly and any other farmer is precluded from turning his land to that purpose.

And recently still further powers were demanded from the Congress by which the last details of complete coercion and dictation might be exerted not alone to farmers but to everyone who manufactures and distributes farm products. That all this is marching to full regimentation of thirty millions of our agricultural population is obvious enough.

But we are told that the farmer must, in the future, sacrifice Liberty to economic comfort. The economic comfort up to date may be questioned, as likewise the longevity of any comfort, for the basic premise is not tenable.

The stark fact is that if part of Liberty to a particular farmer is removed, the program must move quickly into complete dictation, for there are here no intermediate stages. The nature of agriculture makes it impossible to have regimentation up to a point and freedom of action beyond that point. Either the farmer must use his own judgment, must be free to plant and sell as he wills, or he must take orders from the corporal put above him.

The whole thesis behind this program is the very theory that man is but the pawn of the state. It is a usurpation of the primary liberties of men by government.

The deliberate entry of the government into business in competition with the citizen, or in replacement of private enterprise, (other than as a minor incident to some major public purpose), is regimentation of the people directly into a bureaucracy. That, of course, is Socialism in the connotation of any sociologist or economist and is confirmed as such today by the acclaim of the Socialists.

As an instance we may cite the Tennessee Valley Authority, where the major purpose of the government is the purchase, construction, operation, transmission, and sale of electricity in the Tennessee Valley and neighborhood, together with the manufacture and merchandising of appliances, fertilizers, chemicals, and other commodities. Other instances occur where Public Works money has been allotted to the erection of dams and reservoirs, and to the construction of power plants, the major purpose of which is to undertake the production and sale of electricity in competition with the citizen. . . .

How far the Regimentation of banking and the government dictation of credit through various government agencies may extend is not yet clear. There are national stresses in which the government must support private financial institutions, but it is unnecessary for it to enter into competitive business to accomplish this. And lest the government step over the line into Socialism this support must be limited to activities where there is no competition, or so organized as ultimately to be absorbed into the hands of private ownership. The original Reconstruction Finance Corporation is an example of the former and the Federal Reserve Banks, the Home Loan Banks, the Federal Land Banks, of the latter. There are, however, some of the new financial agencies and some uses being made of the old agencies which forecast occupation beyond these fields, and threaten dictation as to who may and who may not have credit. The threat to farmers of withholding credit to force them to sign crop contracts with the government is a current example of possibilities.

The reduction of the independence of the Federal Reserve Board and the Farm Loan System to dependency upon the political administration, the provisions for appointment of officials in the banks by government agencies, and certain provisions in the new regulatory acts, all at least give enormous powers of "managed credit."

If the purpose of all these activities is to enable the government to dictate which business or individual shall have credit and which shall not, we will witness a tyranny never before contemplated in our history.

The wounds to Liberty—and to justice upon which Liberty rests—in these monetary actions and policies are thus myriad. It is again a specific demonstration of a social philosophy defensible only on the ground that the citizen is but the pawn of the state—the negation of the whole philosophy of Liberty. Executive power over the coin is one of the oldest components of despotism. . . .

This brief survey of examples of experience up to this time is sufficient to make clear the definition and nature of National Regimentation and its progress in the United States. There are other channels in which our economic and social life is being regimented which could be developed. These instances are certainly sufficient to show that its very spirit is government direction, management, and dictation of social and economic life. It is a vast shift from the American concept of human rights which even the government may not infringe to those social philosophies where men are wholly subjective to the state. It is a vast casualty to Liberty if it shall be continued.

8. JOHN STEINBECK, "DUBIOUS BATTLE IN CALIFORNIA"

THE publication in 1939 of the novel, The Grapes of Wrath, *evoked instantaneous acclaim from a nation that had endured a decade of hardship. John Steinbeck's sensitive but realistic treatment of an American tragedy—the desperate flight to the promised land of California by the disinherited dirt farmers of Oklahoma—became an important American novel. In describing the hardships encountered by the family of Tom Joad on Route 66 and in the fertile San Joaquin Valley, Steinbeck drew upon firsthand observation. In 1936, he published a revealing essay on the California farm-labor situation, which provided one of the foundations for his novel.*

SOURCE. John Steinbeck, "Dubious Battle in California," in *The Nation,* Vol. 143, September 12, 1936, pp. 302–304. Copyright 1963 by *The Nation.* Reprinted by permission of *The Nation.*

In sixty years a complete revolution has taken place in California agriculture. Once its principal products were hay and cattle. Today fruits and vegetables are its most profitable crops. With the change in the nature of farming there has come a parallel change in the nature and amount of the labor necessary to carry it on. Truck gardens, while they give a heavy yield per acre, require much more labor and equipment than the raising of hay and livestock. At the same time these crops are seasonal, which means that they are largely handled by migratory workers. Along with the intensification of farming made necessary by truck gardening has come another important development. The number of large-scale farms, involving the investment of thousands of dollars, has increased; so has the number of very small farms of from five to ten acres. But the middle farm, of from 100 to 300 acres is in process of elimination.

There are in California, therefore, two distinct classes of farmers widely separated in standard of living, desires, needs, and sympathies: the very small farmer who more often than not takes the side of the workers in disputes and the speculative farmer, like A. J. Chandler, publisher of the Los Angeles *Times*, or like Herbert Hoover and William Randolph Hearst, absentee owners who possess huge sections of land. Allied with these large individual growers have been the big incorporated farms, owned by their stockholders and farmed by instructed managers, and a large number of bank farms, acquired by foreclosure and operated by superintendents whose labor policy is dictated by the bank. For example, the Bank of America is very nearly the largest farm owner and operator in the state of California.

These two classes have little or no common ground; while the small farmer is likely to belong to the grange, the speculative farmer belongs to some such organization as the Associated Farmers of California, which is closely tied to the state Chamber of Commerce. This group has as its major activity resistance to any attempt of farm labor to organize. Its avowed purpose has been the distribution of news reports and leaflets tending to show that every attempt to organize agricultural workers was the work of red agitators and that every organization was Communist inspired.

The completion of the transcontinental railroads left in the country many thousands of Chinese and some Hindus who had been imported for the work. At about the same time the increase of fruit crops, with their heavy seasonal need for pickers, created a demand for this mass of cheap labor. These people, however, did not long remain on the land. They migrated to the cities, rented small plots of land there, and, worst of all, organized in the so-called "Tongs," which were able to direct their efforts as a group. Soon the whites were inflamed to race hatred, riots broke out against the Chinese, and repressive activities were undertaken all over the state, until these people, who had been a tractable and cheap source of labor, were driven from the fields.

To take the place of the Chinese, the Japanese were encouraged to come into California; and they, even more than the Chinese, showed an ability not only to obtain land for their subsistence but to organize. The "Yellow Peril" agitation was the result. Then, soon after the turn of the century Mexicans were imported in great numbers. For a while they were industrious workers, until the process of importing twice as many as were needed in order to depress wages made their earnings drop below any conceivable living standard. In such conditions they did what the others had done; they began to organize. The large growers immediately opened fire on them. The newspapers were full of the radicalism of the Mexican unions. Riots became common in the Imperial Valley and in the grape country in and adjacent to Kern County. Another wave of importations was arranged, from the Philippine Islands, and the cycle was repeated—wage depression due to abundant labor, organization, and the inevitable race hatred and riots.

This brings us almost to the present. The drought in the Middle West has very recently made available an enormous amount of cheap labor. Workers have been coming to California in nondescript cars from Oklahoma, Nebraska, Texas, and other states, parts of which have been rendered uninhabitable by drought. Poverty-stricken after the destruction of their farms, their last reserves used up in making the trip, they have arrived so beaten and destitute that they have been willing at first to work under any conditions and for any wages offered. This migration started on a considerable scale about two years ago and is increasing all the time.

For a time it looked as though the present cycle would be identical with the earlier ones, but there are several factors in this influx which differentiate it from the others. In the first place, the migrants are undeniably American and not deportable. In the second place, they were not lured to California by a promise of good wages, but are refugees as surely as though they had fled from destruction by an invader. In the third place, they are not drawn from a peon class, but have either owned small farms or been farm hands in the early American sense, in which the "hand" is a member of the employing family. They have one fixed idea, and that is to acquire land and settle on it. Probably the most important difference is that they are not easily intimidated. They are courageous, intelligent, and resourceful. Having gone through the horrors of the drought and with immense effort having escaped from it, they cannot be herded, attacked, starved, or frightened as all the others were.

Let us see what the emigrants from the dust bowl find when they arrive in California. The ranks of permanent and settled labor are filled. In most cases all resources have been spent in making the trip from the dust bowl. Unlike the Chinese and the Filipinos, the men rarely come alone. They bring wives and children, now and then a few chickens and their pitiful household goods, though in most cases these have been sold to buy gasoline for the trip. It is quite usual for a man, his wife, and from three to eight children to arrive in

California with no possessions but the rattletrap car they travel in and the ragged clothes on their bodies. They often lack bedding and cooking utensils.

During the spring, summer, and part of the fall the man may find some kind of agricultural work. The top pay for a successful year will not be over $400, and if he has any trouble or is not agile, strong, and quick it may well be only $150. It will be seen that rent is out of the question. Clothes cannot be bought. Every available cent must go for food and a reserve to move the car from harvest to harvest. The migrant will stop in one of two federal camps, in a state camp, in houses put up by the large or small farmers, or in the notorious squatters' camps. In the state and federal camps he will find sanitary arrangements and a place to pitch his tent. The camps maintained by the large farmers are of two classes—houses which are rented to the workers at what are called nominal prices, $4 to $8 a month, and camp grounds which are little if any better than the squatters' camps. Since rent is such a problem, let us see how the houses are fitted. Ordinarily there is one room, no running water; one toilet and one bathroom are provided for two or three hundred persons. Indeed, one large farmer was accused in a Growers' Association meeting of being "kind of communistic" because he advocated separate toilets for men and women. Some of the large ranches maintain what are called model workers' houses. One such ranch, run by a very prominent man, has neat single-room houses built of whitewashed adobe. They are said to have cost $500 apiece. They are rented for $5 a month. This ranch pays twenty cents an hour as opposed to the thirty cents paid at other ranches and indorsed by the grange in the community. Since this rugged individual is saving $33\frac{1}{3}$ percent of his labor cost and still charging $5 a month rent for his houses, it will be readily seen that he is getting a very fair return on his money besides being generally praised as a philanthropist. The reputation of this ranch, however, is that the migrants stay only long enough to get money to buy gasoline with, and then move on.

The small farmers are not able to maintain camps of any comfort or with any sanitary facilities except one or two holes dug for toilets. The final resource is the squatters' camp, usually located on the bank of some watercourse. The people pack into them. They use the watercourse for drinking, bathing, washing their clothes, and to receive their refuse, with the result that epidemics start easily and are difficult to check. Stanislaus County, for example, has a nice culture of hookworm in the mud by its squatters' camp. The people in these camps, because of long-continued privation, are in no shape to fight illness. It is often said that no one starves in the United States, yet in Santa Clara County last year five babies were certified by the local coroner to have died of "malnutrition," the modern word for starvation, and the less shocking word, although in its connotation it is perhaps more horrible since it indicates that the suffering has been long drawn out.

In these squatters' camps the migrant will find squalor beyond anything he has yet had to experience and intimidation almost unchecked. At one camp it is the custom of deputy sheriffs, who are also employees of a great ranch nearby, to drive by the camp for hours at a time, staring into the tents as though trying to memorize faces. The communities in which these camps exist want migratory workers to come for the month required to pick the harvest, and to move on when it is over. If they do not move on, they are urged to with guns.

These are some of the conditions California offers the refugees from the dust bowl. But the refugees are even less content with the starvation wages and the rural slums than were the Chinese, the Filipinos, and the Mexicans. Having their families with them, they are not so mobile as the earlier immigrants were. If starvation sets in, the whole family starves, instead of just one man. Therefore they have been quick to see that they must organize for their own safety.

Attempts to organize have been met with a savagery from the large growers beyond anything yet attempted. In Kern County a short time ago a group met to organize under the A. F. of L. They made out their form and petition for a charter and put it in the mail for Washington. That night a representative of Associated Farmers wired Washington for information concerning a charter granted to these workers. The Washington office naturally replied that it had no knowledge of such a charter. In the Bakersfield papers the next day appeared a story that the A. F. of L. denied the affiliation; consequently the proposed union must be of Communist origin.

But the use of the term communism as a bugbear has nearly lost its sting. An official of a speculative-farmer group, when asked what he meant by a Communist replied: "Why, he's the guy that wants twenty-five cents an hour when we're paying twenty." This realistic and cynical definition has finally been understood by the workers, so that the term is no longer the frightening thing it was. And when a county judge said, "California agriculture demands that we create and maintain a peonage," the future of unorganized agricultural labor was made clear to every man in the field.

The usual repressive measures have been used against these migrants: shooting by deputy sheriffs in "self-defense," jailing without charge, refusal of trial by jury, torture and beating by night riders. But even in the short time that these American migrants have been out here there has been a change. It is understood that they are being attacked not because they want higher wages, not because they are Communists, but simply because they want to organize. And to the men, since this defines the thing not to be allowed, it also defines the thing that is completely necessary to the safety of the workers.

This season has seen the beginning of a new form of intimidation not used before. It is the whispering campaign which proved so successful among business rivals. As in business, it is <u>particularly deadly here because its source cannot be traced</u> and because it is easily spread. One of the items of this campaign is the rumor that in the event of labor troubles the deputy sheriffs inducted to break up picket lines will be armed not with tear gas but with poison gas. The second is aimed at the women and marks a new low in tactics. It is to the effect that in the event of labor troubles the water supply used by strikers will be infected with typhoid germs. The fact that these bits of information are current over a good part of the state indicates that they have been widely planted.

The effect has been far from that desired. There is now in California anger instead of fear. The stupidity of the large grower has changed terror into defensive fury. The granges, working close to the soil and to the men, and knowing the temper of the men of this new race, have tried to put through wages that will allow a living, however small. But the large growers, who have been shown to be the only group making a considerable profit from agriculture, are devoting their money to tear gas and rifle ammunition. The men will organize and the large growers will meet organization with force. It is easy to prophesy this. In Kern County the grange has voted $1 a hundred pounds for cotton pickers for the first picking. The Associated Farmers have not yielded from seventy-five cents. There is tension in the valley, and fear for the future.

It is fervently to be hoped that the great group of migrant workers so necessary to the harvesting of California's crops may be given the right to live decently, that they may not be so badgered, tormented, and hurt that in the end they become avengers of the hundreds of thousands who have been tortured and starved before them.

9. BRUCE BLIVEN, JR., "SHALL THEY STARVE?"

THE problem of providing adequate relief not only created problems for the Hoover Administration, but it also posed a perplexing dilemma for the New Deal. Although various New Deal relief agencies spent over twenty-five billion dollars for relief, the federal programs never came close to meeting the national need. In fact, Roosevelt was sincerely uneasy about the correctness of federal relief and determined that it never should become a permanent federal responsibility. Sounding not unlike Herbert Hoover, Roosevelt told the Congress on January 4, 1935, "Continued dependence upon relief

SOURCE. Bruce Bliven, Jr., "Shall They Starve?", in *The New Republic*, Vol. 94, April 13, 1938, pp. 299–301. Copyright 1938 by *The New Republic*. Reprinted by permission of *The New Republic* and the author.

induces a spiritual and moral disintegration fundamentally destructive to the national
fibre. To dole out relief in this way is to administer a narcotic, a subtle destroyer of the
human spirit. . . . The federal government must and shall quit this business of
relief."

This was not merely political pap designed to placate the conservatives. Each time
he sought to reduce the federal commitment to relief, however, Roosevelt came up against
the harsh reality of the millions of unemployed; private charity was overwhelmed, and
the various states lacked the resources with which to meet the huge need. Although the
conservatives constantly attacked the size of the relief programs, many liberals, such as
Bruce Bliven, Jr., of The New Republic, were very critical of the Administration for its
failure to provide jobs or relief for all. The following essay was written more than five
years after the New Deal came to power.

Few people realize how desperate the relief problem in the United States
has become. Few people, that is to say, beside the twenty million or more
men, women and children who depend upon local, state or federal government assistance for the necessities of life. The fact is that the present depression has thrown us into an emergency very nearly as serious as the breakdown
of relief administration this country experienced in 1931 and 1932. The widespread layoffs in industry since the fall have flooded relief agencies all over
the country with applications they have neither the funds nor the personnel
to handle. And while the pleas for government aid grow more and more
insistent, the relief bureaus are under heavy pressure to cut down on their
budgets. Nowhere in the United States are the unemployed and the destitute
getting adequate help. Unless some drastic emergency aid is given them, the
prospects for the near future are even worse.

There was no provision for the wholesale unemployment that came after
1929. There were no agencies equipped to handle the administration of relief
other than private charities and the hit-or-miss local systems of poor relief.
There was no money to meet the cost of keeping millions of helpless Americans alive. Public opinion had not even agreed that it is the government's
duty to provide for those the industrial economy does not support. By 1932
the federal government had begun to assist local agencies with their insur-
mountable problems: the Reconstruction Finance Corporation lent them
money and in 1933 the Federal Emergency Relief Administration was created
to help out in the crisis that was supposed to disappear in the course of a
relatively short time. Anyone who suggested that the unemployment problem
might hang on indefinitely was regarded as a professional pessimist. Yet
today the crisis is here again and we are just about as surprised and unprepared as we were in the winters of 1929 and '30.

With the arrival of some measure of recovery in 1934 and 1935 and the
creation of the Works Progress Administration in the fall of 1935, we returned

to the method of letting local agencies handle their own relief problems. The theory was that the federal government would provide work for all employables on the relief rolls while the cities and states maintained those who were too young or too old to work, or physically handicapped. The theory has never been put into actual practice. There have continuously been a large number of employables on direct relief for whom the WPA had no place, who therefore had to be cared for by their local agencies or not at all. But the theory was that the peak of the emergency had been passed by 1935 and that it was time to return to the traditional policy of care by the community for its own citizens.

Today we are administering relief in the United States according to the same principle, even though the cities and states are obviously unable to carry their share of the burden. The most conservative estimates put the total figure for unemployment at 12,000,000 and it is probably closer to 14,000,000 in reality. And while the rolls of relief applicants grow (often double, sometimes treble), the appropriations for relief are everywhere being curtailed. Everybody is sick of the problem. The emergency of 1932 has not been passed, but the public enthusiasm over meeting the crisis has largely died down. When a state legislature is asked to increase its appropriation for relief, its attitude is likely to be a cold one. The legislators can't remain steamed up over the question for six years and, because so much has to be done and there's so little to show for all the money and energy that have been poured into the breach, the legislators are tempted to fall into the easy answer: the unemployed are bums anyway; they could get jobs if they really tried. Why worry about a pack of bums?

In some respects the problem today is more difficult than it was in 1932. The prosperity that preceded the depression of 1929 had enabled a great many families to build up some sort of reserve to fall back on in case the income source should be cut off. Men who had held jobs all their lives, who had built up savings accounts and bought homes and automobiles, were able to carry on for several years, in many cases, after they were fired. They sold their possessions, borrowed money on their homes and insurance policies until every last resource had been tapped and they were forced to make application at the relief bureau. That was the type of case that began to come into the relief picture in about 1933. It was also the type of case that was the first to leave the relief rolls when recovery began. But although many of the heads of these families were able to get their jobs back, or to find new ones in 1935 and 1936, there has been no time for them to build up any reserves.

One important advance since 1932 is the organization that has been set up to administer relief, even though all the organization in the world cannot make up for lack of funds. The experience we have gained is a valuable asset. What we need is a realization of how serious the present emergency is and of how much money will be needed to meet it. . . .

The survey made by the American Association of Social Workers uncovered a picture of unbelievable destitution throughout the country. In Douglas County, Nebraska, for example, the average amount of relief per family is $6.90 a month and only about 20 percent of the families that need help are getting it. In Chicago, where the city's entire appropriation for 1938 is already nearly exhausted, the Association studied the clothing needs of one hundred men, picked at random from the relief rolls. Out of the whole lot only enough decent shoes, underwear, jackets and overcoats could be collected to clothe twenty-eight of them.

In Arkansas the average monthly relief allowance for a family is $6. In Little Rock, during February, it was discovered that two thousand families without any income were receiving no aid whatsoever and were on the verge of starvation.

In California, the woeful tale of relief problems is complicated by the plight of the migratory farm workers in the San Joaquin Valley and in other agricultural regions. Migratory families are ineligible for either county or state relief, and there are about 13,000 of them, most of them from the Oklahoma and Texas dust bowls, living in tents and squatter shacks in their ditchbank camps, facing a completely blank future.

In Louisiana, where relief funds are hopelessly inadequate, the custom is to give 75 percent of the money needed to supply a family's basic needs. If, for example, the minimum on which a family of four can buy food, fuel, household supplies and pay the rent is $50, the relief check is made out for $38.

In St. Louis, the Board of Education reports that out of the 70,000 school children given physical examinations during the past year, 6,000, or about eight percent, are undernourished. This in spite of the fact that the schools give free milk and balanced free lunches to counteract the poor food the children get at home. The crop of new children entering school for the first time each year keeps the percentage up, because so many of them have not been getting enough of the right things to eat.

It hardly matters what community you examine. In every case the problem is the same: growing lists of families who are desperately in need of help matched against curtailed relief budgets and constant pressure to cut down on the aid that is being given. The people who are lucky enough to be getting relief at all are not getting enough. And on top of that problem you have to add the hundreds of thousands of families who are just outside the pale of eligibility, who should be getting help now, because in the course of a short time they will have bogged down into the class of the completely helpless. To qualify for relief a family must be entirely destitute. Nobody can even think about the problem of rescuing the families that are scraping along somehow for the time being, but are headed inevitably for the relief-application bureau. All we are doing at present is fighting to keep the very worst cases from starvation, and right now we don't seem to be winning even that battle.

10. GEORGE FORT MILTON, "A CONSUMER'S VIEW OF TVA"

THE concept of regional planning as embodied in the creative multipurpose design of the Tennessee Valley Authority held out tremendous possibilities for the seven state area through which the Tennessee River meanders. Exploited by previous generations, the Tennessee Valley was an impoverished region with equally impoverished inhabitants. As originally conceived, the TVA had four goals: the development of a navigable river system; the establishment of a far-flung flood control system; the creation of a huge recreational area of lakes and parks; and the production of inexpensive hydroelectrical power. It was this last goal that created heated political controversy throughout the 1930's and well into the next decade as well. The TVA, critics charged, would be an opening step to "sovietize" the United States. Most residents of the area, however, favored TVA even if it did have strong "socialistic" overtones. George Fort Milton, a prominent Tennessee journalist and a competent historian, presented the consumer's viewpoint in an essay published late in 1937.

I have in my family treasures a letter from my great-grandfather, Dr. Tomlinson Fort, written to his wife in 1842, eagerly reporting that "at last I believe, the government at Washington is going to do something about Muscle Shoals. . . ." For at least a century the property holders and citizens of the Tennessee Valley have waited for the government to "do something" about their great river—too large a task for their own unaided hands.

As I say, we were born sighing for something to be done about our river; and yet, now that something *is* being done about it, some of us feel as though we were guinea pigs in a vivisection laboratory; indeed, as though we were guinea pigs doomed to be the spoils of a struggle between the angry savants of two rival schools of vivisectionists, who have hold of different parts of our devoted carcasses and are pulling and hauling our whole bodies, one enjoining the other in the courts of law on the theory that the God in his Heaven had dedicated all guinea pigs to his privately owned dissecting knife. So we wonder if the prizes of this titanic struggle are to be deprived of all voice in electing which shall wield the sacrificial knife.

As editor of a newspaper in Chattanooga, it has been my journalistic lot to

SOURCE. George Fort Milton, "A Consumer's View of TVA," in *The Atlantic Monthly*, Vol. 160, November 1937, pp. 653–658. Copyright 1937, 1965, by The Atlantic Monthly Company, Boston, Massachusetts. Reprinted by permission of *The Atlantic Monthly*.

see, at close range, many exciting episodes of this struggle; to take part in some of them, and to sense the feeling of the Valley folk about the controversy. Perhaps I should preface my remarks by saying that while I am delighted at the prospect, and reasonably pleased with the performance of TVA, still I abhor both of the mutually exclusive theses: the first, that the distribution of electricity must never be "of the people, by the people, and for the people"; the second, the equally uncomfortable ideological strait-jacket that all power must be public, because all private utilities always indulge in frenzied finance, corrupt local politics, and exploit the hapless consumers.

Neither of these theories seems to me exclusively tenable; much better is it for us here in this Valley to eschew absolutist contentions, and to consider the debate from the standpoint of the welfare and development of the region itself. And for us the question is not merely one of whether power shall be private or public; we are chiefly concerned about the economic development and social progress of the Valley and its people.

This Tennessee Valley watershed, covering some 40,000 square miles, embraces parts of seven States. A significant thing about it is that its annual rainfall is among the heaviest in the United States. Carrying this to the Mississippi, the Tennessee River falls 600 feet in 200 miles—and there is power in the fall. The Tennessee system as a whole may be made to yield three million kilowatts of electric energy. The power in these streams belongs to the people—is among their last great unalienated natural resources. Now the Government is undertaking to develop this power by an integrated system, and to use it as an energizing agent to quicken the economic competence and to raise the living levels of the whole area.

This basin has immense natural resources. After water power, at the head of the list, comes coal, in great abundance; iron ore and the limestone to flux it; zinc, and other metals; bauxite to make aluminum; marble, building stones, and many of the nonmetallic minerals. Forest products are bountiful. The region has a diversified agricultural yield, and its human stuff is of sturdy, independent Anglo-Saxon stock.

Here in the Tennessee Valley area we have the whole Southern problem in microcosm. We have poverty in the midst of potential plenty; we have rivers running to waste that should be harnessed; we have rich resources needing development; we have people of low incomes with all the qualities needed to do skilled tasks and to build a civilization of high degree. The Tennessee Valley is particularly suitable for a demonstration of the coördinated development of human and material resources. The Tennessee Valley should become the American Ruhr.

Furthermore, TVA is at grips with the region's vital problems. Take soil erosion. The experts say it was not Alexander, nor Tamerlane, nor Genghis Khan, who destroyed the ancient civilizations on the fertile Tigris and

Euphrates plains; not they, but soil erosion, made a desert out of a paradise. We Americans should remember this. It is estimated that in 1931 soil erosion destroyed enough land in West Tennessee alone to equal 10,000 farms of thirty acres each. This illustrates why it is one of our worst national menaces. The Authority considers soil conservation and erosion control among its most important jobs. It is now setting up in each county in its area a unit which can aid the farmers to terrace their land and, through crop adjustment, to preserve it.

A second major activity is in fertilizer. The old World War nitrate plant at Muscle Shoals has been transformed into a plant for reducing the acids needed for fertilizer. The rich phosphate beds of Middle Tennessee are near by; new reduction processes are expected to yield better fertilizer at much less cost. New methods of distribution through farmers' fertilizer coöperative groups could cut the delivered cost. This is only one of many examples that could be offered of the experimentation and research by the Authority, as a result of which many new methods and processes have already been developed, to save time and money, and occasionally to give an open-sesame to new enterprises.

Another important phase is the development of the river which will make it available for year-round navigation from Paducah, Kentucky, to Knoxville, Tennessee—an immense boon to interior transportation of heavy-burden freights. Incidentally, one of the South's great disadvantages in the interregional competition is the higher levels of freight rates we must pay in comparison with those charged to the north of us. TVA has already taken steps to bring some redress to this disadvantage.

Then the TVA is devoting itself to bringing about a companionship of industry and agriculture. With huge quantities of power to wholesale, it must look for customers, and one place it seeks them is on the farm. TVA is taking electricity to the farmers, who are themselves organizing county coöperatives to run their rural lines. Several such have been formed, and they have succeeded from the word "go." Rural electrification stimulates farmers to increase their income. It lightens the farm wife's backbreaking burden. Running water, modern plumbing, electric lights, and refrigeration—all these things add new satisfactions to rural life.

TVA likewise seeks increased residential load in the towns and cities. Although it does not distribute directly, through its wholesale power contract it retains control over the retailer's rates. This control is essential, because the Authority sees its problem as one of procuring the widest possible use of electricity, and it is operating on the sound theory that lower rates bring great volume increases, which in turn enable costs to be cut to the bone—the path Ford took to make the automobile a necessity for the common man. This programme is working wonders. In little Tupelo, Mississippi, for example, power use has doubled and trebled, householders are paying no more cash than before, and the city is paying itself taxes, retiring its debt, and showing a profit. The sale of electric refrigerators, stoves, heaters, and so forth, in the Valley is prodigious. The TVA rate structure, directed toward more power use, not less, ties right in with an abundance economy.

Then TVA does not overlook industrial use of electricity. With such quantities of current, thermal as well as mechanical users must be had. But the Authority has carefully avoided trying to siphon these new users out of other areas. It is making an earnest effort to find completely new industries to establish here to use its power. Within the last year it has made contracts with great industries involving the sale of huge blocks of secondary power, at prices which yield the Authority an income of about $4,000,000 a year.

Perhaps more important than anything I have mentioned is that TVA may give us the key to the efficient public performance of economic function. All over the world, government seems on the move from performing services of a merely political or ministerial type to the performance of economic function. We may praise or deplore the tendency, but the essential fact is that it is under way. Our public operations are becoming increasingly important and we must find the way to have them well done. The competence of American public service has suffered both from the unwieldy size of the government machine and from the indifference of the public personnel. This last began over a century ago, when our mystic Democracy claimed every man was a popular sovereign and hence competent to hold any sort of public post, no matter how technical might be its tasks. Our civil-service reformers sought to correct it by substituting a rigidly frozen system of status and rights, without any workable mechanism for discovering and rewarding the worker who has energy, imagination, and intelligence. Therefore incentive for good work was lacking.

TVA is an approach to both these problems. Because of the restricted zone of operation, it permits both immediacy and flexibility of control. Its directors are seeking to set up the apparatus for discovering and then promptly advancing the men of promise. From the start, it has made political backing a disadvantage in getting jobs. This policy, commanded by the law of its establishment, has had the backing of its Chairman from the beginning. The Authority's personnel policies cut through the rigidities of civil service and come closer to affording those rewards for initiative which make men really work. . . .

If I read aright the feelings of the general run of folks here in the Valley, it is about like this:—

First, they do not feel that the private power companies can ever do one quarter as much for building the region as can the Federal Government through TVA, and therefore they want TVA to do the job. But in doing so they would like the TVA to take over the generation and transmission of electric power in the Valley, purchasing the area's existing private utilities' transmitting and generating facilities.

Second, they are anxious for the TVA to acquire, at a fair price, the existing power facilities. This price should represent the real remaining investment value, and not any "wind and water" of fictitious write-ups. There are tens of millions of dollars of legitimately made private investments in bonds and preferred stocks of Valley operating subsidiaries. Except for rare extremists, the Valley public does not want these values wiped out. They favor no confiscation; indeed, they are willing that the price paid perhaps shall be a little above the real value, in order quickly to unsnarl the tangle and get TVA to work. As Chairman Morgan says, condemnation is not necessarily the most appropriate procedure. Indeed, assuming that both parties to a potential purchase went into the conference room with a real desire to effect a meeting of the minds, there is no valid reason why either an upset price, or at least a mechanism for achieving one, could not be directly agreed upon.

Third, in the event of any "dog in the manger" refusal by the private-power people to negotiate upon any other than a fantastic basis, the public would, by a vigorous majority, insist that TVA go ahead, erect the necessary public-power transmission lines, and bring its power to competing public systems in the towns and cities of the Valley. In such event, the wreckage of private investors' securities would be chargeable to a blind Bourbonism on the part of private-power magnates.

Fourth, the actual distribution within cities, towns, and for coöperative rural lines, should be undertaken by the appropriate public agencies in the units. For example, in the City of Chattanooga, the distribution network would be run by the Electric Power Board of Chattanooga, an agency authorized by the public at election and established by legislative charter. This agency has already sought—in vain—to secure any sort of conference with the private-power owners of the present Chattanooga distribution network to consider the latter's purchase. The people of Chattanooga want the Electric Power Board to buy the existing private properties, at a fair price. Still they want public power and TVA. This attitude typifies the feeling of the public in most of the towns and cities of the Valley.

The result of such a programme would be a great system, under which TVA would generate and wholesale power; the cities and towns would buy it at city gates and distribute it within their retail areas, and the Valley would progress amazingly. This is the ideal and logical goal for TVA in the Valley. Incidentally, this is a programme in which the dominant management influences in TVA itself would be happy to coöperate. It is greatly to be hoped that the controlling private-power interests in New York will at some stage be willing to cease their guerrilla war and talk common sense.

2nd
hourly

PART V

The Second World War

THE fascination of the American people with World War II seems to have no limit. The dramatic spectacle of America's gigantic global struggle against the forces of fascism has provided innumerable themes for motion pictures, novels, military histories, and television programs. It seems that no major battle remains for Walter Cronkite to narrate or for a heroic John Wayne to re-create in bloody technicolor. The sensational qualities of the stirring military epic, however, have tended to obscure other historical developments of far-reaching importance. Although historians have only begun to research topics outside of diplomatic or military history, it is already quite clear that the war produced wide-sweeping changes in American life.

The triumph of internationalism in American foreign policy is the most obvious change produced by the war. The reluctant breakdown of political isolationism underscores the revolutionary nature of this change. While the nation had long followed an active policy of seeking economic opportunities abroad, the nation balked at political entanglements and diplomatic commitments that would require the use of force outside the Western Hemisphere. Consequently, she had fought in World War I as an "Associated Power," and during the 1920's had refused to join the League of Nations and the World Court while simultaneously pursuing an ambitious program of economic expansionism. During the 1930's, political isolationism was tested as never before as the militant and expansionistic Germany and Italy altered the *status quo* in Europe and as Japan began to "close" the nation's traditional "Open Door" policy in China. Still the American people and their leaders clung to the traditional policy of "no entangling alliances" and gave little

273

serious thought to the need for a fundamental change in long-accepted diplomatic or defense policies.

The war, however, shattered the strong hold on American thought by the doctrines of political isolationism and unilateralism and drove home the lesson that America's age of free security had ended. For the century after the War of 1812, as C. Vann Woodward has pointed out, the blessings of geography had enabled the United States to follow a policy of diplomatic isolationism—at least when it so desired. The Atlantic, Pacific, and Arctic Oceans protected the United States like a moat around a medieval castle but, by 1940, responsible leaders understood that military technology was about to make "Fortress America" obsolete. Moreover, America's defenses in the future would demand the expenditure of vast sums and far-flung political, economic, and military commitments around the globe.

The startling successes of Adolph Hitler's *blitzkreig* in the spring of 1940 forced President Roosevelt to seek security in an unprecedented peacetime mobilization. In May he announced a major military buildup and in October the nation inaugurated its first peacetime draft. The swift collapse of France in June not only prompted Roosevelt to advocate preparedness, but it forced the Republican party to reject the popular conservative isolationist, Robert A. Taft, and to nominate the relatively unknown but ardent internationalist, Wendell Willkie.

Roosevelt moved the United States away from its traditional policy of unilateralism and toward collective security as rapidly as he dared. In September he announced that he had concluded an executive agreement with Great Britain whereby the United States would give that beleaguered island nation fifty outdated destroyers in return for ninety-nine year leases to military bases on Newfoundland and in the Caribbean (ostensibly to defend the Panama Canal). Then in December, following his victory over Willkie, Roosevelt proposed a program of "lend-lease" to strengthen further England's defenses. In a fireside chat, he told the American people that, "There is far less chance of the United States getting into the war, if we do all we can now to support the nations defending themselves against attack by the Axis than if we acquiesce in their defeat, submit tamely to an Axis victory, and wait our turn to be the object of attack in another war later on." The Lend-Lease proposal infuriated the isolationists but, by this time, their shrill opposition was undermined when Willkie supported Lend-Lease, and Congress approved by substantial majorities the unprecedented program that funneled millions of dollars of urgently needed military supplies to England; when Hitler launched his surprise attack on Russia on June 22, 1941, Lend-Lease was extended to the Soviets.

In August, 1941, Roosevelt moved yet another step away from isolation when he and Prime Minister Winston Churchill jointly issued the Atlantic

Charter. Similar in content to the Fourteen Points of Woodrow Wilson, the Charter called for "the final destruction of the Nazi tyranny." Although Roosevelt placed the moral and financial support of the United States behind Great Britain, he could not have convinced the Congress of the necessity of intervening directly, even if he personally desired to do so.

Pearl Harbor ended his dilemma. The surprise attack on the American naval base on December 7, 1941, climaxed a steady deterioration of Japanese-American relations created by conflicting interests in East Asia and the South Pacific. The attack effectively silenced the acrimonious debate that had raged within the United States between the isolationists and internationalists. In less than an hour after President Roosevelt asked the joint session of Congress on December 8 for a resolution of war, the Congress approved with only one dissenting vote. On December 11, Italy and Germany declared war on the United States; that same afternoon Congress unanimously declared war on them, and the battle was joined.

The clear recognition that Nazism stood for all that was repugnant to American values served to unify further the American people. Adolph Hitler's version of fascism advocated not only the complete subordination of the individual to the state, but also a frightening and deranged racism that exalted the purity and superiority of the so-called "Aryan" race. He not only preached this philosophy, but sought to put it into practice. He identified the Jew as the source of Germany's past difficulties and established death camps in an attempt to exterminate the source of Germany's racial "impurity." By 1945, an estimated 6,000,000 Jews had been murdered. The horrors and barbarism of Buchenwald and Auschwitz are beyond imagination. The Nazi plan of genocide for all Jews and the expressed goal of world domination caused the American people to redouble their resolve to defeat the Axis. Never before (or since) had the American people been so unified in time of war.

During the course of the war the internationalists strengthened their position. By 1943, a strong bipartisan movement for American participation in an international security organization had developed. Even in the Midwest, traditionally an area of strong isolationist sentiment, spokesmen for a postwar organization found a receptive audience. The "One World" concept advocated by Wendell Willkie spearheaded a reversal by his party of its traditional isolationism; led by one-time isolationist leader, Senator Arthur H. Vandenberg, a special Republican leadership conference held on Mackinac Island in September, 1943, adopted a statement to the effect that the United States had to assume a position of world leadership following the war, including membership in a strong international organization. The 1944 Republican platform, in paraphrase of the Mackinac statement, called for "responsible participation by the United States in a postwar cooperative organization among sovereign nations to prevent military aggression and to attain permanent peace with organized justice in a free world."

Recognizing the growing strength of internationalist sentiment, Congress responded by passing a resolution by a resounding margin calling upon the Roosevelt Administration to take the leadership in the creation of such an organization at "the earliest practicable date." Roosevelt needed little urging, and he enthusiastically pushed the creation of the United Nations. At Dumbarton Oaks in the fall of 1944, the representatives of the Big Three hammered out a set of proposals that provided the basis for the formal *Charter*, which was drafted the following spring in San Francisco. The Senate quickly ratified the *Charter* by a vote of 89-2 on July 28, 1945. The triumph of internationalism was virtually complete.

The American war effort reflected the new internationalism as well. Unlike World War I, when the nation had fought as an "Associated Power," the United States now assumed the dominant position among the Big Three. The willingness of the United States to cooperate to the fullest with her allies illustrates an important new tack of national policy. Although the American people desired to revenge Pearl Harbor, first priority was placed upon defeating Germany. Reasoning that Germany was a greater threat to American security than Japan and, anxious to aid her hard-pressed allies, the American strategists wisely decided to fight a holding action in the Pacific while relentlessly prosecuting the war in Europe. In this effort, cooperation with Great Britain could scarcely have been better. Military plans were jointly prepared, and the few major differences that did appear were amicably resolved.

Cooperation with the other member of the Big Three, however, was another matter. Throughout the war, Roosevelt publicly affirmed his belief that Russia would prove to be a long-time friend of the United States. His optimism had little foundation in reality because, from the first, major differences developed between the two Powers. The hard-headed realism that would characterize Soviet diplomacy throughout the war was manifest as early as the talks between Foreign Minister Anthony Eden of Great Britain and Stalin in December, 1941. At that time, with his armies extremely hard pressed to withstand the German invasion, Stalin had the temerity to ask that Britain agree to an extension of Soviet boundaries to include all of Lithuania, Latvia, and Estonia, and sizeable portions of Poland and Finland. Roosevelt, convinced that Russia's cooperation was vital in the creation of a peaceful world order, worked toward that desired end. It was mutual necessity, however, and not common long-range objectives, that kept the Grand Alliance from becoming a dual alliance.

One of the major issues disrupting American-Soviet relations was that of a second front. Early in 1942, Russian Foreign Minister Molotov came to Washington to present the Soviet demand for an invasion of France no later than the end of the year; quite understandably, the Soviets wanted the pressure on their retreating armies reduced. Churchill strongly opposed such a demand as much too premature. Instead, he convinced Roosevelt of the importance of invading North Africa to relieve Nazi pressure on the Suez Canal. Stalin viewed the resulting North Africa campaign as an insidious attempt by his two capitalist allies to allow the Russian military to suffer heavy losses. When Roosevelt met with Churchill at Casablanca in January of 1943, he decided against the recommendation of General George C. Marshall, his Chief-of-Staff, to proceed with the invasion so strongly desired by Stalin, in favor of Churchill's plan to invade Sicily and Italy. This decision only intensified Soviet distrust of American intentions, and the seeds of the Cold War had been sown.

The Casablanca "summit" meeting also produced the highly controversial demand for "unconditional surrender." In making the announcement that "Peace can come to the world only by the total elimination of German and Japanese war power," Roosevelt apparently believed that only by completely eradicating fascism from the world could the postwar reconstruction begin. The proclamation was at least partially designed to reassure Stalin of his and Churchill's good intentions. Instead of a cross-channel invasion of France, Stalin received merely a pledge from his Allies to destroy the enemy. In retrospect, the proclamation stands as a monument to Roosevelt's failure to develop detailed plans for the inevitable postwar era. As Professor Gaddis Smith observes, "The harm was in the impact of the slogan on the formulation of American policy. Unconditional surrender was in spirit the antithesis of careful long-range planning. It encouraged the delusion that once the Axis was defeated there would be few obstacles in the way of establishing the wonderful world of peace."

Critics later charged that the unconditional surrender ultimatum caused Germany to stiffen her resistance, thus prolonging the war. It should be remembered, however, that Roosevelt explicitly stated that the policy "does not mean the destruction of the population of Germany, Italy or Japan, but it does mean the destruction of the philosophies in those countries which are based on conquest and the subjugation of other people." Together with Roosevelt's temporary endorsement of the Morgenthau Plan in the autumn of 1944, which would have stripped Germany of its mines and factories and created an impotent pastoral society incapable of waging war, unconditional surrender provided the German leaders with effective propaganda with which to urge the German people to continue the fight.

The tide of the war had turned by mid-1943. The Russian Army stopped the Germans just thirty miles from the outskirts of Moscow in December 1941 and slowly began to push them backwards. Germany's loss of nearly 90,000 troops at Stalingrad crippled her military power to such an extent that Hitler was thereafter unable to launch a sustained offensive. Victory in North Africa was complete by May and hard-earned successes in Sicily led to the withdrawal of Italy from the war. Nazi troops, however, remained in Italy and offered fierce resistance to the invading Allied troops until the end of the war in Europe. Perhaps most significant of all was the allied victory over the German submarines in the North Atlantic. By mid-1943, the three-year Battle of the Atlantic had been won and, thereafter, men and supplies flowed in an ever-increasing stream across the ocean.

Encouraged by these successes, Roosevelt and Churchill turned their attention to the long-delayed cross-channel invasion. During the Quebec conference in August, 1943, they instructed General Eisenhower to prepare for OVERLORD by May 1, 1944. The lack of sufficient landing ships caused a temporary delay but, on June 6, the biggest military operation in history began on the desolate beaches west of Normandy. It was the beginning of the end for Adolph Hitler.

The Allies could not have won the war without the fantastic production by American industry. Fortunately, the Roosevelt Administration had inaugurated a substantial preparedness program in 1940. Without it the war would have lasted much longer. "Our task is hard—our task is unprecedented—and the time is short," Roosevelt told Congress a month following Pearl Harbor. "We must strain every existing armament-producing facility to the utmost. We must convert every plant and tool to war production."

To a remarkable degree, this was accomplished. The result was staggering—80,000 tanks, 276,000 airplanes, 71,000 naval vessels, and millions of hand weapons. The problems of coordinating production were tremendous and it was not until 1943, when the Office of War Mobilization was created, under the chairmanship of James F. Byrnes, that the problems were solved. Like the War Industries Board of World War I, the O. W. M. wielded tremendous powers over all aspects of war production. Priorities over materials were rigidly enforced and rationing of scarce commodities, such as sugar, meat, gasoline, rubber, and shoes, was established; even a national speed limit of 35 mph was set in an attempt to conserve fuel and tires. Civilian Americans planted Victory Gardens, conducted scrap drives, and participated in Civilian Defense programs with patriotic enthusiasm. Black-market operations were kept to a minimum, but the ingenuity demonstrated by the American women in locating extremely scarce nylon stockings was often amazing.

The price of survival was high—291,557 Americans were killed and more than a half million others were wounded in action. The war also cost the American taxpayer dearly—over $320 billion. This was twice as much spent by the nation throughout its entire history up to 1941. For the first time, the average American citizen paid a tax on his income as Congress placed some of the burden of the war upon those with small incomes. Just 7,500,000 Americans had filed income tax returns in 1939, but 50,000,000 did so in 1945. High taxes on inheritance, luxuries, and amusements were collected as Congress sought to locate new sources of revenue. Even so, 60 percent of the war cost was financed by borrowing from the American people through the sale of Series "E" savings bonds. At war's end, the United States carried an indebtedness of $258 billion; in 1940, the national debt had stood at just $43 billion.

The tremendous increase in government spending accomplished what the New Deal could not—the restoration of full employment. Lord Keynes had been correct—massive injections of federal dollars into the economy quickly ended the depression and set off an era of economic growth, which continued far into the postwar era. The Gross National Product jumped 113 percent between 1940 and 1945; by 1944, the national unemployment level was below 2 percent. With a peak strength of 12,300,000 men in uniform, many leaders feared that the end of the war would cause a resumption of the depression, but their concern was proven unfounded by the rapid expansion of the economy during the postwar years.

Millions of Americans improved their economic position substantially during the war. Skilled workers, technicians, and farmers were among the chief beneficiaries. In fact, many workers benefitted from substantial overtime pay and some even held two jobs. Income for industrial workers increased by 86 percent between 1939 and 1945, while inflation raised the cost of living just 28 percent. By 1942, farm policy had been changed from restriction of production to encouragement of maximum yield, and per capita income for farmers increased over 300 percent during the war. Ironically, those 15,000,000 men and women who served in the armed forces were generally unable to participate in the new prosperity, although a politically alert Congress, responding to the prodding of the veterans' lobby, provided G. I. Joe with substantial education and housing benefits designed to help ease his return to civilian life.

The benefits received by the workers and farmers, however, paled in comparison to those reaped by big business. In its efforts to stimulate production, the government granted corporations involved in defense extremely favorable tax advantages, awarded lucrative "cost-plus" contracts, and even provided the corporations with new equipment and facilities. A special Senate Committee headed by Harry S. Truman saved the taxpayers billions by investigating waste and duplication of programs in the gigantic defense program but, despite its best efforts, the committee proved incapable of securing many contracts for small firms. The close present-day relationship between the military and big business was firmly cemented during the war. Of the approximate $175 billion of prime defense contracts awarded by the government, the one hundred largest corporations received about 70 percent. "No wonder," sociologist C. Wright Mills concluded, "that in World War II, little fortunes became big and many new little ones were created."

One of the most portentous side effects of the economic expansion was the revival of urban growth. Quite naturally the cities on the eastern and western coasts grew rapidly as the American war machine funneled men and supplies through their several ports. Los Angeles, for example, gained nearly 25 percent in population during the decade; nearly one and a half million persons migrated to the West Coast during the war to work in the defense establishments in such cities as Long Beach, Oakland, and Seattle. Throughout the nation, families left the small towns and marginal farms to seek the high wages available in the burgeoning defense industries. By war's end, the United States stood on the brink of the new age of megalopolis.

Of all social institutions, the family underwent the most significant change. Under the pressures of war, the marriage rate rose markedly as did the birthrate (especially after 1943). The tensions and anxieties created by the prolonged separation of nearly four million families as sons, fathers, and husbands served in the armed forces were manifest in the shocking increases of illegitimacy, juvenile delinquency, and divorce (which nearly doubled between 1940 and 1945).

Nowhere was the impact of the war more evident than in the large cities where collisions of whites and blacks occurred under the extraordinary frustrations and tensions created by total war. In Detroit the result was a violent race riot, which lasted for three days. Well before the turn of the twentieth century, Negroes had begun to migrate to the north and west in search of economic opportunity, and World War I had intensified this process. Between 1940 and 1945, however, nearly one million blacks left the South. One hundred thousand moved into Chicago alone, and 250,000 to West Coast cities. Equally significant, but less evident, was the fact that in the South 300,000 Negroes left their sharecroppers' shacks and moved to the ghettos of such rapidly expanding cities as Birmingham, Memphis, and Houston. By 1945, the question of race could no longer be considered merely regional in scope.

While the United States battled the racist doctrines of Adolph Hitler, civil rights leaders did not hesitate to point out the paradox of the condition of one tenth of the American people. As Roy Wilkins of the NAACP sardonically noted, "Hitler jammed our white people into the logically untenable position. Forced to oppose him for the sake of the life of the nation, they were jockeyed into declaring against his racial theories—publicly." Within the black community there emerged a new determination and a new sense of urgency and militancy. "There is bound to be a redefinition of the Negro's status in America as a result of the war," Gunnar Myrdal correctly predicted in 1944;

the revolution in race relations, which occurred in postwar America, grew out of the milieu of the war.

The long-developing revolution in science and technology also received a stimulus from the war. Mobilization of resources for military purposes was mandatory and, in 1941, President Roosevelt created the Office of Scientific Research and Development under the chairmanship of Dr. Vannevar Bush. Under his direction, two divisions were created. The National Defense Research Committee devoted its attention to weaponry development and produced such lethal devices as proximity fuses (which turned antiaircraft near-misses into hits) and new and sophisticated rockets, including the bazooka. The development of radar and innumerable electronic devices associated with air travel were other achievements. The Committee on Medical Research concerned itself with the problems of military medicine. Its accomplishments included the development of blood plasma, the further development of the British-discovered penicillin, and improved efficiency in the methods of treating battle wounds; during World War I, 8 percent of the wounded Americans died, but this was reduced to just 3 percent in World War II. In addition, the Office of Production Research and Development under the Office of War Mobilization studied the scientific and technical problems related to industrial production and made significant advances in synthetic rubber and the production of magnesium, aluminum, and motor fuels.

The development of the atomic bomb, of course, overshadows all of the other scientific achievements. President Roosevelt authorized the development of such a weapon at the insistence of Albert Einstein and other leading scientists who correctly believed that Germany had its own scientists at work on developing a nuclear weapon. At a cost of two billion dollars, the super-secret Manhattan Project produced a nuclear explosion on July 16, 1945, over the New Mexico desert. Twenty-one days later a larger version of the bomb, with a force equal to 20,000 tons of TNT, was detonated over Hiroshima. It killed an estimated 80,000 Japanese and maimed an untold number of others. When the Japanese leaders failed to surrender, an even more powerful bomb was dropped on Nagasaki three days later. The next day Emperor Hirohito overruled the fanatic and resolute military and sued for peace. On September 2, 1945, General Douglas MacArthur accepted the Japanese surrender on the deck of the *U.S.S. Missouri* in Tokyo Bay.

The use of the two atomic bombs immediately became a major controversy. President Truman defended his decision by arguing that their use saved thousands of American and Japanese lives by shortening the war and making an invasion of the Japanese mainland unnecessary. His decision rested upon a recommendation by a special "interim" committee headed by Secretary of War Henry L. Stimson, which urged that the bomb be used on a target that would produce the maximum psychological effect. A large group of nuclear scientists who had worked on the Manhattan Project, however, submitted a report to the White House urging that it not be used, at least not until a demonstration bomb had been detonated over a deserted island so that the Japanese leaders could see the consequences of prolonging the war. Truman, however, for still puzzling reasons, never saw this report, and his decision to use the bomb upon essentially civilian targets has haunted many Americans ever since.

President Truman has explained that he looked upon the atomic bomb solely from within a military context and primarily as a device to save American lives: "I had realized, of course, that an atomic bomb would inflict damage and casualties beyond imagination. . . . The final decision of where and when to use the atomic bomb was up to me. Let there be no mistake about it. I regarded the bomb as a military weapon and never had any doubt that it should be used. The top military advisors to the President recommended its use, and when I talked to Churchill he unhesitatingly told me that he favored the use of the atomic bomb if it might aid to end the war."

Several "revisionist" historians, however, have been unwilling to accept Mr. Truman's simple explanation. They have pointed out in several books and articles that the planned invasion of the Japanese mainland was not scheduled until November 1, 1945, and that by the summer of 1945 the ability of the Japanese to sustain their military efforts had been seriously impaired. With American lives not immediately endangered and the Japanese military incapable of offensive action, they conclude, Truman must have had another motivation to use the bombs with such haste. They found it in the important American diplomatic objectives of preventing the Soviet Union from establishing a foothold in the Far East and of forcing her acquiescence to an American solution to the reconstruction of Europe. By demonstrating her willingness to use the new superweapon, the revisionists imply, the United States hoped to blackmail the Russians into accepting the American formula for postwar settlement. Such crude atomic diplomacy, together with other examples of American bellicosity, naturally created a Soviet response. Thus the Truman Administration must be held primarily responsible for starting the Cold War.

Critics of this startling interpretation, however, have contended that if the Truman Administration did, in fact, use the atomic bomb to intimidate the Russians, then it failed miserably. Atomic monopoly or no, the United States suffered serious diplomatic reversals at the hands of the bombless Soviets in 1945 and 1946.

Whatever the motivation, however, the bombs did in fact end the greatest war in history. War had reshuffled the world order—once mighty England and haughty France were now reduced to the status of second-rate powers, and

Germany and Japan lay prostrate at the feet of the Allied occupying forces. The United States and the Soviet Union now controlled the balance of power in the world, and their rival philosophies of capitalism and communism, democracy and authoritarianism, confronted each other in an atomic age. The way in which the American people would live had also been transformed. By stimulating the civil rights movement, by accelerating the rate of scientific and technological advance, by increasing the rate of urban growth and by placing new stresses upon social institutions, the war had sculptured the pattern for postwar America.

SECONDARY SOURCES

1. HERBERT FEIS, "WAR CAME AT PEARL HARBOR: SUSPICIONS RECONSIDERED"

SHORTLY after sunrise on Sunday morning, December 7, 1941, a wave of Japanese fighter planes swept down upon the unsuspecting American naval base at Pearl Harbor. Catching the sleepy Americans completely by surprise, the Japanese shattered the Pacific fleet. Fortunately, the attackers did not bother to bomb the huge oil reserves and the permanent installations on the island. And the all-important aircraft carriers attached to the Pacific Fleet were out on maneuvers and thus escaped the bombardment. Even then, the attack was a tremendous success. Few American aircraft managed to become airborne to challenge the attacking Zeroes, and most antiaircraft batteries remained silent. More than 50 percent of the aircraft on the island of Oahu were damaged or destroyed; five battleships were sunk and several others severely damaged. More than 2400 Americans were killed and 1178 wounded. So great were the losses that the government did not release full reports until much later in order to prevent panic among the American people.

This ruthless attack, however, served the purpose of swiftly uniting the American nation. The rancorous debate over foreign policy ended abruptly with the news of the attack (staunch isolationist Senator Gerald P. Nye, in fact, halted his criticism of Roosevelt's policies in the middle of a Pittsburgh speech). Shock and dismay soon gave way to anger and resolution as a united people girded for war.

Following the Axis defeat in 1945, several writers, including historians Charles A. Beard and Charles C. Tansill, sought to place the blame for Pearl Harbor on President

SOURCE. Herbert Feis, "War Came at Pearl Harbor: Suspicions Reconsidered," in *The Yale Review*, Vol. 45, Spring 1956, pp. 378–390. Copyright 1965 by Yale University Press. Reprinted by permission of *The Yale Review* and the author.

Roosevelt. Although the arguments of these "revisionists" vary somewhat, the general theme of their writings is that President Roosevelt was unable to convince the American people or the Congress of the importance of intervening in the European conflict to defeat Nazi Germany and had needlessly exposed the fleet at Pearl Harbor in an attempt to invite attack. One of the key bits of evidence used to support this contention is the entry in the Diary *of Secretary of War Henry L. Stimson, which related how the Roosevelt Cabinet on November 25 discussed "the question of how we should maneuver them (the Japanese) into the position of firing the first shot without allowing too much danger to ourselves." Thus the Roosevelt critics concluded that the President maneuvered the United States through "the back door to war" in the Pacific in order to bring the nation into the European war to save England.*

The overwhelming rejection by professional historians of this "devil" interpretation of America's entrance into the war does not mean, however, that the policies followed by the Roosevelt Administration were necessarily correct. Professor Paul Schroeder, for example, has brilliantly argued that war with Japan could possibly have been avoided had the Roosevelt Administration not taken an unrealistic position of demanding the liberation of China. By mounting a strong diplomatic and economic offensive, which sought to force Japan to withdraw her troops from China, Schroeder argues, the United States left Japan with no alternative but to attack the United States. By freezing Japanese assets in the United States and by placing a crippling embargo upon strategic materials, he concludes, the United States made inevitable "an unnecessary and avoidable war—an outcome which constitutes the ultimate failure of diplomacy."

Schroeder's carefully documented and reasoned analysis, however, has not attracted much attention outside of scholarly circles. Instead, those advocating the sensational conspiratorial thesis have received the attention of the general public. It was this unhappy situation which prompted Herbert Feis to challenge the false assumptions and juggling of evidence that characterizes these studies. Feis is a former member of the State Department and the author of several volumes that are characterized by their favorable treatment of the diplomacy of Franklin D. Roosevelt.

Ten years after victory, we look ruefully at the way the world has gone. It is right and natural to search out any errors of judgment or faults of character that have led us to our present pass. But such self-scrutiny can go awry if governed by a wish to revile rather than a wish to understand. Unless we are alert, that could happen as a result of the suspicions that have come to cluster around the way in which the United States became engaged in the Second World War—torch-lit by the Pearl Harbor disaster.

The more recently available sources have added but little to our knowledge of the events that led to our entry into the war. The books of memoirs written by Japanese witnesses have told us something more, especially about the struggle within the Japanese Government. But in my reading, while they may improve our knowledge of details, they do not change the fundamental view of this experience or its main features. In American and British records still kept secret there may be information or explanations that would do so. But even this I doubt. With no new great revealing facts to display, and no great new insights to impart, the most useful service would seem to be to act as caretaker of what is known, and in particular to deal with certain warped comments and inferences that seasonally must feel the straightening edge of evidence.

Of all the accusations made, the one most shocking to me is that Roosevelt and his chief advisers deliberately left the Pacific Fleet and base at Pearl Harbor exposed as a lure to bring about a direct Japanese attack upon us.

This has been diffused in the face of the fact that the Japanese High Military Command conference before the Imperial Throne on September 6, 1941, resolved that "If by the early part of October there is no reasonable hope of having our demands agreed to in the diplomatic negotiations mentioned above, we will immediately make up our minds to get ready for war against America (and England and Holland)." This is September 6. The plan for the attack on Pearl Harbor was not approved and adopted until October; and Secret Operation Order #1, the execution of the plan, was not issued until November 5. The presence of the Pacific Fleet at Pearl Harbor was not a lure but an obstacle.

The literature of accusation ignores or rejects the real reasons why the Pacific Fleet was kept in Hawaii. It must do so, since one of the main reasons was the hope that its presence there would deter the Japanese from making so threatening a move south or north that American armed forces might have to join in the war. It scorns the fact that the American military plans—to be executed in the event that we became engaged in war—assigned vital tasks to this Pacific Fleet. A mind must indeed be distracted if it can believe that the American Government could, at one and the same time, use the Pacific Fleet as a target and count on having it as part of its main defending force.

A variant of this accusation, which at least does not require such a willingness to believe the worst, might also be noted—that despite ample knowledge that Pearl Harbor was about to be attacked, the American Government purposefully left it exposed and allowed the event to happen.

Those who do not find such an idea at odds with their view of the sense of duty and regard for human life of President Roosevelt and his chief advisers can find striking points about the occurrence that may be construed to correspond with this conception. How they glare out of the record in hindsight: Ambassador Grew's warnings; Secretary Hull's acute gleam put into words at least three times in Cabinet Councils in November that the Japanese attack might come "at any moment, anywhere"; the intercepted Japanese messages telling of the Japanese effort to secure minute information as to the location of the ships of our Pacific Fleet in the Harbor; carelessness in checking up on the protective measures taken by the local commanders; failure to use the chance to give an effective last-minute warning to Hawaii. How else, it is asked, can these be explained except in terms of secret and conscious purpose?

However, just as hindsight makes the failure of perception plain, so it also makes it understandable—but only by bringing back to mind the total circumstances. That can be done here only in the barest way. Up to then Japanese strategy had been wary, one small creeping step after another, from Manchuria to North China into China and down into Indo-China. American military circles came to take it for granted that it would go on that way. Then there was the fact that Japan's basic objectives lay to the south and southeast; there and there only it could get what it needed—raw materials, oil, and island bases to withstand the attack from the West. Expectation already set in that direction was kept there by impressive and accurate intelligence reports of movements under way. Against this flow of preconception, the signs pointing to Pearl Harbor were not heeded.

Such features of contemporary thinking within the American Government explain, though they do not excuse, the failure to discern that Pearl Harbor was going to be attacked. To think the contrary is to believe that the President and the heads of the American Army, Navy, and Air Force were given to deep deception, and in order to have us enter the war were ready to sacrifice not only the Pacific Fleet but the whole war plan for the Pacific. This, I think, is the difference between history and police court history.

I have taken note of these accusations that have been built about the disaster at Pearl Harbor because they appeal to the sense of the sinister which is so lively in our times. But I am glad to turn to ideas and interpretations of broader historical import.

The first of these is that Roosevelt and the Joint Chiefs of Staff were obligated by secret agreements with Churchill and their British colleagues to enter the war at some time or other, in one way or other. Therefore, it is further supposed, the American authors of this agreement had to cause either Germany or Japan, or both, to attack us.

This view derives encouragement from the fact that the American Government *did* enter into a secret agreement about strategy with the British. The accord, known as ABC-1 Staff Agreement, adopted at Washington in March, 1941, set down the respective missions of the British and American elements in the event that the United States should be at war with Germany or Japan, or both; and subsequently the American basic joint war plan, Rainbow-5, was adjusted to fit this combined plan of operations. An attempt was made at a similar conference in Singapore soon after to work out a more detailed United States–British–Dutch operating plan for the Pacific. This attempt failed; but the discussion that took place there left a lasting mark on American official thinking, for the conferees defined the limits on land and sea beyond which Japanese forces could not be permitted to go without great risk to the defenders.

The ABC-1 agreement did not place the Roosevelt Administration under *political* obligation to enter the war against either Germany or Japan, not even if Japan attacked British or Dutch areas in the Far East. Nor did Roosevelt give a promise to this effect to Churchill when they met at Newfoundland in August, 1941. Up to the very eve of the Japanese assault the President refused to tell the British or Dutch what we would do. In short, the Government kept itself officially free from any obligation to enter the war, certainly free of any obligation to thrust itself into the war.

But I do think this accord conveyed responsibilities of a moral sort. After ABC-1 was adopted, production of weapons in the United States and the British Commonwealth took it into account; and the allocation of weapons, troops, ships, and planes as between threatened areas was based on the expectation that the United States would carry out the assignments set down in the plan.

Thus, it may be fairly thought, Roosevelt and his administration were obligated to try to gain the consent of Congress and the American people to play the part designated in the joint plans if Japanese assaults crossed the land and sea boundaries of resistance that were defined at these joint staff conferences. In the last November weeks when the end of the diplomatic talks with Japan came into sight, and General Marshall and Admiral Stark were asked what measures should be taken in face of the threatened Japanese advances, they advised the President to declare the limits defined at Singapore, and to warn the Japanese that we would fight if these were crossed. There is much reason to think this would have been done even had the Japanese not struck at Pearl Harbor and the Philippines, and this boundary would have been the line between peace and war. But this reaffirmation was made not as a measure required to carry out a secret accord, but because it was believed to be the best course.

A variant explanation of the way we dealt with Japan runs somewhat as follows: that Roosevelt was determined to get into the war against Germany; that he had to find a release from his public promises that the United States would not enter "foreign wars" unless attacked; that his efforts to do so by unneutral aid to Britain and the Soviet Union had failed because Hitler had refused to accept the challenge; and so he sought another door into war, a back door, by inviting or compelling the Japanese attack.

This interpretation, with its kick at the end, twists the record around its own preconception. The actions taken did not flow from a settled wish to get us into war. They trailed along the rim of necessity of the true purpose—which was to sustain resistance against the Axis. How many times the American Government refused to do what the British, French, Chinese, Russians, Dutch asked it to do, because it might involve us in actual combat!

This slant of reasoning about American action passes by the course of Japanese conduct which aroused our fears and stimulated our opposition: the way in which, despite all our pleas and warnings, Japan pressed on. By not recognizing that these Japanese actions called for American counter-action, it excuses them. Thus our resistance is made to appear as nothing else but a deceitful plot to plunge us into war. Furthermore, it dismisses as insincere the patient attempt to calm Japan by diplomatic talks, by offers to join in safeguarding its security.

There were influential individuals in the Roosevelt Administration who wanted to get into the war and indifferent as to how we got into it. Of these, Secretary of the Interior Ickes was, I believe, the most candid, at any rate in his diary entries. Secretary of the Treasury Morgenthau and his staff also had a positive wish that we should engage in war—but against Germany, not against Japan, for that might have brought a diversion of forces to the Pacific. Secretary of War Stimson thought that it would not be possible for Great Britain to sustain the fight unless we entered it; but toward the very end, particularly as it was becoming plain that the Soviet Union was going to survive the Nazi assault, he began to wish for delay. However, time and time again the memoirs and diaries record the impatience of these officials, and those who thought like them, with Hull's caution and Roosevelt's watchful indirection.

The most genuine point made by those who dissent, one that merits thorough analysis, is that the American Government, in conjunction with the British and Dutch, refused to continue to supply Japan with machines and materials vital to it—especially oil. It is contended that they thereby compelled Japan to resort to war, or at least fixed a time period in which Japan was faced with the need of deciding to yield to our terms or go to war.

In reflecting upon this action, the reasons for it must not be confused with the Japanese response to it. Japan showed no signs of curbing its aggressive course. It paid no heed to repeated and friendly warnings that unless it did, the threatened countries would have to take counter-measures. As when on February 14, 1941, while the Lend-Lease Act was being argued in Congress, Dooman, Counsellor of the American Embassy in Japan and known to be a firm and straightforward friend of that country, carried back from Washington the message for the Vice-Minister for Foreign Affairs: that the American people were determined to support Britain even at the risk of war; that if Japan or any other country menaced that effort "it would have to expect to come in conflict with the United States"; and that the United States had abstained from an oil embargo in order not to impel Japan to create a situation that could only lead to the most serious outcome. Japan's answer over the following months had been to force its way further into Indo-China and threaten the Dutch East Indies.

This sustained proof that Japan was going on with its effort to dominate Asia, and the alliance pledging it to stand by Germany if that country got into war with the United States, made a continuation of trade with Japan an act of meekness on our part. Japan was concentrating its foreign purchases on products needed for war, while reducing civilian use by every means, and was thus accumulating great reserve stocks. These were enabling it to maintain its invasion of China without much strain, while continuing to expand its war-making power. Had *effective* restraints—note that I do not say *total* restraints—not been imposed, the American Government would have been in the strange position of having declared an unlimited national emergency, of calling upon the American people to strengthen their army, navy, and air force in great urgency, while at the same time nourishing the opponent that might have to be met in battle. This was a grave, if not intolerable, responsibility.

It is hard to tell how squarely the American and British Governments faced the possible consequence of their restrictive measures. My impression is that they knew the danger of war with Japan was being increased; that Japan might try to get by force the means denied it. The Japanese Government served plain warnings that this game of thrust and counterthrust might so end. These were soberly regarded, but did not weaken the will that Japan was not to have its way by threat.

Mingled with the anxiety lest these restrictive measures would make war more likely, there was a real hope that they might be a deterrent to war. Conceivably they would bring home to the Japanese people that if it came to war, they might soon run out of the means for combat, while the rapid growth of American military strength would make it clear that they could not in the end win. And, as evidence of these probabilities became plain, the conciliatory elements in the Japanese Government would prevail over the more militant ones.

This almost happened. But the reckless ones, those who would rather court fatality than accept frustration, managed to retain control of Japanese decision. The pressure applied by us did not prevent war, and may have brought the time of decision for war closer. The valid question, however, is not whether the American Government resorted to these restrictions *in order* to drive Japan to attack; it is whether the American Government failed to grasp a real chance, after the restraints had begun to leave their mark in Japanese official circles, to arrive at a satisfactory understanding that would have averted war. Twice, in the opinion of some qualified students of the subject, such a chance emerged, or at least appeared on the horizon of diplomacy. Were they real opportunities or merely mirages or decoys?

The first of these was the occasion when in the autumn of 1941, the Japanese Prime Minister, Prince Konoye, sought a personal meeting with the President. It is averred that the President's failure to respond lost a chance to avert the war without yielding any American principle or purpose. Some think the reason was that American diplomacy was inflexible, dull in its insight, and too soaked in mistrust. Others, more accusatory, explain the decision by a lack of desire for an agreement that would have thwarted the design for war.

Since there is no conclusive evidence of what Konoye intended to propose or could have achieved, comment on this subject must enter into the "boggy ground of what-might-have-been." Some observers, including Ambassador Grew, believe that Konoye could have made a real, and an irreversible, start toward meeting American terms. It will always be possible to think that this is so. But to the Americans in authority, the chance seemed small. Konoye was a man who in every past crisis had allowed himself to flounder between criss-crossed promises; hence there was good reason to fear an attempt at deception. Such glimpses as we have of what he might have proposed do not support the view that he could have offered a suspension or end of the fight against China. His freedom to negotiate would have been subject to the conditions stated by those who had controlled Japan's course up to then—their price for allowing him to go to meet the President.

Even so, to repeat, it is possible that skilled and more daring American diplomacy might have handled the meeting so as to get a satisfactory accord; or, failing that—and this is the more likley chance—to bring about so deep a division within the Japanese circle of decision as to have prevented warlike action. These alluring historical queries will continue to roam in the land of might-have-been.

But the risks were great. The echoes of Munich and its aftermath were still loud. The American Government might have found itself forced to make a miserable choice: either to accept an accord which would have left Japan free to complete its conquest of China and menace the rest of Asia, or to face a deep division among the American people. Any understanding with Japan that was not clear and decisive would have had unpredictable consequences. The Chinese Government might have felt justified in making a deal following our own. The Soviet Union, at this time just managing with the greatest effort and agony to prevent German victory, might also have chosen to compromise with Hitler rather than to fight it out. Speculations such as these must leave the subject unsettled. But in any case I think it clear that the American decision was one of judgment, not of secret intent. Konoye was not told that the President would not meet with him; he was told that he would not do so until more progress had been made toward defining what the Japanese Government was prepared to propose.

The same basic question had to be faced in the final crisis of negotiation in November, 1941: whether to relax restraints on Japan and leave it in a position to keep on trying to control much of Asia in return for a promise not to press on farther for the time being.

The opinion that the Japanese truce offer made at this last juncture accepted the main purposes and principles for which the American Government had been standing may be summarily dismissed. It was ambiguously worded, it was silent about the alliance with Germany, and it would have required the American Government to end its support of China—for the last of its numbered five points read: "The Government of the United States undertakes to refrain from such measures and actions as will be prejudicial to the endeavors for the restoration of general peace between Japan and China." This scant and unclear proposal was at once deemed "entirely unacceptable." Furthermore, there seemed little use and much possible damage in making a counter truce-offer of the same variety. The intercepted Japanese messages stated flatly that this was Japan's last and best offer. They told of the swift dismissal of a much more nearly acceptable one that Nomura and Korusu asked their superiors in Tokyo to consider. A deadline had been set. Thus it was all but sure that the reduced counter-order which had been patched together in Washington would be unheeded. But it might shake the coalition to which by then the opponents of the Axis had pledged their lives and national destinies.

This seems to have been the thought uppermost in Hull's mind in recommending to the President that the counter truce-offer be withheld. As set down in his historic memo of November 26, he had been led to this conclusion by the opposition of the Chinese, the half-hearted support or actual opposition of the British, Dutch, and Australian governments, and the further excited opposition to be expected because of lack of appreciation of the importance and value of a truce. This I believe to have been the true determining reason for a decision reluctantly taken. Even if by then Japan was genuinely ready to reform, the repentance had come too late. The situation had grown too entangled by then for minor measures, its momentum too great. Germany-Italy-Japan had forced the creation of a defensive coalition more vast than the empire of the Pacific for which Japan plotted. This was not now to be quieted or endangered by a temporary halt along the fringe of the Japanese advance.

Even though these reasons for dropping the idea of a truce may seem sufficient, they leave the question why the American Government could not have given a softer and less declaratory answer. Why had it to give one so "bleakly uncompromising"? It could have said simply that the Japanese offer did not convey the assurances that would warrant us and the alliance for which we spoke to resume the shipment of war materials to Japan and end our aid to China. Why was it deemed advisable or essential at this juncture to state fully and forcibly our maximum terms for a settlement in the Pacific? Was it foreseen that, scanned with mistrust as it would almost surely be, this would be construed as a demand for the swift abandonment of Japan's whole program? Was it done, as the accusation runs, with the deliberate intent of banning any last chance for an accord? Of propelling the Japanese attack?

That this was not the reason I am as sure as anyone can be on a matter of this sort; but I can offer only conjecture as to what the inspiring purposes were. Perhaps to vindicate past actions and decisions. Perhaps a wish to use the dramatic chance to put in the record a statement of the aims for which the risk of war was being accepted, and of the basis on which the Americans would found the peace when the time came. Such an idea was in accord with the usual mode of thought of the men in charge of the Executive Branch of the Government and of most of the American people. It gave vent to the propensity exemplified in Hull to find a base in general principles meant to be at once political standards and moral ideals. After long caution, it appealed as a defiant contradiction of the Axis program. All this, however, is surmise rather than evidenced history.

But I think it is well within the realm of evidenced history that the memo of November 26 was not in any usual sense of the word an ultimatum. It did not threaten the Japanese with war or any other form of forceful punishment if our terms were not accepted. It simply left them in the state of distress in which they were, with the prospect that they might later have to submit to our requirements. The Japanese Government could have, as Konoye and Nomura pleaded with it to do, allowed the situation to drag along, with or without resuming talks with the American Government. Its power to make war would have been depleted, but neither quickly nor crucially. The armed forces and even the position in China could have been maintained.

Notably, the final Japanese answer which ended negotiations on December 7, 1941, does not accuse the American Government of confronting it with an ultimatum, but only of thwarting the larger Japanese aims. Part 14—the clinching part of this note—reads: "Obviously it is the intention of the American Government to conspire with Great Britain and other countries to obstruct Japan's efforts toward the establishment of peace through the creation of a New Order in East Asia and especially to preserve Anglo-American rights and interests by keeping Japan and China at war. This intention has been revealed clearly during the course of the present negotiations. Thus, the earnest hope of the Japanese Government to adjust Japanese-American relations and to preserve and promote the peace of the Pacific through cooperation with the American Government has finally been lost."

This is a more nearly accurate description of the purposes of the American Government under Roosevelt than those attributed to it by hostile and suspicious American critics. Our Government did obstruct Japanese efforts, believing them to be unjust, cruel, and a threat to our national security, especially after Japan became a partner with Hitler's Germany and Mussolini's Italy and bent its efforts toward bringing the world under their combined control.

This determination stood on the proposition that it was better to take the risks of having to share in the suffering of the war than of finding ourselves moved or compelled to fight a more desperate battle against the Axis later on. The American Government, I believe, knew how serious a risk of war was being taken. But in its addresses to the American people it chose to put in the forefront the perils we would face if the Axis won, and to leave in the background, even to camouflage, the risks of finding ourselves plunged into wars which during the election campaign it had promised would not occur. Whether any large number of Americans were fooled by this, or whether most of them, in reality, were content to have the prospect presented that way rather than in a more blunt and candid way, I do not know.

This essay in interpretation has compelled me to recall and stress the aggressive Japanese assault—though I should have been glad to let that slip into the past. The passage of time does not alter facts, but it can bring a fuller and calmer understanding of them. It frees the mind for fairer appreciation of the causes and circumstances which impelled Japan along its tragic course and which impelled us to resist it. For both countries there are many common lessons. One of them is that continued friendliness requires mutual effort to relieve the other, to the extent it can, of deep cause for anxiety—the Japanese people of their anxiety over the means of living decently, the American people of anxiety about their security and power to defend the free world. Another is that they must both feel, speak, and act so honestly and steadily that their view of each other will be cleared of mistrust, and brightened by trust.

2. GADDIS SMITH, "THE NATURE OF WARTIME DIPLOMACY"

WHEN President Roosevelt returned from the Yalta Conference in February of 1945, he expressed high hopes for the future. The Conference, he said, would lead to "the end of the system of unilateral action, the exclusive alliances, the spheres of influence, the bal-

SOURCE. Gaddis Smith, *American Diplomacy During the Second World War*, New York: John Wiley & Sons, 1965, pp. 1–17. Copyright 1965 by John Wiley & Sons, Inc. Reprinted by permission of the author.

ances of power, and all the other expedients that have been tried for centuries—and failed. We propose to substitute for all these a universal organization in which all peace-loving Nations will finally have a chance to join." Roosevelt's dreams of the establishment of a new world order based on cooperation, democracy, and peace soon faded before the reality of Russian intransigence. In the weeks following Yalta, as the defeat of Germany grew closer, Marshal Joseph Stalin grew less cooperative and more cantankerous. Roosevelt himself recognized this, and only hours before his death sent a message to Churchill that he was growing apprehensive about "the general Soviet problem." Roosevelt told the Prime Minister, "We must be firm, however, and our course thus far is correct."

Just how much Roosevelt's conduct of wartime diplomacy contributed to America's postwar international difficulties is impossible to determine. What is clear, however, is that his own personality shaped the manner in which he dealt with other world powers. Forever optimistic about the future, and devoted to the establishment of a world order based on the vision of Woodrow Wilson, Roosevelt was much more interested in discussing broad humitarian goals than in hammering out detailed policies. Anxious to avoid fundamental differences among the Big Three, he contented himself with having Churchill and Stalin agree "in principle" to his lofty but imprecise vision of the postwar world, which had as its central theme the establishment of the United Nations. For the most part, Roosevelt was unwilling to use his superior bargaining power to force Stalin to commit himself to specific policies for fear that Russia might pull out of the war as it had in 1918. By the spring of 1945, therefore, Roosevelt's hopes for cooperation between the United States and the Soviet Union began to fade, and it was Harry S. Truman who would have to try to put the pieces together again.

The assumptions on which Roosevelt built his wartime diplomacy have been given careful scrutiny by Professor Gaddis Smith of Yale University. Despite his rigorous criticism of Roosevelt's diplomacy, Smith nevertheless concludes his study on a balanced and thoughtful note: "Would the postwar world have been a happier and more secure place for the United States and for all mankind if Roosevelt had behaved differently during the war? Possibly. It also might have been worse. Russia treated as an adversary rather than friend might, as men feared at the time, have reached a truce with Hitler. This seems unlikely, but the possibility was there. Or Stalin in the face of the type of opposition which Churchill recommended in 1945 might have acted with less rather than more restraint in Europe and Asia. Who knows? The critic who denounces Roosevelt as a fool or worse and then says that such-and-such an alternative strategy in Europe and Asia, or both, would have altered the world for the better can never be convincing." The following selection is taken from the introductory chapter of Professor Smith's "American Diplomacy during the Second World War."

In the first half of the twentieth century man approximately doubled his population, quadrupled his industrial production, and radically altered the form of government over most of the earth. He also increased a thousandfold his power to kill. Chronic, dangerous instability was the result. World security depended as never before on international cooperation, but suspicion and hostility were the rule between states. Some nations longed for peace but prepared fearfully for war. Other nations gloried in the use of force because amoral leaders preferred to steal what they were unable to build in peace.

At first the United States considered itself blessedly immune from the world's violence and suffering. In 1914 President Woodrow Wilson urged unconditional neutrality as the way to safety during the European war. Neutrality was impossible; the United States joined the war and tipped the balance of opposing forces sufficiently to bring about the military defeat of Germany and an armistice in November 1918. Wilson then said that the unconditional acceptance by all nations of the ideals of altruism, democracy, and the League of Nations was the only way to secure lasting peace. The American people, however, denounced the League of Nations, and other countries felt that idealism was scant protection against the economic and political chaos of the time. By 1936 the League was dying, and the American Congress was busy passing laws designed to preserve absolute isolation when the next war, ominously visible on the horizon, swept over Europe.

War broke out in 1939 when Great Britain and France declared war on Germany for invading Poland. Germany and Soviet Russia, in cynical collusion, divided Poland and the Baltic states. Hitler soon struck to the west. Italy, stabbing France in the back, joined her Nazi ally. In June 1940 France fell. Hitler dominated western Europe and was planning to invade Great Britain. In Asia Japan intensified her war against China, entered into formal anti-American alliance with Germany and Italy, and prepared to extend her conquests.

American public opinion changed before the spectacle of unchecked Nazi aggression. President Franklin D. Roosevelt won support for military and naval preparedness and material aid to Great Britain. The United States became the "arsenal of democracy." Congress put aside the neutrality laws and passed the lend-lease program in March 1941. Three months later Hitler attacked Russia. Americans forgot their dislike for the Soviet state and extended aid. Roosevelt claimed that his aim was to keep the United States out of war, but by late 1941 the American people realized that the higher aim of checking Axis aggression might soon make entry into war inevitable. On the Atlantic the American navy was skirmishing with German U-boats. In the Pacific Japan might strike at any moment against the tightening web of American economic warfare. The blow came at Pearl Harbor, December 7,

1941. The United States was at war with Japan. Germany and Italy immediately declared war on the United States. The period of equivocal undeclared war was over.

Repeatedly and without success the United States had tried various unconditional approaches to peace and security: neutrality in 1914, idealism in 1918, isolation in the 1930's. Now the nation sought security by the unconditional defeat of the enemy. Since the enemy's existence was deemed the only significant cause of insecurity, men now assumed that a world consistent with American ideals and interests would emerge once the Axis powers were destroyed. Freed from enslavement and the fear of Axis aggression, all nations would embrace American ideals of democracy and peaceful conduct. If a misguided ally—Great Britain, for example—showed a tendency to stray from these ideals, a little friendly diplomatic persuasion would be sufficient to return her to the paths of righteousness. Absolute victory was achieved after four years and some effort had been made to change the behavior of allies, but Americans discovered in sorrow that peace was still unsecured. At the moment of victory in 1945 American leaders were on the verge of the realization that there were no unconditional solutions and that final, complete security in the twentieth century was unattainable.

The first diplomatic objective on the road to unconditional victory was coordination of the American, British, and Russian efforts. This was the task of the three heads of government: President Roosevelt, Prime Minister Winston S. Churchill, and Premier Josef V. Stalin. While the Big Three at the summit decided grand strategy and ambiguously discussed fundamental objectives of the war, their subordinates bargained to allocate materials, provide shipping, build bases, assign troops, and develop new weapons. The great decisions were tied to the outcome of the lesser and all required international negotiation. Diplomacy, instead of retiring to the sidelines until the fighting was over, became indispensable to every aspect of the war and thus to the life of the United States.

In December 1941 the potential power of the United States was great, but the immediate outlook was disastrous, far more disastrous than the American public realized. The navy was crippled; the army was an expanding swarm of civilians without sufficient equipment, training, or experienced officers; and industry was only partially converted from peacetime production. Germany controlled western Europe and her armies were wintering deep in Russia. Who dared predict that Russia could withstand the onslaught through another summer? Elsewhere German armies seemed on the verge of driving the British from Egypt and taking the vital Suez Canal. At any moment Franco in Spain might snatch Gibraltar. Hitler could then close the Mediterranean, dominate North Africa and the Middle East while choking the United Kingdom with a cordon of submarines in the Atlantic. The western hemisphere would be directly threatened. In Asia and the Pacific the only limit to Japan's wave of conquest was her own decision not to move beyond certain lines. Half of China, the Philippines, Indochina, Burma, Malaya, the Netherlands East Indies, and scores of smaller island groups were in her grasp. Would she seize India, Australia, Siberia, Hawaii? What could stop her? Anything was conceivable.

Fortunately, American diplomacy responded less to the immediate military peril, which might have been paralyzing, than to an optimistic view of the nation's historical experience and to the buoyantly confident personality of the commander-in-chief, Franklin D. Roosevelt. Americans later were to be led astray by too much optimism, but, on the dark morrow of Pearl Harbor, optimism enabled men to begin planning for victory. Notwithstanding the pain and humiliation of retreat in the Pacific, attention was turned first to coordinating strategy for the defeat of Germany. This priority was maintained on the sound assumption that Germany without Japan would be as strong as ever, whereas Japan without Germany could not long stand alone.

The remembered experience of the First World War exercised a profound effect on the diplomacy of European strategy. Americans had misleading and rather happy memories. In the summer of 1918 large numbers of American troops faced the enemy for the first time. By November the war was over. Admittedly, circumstances were now radically different, but the experience of 1918 combined with a natural optimism led Americans to favor a strategy of direct attack as soon as possible (preferably 1942 but certainly 1943) across the Channel on the center of German power.

The favored strategy of Great Britain, also based in large measure on experience of the First World War, was totally different. From the autumn of 1914 until the summer of 1918, while the United States remained neutral or in a state of preparation, Great Britain and France had seen an entire generation of young manhood die in the stinking trenches of the western front. For four years gains and losses were measured in yards, casualties in millions. Now, twenty-five years later, France was conquered and Britain, having narrowly rescued her small army at Dunkirk, stood alone in Europe. What Englishman could advocate a deliberate return to the horrors of the continent before all other methods of attacking the enemy had been exhausted and victory assured? Certainly not Churchill, who had in the First War been a leading, if unsuccessful, critic of the stationary slaughter of the trenches. In the Second War Churchill, expressing his own and his nation's convictions, argued tirelessly against a premature frontal attack. By no means all of his alternative proposals were adopted, but he did succeed in postponing the main attack until Anglo-American strength was overwhelming. Until that attack came, in June 1944, the competition between the two strategies—the massive direct assault versus shifting operations on the periphery—was a central theme in Anglo-American diplomacy to which all other issues were in some way related.

Russia, the third great ally, had only one possible strategy: maximum defensive pressure against Germany while urging the United States and Great Britain to open the second front in Europe without delay and simultaneously hoping that Japan, a neutral in the Russo-German war, would not attack in Siberia. The keynote of Russian diplomacy was surly suspicion compounded from Marxist-Leninist-Stalinist theories, Russia's warped memory and interpretation of events since 1917, and anticapitalist propaganda which Soviet leaders no doubt had come themselves to believe. Accordingly to the Russian view, the capitalist nations had sought to strangle the Soviet Union at birth from 1917 to 1920 but having failed had sought in the 1930's to save their own necks by turning Hitler against Russia. Current Anglo-American friendliness was, in Soviet eyes, the product of fear and the mask to a continuing hope that Russia would bleed to death. Postponement of the second front in Europe was simply an expression of this hope.

British and American leaders were angered and hurt by the Soviet calumny, but they differed in their opinions of how to deal with it. The British were relatively unruffled and stoical. Russian suspicions were a fact of life to the British. Russian demands for an immediate second front were understandable, but must be firmly refused until the time was ripe. The idea that Russia might make a separate peace with Germany, as at Brest-Litovsk in 1918, if she did not receive full satisfaction from the West was dismissed by the British as nonsense. Similarly, the British argued that Russian cooperation or the lack of it in the postwar world would depend on the power structure at the time and not on fanciful Russian gratitude for favors which the West could not afford to grant.

The American attitude toward Russia was not monolithic, but the dominant view, to which President Roosevelt subscribed, was conciliatory, indulgent, and tinged with the vague fear that an unappeased Russia might make a separate peace. Roosevelt and his closest advisors were far readier than the British to meet Russian demands, to see an element of truth in Russian distortion of the past, and to insist that the way to win Russian trust was to begin by trusting, and making every possible allowance for Russian unpleasantness. Furthermore, Americans proclaimed time and again that the future peace of the world depended not on the balance of power but on the closest possible cooperation with Russia. That cooperation could and must be assured while the war was still in progress. In short, Americans were pessimistic concerning what Russia might do if her wishes were not met, but they were essentially optimistic in their belief that Western attitudes could shape Russian behavior both during and after the war. The ramifications of this Anglo-American-Soviet interplay appear everywhere in the diplomacy of the war. They affected the debate over grand strategy and they touched such questions as shipping and allocation of supplies. They lay behind the formulation of war aims for Europe, for Asia, and for the nature of the United Nations. In that interplay can be found some of the origins of the Cold War.

American optimism extended to the war against Japan. This segment of the conflict remained second priority until the day of victory in Europe, but it absorbed an increasing amount of diplomatic energy and military resources. The ocean war on the Pacific was an American show and required few diplomatic arrangements, but on the mainland of Asia diplomacy encountered its most complicated, difficult, and frustrating task: the support of China. Of all the allies of the United States, China excited the highest hopes and ultimately provided the most crushing disappointment. The reasons are embedded in both Chinese and American history as well as in the hard realities of geography and military power during the war. Had the China of Chiang Kai-shek conformed to the romantic image cherished widely in the United States all would have been well. According to this image, which had flourished since the early nineteenth century, China was yearning and able to follow in the ways of its one benefactor and friend, the United States. If China could only be freed from the bondage of foreign oppression, an efficient, modern democracy would emerge. The Japanese occupation was a serious obstacle on this road to freedom, but, according to American illusion, the full moral support of the United States plus whatever equipment could be spared would bring ultimate triumph and a united, independent China, one of the four great powers (along with the United States, Russia, and Britain) upon whose permanent friendship the peace of the world would depend.

Such was the dream. Before long it became a nightmare. First, as in other areas of war, came the conflict of basic strategies. Naturally, Chiang Kai-shek considered that the center of the war was in China and that he should receive as much American support as he needed in order to preserve his position against the Communists and other domestic foes and then defeat the Japanese. For the United States, however, world strategy placed China fourth in line as a recipient of supplies: behind Anglo-American operations in Europe, behind Russia, and behind the naval war in the Pacific; and at no time was the United States willing to see its limited aid to China used for any purpose except the waging of war against Japan. Next came the problem of geography and logistics. Because Japan soon controlled all the land and water routes into China, every ton of supplies had to be transported first to northeastern India and then flown "over the Hump" at astronomical expense. For equal expenditure the United States could deliver hundreds of tons of supplies to England for every ton delivered in China. Last and most important was the relationship of the irreconcilable conflict between Chiang's government and the Communists. Few Americans could comprehend the murderous bitterness of this antagonism or why the Chinese could not forget their differences, like good Democrats and Republicans in the United States, in the patriotic struggle against Japan. Throughout the war and for more than a year afterward, it was American policy to seek to unify the Chinese factions. Seldom has an effort been so futile.

But in the days after Pearl Harbor none of these dismal facts about China was understood. Roosevelt, his advisers, and the American people looked forward to a triumphant partnership. Thus, in every quarter of the globe American diplomacy, sustained by an optimistic reading of the past and an unreal attitude toward the present, began its wartime tasks.

A factor that influenced the style and results of American wartime diplomacy as much as the nation's optimistic interpretation of the past was the personality of President Roosevelt. He took crucial diplomatic negotiations more completely into his own hands than any president before or since. One way to examine Roosevelt's qualities as a diplomat is to compare him with Woodrow Wilson. There was nothing cheerful about Wilson's solemn crusade of Christian good against the forces of evil. Roosevelt, in contrast, always gave the appearance of a happy man, sometimes to the point of an unbecoming and inappropriate frivolity. Wilson found it hard to like the individuals with whom he was forced to deal; Roosevelt's first instinct was to like everybody. Wilson was solitary; Roosevelt loved the crowd, huge parties, the feeling of presiding over a numerous family.

Associates found both Wilson and Roosevelt difficult to work with, but for different reasons. Wilson enjoyed admitting that he had a "one track mind." For long periods he would concentrate on a single issue and ignore others of equal importance. Roosevelt's mind, in contrast, was trackless. He would dabble in a dozen questions simultaneously and acquire a superficial acquaintance with thousands of details in which Wilson would have had no interest. Subordinates found it difficult to keep Roosevelt's mind focused for long on any one problem. He loved to ramble and he seldom studied deeply.

Wilson was stubborn and opinionated; his dislike for advice that did not conform with his own conclusions often became dislike for the adviser. Roosevelt, on the other hand, had a compulsion to be liked. In dealing with others he would feign agreement with an opinion rather than produce disappointment. In domestic politics this habit of trying to please everyone caused confusion but no lasting harm. When Roosevelt's final views on an issued emerged, the man who had been misled could resign. Many did.

But this Rooseveltian technique had doleful results when applied to international affairs, where all the favorable conditions that Roosevelt enjoyed at home were missing. Disagreements in domestic affairs were over means, not basic objectives. All Americans desired a healthy economy, an end to unemployment, and a broadening of security among the whole population. There were no disagreements that could not be faced and thrashed out by reasonable men of good will. But how different the conduct of international affairs, especially in the emergency conditions of a world war. The nations in uneasy coalition against the Axis disagreed not only on the means of winning the war, but also on fundamental objectives for the future. Differences were too profound to be dissolved by geniality, and disgruntled allies, unlike subordinates, could not be ignored. Roosevelt either forgot these truths, or else believed that his power to make friends was so irresistible that all opposition could be charmed out of existence. He was wrong.

There was another unfortunate connection between domestic politics and Roosevelt's diplomacy. As the most successful American politician of the century, Roosevelt had a superb sense of how much support he could command for his domestic programs. But in his understanding of what the people would accept in foreign affairs he was timid and unsure. Often he shied away from problems that needed to be confronted—Russian treatment of Poland, for example—because he feared that publicity might lose votes. He overestimated the strength of isolationism and underestimated the ability of the American people to absorb bad news and undertake new responsibility. As a result Roosevelt sometimes gave the public a falsely optimistic picture of our diplomacy, especially in regard to Russia and China. He also gave the Russians the impression that the United States would probably withdraw into partial isolation after victory and that Russia, therefore, need not worry about American opposition to her postwar ambitions in Europe.

Two further traits of Roosevelt's character should be noted. The President had a small boy's delight in military and naval problems. Under the Constitution he was commander-in-chief of the armed forces and he set out to give practical as well as theoretical meaning to the title. Much of his time was spent in close consultation with military and naval authorities. Usually, he took the advice of the chiefs of staff, but on occasion he made important military decisions independently. Roosevelt's fascination with strategy and tactics intensified the American emphasis on military objectives to the neglect of those long-range political conditions to which military operations should always be subordinate. For example, in 1944 and 1945 Roosevelt concentrated so hard on the military objective of bringing Russia into the war against Japan that he seriously weakened American bargaining power in the settlement of permanent political objectives in Europe and Asia.

Finally, Roosevelt, unlike Wilson, was a pragmatist who lived in a world in which good and bad were somewhat mixed. He had no qualms about further blending the two, and for settling by way of compromise for the best that seemed available. Roosevelt was no metaphysician losing sleep by wondering if evil means could contaminate a worthy end. He was more inclined to act and let the historians worry about the philosophical problems involved in his behavior. The historian must conclude, however, that much of Roosevelt's diplomacy fails of justification even on its own terms. Too often the means were questionable and the results worse.

Roosevelt's character produced the worst results in his diplomacy with Stalin; with Churchill the best. Churchill and Roosevelt enjoyed the closest personal and official relationship that has ever existed between an American president and the head of another government. It was not, however, a relationship of equality. Roosevelt had the power and Churchill the ideas. Churchill, acutely aware of the British Empire's dependence on the United States, kept Roosevelt informed and entertained with an almost daily stream of imcomparably lucid and persuasive letters and telegrams. Frequently, he traveled to meet Roosevelt in Washington, at Hyde Park, or in Canada. Roosevelt never went to Churchill in Great Britain, although both Roosevelt and Churchill did meet Stalin on or near his home ground. Churchill's sincere liking for Roosevelt, his understanding of the President's character, and above all the range and penetration of his intellect served the British Empire and the Anglo-American cause well. No other man could have won Roosevelt's approval to such a large measure of British policy. But sometimes Roosevelt and his advisers did refuse Churchill's requests. On those occasions Churchill gave way with a grace that was as uncharacteristic of his past political behavior as it was serviceable for the preservation of the even tenor of Anglo-American relations.

Roosevelt's personal relations with Stalin were the least effective aspect of his diplomacy. The President met Stalin's displays of temper, suspicion, and churlish obstructionism with redoubled efforts at conciliation. Early in the war he tried to please Stalin by an implied promise of an immediate second front, and later he remained silent in the face of barbarous Soviet conduct in Poland. Sometimes he tried to win Stalin's confidence by ridiculing Churchill and hinting at a Soviet-American alignment against British colonialism. In personal relations and in diplomacy it is unwise and dangerous to pretend to denounce a proven friend in order to ingratiate oneself with a third party. Churchill bore the humiliation manfully; Stalin was not fooled. He listened to Roosevelt's chatter, said little himself, and coolly pushed the Soviet advantage in Europe and Asia without regard to the idealistic principles of political liberty to which Russia, as one of the United Nations, had subscribed. Stalin acted on the assumption, which Roosevelt's words and behavior amply confirmed, that the United States would raise no effective opposition to hostile Russian expansion. By the time Roosevelt's policy was reversed after the war, the Russian position had been consolidated, and the lines of the Cold War drawn.

The results of Roosevelt's personal diplomatic contact with the proud and haughty leaders who ranked just below the triumvirate, Chiang Kai-shek of China and Charles de Gaulle of France, were poor. Chiang and de Gaulle were similar in many ways. Each claimed to represent a great power suffering from temporary adversity; each was quick to resent the slightest reflection on his personal prestige or the sovereign prerogatives of his nation. Roosevelt, however, treated the two leaders in opposite fashion, acting more in terms of his preconceived notions about France and China than the actual situation. The President was an infatuated captive of the myth that China under Chiang Kai-shek was one of the world's great powers and deserved to be treated as such. He even toyed with the idea of giving Chiang a voice in the settlement of European affairs. No amount of evidence concerning Chiang's maladministration, the disunity of the country, the strength of the opposition, or the inefficiency of the Kuomintang armies appeared capable of shaking Roosevelt's illusion, at least until the closing months of the war.

For modern France, in contrast, Roosevelt had acquired an attitude of contempt as extreme as his admiration for China. He considered France a source of decay in the world, a politically and socially sick nation which by laying down before Hitler and giving way to the Japanese in Indochina had forfeited the right to be respected. Roosevelt saw de Gaulle as a pompous adventurer who represented only a clique of followers and who secretly intended to assume the dictatorship of his country after the liberation. Ultimately, Roosevelt's attitudes led to severe friction with France and to bitter misunderstandings on the part of the American people when Chiang Kai-shek collapsed so ignominiously in his civil war with the Communists.

Although wartime diplomacy, pervasively influenced by the personality of President Roosevelt, dealt principally with military operations, one overriding question was always present: what kind of world did each of the three major allies desire after the war? Each power sought, first of all, a victory that would prevent recurrence of a war as catastrophic as the one in which the world was then involved. American leaders gradually developed among themselves some broad ideas on how this might be done, but they believed that their objectives could best be achieved if specific discussions concerning the future were postponed until the fighting was over. Assuming that no postwar problem could be as important or difficult as the defeat of the Axis and that there would be time enough after victory to make detailed arrangements, they were insensitive to the way in which the conduct of war can prejudice the results.

From the American point of view, there were several ways that the goal of postwar security might be sought. Isolation had failed and was now discredited, more thoroughly than Roosevelt realized. A unilateral armed *Pax Americana* in which every threat to security was instantaneously smashed by the exercise of the superior force of the United States was technically worth considering, but was not politically or morally tolerable. A *Pax Anglo-Americana* in which the United States and Great Britain together ran the world had appeal for some Americans, and briefly for President Roosevelt, but it, too, was not feasible. Roosevelt until 1944 favored a peace secured by the armed cooperation of "the Four Policemen": the United States, Russia, China, and Great Britain—in that order of importance. Little countries would be required to keep quiet and take orders. This concept had numerous flaws. A power vacuum would be left in western Europe where, according to Roosevelt, neither Germany nor France would again be factors in world politics. This would be especially dangerous if Roosevelt's assumption of an identity of interest between Russia and the West proved unfounded. In Asia there was considerable doubt whether the Chiang Kai-shek regime in China could survive, much less serve as a policeman for others. In addition, the outcry of small nations at being herded about by the great powers would be too loud to ignore in the United States and Great Britain, countries which prided themselves on respecting the rights of others.

Churchill felt that Roosevelt intended to relegate Great Britain to a position of undeserved and unrealistic inferiority while encouraging the disintegration of the British Empire, a development which Churchill resisted with skill and energy. The Prime Minister's own program for securing the peace was equally objectionable to most Americans. Churchill, a strong believer in the traditional British reliance on the balance of power, assumed that the fate of Europe still determined the fate of the world; that there was a basic conflict of interest between Russia and the West; that these differences should be faced openly and realistically; that western Europe had to be rehabilitated as quickly as possible with France and eventually Germany rejoining the continent's power structure; that the United States ought to cooperate with Britain in rebuilding Europe and be prepared, if necessary, to oppose Russian ambitions. Churchill believed that colonial peoples should receive increased self-government, but that the imperial powers should continue to exercise responsibility for their colonies in the interests of world stability.

Roosevelt abandoned the concept of "the Four Policemen" in favor not of Churchill's balance of power program but in response to the rising enthusiasm in the United States for the formation of a universal collective security organization, the United Nations. Secretary of State Cordell Hull, for example, argued that postwar antagonism between Russia and the West was unthinkable and that a third world war was the only conceivable alternative to full cooperation. Great power cooperation must be embedded in a world organization, a resurrection of the Wilsonian League of Nations. From 1944 onward Roosevelt and his advisers were fully committed to the early establishment of the United Nations as the only way to lasting peace. They became increasingly suspicious of Churchill's ideas. Ironically, many Americans came to believe that British imperialism and continued adherence to the idea of the balance of power were greater threats to security than anything Soviet Russia might do.

This does not mean that American leaders were hostile to Great Britain; rather they looked upon Britain as a misguided friend unfortunately wedded to dangerous and outmoded patterns of behavior. It was the duty of the United States to set this friend right for her own good and the good of the world. Russia, in contrast, was seen as the unfairly maligned giant, a bear too long harassed by an unsympathetic world. Russia had been so badly treated in the past that it was now necessary for the United States and Great Britain to make an extra effort to be warm and understanding. . . .

Roosevelt thought that Russia wanted nothing but security from attack and that this could easily be granted. . . . Roosevelt tended to assume that national security meant approximately the same thing in Moscow as it did in Washington. . . . Russia's minimum territorial objectives were clearly stated. They included restoration of the June 1941 boundary, which meant that Russia would enjoy the full fruits of the 1939 Nazi-Soviet pact, specifically the annexation of the three Baltic states, nearly half of prewar Poland, and pieces of Finland and Rumania. Germany was to be dismembered into a cluster of weak separate states and hunks of territory were to be given to Poland and Russia. Politically, Russia insisted on "friendly" governments along her central European borders. In practice this came to mean Communist regimes imposed by totalitarian means. In Asia the Soviets sought the expulsion of Japan from the mainland and the restoration of Russia's position as it existed at the height of Tsarist imperial power in 1904. This would entail serious limitations on Chinese sovereignty in Manchuria.

The United States shared these aims as far as they applied directly to Germany and Japan, but everything beyond that was in actual or potential conflict with the Atlantic Charter. By postponing decisions on these conflicts, Roosevelt convinced himself that he was preventing discord with Russia without making concessions that violated the Charter. But inwardly the President was quite prepared to concede these Russian aims on the assumption that once they were attained Russia would feel secure and would cooperate without reservations in the new world organization.

In retrospect it seems clear that Roosevelt's basic assumption was false. The evidence indicates that Soviet leaders believed that their state and ideology could never be secure as long as the world contained any large concentration of non-Communist power. Defensively they could assign no limits to the requirements of security; offensively they were under a compulsion rooted in Russian history as well as Communist ideology to expand the area of their domination wherever practical. Russian security and expansion were two sides of the same coin. A collective security organization was for the Russians an instrument to be joined or abandoned solely in terms of its usefulness in advancing Russian power in a world of irreconcilable conflict between capitalism and Communism; it was not the beneficent organization of universal cooperation envisioned by the more idealistic Americans.

Historically, most wars have been accompanied by considerable diplomatic contact between enemies; the two sides test each other's determination and bargain quietly over terms while the guns are still firing. In the Second World War, the war of unconditional surrender, the United States engaged in little diplomacy of this type. Germany and Japan, however, carried on negotiations within their spheres which significantly influenced the outcome of the war. To generalize, the Axis lost through blundering many of the advantages gained by force of arms. Had Germany and Japan been as skilled at dealing with each other, with neutrals, and with conquered peoples as they were in launching military offensives, the plight of the Allies would have been far more drastic than it was. Instead, Axis diplomacy was one of the greatest assets enjoyed by the Allies.

Hitler and the militarists of Japan came to power because the German and Japanese people were dissatisfied with the conditions that prevailed after the First World War and found a totalitarian new order appealing. In like manner, Germany and Japan scored great initial military success because many of their adversaries lacked the will to take risks in defense of an international status quo which had not brought security, prosperity, or happiness. In order to exploit this advantage it was necessary for Germany and Japan to coordinate their activities and to convince the neutrals and the conquered that, as their propaganda claimed, the new orders for Europe and Asia offered genuine benefits for those willing to cooperate. They failed utterly on both counts.

In every war between coalitions one group seeks to drive wedges into the other. It was not necessary for the Allies to seek to separate Germany and Japan because they were never together, notwithstanding the alliance signed in September 1940. The two countries were profoundly suspicious of each other and withheld information with a fervor of secrecy more appropriate among enemies. The major, fateful decisions of each—Germany's invasion of Russia and Japan's attack on the United States—were made without informing the other in advance. Ultimately, these decisions meant defeat; perhaps it could not have been otherwise given the inferiority of the Axis in population and economic resources. But true coordination diplomatically arranged might have placed the outcome in doubt.

Geographical separation was, of course, a huge obstacle to coordination, but military action might have brought the two countries into contact. Far more divisive was ideological antipathy. Japanese propaganda stressed opposition to European imperialism and appealed to the idea of Asia for the Asians. It was thus most difficult to sympathize with the boundless growth of German power. Would Germany insist on acquiring new imperial status in the Far East? The Japanese could not be sure. Hitler's ideological dislike for the Japanese was even stronger. He was a believer in "the Yellow Peril" and found the spectacle of Japanese victories over white people most disturbing even when the whites were his enemies. In short, there was "a fundamental inconsistency in the alliance between Nazi Germany, the champion of the concept of Nordic racial superiority, and Japan, the self-appointed defender of Asia against Western imperialism." In March 1942, to illustrate this point, Hitler is reported to have indulged in the thought that it would be satisfying to send England twenty divisions to help throw back the yellow horde.

Few countries have ever been as brutally and selfishly nationalistic as Germany and Japan during the Second World War. They went to war to satisfy that nationalism and lost partly because their nationalism prevented their cooperation. Still less could they cooperate with smaller countries and colonial peoples who had no love for the Allies and who might have been made into effective collaborators if the Axis had tried seduction instead of rape. In Europe Hitler had an opportunity of winning support from anti-Communists in the Balkans, Poland, and the Ukraine. But he imposed slavery where he might have made friends. He could have had far greater support from Vichy France and Franco's Spain if he had decided to offer them advantages in the new Europe. Different diplomacy and military strategy could have brought Hitler control of the Mediterranean and all of North Africa. He then might have exploited anti-British sentiment in the Middle East and brought that sparsely defended and crucial area into his orbit. India was also susceptible to anti-British appeals and if India fell, Germany and Japan would be united in control of the southern rim of Eurasia. This would have brought incalculable adversity to the Allies.

Similarly, in Asia Japan had great opportunities as she conquered colonies whose populations longed to be rid of European rule. By acting genuinely in tune with their propaganda and granting some scope to the national aspirations of these peoples, the Japanese might have forged a chain of allies across Southeast Asia. In many places they did receive a tentative welcome at first, but soon the arrogance and brutality of conquerors produced bitter hatred. The colonial peoples knew that European imperialism was bad, but Japanese imperialism was worse.

12

3. RICHARD DALFIUME, "THE 'FORGOTTEN YEARS' OF THE NEGRO REVOLUTION"

AS historians gain the necessary perspective, they are increasingly pointing to World War II as a major turning point in the civil rights movement. It was during this time that the Negro movement took on new purpose and intensity; by 1945, its leadership had determined upon a full-scale drive to gain equality of opportunity and treatment for the Negro.

Several factors contributed to this new attitude. There occurred, first, a growing awareness of the racist attitudes that pervaded American society. Second, the publication in 1944 of the monumental two-volume work, The American Dilemma, *by Swedish sociologist Gunnar Myrdal, demonstrated convincingly the manner in which the Negro was caught up in a "vicious cycle" of second-rate education, substandard housing, job discrimination, and segregated public facilities. Throughout his massive study, Myrdal repeatedly hammered home his thesis that "the great American Dilemma" was the all-too-apparent conflict between "the ideals of liberty and equality to which the nation was pledged" and the reality of racial discrimination.*

Moreover, the incongruity of a nation valiantly struggling against the deranged racist doctrines of Adolph Hitler's Germany with its own armed forces segregated on the basis of race was all too obvious. How could the United States fight in the name of freedom and democracy when it had a racial caste system of its own? This paradox was not lost upon Negro leaders, and they determined to make the most of the situation. When Negro labor leader A. Philip Randolph threatened to lead a march on Washington in 1941 of fifty thousand blacks to protest hiring discrimination in defense industries, members of Roosevelt's cabinet were reportedly to have asked, "What will they say about us in Berlin?" In the face of this display of Negro determination, Roosevelt reluctantly issued Executive Order, number 8802, forbidding racial discrimination in defense industries. Triumphant, Randolph called off the march.

The forceful leadership of Randolph perhaps best illustrates the new militancy of the American Negro, which emerged during the war years; his rhetoric anticipated the Black Power movement of the sixties. "Negroes have a stake in National Defense," he

SOURCE. Richard Dalfiume, "The 'Forgotten Years' of the Negro Revolution," in the *Journal of American History*, Vol. LV, June 1968, pp. 90–106. Copyright 1968 by the Organization of American Historians. Reprinted by permission of the *Journal of American History* and the author.

exhorted his followers in 1941. "The stake involves jobs. It involves equal employment opportunities. It involves equal opportunity for integration in the Armed Forces of the nation. . . . Hence, let the Negro masses fight! . . . Only the masses possess power. Only the voice of the masses will be heard and heeded—Negro America has never yet spoken as a mass, an organized mass. . . . Then, let the Negro masses speak!"

In the following selection, Professor Richard Dalfiume of the State University of New York at Binghamton describes the "forgotten years" of the civil rights movement that preceded the victories of the fifties and sixties.

A recent president of the American Sociological Society addressed himself to a puzzling question about what we know as the Civil Rights Revolution: "Why did social scientists—and sociologists in particular—not foresee the explosion of collective action of Negro Americans toward full integration into American society?" He pointed out that "it is the vigor and urgency of the Negro demand that is new, not its direction or supporting ideas." Without arguing the point further, the lack of knowledge can be attributed to two groups—the ahistorical social scientists, and the historians who, until recently, have neglected modern Negro history.

The search for a "watershed" in recent Negro history ends at the years that comprised World War II, 1939–1945. James Baldwin has written of this period: "The treatment accorded the Negro during the Second World War marks, for me, a turning point in the Negro's relation to America. To put it briefly, and somewhat too simply, a certain hope died, a certain respect for white Americans faded." Writing during World War II, Gunnar Myrdal predicted that the war would act as a "stimulant" to Negro protest, and he felt that "There is bound to be a redefinition of the Negro's status in America as a result of this War." The Negro sociologist E. Franklin Frazier states that World War II marked the point where "The Negro was no longer willing to accept discrimination in employment and in housing without protest." Charles E. Silberman writes that the war was a "turning point" in American race relations, in which "the seeds of the protest movements of the 1950s and 1960s were sown." While a few writers have indicated the importance of these years in the recent Negro protest movement, the majority have failed to do so. Overlooking what went before, most recent books on the subject claim that a Negro "revolution" or "revolt" occurred in 1954, 1955, 1960, or 1963. Because of the neglect of the war period, these years of transition in American race relations comprise the "forgotten years" of the Negro revolution.

To understand how the American Negro reacted to World War II, it is necessary to have some idea of the discrimination he faced. The defense build-up begun by the United States in 1940 was welcomed by Negroes who were disproportionately represented among the unemployed. Employment discrimination in the revived industries, however, was rampant. When Negroes sought jobs at aircraft factories where employers begged for workers, they were informed that "the Negro will be considered only as janitors and in other similar capacities. . . ." Government financed training programs to overcome the shortages of skilled workers discriminated against Negro trainees. When government agencies issued orders against such discrimination, they were ignored.

Increasing defense preparations also meant an expansion of the armed forces. Here, as in industry, however, Negroes faced restrictions. Black Americans were assigned a minimal role and rigidly segregated. In the navy, Negroes could enlist only in the all-Negro messman's branch. The marine and the air corps excluded Negroes entirely. In the army, black Americans were prevented from enlisting, except for a few vacancies in the four regular army Negro units that had been created shortly after the Civil War; and the strength of these had been reduced drastically in the 1920s and 1930s.

Although the most important bread-and-butter issue for Negroes in this period was employment discrimination, their position in the armed forces was an important symbol. If one could not participate fully in the defense of his country, he could not lay claim to the rights of a full-fledged citizen. The NAACP organ, the *Crisis*, expressed this idea in its demand for unrestricted participation in the armed forces: "this is no fight merely to wear a uniform. This is a struggle for status, a struggle to take democracy off of parchment and give it life." Herbert Garfinkel, a student of Negro protest during this period, points out that "in many respects, the discriminatory practices against Negroes which characterized the military programs . . . cut deeper into Negro feelings than did employment discrimination."

Added to the rebuffs from industry and the armed services were a hundred others. Negroes, anxious to contribute to the Red Cross blood program, were turned away. Despite the fact that white and Negro blood is the same biologically, it was deemed inadvisable "to collect and mix caucasian and Negro blood indiscriminately." When Negro citizens called upon the governor of Tennessee to appoint some black members to the state's draft boards, he told them: "This is a white man's country. . . . The Negro had nothing to do with the settling of America." At a time when the United States claimed to be the last bulwark of democracy in a war-torn world, the legislature of Mississippi passed a law requiring different textbooks for Negro schools: all references to voting, elections, and democracy were to be excluded from the black student's books.

The Negro's morale at the beginning of World War II is also partly explained by his experience in World War I. Black America had gone into that war with high morale, generated by the belief that the democratic slogans literally meant what they said. Most Negroes succumbed to the "close ranks" strategy announced by the crusading NAACP editor, W. E. B. Du Bois, who advocated subduing racial grievances in order to give full support to winning the war. But the image of a new democratic order was smashed by the race riots, lynchings, and continued rigid discrimination. The result was a mass trauma and a series of movements among Negroes in the 1920s which were characterized by a desire to withdraw from a white society which wanted little to do with them. When the war crisis of the 1940s came along, the bitter memories of World War I were recalled with the result that there was a built-in cynicism among Negroes toward the democratic slogans of the new war.

Nevertheless, Negroes were part of the general population being stimulated to come to the defense of democracy in the world. When they responded and attempted to do their share, they were turned away. The result was a widespread feeling of frustration and a general decline of the Negro's morale toward the war effort, as compared with the rest of American society. But paradoxically, the Negro's general morale was both low and high.

While the morale of the Negro, as an American, was low in regard to the war effort, the Negro, as a member of a minority group, had high morale in his heightened race consciousness and determination to fight for a better position in American society. The same slogans which caused the Negro to react cynically also served to emphasize the disparity between the creed and the practice of democracy as far as the Negro in America was concerned. Because of his position in society, the Negro reacted to the war both as an American and as a Negro. Discrimination against him had given rise to "a sickly, negative attitude toward national goals, but at the same time a vibrantly positive attitude toward racial aims and aspirations."

When war broke out in Europe in 1939, many black Americans tended to adopt an isolationist attitude. Those taking this position viewed the war as a "white man's war." George Schuyler, the iconoclastic columnist, was a typical spokesman for this view: "So far as the colored peoples of the earth are concerned," Schulyer wrote, "it is a toss-up between the 'democracies' and the dictatorships. . . . [W]hat is there to choose between the rule of the British in Africa and the rule of the Germans in Austria?" Another Negro columnist claimed that it was a blessing to have war so that whites could "mow one another down" rather than "have them quietly murder hundreds of thousands of Africans, East Indians and Chinese. . . ." This kind of isolationism took the form of anti-colonialism, particularly against the British. There was some sympathy for France, however, because of its more liberal treatment of black citizens.

Another spur to isolationist sentiment was the obvious hypocrisy of calling for the defense of democracy abroad while it was not a reality at home. The NAACP bitterly expressed this point:

The Crisis is sorry for brutality, blood, and death among the peoples of Europe, just as we were sorry for China and Ethiopia. But the hysterical cries of the preachers of democracy for Europe leave us cold. We want democracy in Alabama and Arkansas, in Mississippi and Michigan, in the District of Columbia—*in the Senate of the United States.*

The editor of the Pittsburgh *Courier* proclaimed that Negroes had their "own war" at home "against oppression and exploitation from without and against disorganization and lack of confidence within"; and the Chicago *Defender* thought that "peace at home" should be the main concern of black Americans.

Many Negroes agreed with columnist Schulyer that "Our war is not against Hitler in Europe, but against the Hitlers in America." The isolationist view of the war in Europe and the antagonism toward Great Britain led to an attitude that was rather neutral toward the Nazis and the Japanese, or, in some extreme cases, pro-Axis. Appealing to this latent feeling, isolationist periodicals tried to gain Negro support in their struggle against American entrance into the war. By 1940 there were also Negro cults such as the Ethiopian Pacific Movement, the World Wide Friends of Africa, the Brotherhood of Liberty for the Black People of America, and many others, which preached unity among the world's darker people, including Japanese. Many of these groups exploited the latent anti-semitism common among Negroes in the urban ghettos by claiming that the racial policies of Germany were correct.

Reports reached the public that some black Americans were expressing a vicarious pleasure over successes by the "yellow" Japanese and by Germany. In a quarrel with her employer in North Carolina, a Negro woman retorted: "I hope Hitler does come, because if he does he will get you first!" A Negro truck driver in Philadelphia was held on charges of treason after he was accused of telling a Negro soldier that he should not be in uniform and that "This is a white man's government and war and it's no damned good." After Pearl Harbor, a Negro share cropper told his landlord: "By the way, Captain, I hear the Japs done declared war on you white folks." Another Negro declared that he was going to get his eyes slanted so that the next time a white man shoved him around he could fight back.

It is impossible to determine the extent of this kind of pro-Axis sentiment among Negroes, but it was widespread enough for the Negro press to make rather frequent mention of it. In 1942 and 1943 the federal government did arrest the members of several pro-Japanese Negro cults in Chicago, New York, Newark, New Jersey, and East St. Louis, Illinois. Although the numbers involved were small, the evidence indicated that Japanese agents had been at work among these groups and had capitalized on Negro grievances.

By the time of the Pearl Harbor attack, certain fundamental changes were taking place among American Negroes. Nowhere is this more evident than in a comparison of Negroes' reactions to World Wars I and II. The dominant opinion among them toward World War I was expressed by Du Bois. In World War II, most Negroes looked upon the earlier stand as a great mistake. The dominant attitude during World War II was that the Negro must fight for democracy on two fronts—at home as well as abroad. This opinion had first appeared in reaction to the discriminatory treatment of Negro soldiers; but with the attack on Pearl Harbor, this idea, stated in many different ways, became the slogan of black America.

American Negroes took advantage of the war to tie their racial demands to the ideology for which the war was being fought. Before Pearl Harbor, the Negro press frequently pointed out the similarity of American treatment of Negroes and Nazi Germany's treatment of minorities. In 1940, the Chicago *Defender* featured a mock invasion of the United States by Germany in which the Nazis were victorious because a fifth column of southern senators and other racists aided them. Later the *Crisis* printed an editorial which compared the white supremacy doctrine in America to the Nazi plan for Negroes, a comparison which indicated a marked similarity. Even the periodical of the conservative Urban League made such comparisons.

Many Negroes adopted a paradoxical stand on the meaning of the war. At the same time that it was labeled a "white man's war," Negroes often stated that they were bound to benefit from it. For example, Schuyler could argue that the war was not for democracy, but "Peace means . . . a continuation of the status quo . . . which must be ended if the Negro is to get free." And accordingly, the longer the war the better: "Perhaps in the shuffle we who have been on the bottom of the deck for so long will find ourselves at the top."

Cynicism and hope existed side by side in the Negro mind. Cynicism was often the attitude expressed after some outrageous example of discrimination. After Pearl Harbor, however, a mixture of hope and certainty—great changes favorable to the Negro would result from the war and things would never be the same again—became the dominant attitude. Hope was evident in the growing realization that the war provided the Negro with an excellent opportunity to prick the conscience of white America. "What an opportunity the crisis has been . . . for one to persuade, embarrass, compel and shame our government and our nation . . . into a more enlightened attitude toward a tenth of its people!" the Pittsburgh *Courier* proclaimed. Certainty that a better life would result from the war was based on the belief that revolutionary forces had been released throughout the world. It was no longer a "white man's world," and the "myth of white invincibility" had been shattered for good.

[There was a growing protest against the racial status quo by black Americans; this was evidenced by the reevaluation of segregation in all sections of the country. In the North there was self-criticism of past acceptance of certain forms of segregation. Southern Negroes became bolder in openly questioning the sacredness of segregation.] In October 1942, a group of southern Negro leaders met in Durham, North Carolina, and issued a statement on race relations. In addition to endorsing the idea that the Negro should fight for democracy at home as well as abroad, these leaders called for complete equality for the Negro in American life. While recognizing the "strength and age" of the South's racial customs, the Durham meeting was "fundamentally opposed to the principle and practice of compulsory segregation in our American society." In addition, there were reports of deep discontent among southern Negro college students and evidence that political activity among the blacks of the South, particularly on the local level, was increasing.

The American Negro, stimulated by the democratic ideology of the war, was reexamining his position in American society. "It cannot be doubted that the spirit of American Negroes in all classes is different today from what it was a generation ago," Myrdal observed. Part of this new spirit was an increased militancy, a readiness to protest loud and strong against grievances. The crisis gave Negroes more reason and opportunity to protest. Representative of all of the trends of black thought and action—the cynicism, the hope, the heightened race consciousness, the militancy—was the March on Washington Movement (MOWM).

The general idea of exerting mass pressure upon the government to end defense discrimination did not originate with A. Philip Randolph's call for a march on Washington, D.C., in early 1941. [Agitation for mass pressure had grown since the failure of a group of Negro leaders to gain any major concessions from President Franklin D. Roosevelt in September 1940.] Various organizations, such as the NAACP, the Committee for Participation of Negroes in the National Defense, and the Allied Committees on National Defense, held mass protest meetings around the country in late 1940 and early 1941. The weeks passed and these efforts did not seem to have any appreciable impact on the government; Walter White, Randolph, and other Negro leaders could not even secure an appointment to see the President. "Bitterness grew at an alarming pace throughout the country," White recalled.

It remained, however, for Randolph to consolidate this protest. In January 1941, he wrote an article for the Negro press which pointed out the failure of committees and individuals to achieve action against defense discrimination. "Only power can effect the enforcement and adoption of a given policy," Randolph noted; and "Power is the active principle of only the organized masses, the masses united for a definite purpose." To focus the weight of the black masses, he suggested that 10,000 Negroes march on Washington, D.C., with the slogan: "We loyal Negro-American citizens demand the right to work and fight for our country."

[This march appeal led to the formation of one of the most significant—though today almost forgotten—Negro protest movements. The MOWM pioneered what has become the common denominator of today's Negro revolt—"the spontaneous involvement of large masses of Negroes in a political protest."] Furthermore, as August Meier and Elliott Rudwick have recently pointed out, the MOWM clearly foreshadowed "the goals, tactics, and strategy of the mid-twentieth-century civil rights movement." Whites were excluded purposely to make it an all-Negro movement; its main weapon was direct action on the part of the black masses. Furthermore, the MOWM took as its major concern the economic problems of urban slum-dwellers.

Randolph's tactic of mass pressure through a demonstration of black power struck a response among the Negro masses. [The number to march on Washington on July 1, 1941, was increased to 50,000, and only Roosevelt's agreement to issue an executive order establishing a President's Committee on Fair Employment Practices led to a cancellation of the march.] Negroes then, and scholars later, generally interpreted this as a great victory. But the magnitude of the victory is diminished when one examines the original MOWM demands: an executive order forbidding government contracts to be awarded to a firm which practiced discrimination in hiring, an executive order abolishing discrimination in government defense training courses, an executive order requiring the United States Employment Service to supply workers without regard to race, an executive order abolishing segregation in the armed forces, an executive order abolishing discrimination and segregation on account of race in all departments of the federal government, and a request from the President to Congress to pass a law forbidding benefits of the National Labor Relations Act to unions denying Negroes membership. Regardless of the extent of the success of the MOWM, however, it represented something different in black protest. Unlike the older Negro movements, the MOWM had captured the imagination of the masses.

Although overlooked by most recent writers on civil rights, a mass militancy became characteristic of the American Negro in World War II. This was symbolized by the MOWM and was the reason for its wide appeal. Furthermore, older Negro organizations found themselves pushed into militant stands. For example, the NAACP underwent a tremendous growth in its membership and became representative of the Negro masses for the first time in its history. From 355 branches and a membership of 50,556 in

1940, the NAACP grew to 1,073 branches with a membership of slightly less than 450,000 in 1946. The editors of the Pittsburgh *Courier* recognized that a new spirit was present in black America. In the past, Negroes

made the mistake of relying entirely upon the gratitude and sense of fair play of the American people. Now we are disillusioned. We have neither faith in promises, nor a high opinion of the integrity of the American people, where race is involved. Experience has taught us that we must rely primarily upon our own efforts. . . . That is why we protest, agitate, and demand that all forms of color prejudice be blotted out. . . .

By the time of the Japanese attack on Pearl Harbor, many in America, both inside and outside of the government, were worried over the state of Negro morale. There was fear that the Negro would be disloyal. The depth of white ignorance about the causes for the Negro's cynicism and low morale is obvious from the fact that the black press was blamed for the widespread discontent. The double victory attitude constantly displayed in Negro newspapers throughout the war, and supported by most black Americans, was considered as verging on disloyalty by most whites. White America, ignorant of the American Negroes' reaction to World War I, thought that black citizens should subdue their grievances for the duration.

During World War II, there was pressure upon the White House and the justice department from within the federal government to indict some Negro editors for sedition and interference with the war effort. President Roosevelt refused to sanction this, however. There was also an attempt to deny newsprint to the more militant Negro newspapers, but the President put an end to this when the matter was brought to his attention. The restriction of Negro newspapers from military installations became so widespread that the war department had to call a halt to this practice in 1943. These critics failed to realize that, although serving to unify black opinion, the Negro press simply reflected the Negro mind.

One of the most widely publicized attacks on the Negro press was made by the southern white liberal, Virginius Dabney, editor of the Richmond *Times Dispatch*. He charged that "extremist" Negro newspapers and Negro leaders were "demanding an overnight revolution in race relations," and as a consequence they were "stirring up interracial hate." Dabney concluded his indictment by warning that "it is a foregone conclusion that if an attempt is made forcibly to abolish segregation throughout the South, violence and bloodshed will result." The Negro press reacted vigorously to such charges. Admitting that there were "all-or-nothing" Negro leaders, the Norfolk *Journal and Guide* claimed they were created by the "nothing-at-all" attitude of whites. The Chicago *Defender* and Baltimore *Afro-American* took the position that they were only pointing out the shortcomings of

American democracy, and this was certainly not disloyal. The NAACP and the Urban League claimed that it was patriotic for Negroes to protest against undemocratic practices, and those who sought to stifle this protest were the unpatriotic ones.

The Negro masses simply did not support a strategy of moderating their grievances for the duration of the war. After attending an Office of Facts and Figures conference for Negro leaders in March 1942, Roy Wilkins of the NAACP wrote:

. . . it is a plain fact that no Negro leader with a constituency can face his members today and ask full support for the war in the light of the atmosphere the government has created. Some Negro educators who are responsible only to their boards or trustees might do so, but the heads of no organized groups would dare do so.

By 1942, the federal government began investigating Negro morale in order to find out what could be done to improve it. This project was undertaken by the Office of Facts and Figures and its successor, the Office of War Information. Surveys by these agencies indicated that the great amount of national publicity given the defense program only served to increase the Negro's awareness that he was not participating fully in that program. Black Americans found it increasingly difficult to reconcile their treatment with the announced war aims. Urban Negroes were the most resentful over defense discrimination, particularly against the treatment accorded black members of the armed forces. Never before had Negroes been so united behind a cause: the war had served to focus their attention on their unequal status in American society. Black Americans were almost unanimous in wanting a show of good intention from the federal government that changes would be made in the racial status quo.

The government's inclination to take steps to improve Negro morale, and the Negro's desire for change, were frustrated by the general attitude of white Americans. In 1942, after two years of militant agitation by Negroes, six out of ten white Americans felt that black Americans were satisfied with things the way they were and that Negroes were receiving all of the opportunities they deserved. More than half of all whites interviewed in the Northeast and West believed that there should be separate schools, separate restaurants, and separate neighborhoods for the races. A majority of whites in all parts of the country believed that the Negro would not be treated any better after the war than in 1942 and that the Negro's lesser role in society was due to his own shortcomings rather than anything the whites had done. The white opposition to racial change may have provided the rationale for governmental inactivity. Furthermore, the white obstinance must have added to the bitterness of black Americans.

Although few people recognized it, the war was working a revolution in

American race relations. Sociologist Robert E. Park felt that the racial structure of society was "cracking," and the equilibrium reached after the Civil
War seemed "to be under attack at a time and under conditions when it is
particularly difficult to defend it." Sociologist Howard W. Odum wrote from
the South that there was "an unmeasurable and unbridgeable distance
between the white South and the reasonable expectation of the Negro."
White southerners opposed to change in the racial mores sensed changes
occurring among "their" Negroes. "Outsiders" from the North, Mrs.
Franklin Roosevelt, and the Roosevelt Administration were all accused of
attempting to undermine segregation under the pretense of wartime necessity.

Racial tensions were common in all sections of the country during the war.
There were riots in 1943. Tensions were high because Negro Americans were
challenging the status quo. When fourteen prominent Negroes, conservatives
and liberals, southerners and northerners, were asked in 1944 what they
thought the black American wanted, their responses were almost unanimous.
Twelve of the fourteen said they thought that Negroes wanted full political
equality, economic equality, equality of opportunity, and full social equality
with the abolition of legal segregation. The war had stimulated the race
consciousness and the desire for change among Negroes.

Most American Negroes and their leaders wanted the government to institute a revolutionary change in its race policy. Whereas the policy had been
acquiescence in segregation since the end of Reconstruction, the government
was now asked to set the example for the rest of the nation by supporting
integration. This was the demand voiced by the great majority of the Negro
leaders called together in March 1942 by the Office of Facts and Figures.
Crisis magazine summarized the feelings of many black Americans: Negroes
have "waited thus far in vain for some sharp and dramatic notice that this
war is not to maintain the status quo here."

The White House, and it was not alone, failed to respond to the revolutionary changes occurring among the nation's largest minority. When the
Fraternal Council of Negro Churches called upon President Roosevelt to end
discrimination in the defense industries and armed forces, the position taken
was that "it would be very bad to give encouragement beyond the point
where actual results can be accomplished." Roosevelt did bestir himself over
particularly outrageous incidents. When Roland Hayes, a noted Negro singer,
was beaten and jailed in a Georgia town, the President dashed off a note to
his attorney general: "Will you have someone go down and check up . . .
and see if any law was violated. I suggest you send a northerner."

Roosevelt was not enthusiastic about major steps in the race relations field
proposed by interested individuals within and without the government. In
February 1942 Edwin R. Embree of the Julius Rosenwald Fund, acutely
aware of the growing crisis in American race relations, urged Roosevelt to
create a commission of experts on race relations to advise him on what steps

the government should take to improve matters. FDR's answer to this pro-posal indicates that he felt race relations was one of the reform areas that had to be sacrificed for the present in order to prosecute the war. He thought such a commission was "premature" and that "we must start winning the war . . . before we do much general planning for the future." The President believed that "there is a danger of such long-range planning becoming projects of wide influence in escape from the realities of war. I am not convinced that we can be realists about the war and planners for the future at this critical time."

After the race riots of 1943, numerous proposals for a national committee on race relations were put forward; but FDR refused to change his position. Instead, the President simply appointed Jonathan Daniels to gather informa-tion from all government departments on current race tensions and what they were doing to combat them. This suggestion for what would eventually become a President's Committee on Civil Rights would have to wait until a President recognized that a revolution in race relations was occurring and that action by the government could no longer be put off. In the interim, many would share the shallow reasoning of Secretary of War Stimson that the cause of racial tension was "the deliberate effort . . . on the part of certain radical leaders of the colored race to use the war for obtaining . . . race equality and interracial marriages. . . ."

The hypocrisy and paradox involved in fighting a world war for the four freedoms and against aggression by an enemy preaching a master race ide-ology, while at the same time upholding racial segregation and white suprem-acy, were too obvious. The war crisis provided American Negroes with a unique opportunity to point out, for all to see, the difference between the American creed and practice. The democratic ideology and rhetoric with which the war was fought stimulated a sense of hope and certainty in black Americans that the old race structure was destroyed forever. In part, this confidence was also the result of the mass militancy and race consciousness that developed in these years. When the expected white acquiescence in a new racial order did not occur, the ground was prepared for the civil rights revolution of the 1950s and 1960s; the seeds were indeed sown in the World War II years.

CONTEMPORARY SOURCES

4. FRANKLIN D. ROOSEVELT, ADDRESS TO CONGRESS, MAY 16, 1940

ON April 9, 1940, Adolph Hitler ended the suspense which had hung over Europe by invading Denmark and Norway. Following this first success, on May 10 he unleashed

SOURCE. *Congressional Record*, 76th Congress, 3rd Session, pp. 6243–6244.

his blitzkreig upon Belgium, Luxemburg and the Netherlands. The next day he invaded France. It would be only a matter of weeks before France would fall to the Nazis.

Fearful that the United States would have to play an important role in the war, and concerned for America's security, President Roosevelt went before Congress on May 16 to present a call for immediate military preparedness, including the seemingly impossible goal of 50,000 airplanes within a year. Recognizing that new military technology was rapidly outstripping America's geographical security, and fearful that Germany might soon capture the British navy, President Roosevelt began to move the nation in the direction of a policy of preparedness.

The PRESIDENT. Mr. Vice President, Mr. Speaker, Members of the Senate and House of Representatives, these are ominous days—days whose swift and shocking developments force every neutral nation to look to its defenses in the light of new factors. The brutal force of modern offensive war has been loosed in all its horror. New powers of destruction, incredibly swift and deadly, have been developed; and those who wield them are ruthless and daring. No old defense is so strong that it requires no further strengthening and no attack is so unlikely or impossible that it may be ignored.

Let us examine, without self-deception, the dangers which confront us. Let us measure our strength and our defense without self-delusion.

The clear fact is that the American people must recast their thinking about national protection.

Motorized armies can now sweep through enemy territories at the rate of 200 miles a day. Parachute troops are dropped from airplanes in large numbers behind enemy lines. Troops are landed from planes in open fields, on wide highways, and at local civil airports.

We have seen the treacherous use of the "fifth column" by which persons supposed to be peaceful visitors were actually a part of an enemy unit of occupation. Lightning attacks, capable of destroying airplane factories and munition works hundreds of miles behind the lines, are part of the new technique of modern war.

The element of surprise which has ever been an important tactic in warfare has become the more dangerous because of the amazing speed with which modern equipment can reach and attack the enemy's country.

Our own vital interests are widespread. More than ever the protection of the whole American Hemisphere against invasion or control or domination by non-American nations has the united support of the 21 American Republics, including the United States. More than ever this protection calls for ready-at-hand weapons capable of great mobility because of the potential speed of modern attack.

The Atlantic and Pacific Oceans were reasonably adequate defensive barriers when fleets under sail could move at an average speed of 5 miles an hour. Even then by a sudden foray it was possible for an opponent actually to burn our National Capitol. Later the oceans still gave strength to our defense when fleets and convoys propelled by steam could sail the oceans at 15 or 20 miles an hour.

But the new element—air navigation—steps up the speed of possible attack to 200, to 300, miles an hour.

Furthermore, it brings the new possibilities of the use of nearer bases from which an attack or attacks on the American Continents could be made. From the fiords of Greenland it is 4 hours by air to Newfoundland; 5 hours to Nova Scotia, New Brunswick, and Quebec; and only 6 hours to New England.

The Azores are only 2,000 miles from parts of our eastern seaboard, and if Bermuda fell into hostile hands it is a matter of less than 3 hours for modern bombers to reach our shores.

From a base in the outer West Indies the coast of Florida could be reached in 200 minutes. . . .

Surely the developments of the past few weeks have made it clear to all of our citizens that the possibility of attack on vital American zones ought to make it essential that we have the physical, the ready, ability to meet those attacks and to prevent them from reaching their objectives.

This means military implements—not on paper—which are ready and available to meet any lightning offensive against our American interest. It means also that facilities for production must be ready to turn out munitions and equipment at top speed.

We have had the lesson before us over and over again—nations that were not ready and were unable to get ready found themselves overrun by the enemy. So-called impregnable fortifications no longer exist. A defense which allows an enemy to consolidate his approach without hindrance will lose. A defense which makes no effective effort to destroy the lines of supplies and communications of the enemy will lose.

An effective defense, by its very nature, requires the equipment to attack an aggressor on his route before he can establish strong bases within the territory of American vital interests.

Loose talking and thinking on the part of some may give the false impression that our own Army and Navy are not first rate, or that money has been wasted on them.

Nothing could be further from the truth.

In recent years the defensive power of our Army, Navy, and Marine Corps has been very greatly improved.

The Navy is stronger today than at any time in the Nation's history. Today also a large program of new construction is well under way. Ship for ship, ours are equal to or better than the vessels of any foreign power.

The Army likewise is at its greatest peacetime strength. Its equipment in quality and quantity has been greatly increased and improved.

The National Guard and the Reserve strength of the two services are better equipped and better prepared than during any other peacetime period.

On the other side of the picture we must visualize the outstanding fact that since the 1st day of September 1939 every week that has passed has brought new lessons learned from actual combat on land and sea.

I cite examples. Where naval ships have operated without adequate protection by defending aircraft, their vulnerability to air attack has increased. All nations are hard at work studying the need of additional antiaircraft protection.

Several months ago the use of a new type of magnetic mine made many unthinking people believe that all surface ships were doomed. Within a few weeks a successful defensive device against these mines was placed in operation; and it is a fact that the sinkings of merchant ships by torpedo, by mine, or by airplane are definitely much lower than during the similar period in 1915.

Combat conditions have changed even more rapidly in the air. With the amazing progress in the design of planes and engines, the airplane of a year ago is out of date now. It is too slow, it is improperly protected, it is too weak in gunpower.

In types of planes we are not behind the other nations of the world. Many of the planes of the belligerent powers are at this moment not of the latest models. But one belligerent power not only has many more planes than all their opponents combined, but also appears to have a weekly production capacity at the moment that is far greater than that of their opponents.

From the point of view of our own defense, therefore, great additional production capacity is our principal air requisite.

For the permanent record, I ask the Congress not to take any action which would in any way hamper or delay the delivery of American-made planes to foreign nations which have ordered them, or seek to purchase more planes. That, from the point of view of our own national defense, would be extremly short-sighted.

During the past year American production capacity for war planes, including engines, has risen from approximately 6,000 planes a year to more than double that number, due in greater part to the placing of foreign orders.

Our immediate problem is to superimpose on this production capacity a greatly increased additional production capacity. I should like to see this Nation geared up to the ability to turn out at least 50,000 planes a year. Furthermore, I believe that this Nation should plan at this time a program that would provide us with 50,000 military and naval planes. . . .

There are some who say that democracy cannot cope with the new techniques of government developed in recent years by a few countries—by a few countries which deny the freedoms which we maintain are essential to our democratic way of life. This I reject.

I know that our trained officers and men know more about fighting and the weapons and equipment needed for fighting than any of us laymen; and I have confidence in them.

I know that to cope with present dangers we must be strong in heart and hand; strong in our faith—strong in faith in our way of living.

I, too, pray for peace—that the ways of aggression and force may be banished from the earth—but I am determined to face the fact realistically that this Nation requires a toughness of moral and physical fiber. Those qualities, I am convinced, the American people hold to a high degree.

Our task is plain. The road we must take is clearly indicated. Our defenses must be invulnerable, our security absolute. But our defense as it was yesterday, or even as it is today, does not provide security against potential developments and dangers of the future. . . .

Our ideal, our objective, is still peace—peace at home and peace abroad. Nevertheless, we stand ready not only to spend millions for defense but to give our service and even our lives for the maintenance of our American liberties. . . .

These are the characteristics of a free people, a people devoted to the institutions they themselves have built, a people willing to defend a way of life that is precious to them all, a people who put their faith in God.

5. BURTON K. WHEELER, ADDRESS ON THE AMERICAN RADIO FORUM OF THE AIR, JANUARY 12, 1941

FOLLOWING the brutal westward thrust by the German Wehrmacht in the spring of 1940, American public opinion shifted away from the isolationism of the 1930's toward a recognition that German domination of all Europe threatened American interests. Shortly after the British army's miraculous escape at Dunkirk, the Committee to Defend

SOURCE. *Congressional Record*, 77th Congress, 1st Session, Appendix, pp. 178–179.

America by Aiding the Allies was established under the chairmanship of William Allen White. The Committee, which believed that it was in the national interest to prevent the fall of Britain, found a sympathetic listener in Franklin D. Roosevelt.

Conversely, as public opinion continued to abandon political isolationism, anti-interventionists founded the America First Committee under the chairmanship of General Robert E. Wood, President of Sears, Roebuck and Company. The America First Committee advocated a hemispheric defense system and vigorously opposed any American aid to Britain for fear that it would pull the United States into the European conflict. The Destroyers-for-Bases deal in September, 1940, caused the isolationists alarm, but their full thunder descended upon F.D.R. when he proposed in December that the United States become the "arsenal for Democracy" by establishing a lend-lease program to aid England gird for the threatened Nazi cross-channel invasion. In the following radio address, arch isolationist Burton K. Wheeler, a Democratic Senator from Montana, condemned Roosevelt's proposal with all of the invective he could summon.

The lend-lease policy, translated into legislative form, stunned a Congress and a nation wholly sympathetic to the cause of Great Britain. The Kaiser's blank check to Austria-Hungary in the first World War was a piker compared to the Roosevelt blank check of World War II. It warranted my worst fears for the future of America, and it definitely stamps the President as war-minded.

The lend-lease-give program is the New Deal's triple A foreign policy; it will plow under every fourth American boy.

Never before have the American people been asked or compelled to give so bounteously and so completely of their tax dollars to any foreign nation. Never before has the Congress of the United States been asked by any President to violate international law. Never before has this Nation resorted to duplicity in the conduct of its foreign affairs. Never before has the United States given to one man the power to strip this Nation of its defenses. Never before has a Congress coldly and flatly been asked to abdicate.

If the American people want a dictatorship—if they want a totalitarian form of government and if they want war—this bill should be steam-rollered through Congress, as is the wont of President Roosevelt.

Approval of this legislation means war, open and complete warfare. I, therefore, ask the American people before they supinely accept it, Was the last World War worth while?

If it were, then we should lend and lease war materials. If it were, then we should lend and lease American boys. President Roosevelt has said we would be repaid by England. We will be. We will be repaid, just as England repaid her war debts of the first World War—repaid those dollars wrung from the sweat of labor and the toil of farmers with cries of "Uncle Shylock." Our boys will be returned—returned in caskets, maybe; returned with bodies maimed; returned with minds warped and twisted by sights of horrors and the scream and shriek of high-powered shells.

Considered on its merits and stripped of its emotional appeal to our sympathies, the lend-lease-give bill is both ruinous and ridiculous. Why should we Americans pay for war materials for Great Britain who still has $7,000,000,000 in credit or collateral in the United States? Thus far England has fully maintained rather than depleted her credits in the United States. The cost of the lend-lease-give program is high in terms of American tax dollars, but it is even higher in terms of our national defense. Now it gives to the President the unlimited power to completely strip our air forces of its every bomber, of its every fighting plane.

It gives to one man—responsible to no one—the power to denude our shores of every warship. It gives to one individual the dictatorial power to strip the American Army of our every tank, cannon, rifle, or antiaircraft gun. No one would deny that the lend-lease-give bill contains provisions that would enable one man to render the United States defenseless, but they will tell you, "The President would never do it." To this I say, "Why does he ask the power if he does not intend to use it?" Why not, I say, place some check on American donations to a foreign nation?

Is it possible that the farmers of America are willing to sell their birthright for a mess of pottage?

Is it possible that American labor is to be sold down the river in return for a place upon the Defense Commission, or because your labor leaders are entertained at pink teas?

Is it possible that the American people are so gullible that they will permit their representatives in Congress to sit supinely by while an American President demands totalitarian powers—in the name of saving democracy?

I say in the kind of language used by the President—shame on those who ask the powers—and shame on those who would grant them.

You people who oppose war and dictatorship, do not be dismayed because the war-mongers and interventionists control most of the avenues of propaganda, including the motion-picture industry.

Do not be dismayed because Mr. Willkie, of the Commonwealth & Southern, agrees with Mr. Roosevelt. This merely puts all the economic and foreign "royalists" on the side of war.

Remember, the interventionists control the money bags, but you control the votes.

6. A. G. MEZERIK, "THE FACTORY MANAGER LEARNS THE FACTS OF LIFE"

THE scope of industrial mobilization during the war staggers the imagination. For a nation that had just limped through the decade-long depression, wartime productivity was astounding. The great task faced by industry demanded an expanded labor force. By 1945, over seven million new workers had entered the job market to swell the number of employed Americans to over 53,000,000. At the same time, the armed forces numbered over 12,000,000. One of the new sources of labor for industry was the American woman; over 4,000,000 women held full-time positions during the war, many of them in heretofore all-male industries. "Rosie the Riveter" became the national symbol for a womanhood that had learned the skills of ship construction and assembly-line production. The dedication of the women war workers was frequently cited as an example of the nation's determination to "back the boys" on the front lines. Women proved to be effective workers, and they received much publicity for their efforts. The invasion of the factory and shipyard by glamor in overalls, however, created many new and sometimes humorous problems for the plant manager, as the following selection demonstrates.

The mass-production industries never liked the idea of employing women. In peacetime, with plenty of men available, the factory manager would not have dreamed of placing women on the assembly line. He had no special objection to using them in offices but, aside from that, it seemed to him that they ought to stay home and take care of the men and the children. The war has changed that.

Four million women are now employed in munitions and essential industries. Before the end of 1943 another million will be added. To the plant manager this adds up to a situation for which he was almost completely unprepared. He has had to learn nearly all the facts of life directly from the women. And he is still learning the hard way, which seems to be the American way—every manager for himself and with almost no research into how his current problems were met during the last war or how other companies are solving them in this one.

SOURCE. A. G. Mezerik, "The Factory Manager Learns the Facts of Life," in *Harper's Magazine*, Vol. 187, September 1943, pp. 289–290 and 295–296. Copyright 1943 by Harper's Magazine, Inc. Reprinted by permission of *Harper's Magazine* and the author.

The first question he had to face was "Can a woman do a man's work?" At first the manager tended to assume that all women are weak and can do only light work. But as the shortage of male workers intensified he was forced, willy-nilly, to let women try other jobs—with surprising results. At Sperry Gyroscope, making precision devices, 13,000 women work beside 17,000 men and there is no type of job in the whole plant that women are not doing. In steel, heaviest of all industries, women work at the open hearth and alongside the blast furnaces, tear down and rebuild steel furnaces, and work as laborers in many other jobs. In the Bethlehem plant they swing eight-pound bricks to waiting bricklayers—this in spite of the fact that women are supposed to be unable to lift. In shipyards women comprise 15 percent of the total work force and in some large yards the percentage is 25 percent.

Experience is proving to the plant manager that a woman can do almost all of the jobs he thought were exclusively masculine. But he does run into limitations on heavy lifting and continuous muscular strains, and here he begins to utilize his experience and turn to the making of job classifications so that he can fit the job to the worker instead of the worker to the job. The fact that, pound for pound of body weight, a woman can lift only a little more than half as much as a man is canceled if the woman is given a mechanical hoist to lift the work up to her. Once the work is in place she will do the job as well as a man—better if it is routine, monotonous, repetitive, painstaking, and intricate, as most mass-production jobs are.

But the mere fitting of work to women does not solve the manager's problem. The differences between men and women are not only physical; they are psychological and social as well. The plant manager first caught on to that when he dealt summarily with women about their defective work or about their dress. He was met with tears and he did not understand them any better than he does his wife's or his daughter's. The barrage of tears was so effective that, in desperation, the manager began to employ women as counselors. Most of these women had little to go on except tact and a college education. But they knew that a woman will cry under most of the stresses which cause her male fellow worker to curse—a piece of work that won't shape up right or a foreman's ridicule. Starting with these counselors, a whole new classification of administration has sprung into being. Women are now installed as personnel executives, and under them there are counselors who roam the plant floor, straightening out snarls before they cause tears, acting as the working woman's agent in getting household help, housing, and child care for her, and even filling the role of adviser on pregnancy and marriage problems. The plant manager made a ten-strike when he stumbled into hiring women counselors, for more than any other factor they ease the way for him. But there are, as yet, too few of them to affect the situation profoundly. The problems are still with the manager. . . .

The plant manager's knowledge of women is not complete until he has learned about two cardinal facts of life—pregnancy and abortion. He has to be prepared for both. In every large factory pregnancy and abortion are constant topics of discussion among workers and also among members of the management. The workers talk about pregnancy and how to avoid it for the obvious reason that women like and need the money they earn, do not want to have to leave or be fired because they are pregnant—and in most cases will be fired. The management talks about the subject because nearly every large plant is staggered by the problem of pregnancy and only a few have worked out any policy to cope with it.

Of 73 plants employing 273,000 people observed by Dr. Charlotte Silverman of the Children's Bureau, 64 did something about pregnancy—but what they did was not very enlightened. Thirty-two discharged the employees as soon as they heard they were pregnant or within the next three months. Three plants discharged pregnant women on their physicians' advice. Only one gave leaves of absence. Of the 73, only 26 could furnish any record of the extent of pregnancy in the plant. How big the problem is can be gaged from a dependable estimate that each month as many as five out of every 1,000 women in the war industries become pregnant.

7. ERNIE PYLE, "THE TOUGHEST BEACHHEAD IN THE WORLD"

ON June 6, 1944, an Allied task force under the command of General Dwight D. Eisenhower launched the long-awaited invasion of France. It was the biggest military operation in history. Eisenhower commanded 2,870,000 men and officers. Effectively utilizing 5000 ships and landing craft, 29,000 paratroopers, and extensive naval and aerial bombardment, the Allies caught the German defenders by surprise, making the initial landing on the Normandy peninsula instead of in the more likely Calais area to the north. Suspecting that the Normandy invasion was merely a feint before the major assault, the Germans withheld several divisions for more than a week. Even then, 7300 of the 34,000 Americans who stormed ashore onto Utah and Omaha Beaches that first morning were killed. After brutal fighting at the water's edge, beachheads were estab-

SOURCE. Ernie Pyle, "The Toughest Beachhead in the World," in *Science Digest*, Vol. 16, September 1944, pp. 13–14. Condensed from *Brave Men* by Ernie Pyle. Copyright 1943, 1944 by Scripps-Howard Newspaper Alliance and Holt, Rinehart & Winston, Inc. Reprinted by permission of Holt, Rinehart & Winston, Inc.

lished. It was not until June 27, however, that the strategic port city of Cherbourg was captured, and yet another month before a general breakthrough occurred. Meticulous planning by General Eisenhower and his staff, together with considerable good fortune, brought victory. With the German army reeling in retreat toward the borders of Germany, the days of Nazi domination of Europe were nearing an end.

The slaughter of war, however, cannot be forgotten. At such unlikely places as Anzio, Guadalcanal, and Iwo Jima, thousands of young Americans made the supreme sacrifice. Among the fatalities was Ernie Pyle, the nation's most widely read war correspondent. He was killed in mid-April of 1945 by a burst of Japanese machine-gun fire on the tiny and insignificant Pacific island of Ie. As did the imaginative young cartoonist, Bill Mauldin, Pyle succeeded in capturing the soldier's view of the war. The following is Pyle's first report from France, cabled only twenty-four hours after the first assault wave had hit bloody Omaha Beach.

Now that it is over, it seems to me a pure miracle we ever took the beach at all. For some it was easy, but in this special sector where I now am, our troops faced such odds that our getting to shore would be like me whipping Joe Louis down to a pulp.

Ashore, facing us were more enemy troops than we had in our assault waves. The advantages were all theirs. The disadvantages all ours.

The Germans were dug into positions they had been working on for months. Still they weren't yet all complete. A 100-foot bluff a couple of hundred yards back from the beach had great concrete gun emplacements built right into the hilltops. They opened to the sides instead of the front, thus making it very hard for naval fire from the ships to reach them, and enabling the Germans to shoot parallel with the beach and cover every foot of it for miles with artillery fire.

Then they had hidden machine-gun nests on the forward slopes with crossfire taking in every inch of the beach. These nests are connected with the networks of trenches so that German gunners could move about without exposing themselves.

Throughout the length of the beach, running zigzag a couple of hundred yards back from the shoreline, was an immense V-shaped ditch, 15 deep feet. Nothing could cross it, not even men on foot, until it had been partially filled.

And in other places at the far ends of the beach where the ground was flatter they had great concrete walls which had been blasted by naval gunfire or by hand-set explosives after we got ashore. Our only exits from the beach were several valleys, each about 100 yards wide.

The Germans made the most of these funnellike traps, literally sowing their bottom sides with buried mines. They contained, too, barbed-wire

330 The Second World War

entanglements with mines attached, hidden ditches and machine guns firing from the slopes. That is what was on shore.

But our men had to go through a maze nearly as deadly before they even got ashore. The underwater obstacles were terrific. The Germans had whole fields of evil devices under the water to catch our boats.

The Germans had masses of those great six-pronged spiders made of railroad iron and standing shoulder high in places just beneath the surface of the water for our landing craft to run into. They also had huge logs, buried in the sand, pointing upward and outward, their tops just below the water. Attached to these logs were mines.

In addition to these obstacles, they had floating mines in the beach waters, land mines buried on the sand beach, and more mines in checkerboard rows in the tall grass beyond the sand. And the enemy had four men on shore for every three men we had approaching shore.

And yet we got on.

Now that the fighting has moved inland, human litter extends in a thin little line, just like a high water mark, for miles along the beach. This is the strewn personal gear, gear that will never be needed again, of those who fought and died to give us our entrance into Europe.

Here in a jumbled row for mile on mile are soldiers' packs. Here are socks and shoe polish, sewing kits, diaries, Bibles and hand grenades. Here are the latest letters from home, with the address on each one neatly razored out—one of the security precautions enforced before the boys embarked.

Here are toothbrushes and razors and snapshots of families back home staring up at you from the sand. Here are pocketbooks, metal mirrors, extra trousers, and bloody, abandoned shoes. Here are broken-handled shovels, and portable radios smashed almost beyond recognition, and mine detectors twisted and ruined.

Soldiers carry strange things ashore with them. In every invasion you'll find at least one soldier hitting the beach at H-Hour with a banjo slung over his shoulder. The most ironic piece of equipment marking our beach—this beach of first despair, then victory—is a tennis racket that some soldier had brought along.

Two of the most dominant items in the beach refuse are cigarettes and writing paper. Each soldier was issued a carton of cigarettes just before he started. Today these cartons by the thousand, water-soaked and spilled out, mark the line of our first savage blow.

Writing paper and air-mail envelopes come second. The boys had intended to do a lot of writing in France. Letters that would have filled those blank, abandoned pages.

The strong, swirling tides of the Normandy coastline shift the contours of the sandy beach as they move in and out. They carry soldiers' bodies out to sea, and later they return them. They cover the bodies of heroes with sand, and then in their whims they uncover them.

As I plowed out over the wet sand of the beach on that first day ashore, I walked around what seemed to be a couple of pieces of driftwood sticking out of the sand.

They were a soldier's two feet. He was completely covered by the shifting sands except for his feet. The toes of his G.I. shoes pointed toward the land he had come so far to see, and which he saw so briefly.

8. FRANKLIN D. ROOSEVELT, STATE OF THE UNION MESSAGE, JANUARY 11, 1944

SHORTLY after the war began, President Roosevelt announced that "Dr. Win-the-War" had replaced "Dr. New Deal." This announcement was ostensibly made in the spirit of achieving national unity in the face of a resurgence of conservatism. Many liberals saw the war as a means of extending social and economic reform and, by 1943, their efforts had become intricately involved in the question of postwar planning. In response to the liberal demand for postwar planning, the National Resources Planning Board drew up a tentative set of postwar goals, which included a substantial extension of federal responsibility in the area of social welfare. Conservatives in the House of Representatives, however, angrily voted to deny the planning body further operation funds, thereby abolishing the liberals' vehicle for planning.

In his State of the Union Message on January 11, 1944, President Roosevelt, with one eye on the upcoming presidential election and the other on postwar America, sketched to the Congress his plans for the future. This "Economic Bill of Rights" drew heavily upon the Resources Planning Board's report and shocked the conservatives for its advanced liberalism. The President quite obviously intended that his fourth term would bring the New Deal to completion. He apparently expected "Dr. New Deal" to return to power as soon as "Dr. Win-the-War" had completed his task.

To the Congress of the United States:

This Nation in the past two years has become an active partner in the world's greatest war against human slavery.

SOURCE. Samuel E. Rosenman, ed., *The Public Papers and Addresses of Franklin D. Roosevelt,* Vol. 13, New York: Random House, pp. 32–44.

We have joined with like-minded people in order to defend ourselves in a world that has been gravely threatened with gangster rule.

But I do not think that any of us Americans can be content with mere survival. Sacrifices that we and our allies are making impose upon us all a sacred obligation to see to it that out of this war we and our children will gain something better than mere survival.

We are united in determination that this war shall not be followed by another interim which leads to new disaster—that we shall not repeat the tragic errors of <u>ostrich isolationism</u>—that we shall not repeat the excesses of the wild twenties when this Nation went for a joyride on a roller coaster which ended in a tragic crash. . . .

It is our duty now to begin to lay the plans and determine the strategy for the winning of a lasting peace and the establishment of an American standard of living higher than ever before known. We cannot be content, no matter how high that general standard of living may be, if some fraction of our people—whether it be one-third or one-fifth or one-tenth—is ill-fed, ill-clothed, ill-housed, and insecure.

This Republic had its beginning, and grew to its present strength, under the protection of certain inalienable political rights—among them the right of free speech, free press, free worship, trial by jury, freedom from unreasonable searches and seizures. They were our rights to life and liberty.

As our Nation has grown in size and stature, however—as our industrial economy expanded—these political rights proved inadequate to assure us equality in the pursuit of happiness.

We have come to a clear realization of the fact that true individual freedom cannot exist without economic security and independence. "Necessitous men are not free men." People who are hungry and out of a job are the stuff of which dictatorships are made.

In our day these economic truths have been accepted as self-evident. We have accepted, so to speak, a second Bill of Rights under which a new basis of security and prosperity can be established for all—regardless of station, race, or creed.

Among these are:

The right to a useful and remunerative job in the industries or shops or farms or mines of the Nation;

The right to earn enough to provide adequate food and clothing and recreation;

The right of every farmer to raise and sell his products at a return which will give him and his family a decent living;

The right of every businessman, large and small, to trade in an atmosphere of freedom from unfair competition and domination by monopolies at home or abroad;

The right of every family to a decent home;

The right to adequate medical care and the opportunity to achieve and enjoy good health;

The right to adequate protection from the economic fears of old age, sickness, accident, and unemployment;

The right to a good education.

All of these rights spell security. And after this war is won, we must be prepared to move forward, in the implementation of these rights, to new goals of human happiness and well-being.

America's own rightful place in the world depends in large part upon how fully these and similar rights have been carried into practice for our citizens. For unless there is security here at home there cannot be lasting peace in the world.

One of the great American industrialists of our day—a man who has rendered yeoman service to his country in this crisis—recently emphasized the grave dangers of rightist reaction in this Nation. All clear-thinking businessmen share his concern. Indeed, if such reaction should develop—if history were to repeat itself and we were to return to the so-called normalcy of the 1920's—then it is certain that, even though we shall have conquered our enemies on the battlefields abroad, we shall have yielded to the spirit of fascism here at home.

I ask the Congress to explore the means for implementing this economic bill of rights—for it is definitely the responsibility of the Congress so to do. Many of these problems are already before committees of the Congress in the form of proposed legislation. I shall from time to time communicate with the Congress with respect to these and further proposals. In the event that no adequate program of progress is evolved, I am certain that the Nation will be conscious of the fact.

Our fighting men abroad—and their families at home—expect such a program and have the right to insist upon it. It is to their demands that this Government should pay heed rather than to the whining demands of selfish pressure groups who seek to feather their nests while young Americans are dying.

The foreign policy that we have been following—the policy that guided us at Moscow, Cairo, and Teheran—is based on the common-sense principle which was best expressed by Benjamin Franklin on July 4, 1776: "We must all hang together, or assuredly we shall all hang separately."

I have often said that there are no two fronts for America in this war. There is only one front. There is one line of unity which extends from the hearts of the people at home to the men of our attacking forces in our farthest outposts. When we speak of our total effort, we speak of the factory and the field and the mine as well as of the battleground—we speak of the soldier and the civilian, the citizen and his Government.

Each and every one of us has a solemn obligation under God to serve this Nation in its most critical hour—to keep this Nation great—to make this Nation greater in a better world.

9. I. F. STONE, "FAREWELL TO F. D. R."

FRANKLIN D. ROOSEVELT brought the Presidency closer to the people than ever before in history. His effective use of the radio, extensive travel, and his almost unerring ability to recognize changing national moods helped make him a President with whom a broad spectrum of the American people could identify. On April 12, 1945, he suddenly died of a massive stroke. The shock of disbelief gave way to heartfelt national mourning as the nation paid tribute to the man who had rekindled America's faith in itself during the depression and had provided courageous wartime leadership.

F. D. R. died at an inopportune moment. Germany had not yet surrendered, Japan was far from subdued, the atomic bomb was nearing a successful test, and matters of far-reaching consequence for the future of Europe and Asia awaited presidential decision. At this critical juncture of history, a relatively unknown and untested Harry S. Truman was thrust into the Presidency. "Boys, if you ever pray, pray for me now," he told reporters. "I've got the most terribly responsible job a man ever had." Because of his obscure political origins and his modest physical appearance and awkward speaking style, Truman caused many persons to fear the worst. Those who knew the doughty Missourian, however, recognized that he was a man of uncommon abilities and courage, with a potential for leadership. Liberal journalist I. F. Stone, who had become familiar with Truman's qualities as a Senator, sought to remove some of the gloom and doom which resulted from Roosevelt's death.

Washington, April 14

Mr. Roosevelt's body was brought back to Washington today for the last time. The crowds began to gather early in Lafayette Park opposite the White House, as they did all along the line of the procession from Union Station. I got down to the park early and stood with many others waiting. Some small boys climbed into a tree for a better view. The gray tip of the Washington Monument showed above the White House. The trees were in full green; tulips bloomed on the lawn. Outside on the sidewalk there were soldiers in helmets every few feet, and we could hear the harsh tones of command as the guard of honor lined up on the White House lawn. Florists' trucks pulled

SOURCE. I. F. Stone, "Farewell to F. D. R.," in *The Nation*, Vol. 160, April 21, 1945, pp. 436–437. Reprinted by permission of *I. F. Stone's Weekly*.

up at the door, and huge wreaths were taken inside. Cameras were set up on the front porch, and camera men were perched on high ladders on the sidewalks and among us in the park. Birds sang, but the crowd was quiet.

In the park I recognized a group of girls from the C. I. O. offices in nearby Jackson Place, Walter Lippmann, and an Army and Navy Club bellboy with a sensitive Negro face. There were soldiers and sailors, Waves and Wacs. There were many Negroes, some of them quite obviously housemaids. There were well-dressed women and men in shirt sleeves. I noticed a small middle-aged priest, several grave and owlish Chinese, many service men with their wives or sweethearts, a tired man in overalls and blue-denim work cap. A tall gangling Negro boy in jitterbug jacket and pork-pie hat towered above the crowd in front of me. A man who seemed to be a hobo, unshaven and dirty, jarred the silence with a loud laugh at something a child behind him had said. There were close-mouthed New England faces, Jewish faces, Midwestern faces; workers and business men and housewives, all curiously alike in their patience and in the dumb stolidity that is often sorrow's aspect.

A truck sped by on Pennsylvania Avenue. On the roof of the truck two navy men operated a movie camera, taking pictures of the crowd. Far above us, twenty-four Flying Fortresses roared across the skies in proud formation. One remembered the President's 50,000-plane speech, and choked. Motorcycle police heralded the procession's approach. The marching men, the solemn bands, the armored cars, the regiment of Negro soldiers, the uniformed women's detachments, the trucks filled with soldiers, and the black limousines carrying officials and the President's family went by slowly. They seemed part of an unreal pageant by comparison with the one glimpse of what we had come to see—the coffin covered with a flag. Many faces in the crowd puckered as it went past. In that one quick look thousands of us said our goodbys to a great and good man, and to an era.

I was at the *PM* office in New York Thursday when it happened. There was a commotion in the newsroom. A copyboy ran out of the wire-room with a piece of United Press copy in his hand. That first flash, "The President died this afternoon," seemed incredible; like something in a nightmare, far down under the horror was the comfortable feeling that you would wake to find it was all a dream. The Romans must have felt this way when word came that Caesar Augustus was dead. Later, when work was done, I went to a meeting of liberals in an apartment on Washington Square. It was a gloomy gathering, much too gloomy to honor so buoyant a spirit as Mr. Roosevelt's. Some felt that with his passing the Big Three would split up, that hope of a new world organization was dim. One of those present reported, apropos, that an automobile-company official in Detroit had told a delegation of visiting French newspaperman, "Next we fight the Soviet Union." Some thought the Nazis would be encouraged to hold out, that the war had been lengthened by the President's passing. Everyone seemed to feel that trouble, serious trouble, lay ahead.

I don't want to sound like Pollyanna, but I can remember so many crepe-hanging sessions of this kind since 1932. The Roosevelt era, for folk who scare easily, was a series of scares. Just before he took office, when the bonus marchers were driven out of Washington, revolution seemed to be around the corner. There was the banking crisis. The NRA was suspected of being the beginning of fascism; one of my friends in New York cautiously erased his name from the volumes of Marx and Lenin he owned; he felt the men with the bludgeons might be in his apartment any day. The Supreme Court knocked one piece of reform legislation after another on the head, and Mr. Roosevelt, when he set out to fight back, showed a deplorable disrespect for the constitution amenities. There were the Chicago massacre and the Little Steel strike. There was Hitler. France fell when our armed forces were in good shape for a war with Nicaragua. The Japs sank most of the fleet at Pearl Harbor. It was a lush era for Cassandras.

Somehow we pulled through before, and somehow we'll pull through again. In part it was luck. In part it was Mr. Roosevelt's leadership. In part it was the quality of the country and its people. I don't know about the rest of the four freedoms, but one thing Mr. Roosevelt gave the United States in one crisis after another, and that was freedom from fear. Perhaps his most important contribution was the example, the superlative example, of his personal courage. Perhaps some of us will feel less gloomy if we remember it. Perhaps some of us will be more effective politically if we also learn from Mr. Roosevelt's robust realism, his ability to keep his eye on the main issue and not worry too much about the minor details.

I found the mood of the intellectuals and New Dealers in Washington this week-end quite different from that in New York. There has been much swapping of information and sidelights, and there is a good deal of confidence in the new President. No one, least of all Mr. Truman, an impressively modest man, expects him fully to fill Mr. Roosevelt's shoes. But the general feeling among those who know Mr. Truman is that he will surprise the skeptical. I can only record my own impression for whatever it is worth. I talked with Mr. Truman several years ago and liked him immediately and instinctively. The Presidency is a terrific job, and it remains to be seen how he will stand up under its pressure. But he is a good man, an honest man, a devoted man. Our country could be far more poorly served. Mr. Truman is a hard worker, decisive, a good executive. He works well with people. He is at once humble about his own knowledge and capacities, as a wise man should be, and quietly confident about his ability to learn and to rise to the occasion.

I hate to confess it, but I think Mr. Roosevelt was astute and farsighted in picking Mr. Truman rather than Mr. Wallace as his successor. At this particular moment in our history, Mr. Truman can do a better job. Mr. Wallace's accession might have split the country wide open, not because of Mr. Wallace but because of the feeling against him on the right. Mr. Truman has the good-will of both sides and is in a position to capitalize on the sobering influence of Mr. Roosevelt's passing. The heaviest task of the President lies in the field of foreign relations, and the biggest obstacle to its accomplishment is in the Senate. It is fortunate that Mr. Truman's greatest and most obvious political assets are his relations with the Senate. He is a friendly person, and was well liked on both sides of the aisle. Isolationists like Wheeler and La Follette are among his friends, and he may be able to exert an influence with them that circumstances and the momentum of past events denied to Mr. Roosevelt. The chances of a two-thirds' vote in the Senate for the new peace organization are improved by the shift in the Presidency. I say this with no disrespect to our great departed leader.

I think Mr. Truman will carry on Mr. Roosevelt's work. He had been very effective in support of Mr. Roosevelt in the Senate. I can authoritatively report that the famous B2H2 resolution originated in Mr. Truman's office. Three of the sponsors, Senators Ball, Burton, and Hatch, were members of the Truman committee. Mr. Truman's closest personal friends in the Senate were Kilgore of West Virginia and Wallgren of Washington, both sturdy progressives and good New Dealers. There will be changes in the Cabinet, perhaps some for the better. On domestic policy Mr. Truman's record is an excellent one, and labor has nothing to fear from him. The shock of Mr. Roosevelt's death has created an atmosphere in which the new President may be able to unite the nation more closely than ever and carry it forward to that stable peace Mr. Roosevelt so deeply desired.

PART VI

Postwar America

THE forces unleashed by World War II have shaped in an indelible fashion
the structure of postwar America. The war itself stands as the continental
divide of the twentieth century, equal in import to the Civil War of the
nineteenth century and the American Revolution of the eighteenth. No
aspect of American life fully escaped the impact of the war. The changes
wrought by the progressive movement or even the New Deal pale in comparison with those that resulted from the experiences of war.

The war gave birth to the Atomic Age, with all its catastrophic dangers and
incalculable peaceful potential. The goals and assumptions that guided
diplomats were fundamentally altered as national leaders recognized that
they could not reasonably resort to total war as a means of accomplishing
their ends. The American people would also have to learn to live with the
frustrations of knowing that atomic superiority brought not only unprecedented national power but also unprecedented restraints upon ever using
that power. Despite optimistic visions of the peaceful uses of the atom, a
quarter of a century after the first nuclear explosion at Alamogordo, the
United States has only begun to benefit from this unlimited potential.

Beyond the dramatic power of the atom, the new military technology, so
evident by war's end, had made obsolete America's geographical security;
consequently, traditional peacetime political isolation yielded to unprecedented internationalism as the United States took the leadership in the
establishment of the United Nations and assumed the responsibility of
leadership in the war-torn world. The new global commitments would soon
lead the United States into a radical departure from traditional unilateralism,

339

when it sought to counter Russian expansionist actions in eastern and central Europe by the employment of collective security. Equally important was the war's acceleration of other historical forces within American society, including the movement of the people to the cities and the growth of suburbia, the Negro's drive for equality, the expansion of the welfare and regulatory functions of the national government, and the rapidity of the advances of science and technology.

The influence of science and technology upon American life must be appreciated, since it provided the moving force for the increased tempo of social and cultural change. The manner in which American life has been altered during the past quarter of a century can be readily recognized if we realize that, in 1945, Americans had not yet eaten a frozen TV dinner; in fact, they had not yet watched a regularly scheduled television program. They were yet to reap the bountiful Neilson harvest of Ed Sullivan, deodorant advertisements, and fraudulent $64,000 questions. Space exploration was still the province of Buck Rogers and other comic strip characters, but in February of 1962, Astronaut John Glenn orbited the earth three times. As the decade drew to a close, the possibility of achieving President John F. Kennedy's goal of placing a man on the moon by 1970 seemed within reach. In 1945, jet airplanes were still in the testing stage but, by 1965, over 50,-000,000 air miles would be traveled by Americans on commercial jets. Medical researchers in 1945 had not yet produced a vaccine for infantile paralysis, heart transplants, or birth control pills, and the laboratories of the nation's corporations were yet to develop transistor radios, styrofoam, or stereophonic sound. The portentous "cybernetics" revolution—the marriage of the computer with automatic machines—was yet to alter American life.

The new technology, however, failed to provide the means of eliminating poverty within the world's most affluent nation. The new advances in science and technology seemed to benefit mainly the middle and upper classes. Automation, in fact, contributed to the rising unemployment rate among the unskilled and poorly educated as machines replaced men in a variety of jobs. Automatic elevators, for example, have replaced over 40,000 operators in New York City alone.

The problems of hard-core poverty in the United States described so vividly by Michael Harrington in his shocking book, *The Other America* (1962), stirred the consciences of its readers and caused President Kennedy to call the problem to the attention of the American people; it ultimately led to the War on Poverty under President Lyndon B. Johnson. Yet in the summer of 1968, the United States government announced that almost 30,000,000 Americans still lived in poverty. The unemployment rate in the black ghettos fluctuated between 30 and 50 percent during the sixties, and Negro income, as compared to that of the whites, has actually fallen since

1954, about the time when the cybernetics movement began to gain momentum. By 1968, the difficulties of ending poverty has frustrated many a citizen and government official.

One of the reasons for the failure to eliminate poverty was that it never received top priority from the national leadership. That was reserved for national defense. Beyond a doubt, one of the great tragedies of American history has been the Cold War. The costs are incalculable, for not only must one consider the loss of life in Korea and Vietnam and the tremendous expense of maintaining a far-flung military establishment, but also the manner in which the Cold War has affected American society.

The frustrations encountered in the struggle with the Communist powers contributed directly to the acrimonious atmosphere of suspicion and distrust, which produced the phenomenon of McCarthyism. By 1952, Senator Joseph McCarthy had opened deep divisions within American by his irresponsible and frequently unsubstantiated charges of Communist influence within the United States government. Supported by the conservative and isolationist wing of the Republican party, McCarthy accused Secretary of State Dean Acheson and even the 1952 Democratic presidential candidate, Adlai E. Stevenson, of having Communist sympathies. McCarthyism had run its course by 1954, but its damage was great. Not only did many responsible and patriotic citizens suffer the agony of being publicly accused of being Communists or "Communist sympathizers," but the demand for rigid anticommunism created a national mood of fear and suspicion, which tended to stultify creative leadership.

The Cold War also profoundly affected the course of economic growth. Defense spending contributed to the inflationary pressures and to the continued expansion of large corporations. By 1968–69, the defense budget exceeded $70 billion. Without defense expenditures, the size of the federal government today would be less than half its present size. Many social critics charged, with considerable justification, that the United States was being transformed into a "warfare state." Even Dwight D. Eisenhower became alarmed by the trend and, in his farewell message to the American people in 1961 as he left the Presidency, warned of the growing danger from "the potential for the disastrous rise of misplaced power" by the "military-industrial complex."

The conflicting objectives of the United States and the Soviet Union were easily recognizable by the time President Truman returned from Potsdam in early August of 1945. To what extent Truman's deep-seated distrust of the Russians contributed to the widening gulf between the two wartime allies is impossible to determine, but it is clear that Truman did not have the patience of President Roosevelt in dealing with the Soviets. Within two weeks after taking office, Truman bluntly told Molotov that the United States expected

Russia to honor all its Yalta pledges and, in particular, its promise to conduct free elections in Poland. Truman scolded Molotov and warned him that friendship between the two nations "could be only on a basis of the mutual observation of agreements and not on the basis of a one-way street."

Throughout 1945 and 1946, the two powers wrangled over the partition of Germany, free elections in Poland, international control of atomic weapons, and the organization of the United Nations. Meanwhile, with the great bulk of the American military force withdrawn from Europe, the Russians ruthlessly brought eastern Europe within its orbit. As one nation after another became part of the Russian satellite system, the Truman Administration sought to establish a firm policy with which to deal with the Soviet Union. It found it in the recommendation of career diplomat George F. Kennan. In an extremely influential article in the July 1947 issue of *Foreign Affairs*, which grew out of his earlier memorandum to the State Department from Moscow, Kennan argued that the policy of the United States "must be that of a long-term, patient but firm and vigilant containment of Russian expansive tendencies." Such containment, he argued, would increase greatly "the strains under which Soviet policy must operate" and ultimately "promote tendencies which must eventually find their outlet in either the break-up or the gradual mellowing of Soviet power. . . ."

On March 12, 1947, President Truman went before Congress to request authority to implement the policy of containment. Pointing out that Communist subversion threatened the security of the Middle East, he requested a $400 million appropriation for military and economic aid for the royalist Greek government which was threatened by Communist guerrilla activities. In his Truman Doctrine speech, however, the President ranged far beyond the Middle East and sketched a grand design that would later lead the United States into such remote places as Korea and Vietnam: "I believe that it must be the policy of the United States to support free peoples who are resisting attempted subjugation by armed minorities or by outside pressures."

A few months later, speaking at the Harvard commencement, Secretary of State George C. Marshall proposed a massive American aid program to enable the shattered European nations to rebuild their economies: "It is logical that the United States would do whatever it is able to do to assist in the return of normal economic health in the world, without which there can be no political stability and no assured peace." When the Russian delegation marched out of the preliminary meetings that led to the European Recovery Program (or "Marshall Plan"), the Cold War had obviously begun. Although several prominent Republicans, led by Senator Robert A. Taft, opposed the Truman Doctrine and the Marshall Plan, they lost by wide margins in their attempt to withhold congressional approval. Political isolationism had been reduced to the status of a loud but ineffective minority.

By 1947, the revolution in American policy, begun in 1941 with Lend-Lease and the Atlantic Charter, had been completed. "Fortress America" was a relic of the past. In 1949, the United States spearheaded the formation of the North Atlantic Treaty Organization and, for the first time since the American Revolution, the United States was a member of an "entangling alliance." Containment was tested in 1950 in Korea when the Truman Administration attempted to fight an unpopular "limited war." When General Douglas MacArthur openly criticized the limited objectives of the Korean War, he was relieved of his command by the resolute Harry Truman while the Republicans, and especially the McCarthyites, sought to use MacArthur for their narrow partisan purposes.

The Cold War reached its zenith in the early 1950's. The McCarthy hysteria, a truculent Stalin, and the Korean War served as a backdrop to the ascendancy of John Foster Dulles as Secretary of State under President Eisenhower. In an attempt to placate the virulent members of his party, Dulles resorted to strident anticommunist rhetoric. Containment, he said, was a defeatist policy; he even condemned the neutrality of such nations as India as "immoral." In the 1952 presidential campaign, his influence upon General Eisenhower was evident when the Republican nominee advocated a new foreign policy of "liberation"—the freeing of the "captive" Communist nations.

As Secretary of State, Dulles emphasized the importance of nuclear retaliation instead of fighting limited wars and advocated a policy of "brinkmanship," which meant that the United States should use its nuclear superiority to force her opponents to abandon their aggressive policies. Dulles' rhetoric did more than aid Republican office seekers. During the 1956 Hungarian revolution, the rebels managed to overthrow their Communist government for four days, but their hopes that the United States would intervene under its "liberation" policy were dashed when President Eisenhower decided against risking an American-Russian military confrontation. In Indo-China in 1954, as in Korea, the Eisenhower administration accepted a negotiated settlement rather than risk nuclear war to gain its limited objectives. Rhetoric aside, the Eisenhower administration did little more than continue unbroken the containment policies of its Democratic predecessor.

The death of Stalin and the Korean truce in 1953, however, led to a gradual, if uneven, lessening of tensions between the two powers. The 1955 "summit" conference between Eisenhower and Premier Bulganin produced no agreement over the crucial question of German unification or nuclear control, but a new spirit of accommodation emerged, which was further strengthened during the 1959 meeting between Eisenhower and Nikita Khrushchev at Camp David in Maryland. In 1956, cultural exchanges were begun and in February of that same year, the Soviets announced a fundamental revision in policy with the adoption of the doctrine of "peaceful coexistence" with her capitalist enemies. Traditional Marxist doctrines needed to be adapted to the realities of an atomic age, Khrushchev said. "There are only two ways, either peaceful coexistence or the most devastating war in history. There is no third alternative."

Following the cordiality created by the "spirit of Camp David," relations turned frigid once more. The shooting down of an American U-2 spy plane in May of 1960 well within Russian borders caused Khrushchev to scuttle the Paris summit meeting and, in the summer of 1961, the East German government caught the United States and her allies flatfooted when it erected the Berlin Wall to stem the embarrassing flow of defectors to the West and threatened to close access to West Berlin. Then in October of 1962, the world lurched precariously close to nuclear war when President Kennedy ordered a naval blockade of Cuba when he learned that offensive missile sites were being built on that island nation within one hundred miles of Florida. The blockade caused Russian ships bound for Cuba, ostensibly carrying offensive missiles and launching equipment, to turn around and return to the Soviet Union. Shortly thereafter, existing missile sites were dismantled and the crisis ended. Relations between East and West slowly improved once more, and the Test Ban Treaty was signed in 1963. Thereafter, the two powers, perhaps recognizing the increasing threat posed to both by the People's Republic of China, sought means of accommodation.

Just as the Cold War caused men of goodwill to fear for man's future, so the drive of the American Negro toward equality inspired their hope. The past quarter century has marked the greatest advance by the American Negro since the abolition of slavery. During World War II, Negro leaders had determined upon a concerted drive for equality at war's end. In response to the resulting pressures, President Truman established a special President's Commission on Civil Rights to make a detailed study of the condition of American minority groups. In the Autumn of 1947, the Commission released its explosive report, *To Secure These Rights.* The eighty-page report calmly but forcefully delineated the pervasive racial discrimination which confronted the Negro and other minorities in housing, education, employment, and public accommodations. President Truman reacted to this impressive report on February 2, 1948, and sent a strongly worded civil rights message to Congress requesting far-reaching remedial legislation. Although the upcoming presidential election provided at least part of Truman's motivation, he nevertheless placed the powers of his office squarely behind the demand for equal treatment: "The Federal Government has a clear duty to see that Constitutional guarantees of individual liberties and of equal protection under the laws are not denied or abridged anywhere in our Union." Thus began what historian C. Vann Woodward has called the "Second Reconstruction."

Congress, however, stalemated on civil rights by the southern bloc, failed to respond, and it was the Supreme Court that became the vehicle for reform. On May 17, 1954, building upon a long series of decisions that originated in 1938, the Court went the full distance and declared that laws in seventeen states requiring segregated public schools were unconstitutional; similarly, laws permitting optional local segregation in four other states were also overturned. The longstanding "separate but equal" doctrine was declared "inherently unequal" by the Court and, in 1955, the states were subsequently ordered to proceed with desegregation of their public schools "with all deliberate speed."

By mid-1956, federal courts had toppled school segregation in Arkansas, Florida, Louisiana, Tennessee, and Texas. Perhaps even more ominous for segregationists was that the Negroes themselves were beginning to demonstrate a new militancy. The Montgomery bus boycott protesting segregated seating proved the ability of the blacks to achieve new rights for themselves; economic boycotts and the direct action "nonviolent" techniques advocated by the Reverend Martin Luther King, Jr., opened up new vistas for changing southern racial practices.

Angered white southerners counterattacked. White Citizens Councils were formed throughout the lower South and by 1959 boasted of membership of more than half a million. In March of 1956, nineteen Senators and eighty-one Congressmen issued a "Southern Manifesto," which praised "those states which have declared the intention to resist forced integration by any lawful means." Openly defiant to the school desegregation order, southerners rallied to the cry of "massive resistance." It came first in the struggle to integrate Little Rock Central High School. Arkansas Governor Orval Faubus used state police and national guardsmen to prevent nine Negro students from enrolling in the autumn of 1957. They were ultimately able to do so only when President Eisenhower, with great reluctance, sent in federal troops to carry out the court order. For the next several years, the nation's newspapers were filled with incidents related to school desegregation. In 1958–59, Prince Edward County, Virginia, closed its public schools to prevent integration and used tax funds to operate "private" schools for white students. Federal troops were required to enroll James Meredith in the University of Mississippi, and Alabama Governor George Wallace "stood in the doorway" in a futile attempt to keep the University of Alabama lily-white. Southern legal experts even dusted off the century-old theory of "interposition," whereby the "sovereign" state government placed itself between the federal government and local governmental units and individual citizens in an attempt to find a constitutional means of preventing school desegregation. Negro parents who sought to enroll their children in all-white schools were made victims of social and economic pressures, and the Ku Klux Klan rose once more to terrorize civil rights workers and "uppity" blacks.

Such resistance, however, only slowed the inevitable, because the early 1960's saw a broadening and strengthening of the civil rights movement. By the end of the decade, legalized segregation was virtually ended in the United States. The dramatic direct-action techniques of college students who openly defied southern custom and law in a wave of sit-ins, freedom rides, and voter registration drives symbolized the emergence of the "new Negro" in America. Rallying to the cry of "Freedom Now!" and chanting "We will overcome!", this new vanguard dismissed the legalistic and legislative approach of the prestigious National Association for the Advancement of Colored People as outdated, as blacks took their movement into the streets to dramatize their grievances. In 1964 Congress responded both to its conscience and to Negro demands in an election year and enacted the far-reaching Civil Rights Act, which abolished segregation in public facilities and established procedures to end discrimination in employment. In 1965, Congress passed a strong bill designed to insure Negroes of the right to vote.

Civil rights legislation, however, did not produce "Freedom Now." While the legal barriers had been toppled, *de facto* segregation remained an obvious fact. As increasing numbers of Negroes were squeezed into the urban ghettos, the United States in practice was becoming two nations within one—black and white. Economically and socially, the Negro still was a second-class citizen. Rising rates of Negro unemployment made a mockery of much of the early rhetoric of the civil rights movement. The perceptive Martin Luther King recognized this and, shortly before his tragic death, had begun to emphasize the economic conditions of his people; in fact, he was in Memphis, Tennessee, to assist the city's Negro garbage collectors in their fight for higher wages when he was assassinated. The Southern Christian Leadership Conference two months later carried out his plans for a Poor Peoples' March on Washington to demonstrate the condition of the nation's poor.

The frustrations bred of a second-class citizenship characterized by the social and economic conditions of the ghettos contributed directly to the greatest outbreak of civil disorder in American history. Throughout 1964, sporadic violence flared in over a dozen cities. Then came Watts. On August 11, 1965, the large Negro section in the heart of sprawling Los Angeles erupted in the violence of fire bombings, sniping, and looting which lasted for nearly a week. Not since Detroit in 1943 had the United States endured such a racial bloodbath. The following year, forty-three disorders and riots occurred, which served as a prologue to the "long, hot summer" of 1967. Newark, Detroit, and Cincinnati suffered major losses in life and property from Negro rioters and all-too-often inept police and military action. By the end of the year nearly 150 cities had been touched by violence; the President's Commission on Civil Disorders later classified forty-one of the outbreaks of violence as either of a "serious" or "major" nature. Eighty-three persons died in the rioting and 1897 were injured. By the presidential election year of 1968, both national parties had recognized that conditions within the cities would severely test the resilience of American institutions.

The racial disorders served to bring into focus the serious conditions of the nation's cities. For decades, social critics had spoken out in vain about the deteriorating central cities as middle-class whites fled to the suburbs. A rural-dominated Congress and numerous state legislatures, however, refused to act to meet the growing crisis. By 1965, as the skies of Los Angeles grew black with smoke, it seemed to many that it already was too late. Contenting itself with a few limited programs to build public housing or to clear ugly slums, Congress never forced itself to face the urban crisis directly. Only in 1965 did it create a cabinet-level Department of Housing and Urban Development, over one hundred years after the establishment of the Department of Agriculture. Appropriately, President Johnson named as the first Secretary of the new department, Robert Weaver, a Negro whose expertise in urban affairs was internationally recognized.

The problems facing the new Secretary were enormous and, perhaps, beyond complete solution: inadequate housing for millions of the urban poor, lack of sufficient public services and facilities, antiquated governmental structures, snarled transportation systems, growing unemployment in the ghettos, polluted air and water, spiralling crime rates and the flight of the whites to the suburbs away from the centers of social disintegration. By 1968, some responsible national leaders were advocating a domestic Marshall Plan, which would cost approximately $50 billion to save the cities from self-destruction.

Such a program, no matter how urgent, was rejected by the Johnson Administration as impossible because of the cost of the Vietnam war. By that year, Johnson no longer could argue that the United States could fight the war and continue to build a Great Society at home. As $30 billion were funneled annually into the war, the Great Society became a mirage. From the commitment of 12,000 American soldiers in Vietnam in 1963, President Johnson escalated the American effort to more than a half million men and officers by 1967. Vietnam had become the fourth largest war in the nation's history. By the time the two national parties gathered for their nominating conventions in August of 1968, over 26,000 Americans had been killed and 131,000 wounded.

It also was the nation's most unpopular war. As the United States enlarged the scope of the war in early 1965 and as the futility of defeating an enemy that had substantial support among the South Vietnamese became evident, Johnson steadily lost public support. He soon discovered that the sources of support for the war were those that stood in opposition to his domestic program—primarily southern members of his own party and conservative

Republicans. By 1967, such leading senators as Robert F. Kennedy, William Fulbright, and Eugene McCarthy were in open rebellion, as was much of the liberal wing of the Democratic party. The bombing of civilian targets, the interference in what many Americans believed to be a civil war, and a growing belief that Vietnam was not vital to American security led to massive antiwar demonstrations—especially among the idealistic youth of the nation. When they found that they could not alter Johnson's course, they felt alienated from American society. Some even fled to Canada to escape the draft, while others contented themselves with symbolic draft-card burnings and mass demonstrations against Administration policy. The harrassed President himself became the symbol to the rebels of their grievances with their society. Appalled by what they believed to be senseless and oppressive poverty, by racial barbarism and the blatant materialism of their society, the youthful radicals believed that Vietnam was the logical product of a sick society.

By 1967, however, not only the young were in opposition. Johnson's support among liberals had been spent, and many white moderates in the suburbs even bestirred themselves to join in the protest. Senator McCarthy's surprising victory over Johnson in the New Hampshire primary, the entrance of Senator Robert Kennedy into the race, and the results of several opinion polls led Johnson to withdraw unexpectedly from the 1968 presidential race on March 31. The huge majority he had won in the 1964 election over conservative Barry Goldwater had been spent, and his prized "consensus," along with the Great Society, had been destroyed by Vietnam. In the words of Journalist Tom Wicker, Johnson had crossed the wrong Rubicon.

SECONDARY SOURCES

1. ARTHUR M. SCHLESINGER, JR., "THE ORIGINS OF THE COLD WAR"

THE cordiality which outwardly characterized the relationship between the United States and the Soviet Union during World War II began to deteriorate shortly after the conclusion of the Yalta Conference in February, 1945. Upon taking office on April 12, 1945, following the sudden death of Franklin Roosevelt, President Harry S. Truman promised Premier Stalin that he would continue the policy of mutual cooperation and accommodation that had been practiced by President Roosevelt. Within a short time,

SOURCE. Arthur M. Schlesinger, Jr., "The Origins of the Cold War," in *Foreign Affairs*, Vol. 46, October 1967, pp. 22–52. Copyright 1967 by the Council on Foreign Relations, Inc., New York. Reprinted by permission of *Foreign Affairs* and the author.

however, it was evident that Truman was not as inclined toward tolerating Russian intransigence as Roosevelt had been. Despite the efforts of the United States to reach fundamental agreements with Russia on the settlement of postwar Europe, Soviet-American relations had polarized by 1947. Truman bluntly accused the Soviets of duplicity and insisted that the U.S.S.R. honor her pledges of establishing free governments in Poland, Rumania, and Hungary.

The sources of American-Russian distrust go back at least to the Bolshevik Revolution of 1917. Perhaps the conflicting ideologies of the two powerful nations made conflict inevitable, but had Russia not reneged on her pledges at Yalta and had the United States not taken such an inflexible position, an accord could possibly have been reached. But just as President Truman told a cabinet meeting on April 23, 1945, that negotiations with the Russians "had so far been a one-way street," and that he was going to change that situation immediately, so the Russians refused to participate in the Baruch Plan that would have divested the United States of her nuclear monopoly and placed all atomic weapons under international control.

The responsibility for the Cold War has understandably become a subject of controversy among scholars. Following essentially the position of Secretary of Commerce Henry A. Wallace, who broke with the Truman Administration over foreign policy, a small but articulate group of scholars has placed the blame squarely upon the United States. They contend that President Truman unnecessarily followed a harsh line, that his abrupt curtailment of lend-lease shortly after the war served only to confirm Russian fears of the intentions of her capitalistic ally, and that Truman sought to use the American atomic monopoly to force the Russians to accept American solutions to postwar reconstruction in Europe and Asia. Although the "revisionist" position is apparently gaining new converts, most historians have thus far rejected it and have followed a more traditional approach by pointing to Russia's repeated violations of her Yalta pledges and her refusal to cooperate in the creation of a stable and democratic postwar world. The United States was merely responding to hostile Russian actions.

In assessing both the traditionalist and revisionist positions, Professor Arthur M. Schlesinger, Jr., seeks to diffuse responsibility and calls for a balanced approach to the complex question of causation. While he vigorously attacks the revisionists, he nevertheless points out that American policy and attitudes contributed substantially to the impasse which led the world to the brink of nuclear war and into a Cold War that has endured for a quarter of a century.

The Cold War in its original form was a presumably mortal antagonism, arising in the wake of the Second World War, between two rigidly hostile blocs, one led by the Soviet Union, the other by the United States. For nearly two somber and dangerous decades this antagonism dominated the fears of mankind; it may even, on occasion, have come close to blowing up the planet. In recent years, however, the once implacable struggle has lost its familiar clarity of outline. With the passing of old issues and the emergence of new conflicts and contestants, there is a natural tendency, especially on the part of the generation which grew up during the Cold War, to take a fresh look at the causes of the great contention between Russia and America.

Some exercises in reappraisal have merely elaborated the orthodoxies promulgated in Washington or Moscow during the boom years of the Cold War. But others, especially in the United States (there are no signs, alas, of this in the Soviet Union), represent what American historians call "revisionism"—that is, a readiness to challenge official explanations. No one should be surprised by this phenomenon. Every war in American history has been followed in due course by skeptical reassessments of supposedly sacred assumptions. So the War of 1812, fought at the time for the freedom of the seas, was in later years ascribed to the expansionist ambitions of Congressional war hawks; so the Mexican War became a slaveholders' conspiracy. So the Civil War has been pronounced a "needless war," and Lincoln has even been accused of manœuvring the rebel attack on Fort Sumter. So too the Spanish-American War and the First and Second World Wars have, each in its turn, undergone revisionist critiques. It is not to be supposed that the Cold War would remain exempt.

In the case of the Cold War, special factors reinforce the predictable historiographical rhythm. The outburst of polycentrism in the communist empire has made people wonder whether communism was ever so monolithic as official theories of the Cold War supposed. A generation with no vivid memories of Stalinism may see the Russia of the forties in the image of the relatively mild, seedy and irresolute Russia of the sixties. And for this same generation the American course of widening the war in Viet Nam—which even non-revisionists can easily regard as folly—has unquestionably stirred doubts about the wisdom of American foreign policy in the sixties which younger historians may have begun to read back into the forties.

It is useful to remember that, on the whole, past exercises in revisionism have failed to stick. Few historians today believe that the war hawks caused the War of 1812 or the slaveholders the Mexican War, or that the Civil War was needless, or that the House of Morgan brought America into the First World War or that Franklin Roosevelt schemed to produce the attack on Pearl Harbor. But this does not mean that one should deplore the rise of Cold War revisionism.[1] For revisionism is an essential part of the process by which history, through the posing of new problems and the investigation of new possibilities, enlarges its perspectives and enriches its insights.

[1] As this writer somewhat intemperately did in a letter to *The New York Review of Books*, October 20, 1966.

More than this, in the present context, revisionism expresses a deep, legitimate and tragic apprehension. As the Cold War has begun to lose its purity of definition, as the moral absolutes of the fifties become the moralistic clichés of the sixties, some have begun to ask whether the appalling risks which humanity ran during the Cold War were, after all, necessary and inevitable; whether more restrained and rational policies might not have guided the energies of man from the perils of conflict into the potentialities of collaboration. The fact that such questions are in their nature unanswerable does not mean that it is not right and useful to raise them. Nor does it mean that our sons and daughters are not entitled to an accounting from the generation of Russians and Americans who produced the Cold War.

II

The orthodox American view, as originally set forth by the American government and as reaffirmed until recently by most American scholars, has been that the Cold War was the brave and essential response of free men to communist aggression. Some have gone back well before the Second World War to lay open the sources of Russian expansionism. Geopoliticians traced the Cold War to imperial Russian strategic ambitions which in the nineteenth century led to the Crimean War, to Russian penetration of the Balkans and the Middle East and to Russian pressure on Britain's "lifeline" to India. Ideologists traced it to the Communist Manifesto of 1848 ("the violent overthrow of the bourgeoisie lays the foundation for the sway of the proletariat"). Thoughtful observers (a phrase meant to exclude those who speak in Dullese about the unlimited evil of godless, atheistic, militant communism) concluded that classical Russian imperialism and Pan-Slavism, compounded after 1917 by Leninist messianism, confronted the West at the end of the Second World War with an inexorable drive for domination.[1]

The revisionist thesis is very different.[2] In its extreme form, it is that, after

[1] Every student of the Cold War must acknowledge his debt to W. H. McNeill's remarkable account, "America, Britain and Russia: Their Cooperation and Conflict, 1941–1946" (New York, 1953) and to the brilliant and indispensable series by Herbert Feis: "Churchill, Roosevelt, Stalin: The War They Waged and the Peace They Sought" (Princeton, 1957); "Between War and Peace: The Potsdam Conference" (Princeton, 1960); and "The Atomic Bomb and the End of World War II" (Princeton, 1966). Useful recent analyses include André Fontaine, "Histoire de la Guerre Froide" (2 v., Paris, 1965, 1967); N. A. Graebner, "Cold War Diplomacy, 1945–1960" (Princeton, 1962); L. J. Halle, "The Cold War as History" (London, 1967); M. F. Herz, "Beginnings of the Cold War" (Bloomington, 1966) and W. L. Neumann, "After Victory: Churchill, Roosevelt, Stalin and the Making of the Peace" (New York, 1967).

[2] The fullest statement of this case is to be found in D. F. Fleming's voluminous "The Cold War and Its Origins" (New York, 1961). For a shorter version of this argument, see David Horowitz, "The Free World Colossus" (New York, 1965); the most subtle and ingenious statements come in W. A. Williams' "The Tragedy of American Diplomacy"

the death of Franklin Roosevelt and the end of the Second World War, the United States deliberately abandoned the wartime policy of collaboration and, exhilarated by the possession of the atomic bomb, undertook a course of aggression of its own designed to expel all Russian influence from Eastern Europe and to establish democratic-capitalist states on the very border of the Soviet Union. As the revisionists see it, this radically new American policy— or rather this resumption by Truman of the pre-Roosevelt policy of insensate anti-communism—left Moscow no alternative but to take measures in defense of its own borders. The result was the Cold War.

These two views, of course, could not be more starkly contrasting. It is therefore not unreasonable to look again at the half-dozen critical years between June 22, 1941, when Hitler attacked Russia, and July 2, 1947, when the Russians walked out of the Marshall Plan meeting in Paris. Several things should be borne in mind as this reëxamination is made. For one thing, we have thought a great deal more in recent years, in part because of writers like Roberta Wohlstetter and T. C. Schelling, about the problems of communication in diplomacy—the signals which one nation, by word or by deed, gives, inadvertently or intentionally, to another. Any honest reappraisal of

---

(rev. ed., New York, 1962) and in Gar Alperowitz's "Atomic Diplomacy: Hiroshima and Potsdam" (New York, 1965) and in subsequent articles and reviews by Mr. Alperowitz in *The New York Review of Books*. The fact that in some aspects the revisionist thesis parallels the official Soviet argument must not, of course, prevent consideration of the case on its merits, nor raise questions about the motives of the writers, all of whom, so far as I know, are independent-minded scholars.

I might further add that all these books, in spite of their ostentatious display of scholarly apparatus, must be used with caution. Professor Fleming, for example, relies heavily on newspaper articles and even columnists. While Mr. Alperowitz bases his case on official documents or authoritative reminiscences, he sometimes twists his material in a most unscholarly way. For example, in describing Ambassador Harriman's talk with President Truman on April 20, 1945, Mr. Alperowitz writes, "He argued that a reconsideration of Roosevelt's policy was necessary" (p. 22, repeated on p. 24). The citation is to p. 70–72 in President Truman's "Years of Decision." What President Truman reported Harriman as saying was the exact opposite: "Before leaving, Harriman took me aside and said, 'Frankly, one of the reasons that made me rush back to Washington was the fear that you did not understand, as I had seen Roosevelt understand, that Stalin is breaking his agreements.' " Similarly, in an appendix (p. 271) Mr. Alperowitz writes that the Hopkins and Davies missions of May 1945 "were opposed by the 'firm' advisers." Actually the Hopkins mission was proposed by Harriman and Charles E. Bohlen, who Mr. Alperowitz elsewhere suggests were the firmest of the firm—and was proposed by them precisely to impress on Stalin the continuity of American policy from Roosevelt to Truman. While the idea that Truman reversed Roosevelt's policy is tempting dramatically, it is a myth. See, for example, the testimony of Anna Rosenberg Hoffman, who lunched with Roosevelt on March 24, 1945, the last day he spent in Washington. After luncheon, Roosevelt was handed a cable. "He read it and became quite angry. He banged his fists on the arms of his wheelchair and said, 'Averell is right; we can't do business with Stalin. He has broken every one of the promises he made at Yalta.' He was very upset and continued in the same vein on the subject."

the origins of the Cold War requires the imaginative leap—which should in any case be as instinctive for the historian as it is prudent for the statesman—into the adversary's viewpoint. We must strive to see how, given Soviet perspectives, the Russians might conceivably have misread our signals, as we must reconsider how intelligently we read theirs.

For another, the historian must not overindulge the man of power in the illusion cherished by those in office that high position carries with it the easy ability to shape history. Violating the statesman's creed, Lincoln once blurted out the truth in his letter of 1864 to A. G. Hodges: "I claim not to have controlled events, but confess plainly that events have controlled me." He was not asserting Tolstoyan fatalism but rather suggesting how greatly events limit the capacity of the statesman to bend history to his will. The physical course of the Second World War—the military operations undertaken, the position of the respective armies at the war's end, the momentum generated by victory and the vacuums created by defeat—all these determined the future as much as the character of individual leaders and the substance of national ideology and purpose.

Nor can the historian forget the conditions under which decisions are made, especially in a time like the Second World War. These were tired, overworked, aging men: in 1945, Churchill was 71 years old, Stalin had governed his country for 17 exacting years, Roosevelt his for 12 years nearly as exacting. During the war, moreover, the importunities of military operations had shoved postwar questions to the margins of their minds. All—even Stalin, behind his screen of ideology—had become addicts of improvisation, relying on authority and virtuosity to conceal the fact that they were constantly surprised by developments. Like Eliza, they leaped from one cake of ice to the next in the effort to reach the other side of the river. None showed great tactical consistency, or cared much about it; all employed a certain ambiguity to preserve their power to decide big issues; and it is hard to know how to interpret anything any one of them said on any specific occasion. This was partly because, like all princes, they designed their expressions to have particular effects on particular audiences; partly because the entirely genuine intellectual difficulty of the questions they faced made a degree of vacillation and mind-changing eminently reasonable. If historians cannot solve their problems in retrospect, who are they to blame Roosevelt, Stalin and Churchill for not having solved them at the time?

III

Peacemaking after the Second World War was not so much a tapestry as it was a hopelessly raveled and knotted mess of yarn. Yet, for purposes of clarity, it is essential to follow certain threads. One theme indispensable to an understanding of the Cold War is the constrast between two clashing views of world order: the "universalist" view, by which all nations shared a common interest in all the affairs of the world, and the "sphere-of-influence" view, by which each great power would be assured by the other great powers of an acknowledged predominance in its own area of special interest. The universalist view assumed that national security would be guaranteed by an international organization. The sphere-of-interest view assumed that national security would be guaranteed by the balance of power. While in practice these views have by no means been incompatible (indeed, our shaky peace has been based on a combination of the two), in the abstract they involved sharp contradictions.

The tradition of American thought in these matters was universalist—*i.e.* Wilsonian. Roosevelt had been a member of Wilson's subcabinet; in 1920, as candidate for Vice President, he had campaigned for the League of Nations. It is true that, within Roosevelt's infinitely complex mind, Wilsonianism warred with the perception of vital strategic interests he had imbibed from Mahan. Moreover, his temperamental inclination to settle things with fellow princes around the conference table led him to regard the Big Three—or Four—as trustees for the rest of the world. On occasion, as this narrative will show, he was beguiled into flirtation with the sphere-of-influence heresy. But in principle he believed in joint action and remained a Wilsonian. His hope for Yalta, as he told the Congress on his return, was that it would "spell the end of the system of unilateral action, the exclusive alliances, the spheres of influence, the balances of power, and all the other expedients that have been tried for centuries—and have always failed."

Whenever Roosevelt backslid, he had at his side that Wilsonian fundamentalist, Secretary of State Cordell Hull, to recall him to the pure faith. After his visit to Moscow in 1943, Hull characteristically said that, with the Declaration of Four Nations on General Security (in which America, Russia, Britain and China pledged "united action . . . for the organization and maintenance of peace and security"), "there will no longer be need for spheres of influence, for alliances, for balance of power, or any other of the special arrangements through which, in the unhappy past, the nations strove to safeguard their security or to promote their interests."

Remembering the corruption of the Wilsonian vision by the secret treaties of the First World War, Hull was determined to prevent any sphere-of-influence nonsense after the Second World War. He therefore fought all proposals to settle border questions while the war was still on and, excluded as he largely was from wartime diplomacy, poured his not inconsiderable moral energy and frustration into the promulgation of virtuous and spacious general principles.

In adopting the universalist view, Roosevelt and Hull were not indulging personal hobbies. Sumner Welles, Adolf Berle, Averell Harriman, Charles Bohlen—all, if with a variety of nuances, opposed the sphere-of-influence approach. And here the State Department was expressing what seems clearly to have been the predominant mood of the American people, so long mistrustful of European power politics. The Republicans shared the true faith. John Foster Dulles argued that the great threat to peace after the war would lie in the revival of sphere-of-influence thinking. The United States, he said, must not permit Britain and Russia to revert to these bad old ways; it must therefore insist on American participation in all policy decisions for all territories in the world. Dulles wrote pessimistically in January 1945, "The three great powers which at Moscow agreed upon the 'closest coöperation' about European questions have shifted to a practice of separate, regional responsibility."

It is true that critics, and even friends, of the United States sometimes noted a discrepancy between the American passion for universalism when it applied to territory far from American shores and the preëminence the United States accorded its own interests nearer home. Churchill, seeking Washington's blessing for a sphere-of-influence initiative in Eastern Europe, could not forbear reminding the Americans, "We follow the lead of the United States in South America;" nor did any universalist of record propose the abolition of the Monroe Doctrine. But a convenient myopia prevented such inconsistencies from qualifying the ardency of the universalist faith.

There seem only to have been three officials in the United States Government who dissented. One was the Secretary of War, Henry L. Stimson, a classical balance-of-power man, who in 1944 opposed the creation of a vacuum in Central Europe by the pastoralization of Germany and in 1945 urged "the settlement of all territorial acquisitions in the shape of defense posts which each of these four powers may deem to be necessary for their own safety" in advance of any effort to establish a peacetime United Nations. Stimson considered the claim of Russia to a preferred position in Eastern Europe as not unreasonable: as he told President Truman, "he thought the Russians perhaps were being more realistic than we were in regard to their own security." Such a position for Russia seemed to him comparable to the preferred American position in Latin America; he even spoke of "our respective orbits." Stimson was therefore skeptical of what he regarded as the prevailing tendency "to hang on to exaggerated views of the Monroe Doctrine and at the same time butt into every question that comes up in Central Europe." Acceptance of spheres of influence seemed to him the way to avoid "a head-on collision."

A second official opponent of universalism was George Kennan, an eloquent advocate from the American Embassy in Moscow of "a prompt and clear recognition of the division of Europe into spheres of influence and of a policy based on the fact of such division." Kennan argued that nothing we could do would possibly alter the course of events in Eastern Europe; that we were deceiving ourselves by supposing that these countries had any future but Russian domination; that we should therefore relinquish Eastern Europe to the Soviet Union and avoid anything which would make things easier for the Russians by giving them economic assistance or by sharing moral responsibility for their actions.

A third voice within the government against universalism was (at least after the war) Henry A. Wallace. As Secretary of Commerce, he stated the sphere-of-influence case with trenchancy in the famous Madison Square Garden speech of September 1946 which led to his dismissal by President Truman:

> On our part, we should recognize that we have no more business in the *political* affairs of Eastern Europe than Russia has in the *political* affairs of Latin America, Western Europe, and the United States. . . . Whether we like it or not, the Russians will try to socialize their sphere of influence just as we try to democratize our sphere of influence. . . . The Russians have no more business stirring up native Communists to political activity in Western Europe, Latin America, and the United States than we have in interfering with the politics of Eastern Europe and Russia.

Stimson, Kennan and Wallace seem to have been alone in the government, however, in taking these views. They were very much minority voices. Meanwhile universalism, rooted in the American legal and moral tradition, overwhelmingly backed by contemporary opinion, received successive enshrinements in the Atlantic Charter of 1941, in the Declaration of the United Nations in 1942 and in the Moscow Declaration of 1943.

IV

The Kremlin, on the other hand, thought *only* of spheres of interest; above all, the Russians were determined to protect their frontiers, and especially their border to the west, crossed so often and so bloodily in the dark course of their history. These western frontiers lacked natural means of defense—no great oceans, rugged mountains, steaming swamps or impenetrable jungles. The history of Russia had been the history of invasion, the last of which was by now horribly killing up to twenty million of its people. The protocol of Russia therefore meant the enlargement of the area of Russian influence. Kennan himself wrote (in May 1944), "Behind Russia's stubborn expansion lies only the age-old sense of insecurity of a sedentary people reared on an exposed plain in the neighborhood of fierce nomadic peoples," and he called this "urge" a "permanent feature of Russian psychology."

In earlier times the "urge" had produced the tsarist search for buffer states and maritime outlets. In 1939 the Soviet-Nazi pact and its secret protocol had enabled Russia to begin to satisfy in the Baltic states, Karelian Finland and Poland, part of what it conceived as its security requirements in Eastern Europe. But the "urge" persisted, causing the friction between Russia and

Germany in 1940 as each jostled for position in the area which separated them. Later it led to Molotov's new demands on Hitler in November 1940—a free hand in Finland, Soviet predominance in Rumania and Bulgaria, bases in the Dardanelles—the demands which convinced Hitler that he had no choice but to attack Russia. Now Stalin hoped to gain from the West what Hitler, a closer neighbor, had not dared yield him.

It is true that, so long as Russian survival appeared to require a second front to relieve the Nazi pressure, Moscow's demand for Eastern Europe was a little muffled. Thus the Soviet government adhered to the Atlantic Charter (though with a significant if obscure reservation about adapting its principles to "the circumstances, needs, and historic peculiarities of particular countries"). Thus it also adhered to the Moscow Declaration of 1943, and Molotov then, with his easy mendacity, even denied that Russia had any desire to divide Europe into spheres of influence. But this was guff, which the Russians were perfectly willing to ladle out if it would keep the Americans, and especially Secretary Hull (who made a strong personal impression at the Moscow conference) happy. "A declaration," as Stalin once observed to Eden, "I regard as algebra, but an agreement as practical arithmetic. I do not wish to decry algebra, but I prefer practical arithmetic."

The more consistent Russian purpose was revealed when Stalin offered the British a straight sphere-of-influence deal at the end of 1941. Britain, he suggested, should recognize the Russian absorption of the Baltic states, part of Finland, eastern Poland and Bessarabia; in return, Russia would support any special British need for bases or security arrangements in Western Europe. There was nothing specifically communist about these ambitions. If Stalin achieved them, he would be fulfilling an age-old dream of the tsars. The British reaction was mixed. "Soviet policy is amoral," as Anthony Eden noted at the time; "United States policy is exaggeratedly moral, at least where non-American interests are concerned." If Roosevelt was a universalist with occasional leanings toward spheres of influence and Stalin was a sphere-of-influence man with occasional gestures toward universalism, Churchill seemed evenly poised between the familiar realism of the balance of power, which he had so long recorded as an historian and manipulated as a statesman, and the hope that there must be some better way of doing things. His 1943 proposal of a world organization divided into regional councils represented an effort to blend universalist and sphere-of-interest conceptions. His initial rejection of Stalin's proposal in December 1941 as "directly contrary to the first, second and third articles of the Atlantic Charter" thus did not spring entirely from a desire to propitiate the United States. On the other hand, he had himself already reinterpreted the Atlantic Charter as applying only to Europe (and thus not to the British Empire), and he was, above all, an empiricist who never believed in sacrificing reality on the altar of doctrine.

So in April 1942, he wrote Roosevelt that "the increasing gravity of the war" had led him to feel that the Charter "ought not to be construed so as to deny Russia the frontiers she occupied when Germany attacked her." Hull, however, remained fiercely hostile to the inclusion of territorial provisions in the Anglo-Russian treaty; the American position, Eden noted, "chilled me with Wilsonian memories." Though Stalin complained that it looked "as if the Atlantic Charter was directed against the U.S.S.R.," it was the Russian season of military adversity in the spring of 1942, and he dropped his demands.

He did not, however, change his intentions. A year later Ambassador Standley could cable Washington from Moscow: "In 1918 Western Europe attempted to set up a *cordon sanitaire* to protect it from the influence of bolshevism. Might not now the Kremlin envisage the formation of a belt of pro-Soviet states to protect it from the influences of the West?" It well might; and that purpose became increasingly clear as the war approached its end. Indeed, it derived sustenance from Western policy in the first area of liberation.

The unconditional surrender of Italy in July 1943 created the first major test of the Western devotion to universalism. America and Britain, having won the Italian war, handled the capitulation, keeping Moscow informed at a distance. Stalin complained:

> The United States and Great Britain made agreements but the Soviet Union received information about the results . . . just as a passive third observer. I have to tell you that it is impossible to tolerate the situation any longer. I propose that the [tripartite military-political commission] be established and that Sicily be assigned . . . as its place of residence.

Roosevelt, who had no intention of sharing the control of Italy with the Russians, suavely replied with the suggestion that Stalin send an officer "to General Eisenhower's headquarters in connection with the commission." Unimpressed, Stalin continued to press for a tripartite body; but his Western allies were adamant in keeping the Soviet Union off the Control Commission for Italy, and the Russians in the end had to be satisfied with a seat, along with minor Allied states, on a meaningless Inter-Allied Advisory Council. Their acquiescence in this was doubtless not unconnected with a desire to establish precedents for Eastern Europe.

Teheran in December 1943 marked the high point of three-power collaboration. Still, when Churchill asked about Russian territorial interests, Stalin replied a little ominously, "There is no need to speak at the present time about any Soviet desires, but when the time comes we will speak." In the next weeks, there were increasing indications of a Soviet determination to deal unilaterally with Eastern Europe—so much so that in early February 1944 Hull cabled Harriman in Moscow:

Matters are rapidly approaching the point where the Soviet Government will have to choose between the development and extension of the foundation of international cooperation as the guiding principle of the postwar world as against the continuance of a unilateral and arbitrary method of dealing with its special problems even though these problems are admittedly of more direct interest to the Soviet Union than to other great powers.

As against this approach, however, Churchill, more tolerant of sphere-of-influence deviations, soon proposed that, with the impending liberation of the Balkans, Russia should run things in Rumania and Britain in Greece. Hull strongly opposed this suggestion but made the mistake of leaving Washington for a few days; and Roosevelt, momentarily free from his Wilsonian conscience, yielded to Churchill's plea for a three-months' trial. Hull resumed the fight on his return, and Churchill postponed the matter.

The Red Army continued its advance into Eastern Europe. In August the Polish Home Army, urged on by Polish-language broadcasts from Moscow, rose up against the Nazis in Warsaw. For 63 terrible days, the Poles fought valiantly on, while the Red Army halted on the banks of the Vistula a few miles away, and in Moscow Stalin for more than half this time declined to coöperate with the Western effort to drop supplies to the Warsaw Resistance. It appeared a calculated Soviet decision to let the Nazis slaughter the anti-Soviet Polish underground; and, indeed, the result was to destroy any substantial alternative to a Soviet solution in Poland. The agony of Warsaw caused the most deep and genuine moral shock in Britain and America and provoked dark forebodings about Soviet postwar purposes.

Again history enjoins the imaginative leap in order to see things for a moment from Moscow's viewpoint. The Polish question, Churchill would say at Yalta, was for Britain a question of honor. "It is not only a question of honor for Russia," Stalin replied, "but one of life and death. . . . Throughout history Poland had been the corridor for attack on Russia." A top postwar priority for any Russian régime must be to close that corridor. The Home Army was led by anti-communists. It clearly hoped by its action to forestall the Soviet occupation of Warsaw and, in Russian eyes, to prepare the way for an anti-Russian Poland. In addition, the uprising from a strictly operational viewpoint was premature. The Russians, it is evident in retrospect, had real military problems at the Vistula. The Soviet attempt in September to send Polish units from the Red Army across the river to join forces with the Home Army was a disaster. Heavy German shelling thereafter prevented the ferrying of tanks necessary for an assault on the German position. The Red Army itself did not take Warsaw for another three months. None the less, Stalin's indifference to the human tragedy, his effort to blackmail the London Poles during the ordeal, his sanctimonious opposition during five precious weeks to aerial resupply, the invariable coldness of his explanations ("the Soviet command has come to the conclusion that it must dissociate itself from the War-saw adventure") and the obvious political benefit to the Soviet Union from the destruction of the Home Army—all these had the effect of suddenly drop-ping the mask of wartime comradeship and displaying to the West the hard face of Soviet policy. In now pursuing what he grimly regarded as the minimal requirements for the postwar security of his country, Stalin was inadvertently showing the irreconcilability of both his means and his ends with the Anglo-American conception of the peace.

Meanwhile Eastern Europe presented the Alliance with still another crisis that same September. Bulgaria, which was not at war with Russia, decided to surrender to the Western Allies while it still could; and the English and Americans at Cairo began to discuss armistice terms with Bulgarian envoys. Moscow, challenged by what it plainly saw as a Western intrusion into its own zone of vital interest, promptly declared war on Bulgaria, took over the surrender negotiations and, invoking the Italian precedent, denied its West-ern Allies any role in the Bulgarian Control Commission. In a long and thoughtful cable, Ambassador Harriman meditated on the problems of com-munication with the Soviet Union. "Words," he reflected, "have a different connotation to the Soviets than they have to us. When they speak of insisting on 'friendly governments' in their neighboring countries, they have in mind something quite different from what we would mean." The Russians, he surmised, really believed that Washington accepted "their position that although they would keep us informed they had the right to settle their prob-lems with their western neighbors unilaterally." But the Soviet position was still in flux: "the Soviet Government is not one mind." The problem, as Harriman had earlier told Harry Hopkins, was "to strengthen the hands of those around Stalin who want to play the game along our lines." The way to do this, he now told Hull, was to

be understanding of their sensitivity, meet them much more than half way, encourage them and support them wherever we can, and yet oppose them promptly with the greatest of firmness where we see them going wrong. . . . The only way we can eventually come to an understanding with the Soviet Union on the question of non-interference in the internal affairs of other countries is for us to take a definite interest in the solution of the problems of each individual country as they arise.

As against Harriman's sophisticated universalist strategy, however, Churchill, increasingly fearfull of the consequences of unrestrained competi-tion in Eastern Europe, decided in early October to carry his sphere-of-influence proposal directly to Moscow. Roosevelt was at first content to have Churchill speak for him too and even prepared a cable to that effect. But Hopkins, a more rigorous universalist, took it upon himself to stop the cable and warn Roosevelt of its possible implications. Eventually Roosevelt sent a message to Harriman in Moscow emphasizing that he expected to "retain complete freedom of action after this conference is over." It was now that Churchill quickly proposed—and Stalin as quickly accepted—the celebrated division of southeastern Europe: ending (after further haggling between Eden and Molotov) with 90 percent Soviet predominance in Rumania, 80 percent in Bulgaria and Hungary, fifty-fifty in Yugoslavia, 90 percent British predominance in Greece.

Churchill in discussing this with Harriman used the phrase "spheres of influence." But he insisted that these were only "immediate wartime arrangements" and received a highly general blessing from Roosevelt. Yet, whatever Churchill intended, there is reason to believe that Stalin construed the percentages as an agreement, not a declaration; as practical arithmetic, not algebra. For Stalin, it should be understood, the sphere-of-influence idea did not mean that he would abandon all efforts to spread communism in some other nation's sphere; it did mean that, if he tried this and the other side cracked down, he could not feel he had serious cause for complaint. As Kennan wrote to Harriman at the end of 1944:

> As far as border states are concerned the Soviet government has never ceased to think in terms of spheres of interest. They expect us to support them in whatever action they wish to take in those regions, regardless of whether that action seems to us or to the rest of the world to be right or wrong. . . . I have no doubt that this position is honestly maintained on their part, and that they would be equally prepared to reserve moral judgment on any actions which we might wish to carry out, i.e., in the Caribbean area.

In any case, the matter was already under test a good deal closer to Moscow than the Caribbean. The communist-dominated resistance movement in Greece was in open revolt against the effort of the Papandreou government to disarm and disband the guerrillas (the same Papandreou whom the Greek colonels have recently arrested on the claim that he is a tool of the communists). Churchill now called in British Army units to crush the insurrection. This action produced a storm of criticism in his own country and in the United States; the American Government even publicly dissociated itself from the intervention, thereby emphasizing its detachment from the sphere-of-influence deal. But Stalin, Churchill later claimed, "adhered strictly and faithfully to our agreement of October, and during all the long weeks of fighting the Communists in the streets of Athens not one word of reproach came from *Pravda* or *Izvestia*," though there is no evidence that he tried to call off the Greek communists. Still, when the communist rebellion later broke out again in Greece, Stalin told Kardelj and Djilas of Yugoslavia in 1948, "The uprising in Greece must be stopped, and as quickly as possible."

No one, of course, can know what really was in the minds of the Russian leaders. The Kremlin archives are locked; of the primary actors, only Molotov survives, and he has not yet indicated any desire to collaborate with the Columbia Oral History Project. We do know that Stalin did not wholly surrender to sentimental illusion about his new friends. In June 1944, on the night before the landings in Normandy, he told Djilas that the English "find nothing sweeter than to trick their allies. . . . And Churchill? Churchill is the kind who, if you don't watch him, will slip a kopeck out of your pocket. Yes, a kopeck out of your pocket! . . . Roosevelt is not like that. He dips in his hand only for bigger coins." But whatever his views of his colleagues it is not unreasonable to suppose that Stalin would have been satisfied at the end of the war to secure what Kennan has called "a protective glacis along Russia's western border," and that, in exchange for a free hand in Eastern Europe, he was prepared to give the British and Americans equally free hands in their zones of vital interest, including in nations as close to Russia as Greece (for the British) and, very probably—or at least so the Jugoslavs believe—China (for the United States). In other words, his initial objectives were very probably not world conquest but Russian security.

V

It is now pertinent to inquire why the United States rejected the idea of stabilizing the world by division into spheres of influence and insisted on an East European strategy. One should warn against rushing to the conclusion that it was all a row between hard-nosed, balance-of-power realists and starry-eyed Wilsonians. Roosevelt, Hopkins, Welles, Harriman, Bohlen, Berle, Dulles and other universalists were tough and serious men. Why then did they rebuff the sphere-of-influence solution?

The first reason is that they regarded this solution as containing within itself the seeds of a third world war. The balance-of-power idea seemed inherently unstable. It had always broken down in the past. It held out to each power the permanent temptation to try to alter the balance in its own favor, and it built this temptation into the international order. It would turn the great powers of 1945 away from the objective of concerting common policies toward competition for postwar advantage. As Hopkins told Molotov at Teheran, "The President feels it essential to world peace that Russia, Great Britain and the United States work out this control question in a manner which will not start each of the three powers arming against the others." "The greatest likelihood of eventual conflict," said the Joint Chiefs of Staff in 1944 (the only conflict which the J.C.S., in its wisdom, could then glimpse "in the foreseeable future" was between Britain and Russia), ". . . would seem to grow out of either nation initiating attempts to build up its strength, by seeking to attach to herself parts of Europe to the disadvantage and possible danger of her potential adversary." The Americans were perfectly ready to acknowledge that Russia was entitled to convincing assurance of her national security—but not this way. "I could sympathize fully with Stalin's desire to protect his western borders from future attack," as Hull put it. "But I felt that this security could best be obtained through a strong post-war peace organization."

Hull's remark suggests the second objection: that the sphere-of-influence approach would, in the words of the State Department in 1945, "militate against the establishment and effective functioning of a broader system of general security in which all countries will have their part." The United Nations, in short, was seen as the alternative to the balance of power. Nor did the universalists see any necessary incompatibility between the Russian desire for "friendly governments" on its frontier and the American desire for self-determination in Eastern Europe. Before Yalta the State Department judged the general mood of Europe as "to the left and strongly in favor of far-reaching economic and social reforms, but not, however, in favor of a left-wing totalitarian regime to achieve these reforms." Governments in Eastern Europe could be sufficiently to the left "to allay Soviet suspicions" but sufficiently representative "of the center and *petit bourgeois* elements" not to seem a prelude to communist dictatorship. The American criteria were therefore that the government "should be dedicated to the preservation of civil liberties" and "should favor social and economic reforms." A string of New Deal states—of Finlands and Czechoslovakias—seemed a reasonable compromise solution.

Third, the universalists feared that the sphere-of-interest approach would be what Hull termed "a haven for the isolationists," who would advocate America's participation in Western Hemisphere affairs on condition that it did not participate in European or Asian affairs. Hull also feared that spheres of interest would lead to "closed trade areas or discriminatory systems" and thus defeat his cherished dream of a low-tariff, freely trading world.

Fourth, the sphere-of-interest solution meant the betrayal of the principles for which the Second World War was being fought—the Atlantic Charter, the Four Freedoms, the Declaration of the United Nations. Poland summed up the problem. Britain, having gone to war to defend the independence of Poland from the Germans, could not easily conclude the war by surrendering the independence of Poland to the Russians. Thus, as Hopkins told Stalin after Roosevelt's death in 1945, Poland had "become the symbol of our ability to work out problems with the Soviet Union." Nor could American liberals in general watch with equanimity while the police state spread into countries which, if they had mostly not been real democracies, had mostly not been tyrannies either. The execution in 1943 of Ehrlich and Alter, the Polish socialist trade union leaders, excited deep concern. "I have particularly in mind," Harriman cabled in 1944, "objection to the institution of secret police who may become involved in the persecution of persons of truly democratic convictions who may not be willing to conform to Soviet methods."

(Fifth), the sphere-of-influence solution would create difficult domestic problems in American politics. Roosevelt was aware of the six million or more Polish votes in the 1944 election; even more acutely, he was aware of the broader and deeper attack which would follow if, after going to war to stop the Nazi conquest of Europe, he permitted the war to end with the communist conquest of Eastern Europe. As Archibald MacLeish, then Assistant Secretary of State for Public Affairs, warned in January 1945, "The wave of disillusionment which has distressed us in the last several weeks will be increased if the impression is permitted to get abroad that potentially totalitarian provisional governments are to be set up without adequate safeguards as to the holding of free elections and the realization of the principles of the Atlantic Charter." Roosevelt believed that no administration could survive which did not try everything short of war to save Eastern Europe, and he was the supreme American politician of the century.

(Sixth), if the Russians were allowed to overrun Eastern Europe without argument, would that satisfy them? Even Kennan, in a dispatch of May 1944, admitted that the "urge" had dreadful potentialities: "If initially successful, will it know where to stop? Will it not be inexorably carried forward, by its very nature, in a struggle to reach the whole—to attain complete mastery of the shores of the Atlantic and the Pacific?" His own answer was that there were inherent limits to the Russian capacity to expand—"that Russia will not have an easy time in maintaining the power which it has seized over other people in Eastern and Central Europe unless it receives both moral and material assistance from the West." Subsequent developments have vindicated Kennan's argument. By the late forties, Jugoslavia and Albania, the two East European states farthest from the Soviet Union and the two in which communism was imposed from within rather than from without, had declared their independence of Moscow. But, given Russia's success in maintaining centralized control over the international communist movement for a quarter of a century, who in 1944 could have had much confidence in the idea of communist revolts against Moscow?

Most of those involved therefore rejected Kennan's answer and stayed with his question. If the West turned its back on Eastern Europe, the higher probability, in their view, was that the Russians would use their security zone, not just for defensive purposes, but as a springboard from which to mount an attack on Western Europe, now shattered by war, a vacuum of power awaiting its master. "If the policy is accepted that the Soviet Union has a right to penetrate her immediate neighbors for security," Harriman said in 1944, "penetration of the next immediate neighbors becomes at a certain time equally logical." If a row with Russia were inevitable, every consideration of prudence dictated that it should take place in Eastern rather than Western Europe.

Thus idealism and realism joined in opposition to the sphere-of-influence solution. The consequence was a determination to assert an American interest in the postwar destiny of all nations, including those of Eastern Europe. In the message which Roosevelt and Hopkins drafted after Hopkins had stopped Roosevelt's initial cable authorizing Churchill to speak for the United States at the Moscow meeting of October 1944, Roosevelt now said, "There is in this global war literally no question, either military or political, in which the United States is not interested." After Roosevelt's death Hopkins repeated the point to Stalin: "The cardinal basis of President Roosevelt's policy which the American people had fully supported had been the concept that the interests of the U.S. were worldwide and not confined to North and South America and the Pacific Ocean."

VI

For better or worse, this was the American position. It is now necessary to attempt the imaginative leap and consider the impact of this position on the leaders of the Soviet Union who, also for better or for worse, had reached the bitter conclusion that the survival of their country depended on their unchallenged control of the corridors through which enemies had so often invaded their homeland. They could claim to have been keeping their own side of the sphere-of-influence bargain. Of course, they were working to capture the resistance movements of Western Europe; indeed, with the appointment of Oumansky as Ambassador to Mexico they were even beginning to enlarge underground operations in the Western Hemisphere. But, from their viewpoint, if the West permitted this, the more fools they; and, if the West stopped it, it was within their right to do so. In overt political matters the Russians were scrupulously playing the game. They had watched in silence while the British shot down communists in Greece. In Jugoslavia Stalin was urging Tito (as Djilas later revealed) to keep King Peter. They had not only acknowledged Western preëminence in Italy but had recognized the Badoglio régime; the Italian Communists had even voted (against the Socialists and the Liberals) for the renewal of the Lateran Pacts.

They would not regard anti-communist action in a Western zone as a *casus belli;* and they expected reciprocal license to assert their own authority in the East. But the principle of self-determination was carrying the United States into a deeper entanglement in Eastern Europe than the Soviet Union claimed as a right (whatever it was doing underground) in the affairs of Italy, Greece or China. When the Russians now exercised in Eastern Europe the same brutal control they were prepared to have Washington exercise in the American sphere of influence, the American protests, given the paranoia produced alike by Russian history and Leninist ideology, no doubt seemed not only an act of hypocrisy but a threat to security. To the Russians, a stroll into the neighborhood easily became a plot to burn down the house: when, for example, damaged American planes made emergency landings in Poland and Hungary, Moscow took this as attempts to organize the local resistance. It is not unusual to suspect one's adversary of doing what one is already doing oneself. At the same time, the cruelty with which the Russians executed their idea of spheres of influence—in a sense, perhaps, an unwitting cruelty, since Stalin treated the East Europeans no worse than he had treated the Russians in the thirties—discouraged the West from accepting the equation (for example, Italy = Rumania) which seemed so self-evident to the Kremlin.

So Moscow very probably, and not unnaturally, perceived the emphasis on self-determination as a systematic and deliberate pressure on Russia's western frontiers. Moreover, the restoration of capitalism to countries freed at frightful cost by the Red Army no doubt struck the Russians as the betrayal of the principles for which *they* were fighting. "That they, the victors," Isaac Deutscher has suggested, "should now preserve an order from which they had experienced nothing but hostility, and could expect nothing but hostility . . . would have been the most miserable anti-climax to their great 'war of liberation.' " By 1944 Poland was the critical issue; Harriman later said that "under instructions from President Roosevelt, I talked about Poland with Stalin more frequently than any other subject." While the West saw the point of Stalin's demand for a "friendly government" in Warsaw, the American insistence on the sovereign virtues of free elections (ironically in the spirit of the 1917 Bolshevik decree of peace, which affirmed "the right" of a nation "to decide the forms of its state existence by a free vote, taken after the complete evacuation of the incorporating or, generally, of the stronger nation") created an insoluble problem in those countries, like Poland (and Rumania) where free elections would almost certainly produce anti-Soviet governments.

The Russians thus may well have estimated the Western pressures as calculated to encourage their enemies in Eastern Europe and to defeat their own minimum objective of a protective glacis. Everything still hung, however, on the course of military operations. The wartime collaboration had been created by one thing, and one thing alone: the threat of Nazi victory. So long as this threat was real, so was the collaboration. In late December 1944, von Rundstedt launched his counter-offensive in the Ardennes. A few weeks later, when Roosevelt, Churchill and Stalin gathered in the Crimea, it was in the shadow of this last considerable explosion of German power. The meeting at Yalta was still dominated by the mood of war.

Yalta remains something of an historical perplexity—less, from the perspective of 1967, because of a mythical American deference to the sphere-of-influence thesis than because of the documentable Russian deference to the universalist thesis. Why should Stalin in 1945 have accepted the Declaration on Liberated Europe and an agreement on Poland pledging that "the three governments will jointly" act to assure "free elections of governments responsive to the will of the people?" There are several probable answers: that the war was not over and the Russians still wanted the Americans to intensify their military effort in the West; that one clause in the Declaration premised action on "the opinion of the three governments" and thus implied a Soviet veto, though the Polish agreement was more definite; most of all that the universalist algebra of the Declaration was plainly in Stalin's mind to be construed in terms of the practical arithmetic of his sphere-of-influence agreement with Churchill the previous October. Stalin's assurance to Churchill at Yalta that a proposed Russian amendment to the Declaration would not apply to Greece makes it clear that Roosevelt's pieties did not, in Stalin's mind, nullify Churchill's percentages. He could well have been strengthened in this supposition by the fact that *after* Yalta, Churchill himself repeatedly reasserted the terms of the October agreement as if he regarded it, despite Yalta, as controlling.

Harriman still had the feeling before Yalta that the Kremlin had "two approaches to their postwar policies" and that Stalin himself was "of two minds." One approach emphasized the internal reconstruction and development of Russia; the other its external expansion. But in the meantime the fact which dominated all political decisions—that is, the war against Germany— was moving into its final phase. In the weeks after Yalta, the military situation changed with great rapidity. As the Nazi threat declined, so too did the need for coöperation. The Soviet Union, feeling itself menaced by the American idea of self-determination and the borderlands diplomacy to which it was leading, skeptical whether the United Nations would protect its frontiers as reliably as its own domination in Eastern Europe, began to fulfill its security requirements unilaterally.

In March Stalin expressed his evaluation of the United Nations by rejecting Roosevelt's plea that Molotov come to the San Francisco conference, if only for the opening sessions. In the next weeks the Russians emphatically and crudely worked their will in Eastern Europe, above all in the test country of Poland. They were ignoring the Declaration on Liberated Europe, ignoring the Atlantic Charter, self-determination, human freedom and everything else the Americans considered essential for a stable peace. "We must clearly recognize," Harriman wired Washington a few days before Roosevelt's death, "that the Soviet program is the establishment of totalitarianism, ending personal liberty and democracy as we know and respect it."

At the same time, the Russians also began to mobilize communist resources in the United States itself to block American universalism. In April 1945 Jacques Duclos, who had been the Comintern official responsible for the Western communist parties, launched in *Cahiers du Communisme* an uncompromising attack on the policy of the American Communist Party. Duclos sharply condemned the revisionism of Earl Browder, the American Communist leader, as "expressed in the concept of a long-term class peace in the United States, of the possibility of the suppression of the class struggle in the postwar period and of establishment of harmony between labor and capital." Browder was specifically rebuked for favoring the "self-determination" of Europe "west of the Soviet Union" on a bourgeois-democratic basis. The excommunication of Browderism was plainly the Politburo's considered reaction to the impending defeat of Germany; it was a signal to the communist parties of the West that they should recover their identity; it was Moscow's alert to communists everywhere that they should prepare for new policies in the postwar world.

The Duclos piece obviously could not have been planned and written much later than the Yalta conference—that is, well before a number of events which revisionists now cite in order to demonstrate American responsibility for the Cold War: before Allen Dulles, for example, began to negotiate the surrender of the German armies in Italy (the episode which provoked Stalin to charge Roosevelt with seeking a separate peace and provoked Roosevelt to denounce the "vile misrepresentations" of Stalin's informants); well before Roosevelt died; many months before the testing of the atomic bomb; even more months before Truman ordered that the bomb be dropped on Japan. William Z. Foster, who soon replaced Browder as the leader of the American Communist Party and embodied the new Moscow line, later boasted of having said in January 1944, "A post-war Roosevelt administration would continue to be, as it is now, an imperialist government." With ancient suspicions revived by the American insistence on universalism, this was no doubt the conclusion which the Russians were reaching at the same time. The Soviet canonization of Roosevelt (like their present-day canonization of Kennedy) took place after the American President's death.

The atmosphere of mutual suspicion was beginning to rise. In January 1945 Molotov formally proposed that the United States grant Russia a $6 billion credit for postwar reconstruction. With characteristic tact he explained that he was doing this as a favor to save America from a postwar depression. The proposal seems to have been diffidently made and diffidently received. Roosevelt requested that the matter "not be pressed further" on the American side until he had a chance to talk with Stalin; but the Russians did not follow it up either at Yalta in February (save for a single glancing reference) or during the Stalin-Hopkins talks in May or at Potsdam. Finally the proposal was renewed in the very different political atmosphere of August. This time Washington inexplicably mislaid the request during the transfer of the records of the Foreign Economic Administration to the State Department. It did not turn up again until March 1946. Of course this was impossible for the Russians to believe; it is hard enough even for those acquanited with the capacity of the American government for incompetence to believe; and it only strengthened Soviet suspicions of American purposes.

The American credit was one conceivable form of Western contribution to Russian reconstruction. Another was lend-lease, and the possibility of reconstruction aid under the lend-lease protocol had already been discussed in 1944. But in May 1945 Russia, like Britain, suffered from Truman's abrupt termination of lend-lease shipments—"unfortunate and even brutal," Stalin told Hopkins, adding that, if it was "designed as pressure on the Russians in order to soften them up, then it was a fundamental mistake." A third form was German reparations. Here Stalin in demanding $10 billion in reparations for the Soviet Union made his strongest fight at Yalta. Roosevelt, while agreeing essentially with Churchill's opposition, tried to postpone the matter by accepting the Soviet figure as a "basis for discussion"—a formula which led to future misunderstanding. In short, the Russian hope for major Western assistance in postwar reconstruction foundered on three events which the Kremlin could well have interpreted respectively as deliberate sabotage (the loan request), blackmail (lend-lease cancellation) and pro-Germanism (reparations).

Actually the American attempt to settle the fourth lend-lease protocol was generous and the Russians for their own reasons declined to come to an agreement. It is not clear, though, that satisfying Moscow on any of these financial scores would have made much essential difference. It might have persuaded some doves in the Kremlin that the U.S. government was genuinely friendly; it might have persuaded some hawks that the American anxiety for Soviet friendship was such that Moscow could do as it wished without inviting challenge from the United States. It would, in short, merely have reinforced both sides of the Kremlin debate; it would hardly have reversed deeper tendencies toward the deterioration of political relationships. Economic deals were surely subordinate to the quality of mutual political confidence; and here, in the months after Yalta, the decay was steady.

The Cold War had now begun. It was the product not of a decision but of a dilemma. Each side felt compelled to adopt policies which the other could not but regard as a threat to the principles of the peace. Each then felt compelled to undertake defensive measures. Thus the Russians saw no choice but to consolidate their security in Eastern Europe. The Americans, regarding Eastern Europe as the first step toward Western Europe, responded by asserting their interest in the zone the Russians deemed vital to their security. The Russians concluded that the West was resuming its old course of capitalist encirclement; that it was purposefully laying the foundation for anti-Soviet régimes in the area defined by the blood of centuries as crucial to Russian survival. Each side believed with passion that future international stability depended on the success of its own conception of world order. Each side, in pursuing its own clearly indicated and deeply cherished principles, was only confirming the fear of the other that it was bent on aggression.

Very soon the process began to acquire a cumulative momentum. The impending collapse of Germany thus provoked new troubles: the Russians, for example, sincerely feared that the West was planning a separate surrender of the German armies in Italy in a way which would release troops for Hilter's eastern front, as they subsequently feared that the Nazis might succeed in surrendering Berlin to the West. This was the context in which the atomic bomb now appeared. Though the revisionist argument that Truman dropped the bomb less to defeat Japan than to intimidate Russia is not convincing, this thought unquestionably appealed to some in Washington as at least an advantageous side-effect of Hiroshima.

So the machinery of suspicion and counter-suspicion, action and counter-action, was set in motion. But, given relations among traditional national states, there was still no reason, even with all the postwar jostling, why this should not have remained a manageable situation. What made it unmanageable, what caused the rapid escalation of the Cold War and in another two years completed the division of Europe, was a set of considerations which this account has thus far excluded.

VII

Up to this point, the discussion has considered the schism within the wartime coalition as if it were entirely the result of disagreements among national states. Assuming this framework, there was unquestionably a failure of communication between America and Russia, a misperception of signals and, as time went on, a mounting tendency to ascribe ominous motives to the other side. It seems hard, for example, to deny that American postwar policy created genuine difficulties for the Russians and even assumed a threatening aspect for them. All this the revisionists have rightly and usefully emphasized.

But the great omission of the revisionists—and also the fundamental explanation of the speed with which the Cold War escalated—lies precisely in the fact that the Soviet Union was *not* a traditional national state.[1] This is where the "mirror image," invoked by some psychologists, falls down. For the Soviet Union was a phenomenon very different from America or Britain: it was a totalitarian state, endowed with an all-explanatory, all-consuming

[1] This is the classical revisionist fallacy—the assumption of the rationality, or at least of the traditionalism, of states where ideology and social organization have created a different range of motives. So the Second World War revisionists omit the totalitarian dynamism of Nazism and the fanaticism of Hitler, as the Civil War revisionists omit the fact that the slavery system was producing a doctrinaire closed society in the American South. For a consideration of some of these issues, see "The Causes of the Civil War: A Note on Historical Sentimentalism" in my "The Politics of Hope" (Boston, 1963).

ideology, committed to the infallibility of government and party, still in a somewhat messianic mood, equating dissent with treason, and ruled by a dictator who, for all his quite extraordinary abilities, had his paranoid moments.

Marxism-Leninism gave the Russian leaders a view of the world according to which all societies were inexorably destined to proceed along appointed roads by appointed stages until they achieved the classless nirvana. Moreover, given the resistance of the capitalists to this development, the existence of any noncommunist state was *by definition* a threat to the Soviet Union. "As long as capitalism and socialism exist," Lenin wrote, "we cannot live in peace: in the end, one or the other will triumph—a funeral dirge will be sung either over the Soviet Republic or over world capitalism."

V./MP.

Stalin and his associates, whatever Roosevelt or Truman did or failed to do, were bound to regard the United States as the enemy, not because of this deed or that, but because of the primordial fact that America was the leading capitalist power and thus, by Leninist syllogism, unappeasably hostile, driven by the logic of its system to oppose, encircle and destroy Soviet Russia. Nothing the United States could have done in 1944–45 would have abolished this mistrust, required and sanctified as it was by Marxist gospel—nothing short of the conversion of the United States into a Stalinist despotism; and even this would not have sufficed, as the experience of Jugoslavia and China soon showed, unless it were accompanied by total subservience to Moscow. So long as the United States remained a capitalist democracy, no American policy, given Moscow's theology, could hope to win basic Soviet confidence, and every American action was poisoned from the source. So long as the Soviet Union remained a messianic state, ideology compelled a steady expansion of communist power.

It is easy, of course, to exaggerate the capacity of ideology to control events. The tension of acting according to revolutionary abstractions is too much for most nations to sustain over a long period: that is why Mao Tse-tung has launched his Cultural Revolution, hoping thereby to create a permanent revolutionary mood and save Chinese communism from the degeneration which, in his view, has overtaken Russian communism. Still, as any revolution grows older, normal human and social motives will increasingly reassert themselves. In due course, we can be sure, Leninism will be about as effective in governing the daily lives of Russians as Christianity is in governing the daily lives of Americans. Like the Ten Commandments and the Sermon on the Mount, the Leninist verities will increasingly become platitudes for ritual observance, not guides to secular decision. There can be no worse fallacy (even if respectable people practiced it diligently for a season in the United States) than that of drawing from a nation's ideology permanent conclusions about its behavior.

[A temporary recession of ideology was already taking place during the Second World War when Stalin, to rally his people against the invader, had to replace the appeal of Marxism by that of nationalism.] ("We are under no illusions that they are fighting for us," Stalin once said to Harriman. "They are fighting for Mother Russia.") But this was still taking place within the strictest limitations. The Soviet Union remained as much a police state as ever; the régime was as infallible as ever; foreigners and their ideas were as suspect as ever. "Never, except possibly during my later experience as ambassador in Moscow," Kennan has written, "did the insistence of the Soviet authorities on isolation of the diplomatic corps weigh more heavily on me . . . than in these first weeks following my return to Russia in the final months of the war. . . . [We were] treated as though we were the bearers of some species of the plague"—which, of course, from the Soviet viewpoint, they were: the plague of skepticism.

[Paradoxically, of the forces capable of bringing about a modification of ideology, the most practical and effective was the Soviet dictatorship itself.] If Stalin was an ideologist, he was also a pragmatist. If he saw everything through the lenses of Marxism-Leninism, he also, as the infallible expositor of the faith, could reinterpret Marxism-Leninism to justify anything he wanted to do at any given moment. No doubt Roosevelt's ignorance of Marxism-Leninism was inexcusable and led to grievous miscalculations. But Roosevelt's efforts to work on and through Stalin were not so hopelessly naïve as it used to be fashionable to think. [With the extraordinary instinct of a great political leader, Roosevelt intuitively understood that Stalin was the *only* lever available to the West against the Leninist ideology and the Soviet system. If Stalin could be reached, then alone was there a chance of getting the Russians to act contrary to the prescriptions of their faith.] The best evidence is that Roosevelt retained a certain capacity to influence Stalin to the end; the nominal Soviet acquiescence in American universalism as late as Yalta was perhaps an indication of that. [It is in this way that the death of Roosevelt was crucial—not in the vulgar sense that his policy was then reversed by his successor, which did not happen, but in the sense that no other American could hope to have the restraining impact on Stalin which Roosevelt might for a while have had.]

Stalin alone could have made any difference. Yet Stalin, in spite of the impression of sobriety and realism he made on Westerners who saw him during the Second World War, was plainly a man of deep and morbid obsessions and compulsions. When he was still a young man, Lenin had criticized his rude and arbitrary ways. A reasonably authoritative observer (N. S. Khrushchev) later commented, "These negative characteristics of his developed steadily and during the last years acquired an absolutely insufferable character." His paranoia, probably set off by the suicide of his wife in 1932, led to the terrible purges of the mid-thirties and the wanton murder of thousands of his Bolshevik comrades. "Everywhere and in everything," Khrushchev says of this period, "he saw 'enemies,' 'double-dealers' and 'spies.' " The crisis of war evidently steadied him in some way, though Khrushchev speaks of his "nervousness and hysteria . . . even after the war began." The madness, so rigidly controlled for a time, burst out with new and shocking intensity in the postwar years. "After the war," Khrushchev testifies,

the situation became even more complicated. Stalin became even more capricious, irritable and brutal; in particular, his suspicion grew. His persecution mania reached unbelievable dimensions. . . . He decided everything, without any consideration for anyone or anything.

Stalin's wilfulness showed itself . . . also in the international relations of the Soviet Union. . . . He had completely lost a sense of reality; he demonstrated his suspicion and haughtiness not only in relation to individuals in the USSR, but in relation to whole parties and nations.

A revisionist fallacy has been to treat Stalin as just another Realpolitik statesman, as Second World War revisionists see Hitler as just another Stresemann or Bismarck. But the record makes it clear that in the end nothing could satisfy Stalin's paranoia. His own associates failed. Why does anyone suppose that any conceivable American policy would have succeeded?

An analysis of the origins of the Cold War which leaves out these factors— the intransigence of Leninist ideology, the sinister dynamics of a totalitarian society and the madness of Stalin—is obviously incomplete. It was these factors which made it hard for the West to accept the thesis that Russia was moved only by a desire to protect its security and would be satisfied by the control of Eastern Europe; it was these factors which charged the debate between universalism and spheres of influence with apocalyptic potentiality.

Leninism and totalitarianism created a structure of thought and behavior which made postwar collaboration between Russia and America—in any normal sense of civilized intercourse between national states—inherently impossible. The Soviet dictatorship of 1945 simply could not have survived such a collaboration. Indeed, nearly a quarter-century later, the Soviet régime, though it has meanwhile moved a good distance, could still hardly survive it without risking the release inside Russia of energies profoundly opposed to communist depotism. As for Stalin, he may have represented the only force in 1945 capable of overcoming Stalinism, but the very traits which enabled him to win absolute power expressed terrifying instabilities of mind and temperament and hardly offered a solid foundation for a peaceful world.

VIII

The difference between America and Russia in 1945 was that some Americans fundamentally believed that, over a long run, a modus vivendi with Russia was possible; while the Russians, so far as one can tell, believed in no more than a short-run modus vivendi with the United States.]

Harriman and Kennan, this narrative has made clear, took the lead in warning Washington about the difficulties of short-run dealings with the Soviet Union. But both argued that, if the United States developed a rational policy and stuck to it, there would be, after long and rough passages, the prospect of eventual clearing. "I am, as you know," Harriman cabled Washington in early April, "a most earnest advocate of the closest possible understanding with the Soviet Union so that what I am saying relates only to how best to attain such understanding." Kennan has similarly made it clear that the function of his containment policy was "to tide us over a difficult time and bring us to the point where we could discuss effectively with the Russians the dangers and drawbacks this status quo involved, and to arrange with them for its peaceful replacement by a better and sounder one." The subsequent careers of both men attest to the honesty of these statements.

There is [no corresponding evidence on the Russian side that anyone seriously sought a modus vivendi in these terms.]Stalin's choice was whether his long-term ideological and national interests would be better served by a short-run truce with the West or by an immediate resumption of pressure. In October 1945 Stalin indicated to Harriman at Sochi that he planned to adopt the second course—that the Soviet Union was going isolationist. No doubt the succession of problems with the United States contributed to this decision, but the basic causes most probably lay elsewhere: in the developing situations in Eastern Europe, in Western Europe and in the United States.

In Eastern Europe, Stalin was still for a moment experimenting with techniques of control. But he must by now have begun to conclude that he had underestimated the hostility of the people to Russian dominion. The Hungarian elections in November would finally convince him that the Yalta formula was a road to anti-Soviet governments. At the same time, he was feeling more strongly than ever a sense of his opportunities in Western Europe. The other half of the Continent lay unexpectedly before him, politically demoralized, economically prostrate, militarily defenseless. The hunting would be better and safer than he had anticipated. As for the United States, the alacrity of postwar demobilization must have recalled Roosevelt's offhand remark at Yalta that "two years would be the limit" for keeping American troops in Europe. And, despite Dr. Eugene Varga's doubts about the imminence of American economic breakdown, Marxist theology assured Stalin that the United States was heading into a bitter postwar depression and would be consumed with its own problems. If the condition of Eastern Europe made unilateral action seem essential in the interests of Russian security, the condition of Western Europe and the United States offered new temptations for communist expansion. The Cold War was now in full swing.

It still had its year of modulations and accommodations. Secretary Byrnes conducted his long and fruitless campaign to persuade the Russians that America only sought governments in Eastern Europe "both friendly to the Soviet Union and representative of all the democratic elements of the country." Crises were surmounted in Trieste and Iran. Secretary Marshall evidently did not give up hope of a modus vivendi until the Moscow conference of foreign secretaries of March 1947. Even then, the Soviet Union was invited to participate in the Marshall Plan.

The point of no return came on July 2, 1947, when Molotov, after bringing 89 technical specialists with him to Paris and evincing initial interest in the project for European reconstruction, received the hot flash from the Kremlin, denounced the whole idea and walked out of the conference. For the next fifteen years the Cold War raged unabated, passing out of historical ambiguity into the realm of good versus evil and breeding on both sides simplifications, stereotypes and self-serving absolutes, often couched in interchangeable phrases. Under the pressure even America, for a deplorable decade, forsook its pragmatic and pluralist traditions, posed as God's appointed messenger to ignorant and sinful man and followed the Soviet example in looking to a world remade in its own image.

In retrospect, if it is impossible to see the Cold War as a case of American aggression and Russian response, it is also hard to see it as a pure case of Russian aggression and American response. "In what is truly tragic," wrote Hegel, "there must be valid moral powers on both the sides which come into collision. . . . Both suffer loss and yet both are mutually justified." In this sense, the Cold War had its tragic elements. The question remains whether it was an instance of Greek tragedy—as Auden has called it, "the tragedy of necessity," where the feeling aroused in the spectator is "What a pity it had to be this way"—or of Christian tragedy, "the tragedy of possibility," where the feeling aroused is "What a pity it was this way when it might have been otherwise."

Once something has happened, the historian is tempted to assume that it had to happen; but this may often be a highly unphilosophical assumption. The Cold War could have been avoided only if the Soviet Union had not been possessed by convictions both of the infallibility of the communist word and of the inevitability of a communist world. These convictions transformed an impasse between national states into a religious war, a tragedy of possibility into one of necessity. One might wish that America had preserved the poise and proportion of the first years of the Cold War and had not in time succumbed to its own forms of self-righteousness. But the most rational of American policies could hardly have averted the Cold War. Only today, as Russia begins to recede from its messianic mission and to accept, in practice if not yet in principle, the permanence of the world of diversity, only now can the hope flicker that this long, dreary, costly contest may at last be taking on forms less dramatic, less obsessive and less dangerous to the future of mankind.

\3

2. RICHARD NEUSTADT, "KENNEDY IN THE PRESIDENCY: A PREMATURE APPRAISAL"

JOHN F. KENNEDY brought much to the Presidency that was new and refreshing. Following an era of national inertia characterized by the self-congratulatory attitude of the Eisenhower Administration, Kenndey sought to "get America moving again" to meet "the challenges of the Sixties." The thirty-fifth President was made of the stuff from which myths grow. Not only was he the first Roman Catholic Chief Executive, but he was at age forty-three the youngest man elected to the office. A member of a notable Boston family, a genuine war hero, and the recipient of a Pulitzer Prize in History for his Profiles in Courage, *Kennedy capped a mercurial political career by his razor-thin victory over Richard M. Nixon in the presidential election of 1960.*

Kennedy sought to use the powers of the Presidency to attack what he called the "common enemies of mankind: tyranny, poverty, disease and war itself." In domestic policy he attempted to extend and modernize the New Deal-Fair Deal legacy of his party. In foreign policy he hoped to move beyond the inflexibility and moralism that had characterized much of the diplomacy of the Eisenhower Administration in order to wage a "strategy of peace." To what extent he succeeded in his goals is an open question, and it is compounded by the tragedy of his assassination exactly thirty-four months after taking office. History has tended to deal harshly with short-term Presidents and, to be certain, Kennedy left much unfinished.

He proceeded toward the New Frontier with considerable caution. Elected by the narrowest of margins and confronted by a strongly entrenched conservative coalition in Congress, he was unable to secure the enactment of several major New Frontier programs. By mid-1963, disappointed liberals pointed to defeats on agricultural policy, medicare under Social Security, and the creation of a cabinet level position for urban affairs.

Especially irritating to liberals was his reluctance to embrace fully the growing civil rights movement. His deference to powerful southern Democrats in the Congress and his

SOURCE. Richard Neustadt, "Kennedy in the Presidency: A Premature Appraisal," from Aida Di Pace Donald, ed., *John F. Kennedy and the New Frontier*, New York: Hill and Wang, 1966, pp. 232–246. Copyright, The Academy of Political Science, 1964. Reprinted by permission from the *Political Science Quarterly*, Vol. LXXIX, September 1964 and the author.

unwillingness to champion far-reaching civil rights legislation rankled liberals. As one of his biographers points out, however, Kennedy was a strong believer in the theory that politics is the art of the possible. As such, he looked forward to 1965 as the time to achieve a major breakthrough in social reform. Then he hoped to have the advantages of a strong mandate from the people and a more reform-minded Congress. It would be another Democratic President, however, who would win that landslide victory and enjoy the luxury of such a Congress.

Kennedy's defenders, however, have argued that his domestic record was far from dismal. It was the Kennedy Administration that secured the enactment of the important Trade Expansion Act of 1962 in an effort to update American trade policies in response to the growing strength of the European Common Market. In addition, his Administration launched the ambitious Alliance for Progress for Latin America, created the Peace Corps, committed the United States to a major effort in space exploration, and negotiated and guided to ratification the nuclear Test Ban Treaty. His legislative record also shows enactment of substantial programs for housing, water pollution control, manpower development and public works, as well as a constitutional amendment abolishing the poll tax and a hefty increase in the minimum wage.

accomp. 2

The Kennedy record in foreign policy also included successes and failures. His position as a world leader was badly shaken within a few months after his inauguration by the debacle of the Bay of Pigs. This poorly conceived and even more poorly executed effort to overthrow Fidel Castro failed miserably and only served to cement further his power in Cuba. In seeking to reduce tensions between East and West, Kennedy encountered continued frustrations. At Vienna in the spring of 1961, Premier Khrushchev was unbending and a few months later sought to test the young President by placing new pressures on West Berlin. In August the Berlin Wall was constructed and that autumn the Soviet Union openly defied Kennedy's efforts to halt nuclear testing by exploding a weapon 300 times the magnitude of the bomb dropped on Hiroshima. The following autumn came the Cuban missile crisis, and for a few days the world lurched perilously close to nuclear war. The ratification of the Test Ban Treaty the following summer raised hopes of a possible thaw in the Cold War, but at best it was only a limited step forward.

By late 1963, President Kennedy had begun to plan for the 1964 presidential election. Already the political indicators pointed toward the nomination by the Republicans of the outspoken Arizona conservative, Senator Barry M. Goldwater. An assassin's bullet, however, altered the course of history. The New Frontier died on a Dallas street.

It will be many years before scholars can hope to study the Kennedy Administration with some degree of detachment, but already the outpouring of books and articles is overwhelming. One of the most useful essays has been written by Professor Richard Neustadt of Harvard University, who served as a White House assistant to President Truman and who is an acknowledged authority on the Presidency.

There are many ways to look at the performance of a President of the United States. One way—not the only one—is to assess his operational effectiveness as man in office, a single individual amidst a vast machine. This has been my own approach in previous writings on past Presidents. Regarding our most recent President, John F. Kennedy, it is foolhardy to attempt appraisal in these terms. He died too soon and it is too soon after his death. Still, the *Political Science Quarterly* has asked me to attempt it. And assuming that my readers will indulge the folly, I shall try.

I

In appraising the personal performance of a President it is useful to ask four questions. First, what were his purposes and did these run with or against the grain of history; how relevant were they to what would happen in his time? Second, what was his "feel," his human understanding, for the nature of his power in the circumstances of his time, and how close did he come in this respect to the realities around him (a matter again of relevance)? Third, what was his stance under pressure in office, what sustained him as a person against the frustrations native to the place, and how did his peace-making with himself affect the style and content of his own decision-making? This becomes especially important now that nuclear technology has equipped both Americans and Russians with an intercontinental capability; stresses on the Presidency grow apace. Fourth, what was his legacy? What imprint did he leave upon the office, its character and public standing; where did he leave his party and the other party nationally; what remained by way of public policies adopted or in controversy; what remained as issues in American society, insofar as his own stance may have affected them; and what was the American position in the world insofar as his diplomacy may have affected it?

With respect to each of these four questions, the outside observer looks for certain clues in seeking answers.

First, regarding purpose, clues are found in irreversible commitments to defined courses of action. By "purpose" I mean nothing so particular as an endorsement for, say, "Medicare," or anything so general as a pledge to "peace." (All Presidents desire peace.) By "course of action" I mean something broader than the one but more definable than the other: Harry S. Truman's commitment to "containment," so called, or Dwight D. Eisenhower's to what he called "fiscal responsibility." By "commitment" I mean personal involvement, in terms of what the man himself is seen to say and do, so plain and so direct that politics—and history—will not let him turn back: Truman on civil rights, or Eisenhower on the Army budget.

Second, regarding feel for office, sensitivity to power, clues are drawn from signs of pattern in the man's own operating style as he encounters concrete cases, cases of decision and of follow-through in every sphere of action, legislative and executive, public and partisan, foreign and domestic—

Truman seeking above all to be decisive: Eisenhower reaching for a place above the struggle.

Third, regarding pressure and its consequences, clues are to be drawn again from cases; here one examines crisis situations, seeking signs of pattern in the man's response—Truman at the time of the Korean outbreak, or of Chinese intervention; Eisenhower at the time of Hungary and Suez, or of Little Rock—times like these compared with others just as tough in terms of stress.

And fourth, regarding the man's legacy, one seeks clues in the conduct of the *next* administration. Roosevelt's first New Deal in 1933 tells us a lot about the Hoover Presidency. Truman's troubled turnabout in postwar foreign policy casts shadows on the later Roosevelt Presidency. And Kennedy's complaint at Yale two years ago about the "myths" retarding economic management is testimony to one part of Eisenhower's legacy, that part identified with the redoubtable George Humphrey.

To list these sources of the wherewithal for answers is to indicate the folly of pursuing my four questions when the object of the exercise is Kennedy-in-office. He was President for two years and ten months. Were one to assess Franklin Roosevelt on the basis of performance before January 1936, or Harry Truman on his accomplishments before enactment of the Marshall Plan, or Eisenhower had he not survived his heart attack—or Lincoln, for that matter, had he been assassinated six months after Gettysburg—one would be most unlikely to reach judgments about any of these men resembling current judgments drawn from the full record of their terms. We cannot know what Kennedy's full record would have been had he escaped assassination. Still more important, we can never know precisely how to weigh events in his truncated term.

Truman's seven years and Eisenhower's eight suggest a certain rhythm in the modern Presidency. The first twelve to eighteen months become a learning time for the new President who has to learn—or unlearn—many things about his job. No matter what his prior training, nothing he has done will have prepared him for all facets of that job. Some aspects of the learning process will persist beyond the first year-and-a-half. Most Presidents will go on making new discoveries as long as they hold office (until at last they learn the bitterness of leaving office). But the intensive learning time comes at the start and dominates the first two years. A President's behavior in those years is an uncertain source of clues to what will follow after, unreliable in indicating what will be the patterns of performance "on the job" once learning has been done. Yet the fourth year is also unreliable; traditionally it brings a period of pause, dominated by a special test requiring special effort—the test of reelection. The way that test is taken tells us much about a President, but less about his conduct on the job in other years The seventh year is the beginning of the end—now guaranteed by constitutional amendment—as all eyes turn toward the coming nominations and the *next* administration.

So in the search for signs of pattern, clues to conduct, the key years are the third, the fifth, the sixth. Kennedy had only one of these.

Moreover, in this Presidential cycle, retrospect is an essential aid for sorting evidence. What a man does in his later years sheds light on the significance of what he did in early years, distinguishing the actions which conform to lasting patterns from the aspects of behavior which were transient. The man's early performance will include a host of clues to what is typical throughout his term of office. But it also will include assorted actions which turn out to be unrepresentative. Looking back from later years these become easy to distinguish. But in the second or the third year it is hard indeed to say, "This action, this behavior will be dominant throughout." That is the sort of statement best reserved for retrospect. Kennedy's case leaves no room for retrospect; he was cut off too early in the cycle. (And when it comes to sorting out the legacy he left, Lyndon Johnson has not yet been long enough in office.)

No scholar, therefore, should have the temerity to undertake what follows.

II

Turning to appraise this President in office, I come to my first question, the question of purpose. This is not a matter of initial "ideology," fixed intent; far from it. Franklin Roosevelt did not enter office bent upon becoming "traitor to his class." Truman did not swear the oath with any notion that he was to take this country into the cold war. Lincoln certainly did not assume the Presidency to gain the title of "Great Emancipator." The purposes of Presidents are not to be confused with their intentions at the start; they are a matter, rather, of responses to events. Nor should they be confused with signs of temperament, with "passion." Whether Kennedy was "passionate" or not is scarcely relevant. Truman certainly deserves to have the cause of civil rights cited among his purposes, but were he to be judged in temperamental terms according to the standards of, say, Eastern liberals, he scarcely could be called a man of passion on the point. And F.D.R. goes down historically as "Labor's friend," although his coolness toward the greatest show of that friendship in his time, the Wagner Act, remained until he sensed that it was sure to be enacted. What counts here is not "passion," but the words and acts that lead to irreversible *commitment*.

In his three years of office, what were Kennedy's commitments? Never mind his private thoughts at twenty, or at forty; never mind his preferences for one thing or another; never mind his distaste for a passionate display—taking the real world as he found it, what attracted his commitment in the sense that he identified himself beyond recall?

The record will, I think, disclose at least three purposes so understood: First, above all others, most compelling, most intense, was a commitment to reduce the risk of holocaust by *mutual* miscalculation, to "get the nuclear genie back in the bottle," to render statecraft manageable by statesmen, tolerable for the rest of us. He did not aim at anything so trite (or unachievable) as "victory" in the cold war. His aim, apparently, was to outlast it with American society intact and nuclear risks in check. Nothing, I think, mattered more to Kennedy than bottling that genie. This, I know, was deeply in his mind. It also was made manifest in words, among them his address at American University on June 10, 1963. That speech is seal and symbol of this purpose. But other signs are found in acts, as well, and in more private words accompanying action: from his Vienna interview with Khrushchev, through the Berlin crisis during 1961, to the Cuban missile crisis and thereafter—this commitment evidently deepened with experience as Kennedy responded to events.

Another speech in June of 1963 stands for a second purpose: the speech on civil rights, June 11, and the message to Congress eight days later launched Kennedy's campaign for what became the Civil Rights Act of 1964. Thereby he undertook an irreversible commitment to Negro integration in American society, aiming once again to get us through the effort with society intact. He evidently came to see the risks of social alienation as plainly as he saw the risks of nuclear escalation, and he sought to steer a course toward integration which could hold inside our social order both impatient Negroes and reactive whites—as tough a task of politics as any we have known, and one he faced no sooner than he had to. But he faced it. What Vienna, Berlin, Cuba were to his first purpose, Oxford and then Birmingham were to this second purpose: events which shaped his personal commitment.

A third speech is indicative of still another purpose, a speech less known and a commitment less apparent, though as definite, I think, as both of the others: Kennedy's commencement speech at Yale on June 11, 1962, soon after his short war with Roger Blough. He spoke of making our complex economy, our somewhat *sui generis* economy, function effectively for meaningful growth, and as the means he urged an end-of-ideology in problem-solving. His speech affirmed the notion that the key problems of economic growth are technical, not ideological, to be met not by passion but by intellect, and that the greatest barriers to growth are the ideas in people's heads—"myths" as he called them—standing in the way of reasoned diagnosis and response. Kennedy, I think, was well aware (indeed he was made painfully aware) that only on our one-time Left is ideology defunct. Elsewhere it flourishes, clamping a lid upon applied intelligence, withholding brainpower from rational engagement in the novel problems of our economic management. He evidently wanted most of all to lift that lid.

Failing a response to his Yale lecture, Kennedy retreated to the easier task of teaching one simple economic lesson, the lesson of the recent tax reduction:

well-timed budget deficits can lead to balanced budgets. This, evidently, was the most that he thought he could manage in contesting "myths," at least before election. But his ambition, I believe, was to assault a lot more myths than this, when and as he could. That ambition measures his commitment to effective growth in the economy.

Stemming from this third commitment (and the second) one discerns a corollary which perhaps would have become a fourth: what Kennedy's successor now has named "the war against poverty." During the course of 1963, Kennedy became active in promoting plans for an attack on chronic poverty. His prospective timing no doubt had political utility, but it also had social utility which evidently mattered quite as much. Historically, the "war" is Lyndon Johnson's. All we know of Kennedy is that he meant to make one. Still, for either of these men the effort, if sustained, would lead to irreversible commitment.

Each purpose I have outlined meant commitment to a course of action which engaged the man—his reputation, *amour propre*, and sense of self in history—beyond recall. The question then becomes: how relevant were these, historically? How relevant to Kennedy's own years of actual (and of prospective) office? Here I can only make a judgment, tentative of course, devoid of long perspective. These purposes seem to me entirely relevant. In short perspective, they seem precisely right as the pre-eminent concerns for the first half of this decade.

III

So much for Kennedy as man-of-purpose. What about the man-of-power?

He strikes me as a senator who learned very fast from his confrontation with the executive establishment, particularly after the abortive Cuban invasion which taught him a great deal. On action-issues of particular concern to him he rapidly evolved an operating style which he maintained consistently (and sharpened at the edges) through his years of office. If one looks at Berlin, or Oxford, Mississippi, or the Cuban missile crisis, or at half a dozen other issues of the sort, one finds a pattern: the personal command post, deliberate reaching down for the details, hard questioning of the alternatives, a drive to protect options from foreclosure by sheer urgency or by *ex parte* advocacy, finally a close watch on follow-through. Even on the issues which were secondary to the President and left, perforce, primarily to others, Kennedy was constantly in search of means and men to duplicate at one remove this personalized pattern with its stress on open options and on close control. Numbers of outsiders—Hans Morgenthau and Joseph Alsop for two—sometimes viewed the pattern with alarm and saw this man as "indecisive." But that was to consult *their* preferences, not his performance. Kennedy seemed always keen to single out the necessary from the merely possible. He then decided with alacrity.

Not everything was always done effectively, of course, and even the successes produced side effects of bureaucratic bafflement, frustration, irritation which were not without their costs. Even so, the pattern testifies to an extraordinary feel for the distinction between President and Presidency, an extraordinary urge to master the machine. This took him quite a way toward mastery in two years and ten months. We shall not know how far he might have got.

Kennedy's feel for his own executive position carried over into that of fellow rulers everywhere. He evidently had great curiosity and real concern about the politics of rulership wherever he encountered it. His feel for fine distinctions among fellow "kings" was rare, comparable to the feel of Senate Leader Johnson for the fine distinctions among fellow senators. And with this Kennedy apparently absorbed in his short time a lesson Franklin Roosevelt never learned about the Russians (or de Gaulle): that in another country an *effective* politician can have motives very *different* from his own. What an advantageous lesson to have learned in two years' time! It would have served him well. Indeed, while he still lived I think it did.

The cardinal test of Kennedy as an executive in his own right and also as a student of executives abroad was certainly the confrontation of October 1962, the Cuban missile crisis with Khrushchev. For almost the first time in our foreign relations, the President displayed on that occasion both concern for the psychology of his opponent and insistence on a limited objective. Contrast the Korean War, where we positively courted Chinese intervention by relying on Douglas MacArthur as psychologist and by enlarging our objective after each success. "There is no substitute for victory," MacArthur wrote, but at that time we virtually had a nuclear monopoly and even then our government hastened to find a substitute. Now, with mutual capability, the whole traditional meaning has been taken out of "victory." In nuclear confrontations there is room for no such thing. Kennedy quite evidently knew it. He also knew, as his performance demonstrates, that risks of escalation lurk in high-level misjudgments *and* in low-level momentum. Washington assuredly was capable of both; so, probably, was Moscow. Accordingly, the President outstripped all previous efforts to guard options and assure control. His operating style was tested then as not before or after. It got him what he wanted.

In confrontations with Congress, quite another world than the executive, the key to Kennedy's congressional relations lay outside his feel for power, beyond reach of technique; he won the Presidency by a hair, while in the House of Representatives his party lost some twenty of the seats gained two years earlier. The Democrats *retained* a sizeable majority as they had done in earlier years, no thanks to him. With this beginning, Kennedy's own record of accomplishment in Congress looks enormous, indeterminate, or small, depending on one's willingness to give him credit for enactment of the most divisive, innovative bills he espoused: the tax and civil rights bills passed in Johnson's Presidency. Certainly it can be said that Kennedy prepared the way, negotiating a bipartisan approach, and also that he took the heat, stalling his whole program in the process. Equally, it can be said that with his death—or by it—the White House gained advantages which he could not have mustered. Johnson made the most of these. How well would Kennedy have done without them? My own guess is that in the end, with rancor and delay, both bills would have been passed. But it is a moot point. Accordingly, so is the Kennedy record.

Whatever his accomplishment, does it appear the most he could have managed in his years? Granting the limits set by his election, granting the divisiveness injected after Birmingham with his decisive move on civil rights, did he use to the fullest his advantages of office? The answer may well be "not quite." Perhaps a better answer is, "This man could do no more." For Kennedy, it seems, was not a man enamored of the legislative way of life and legislators knew it. He was wry about it. He had spent fourteen years in Congress and he understood its business, but he never was a "member of the family" on the Hill. "Downtown" had always seemed his native habitat; he was a natural executive. They knew that, too. Besides, he was a young man, very young by Senate standards, and his presence in the White House with still younger men around him was a constant irritant to seniors. Moreover, he was not a "mixer" socially, not, anyway, with most members of Congress and their wives. His manners were impeccable, his charm impelling, but he kept his social life distinct from his official life and congressmen were rarely in his social circle. To know how Congress works but to disdain its joys is an acquired taste for most ex-congressmen downtown, produced by hard experience. Kennedy, however, brought it with him. Many of the difficulties he was to encounter in his day-by-day congressional relations stemmed from that.

But even had he been a man who dearly loved the Congress, even had that feeling been reciprocated, nothing could have rendered their relationship sweetness-and-light in his last year, so long as he persisted with his legislative program. As an innovative President confronting a reluctant Congress, he was heir to Truman, and to Roosevelt after 1936. Kennedy's own manner may have hurt him on the Hill, but these were scratches. Deeper scars had more substantial sources and he knew it.

In confrontations with the larger public outside Washington (again a different world), Kennedy made a brilliant beginning, matched only by the start in different circumstances of his own successor. The "public relations" of transition into office were superb. In three months after his election, Kennedy transformed himself from "pushy," "young," "Catholic," into

President-of-all-the-people, widening and deepening acceptance of his Presidency out of all proportion to the election returns. The Bay of Pigs was a severe check, but his handling of the aftermath displayed again superb feel for the imagery befitting an incumbent of the White House, heir to F.D.R. _and_ Eisenhower. That feel he always had. I think it never failed him.

What he also had was a distaste for preaching, really for the preachiness of politics, backed by genuine mistrust of mass emotion as a tool in politics. These attitudes are rare among American politicians; with Kennedy their roots ran deep into recesses of experience and character where I, as an outsider, cannot follow. But they assuredly were rooted in this man and they had visible effects upon his public style. He delighted in the play of minds, not of emotions. He doted on press conferences, not set performances. He feared "overexposure"; he dreaded overreaction. Obviously he enjoyed responsive crowds, and was himself responsive to a sea of cheering faces, but I think he rarely looked at their reaction—or his own—without a twinge of apprehension. He never seems to have displayed much fondness for the "fireside chat," a form of crowd appeal without the crowd; television talks in evening hours evidently struck him more as duty than as opportunity, and dangerous at that; some words on air-raid shelters in a talk about Berlin could set off mass hysteria—and did. At the moment when he had his largest, most attentive audience, on the climactic Sunday of the Cuban missile crisis, he turned it away (and turned attention off) with a two-minute announcement, spare and dry.

Yet we know now, after his death, what none of us knew before: that with a minimum of preaching, of emotional appeal, or of self-justification, even explanation, he had managed to touch millions in their private lives, not only at home but emphatically abroad. Perhaps his very coolness helped him do it. Perhaps his very vigor, family, fortune, sense of fun, his manners, taste, and sportsmanship, his evident enjoyment of his life and of the job made him the heart's desire of all sorts of people everywhere, not least among the young. At any rate, we know now that he managed in his years to make enormous impact on a world-wide audience, building an extraordinary base of public interest and affection (interspersed, of course, with doubters and detractors). What he might have made of this or done with it in later years, nobody knows.

IV

So much for power; what of pressure? What sustained this man in his decisions, his frustrations, and with what effect on his approach to being President? For an answer one turns to the evidence of crises, those already mentioned among others, and the _surface_ signs are clear. In all such situations it appears that Kennedy was cool, collected, courteous, and terse. This does not mean that he was unemotional. By temperament I think he was a man of mood and passion. But he had schooled his temperament. He kept his own emotions under tight control. He did not lose his temper inadvertently, and never lost it long. He was observer and participant combined; he saw himself as coolly as all others—and with humor. He always was a witty man, dry with a bit of bite and a touch of self-deprecation. He could laugh at himself, and did. Often he used humor to break tension. And in tight places he displayed a keen awareness of the human situation, human limits, his included, but it did not slow his work.

Readers over forty may recognize this portrait as "the stance of junior officers in the Second World War"; Elspeth Rostow coined that phrase and, superficially at least, she is quite right. This was the Kennedy stance and his self-confidence, his shield against frustration, must have owed a lot to his young manhood in that war.

This tells us a good deal but not nearly enough. At his very first encounter with a crisis in the Presidency, Kennedy's self-confidence seems to have been severely strained. The Bay of Pigs fiasco shook him deeply, shook his confidence in methods and associates. Yet he went on governing without a break, no change in manner, or in temper, or in humor. What sustained him? Surely much that went beyond experience of war.

What else? I cannot answer. I can only conjecture. His family life and rearing have some part to play, no doubt. His political successes also: in 1952 he bucked the Eisenhower tide to reach the Senate; in 1960 he broke barriers of youth and of religion which had always held before; on each occasion the Conventional Wisdom was against him: "can't be done." Beyond these things, this man had been exceptionally close to death, not only in the war but ten years after. And in his Presidential years his back was almost constantly a source of pain; he never talked about it but he lived with it. All this is of a piece with his behavior in a crisis. His control, his objectivity, his humor, and his sense of human limits, these were but expressions of his confidence; its sources must lie somewhere in this ground.

Whatever the sources, the results were rewarding for this President's performance on the job. In the most critical, nerve-straining aspects of the office, coping with its terrible responsibility for use of force, Kennedy's own image of himself impelled him neither to lash out nor run for cover. Rather, it released him for engagement and decision as a reasonable man. In some of the less awesome aspects of the Presidency, his own values restrained him, kept him off the pulpit, trimmed his guest list, made him shy away from the hyperbole of politics. But as a chief *executive*, confronting action-issues for decision and control, his duty and his confidence in doing it were nicely matched. So the world discovered in October 1962.

V

Now for my last question. What did John Kennedy leave behind him? What was the legacy of his short years? At the very least he left a myth: the vibrant, youthful leader cut down senselessly before his time. What this may come to signify as the years pass, I cannot tell. He left a glamorous moment, an engaging, youthful time, but how we shall remember it depends on what becomes of Lyndon Johnson. He left a broken promise, that "the torch has been passed to a new generation," and the youngsters who identified with him felt cheated as the promise, like the glamor, disappeared. What do their feelings matter? We shall have to wait and see.

May this be all that history is likely to record? Perhaps, but I doubt it. My guess is that when the observers can appraise the work of Kennedy's successors, they will find some things of substance in his legacy. Rashly, let me record what I think these are.

To begin with, our first Catholic President chose and paved the way for our first Southern President since the Civil War. (Woodrow Wilson was no Southerner *politically;* he came to the White House from the State House of New Jersey.) While Texas may be suspect now in Southern eyes, it certainly is of the South in Northern eyes, as Johnson found so painfully in 1960. Kennedy made him President. How free the choice of Johnson as Vice-Presidential candidate is subject to some argument. But what appears beyond dispute is that once chosen, Johnson was so treated by his rival for the White House as to ease his way enormously when he took over there. Johnson may have suffered great frustration as Vice-President, but his public standing and his knowledge of affairs were nurtured in those years. From this he gained a running start. The credit goes in no small part to Kennedy.

Moreover, Kennedy bequeathed to Johnson widened options in the sphere of foreign relations: a military posture far more flexible and usable than he himself inherited; a diplomatic posture more sophisticated in its whole approach to neutralists and leftists, markedly more mindful of distinctions in the world, even among allies.

On the domestic side, Kennedy left a large inheritance of controversies, opened by a youthful, Catholic urbanite from the Northeast, which his Southwestern, Protestant successor might have had more trouble stirring at the start, but now can ride and maybe even "heal." This may turn out to have been a productive division of labor. However it turns out, Kennedy lived long enough to keep at least one promise. He got the country "moving again." For in our politics, the *sine qua non* of innovative policy is controversy. By 1963 we were engaged in controversy with an openness which would have been unthinkable, or at least "unAmerican," during the later Eisenhower years.

Events, of course, have more to do with stirring controversy than a President. No man can make an issue on his own. But Presidents will help to shape the meaning of events, the terms of discourse, the attention paid, the noise-level. Eisenhower's years were marked by a pervasive fog of self-congratulation, muffling noise. The fog-machine was centered in the White House. Perhaps there had been need for this after the divisive Truman years. By the late nineteen-fifties, though, it fuzzed our chance to innovate in time. Kennedy broke out of it.

Finally, this President set a new standard of performance on the job, suitable to a new state of Presidential being, a state he was the first to face throughout his term of office: the state of substantial, deliverable, nuclear capability in other hands than ours. Whatever else historians may make of Kennedy, I think them likely to begin with this. There can be little doubt that his successors have a lighter task because *he* pioneered in handling nuclear confrontations. During the Cuban missile crisis and thereafter, he did something which had not been done before, did it well, and got it publicly accepted. His innovation happened to be timely, since the need for innovation was upon us; technology had put it there. But also, in his reach for information and control, his balancing of firmness with caution, his sense of limits, he displayed and dramatized what Presidents must do to minimize the risk of war through mutual miscalculation. This may well be the cardinal risk confronting his successors. If so, he made a major contribution to the Presidency.

CONTEMPORARY SOURCES 52

3. HARRY S. TRUMAN, ACCEPTANCE SPEECH, JULY 15, 1948

BY the time President Harry S. Truman appeared before the listless Democratic convention in Philadelphia at 2 A.M. on July 15, 1948, to accept a nomination few party leaders wanted him to have, the election of Republican Thomas E. Dewey seemed virtually assured. The Administration had been badly hurt by its mediocre record of dealing with postwar economic turbulence, and its foreign policy of containment had aroused great apprehension from both the right and left sides of the political spectrum. The defection of former Vice-President Henry Wallace threatened to cost Truman millions of votes and, during the convention, several angry southern delegations had marched out in protest over a strong civil rights plank in the platform.

Recognizing the desperate need to pump new life into his moribund party, Truman took a big gamble and told the convention that he was going to call the Republican-controlled

SOURCE. *Public Papers of the Presidents of the United States, Harry S. Truman, 1948*, Washington, D.C.: United States Government Printing Office, 1960, pp. 406–407 and 409–410.

Eightieth Congress into a special session to act on several of his domestic reform programs.
He wanted to give the voters an opportunity to see if "there is any reality behind the
Republican platform," which had in effect endorsed most of his domestic policies. The
reconvened Congress did as Truman expected—it refused to act. Truman then had his
winning issue, the "do-nothing" Eightieth Congress. Wrapping himself in the mantle of
Franklin Roosevelt, he charged that the Republican party would repeal most of the New
Deal reforms. Truman stumped the country to give 354 "give 'em hell" speeches. His
electric acceptance speech had turned the entire campaign strategy to his advantage, and
the veteran Missouri campaigner made the most of it.

I can't tell you how very much I appreciate the honor which you have just conferred upon me. I shall continue to try to deserve it.

I accept the nomination. . . .

We have been working together for victory in a great cause. Victory has become a habit of our party. It has been elected four times in succession, and I am convinced it will be elected a fifth time next November.

The reason is that the people know that the Democratic Party is the people's party, and the Republican Party is the party of special interest, and it always has been and always will be.

The record of the Democratic Party is written in the accomplishments of the last 16 years. I don't need to repeat them. They have been very ably placed before this convention by the keynote speaker, the candidate for Vice President, and by the permanent chairman.

Confidence and security have been brought to the people by the Democratic Party. Farm income has increased from less than $2\frac{1}{2}$ billion in 1932 to more than $18 billion in 1947. Never in the world were the farmers of any republic or any kingdom or any other country as prosperous as the farmers of the United States; and if they don't do their duty by the Democratic Party, they are the most ungrateful people in the world!

Wages and salaries in this country have increased from 29 billion in 1933 to more than $128 billion in 1947. That's labor, and labor never had but one friend in politics, and that is the Democratic Party and Franklin D. Roosevelt.

And I say to labor what I have said to the farmers: they are the most ungrateful people in the world if they pass the Democratic Party by this year.

The total national income has increased from less than $40 billion in 1933 to $203 billion in 1947, the greatest in all the history of the world. These benefits have been spread to all the people, because it is the business of the Democratic Party to see that the people get a fair share of these things.

This last, worst 80th Congress proved just the opposite for the Republicans.

The record on foreign policy of the Democratic Party is that the United States has been turned away permanently from isolationism, and we have converted the greatest and best of the Republicans to our viewpoint on that subject. . . .

Now the Republicans came here a few weeks ago, and they wrote a platform. I hope you have all read that platform. They adopted the platform, and that platform had a lot of promises and statements of what the Republican Party is for, and what they would do if they were in power. They promised to do in that platform a lot of things I have been asking them to do that they have refused to do when they had the power.

The Republican platform cries about cruelly high prices. I have been trying to get them to do something about high prices ever since they met the first time.

Now listen! This is equally as bad, and as cynical. The Republican platform comes out for slum clearance and low-rental housing. I have been trying to get them to pass that housing bill ever since they met the first time, and it is still resting in the Rules Committee, that bill.

The Republican platform favors educational opportunity and promotion of education. I have been trying to get Congress to do something about that ever since they came there, and that bill is at rest in the House of Representatives.

The Republican platform is for extending and increasing social security benefits. Think of that! Increasing social security benefits! Yet when they had the opportunity, they took 750,000 off the social security rolls!

I wonder if they think they can fool the people of the United States with such poppycock as that!

There is a long list of these promises in that Republican platform. If it weren't so late, I would tell you all about them. I have discussed a number of these failures of the Republican 80th Congress. Every one of them is important. Two of them are of major concern to nearly every American family. They failed to do anything about high prices, they failed to do anything about housing.

My duty as President requires that I use every means within my power to get the laws the people need on matters of such importance and urgency.

I am therefore calling this Congress back into session July 26th.

On the 26th day of July, which out in Missouri we call "Turnip Day," I am going to call Congress back and ask them to pass laws to halt rising prices, to meet the housing crisis—which they are saying they are for in their platform.

At the same time I shall ask them to act upon other vitally needed measures such as aid to education, which they say they are for; a national health program; civil rights legislation, which they say they are for; an increase in the minimum wage, which I doubt very much they are for; extension of the social security coverage and increased benefits, which they say they are for;

funds for projects needed in our program to provide public power and cheap electricity. By indirection, this 80th Congress has tried to sabotage the power policies the United States has pursued for 14 years. That power lobby is as bad as the real estate lobby, which is sitting on the housing bill.

I shall ask for adequate and decent laws for displaced persons in place of this anti-Semitic, anti-Catholic law which this 80th Congress passed.

Now, my friends, if there is any reality behind that Republican platform, we ought to get some action from a short session of the 80th Congress. They can do this job in 15 days, if they want to do it. They will still have time to go out and run for office.

They are going to try to dodge their responsibility. They are going to drag all the red herrings they can across this campaign, but I am here to say that Senator Barkley and I are not going to let them get away with it.

Now, what that worst 80th Congress does in this special session will be the test. The American people will not decide by listening to mere words, or by reading a mere platform. They will decide on the record, the record as it has been written. And in the record is the stark truth, that the battle lines of 1948 are the same as they were in 1932, when the Nation lay prostrate and helpless as a result of Republican misrule and inaction.

In 1932 we were attacking the citadel of special privilege and greed. We were fighting to drive the money changers from the temple. Today, in 1948, we are now the defenders of the stronghold of democracy and of equal opportunity, the haven of the ordinary people of this land and not of the favored classes or the powerful few. The battle cry is just the same now as it was in 1932, and I paraphrase the words of Franklin D. Roosevelt as he issued the challenge, in accepting nomination in Chicago: "This is more than a political call to arms. Give me your help, not to win votes alone, but to win in this new crusade to keep America secure and safe for its own people."

4. JOSEPH R. McCARTHY, NATIONWIDE RADIO ADDRESS, OCTOBER 27, 1952

ON February 9, 1950, the relatively obscure junior senator from Wisconsin, Joseph R. McCarthy, startled the nation with his charge that, "I have here in my hand a list of 205—a list of names that were known to the Secretary of State as being members of the

SOURCE. *The New York Times*, October 28, 1952, p. 26.

Communist Party and who nevertheless are still working and shaping policy in the State Department." By the time that the senator made this charge in Wheeling, West Virginia, millions of Americans were ready to believe his unsupported statement. They were looking for a convenient scapegoat to explain away the Cold War difficulties being endured by the United States. The fall of China, the exposure of a very efficient Soviet spy system that had penetrated even the atomic energy program, the confusions over the Yalta agreements, and the sensational perjury conviction of the former influential New Dealer, Alger Hiss, had created a national mood of uneasiness and distrust.

This undercurrent of frustration and suspicion created the phenomenon known as McCarthyism. Urged on by unhappy Republicans who longed for a return to power, McCarthy sought to connect the New Deal to communism with his charge of "Twenty years of treason." ("If one case doesn't work, then bring up another," Senator Robert A. Taft advised him.) Unwilling to be muzzled following the election of a Republican to the Presidency in 1952, McCarthy ultimately bruised too many Senators with his cruel and often irrelevant charges against responsible and loyal national leaders, and was censored by the Senate in November, 1954. Typical of his demagogic technique was his national telecast shortly before the 1952 election when he sought to connect "Alger— I mean Adlai" Stevenson with the Communist movement.

Thank you, fellow Americans. I am deeply grateful, very deeply grateful to all of you who have made this night possible.

We are at war tonight—a war which started decades ago, a war which we did not start, a war which we cannot stop except by either victory or death. The Korean war is only one phase of this war between international atheistic communism and our free civilization.

And we've been losing, we've been losing that war since the shooting part of World War II ended, losing it at an incredibly fantastic rate of 100,000,000 people a year.

And for the past two and a half years I've been trying to expose and force out of high positions in Government those who are in charge of our deliberate planned retreat from victory.

Now this fight, this fight against international communism, should not be a contest between America's two great political parties. Certainly, after all the millions of Americans who've long voted the Democratic ticket are just as loyal, they love America just as much, they hate communism just as much as the average Republican.

Unfortunately, the millions of loyal Democrats no longer have a party in Washington. And tonight, tonight I shall give you the history of the Democratic candidate for the Presidency who endorsed and could continue the suicidal Kremlin-directed policies of the nation.

Now I'm not going to give you a speech tonight. Tonight I'm a lawyer giving you the facts on the evidence in the case of Stevenson vs. Stevenson.

Let me make it clear that I'm only covering his history in so far as it deals with his aid to the Communist cause and the extent, the extent to which he is part and parcel of the Acheson-Hiss-Lattimore group. Now I perform the unpleasant task because the American people are entitled to have the coldly-documented history of this man who says, "I want to be your President." . . .

Now these facts, my good friends, cannot be answered—cannot be answered by screams of smears and lies. These facts can only be answered by facts. And we call upon Adlai of Illinois to so answer those facts.

The time is short, so let me get about the task of looking at his record. The Democratic candidate has said, and I quote him verbatim. He said, "As evidence of my direction I have established my headquarters here in Springfield with people of my own choosing." In other words he says, judge me, judge me by the advisers whom I have selected. Good, let's do that. Let's examine a few of those advisers first.

First is Wilson Wyatt, his personal manager. Now Wilson Wyatt is a former head of the left-winger A.D.A., the Americans for Democratic Action. The A.D.A. has five major points in its program. Listen to these and remember them if you will.

Point No. 1. Repeal of the Smith Act, which makes it a crime to conspire to overthrow this Government,

No. 2. Recognition of Red China,

No. 3. Opposition to the loyalty oath,

No. 4. Condemnation of the F.B.I. for exposing traitors like Coplon and Gubitchev, and

No. 5. Continuous all-out opposition to the House Committee on Un-American Activities.

Let me speak to you about that platform. They publish it day after day.

Now, according to an article in The New York *Times*, and I have that which I hold in my hands—the Democratic candidate's campaign manager Wyatt condemns the Government's loyalty program and here's the proof—it condemns the loyalty program in the most vicious terms. Strangely Alger—I mean Adlai—Adlai in 1952, now that he's running for President, says, I will dig out the Communists using as my weapon the loyalty program which my campaign manager damns and condemns.

Next, and perhaps the key figure in the Stevenson camp is his speech writer, Arthur Schlesinger Jr., former vice chairman of the same A.D.A. Now, Schlesinger has been a writer, incidentally, for The New York *Post*— New York *Post* whose editor and his wife admit, admit that they were members of the Young Communist League.

Now in 1946, Stevenson's speech writer wrote that the present system in the United States makes, and I quote. Listen to this, here's his speech writer, he says, "The present system in the United States makes even freedom-loving Americans look wistfully at Russia." I wonder if there's anyone in the audience tonight who's looking wistfully at Russia. And I wonder, also, if some calamity would happen and Stevenson would be elected, what job this man would have.

Perhaps the most revealing article written by Stevenson's speech writer appeared in the The New York *Times* on Dec. 11, 1949, on Page 3, and listen to this if you will. I quote, he says, "I happen to believe that the Communist party should be granted the freedom of political action and that Communists should be allowed to teach in universities."

Nothing secret, nothing's secret about it, it's in The New York *Times*, Dec. 11, 1949. Stevenson's speech writer saying I think that Communists should be allowed to teach your children, my good friends. And he says, Oh but judge me, judge me by the advisers whom I select.

Now let's see how Stevenson's speech writer feels on the subject of religion. The answer is given in his review of the book of Whittaker Chambers. Whittaker Chambers, the man whose testimony convicted Alger Hiss. Chambers in his book, as you know, maintained that a belief in God was the hope of the free world—the feeling which most Americans have regardless of whether they're Protestant, Jewish or Catholic. Well, Schlesinger wrote about that. What did he say?

He says this—let me quote him verbatim. He says: "The whole record, the whole record of history, indeed gives proof that a belief in God has created human vanity as overweening and human arrogance as intolerable as the vanity and arrogance of . . . Communists." . . .

Another of the men in the Democratic candidate's camp is Archibald MacLeish. Stevenson's biography, on Page 77, states that MacLeish was the man who brought him into the State Department—it's his own biography. Now Stevenson has him as an adviser.

Well, how does this man MacLeish—he's got that—the longest record of affiliation with Communist fronts of any man that I have ever named in Washington. And Adlai says, Judge me by the friends I select. To that I say, "Amen, Adlai, amen." . . .

While you think, while you may think that there could be no connection between the debonair Democratic candidate and a dilapidated Massachusetts barn, I want to show you a picture of this barn and explain the connection. Here's the outside of a barn. Give me a picture showing the inside of the barn.

Here's the outside of a barn up at Lee, Mass. Looks like it couldn't house a farmer's cow or goat from the outside. Here's the inside. A beautifully paneled conference room with maps of the Soviet Union. Now in what way does Stevenson tie up with this?

My investigators went up and took pictures of this barn after we had been tipped off about what was in it, tipped off that there was in this barn all of the missing documents from the Communist front I.P.R. [Institute of Pacific Relations], the I.P.R. which has been named by the McCarran Committee, named before the McCarran Committee as a cover shop for Communist espionage. We went up and we found in the room adjoining this conference room 200,000—200,000 of the missing I.P.R. documents. The hidden files showing the vouchers, among other things, showing money from Moscow. Men—a group of Communists.

We now come to the much-discussed testimony by Adlai Stevenson in the trial of Alger Hiss. Now, my good friends, I haven't considered, I have not considered this part standing alone as overly important in the Stevenson record. It is only a link in the chain of events that proves a case in Stevenson vs. Stevenson.

Now what does impress me, however, is the deathly fear that Governor Stevenson displays when additional links tying him to Alger Hiss are brought forth. We find that he very cleverly attempts to imply that his knowledge of Hiss was casual, remote and that he is not vouching for Hiss' character at the trial.

And I hold in my hand a petition which has never been made public before, either in the New York courts, a petition by the Hiss lawyers when they asked the court to admit Stevenson's statement. You will recall Stevenson said, I will sign a statement but I will not go to New York and run the risk of being put under cross-examination.

And Senator McCarran's committee, unanimously found that the I.P.R. was Communist-controlled. Communist-dominated and shaping our foreign policy.

Now let's take a look at a photostat of a document taken from that Massachusetts barn. One of those documents that was never supposed to see the light of day, rather interesting it is, this is the document that shows that Alger Hiss and Frank Coe recommended Adlai Stevenson to the Mont Tremblant conference which was called for the purpose of establishing foreign policy— post-war foreign policy in Asia.

Now as you know Alger Hiss is a convicted traitor. Frank Coe was the man [named] under oath before Congressional committees seven times as a member of the Communist party. Why, why do Hiss and Coe find that Adlai Stevenson is the man they want representing them at this conference. I don't know, perhaps Adlai knows.

Let me read this one small section of this affidavit to you, and the entire affidavit's available to the press. Here's the affidavit of the Hiss lawyer:

Gov. Adlai Stevenson of Illinois has been closely associated with Alger Hiss in the course of certain international diplomatic undertakings. They were together at the San Francisco conference of the United Nations at which the Charter of the United

Nations was adopted and they were together at the London conference which preceded and prepared the agenda for the San Francisco conference.

They say this: "The testimony of Governor Stevenson would be of great importance to Alger Hiss." Now I want you to examine closely the statement Governor Stevenson made at Cleveland, Ohio, about two days ago, the twenty-third, in which he attempted to defend his support of the reputation of Hiss—Hiss, the arch-traitor of our times. Stevenson said this last Thurday. I quote him. He said: "I said his reputation was good. I did not say that his reputation was very good."

Now here we have a man who says I want to be your President, saying that Hiss' reputation was good but not very good.

Now I say, my good friends, that if he had such misgivings he should not have vouched for Hiss at all. There are no degrees of loyalty in the United States. A man is either loyal or he's disloyal. There is no such thing—there is no such thing as being a little bit disloyal or being partly a traitor.

Now I note that the television man is holding up a sign, saying thirty seconds to go—I have much, much more of the documentation here. I'm sorry we can't give it to our television audience and I want our audience to know it was not the fault of the television station—we've only arranged for half an hour and that half an hour's about up.

But with your permission my good friends, when we go off the air I would like to complete for this audience the documentation.

5. BEN B. SELIGMAN, "MAN, WORK, AND THE AUTOMATED FEAST"

EACH week automation eliminates between 40,000 and 50,000 jobs, a president of one of the leading electrical equipment manufacturing firms told a congressional committee in 1963. The loss of nearly two and a half million jobs each year, when nearly 4,000,000 young people annually enter the job market, constitutes one of the more serious problems confronting American society. Automation, its defenders optimistically contend, is here "to liberate us," and thus far the maintenance of relatively high levels of employment

SOURCE. Ben B. Seligman, "Man, Work, and the Automated Feast," in *Commentary*, Vol. 34, July 1962, pp. 9–16 and 18–19. Copyright 1962 by The American Jewish Committee; 1966 by Ben B. Seligman. Reprinted by permission of *Commentary* and the author.

seem to bear out this claim. In fact, in each city, while thousands go jobless because of the lack of technical skills, even more jobs go begging for want of qualified applicants.

Perhaps the major threat to American civilization is not automated unemployment, but that the electronic computer will become man's master. The computer is capable of retrieving fantastic amounts of "stored" data within seconds and utilizing that information to carry out a vast array of programmed assignments. Already computers are guiding space vehicles, cross-checking income tax returns, projecting election returns, and registering college students. The possibilities for problem solving are just now beginning to be recognized; when the computer is united with the automatic machine, then the cybernetics revolution takes on tremendous implications for the American people. The first electronic digital computer was introduced shortly after World War II, and already the impact of its more sophisticated successors is impressive. It is sobering to realize that we are actually still in the Model-T stage of the computer age.

Automation is said to have ancient beginnings. To be sure, the technology from which it stems goes back several centuries, at least. Automatic devices in the middle 18th century included a mechanical loom for the manufacture of figured silks; James Watt's steam engine utilized a fly-ball governor which controlled the speed at which his contrivance operated; and it has been suggested that automation's basic concept—the linkage of machines—is evident in the detachable harpoon head of the Eskimo. Yet to assert that automation is simply the latest link in a great chain of industrial history obscures what is patently a new phenomenon. In the old days, industrial change developed through fission: division of labor was the key to progress and work was made available to a huge pool of unskilled persons who in the main had been forced to migrate from farm to city. Today, it is precisely these unskilled, together with semi-skilled and even some of management's people, who are displaced and poured back into the pool. Furthermore, automation represents a marked acceleration of change with so cumulative a force that this alone spells a profound difference from what went on before.

Automation is already moving with a rapidity that threatens to tear apart existing social and organizational structures; according to some observers, it will even alter the habits of thought that men have up to now prided themselves on. Such a prospect is perhaps not surprising when we consider the cataclysmic results of the 18th century's Industrial Revolution: the changes then were so swift as to constitute a whole new phenomenon. And Marx and Weber and Sombart had shown convincingly how human and social transformation accompanied technological transformation.

Now, new industrial functions, new economic forms, new work habits, and new social headaches are being created in ways that signify a kind of dialectic leap. Even John Diebold, who claims to have invented the word "automation" and whose ebullient advocacy of computer technology has done much to spread the gospel, confesses: "I believe that [automation] marks a break with past trends, a qualitative departure from the more conventional advance of technology that began with jagged pieces of flint and progressed up to the steam engine."

Why is this so? Up to recent times, technology simply sought to substitute natural force for animal or human force. In the early days, primacy of place was given to windmills and waterfalls. Then came metallurgical discoveries; and the screw and the lathe made possible the machine, essentially a contrivance which man could watch in action. But man remained at the center of the whole business, essential to both operation and control, still more or less the maker and master of materials. With automation, man not only loses irrevocably his function as *homo faber;* he no longer even possesses the character of *animal laborans.* At best, he is a sometime supervisor of a flow process. Actual control is removed from him and given to an electronic contraption whose feedbacks and servomechanisms make it possible to produce goods and manipulate information in a continuous system, without human participation.

To realize what automation implies, we must examine the kinds of machines employed and see what they do to people and organizations. Essentially, today's scientific upheaval comprises four aspects: the conversion of industrial materials into a flow; the setting of uniform standards so that output can be treated as a flow; the utilization of electronic computers with build-in feedbacks to enable the exercise of automatic control; and the application of new energy sources to the whole process. Thus, raw materials, which represent the "input" of an industry, must be handled without human hands, as in a modern meat-packing plant. Production, at one time a series of discrete steps, is completely integrated by means of transfer machines. In some cases, computers tied to cams or templates can make the producing machine follow a predetermined pattern with greater accuracy and sharper tolerances than were dreamed possible in the heyday of the skilled machinist. Computers, into which all sort of complex information can be fed by "programmers," automatically correct errors. A wide range of goods is now produced in this startling manner—chemicals, automobiles, steel, glassware, electric bulbs, television sets, beverages, and drugs, to name a few. Factories are able to function 24 hours a day, 365 days a year, while manpower needs are reduced dramatically. And with the development of nuclear energy for industrial power, manufacturers no longer need to be near their source of raw materials; they can set up their plants closer to markets, or—if they are seeking to escape the union organizer—in the most isolated of places. Yet one industry necessarily must relate itself more intimately with the next; a seamless web envelops all the entrepreneurs and their works. . . .

The automobile industry illustrates how an integrated set of machines can function. There the engine production line, for example, consists of a series of drilling, boring, and milling operations connected by transfer machines which move the engine blocks from one point to the next. Tolerances are checked automatically; if something is awry, the whole line is stopped by an electronic device. Or one can see an automatic assembly machine put the components of a television set on a printed board and then solder them into place. These are repetitive operations and their economic justification stems from the replacement market. There is not much of a style factor here and such model changes as do occur can be handled with relative ease. Yet even where variation in the product is essential, as in machine tools, the operation still can be made automatic. . . .

The key here is feedback, the simplest case of which is the home thermostat turning a furnace on and off in order to maintain a constant room temperature. In essence, signals are sent from one part of the automated line to another, correcting errors, shifting power loads, or modifying the speed of the line. No human need adjust gauges or read thermometers or press buttons. Feedback or servomechanisms do a better control job than humans, especially when many elements are involved. Whereas the human eye can follow the motion of a gauge at about two cycles a second, a servomechanism does about 100 a second. Now, marry feedback to a computer and automation is complete. The computers, really giant adding machines and calculators, receive information from the gauges and thermometers, analyze the data, and then transmit new instructions to other gauges and instruments.

Computers, whose basic concept goes back to Blaise Pascal, were developed in their electronic form during World War II to help guns hit their targets more efficiently. There are two basic types—the analog and digital computer. The former is a kind of electronic slide rule able to apply higher mathematics to problems of rates of change in various flows. However fast it might have been, for the engineer, mathematician, and operations researcher it was not fast enough. So the digital computer was devised, a machine that employs the binary number system and consequently can only add and subtract. This is no impediment, for like an electronic abacus, the digital computer sends its impulses forward at an unbelievable speed, giving it a marked advantage over the analog machine. Moreover, digital computers have "memory" drums in which data can be stored for future use. The electrical pulses in a digital computer last less than one-millionth of a second. Information can be extracted from the memory drum in about ten-millionths of a second. . . .

By now "Detroit" automation is quite well known. Automatic machines, linked by transfer equipment, move engine blocks through a complete manufacturing process, performing 530 precision cutting and drilling operations in $14\frac{1}{2}$ minutes as compared to 9 hours in a conventional plant. The

Chrysler Corporation's recent breakthrough on computer "balancing" of assembly lines, essentially a "combinatorial" problem, now defines each job so rigidly that little liberties like a worker's taking a few minutes out for a smoke become serious impediments to the smooth flow of cars. An automated power plant in Louisiana saved $175,000 in fuel, $100,000 in maintenance, $1.5 million in eliminating delays and mishaps, and $500,000 in labor. A Jones & Laughlin sheet-plate mill turns out strip at the speed of 70 miles an hour with no labor other than the supervision of engineers. Punch-card systems in a reversing roughing mill modify ingot shapes, and the computer even "remembers" what to do when the forms have to be changed. Foundry work, traditionally a hand operation, is now being tied to the computer. In petroleum and chemicals, the story is almost ancient: as far back as 1949 catalytic cracking plants were turning out 41,000 barrels a day with instruments and only a few workers to watch gauges. In a Texaco refinery the computer controls 26 flow rates, 72 temperatures, 3 pressure levels, and 3 gas combinations. General Electric uses segmented "automation," that is, batch production, for motors of varying models up to 30 horsepower. Ribbon machines make 800 electric bulb blanks a minute, running without end, and requiring only one worker who stands by to make an occasional adjustment. . . .

In retailing, automation starts with inventory and accounting records. Sales data are transmitted to control centers where billing, inventory, and credit information is stored. Bad credit risks are automatically checked and information returned to the sales clerk before the package can be wrapped. Sylvania and IBM have been working on automatic check-out counters for supermarkets—the number of cash registers would be reduced, as well as the number of workers. Ferris wheels, conveyor belts, chutes, and slides, all controlled by electronic computers, deliver garments from receiving platforms to stockrooms and even return the merchandise to the ground floor if necessary. Eventually we will pay our traffic penalties to a computer: in Illinois, records of driver violations are stored in a computer and the fines calculated by machine.

This, then, is the automated feast. Tasks are accomplished with unimaginable speed. Decisions are made by coded instructions and errors quickly detected. Facts are stored and extracted from memory drums. The machines learn and "perceive": they analyze stock market conditions; establish rocket flight patterns before the shot is fired into space; write television scripts that compare favorably with what is now available; compose music; translate; and play games. They combine high technical competence with just enough of an I.Q. to keep them tractable. They do precisely the kind of work to which junior executives and semi-skilled employees are usually assigned. . . .

Between 1953 and 1960, a million and a half jobs disappeared. In one plant, studied by Floyd Mann of Michigan State University, automation reduced the work force by half. In the electrical industry, output increased 21 per cent between 1953 and 1961, while employment declined 10 percent. There was a loss of 80,000 production jobs in steel during the decade of the 50's. In the shift from aircraft to missiles, 200,000 jobs went down the technological drain. For the 5-year period 1955–1960, production workers in automobile factories were down 21 percent. All this displacement occurred in an affluent society that itself went through four postwar recessions each of which left behind an increasingly hard-core residue of unemployment—3 percent in 1951–53; 4 percent in 1955–57; and 5 percent in 1959–60.

Full employment for the next 10 years means creating 12 million new jobs—25,000 a week, or almost double the number of new openings in the 1947–57 decade. Extending the period to 1961, we find that output rose 65 percent while the number of production and maintenance jobs declined. True, white collar workers increased 7 percent, but now automation is making them just as insecure. If we assume that demand in the 60's will expand at the same rate as it did in 1947–57, then output by 1970 may very well be 50 percent greater. However, if the present rate of productivity is maintained, then the number of required man-hours will have increased by 12 percent, providing only 75 million jobs at the end of the decade. Thus, about 8 million persons, 10 percent of the labor force, will have no work. And this is a moderate forecast, for should the secular growth rate fall below 3 percent per annum, as is conceivable, output will have gone up about 40 percent. Add to this the effects of automation, and the job increase by 1970 may be only 2 million, leaving a residue of perhaps 10 million persons without jobs. . . .

What is the solution? Frankly, there is none, at least none of a definitive character. The numerous suggestions for dealing with the pressing problems that stem from automation are all piecemeal, pecking at a spot here and a point there. No amount of federal fiscal tinkering will meet the immediate needs of those who are attached to a dying industry. Economic growth, while essential, will not of itself put to work again the idle coal miner, exmachinist, and troubled bookkeeper whose jobs have vanished like the first atom bomb tower. Administration economists believe that automated unemployment can be solved by turning on ordinary Keynesian tap valves: it's all a matter of failing effective demand, they assert. There seems little awareness in important circles that the American economy is undergoing deep-rooted and subtle structural changes and that it will take massive economic and social therapy to assuage the hurt. . . .

. . . One comes back to an immediate step, which though not by any means a "solution," nevertheless offers a practicable way for mitigating some of the effects of automation—the shorter work week. Mere mention of this is apt to send a shudder down the backs of administration economists and devotees of the conventional wisdom. Expressing their horror at the thought that man should have even more leisure than he now enjoys, the latter urge that a shorter work week means less production and higher costs. And in the present context of growthmanship, this is unthinkable. Arthur Goldberg, whose grasp of legal subtleties contrasts sharply with his simplistic formulations of economic issues, warned the International Ladies' Garment Workers' Union recently that fewer hours per week would ". . . impair adversely our present stable price structure [and] make our goods less competitive both at home and abroad. . . ." The enormous productive capacity of America's industry was conveniently forgotten, a capacity so enhanced by automation that it can more than compensate for the alleged loss of output. And this is to say nothing about the quality and content of contemporary "production"—that would require another essay. The point to observe now is the curious inner tension of an industrial system whose fundamental Puritan outlook demands an incessant, unremitting outpouring of goods (for what?) while at the same time it imposes dreary idleness and dismal futures on those to whom the cornucopia is directed. We may well ask, what is the feedback in this insane circle?

But to return to the shorter work week—a cursory review of its history would demonstrate how completely reasonable it is. Prior to 1860, the rule was dawn to dusk with as much as 72 hours as the weekly standard. Demands for a shorter span were met with the contention that 12 hours a day, 6 days a week had been divinely ordained in order to strengthen worker morality. Three decades later the work week had been shortened by 12 hours. In 1910, the average ranged from 51 to 55 hours, and at that time a work force of 34 million produced a Gross National Product of about $37 billion. The work week continued to shrink: in 1920, it was 48 hours; in 1929, 44 hours; and since 1946, 40 hours. By 1955, the labor force had almost doubled while GNP increased 10-fold as compared to 1910. And all the time the work week kept declining, about 13 hours in a 45-year span, or roughly 15 minutes a year.

Was anyone hurt? Did productivity lag? Has technology been impeded? The depression years aside, whatever unemployment did occur would have been unquestionably greater without the steady drop in hours. A continuation of this secular decline would cut back the normal work week by one hour every four years. According to one estimate, this might create about a million jobs a year which, together with the normal increase in job openings, could really begin to cut into the displacement caused by automation. When Harry van Arsdale of the New York electricians' union obtained a 5-hour day, he was savagely flayed for selfishness and lack of patriotism. Even the labor movement felt embarrassed. Arsdale insisted that he was only seeking to "spread the work." Now it seems, according to Theodore Kheel, the industry's arbitrator, that well over 1,000 new jobs will be made available as a result of the union's action. . . .

It is of course a common cliché that scientific advances have outrun our capacity to deal with them. Technology, the practical and material basis of life, has acquired a tidal force of its own which threatens to inundate human thought. Moreover, modern technology, as evidenced by automation, manifests no orderly growth. Its leads and lags, its uneven development, create new power centers that result in unaccustomed strains. To be sure, this has happened before, but always at immense human cost. It is this that the high priests of automation fail to grasp, while those of us who are merely bystanders can only hope that society will eventually catch up with the engineers and scientists and archons of industry who see only a handsome profit in what the machine can do.

6. MICHAEL HARRINGTON, "THE INVISIBLE LAND"

DURING the 1960 presidential campaign, John F. Kennedy frequently discussed the complex problems faced by America's poor. When he reported in one speech that 17,000,000 Americans went to bed each night hungry, middle-class voters scoffed in disbelief. Conditioned by their suburban environment, they dismissed Kennedy's statement as campaign rhetoric. The subsequent publication of The Other America *by Michael Harrington, however, demonstrated beyond doubt the existence of widespread poverty within America's "affluent society." In an impassioned but disciplined style, the young social critic described in vivid terms the conditions of poverty in the United States. Harrington had a profound influence on President Kennedy and Lyndon Johnson, after assuming the Presidency, made abolition of poverty a major objective of his Great Society.*

The much-hailed War on Poverty, however, proved to be merely a minor skirmish. Never did the Johnson Administration commit itself to a massive attack on the underlying conditions that produce poverty. The War soon became bogged down in a nightmare of bureaucratic trivia, and incessant combat with local officials, political critics, and even between rival antipoverty agencies. The other war—that in Vietnam—received the top priority of the Administration. When Johnson left office in January 1969, little of a

SOURCE. Michael Harrington, *The Other America*, New York: The Macmillan Company, 1962, pp. 1–7, 9–11, and 14–18. Copyright 1962 by Michael Harrington. Reprinted by permission the The Macmillan Company and the author.

substantive nature had been accomplished toward abolishing poverty from the land of
plenty. The following selection is taken from the introduction of Michael Harrington's
The Other America.

There is a familiar America. It is celebrated in speeches and advertised on television and in the magazines. It has the highest mass standard of living the world has ever known.

In the 1950's this America worried about itself, yet even its anxieties were products of abundance. The title of a brilliant book was widely misinterpreted, and the familiar America began to call itself "the affluent society." There was introspection about Madison Avenue and tail fins; there was discussion of the emotional suffering taking place in the suburbs. In all this, there was an implicit assumption that the basic grinding economic problems had been solved in the United States. In this theory the nation's problems were no longer a matter of basic human needs, of food, shelter, and clothing. Now they were seen as qualitative, a question of learning to live decently amid luxury.

While this discussion was carried on, there existed another America. In it dwelt somewhere between 40,000,000 and 50,000,000 citizens of this land. They were poor. They still are.

To be sure, the other America is not impoverished in the same sense as those poor nations where millions cling to hunger as a defense against starvation. This country has escaped such extremes. That does not change the fact that tens of millions of Americans are, at this very moment, mained in body and spirit, existing at levels beneath those necessary for human decency. If these people are not starving, they are hungry, and sometimes fat with hunger, for that is what cheap foods do. They are without adequate housing and education and medical care. . . .

The millions who are poor in the United States tend to become increasingly invisible. Here is a great mass of people, yet it takes an effort of the intellect and will even to see them. . . .

The other America, the America of poverty, is hidden today in a way that it never was before. Its millions are socially invisible to the rest of us. No wonder that so many misinterpreted Galbraith's title and assumed that "the affluent society" meant that everyone had a decent standard of life. The misinterpretation was true as far as the actual day-to-day lives of two-thirds of the nation were concerned. Thus, one must begin a description of the other America by understanding why we do not see it.

There are perennial reasons that make the other America an invisible land.

Poverty is often off the beaten track. It always has been. The ordinary tourist never left the main highway, and today he rides interstate turnpikes. He does not go into the valleys of Pennsylvania where the towns look like movie sets of Wales in the thirties. He does not see the company houses in rows, the rutted roads (the poor always have bad roads whether they live in the city, in towns, or on farms), and everything is black and dirty. And even if he were to pass through such a place by accident, the tourist would not meet the unemployed men in the bar or the women coming home from a runaway sweatshop.

Then too, beauty and myths are perennial masks of poverty. The traveler comes to the Appalachians in the lovely season. He sees the hills, the streams, the foliage—but not the poor. Or perhaps he looks at a run-down mountain house and, remembering Rousseau rather than seeing with his eyes, decides that "those people" are truly fortunate to be living the way they are and that they are lucky to be exempt from the strains and tensions of the middle class. The only problem is that "those people," the quaint inhabitants of those hills, are undereducated, underprivileged, lack medical care, and are in the process of being forced from the land into a life in the cities, where they are misfits.

These are normal and obvious causes of the invisibility of the poor. They operated a generation ago; they will be functioning a generation hence. It is more important to understand that the very development of American society is creating a new kind of blindness about poverty. The poor are increasingly slipping out of the very experience and consciousness of the nation.

If the middle class never did like ugliness and poverty, it was at least aware of them. "Across the tracks" was not a very long way to go. There were forays into the slums at Christmas time; there were charitable organizations that brought contact with the poor. Occasionally, almost everyone passed through the Negro ghetto or the blocks of tenements, if only to get downtown to work or to entertainment.

Now the American city has been transformed. The poor still inhabit the miserable housing in the central area, but they are increasingly isolated from contact with, or sight of, anybody else. Middle-class women coming in from Suburbia on a rare trip may catch the merest glimpse of the other America on the way to an evening at the theater, but their children are segregated in suburban schools. The business or professional man may drive along the fringes of slums in a car or bus, but it is not an important experience to him. The failures, the unskilled, the disabled, the aged, and the minorities are right there, across the tracks, where they have always been. But hardly anyone else is.

In short, the very development of the American city has removed poverty from the living, emotional experience of millions upon millions of middle-class Americans. Living out in the suburbs, it is easy to assume that ours is, indeed, an affluent society.

This new segregation of poverty is compounded by a well-meaning ignorance. A good many concerned and sympathetic Americans are aware that there is much discussion of urban renewal. Suddenly, driving through the city, they notice that a familiar slum has been torn down and that there are towering, modern buildings where once there had been tenements or hovels. There is a warm feeling of satisfaction, of pride in the way things are working out: the poor, it is obvious, are being taken care of.

The irony in this (as the chapter on housing will document) is that the truth is nearly the exact opposite to the impression. The total impact of the various housing programs in postwar America has been to squeeze more and more people into existing slums. More often than not, the modern apartment in a towering building rents at $40 a room or more. For, during the past decade and a half, there has been more subsidization of middle- and upper-income housing than there has been of housing for the poor. . . .

Then, many of the poor are the wrong age to be seen. A good number of them (over 8,000,000) are sixty-five years of age or better; an even larger number are under eighteen. The aged members of the other America are often sick, and they cannot move. Another group of them live out their lives in loneliness and frustration: they sit in rented rooms, or else they stay close to a house in a neighborhood that has completely changed from the old days. Indeed, one of the worst aspects of poverty among the aged is that these people are out of sight and out of mind, and alone.

The young are somewhat more visible, yet they too stay close to their neighborhoods. Sometimes they advertise their poverty through a lurid tabloid story about a gang killing. But generally they do not disturb the quiet streets of the middle class.

And finally, the poor are politically invisible. It is one of the cruelest ironies of social life in advanced countries that the dispossessed at the bottom of society are unable to speak for themselves. The people of the other America do not, by far and large, belong to unions, to fraternal organizations, or to political parties. They are without lobbies of their own; they put forward no legislative program. As a group, they are atomized. They have no face; they have no voice.

Thus, there is not even a cynical political motive for caring about the poor, as in the old days. Because the slums are no longer centers of powerful political organizations, the politicians need not really care about their inhabitants. The slums are no longer visible to the middle class, so much of the idealistic urge to fight for those who need help is gone. Only the social agencies have a really direct involvement with the other America, and they are without any great political power.

To the extent that the poor have a spokesman in American life, that role is played by the labor movement. The unions have their own particular idealism, an ideology of concern. More than that, they realize that the existence of a reservoir of cheap, unorganized labor is a menace to wages and working conditions throughout the entire economy. Thus, many union legislative proposals—to extend the coverage of minimum wage and social security, to organize migrant farm laborers—articulate the needs of the poor.

That the poor are invisible is one of the most important things about them. They are not simply neglected and forgotten as in the old rhetoric of reform; what is much worse, they are not seen. . . .

Out of the thirties came the welfare state. Its creation had been stimulated by mass impoverishment and misery, yet it helped the poor least of all. Laws like unemployment compensation, the Wagner Act, the various farm programs, all these were designed for the middle third in the cities, for the organized workers, and for the upper third in the country, for the big market farmers. If a man works in an extremely low-paying job, he may not even be covered by social security or other welfare programs. If he receives unemployment compensation, the payment is scaled down according to his low earnings.

One of the major laws that was designed to cover everyone, rich and poor, was social security. But even here the other Americans suffered discrimination. Over the years social security payments have not even provided a subsistence level of life. The middle third have been able to supplement the Federal pension through private plans negotiated by unions, through joining medical insurance schemes like Blue Cross, and so on. The poor have not been able to do so. They lead a bitter life, and then have to pay for that fact in old age.

Indeed, the paradox that the welfare state benefits those least who need help most is but a single instance of a persistent irony in the other America. Even when the money finally trickles down, even when a school is built in a poor neighborhood, for instance, the poor are still deprived. Their entire environment, their life, their values, do not prepare them to take advantage of the new opportunity. The parents are anxious for the children to go to work; the pupils are pent up, waiting for the moment when their education has compiled with the law.

Today's poor, in short, missed the political and social gains of the thirties. They are, as Galbraith rightly points out, the first minority poor in history, the first poor not to be seen, the first poor whom the politicians could leave alone.

The first step toward the new poverty was taken when millions of people proved immune to progress. When that happened, the failure was not individual and personal, but a social product. But once the historic accident takes place, it begins to become a personal fate.

The new poor of the other America saw the rest of society move ahead. They went on living in depressed areas, and often they tended to become depressed human beings. In some of the West Virginia towns, for instance, an entire community will become shabby and defeated. The young and the adventurous go to the city, leaving behind those who cannot move and those who lack the will to do so. The entire area becomes permeated with failure, and that is one more reason the big corporations shy away.

Indeed, one of the most important things about the new poverty is that it cannot be defined in simple, statistical terms. Throughout this book a crucial term is used: aspiration. If a group has internal vitality, a will—if it has aspiration—it may live in dilapidated housing, it may eat an inadequate diet, and it may suffer poverty, but it is not impoverished. So it was in those ethnic slums of the immigrants that played such a dramatic role in the unfolding of the American dream. The people found themselves in slums, but they were not slum dwellers.

But the new poverty is constructed so as to destroy aspiration; it is a system designed to be impervious to hope. The other America does not contain the adventurous seeking a new life and land. It is populated by the failures, by those driven from the land and bewildered by the city, by old people suddenly confronted with the torments of loneliness and poverty, and by minorities facing a wall of prejudice.

In the past, when poverty was general in the unskilled and semiskilled work force, the poor were all mixed together. The bright and the dull, those who were going to escape into the great society and those who were to stay behind, all of them lived on the same street. When the middle third rose, this community was destroyed. And the entire invisible land of the other Americans became a ghetto, a modern poor farm for the rejects of society and of the economy.

It is a blow to reform and the political hopes of the poor that the middle class no longer understands that poverty exists. But, perhaps more important, the poor are losing their links with the great world. If statistics and sociology can measure a feeling as delicate as loneliness (and some of the attempts to do so will be cited later on), the other America is becoming increasingly populated by those who do not belong to anybody or anything. They are no longer participants in an ethnic culture from the old country; they are less and less religious; they do not belong to unions or clubs. They are not seen, and because of that they themselves cannot see. Their horizon has become more and more restricted; they see one another, and that means they see little reason to hope. . . .

There are mighty historical and economic forces that keep the poor down; and there are human beings who help out in this grim business, many of them unwittingly. There are sociological and political reasons why poverty is not seen; and there are misconceptions and prejudices that literally blind the eyes. The latter must be understood if anyone is to make the necessary act of intellect and will so that the poor can be noticed.

Here is the most familiar version of social blindness: "The poor are that way because they are afraid of work. And anyway they all have big cars. If they were like me (or my father or my grandfather), they could pay their own way. But they prefer to live on the dole and cheat the taxpayers."

This theory, usually thought of as a virtuous and moral statement, is one of the means of making it impossible for the poor ever to pay their way. There are, one must assume, citizens of the other America who choose impoverishment out of fear of work (though, writing it down, I really do not believe it). But the real explanation of why the poor are where they are is that they made the mistake of being born to the wrong parents, in the wrong section of the country, in the wrong industry, or in the wrong racial or ethnic group. Once that mistake has been made, they could have been paragons of will and morality, but most of them would never even have had a chance to get out of the other America.

There are two important ways of saying this: The poor are caught in a vicious circle; or, The poor live in a culture of poverty.

In a sense, one might define the contemporary poor in the United States as those who, for reasons beyond their control, cannot help themselves. All the most decisive factors making for opportunity and advance are against them. They are born going downward, and most of them stay down. They are victims whose lives are endlessly blown round and round the other America.

Here is one of the most familiar forms of the vicious circle of poverty. The poor get sick more than anyone else in the society. That is because they live in slums, jammed together under unhygienic conditions; they have inadequate diets, and cannot get decent medical care. When they become sick, they are sick longer than any other group in the society. Because they are sick more often and longer than anyone else, they lose wages and work, and find it difficult to hold a steady job. And because of this, they cannot pay for good housing, for a nutritious diet, for doctors. At any given point in the circle, particularly when there is a major illness, their prospect is to move to an even lower level and to begin the cycle, round and round, toward even more suffering.

This is only one example of the vicious circle. Each group in the other America has its own particular version of the experience, and these will be detailed throughout this book. But the pattern, whatever its variations, is basic to the other America.

The individual cannot usually break out of this vicious circle. Neither can the group, for it lacks the social energy and political strength to turn its misery into a cause. Only the larger society, with its help and resources, can really make it possible for these people to help themselves. Yet those who could make the difference too often refuse to act because of their ignorant, smug moralisms. They view the effects of poverty—above all, the warping of the will and spirit that is a consequence of being poor—as choices. Understanding the vicious circle is an important step in breaking down this prejudice.

There is an even richer way of describing this same, general idea: Poverty in the United States is a culture, an institution, a way of life.

There is a famous anecdote about Ernest Hemingway and F. Scott Fitzgerald. Fitzgerald is reported to have remarked to Hemingway, "The rich are different." And Hemingway replied, "Yes, they have money." Fitzgerald had much the better of the exchange. He understood that being rich was not a simple fact, like a large bank account, but a way of looking at reality, a series of attitudes, a special type of life. If this is true of the rich, it is ten times truer of the poor. Everything about them, from the condition of their teeth to the way in which they love, is suffused and permeated by the fact of their poverty. And this is sometimes a hard idea for a Hemingway-like middle-class America to comprehend.

The family structure of the poor, for instance, is different from that of the rest of the society. There are more homes without a father, there are less marriage, more early pregnancy and, if Kinsey's statistical findings can be used, markedly different attitudes toward sex. As a result of this, to take but one consequence of the fact, hundreds of thousands, and perhaps millions, of children in the other America never know stability and "normal" affection.

Or perhaps the policeman is an even better example. For the middle class, the police protect property, give directions, and help old ladies. For the urban poor, the police are those who arrest you. In almost any slum there is a vast conspiracy against the forces of law and order. If someone approaches asking for a person, no one there will have heard of him, even if he lives next door. The outsider is "cop," bill collector, investigator (and, in the Negro ghetto, most dramatically, he is "the Man").

While writing this book, I was arrested for participation in a civil-rights demonstration. A brief experience of a night in a cell made an abstraction personal and immediate: the city jail is one of the basic institutions of the other America. Almost everyone whom I encountered in the "tank" was poor: skid-row whites, Negroes, Puerto Ricans. Their poverty was an incitement to arrest in the first place. (A policeman will be much more careful with a well-dressed, obviously educated man who might have political connections than he will with someone who is poor.) They did not have money for bail or for lawyers. And, perhaps most important, they waited their arraignment with stolidity, in a mood of passive acceptance. They expected the worst, and they probably got it.

There is, in short, a language of the poor, a psychology of the poor, a world view of the poor. To be impoverished is to be an internal alien, to grow up in a culture that is radically different from the one that dominates the society.

The poor can be described statistically; they can be analyzed as a group. But they need a novelist as well as a sociologist if we are to see them. They need an American Dickens to record the smell and texture and quality of their lives. The cycles and trends, the massive forces, must be seen as affecting persons who talk and think differently.

I am not that novelist. Yet in this book I have attempted to describe the faces behind the statistics, to tell a little of the "thickness" of personal life in the other America. Of necessity, I have begun with large groups: the dispossessed workers, the minorities, the farm poor, and the aged. Then, there are three cases of less massive types of poverty, including the only single humorous component in the other America. And finally, there are the slums, and the psychology of the poor.

Throughout, I work on an assumption that cannot be proved by Government figures or even documented by impressions of the other America. It is an ethical proposition, and it can be simply stated: In a nation with a technology that could provide every citizen with a decent life, it is an outrage and a scandal that there should be such social misery. Only if one begins with this assumption is it possible to pierce through the invisibility of 40,000,000 to 50,000,000 human beings and to see the other America. We must perceive passionately, if this blindness is to be lifted from us. A fact can be rationalized and explained away; an indignity cannot.

What shall we tell the American poor, once we have seen them? Shall we say to them that they are better off than the Indian poor, the Italian poor, the Russian poor? That is one answer, but it is heartless. I should put it another way. I want to tell every well-fed and optimistic American that it is intolerable that so many millions should be maimed in body and in spirit when it is not necessary that they should be. My standard of comparison is not how much worse things used to be. It is how much better they could be if only we were stirred.

7. STUDENTS FOR A DEMOCRATIC SOCIETY, "THE PORT HURON STATEMENT"

THE college students of the 1950's reflected the placidity of the Eisenhower Equilibrium. When their professors chastised them for their indifference, they merely yawned. By the late 1960's, however, many a mystified parent and harrassed university administrator yearned

SOURCE. Paul Jacobs and Saul Landau, eds., *The New Radicals*, New York: Vintage Books, 1966, pp. 150–151 and 155–162. Copyright 1966 by Students for a Democratic Society. Reprinted by permission.

for the peace of the Apathetic Generation. Idealistic young Americans, deeply disturbed by what they considered unnecessary racial discrimination, poverty, materialism, and militarism within American society, sought to correct these social ills. Some Americans believed reform impossible and simply dropped out of society to do their thing by joining the world of the Hippy, but most of them turned to social protest as the means of expressing their alienation.

By the late 1960's, the most important vehicle for mobilizing the new radicalism was the loosly organized <u>Students for a Democratic Society</u>. It <u>dismissed Marx as irrelevant</u> and <u>drew upon Emerson and Thoreau</u> for what little ideology it needed. It <u>condemned the</u> <u>"racism, militarism and imperialism"</u> <u>that it saw in American society while it advanced</u> <u>its vague, even romantic goal of a "participatory democracy."</u> Many leaders within the S.D.S. were willing to destroy American society if necessary in order to create a society based upon social justice. In 1968, the S.D.S. moved from "protest to resistance" and, in its first direct assault on the "Establishment," brought to a complete halt the activities of prestigious Columbia University when its members and their recruits took physical possession of key university buildings. To these young militants, Columbia's refusal to respond to student demands for reform and its acceptance of military research contracts symbolized the moral decay of American society. "Our goal is not to create a free university within an unfree society," one S.D.S. leader said. "Our goal is to create a free society."

To many Americans, S.D.S. was a revolutionary force to be feared and forcefully destroyed but, to others, it symbolized a rejuvenated moral spirit among American youth. The following selection is taken from the manifesto of the S.D.S., which was drafted in the summer of 1962 at a student conference near Port Huron, Michigan. Like much of the S.D.S. movement since then, the manifesto is characterized by what is wrong with American society, rather than what the organization intends to do about it.

We are people of this generation, bred in at least modest comfort, housed now in universities, looking uncomfortably to the world we inherit.

When we were kids the United States was the wealthiest and strongest country in the world; the only one with the atom bomb, the least scarred by modern war, an initiator of the United Nations that we thought would distribute Western influence throughout the world. Freedom and equality for each individual, government of, by, and for the people—these American values we found good, principles by which we could live as men. Many of us began maturing in complacency.

As we grew, however, our comfort was penetrated by events too troubling to dismiss. First, the permeating and victimizing fact of human degradation, symbolized by the Southern struggle against racial bigotry, compelled most of us from silence to activism. Second, the enclosing fact of the Cold War, symbolized by the presence of the Bomb, brought awareness that we ourselves, and our friends, and millions of abstract "others" we knew more directly because of our common peril, might die at any time. We might deliberately ignore, or avoid, or fail to feel all other human problems, but not these two, for these were too immediate and crushing in their impact, too challenging in the demand that we as individuals take the responsibility for encounter and resolution.

While these and other problems either directly oppressed us or rankled our consciences and became our own subjective concerns, we began to see complicated and disturbing paradoxes in our surrounding America. The declaration "all men are created equal . . ." rang hollow before the facts of Negro life in the South and the big cities of the North. The proclaimed peaceful intentions of the United States contradicted its economic and military investments in the Cold War status quo.

We witnessed, and continue to witness, other paradoxes. With nuclear energy whole cities can easily be powered, yet the dominant nation-states seem more likely to unleash destruction greater than that incurred in all wars of human history. Although our own technology is destroying old and creating new forms of social organization, men still tolerate meaningless work and idleness. While two-thirds of mankind suffers undernourishment, our own upper classes revel amidst superfluous abundance. Although world population is expected to double in forty years, the nations still tolerate anarchy as a major principle of international conduct and uncontrolled exploitation governs the sapping of the earth's physical resources. Although mankind desperately needs revolutionary leadership, America rests in national stalemate, its goals ambiguous and tradition-bound instead of informed and clear, its democratic system apathetic and manipulated rather than "of, by, and for the people."

Not only did tarnish appear on our image of American virtue, not only did disillusion occur when the hypocrisy of American ideals was discovered, but we began to sense that what we had originally seen as the American Golden Age was actually the decline of an era. The worldwide outbreak of revolution against colonialism and imperialism, the entrenchment of totalitarian states, the menace of war, overpopulation, international disorder, supertechnology—these trends were testing the tenacity of our own commitment to democracy and freedom and our abilities to visualize their application to a world in upheaval. . . .

We would replace power rooted in possession, privilege, or circumstance by power and uniqueness rooted in love, reflectiveness, reason, and creativity. As a *social system* we seek the establishment of a democracy of individual participation, governed by two central aims: that the individual share in those social decisions determining the quality and direction of his life; that society be organized to encourage independence in men and provide the media for their common participation.

In a participatory democracy, the political life would be based in several root principles:

that decision-making of basic social consequence be carried on by public groupings;

that politics be seen positively, as the art of collectively creating an acceptable pattern of social relations;

that politics has the function of bringing people out of isolation and into community, thus being a necessary, though not sufficient, means of finding meaning in personal life;

that the political order should serve to clarify problems in a way instrumental to their solution; it should provide outlets for the expression of personal grievance and aspiration; opposing views should be organized so as to illuminate choices and facilitate the attainment of goals; channels should be commonly available to relate men to knowledge and to power so that private problems—from bad recreation facilities to personal alienation—are formulated as general issues.

The economic sphere would have as its basis the principles:

that work should involve incentives worthier than money or survival. It should be educative, not stultifying; creative, not mechanical; self-directed, not manipulated, encouraging independence, a respect for others, a sense of dignity and a willingness to accept social responsibility, since it is this experience that has crucial influence on habits, perceptions and individual ethics;

that the economic experience is so personally decisive that the individual must share in its full determination;

that the economy itself is of such social importance that its major resources and means of production should be open to democratic participation and subject to democratic social regulation.

Like the political and economic ones, major social institutions—cultural, educational, rehabilitative, and others—should be generally organized with the well-being and dignity of man as the essential measure of success.

In social change or interchange, we find violence to be abhorrent because it requires generally the transformation of the target, be it a human being or a community of people, into a depersonalized object of hate. It is imperative that the means of violence be abolished and the institutions—local, national, international—that encourage nonviolence as a condition of conflict be developed.

These are our central values, in skeletal form. It remains vital to understand their denial or attainment in the context of the modern world. . . .

"Students don't even give a damn about the apathy," one has said. Apathy toward apathy begets a privately constructed universe, a place of systematic study schedules, two nights each week for beer, a girl or two, and early marriage; a framework infused with personality, warmth, and under control, no matter how unsatisfying otherwise.

Under these conditions university life loses all relevance to some. Four hundred thousand of our classmates leave college every year.

But apathy is not simply an attitude; it is a product of social institutions, and of the structure and organization of higher education itself. The extracurricular life is ordered according to *in loco parentis* theory, which ratifies the administration as the moral guardian of the young.

The accompanying "let's pretend" theory of student extracurricular affairs validates student government as a training center for those who want to spend their lives in political pretense, and discourages initiative from the more articulate, honest, and sensitive students. The bounds and style of controversy are delimited before controversy begins. The university "prepares" the student for "citizenship" through perpetual rehearsals and, usually, through emasculation of what creative spirit there is in the individual.

The academic life contains reinforcing counterparts to the way in which extracurricular life is organized. The academic world is founded on a teacher-student relation analogous to the parent-child relation which characterizes *in loco parentis*. Further, academia includes a radical separation of the student from the material of study. That which is studied, the social reality, is "objectified" to sterility, dividing the student from life—just as he is restrained in active involvement by the deans controlling student government. The specialization of function and knowledge, admittedly necessary to our complex technological and social structure, has produced an exaggerated compartmentalization of study and understanding. This has contributed to an overly parochial view, by faculty, of the role of its research and scholarship, to a discontinuous and truncated understanding, by students, of the surrounding social order; and to a loss of personal attachment, by nearly all, to the worth of study as a humanistic enterprise.

There is, finally, the cumbersome academic bureaucracy extending throughout the academic as well as the extracurricular structures, contributing to the sense of outer complexity and inner powerlessness that transforms the honest searching of many students to a ratification of convention and, worse, to a numbness to present and future catastrophes. The size and financing systems of the university enhance the permanent trusteeship of the administrative bureaucracy, their power leading to a shift within the university toward the value standards of business and the administrative mentality. Huge foundations and other private financial interests shape the under-financed colleges and universities, not only making them more commercial, but less disposed to diagnose society critically, less open to dissent. Many social and physical scientists, neglecting the liberating heritage of higher learning, develop "human relations" or "morale-producing" techniques for the corporate economy, while others exercise their intellectual skills to accelerate the arms race. . . .

The American political system is not the democratic model of which its glorifiers speak. In actuality it frustrates democracy by confusing the individual citizen, paralyzing policy discussion, and consolidating the irresponsible power of military and business interests.

A crucial feature of the political apparatus in America is that greater differences are harbored within each major party than the differences existing between them. Instead of two parties presenting distinctive and significant differences of approach, what dominates the system is a natural interlocking of Democrats from Southern states with the more conservative elements of the Republican Party. This arrangement of forces is blessed by the seniority system of Congress which guarantees Congressional committee domination by conservatives—ten of seventeen committees in the Senate and thirteen of twenty-one in the House of Representatives are chaired currently by Dixiecrats.

The party overlap, however, is not the only structural antagonist of democracy in politics. First, the localized nature of the party system does not encourage discussion of national and international issues: thus problems are not raised by and for people, and political representatives usually are unfettered from any responsibilities to the general public except those regarding parochial matters. Second, whole constituencies are divested of the full political power they might have: many Negroes in the South are prevented from voting, migrant workers are disenfranchised by various residence requirements, some urban and suburban dwellers are victimized by gerrymandering, and poor people are too often without the power to obtain political representation. Third, the focus of political attention is significantly distorted by the enormous lobby force, composed predominantly of business interests, spending hundreds of millions each year in an attempt to conform facts about productivity, agriculture, defense, and social services, to the wants of private economic groupings.

What emerges from the party contradiction and insulation of privately held power is the organized political stalemate: calcification dominates flexibility as the principle of parliamentary organization, frustration is the expectancy of legislators intending liberal reform, and Congress becomes less and less central to national decision-making, especially in the area of foreign policy. In this context, confusion and blurring is built into the formulation of issues, long-range priorities are not discussed in the rational manner needed for policy-making, the politics of personality and "image" become a more important mechanism than the construction of issues in a way that affords each voter a challenging and real option. The American voter is buffeted from all directions by pseudo-problems, by the structurally initiated sense that nothing political is subject to human mastery. Worried by his mundane problems which never get solved, but constrained by the common belief that politics is an agonizingly slow accommodation of views, he quits all pretense of bothering.

A most alarming fact is that few, if any, politicians are calling for changes in these conditions. Only a handful even are calling on the President to "live up to" platform pledges; no one is demanding structural changes, such as the shuttling of Southern Democrats out of the Democratic Party. Rather than protesting the state of politics, most politicians are reinforcing and aggravating that state. While in practice they rig public opinion to suit their own interests, in word and ritual they enshrine "the sovereign public" and call for more and more letters. Their speeches and campaign actions are banal, based on a degrading conception of what people want to hear. They respond not to dialogue, but to pressure: and knowing this, the ordinary citizen sees even greater inclination to shun the political sphere. The politician is usually a trumpeter to "citizenship" and "service to the nation," but since he is unwilling to seriously rearrange power relationships, his trumpetings only increase apathy by creating no outlets. Much of the time the call to "service" is justified not in idealistic terms, but in the crasser terms of "defending the free world from Communism"—thus making future idealistic impulses harder to justify in anything but Cold War terms.

In such a setting of status quo politics, where most if not all government activity is rationalized in Cold War anti-Communist terms, it is somewhat natural that discontented, super-patriotic groups would emerge through political channels and explain their ultra-conservatism as the best means of Victory over Communism. They have become a politically influential force within the Republican Party, at a national level through Senator Goldwater, and at a local level through their important social and economic roles. Their political views are defined generally as the opposite of the supposed views of Communists: complete individual freedom in the economic sphere, nonparticipation by the government in the machinery of production. But actually "anti-Communism" becomes an umbrella by which to protest liberalism, internationalism, welfareism, the active civil rights and labor movements. It is to the disgrace of the United States that such a movement should become a prominent kind of public participation in the modern world —but, ironically, it is somewhat to the interests of the United States that such a movement should be a public constituency pointed toward realignment of the political parties, demanding a conservative Republican Party in the South and an exclusion of the "leftist" elements of the national G.O.P.

8. STOKLEY CARMICHAEL, "WHAT WE WANT"

BEGINNING with the sit-ins and freedom rides at the onset of the 1960's, the drive for Negro equality took on new urgency and meaning. "Freedom Now!" became the rallying cry for a determined group of black students and their white allies. The march on Washington on August 28, 1963, by over 200,000 persons and the subsequent enactment of the far-reaching civil rights acts of 1964 and 1965 climaxed successfully this phase of the movement.

As the realization that demonstrations and civil rights legislation alone would not lift the great majority of blacks out of their impoverished position, the movement became more diversified in tactics and goals. One segment of the black community veered sharply away from the nonviolent techniques preached by Dr. Martin Luther King, Jr., and condemned the gradualist approach of the NAACP. A new vanguard of leaders emerged. They were young, educated, and extremely angry. Calling for "Black Power," they argued that only blacks could advance themselves.

"The extremists of this country are the white people who force us to live the way we live," Student Nonviolent Coordinating Committee Chairman Stokley Carmichael proclaimed. Echoing the teachings of the martyred Malcolm X, he argued that, "We are the only people who have to protect themselves from our protectors." Only through Black Power, this bitter young man said, could the black man escape his present condition. "We have got to organize to speak from a position of strength and to stop begging people to look kindly upon us. We are going to build a movement in this country based on the color of our skin that is going to free us from our oppressors and we have to do that ourselves."

One of the tragedies of the struggle against racism is that up to now there has been no national organization which could speak to the growing militancy of young black people in the urban ghetto. There has been only a civil rights movement, whose tone of voice was adapted to an audience of liberal whites. It served as a sort of buffer zone between them and angry young blacks. None of its so-called leaders could go into a rioting community and be

SOURCE. Stokley Carmichael, "What We Want," in *The New York Review of Books*, Vol. 7, September 22, 1966, pp. 5–6 and 8. Copyright 1966, *The New York Review of Book*, Reprinted by permission of the Student Nonviolent Coordinating Committee.

listened to. In a sense, I blame ourselves—together with the mass media—for what has happened in Watts, Harlem, Chicago, Cleveland, Omaha. Each time the people in those cities saw Martin Luther King get slapped, they became angry; when they saw four little black girls bombed to death, they were angrier; and when nothing happened, they were steaming. We had nothing to offer that they could see, except to go out and be beaten again. We helped to build their frustration.

For too many years, black Americans marched and had their heads broken and got shot. They were saying to the country, "Look, you guys are supposed to be nice guys and we are only going to do what we are supposed to do— why do you beat us up, why don't you give us what we ask, why don't you straighten yourselves out?" After years of this, we are at almost the same point—because we demonstrated from a position of weakness. We cannot be expected any longer to march and have our heads broken in order to say to whites: come on, you're nice guys. For you are not nice guys. We have found you out.

An organization which claims to speak for the needs of a community—as does the Student Nonviolent Coordinating Committee—must speak in the tone of that community, not as somebody else's buffer zone. This is the significance of black power as a slogan. For once, black people are going to use the words they want to use—not just the words whites want to hear. And they will do this no matter how often the press tries to stop the use of the slogan by equating it with racism or separatism.

An organization which claims to be working for the needs of a community —as SNCC does—must work to provide that community with a position of strength from which to make its voice heard. This is the significance of black power beyond the slogan.

Black power can be clearly defined for those who do not attach the fears of white America to their questions about it. We should begin with the basic fact that black Americans have two problems: they are poor and they are black. All other problems arise from this two-sided reality: lack of education, the so-called apathy of black men. Any program to end racism must address itself to that double reality.

Almost from its beginning, SNCC sought to address itself to both conditions with a program aimed at winning political power for impoverished Southern blacks. We had to begin with politics because black Americans are a propertyless people in a country where property is valued above all. We had to work for power, because this country does not function by morality, love, and nonviolence, but by power. Thus we determined to win political power, with the idea of moving on from there into activity that would have economic effects. With power, the masses could *make or participate in making* the decisions which govern their destinies, and thus create basic change in their day-to-day lives.

But if political power seemed to be the key to self-determination, it was also obvious that the key had been thrown down a deep well many years earlier. Disenfranchisement, maintained by racist terror, made it impossible to talk about organizing for political power in 1960. The right to vote had to be won, and SNCC workers devoted their energies to this from 1961 to 1965. They set up voter registration drives in the Deep South. They created pressure for the vote by holding mock elections in Mississippi in 1963 and by helping to establish the Mississippi Freedom Democratic Party (MFDP) in 1964. That struggle was eased, though not won, with the passage of the 1965 Voting Rights Act. SNCC workers could then address themselves to the question: "Who can we vote for, to have our needs met—how do we make our vote meaningful?"

SNCC had already gone to Atlantic City for recognition of the Mississippi Freedom Democratic Party by the Democratic convention and been rejected; it had gone with the MFDP to Washington for recognition by Congress and been rejected. In Arkansas, SNCC helped thirty Negroes to run for School Board elections; all but one were defeated, and there was evidence of fraud and intimidation sufficient to cause their defeat. In Atlanta, Julian Bond ran for the state legislature and was elected—twice—and unseated—twice. In several states, black farmers ran in elections for agricultural committees which make crucial decisions concerning land use, loans, etc. Although they won places on a number of committees, they never gained the majorities needed to control them.

All of the efforts were attempts to win black power. Then, in Alabama, the opportunity came to see how blacks could be organized on an independent party basis. An unusual Alabama law provides that any group of citizens can nominate candidates for county office and, if they win 20 percent of the vote, may be recognized as a county political party. The same then applies on a state level. SNCC went to organize in several counties such as Lowndes, where black people—who form 80 percent of the population and have an average annual income of $943—felt they could accomplish nothing within the framework of the Alabama Democratic Party because of its racism and because the qualifying fee for this year's elections was raised from $50 to $500 in order to prevent most Negroes from becoming candidates. On May 3, five new county "freedom organizations" convened and nominated candidates for the offices of sheriff, tax assessor, members of the school boards. These men and women are up for election in November—if they live until then. Their ballot symbol is the black panther: a bold, beautiful animal, representing the strength and dignity of black demands today. A man needs a black panther on his side when he and his family must endure—as hundreds of Alabamians have endured—loss of job, eviction, starvation, and sometimes death, for political activity. He may also need a gun and SNCC reaffirms the right of black men everywhere to defend themselves when threatened or attacked. As for initiating the use of violence, we hope that such programs as ours will make that unnecessary; but it is not for us to tell black communities whether they can or cannot use any particular form of action to resolve their problems. Responsibility for the use of violence by black men, whether in self-defense or initiated by them, lies with the white community.

This is the specific historical experience from which SNCC's call for "black power" emerged on the Mississippi march last July. But the concept of "black power" is not a recent or isolated phenomenon: It has grown out of the ferment of agitation and activity by different people and organizations in many black communities over the years. Our last year of work in Alabama added a new concrete possibility. In Lowndes county, for example, black power will mean that if a Negro is elected sheriff, he can end police brutality. If a black man is elected tax assessor, he can collect and channel funds for the building of better roads and schools serving black people—thus advancing the move from political power into the economic arena. In such areas as Lowndes, where black men have a majority, they will attempt to use it to exercise control. This is what they seek: control. Where Negroes lack a majority, black power means proper representation and sharing of control. It means the creation of power bases from which black people can work to change statewide or nationwide patterns of oppression through pressure from strength—instead of weakness. Politically, black power means what it has always meant to SNCC: the coming-together of black people to elect representatives and to force those representatives to speak to their needs. It does not mean merely putting black faces into office. A man or woman who is black and from the slums cannot be automatically expected to speak to the needs of black people. Most of the black politicians we see around the country today are not what SNCC means by black power. The power must be that of a community, and emanate from there.

SNCC today is working in both North and South on programs of voter registration and independent political organizing. In some places, such as Alabama, Los Angeles, New York, Philadelphia, and New Jersey, independent organizing under the black panther symbol is in progress. The creation of a national "black panther party" must come about; it will take time to build, and it is much too early to predict its success. We have no infallible master plan and we make no claim to exclusive knowledge of how to end racism; different groups will work in their own different ways. SNCC cannot spell out the full logistics of self-determination but it can address itself to the problem by helping black communities define their needs, realize their strength, and go into action along a variety of lines which they must choose for themselves. Without knowing all the answers, It can address itself to the basic problem of poverty; to the fact that in Lowndes County, 86 white families own 90 percent of the land. What are black people in that county going to do for jobs, where are they going to get money? There must be reallocation of land, of money.

Ultimately, the economic foundations of this country must be shaken if black people are to control their lives. The colonies of the United States—and this includes the black ghettoes within its borders, north and south—must be liberated. For a century, this nation has been like an octopus of exploitation, its tentacles stretching from Mississippi and Harlem to South America, the Middle East, southern Africa, and Vietnam; the form of exploitation varies from area to area but the essential result has been the same—a powerful few have been maintained and enriched at the expense of the poor and voiceless colored masses. This pattern must be broken. As its grip loosens here and there around the world, the hopes of black Americans become more realistic. For racism to die, a totally different America must be born.

This is what the white society does not wish to face; this is why that society prefers to talk about integration. But integration speaks not at all to the problem of poverty, only to the problem of blackness. Integration today means the man who "makes it," leaving his black brothers behind in the ghetto as fast as his new sports car will take him. It has no relevance to the Harlem wino or to the cottonpicker making three dollars a day. As a lady I know in Alabama once said, "the food that Ralph Bunche eats doesn't fill my stomach."

Integration, moreover, speaks to the problem of blackness in a despicable way. As a goal, it has been based on complete acceptance of the fact that *in order to have* a decent house or education, blacks must move into a white neighborhood or send their children to a white school. This reinforces, among both black and white, the idea that "white" is automatically better and "black" is by definition inferior. This is why integration is a subterfuge for the maintenance of white supremacy. It allows the nation to focus on a handful of Southern children who get into white schools, at great price, and to ignore the 94 percent who are left behind in unimproved all-black schools. Such situations will not change until black people have power—to control their own school boards, in this case. Then Negroes become equal in a way that means something, and integration ceases to be a one-way street. Then integration doesn't mean draining skills and energies from the ghetto into white neighborhoods; then it can mean white people moving from Beverly Hills into Watts, white people joining the Lowndes County Freedom Organization. Then integration becomes relevant.

Last April, before the furor over black power, Christopher Jencks wrote in a *New Republic* article on white Mississippi's manipulation of the anti-poverty program:

The war on poverty has been predicated on the notion that there is such a thing as *a community* which can be defined geographically and mobilized for a collective effort to help the poor. This theory has no relationship to reality in the Deep South. In every Mississippi county there are *two* communities. Despite all the pious platitudes of the moderates on both sides, these two communities habitually see their interests in terms of conflict rather than cooperation. Only when the Negro community can muster enough political, economic and professional strength to compete on somewhat equal terms, will Negroes believe in the possibility of true cooperation and whites accept its necessity. En route to integration, the Negro community needs to develop greater independence—a chance to run its own affairs and not cave in whenever "the man" barks. . . . Or so it seems to me, and to most of the knowledgeable people with whom I talked in Mississippi. To OEO, this judgment may sound like black nationalism . . . .

Mr. Jencks, a white reporter, perceived the reason why America's anti-poverty program has been a sick farce in both North and South. In the South, it is clearly racism which prevents the poor from running their own programs; in the North, it more often seems to be politicking and bureaucracy. But the results are not so different: In the North, non-whites make up 42 percent of all families in metropolitan "poverty areas" and only 6 percent of families in areas classified as not poor. SNCC has been working with local residents in Arkansas, Alabama, and Mississippi to achieve control by the poor of the program and its funds; it has also been working with groups in the North, and the struggle is no less difficult. Behind it all is a federal government which cares far more about winning the war on the Vietnamese than the war on poverty; which has put the poverty program in the hands of self-serving politicians and bureaucrats rather than the poor themselves; which is unwilling to curb the misuse of white power but quick to condemn black power.

To most whites, black power seems to mean that the Mau Mau are coming to the surburbs at night. The Mau Mau are coming, and whites must stop them. Articles appear about plots to "get Whitey," creating an atmosphere in which "law and order must be maintained." Once again, responsibility is shifted from the oppressor to the oppressed. Other whites chide, "Don't forget—you're only 10 percent of the population; if you get too smart, we'll wipe you out." If they are liberals, they complain, "what about me?—don't you want my help any more?" These are people supposedly concerned about black Americans, but today they think first of themselves, of their feelings of rejection. Or they admonish, "you can't get anywhere without coalitions," without considering the problems of coalition with whom?; on what terms? (coalescing from weakness can mean absorption, betrayal); when? Or they accuse us of "polarizing the races" by our calls for black unity, when the true responsibility for polarization lies with whites who will not accept their responsibility as the majority power for making the democratic process work.

White America will not face the problem of color, the reality of it. The well-intended say: "We're all human, everybody is really decent, we must forget color." But color cannot be "forgotten" until its weight is recognized and dealt with. White America will not acknowledge that the ways in which this country sees itself are contradicted by being black—and always have been. Whereas most of the people who settled this country came here for freedom or for economic opportunity, blacks were brought here to be slaves. When the Lowndes County Freedom Organization chose the black panther as its symbol, it was christened by the press "the Black Panther Party"—but the Alabama Democratic Party, whose symbol is a rooster, has never been called the White Cock Party. No one ever talked about "white power" because power in this country *is* white. All this adds up to more than merely identifying a group phenomenon by some catchy name or adjective. The furor over that black panther reveals the problems that white America has with color and sex; the furor over "black power" reveals how deep racism runs and the great fear which is attached to it.

Whites will not see that I, for example, as a person oppressed because of my blackness, have common cause with other blacks who are oppressed because of blackness. This is not to say that there are no white people who see things as I do, but that it is black people I must speak to first. It must be the oppressed to whom SNCC addresses itself primarily, not to friends from the oppressing group.

From birth, black people are told a set of lies about themselves. We are told that we are lazy—yet I drive through the Delta area of Mississippi and watch black people picking cotton in the hot sun for fourteen hours. We are told, "If you work hard, you'll succeed"—but if that were true, black people would own this country. We are oppressed because we are black—not because we are ignorant, not because we are lazy, not because we're stupid (and got good rhythm), but because we're black.

I remember that when I was a boy, I used to go to see Tarzan movies on Saturday. White Tarzan used to beat up the black natives. I would sit there yelling, "Kill the beasts, kill the savages, kill 'em!" I was saying: Kill *me*. It was as if a Jewish boy watched Nazis taking Jews off to concentration camps and cheered them on. Today, I want the chief to beat hell out of Tarzan and send him back to Europe. But it takes time to become free of the lies and their shaming effect on black minds. It takes time to reject the most important lie; that black people inherently can't do the same things white people can do, unless white people help them.

The need for psychological equality is the reason why SNCC today believes that blacks must organize in the black community. Only black people can convey the revolutionary idea that black people are able to do things themselves. Only they can help create in the community an aroused and continuing black consciousness that will provide the basis for political strength. In the past, white allies have furthered white supremacy without the whites involved realizing it—or wanting it, I think. Black people must do things for themselves; they must get poverty money they will control and spend themselves, they must conduct tutorial programs themselves so that black children can identify with black people. This is one reason Africa has such importance: The reality of black men ruling their own nations gives blacks elsewhere a sense of possibility, of power, which they do not now have.

This does not mean we don't welcome help, or friends. But we want the right to decide whether anyone is, in fact, our friend. In the past, black Americans have been almost the only people whom everybody and his momma could jump up and call their friends. We have been tokens, symbols, objects—as I was in high school to many young whites, who liked having "a Negro friend." We want to decide who is our friend, and we will not accept someone who comes to us and says: "If you do X, Y, and Z, then I'll help you." We will not be told whom we should choose as allies. We will not be isolated from any group or nation except by our own choice. We cannot have the oppressors telling the oppressed how to rid themselves of the oppressor.

I have said that most liberal whites react to "black power" with the question, What about me?, rather than saying: Tell me what you want me to do and I'll see if I can do it. There are answers to the right question. One of the most disturbing things about almost all white supporters of the movement has been that they are afraid to go into their own communities—which is where the racism exists—and work to get rid of it. They want to run from Berkeley to tell us what to do in Mississippi; let them look instead at Berkeley. They admonish blacks to be nonviolent; let them preach nonviolence in the white community. They come to teach me Negro history; let them go to the suburbs and open up freedom schools for whites. Let them work to stop America's racist foreign policy; let them press this government to cease supporting the economy of South Africa.

There is a vital job to be done among poor whites. We hope to see, eventually, a coalition between poor blacks and poor whites. That is the only coalition which seems acceptable to us, and we see such a coalition as the major internal instrument of change in American society. SNCC has tried several times to organize poor whites; we are trying again now, with an initial training program in Tennessee. It is purely academic today to talk about bringing poor blacks and whites together, but the job of creating a poor-white power bloc must be attempted. The main responsibility for it falls upon whites. Black and white can work together in the white community where possible; it is not possible, however, to go into a poor Southern town and talk about integration. Poor whites everywhere are becoming more hostile—not less—partly because they see the nation's attention focused on black poverty and nobody coming to them. Too many young middle-class Americans, like some sort of Pepsi generation, have wanted to come alive through the black community; they've wanted to be where the action is—and the action has been in the black community.

Black people do not want to "take over" this country. They don't want to "get whitey"; they just want to get him off their backs, as the saying goes. It was for example the exploitation by Jewish landlords and merchants which first created black resentment toward Jews—not Judaism. The white man is irrelevant to blacks, except as an oppressive force. Blacks want to be in his place, yes, but not in order to terrorize and lynch and starve him. They want to be in his place because that is where a decent life can be had.

But our vision is not merely of a society in which all black men have enough to buy the good things of life. When we urge that black money go into black pockets, we mean the communal pocket. We want to see money go back into the community and used to benefit it. We want to see the cooperative concept applied in business and banking. We want to see black ghetto residents demand that an exploiting landlord or storekeeper sell them, at minimal cost, a building or a shop that they will own and improve cooperatively; they can back their demand with a rent strike, or a boycott, and a community so unified behind them that no one else will move into the building or buy at the store. The society we seek to build among black people, then, is not a capitalist one. It is a society in which the spirit of community and humanistic love prevail. The word love is suspect; black expectations of what it might produce have been betrayed too often. But those were expectations of a response from the white community, which failed us. The love we seek to encourage is within the black community, the only American community where men call each other "brother" when they meet. We can build a community of love only where we have the ability and power to do so: among blacks.

As for white America, perhaps it can stop crying out against "black supremacy," "black nationalism," "racism in reverse," and begin facing reality. The reality is that this nation, from top to bottom, is racist; that racism is not primarily a problem of "human relations" but of an exploitation maintained—either actively or through silence—by the society as a whole. Camus and Sartre have asked, can a man condemn himself? Can whites, particularly liberal whites, condemn themselves? Can they stop blaming us, and blame their own system? Are they capable of the shame which might become a revolutionary emotion?

We have found that they usually cannot condemn themselves, and so we have done it. But the rebuilding of this society, if at all possible, is basically the responsibility of whites—not blacks. We won't fight to save the present society, in Vietnam or anywhere else. We are just going to work, in the way *we* see fit, and on goals *we* define, not for civil rights but for all our human rights.

9. LYNDON B. JOHNSON, "THE GREAT SOCIETY"

WHEN Lyndon Johnson entered the House of Representatives in 1937, he soon became a favorite protégé of Franklin Roosevelt. The influence of Roosevelt upon Johnson is unmistakable. An heir of Texas populism and a staunch New Dealer, Johnson sought to extend and expand upon the social and economic programs of the New Deal during his own Presidency. Johnson's conception of a Great Society, however, went beyond the somewhat limited boundaries of the New Deal and sought to improve the quality of American life. The emphasis on preserving the beauty of America and obliterating the ugliness, the revitalization of the cities, and improved educational opportunities reflected the new directions taken by postwar liberalism. Assuming that America's abundance could ultimately be extended to all citizens, Johnson raised the crucial question of "whether we have the wisdom to use that wealth to enrich and elevate our national life, and to advance the quality of our American civilization." It seemed to many social critics that the seemingly unsophisticated Texan would lead the United States into a new era of social and esthetic concern. Unfortunately, the President's dreams of a Great Society were destroyed by the harsh realities of war in Vietnam. That military effort siphoned off important resources, split the Johnsonian consensus, and severely drained the American people of their idealism. Like the more than 31,000 American soldiers killed in Vietnam, the Great Society became another war casualty.

I have come today from the turmoil of your Capital to the tranquility of your campus to speak about the future of your country.

The purpose of protecting the life of our Nation and preserving the liberty of our citizens is to pursue the happiness of our people. Our success in that pursuit is the test of our success as a Nation.

For a century we labored to settle and to subdue a continent. For half a century we called upon unbounded invention and untiring industry to create an order of plenty for all of our people.

The challenge of the next half century is whether we have the wisdom to use that wealth to enrich and elevate our national life, and to advance the quality of our American civilization.

Your imagination, your initiative, and your indignation will determine

SOURCE. Lyndon B. Johnson, Address at Ann Arbor, Michigan, May 22, 1964, in *Public Papers of the Presidents of the United States, Lyndon B. Johnson, 1964*, Washington, D.C.: United States Printing Office, pp. 704–707.

whether we build a society where progress is the servant of our needs, or a society where old values and new visions are buried under unbridled growth. For in your time we have the opportunity to move not only toward the rich society and the powerful society, but upward to the Great Society.

The Great Society rests on abundance and liberty for all. It demands an end to poverty and racial injustice, to which we are totally committed in our time. But that is just the beginning.

The Great Society is a place where every child can find knowledge to enrich his mind and to enlarge his talents. It is a place where leisure is a welcome chance to build and reflect, not a feared cause of boredom and restlessness. It is a place where the city of man serves not only the needs of the body and the demands of commerce but the desire for beauty and the hunger for community.

It is a place where man can renew contact with nature. It is a place which honors creation for its own sake and for what it adds to the understanding of the race. It is a place where men are more concerned with the quality of their goals than the quantity of their goods.

But most of all, the Great Society is not a safe harbor, a resting place, a final objective, a finished work. It is a challenge constantly renewed, beckoning us toward a destiny where the meaning of our lives matches the marvelous products of our labor.

So I want to talk to you today about three places where we begin to build the Great Society—in our cities, in our countryside, and in our classrooms.

Many of you will live to see the day, perhaps 50 years from now, when there will be 400 million Americans—four-fifths of them in urban areas. In the remainder of this century urban population will double, city land will double, and we will have to build homes, highways, and facilities equal to all those built since this country was first settled. So in the next 40 years we must rebuild the entire urban United States.

Aristotle said: "Men come together in cities in order to live, but they remain together in order to live the good life." It is harder and harder to live the good life in American cities today.

The catalog of ills is long: there is the decay of the centers and the despoiling of the suburbs. There is not enough housing for our people or transportation for our traffic. Open land is vanishing and old landmarks are violated.

Worst of all expansion is eroding the precious and time honored values of community with neighbors and communion with nature. The loss of these values breeds loneliness and boredom and indifference.

Our society will never be great until our cities are great. Today the frontier of imagination and innovation is inside those cities and not beyond their borders.

New experiments are already going on. It will be the task of your generation to make the American city a place where future generations will come, not only to live but to live the good life.

I understand that if I stayed here tonight I would see that Michigan students are really doing their best to live the good life.

This is the place where the Peace Corps was started. It is inspiring to see how all of you, while you are in this country, are trying so hard to live at the level of the people.

A second place where we begin to build the Great Society is in our countryside. We have always prided ourselves on being not only America the strong and America the free, but America the beautiful. Today that beauty is in danger. The water we drink, the food we eat, the very air that we breathe, are threatened with pollution. Our parks are overcrowded, our seashores overburdened. Green fields and dense forests are disappearing.

A few years ago we were greatly concerned about the "Ugly American." Today we must act to prevent an ugly America.

For once the battle is lost, once our natural splendor is destroyed, it can never be recaptured. And once man can no longer walk with beauty or wonder at nature his spirit will wither and his sustenance be wasted.

A third place to build the Great Society is in the classrooms of America. There your children's lives will be shaped. Our society will not be great until every young mind is set free to scan the farthest reaches of thought and imagination. We are still far from that goal.

Today, 8 million adult Americans, more than the entire population of Michigan, have not finished 5 years of school. Nearly 20 million have not finished 8 years of school. Nearly 54 million—more than one-quarter of all America—have not even finished high school.

Each year more than 100,000 high school graduates, with proved ability, do not enter college because they cannot afford it. And if we cannot educate today's youth, what will we do in 1970 when elementary school enrollment will be 5 million greater than 1960? And high school enrollment will rise by 5 million. College enrollment will increase by more than 3 million.

In many places, classrooms are overcrowded and curricula are outdated. Most of our qualified teachers are underpaid, and many of our paid teachers are unqualified. So we must give every child a place to sit and a teacher to learn from. Poverty must not be a bar to learning, and learning must offer an escape from poverty.

But more classrooms and more teachers are not enough. We must seek an educational system which grows in excellence as it grows in size. This means better training for our teachers. It means preparing youth to enjoy their hours of leisure as well as their hours of labor. It means exploring new techniques of teaching, to find new ways to stimulate the love of learning and the capacity for creation.

These are three of the central issues of the Great Society. While our Government has many programs directed at those issues, I do not pretend that we have the full answer to those problems.

But I do promise this: We are going to assemble the best thought and the broadest knowledge from all over the world to find those answers for America. I intend to establish working groups to prepare a series of White House conferences and meetings—on the cities, on natural beauty, on the quality of education, and on other emerging challenges. And from these meetings and from this inspiration and from these studies we will begin to set our course toward the Great Society.

The solution to these problems does not rest on a massive program in Washington, nor can it rely solely on the strained resources of local authority. They require us to create new concepts of cooperation, a creative federalism, between the National Capital and the leaders of local communities.

Woodrow Wilson once wrote: "Every man sent out from his university should be a man of his Nation as well as a man of his time."

Within your lifetime powerful forces, already loosed, will take us toward a way of life beyond the realm of our experience, almost beyond the bounds of our imagination.

For better or for worse, your generation has been appointed by history to deal with those problems and to lead America toward a new age. You have the chance never before afforded to any people in any age. You can help build a society where the demands of morality, and the needs of the spirit, can be realized in the life of the Nation.

So, will you join in the battle to give every citizen the full equality which God enjoins and the law requires, whatever his belief, or race, or the color of his skin?

Will you join in the battle to give every citizen an escape from the crushing weight of poverty?

Will you join in the battle to make it possible for all nations to live in enduring peace—as neighbors and not as mortal enemies?

Will you join in the battle to build the Great Society, to prove that our material progress is only the foundation on which we will build a richer life of mind and spirit?

There are those timid souls who say this battle cannot be won; that we are condemned to a soulless wealth. I do not agree. We have the power to shape the civilization that we want. But we need your will, your labor, your hearts, if we are to build that kind of society.

Those who came to this land sought to build more than just a new country. They sought a new world. So I have come here today to your campus to say that you can make their vision our reality. So let us from this moment begin our work so that in the future men will look back and say: It was then, after a long and weary way, that man turned the exploits of his genius to the full enrichment of his life.

Thank you. Goodby.

10. UNITED STATES RIOT COMMISSION REPORT, "WHY DID IT HAPPEN? THE BASIC CAUSES"

BETWEEN August 11 and August 16, 1965, the Negro section of Los Angeles was turned into a nightmarish battleground. The statistics of that blazing racial inferno are staggering: thirty-four dead, 1032 injured, 3438 arrested, property losses over $40,000,-000. This, however, was just the beginning; in the "long hot summer" of 1967, the same story was repeated in Newark and Detroit, and scores of other cities were hit by lesser levels of violence. The sources of the disorders, as the following selection indicates, are many and varied: Inferior housing, unemployment, police conduct, and a pervasive white racism have been singled out as major factors by the President's Commission on Civil Disorders.

Behind all of the theories and statistics, however, lies the fundamental fact that the American Negro is unwilling to accept the degrading social and economic conditions of the black ghettos into which he has been forced. And he knows that Whitey is to blame: "What white Americans have never fully understood—but what the Negro can never forget—is that white society is deeply implicated in the ghetto," the Commission concludes. "White institutions created it, white institutions maintain it, and white society condones it." The future of the American cities, which already contain about 70 percent of the American people, is intricately involved with the condition of the Negro. By 1985, the Commission estimates, the Negro population in the cities will rise from its current 12.5 million to 21 million. The newest test of American democracy—and perhaps its most difficult one—now lies festering in the heart of the cities.

We have seen what happened. Why did it happen?

In addressing this question we shift our focus from the local to the national scene, from the particular events of the summer of 1967 to the factors within the society at large which have brought about the sudden violent mood of so many urban Negroes.

The record before this Commission reveals that the causes of recent racial disorders are imbedded in a massive tangle of issues and circumstances—

SOURCE. *Report of the National Advisory Committee on Civil Disorders*, New York: Bantam Books, 1968, pp. 203–206.

social, economic, political, and psychological—which arise out of the historical pattern of Negro-white relations in America.

These factors are both complex and interacting; they vary significantly in
their effect from city to city and from year to year; and the consequences of
one disorder, generating new grievances and new demands, become the
causes of the next. It is this which creates the "thicket of tension, conflicting
evidence and extreme opinions" cited by the President.

Despite these complexities, certain fundamental matters are clear. Of
these, the most fundamental is the racial attitude and behavior of white
Americans toward black Americans. Race prejudice has shaped our history
decisively in the past; it now threatens to do so again. White racism is
essentially responsible for the explosive mixture which has been accumulating in our cities since the end of World War II. At the base of this mixture
are three of the most bitter fruits of white racial attitudes:

Pervasive discrimination and segregation. The first is surely the continuing
exclusion of great numbers of Negroes from the benefits of economic progress
through discrimination in employment and education, and their enforced
confinement in segregated housing and schools. The corrosive and degrading
effects of this condition and the attitudes that underlie it are the source of the
deepest bitterness and at the center of the problem of racial disorder.

Black migration and white exodus. The second is the massive and growing
concentration of impoverished Negroes in our major cities resulting from
Negro migration from the rural South, rapid population growth and the
continuing movement of the white middle-class to the suburbs. The consequence is a greatly increased burden on the already depleted resources of
cities, creating a growing crisis of deteriorating facilities and services and
unmet human needs.

Black ghettos. Third, in the teeming racial ghettos, segregation and poverty
have intersected to destroy opportunity and hope and to enforce failure. The
ghettos too often mean men and women without jobs, families without men,
and schools where children are processed instead of educated, until they
return to the street—to crime, to narcotics, to dependency on welfare, and to
bitterness and resentment against society in general and white society in
particular.

These three forces have converged on the inner city in recent years and on
the people who inhabit it. At the same time, most whites and many Negroes
outside the ghetto have prospered to a degree unparalleled in the history of
civilization. Through television—the universal appliance in the ghetto—and
the other media of mass communications, this affluence has been endlessly
flaunted before the eyes of the Negro poor and the jobless ghetto youth.

As Americans, most Negro citizens carry within themselves two basic aspirations of our society. They seek to share in both the material resources of our system and its intangible benefits—dignity, respect and acceptance. Outside the ghetto many have succeeded in achieving a decent standard of life, and in developing the inner resources which give life meaning and direction. Within the ghetto, however, it is rare that either aspiration is achieved.

Yet these facts alone—fundamental as they are—cannot be said to have caused the disorders. Other and more immediate factors help explain why these events happened now.

Recently, three powerful ingredients have begun to catalyze the mixture.

Frustrated hopes. The expectations aroused by the great judicial and legislative victories of the civil rights movement have led to frustration, hostility and cynicism in the face of the persistent gap between promise and fulfillment. The dramatic struggle for equal rights in the South has sensitized Northern Negroes to the economic inequalities reflected in the deprivations of ghetto life.

Legitimation of violence. A climate that tends toward the approval and encouragement of violence as a form of protest has been created by white terrorism directed against nonviolent protest, including instances of abuse and even murder of some civil rights workers in the South; by the open defiance of law and federal authority by state and local officials resisting desegregation; and by some protest groups engaging in civil disobedience who turn their backs on nonviolence, go beyond the Constitutionally protected rights of petition and free assembly, and resort to violence to attempt to compel alteration of laws and policies with which they disagree. This condition has been reinforced by a general erosion of respect for authority in American society and reduced effectiveness of social standards and community restraints on violence and crime. This in turn has largely resulted from rapid urbanization and the dramatic reduction in the average age of the total population.

Powerlessness. Finally, many Negroes have come to believe that they are being exploited politically and economically by the white "power structure." Negroes, like people in poverty everywhere, in fact lack the channels of communication, influence and appeal that traditionally have been available to ethnic minorities within the city and which enabled them—unburdened by color—to scale the walls of the white ghettos in an earlier era. The frustrations of powerlessness have led some to the conviction that there is no effective alternative to violence as a means of expression and redress, as a way of "moving the system." More generally, the result is alienation and hostility toward the institutions of law and government and the white society which controls them. This is reflected in the reach toward racial consciousness and solidarity reflected in the slogan "Black Power."

These facts have combined to inspire a new mood among Negroes, particularly among the young. Self-esteem and enhanced racial pride are replacing apathy and submission to "the system." Moreover, Negro youth, who make up over half of the ghetto population, share the growing sense of alienation felt by many white youth in our country. Thus, their role in recent civil disorders reflects not only a shared sense of deprivation and victimization by white society but also the rising incidence of disruptive conduct by a segment of American youth throughout the society.

INCITEMENT AND ENCOURAGEMENT OF VIOLENCE

These conditions have created a volatile mixture of attitudes and beliefs which needs only a spark to ignite mass violence. Strident appeals to violence, first heard from white racists, were echoed and reinforced last summer in the inflammatory rhetoric of black racists and militants. Throughout the year, extremists crisscrossed the country preaching a doctrine of black power and violence. Their rhetoric was widely reported in the mass media; it was echoed by local "militants" and organizations; it became the ugly background noise of the violent summer.

We cannot measure with any precision the influence of these organizations and individuals in the ghetto, but we think it clear that the intolerable and unconscionable encouragement of violence heightened tensions, created a mood of acceptance and an expectation of violence, and thus contributed to the eruption of the disorders last summer.

THE POLICE

It is the convergence of all these factors that makes the role of the police so difficult and so significant. Almost invariably the incident that ignites disorder arises from police action. Harlem, Watts, Newark and Detroit—all the major outbursts of recent years—were precipitated by routine arrests of Negroes for minor offenses by white police.

But the police are not merely the spark. In discharge of their obligation to maintain order and insure public safety in the disruptive conditions of ghetto life, they are inevitably involved in sharper and more frequent conflicts with ghetto residents than with the residents of other areas. Thus, to many Negroes police have come to symbolize white power, white racism and white repression. And the fact is that many police do reflect and express these white attitudes. The atmosphere of hostility and cynicism is reinforced by a widespread perception among Negroes of the existence of police brutality and corruption, and of a "double standard" of justice and protection—one for Negroes and one for whites.

11. HANS J. MORGENTHAU, "WE ARE DELUDING OURSELVES IN VIETNAM"

WITHIN a few days after the death of John F. Kennedy, the new President told Henry Cabot Lodge, "I am not going to lose Vietnam. I am not going to be the President who saw Southeast Asia go the way China went." Consequently, Lyndon B. Johnson made a fateful decision early in 1965—to intervene on a massive scale militarily to prevent the overthrow of the South Vietnamese government by a combination of North Vietnam regulars and South Vietnamese Communist rebels. The position of the Administration was set: it viewed South Vietnam as essential to American security. Communism in Southeast Asia had to be contained and, behind the war in Vietnam, President Johnson reminded the American people, stood "the deepening shadow of Communist China." By 1968, the Administration had committed more than a half million American officers and men to the conflict and had dropped more bombs on enemy positions than were used against Germany during World War II.

From the beginning, the American intervention lacked widespread public support and, as the Administration escalated its effort, opposition increased. Many factors contributed to the growing opposition: the murky origins of the conflict, the vague objectives of America's intervention, the inability of the military to defeat the elusive and capable enemy, the apparent lack of resolve to win the war on the part of the South Vietnamese, the horribly corrupt and inept government of the "democracy" of South Vietnam, and the increasing drain upon American resources.

One of the leading critics of the war effort has been Professor Hans Morgenthau of the University of Chicago. His important essay in the New York Times *Magazine in 1965 stands out as one of the earliest and most accurate stimates of the dangers of Amercain intervention into the troubled waters of Vietnam.*

We are militarily engaged in Viet-Nam by virtue of a basic principle of our foreign policy that was implicit in the Truman Doctrine of 1947 and was put into practice by John Foster Dulles from 1954 onward. This principle is the military containment of communism. Containment had its origins in

SOURCE. Hans J. Morgenthau, "We Are Deluding Ourselves in Vietnam," in *The New York Times Magazine*, April 18, 1965, pp. 25 and 85–87. Copyright 1965 by The New York Times Company. Reprinted by permission of *The New York Times* and the author.

Europe; Dulles applied it to the Middle East and Asia through a series of bilateral and multilateral alliances. Yet what was an outstanding success in Europe turned out to be a dismal failure elsewhere. The reasons for that failure are twofold.

First, the threat that faced the nations of Western Europe in the aftermath of the Second World War was primarily military. It was the threat of the Red Army marching westward. Behind the line of military demarcation of 1945 which the policy of containment declared to be the western-most limit of the Soviet empire, there was an ancient civilization, only temporarily weak and able to maintain itself against the threat of Communist subversion.

The situation is different in the Middle East and Asia. The threat there is not primarily military but political in nature. Weak governments and societies provide opportunities for Communist subversion. Military containment is irrelevant to that threat and may even be counterproductive. Thus the Baghdad Pact did not protect Egypt from Soviet influence and SEATO has had no bearing on Chinese influence in Indonesia and Pakistan.

Second, and more important, even if China were threatening her neighbors primarily by military means, it would be impossible to contain her by erecting a military wall at the periphery of her empire. For China is, even in her present underdeveloped state, the dominant power in Asia. She is this by virtue of the quality and quantity of her population, her geographic position, her civilization, her past power remembered and her future power anticipated. Anybody who has traveled in Asia with his eyes and ears open must have been impressed by the enormous impact which the resurgence of China has made upon all manner of men, regardless of class and political conviction, from Japan to Pakistan.

The issue China poses is political and cultural predominance. The United States can no more contain Chinese influence in Asia by arming South Viet-Nam and Thailand than China could contain American influence in the Western Hemisphere by arming, say, Nicaragua and Costa Rica.

If we are convinced that we cannot live with a China predominant on the mainland of Asia, then we must strike at the heart of Chinese power—that is, rather than try to contain the power of China, we must try to destroy that power itself. Thus there is logic on the side of that small group of Americans who are convinced that war between the United States and China is inevitable and that the earlier that war comes, the better will be the chances for the United States to win it.

Yet, while logic is on their side, practical judgment is against them. For while China is obviously no match for the United States in over-all power, China is largely immune to the specific types of power in which the superiority of the United States consists—that is, nuclear, air and naval power. Certainly, the United States has the power to destroy the nuclear installations and the major industrial and population centers of China, but this destruction would not defeat China; it would only set her development back. To be defeated, China has to be conquered.

Physical conquest would require the deployment of millions of American soldiers on the mainland of Asia. No American military leader has ever advocated a course of action so fraught with incalculable risks, so uncertain of outcome, requiring sacrifices so out of proportion to the interests at stake and the benefits to be expected. President Eisenhower declared on February 10, 1954, that he "could conceive of no greater tragedy than for the United States to become involved in an all-out war in Indochina." General Mac-Arthur, in the Congressional hearings concerning his dismissal and in personal conversation with President Kennedy, emphatically warned against sending American foot soldiers to the Asian mainland to fight China.

If we do not want to set ourselves goals which cannot be attained with the means we are willing to employ, we must learn to accommodate ourselves to the predominance of China on the Asian mainland. It is instructive to note that those Asian nations which have done so—such as Burma and Cambodia—live peacefully in the shadow of the Chinese giant.

This *modus vivendi*, composed of legal independence and various degrees of actual dependence, has indeed been for more than a millennium the persistent pattern of Chinese predominance on the mainland of Asia. The military conquest of Tibet is the sole exception to that pattern. The military operations at the Indian border do not diverge from it, since their purpose was the establishment of a frontier disputed by both sides.

On the other hand, those Asian nations which have allowed themselves to be transformed into outposts of American military power—such as Laos a few years ago, South Viet-Nam, and Thailand—have become the actual or prospective victims of Communist aggression and subversion. Thus it appears that peripheral military containment is counterproductive. Challenged at its periphery by American military power at its weakest—that is, by the proxy of client-states—China or its proxies respond with locally superior military and political power.

In specific terms, accommodation means four things: (1) recognition of the political and cultural predominance of China on the mainland of Asia as a fact of life; (2) liquidation of the peripheral military containment of China; (3) strengthening of the uncommitted nations of Asia by nonmilitary means; (4) assessment of Communist governments in Asia in terms not of Communist doctrine but of their relation to the interests and power of the United States.

In the light of these principles, the alternative to our present policies in Viet-Nam would be this: a face-saving agreement which would allow us to disengage ourselves militarily in stages spaced in time; restoration of the status quo of the Geneva Agreement of 1954, with special emphasis upon all-Vietnamese elections; co-operation with the Soviet Union in support of a Titoist all-Vietnamese Government, which would be likely to emerge from such elections.

This last point is crucial, for our present policies not only drive Hanoi into the waiting arms of Peking, but also make it very difficult for Moscow to pursue an independent policy. Our interests in Southeast Asia are identical with those of the Soviet Union: to prevent the expansion of the *military* power of China. But while our present policies invite that expansion, so do they make it impossible for the Soviet Union to join us in preventing it. If we were to reconcile ourselves to the establishment of a Titoist government in all of Viet-Nam, the Soviet Union could successfully compete with China in claiming credit for it and surreptitiously cooperate with us in maintaining it.

Testing the President's proposals by these standards, one realizes how far they go in meeting them. These proposals do not preclude a return to the Geneva Agreement and even assume the existence of a Titoist government in North Viet-Nam. Nor do they preclude the establishment of a Titoist government for all of Viet-Nam, provided the people of South Viet-Nam have freely agreed to it. They also envision the active participation of the Soviet Union in establishing and maintaining a new balance of power in Southeast Asia. On the other hand, the President has flatly rejected a withdrawal "under the cloak of a meaningless agreement." The controlling word is obviously "meaningless," and only the future can tell whether we shall consider any face-saving agreement as "meaningless" regardless of its political context.

However, we are under a psychological compulsion to continue our military presence in South Viet-Nam as part of the peripheral military containment of China. We have been emboldened in this course of action by the identification of the enemy as "Communist," seeing in every Communist party and regime an extension of hostile Russian or Chinese power. This identification was justified twenty or fifteen years ago when communism still had a monolithic character. Here, as elsewhere, our modes of thought and action have been rendered obsolete by new developments.

It is ironic that this simple juxtaposition of "communism" and "free world" was erected by John Foster Dulles's crusading moralism into the guiding principle of American foreign policy at a time when the national communism of Yugoslavia, the neutralism of the third world, and the incipient split between the Soviet Union and China were rendering that juxtaposition invalid.

Today, it is belaboring the obvious to say that we are faced not with one monolithic communism whose uniform hostility must be countered with equally uniform hostility, but with a number of different communisms whose hostilities, determined by different national interests, vary. In fact, the United States encounters today less hostility from Tito, who is a Communist, than from de Gaulle, who is not.

We can today distinguish four different types of communism in view of the kind and degree of hostility to the United States they represent: a communism identified with the Soviet Union—e.g., Poland; a communism identified with China—e.g., Albania; a communism that straddles the fence between the Soviet Union and China—e.g., Rumania; and independent communism —e.g., Yugoslavia. Each of these communisms must be dealt with in terms of the bearing its foreign policy has upon the interests of the United States in a concrete instance.

It would, of course, be absurd to suggest that the officials responsible for the conduct of American foreign policy are unaware of these distinctions and of the demands they make for discriminating subtlety. Yet it is an obvious fact of experience that these officials are incapable of living up to these demands when they deal with Viet-Nam.

Thus they maneuver themselves into a position which is anti-revolutionary *per se* and which requires military opposition to revolution wherever it is found in Asia, regardless of how it affects the interests—and how susceptible it is to the power—of the United States. There is a historic precedent for this kind of policy: Metternich's military opposition to liberalism after the Napoleonic Wars, which collapsed in 1848. For better or for worse, we live again in an age of revolution. It is the task of statesmanship not to oppose what cannot be opposed with a chance of success, but to bend it to one's own interests. This is what the President is trying to do with his proposal for the economic development of Southeast Asia.

Why do we support the Saigon government in the civil war against the Viet-Cong? Because the Saigon government is "free" and the Viet-Cong are "Communist." By containing Vietnamese communism, we assume that we are really containing the communism of China.

Yet this assumption is at odds with the historic experience of a millennium and is unsupported by contemporary evidence. China is the hereditary enemy of Viet-Nam, and Ho Chi Minh will become the leader of a Chinese satellite only if the United States forces him to become one.

Furthermore, Ho Chi Minh, like Tito and unlike the Communist governments of the other states of Eastern Europe, came to power not by courtesy of another Communist nation's victorious army but at the head of a victorious army of his own. He is, then, a natural candidate to become an Asian Tito, and the question we must answer is: How adversely would a Titoist Ho Chi Minh, governing all of Viet-Nam, affect the interests of the United States? The answer can only be: not at all. One can even maintain the proposition that, far from affecting adversely the interests of the United States, it would be in the interest of the United States if the western periphery of China were ringed by a chain of independent states, though they would, of course, in their policies take due account of the predominance of their powerful neighbor. . . .

There is an ominous similarity between this technique and that applied to the expedition in the Bay of Pigs. We wanted to overthrow Castro, but for reasons of public relations we did not want to do it ourselves. So it was not done at all, and our prestige was damaged far beyond what it would have suffered had we worked openly and single-mindedly for the goal we had set ourselves.

Our very presence in Viet-Nam is in a sense dictated by considerations of public relations; we are afraid lest our prestige would suffer were we to retreat from an untenable position.

One may ask whether we have gained prestige by being involved in a civil war on the mainland of Asia and by being unable to win it. Would we gain more by being unable to extricate ourselves from it, and by expanding it unilaterally into an international war? Is French prestige lower today than it was eleven years ago when France was fighting in Indochina, or five years ago when she was fighting in Algeria? Does not a great power gain prestige by mustering the wisdom and courage necessary to liquidate a losing enterprise? In other words, is it not the mark of greatness, in circumstances such as these, to be able to afford to be indifferent to one's prestige?

The peripheral military containment of China, the indiscriminate crusade against communism, counterinsurgency as a technically self-sufficient new branch of warfare, the conception of foreign and military policy as a branch of public relations—they are all misconceptions that conjure up terrible dangers for those who base their policies on them.